Richard Sharpe is Reader in Diplomatic in the University of Oxford.

Medieval Irish
Saints' Lives

Medieval Irish Saints' Lives

An Introduction to Vitae Sanctorum Hiberniae

RICHARD SHARPE

CLARENDON PRESS · OXFORD

1991

Oxford University Press, Walton Street, Oxford OX2 6DP
Oxford New York Toronto
Delhi Bombay Calcutta Madras Karachi
Petaling Jaya Singapore Hong Kong Tokyo
Nairobi Dar es Salaam Cape Town
Melbourne Auckland
and associated companies in
Berlin Ibadan

Oxford is a trade mark of Oxford University Press

Published in the United States
by Oxford University Press, New York

British Library Cataloguing in Publication Data
Sharpe, R. (Richard)
Medieval Irish Saints' lives: an introduction to Vitae
Sanctorum Hiberniae.
1. Hagiography—Critical studies
I. Title 809.9352
ISBN 0-19-821582-7

Library of Congress Cataloging in Publication Data
Sharpe, Richard.
Medieval Irish saints' lives: an introduction to vitae sanctorum
Hiberniae/Richard Sharpe.
Includes bibliographical references and index.
1. Christian hagiography. 2. Christian saints—Ireland—
Historiography. 3. Ireland—Church history—Historiography.
I. Title.
BX4662.S52 1990
274.15'0092'2—dc20
ISBN 0-19-821582-7

Set by Joshua Associates Ltd, Oxford
Printed and bound in
Great Britain by Biddles Ltd
Guildford and King's Lynn

Preface

ALTHOUGH some eighty individual Lives of Irish saints from the Latin compilations of the later Middle Ages have been in print since 1910, and many of them since much earlier, there has been little attempt to understand what they have to say. A few writers, many years ago, took a generous attitude in accepting at face value much of what such Lives had to say: Fr. John Ryan was probably the last of this school, and for the last fifty or sixty years a more cautious attitude has prevailed. It has tended to be those with no experience of Irish historical sources who cite these Lives for some item of information, supporting it with wild guesses as to the date or authority of the source.* Writers familiar with the problems are usually extremely circumspect in referring to the *uitae* of the late medieval collections. The reason for this must be, in part, at least, that the editors who published so many of the texts—De Smedt and De Backer in 1887, Plummer in 1910, and Heist revising De Smedt and De Backer in 1965—gave no guidance as to the status of the lives they were publishing. Studies of individual Lives have been attempted from time to time, but in the absence of any well-founded understanding of the collections and their compilers, the results are at best insecure and in some cases quite mistaken.

It is my purpose in this book to establish the foundations for understanding the work of the compilers. My method has been principally to exploit text-historical arguments of a kind not attempted by Plummer in order to appreciate the relationship between the different versions of a *uita* as contained in the collections. On a basis of verbal comparisons I have tried to explain in textual terms how these different versions are related; in assessing the transmission of the *uitae* I investigate how the compilers of the collections approached their work, what materials they shared, and what influenced their differences. As a result I may point the way to where work on individual Lives can safely begin, and where it is likely to yield evidence of historical interest

---

* See, for example, P. J. Geary, *Furta Sacra* (Princeton, NJ, 1978), pp. 141, 183, on St Abbán; I Deug-Su, *L'opera agiographica di Alcuino* (Spoleto, 1983), pp. 39–42.

concerning the saints or the churches which produced the primary texts. It is not an object of this book to say much about the historical or other interest of individual Lives: studies of that kind will be necessary in due course to test some hypotheses advanced here on the basis only of textual and linguistic arguments. For those interested chiefly in early Irish hagiography and not in the later medieval transmission of the texts, Chapter 10 identifies nine Lives which I suggest existed in a single manuscript collection copied no later than the ninth century. If this argument is found convincing, then the date is a *terminus ante quem* for the composition of these Lives. I have not attempted to determine on evidence of content whether they were written in the seventh, eighth, or ninth century, or indeed whether the evidence of content seriously conflicts with my textual and linguistic arguments. All this has yet to be done.

What I have, in effect, done is gone back to where Plummer began, and written in a quite new and different way about the subjects he aimed to cover in the first three chapters of his Introduction to the first volume of *Vitae Sanctorum Hiberniae*. I have in some measure repeated information, especially from his pp. ix–xxiii, but I have taken the analysis much further. Always I have been conscious of following behind him, and it was an enormous help to me to have had the loan from Jesus College, Oxford, of Plummer's copy of De Smedt and De Backer's *Acta Sanctorum Hiberniae* which he had collated both against its manuscript source, *Codex Salmanticensis*, and also in some measure against the related texts in the Oxford collection. I have come to appreciate how he worked and to realize why he overlooked much that I was able to pick up. We both spent nine years on these collections, in his case from 1901 to 1910, in mine from 1978 to 1987. His harvest may be found to exceed mine, but for eighty years it has been a neglected harvest, bound in *Vitae Sanctorum Hiberniae* but with no key. I shall feel content to have produced a key with which to unlock his harvest.

I was helped in my work first by the availability of a concordance to the texts edited by Plummer, produced for my use in July 1980 by the Literary and Linguistic Computing Centre, Cambridge University. My thanks go to Dr John Dawson and the Ven. Yeshe Zangmo for their help. Since 1981 I have derived constant stimulation from the writings and conversation of

Professor Pádraig Ó Riain, who has also helped by lending me photographs of manuscripts and has generously allowed me to read his own work ahead of publication. In the course of my research I received help of various kinds from several quarters. I should like to thank the staff of the Bodleian Library, Oxford, and Royal Library, Brussels, for the facilities they afforded me in using manuscripts. In Dublin the manuscript department of Trinity College Library was my base for many weeks, and I am particularly grateful to William O'Sullivan, sometime Keeper of Manuscripts, for his advice on matters connected with Ussher and Ware. On many visits to Marsh's Library, Mrs M. MacCarthy, the custodian, took a close interest in my work, and she has answered further queries by letter, for which I thank her. At the Franciscan House of Studies, Killiney, and the Bibliothèque des Bollandistes, Brussels, I received similar help, for which I thank Fr. Bartholomew Egan, OFM, and Fr. Joseph Van der Straeten, SJ. Since the book was first written in 1986–7 I have benefited from comments on different parts of it from Dr David Dumville, Dr Anthony Harvey, Professor Michael Lapidge, Mr William O'Sullivan, Professor Michael Reeve, Dr Paul Russell, Dr Patrick Sims-Williams, Dr Jane Stevenson, Dr Alan Thacker, and Dr Michael Winterbottom. My thanks to them all.

Abbreviations

Acta Sanctorum	*Acta Sanctorum quotquot toto orbe coluntur*, ed. J. Bolland *et al.* (Antwerp, Tongerloo, Paris, Brussels, 1643–in progress)
BHL	*Bibliotheca Hagiographica Latina*, [ed. A. Poncelet *et al.*] (Subsidia Hagiographica, 6; Brussels, 1898–1901). *Novum Supplementum*, ed. H. Fros (Brussels, 1986)
BL	British Library
CLA	*Codices Latini Antiquiores. A Palaeographical Guide to Latin Manuscripts prior to the Ninth Century*, ed. E. A. Lowe (11 vols. and suppl.; Oxford, 1934–72)
Colgan, *Acta*	J. Colgan (ed.), *Acta Sanctorum Veteris et Majoris Scotiæ seu Hiberniæ*, vol. i (Louvain, 1645)
Colgan, *Trias*	J. Colgan (ed.), *Triadis Thaumaturgæ seu Divorum Patricii, Columbæ et Brigidæ . . . Acta* (Louvain, 1647)
De Smedt and De Backer, *Acta*	C. De Smedt and J. De Backer (edd.), *Acta Sanctorum Hiberniae ex Codice Salmanticensi nunc primum integre edita* (Edinburgh and London, Bruges and Lille, 1887–8)
Fleming, *Collectanea Sacra*	P. Fleming (ed.), *Collectanea Sacra seu S. Columbani Hiberni Abbatis . . . Acta et Opuscula*, ed. T. Sirinus [Sheeran] (Louvain, 1667)
Heist, *Vitae*	W. W. Heist (ed.) *Vitae Sanctorum Hiberniae e Codice olim Salmanticensi nunc Bruxellensi* (Subsidia Hagiographica, 25; Brussels, 1965)

Kenney, *The Sources*   J. F. Kenney, *The Sources for the Early History of Ireland: Ecclesiastical* (Records of Civilisation; New York, 1929)

MGH   Monumenta Germaniae Historica

Plummer, 'A Tentative Catalogue' C. Plummer, 'A Tentative Catalogue of Irish Hagiography', in *Miscellanea Hagiographica Hibernica*, ed. C. Plummer (Brussels, 1925)

Plummer, *Vitae*   C. Plummer (ed.), *Vitae Sanctorum Hiberniae* (2 vols.; Oxford, 1910)

Ussher, *Whole Works*   J. Ussher, *The Whole Works*, ed. C. Elrington and J. H. Todd (17 vols.; Dublin, 1847–64)

NOTE ON REFERENCES

In referring to Lives of saints from the three collections, I have followed a few conventions. Manuscripts are designated by capital letters (MT, RI, S, V). Text-types characteristic of a particular recension are designated by bold capitals (**D, O, S, SO,V**). Thus **D** represents the texts of M, T, and any number of lost copies of this recension.

Individual saints' names are given in abbreviated form in footnotes and other references: *Abb.* for Abbán, *Ail.* for Ailbe, *&c.* A list of these follows below.

References to the various recensions of a Life may thus take the form *Ail.* **S** §1, **D** §1, *&c.*

Conjectural manuscripts lying behind the existing collections are designated by Greek capitals, Δ, Θ, Φ.

Abbreviated saints' names: *Abb.* Abbán, *Aed* Aed mac Bricc, *Ail.* Ailbe, *Ba.* Bairre or Finnbarr, *Ber.* Berach, *Boe.* Boecius or Buite, *Bren.* Brendan of Clonfert, *Cain.* Cainnech, *Car.* Carthach or Mochutu, *CiC.* Ciarán of Clonmacnoise, *CiS.* Ciarán of Saigir, *Coem.* Coemgen, *ColE.* Colmán Élo, *ColT.* Columba of Terryglass, *Com.* Comgall, *Cron.* Crónán, *Decl.* Declán, *Enda* Énda, *Fech.* Fechin, *FinC.* Fínán Cam of Kinitty, *Finn.* Finnian of Clonard, *FintC.* Fintán of Clonenagh, *Ger.* Gerald, *Ita* Íte, *Las.* Lasrén or Molaisse of Devenish, *Lug.* Luguid or Molua, *Maed.* Aed or Aedán or Maedóc of Ferns, *Mchg.* Mochoemóc, *Moch.* Mochua of Timahoe, *Mol.* Moling, *Mun.* Fintán or Munnu of Taghmon, *Rua.* Ruadán, *Sam.* Samthann, *Tig.* Tigernach.

Contents

PART I

INTRODUCTION

1

The Writing of Saints' Lives in Medieval Ireland

Hibernia, insula sanctorum, sanctis et mirabilibus perplurimis sublimiter plena habetur.

I RELAND, island of saints. This expression is first attested here, in the writings of the Irish chronicler Maelbrigte, composed while he was living in enforced exile as an *inclusus* in the monastery of St Martin at Mainz during the 1070s.[1] His words form an improbable chronicle entry against the year 674, but they clearly do not refer to an event at all. Rather, they indicate an attitude, a way of understanding the Irish church in its early days.

The same phrase, *insula sanctorum*, was known also to Jocelin of Furness in the 1180s as a name for Ireland.[2] A very similar usage is found in a version of the Life of St Abbán, perhaps dating from the late thirteenth century.[3] The usage appears therefore to have been

[1] On Maelbrigte alias Marianus Scottus (1028–82), see B. MacCarthy, *The Codex Palatino-Vaticanus 830* (Todd Lecture Series, 3; Dublin, 1892), pp. 4–7; Kenney, *The Sources*, pp. 614–16. The chronicle is edited in part by Waitz, MGH *Scriptores* V (Hanover, 1844), pp. 481–564 (quotation from p. 544). His text is based on MS Vat. Pal. Lat. 830, dated 1072 × 1082, written by Maelbrigte's assistant and annotated by the author. The date 674 is *anno Domini*; in Maelbrigte's idiosyncratic chronological system, it appears as 696.

[2] Jocelin, *Vita S. Patricii* §152 (*Acta Sanctorum*, Mart. II (1668), p. 575), 'Infra breue igitur temporis spatium, nulla eremus, nullus pene terre angulus aut locus in insula fuit tam remotus, qui perfectis monachis aut monialibus non repleretur, ita ut Hibernia speciali nomine insula sanctorum ubique terrarum iure nominaretur.'

[3] *Vita S. Abbani* (S) §1, 'In hac insula tot uiri eximie sanctitatis fuerunt quod insula sanctorum nomine appropriato dicebatur'; probably based on ibid. (D) §2, 'De illa scilicet gente maximum sanctorum agmen sibi Deus elegit'. See below, p. 350. The phrase is used also in the vernacular, *Éri óg, inis na náemh* 'Virgin Ireland, island of saints': so begins the poem on the kings of Ireland by Gilla Modutu Ó Casaite, written shortly before 1147; the text is printed from the Book of Ballymote by MacCarthy, *The Codex*, p. 408, and the date is discussed by M. Ní

already familiar in the Middle Ages. When Irish Catholic scholars in the seventeenth century found themselves, like Maelbrigte though for different reasons, exiled from Ireland and obliged to work on the Continent, they took up the phrase again.[4] It has since become commonplace, but in origin the idea that Ireland was a nation especially noted for its saints represents a historical judgement in a European context.[5] From the late sixth until well into the twelfth century, so the belief ran, Ireland was so fertile in saints that her *peregrini* spread themselves over all of central Europe, creating a veritable empire of Irish Christian influence. Among these *peregrini* were such leading figures in European religious life and learning as Iohannes Scottus Eriugena at Laon and Sedulius Scottus at Liège. But men noted for their scholarship were greatly outnumbered by those known as saints, of whom the most influential was St Columbanus, founder of Bobbio. Scores of lesser names also, exiles for Christ's sake, have long enjoyed a reputation for sainthood.[6] Those who founded churches—and in many cases their successors—were regarded as saints by their own communities from where the belief spread outwards.[7] So great was the impact of the Irish on European ideas of sainthood that it

Bhrolcháin, 'The Manuscript Tradition of the Banshenchus', *Ériu*, 33 (1982), 109–35 (at p. 110).

[4] Thomas Messingham published at Paris in 1624 his *Florilegium Insulae Sanctorum*; Peter Lombard's *De Regno Hiberniae Sanctorum Insulae Commentarius* was published at Louvain in 1632; John Colgan's great work, also published at Louvain in 1645–7, has in its title the words *Acta Sanctorum Veteris et Maioris Scotiæ seu Hiberniæ, Sanctorum Insulae*.

[5] L. Gougaud, 'The Isle of Saints', *Studies*, 13 (1924), 363–80, traces the history of the phrase from its use by Maelbrigte to a consistorial address of Pius XI in 1923; one could continue it onwards.

[6] See Gougaud, 'The Isle of Saints', pp. 368–71, for evidence from the ninth to the twelfth century of general respect towards the *Scotti peregrini* in Europe. The nearest any Continental author comes to the phrase *insula sanctorum* is in the anonymous *Vita S. Wironis* (*BHL* 8973), §2, 'Scotia, uber sanctorum patrum insula, stellarum numeris sanctorum coequans patrocinia'. On this Life of a 'Hibernized' saint, see W. Levison, *England and the Continent in the Eighth Century* (Oxford, 1946), pp. 82–3 n.

[7] The network of *uitae* for SS. Fursu, Foillán, Ultán, Gertrude, and others, all emanating from the Péronne–Nivelles centre, is a case in point; see Kenney, *The Sources*, pp. 500–8; P. Grosjean, 'Notes d'hagiographie celtique (nos. 37–40)', *AB* 75 (1957), 373–419; and Hughes, [review], *IHS* 12 (1960–1), 61–4.

became a common motif in hagiography to ascribe to almost any little known saint an Irish birthright.[8]

That Ireland was pre-eminently *insula sanctorum* could not be a strictly native concept: it necessarily implies a comparison with the rest of the world.[9] But taken up by Fr. Thomas Messingham, an Irish priest at work in Paris, and by Fr. John Colgan, one of the Irish Franciscans at St Anthony's College, Louvain, the idea came back to Ireland. These and other seventeenth-century antiquaries identified the history of the Irish church with the Lives of its saints.[10] This idea may be said to have lasted into the twentieth century, even in serious discussion.[11] The reasons why the history of saints for so long held a central place in Irish ecclesiastical history—as in Welsh or Cornish or Breton or, to a lesser degree, Scottish history—are various. In the first place, it must be because the cult of numerous local saints had a more lasting, and perhaps greater, importance among the Celtic churches than was the case elsewhere in medieval Christendom. But it has also something to do with the continuity of devotion to these saints long after the Middle Ages.

1.1. *Extent of the Materials*

Whatever the historical or devotional reasons may have been, medieval Ireland produced a great quantity of hagiographical documents. There are known today upwards of one hundred *Latin* Lives of about sixty Irish saints.[12] Some of these survive only

---

[8] On this problem of 'Hibernization' in Irish-Continental hagiography, see M. Koch, *Sankt Fridolin und sein Biograph Balther* (Zürich, 1959), and comments by J. Hennig, *IER*[5] 95 (1961), 136–8.

[9] 'Ipsa enim ratio et praerogativa nominis, qua et a priscis et modernis scriptoribus, SANCTORUM INSULA passim appellatur, sacrae nostrae insulae tantam tamque gloriosam sanctorum multitudinem evincit, ut nec ullam aliam insulam parem, nec gentem, tametsi in plures provincias vel regna diffusam, in hoc encomio superiorem admittat'; Colgan, *Acta*, praefatio ad lectorem, sig. b1.

[10] C. Mooney, 'Father John Colgan', in *Father John Colgan, O.F.M.*, ed. T. O Donnell (Dublin, 1959), 7–40 (at pp. 15–16, 33, 38–9).

[11] R. Sharpe, 'Some Problems Concerning the Organization of the Church in Early Medieval Ireland', *Peritia*, 3 (1984), 230–70 (at pp. 247–8).

[12] Figures based on C. Plummer, 'A Tentative Catalogue of Irish Hagiography', in his *Miscellanea Hagiographica Hibernica* (Subsidia Hagiographica, 15; Brussels, 1925), pp. 171–285. The section on Latin Lives of Irish saints, pp. 234–

in Continental manuscripts, but the majority are known from three great compilations of the thirteenth and fourteenth centuries. These are conventionally known by titles given to them in the seventeenth century as *Codex Kilkenniensis*, represented by two copies in Dublin, *Codex Insulensis* in two manuscripts now in Oxford, and *Codex Salmanticensis*, a volume now in Brussels. None of the three collections is directly dependent on either of the others, but there is enough overlap in their contents to show that they drew on some common sources, small groups of texts gathered into single volumes which may have circulated between the compilers of the three collections. It is the central purpose of this study to investigate the sources available to those compilers and the use they made of them. The Latin Lives written in Ireland, as attested in some early manuscripts, mostly Continental, and in these three collections, range in date from the seventh century to the fourteenth. The latest item in any of the three collections is probably a text translated from Irish for the compilers of the *Salmanticensis*, the Life of St Cuanna.

The number of Lives still extant and composed in *Irish* before the end of the sixteenth century may be put at about fifty, the number of saints at about forty.[13] Some of these saints have Lives in Latin as well as in Irish: of these, some are closely related, others wholly independent. About twenty Lives are known from manuscripts written during the fourteenth, fifteenth, or sixteenth century. Somewhat more are witnessed principally by transcripts made in the early seventeenth century from originals now perished. The published inventory of these Lives also includes Irish texts which are mere eighteenth-century translations made from printed editions of the Latin texts;[14] I have excluded these

54, must be used in conjunction with the Bollandist catalogue, *Bibliotheca Hagiographica Latina* (2 vols.; Brussels, 1898–1901) with supplements (1911 and 1986). Plummer numbers (206–305) the saints for whom Latin Lives were known or thought to be known, including *peregrini* (and some of dubious Irishness), but does not number the Lives.

[13] Plummer, 'A Tentative Catalogue', pp. 179–97, numbers the Lives (1–64), including some for which texts are not now known, and some which are merely modern Irish translations from Latin.

[14] For example, the Life of Gilla Meic Liac or Gelasius, archbishop of Armagh (1137–74), in Dublin, RIA MS 23 O 35 (wr. 1772), pp. 249 ff., is a translation of a 'vita ex variis' compiled by John Colgan, *Acta Sanctorum Hiberniae* (Louvain, 1645), pp. 772–8. No medieval Life in either Latin or Irish exists.

from my reckoning in the same way as I have not counted Latin translations made from Irish texts in the seventeenth century.[15] To this number of Lives, one should add nearly one hundred and twenty short tracts and anecdotes; various martyrologies, with further anecdotes in the scholia; and a considerable tradition of genealogies and saint-lists.[16]

There is a marked divide between a small number of texts which survive in a large number of manuscripts on the Continent of Europe, and to a lesser extent in England, and the great majority of texts which survived in Ireland, where almost all early manuscripts have disappeared. For these texts survival in a late medieval compilation is generally the best one may hope for, and for vernacular texts a seventeenth-century copy on paper is as likely as an older parchment. Survival in late copies, especially in late medieval compendia, raises the question of how much a text has changed in the course of its transmission. Some texts in these late compilations are undoubtedly early, such as the Life of St Brigit in the so-called *Codex Insulensis* at Oxford, a copy, albeit a poor witness to the original, of *Vita I*, which is also known from ninth- and tenth-century manuscripts. Others are manifestly late, such as the thirteenth-century Life of St Gerald in the same collection, 'extremely fabulous', in its view of both English and Irish history.[17] These texts cannot be put to any use until we are able to assign some kind of date, unless we are to take the evasive and in some cases obviously mistaken approach of treating the collections merely as literary monuments of the age of their latest compilers.

Saints' Lives, however, form a very large part of the Latin literature of Ireland, and a significant part of Irish literature. They are also important as historical evidence. 'These biographies and other *acta* of saints,' writes Kenney,[18]

---

[15] For example, Colgan's translation of the Tripartite Life of St Patrick, *Trias Thaumaturga* (Louvain, 1647), pp. 117–69. Such Latin translations are not counted by Plummer, though Irish translations of comparable or later date are.

[16] Plummer, 'A Tentative Catalogue', pp. 198–224 (nos. 65–179), pp. 225–31 (nos. 180–98). The genealogies and saint-lists are now conveniently available in P. Ó Riain, *Corpus Genealogiarum Sanctorum Hiberniae* (Dublin, 1985).

[17] Plummer, *Vitae*, vol. i, p. lxxi.

[18] Kenney, *The Sources*, p. 293.

make up one of the most extensive classes of material relating, *ex prima facie*, to the early history of Ireland. Their magnitude, and the fact that for so much of the past they are the only records, give them importance, but their character is such that they may be used only with special precautions.

Since Kenney wrote these words, awareness of the limitations of hagiographical evidence has grown a good deal, and historical work has sometimes fought shy of using the saints' Lives. This trend is now reversed, and the opportunities which the saints' Lives offer the historian are becoming more and more appreciated. But one must first establish how and to what end this evidence may be used.

A first step is to place the composition of the Lives in context, to consider over what period they were read and copied, and to learn how hagiographical interests and methods changed over the centuries. In attempting now to offer a framework for such a history of hagiography in Ireland, I am fully conscious that the Lives which can be placed in context are greatly outnumbered by those which cannot yet. But I hold that the better we can understand the development of hagiographical practice, the more it will become possible to fit undated Lives into a context.

1.2. *The Earliest Latin Lives*[19]

The oldest Lives of Irish saints still surviving are the Life of St Columbanus by Jonas of Bobbio, who joined the community three years after the saint's death, and the Life of St Fursu by a member of his community at Péronne.[20] Neither was written by an Irishman; neither is known to have been read in Ireland until centuries later. Although the beginnings of hagiography in Ireland belong to the same period—about the middle of the seventh century—the practice that disciples write Lives of their masters to

---

[19] I mention here two survey-articles of interest: L. Bieler, 'The Celtic Hagiographer', *Studia Patristica*, 5 (1959), 243–65, and K. McCone, 'An Introduction to Early Irish Saints' Lives', *The Maynooth Review*, 11 (1984), 26–59.

[20] Jonas's Life of St Columbanus (*BHL* 1898) was edited by B. Krusch, *Ionae Vitae Sanctorum Columbani, Vedastis, Iohannis* (Hanover and Leipzig, 1905), pp. 144–295. The anonymous Life of St Fursu (*BHL* 3209) was edited by Mabillon, *Acta Sanctorum Ordinis S. Benedicti*, ii. 300–9, and incompletely by Krusch, MGH *Script. rerum Meroving.*, iv. 423–51 (which omits the visions).

commemorate them and to canonize them appears never to have taken hold there.

The saints in Ireland always belonged to an older generation, and often to the remote past. The first saints for whom Lives were written in the seventh century were St Patrick and St Brigit. The earliest Lives do not survive, but Lives from the next generation are known, and it is now agreed that their authors had no sure basis of biographical information for St Brigit and none for St Patrick beyond what could be gleaned from his *Confessio*.[21] St Patrick lived in the fifth century.[22] St Brigit seems to have been a euhemerized deity; it is not known when the cult began, but it was probably in the sixth century.[23] It is hardly surprising that hagiographers one or two centuries later had no historical information to go on. It is, however, more surprising that all the saints for whom Lives exist belong to an early period. Only a few seem to have lived after about 640—St Moling died in 697, the shadowy St Samthann in 739; but their Lives show no sign of having more circumstantial information than the Lives of saints long dead.[24] Even Adomnán, unquestionably a historical figure, who died in 704, becomes unrecognizable in his tenth-century Irish Life.

There were undoubtedly other holy men and women who lived in a period when hagiography had become established in Ireland, but they have no *uitae*. Maelruain of Tallaght (d. 792) for example,

[21] See especially D. A. Binchy, 'Patrick and his Biographers, Ancient and Modern', *Studia Hibernica*, 2 (1962), 7–173. Here is not the place to reopen the question of whether seventh-century writers had biographical data concerning Palladius, which they transferred to Patrick, nor whence such data might have come.

[22] Dates at different points in the fifth century have been argued; for example, R. P. C. Hanson, 'The Date of St Patrick', *Bulletin of the John Rylands Library*, 61 (1978–9), 60–77 (early fifth century), or A. C. Thomas, *Christianity in Roman Britain to AD 500* (London, 1981), pp. 307–46 (late fifth century). Objections can be found to all dating-models proposed, but dates lying outside the fifth century are still less convincing.

[23] Brigit appears as the patron saint of the Fothairt, a people of north Leinster, in a poem which probably dates from the early seventh century; the texts of two manuscripts are printed by M. A. O'Brien, *Corpus Genealogiarum Hiberniae*, i. (Dublin, 1962), pp. 80–1, but there is no edited text.

[24] Aspects of St Samthann's Life are discussed by D. A. Bray, 'Motival Derivations in the Life of St Samthann', *Studia Celtica*, 20/21 (1985–6), 78–86. No historical datum is inferred beyond the fact that 'her historicity has not been called in question'.

who inspired a revival of devotional life in Irish monasteries and led a movement which produced several literary works, would seem an obvious subject for a Life to be written by a disciple. But no Life exists.[25] Blathmac, a monk of Iona martyred by Vikings in 825, when he refused to disclose the hiding-place of St Columba's shrine-reliquary, did not become the subject of a Life in his own country—although Walahfrid Strabo commemorated his death in verse.[26] Neither is credited with miracles. Even St Donnan of Eigg, martyred[27] with his monks as early as 617, was commemorated by no more than a short anecdote.[28] One may wonder whether such Lives once existed but have vanished. Perhaps they did. But the hypothesis is improbable, since all the positive signs suggest a complete lack of interest in the heroes of the contemporary church, at least until the twelfth century.

This aspect of Irish hagiography, that it looks back to a distant past, an Age of Saints, separates it from historical criteria of judgement. If we cannot identify with confidence the author of a work, our attempts to place a Life in its context are not helped by any information we may have from annals or martyrologies or place-name dedications about the actual saint. Historical references are likely to be incidental, and contemporary with the author. If these can be pinned down, they are helpful. But for the most part, we must seek a literary or literary-historical context.

To start with the most solid ground we possess, the oldest hagiographical manuscript of Irish origin is the famous Schaff-hausen codex of Adomnán's *Vita S. Columbae*.[29] A colophon

---

[25] There is a short anecdote about him in the Book of Leinster, edited by R. I. Best in J. Fraser *et al.* (edd.), *Irish Texts* (5 vols.; London, 1930–4), i. 34–5, and in R. I. Best *et al.* (edd.), *The Book of Leinster* (6 vols.; Dublin, 1954–83), v. 1246–7.

[26] Kenney, *The Sources*, no. 227.

[27] This term is hardly ever used of Ireland's native saints; indeed, Gerald of Wales could claim that Ireland produced no martyrs, *Topographia Hibernie*, III 28 (ed. Dimock, v. 174). Donnan, however, is called 'martyr' in a relic-list copied in Schlettstadt, Bibliothèque humanistique, MS 14 (104) (Weissenburg, s. ix3/4), f. 45ʳ, edited by B. Bischoff, 'Ein Reliquien Verzeichnis (neunter Jahrhundert)', in his *Anecdota Novissima* (Quellen und Untersuchungen zur lateinischen Philologie des Mittelalters, 8; Stuttgart, 1984), p. 91.

[28] Best *et al.*, *The Book of Leinster*, vi. 1688; this anecdote is in Latin.

[29] Schaffhausen, Stadtbibliothek, MS Generalia 1 (*CLA* vii. 998), on which see A. O. and M. O. Anderson, *Adomnan's Life of Columba* (Edinburgh, 1961), pp. 3–8, 103–5, 164–75; J.-M. Picard, 'The Schaffhausen Adomnán: A Unique Witness to Hiberno-Latin', *Peritia*, 1 (1982), 216–49.

identifies the scribe as Dorbbéne, almost certainly the same man who died as bishop in Iona in October 713.[30] Although Dorbbéne's copy does not exactly represent the archetype, it is closer to the original than any other manuscript of an Irish Life. The Life's author, Adomnán, ninth abbot of Iona, died in 704; he was writing the work during the 690s, and it was probably finished about 700.[31] Adomnán may himself have been responsible for certain passages added to the text after the archetype of our B-texts was written but before Dorbbéne's copy was made.[32] It is a work on a generous scale, in three *libelli*, but follows no biographical pattern. Instead, the stories are grouped by subject—prophecies in Book I, miracles of power in Book II, and angelic visitations or heavenly lights in Book III, and within this framework stories are grouped in short sequences by subject, prophecies about battles (I 7–8) or kings (I 9–15), miracles of vengeance (II 22–5), miracles involving animals (II 26–8), and so on. Adomnán's style is ambitious and he makes some use of literary models, including Sulpicius Severus's Life of St Martin, Evagrius's Life of St Anthony, and Gregory the Great's *Dialogi*.[33] He is often concerned to provide authentication for the miracle stories he tells, and it has been suggested that some effort was made at Iona to collect formal *testimonia* during the early seventh century.[34] Adomnán, however, sometimes cites informants by name even when he is borrowing from a literary source such as Gregory.[35] We cannot be confident of the exact fidelity of Adomnán's account, nor even whether he was concerned to write what he thought to be factually correct. Historical truth has always been alien to the aims of hagiography.

It is a fortunate chance that the Schaffhausen manuscript left Iona and reached a place of security in Continental Europe. But if it had perished, we should still have Adomnán's work, for three manuscripts are known which descend from an equally early

---

[30] S. Mac Airt and G. Mac Niocaill (edd.), *The Annals of Ulster* (Dublin, 1983), s.a. 713. 5: 'Dorbeni Kathedram Iae obtenuit et .u. mensibus peractis in primatu .u. Kl. Nouimbris die Sabbati obiit.'

[31] J.-M. Picard, 'The Purpose of Adomnán's *Vita Columbae*', *Peritia*, 1 (1982), 160–77 (at pp. 167–9).

[32] Anderson and Anderson, *Adomnan's Life*, pp. 7–9.

[33] G. Brüning, 'Adamnans Vita Columbae und ihre Ableitungen', *ZCP* 11 (1916–17), 213–304.

[34] M. Herbert, *Iona, Kells, and Derry* (Oxford, 1988), pp. 13–22.

[35] Adomnán, *Vita S. Columbae*, I 43 (Anderson and Anderson, pp. 302–5).

sister-copy, and there is a fifth manuscript of the complete text
dating from the ninth century.[36] The same cannot be said for the
early Lives of St Patrick. When in 1647 Fr. John Colgan published
the first collection of various *uitae* of St Patrick, he included three
which contain much that is derived verbatim from the seventh-
century works of Muirchú moccu Machthéni and Tírechán. But
Colgan knew nothing of these authors' original works except a few
inadequate quotations which he took from James Ussher's
Britannicarum Ecclesiarum Antiquitates (1639). Colgan had no access
to Ussher's source for these, the Book of Armagh, written at
Armagh in 807.[37] Ussher himself scarcely made the use one would
have expected of the valuable texts on St Patrick in this manuscript, which were not published until 1827.[38]

Muirchú's *Vita S. Patricii* is a highly individual narrative,
composed at about the same period as Adomnán's *Vita S.
Columbae*, in a more dramatic and rhetorical style, describing the
career of St Patrick as the hero-saint who defeated paganism in
Ireland in a direct contest. The exact status of the Book of Armagh
as a witness to Muirchú's text is unclear. There are points of
inconsistency between the text and the capitulation in the manuscript, besides other internal features suggesting that some
reorganization had affected the text.[39] Two fragmentary manuscripts of Muirchú and those later Lives of St Patrick published by
Colgan whose authors used Muirchú's *uita* all point to an arrangement of the text differing in details from the copy in the Book of
Armagh. The differences are sufficient to make it difficult to
produce a satisfactory edition of the work, but do not greatly
hinder a reading of the text.

---

[36] J. Leclercq, 'Un recueil d'hagiographie colombanienne', *AB* 73 (1955), 193–
6; L. Bieler, [review of Anderson and Anderson, *Adomnan's Life of Columba*], *IHS*
13 (1962–3), 175–84.

[37] *CLA*, ii. 270; R. Sharpe, 'Palaeographical Considerations in the Study of the
Patrician Documents in the Book of Armagh', *Scriptorium*, 36 (1982), 3–28.

[38] On Ussher's use of the Book of Armagh, see J. Gwynn (ed.), *Liber Armachanus: The Book of Armagh* (Dublin, 1913), pp. cvii–cviii, cxix–cxxi. The texts
were first edited very inaccurately by Sir W. Betham, *Irish Antiquarian Researches* (2
vols.; Dublin, 1827).

[39] L. Bieler, *The Patrician Texts in the Book of Armagh* (Scriptores Latini
Hiberniae, 10; Dublin, 1979), pp. 62–122, is the best available text. The
difficulties are discussed in the introduction, pp. 1–35, but no satisfactory answer
is reached. Cf. R. Sharpe, 'The Patrician Texts', *Peritia*, 1 (1982), 363–9.

Tírechán's work is if anything even more individual than Muirchú's. Although its literary style is for the most part extremely simple, its narrative is not biographical; instead, it presents a series of stories in which St Patrick founds individual churches, using the saint's supposed itinerary as a linking device.[40] Tírechán's avowed purpose was to establish St Patrick's successors' claim to these churches, and the argument as a whole is advanced with a fair measure of sophistication. The Book of Armagh has the only surviving copy of this work,[41] which has no title and can hardly be regarded as a true *uita*. In the manuscript, it is presented as a sequel or complement to Muirchú's *uita*, and was once thought to be the later work, dated to about 700.[42] But there is now general agreement that Tírechán wrote before Muirchú, at a time not long after the church in Ireland as elsewhere was devastated by plague during the years 664–8.

Muirchú, in the preface to his *Vita S. Patricii*, refers to 'my father Cogitosus'. The relationship between them must have been one of spiritual or literary parentage, for Cogitosus, who is known to us as the author of a *Vita S. Brigitae*, belonged to a different kindred.[43] He wrote this Life at Kildare, St Brigit's principal church, probably around about 680. It is short, with only a rudimentary biographical framework. A few infant miracles are followed by a seemingly inconsequential series of other miracle stories, and the whole is framed by perfunctory references to St Brigit's birth and death. But of greater note are the remarkable passages of contemporary interest, the preface

---

[40] The text is edited by Bieler, *Patrician Texts*, pp. 122–62. For discussion see Binchy, 'Patrick and his Biographers', pp. 58–69, and L. Bieler, 'Tírechán als Erzähler', *Sitzungsberichte der bayerischen Akademie der Wissenschaften*, phil.-hist. Kl. 1974, no. 6.

[41] The reference by Hanson, *Saint Patrick, His Origins and His Career* (Oxford, 1968), p. 75 n. 3, to 'one other manuscript . . . in the Bodleian Library', proves disappointing. It can only refer to the excerpt in Oxford, Bodleian Library, MS Rawl. B. 480 (Clarendon MS 90, 91), f. 81ᵛ; this is a note made by James Ware from the Book of Armagh.

[42] E. MacNeill, 'The Earliest Lives of St Patrick', *JRSAI* 58 (1928), 1–21.

[43] The name Cogitosus was long thought to render Muirchú's supposed 'patronymic' *moccu Machthéni*, but Cogitosus subscribes himself as 'Cogitosus nepos hAedo' in a passage which is generally corrupted in the printed editions. See R. Sharpe, '*Vitae S. Brigitae*: The Oldest Texts', *Peritia*, 1 (1982), 81–106 (at pp. 83–7).

and the concluding chapters, in which Cogitosus writes about Kildare, its ecclesiastical status and its buildings. No happy survival such as the Schaffhausen Adomnán or the Book of Armagh has preserved an Irish copy of Cogitosus's *uita* but it is known from over sixty Continental manuscripts of the ninth century and later, and a further twenty-odd manuscripts contain lections excerpted from Cogitosus.[44]

Here, then, we have four authors known by name, all from the later seventh century, writing Lives of the three principal saints of Ireland—Patrick, Brigit, and Columba. But they differ completely from one another in their approach to their task and in their use of Latin. On this basis, one could not define any set of characteristics of Hiberno-Latin hagiography in the seventh century.

But these four do not represent the sum of our knowledge for that period. We know that there was a book on St Patrick written earlier than both Tírechán and Muirchú; for Tírechán refers to the *plana historia* of his master, Ultán of Ardbraccan, who died in 655.[45] Also, Dorbbéne, in his copy of Adomnán's *Vita S. Columbae*, added a passage quoted from a *Liber de uirtutibus S. Columbae* written by Cumméne Ailbe.[46] This was most likely written before Cumméne became abbot of Iona in 657, and may embody testimony to the saint's miracles collected in the time of Cumméne's uncle, Abbot Ségéne (623–52).[47] It is highly likely that Cogitosus was not the only person to attempt a Life of St Brigit in the seventh century. The same Ultán is credited with one, and so is Ailerán *sapiens* who died during the plagues of the 660s. Neither

---

[44] List by L. Bieler in R. J. Hayes, *Catalogue of the Manuscript Sources of Irish History* (11 vols.; Boston, Mass., 1965), i. 331–9, and Supplement (3 vols.; Boston, Mass., 1979), i. 78–9. The editions listed at *BHL* 1457 are all seriously defective. During the twentieth century editions have been projected by Esposito, Grosjean, Ó Briain, and Bieler, but have come to nothing. During 1977–9 I prepared a working text based on more than twenty manuscripts, but have not had the opportunity to complete the edition. In 1986 the Medieval Academy of Ireland accepted a proposal from Dr Picard and Dr Connolly for a full edition. This Life appears to have a capacity for defeating attempts to edit it.

[45] Tírechán §1.

[46] Quoted to supplement Adomnán, *Vita S. Columbae*, iii 5. The text attributed by Kenney and others to Cumméne (*BHL* 1884) is an abstract from Adomnán; see Anderson and Anderson, *Adomnán's Life*, pp. 13–17, and Brüning, 'Adamnans Vita Columbae', pp. 291–304.

[47] Herbert, *Iona, Kells, and Derry*, pp. 24–5.

claim carries much weight, and it is certainly impossible to identify any text as being the work of either.[48]

A key text, however, is that commonly known as *Vita I S. Brigitae*.[49] This Life can hardly date from much later than about 800, since a copy of it, already significantly corrupt, was written at Benediktbeuern in southern Germany during the first half of the ninth century; this is now London, British Library, MS Add. 34124.[50] How much earlier than 800 it may have been composed is a matter of dispute. Some have argued that the text dates from the seventh century, and that it was one of two sources used by Cogitosus about 680. Others suppose it to be an eighth-century reworking of seventh-century Lives, including that by Cogitosus.[51] But for our present purpose, this difference of opinion is immaterial. The important fact is that *Vita I S. Brigitae* much more nearly resembles the mass of undated Latin Lives, both in form and language, than it resembles the products of our known seventh-century hagiographers. The possibility is therefore opened up that some texts preserved in manuscripts of the fourteenth century, in our three collections which between them contain most of the known Latin Lives of Irish saints, might prove to be datable to the seventh or eighth century. The merely formal argument, from similarity of approach and expression, is a weak one: it has to be backed up by detailed analysis. But the criteria for dating texts in later medieval compilations have yet to be established.

Internal considerations have been used to date the earliest Life of St Darerca alias Monenna to the early part of the seventh century.[52] The date depends on a list of the three successors of St

---

[48] Sharpe, '*Vitae S. Brigitae*', pp. 96–101.

[49] It is so placed in *Acta Sanctorum*, Feb. I (1658), 118–34 (*BHL* 1455), though a better text of the Life is printed as *Vita III* in Colgan, *Trias*, pp. 527–42 (*BHL* 1456). A well-founded edition of this text remains a desideratum.

[50] B. Bischoff, *Die südostdeutschen Schreibschulen und Bibliotheken der Karolingerzeit* (2 vols.; Wiesbaden, 1974–80), ii. 199.

[51] The early date is proposed by M. Esposito, 'Notes on Latin Learning and Literature in Mediaeval Ireland, part IV: On the Early Latin Lives of St Brigid of Kildare', *Hermathena*, no. 49 (1935), 120–65, and defended by Sharpe, '*Vitae S. Brigitae*', pp. 89–96, 102–6. The later date is proposed by F. Ó Briain, 'Brigitana', *ZCP* 36 (1977), 112–37, and defended (in a more complex form) by K. McCone, 'Brigit in the Seventh Century: A Saint with Three Lives?', *Peritia*, 1 (1982), 107–45.

[52] M. Esposito, 'The Sources of Conchubranus' Life of St Monenna', *EHR* 35 (1920), 71–8; Kenney, *The Sources*, pp. 368–9.

Darerca, included in the common source of the extant texts. The last abbess named in it died in 624, and it is argued that the list must have been written in her time, or her successor's. Whether or not the argument is accepted, the supposed Primitive Life is lost to us and we are dependent on later derivatives. Still less satisfactory as a criterion for dating is a passage in the Life of St Íte concerning 'quidam uir, nomine Feargus, cuius filius adhuc uiuit'.[53] Even if one could be sure it came from the common source of the extant recensions of this Life, it would still seem likely to be a fictitious touch, intended to give a semblance of authenticity to the account.

Textual and recensional studies on the Lives of St Patrick have led to several conjectures of lost early texts. Bury thought that Irish sources, dating from as early as the sixth century, lay behind the work of Muirchú, but the case is very weak.[54] He also argued for the existence of a lost text W, conjectured as the common source of *Vita II S. Patricii* (of which the earliest manuscript dates from the eleventh century) and *Vita IV S. Patricii* (of which the only known copy dates from somewhere around 1100). W, he argued, derived principally from Muirchú, but occasionally used independent and more ancient sources.[55] Bieler, who shared Bury's view that a common source was necessary to explain the relationship of *Vita II* and *Vita IV*, suggested as a tentative *terminus ante quem* the year 774.[56] This rests on the same kind of argument as we have seen above, namely that both texts refer in the present tense to the veneration of relics at the church of *Inis Baitheni*, which according to the Annals of Ulster was burnt in that year. But we have no way of knowing whether the destruction was total, though the case of other 'burning' annals suggests it was not; and if it was total, that is not to say that the church, after rebuilding, did not find some means of recovering relics to continue the veneration. With this

[53] *Vita S. Itae* (**D**) §28. (The **A**- and **O**-texts, which are probably based on the same source as the **D**-text, lack the reference to the son.) Colgan, *Acta*, p. 71 n. 2 (*recte* 1) uses this argument to date the *uita* to *c.*640. Kenney, *The Sources*, p. 390 repeats it with a caution about 'such touches of verisimilitude'.

[54] J. B. Bury, 'The Tradition of Muirchú's Text', *Hermathena*, no. 28 (1902), 172–207 (at pp. 198 n. 2, 200); id., 'Sources of the Early Patrician Documents', *EHR*, 19 (1904), 493–503.

[55] Bury, 'The Tradition of Muirchú's Text', pp. 186–205.

[56] L. Bieler, *Four Latin Lives of St Patrick* (Scriptores Latini Hiberniae, 8; Dublin, 1971), pp. 7–13. In Bieler's view, this common source W was dependent on Muirchú, whereas Bury held that W preceded Muirchú.

dating criterion gone, all the evidence for extensive work on the Life of St Patrick in the eighth century disappears, and one is left with older texts being copied into the Book of Armagh in 807.

This leaves no Latin Life of an Irish saint, composed in Ireland, which can be confidently dated after 700 but before the late eleventh century. In effect, as soon as the relatively safe waters of the seventh century are behind us, we are on that 'pelagus immensum ... uiris peritissimis formidandum' of which the hagiographers complain.[57] For the great majority of Irish *uitae*, there are no named and datable authors and no early manuscripts which might provide some fixed point by which to date the texts.

One text, however, may be datable quite closely on internal evidence. It is not really a saint's Life but a romance in the tradition of the voyage tales, *Nauigatio S. Brendani*. For many years, its date has been uncertain, although various views have been put forward. Carl Selmer argued for the early tenth century, and Giovanni Orlandi has more recently suggested the ninth century.[58] The earlier date was also favoured by Professor Carney, who long ago pointed out the shortcomings of Selmer's argument.[59] Now David Dumville has questioned this date, and argued instead for a date not later than the third quarter of the eighth century.[60] His argument rests on the historical context which makes best sense of the statement of St Brendan's family connexions in the opening sentence. The mere fact that the *Nauigatio* opens with such a statement of family links shows that the author was an Irishman, and by implication shows his concern with Irish dynastic politics. The work was presumably copied in Ireland for some time, for its story was well known. But there is no trace of any manuscript tradition of the *Nauigatio* in Ireland. Although there are later medieval copies of Irish provenance, in our three collections of *uitae*, in which the *Nauigatio* is incorporated

---

[57] Cogitosus, *Vita S. Brigitae*, subscriptio; cf. M. Winterbottom, 'Variations on a Nautical Theme', *Hermathena*, no. 120 (1976), 55–8.

[58] C. Selmer (ed.) *Nauigatio Sancti Brendani Abbatis* (Notre Dame, Ind., 1959), pp. xxvii–xxix; G. Orlandi, *Navigatio Sancti Brendani, I: Introduzione* (Milan, 1968), pp. 72–3.

[59] J. Carney, [review of Selmer's edition], *Medium Ævum*, 32 (1963), 37–44 (at pp. 40, 43).

[60] D. N. Dumville, 'Two Approaches to the Dating of *Nauigatio Sancti Brendani*', *Studi medievali*, 3rd ser., 29 (1988), 87–102. I am grateful to Dr Dumville for letting me read the typescript of this essay.

in a more conventional *uita*, the textual affinities of these copies are with branches of the text-tradition which diverged during transmission on the Continent.[61]

The *Nauigatio S. Brendani* is not the only work composed in early medieval Ireland which owes its survival to textual transmission in Continental libraries. No copy of Adomnán survived on Irish soil, nor did Cogitosus's Life of St Brigit, nor *Vita II* and *Vita III S. Patricii*. In fact, the only *uitae* for which we have manuscript evidence in Ireland before 1300 are those in the Patrician section of the Book of Armagh. For the others, we are entirely indebted to the Irishmen who carried their books to the Continent, and the Frankish, German, Italian, and other scholars who copied and kept the texts. We cannot be sure how early copies of these Lives first came into Continental libraries: the fragmentary Vienna copy of Muirchú, the oldest manuscript in this category, was written in an Anglo-Saxon centre on the Continent in the late eighth century.[62] But the ninth and tenth centuries saw a considerable increase in interest.

There are two manuscripts of Cogitosus's Life of St Brigit written in north-east France in the first third of the ninth century.[63] By the end of the tenth century the text was widely distributed, and three distinct manuscript families were already established. *Vita I S. Brigitae* was perhaps less widely known, but this too is represented by several copies of the ninth and tenth centuries.[64] Moreover, one of the Irish scholars who settled in Europe, probably St Donatus of Fiesole, recast her Life in Latin verse for an Italian audience.[65] The Life of St Columba was being copied in

---

[61] Orlandi, *Navigatio*, p. 17 n. 6 (**O** has French connexions), p. 19 (**S**[1] from a French family), p. 24 n. 2 (**D** from a German family).

[62] *CLA*, x. 1514; L. Bieler, 'Studies on the Text of Muirchú, II: The Vienna Fragments', *PRIA* 59C (1959), 181–95.

[63] Reims, Bibliothèque municipale, MS 296 (Reims, s. ix[in]), and Paris, Bibliothèque nationale, MS lat. 2999 (Saint-Amand, s. ix[in]).

[64] London, BL, MS Add. 34124 (Benediktbeuern, s. ix[1]) is the oldest, and a lost manuscript transcribed by Fr. Stephen White at St Magnus, Regensburg, may have been tenth-century; Zürich, Zentralbibliothek MS Rheinau 81 (s. x) and Munich, Staatsbibliothek, Clm. 2531 (s. x).

[65] The verse Life is edited by D. N. Kissane, '*Vita Metrica Sanctae Brigidae*: A Critical Edition', *PRIA* 77C (1977), 57–192. The attribution of this text to Donatus was suggested by Esposito, 'On the Early Lives of St Brigid', pp. 127–9. It is attacked, but not convincingly, by McCone, 'An Introduction to Early Irish Saints' Lives', pp. 40–2.

France in the ninth century, and at the same period the shorter recension of Adomnán's text made its first appearance.[66] This abbreviated text appears to have been produced for Continental circulation. In the 840s Walahfrid Strabo was moved to describe in verse how St Blathmac of Iona was martyred by Scandinavian raiders when he would not give away the hiding-place of St Columba's relics.[67]

1.3. Latin and Irish

There can be little doubt that the seventh and eighth centuries were the heyday of Latin learning in Ireland. Although the greatest of Hiberno-Latin writers belong to the ninth century, the careers of these men were Continental. Obviously, they must have received their early education in Ireland, but there is nothing to suggest that they could enjoy at home the kind of intellectual and literary environment that they found in the schools of the Carolingian empire of the ninth century. By this date, Ireland had effectively exported her Latin culture to Francia. There is, moreover, contemporary evidence from Ireland itself that in the ninth century the active use of Latin as a literary medium fell into decline. The positive evidence is incomplete, but the significant increase in the proportion of entries made in Irish in the Annals of Ulster against those made in Latin dates from the early ninth century.[68] The negative evidence seems overwhelming. Although there are many Latin texts thought to date from the seventh and eighth centuries, hardly any have been assigned dates from the ninth or tenth century. Then in the eleventh and more noticeably the twelfth century we see a revival.

It may perhaps be argued that the survival of some manuscripts

---

[66] Metz, Bibliothèque du Grand Séminaire, MS 1 (Saint-Mihiel, s. ix), has the longer recension of the text. See Leclercq, 'Un recueil d'hagiographie colombanienne', pp. 193–6; Bieler, [review of Anderson and Anderson], pp. 175–84. The Saint-Mihiel manuscript was known to Stephen White and, through him, to Ussher; W. Reeves (ed.), *The Life of St Columba by Adamnan* (Irish Archaeological and Celtic Society, Dublin, 1857; Bannatyne Club, Edinburgh, 1857), p. xxxviii n.

[67] Kenney, *The Sources*, no. 227.

[68] D. N. Dumville, 'Latin and Irish in the *Annals of Ulster*, A.D. 431–1050', in *Ireland in Early Mediaeval Europe*, ed. D. Whitelock *et al.* (Cambridge, 1982), pp. 320–41 (table at p. 336).

from the period undermines this impression. But even among liturgical manuscripts, the number produced in the ninth, tenth, and eleventh centuries seems considerably less than was produced before about 800.

The eighth to ninth century is the first period when we see texts originally written in Latin being turned into Irish. It is the period of the major surviving Irish glosses and commentaries on Latin texts.[69] It is the period when the Lambeth Commentary on Matthew was put into Irish.[70] And the same phenomenon of translation affects the Lives of saints. A Latin text of the Life of St Brigit was incompletely put into Irish, probably in the early ninth century. About one quarter of the text as we have it is still in Latin, and it may be that the translation began as interlinear gloss.[71] Where the gloss existed, it was copied, but in passages where there was no gloss, the original Latin was copied. The Life of St Patrick in Irish, commonly known as the Tripartite Life, has been variously dated. This text is a greatly expanded revision of Tírechán, updating his ecclesiastical interests and introducing a greater attention to political considerations. Although the Tripartite Life is one of the most valuable witnesses to Irish political geography, the historical arguments advanced for its date are unconvincing. Linguistically it is not uniform, but may probably be assigned to the tenth century.[72]

---

[69] The three principal glossed manuscripts are Würzburg, Universitäts-bibliothek, MS p. th. f. 12 (*CLA* ix. 1403), from the late eighth century (Kenney, *The Sources*, no. 461); Milan, Biblioteca Ambrosiana, MS C 301 inf., from the ninth century (Kenney, *The Sources*, no. 47); and St. Gallen, Stiftsbibliothek, MS 904, the 'St Gall Priscian', from the ninth century (Kenney, *The Sources*, no. 533). Some of the glosses in the last of these come from the same source as glosses in another early copy of Priscian, the ninth-century Karlsruhe, Landesbibliothek, MS Augiensis CXXXII.

[70] L. Bieler and J. Carney (edd. and trans.), 'The Lambeth Commentary', *Ériu*, 23 (1972), 1–55. Carney, pp. 7–9, suggests a date in the early eighth century, 'marginally earlier' than the Würzburg Glosses.

[71] D. Ó hAodha, *Bethu Brigte* (Dublin, 1978), p. xix n. 49, hesitates between this view and the possibility of an originally bilingual Life.

[72] K. Mulchrone, 'Die Abfassungszeit und Überlieferung der Vita Tripartita', *ŽCP* 16 (1926–7), 1–94, dated the Urtext of the Tripartite to the reign of Cenn Gécán, king of Cashel (895–901), mentioned in the text. But G. S. Mac Eoin, 'The Dating of Middle Irish Texts', *PBA* 68 (1982), 109–37, has argued that even on its own terms her argument should lead to a date later in the tenth century (pp. 127–34). On linguistic grounds, the Tripartite has been dated to the tenth century by K. H. Jackson, 'The Date of the Tripartite Life of St Patrick', *ŽCP* 41 (1986), 5–45.

The change in the literary milieu, from one in which Latin held its own to one which was bilingual and increasingly moving towards the vernacular, has never been treated as a watershed in the history of Hiberno-Latin hagiography.[73] Kenney, who has suggested dates for more Lives than anyone else, appears not to have been conscious of this divide, though he was aware of the change in the language of learned writing.[74] For him the watershed was the Scandinavian invasions, a notion in which he was under the influence of Heinrich Zimmer.[75] Texts which Kenney thought were 'early' or 'fairly early' he dated to no later than the ninth or tenth century, 'late' texts to the eleventh or twelfth century. But he was quite prepared to contemplate that the Lives of SS. Comgall, Colmán Élo, or Coemgen were written in the tenth century.[76] He offers such a date without prejudice as regards one recension or another. It cannot be established that the Vikings' attacks had any particular impact on the hagiography or on the intellectual activity of Irish schools generally. Although pressure from the activity of Scandinavian invaders may have induced individual scholars to leave Ireland, the argument that this led to the eclipse of Latin as a literary medium in Ireland is impossible to accept. Other reasons must be found to explain why,

---

[73] McCone has come closest to this: 'The earliest Irish saints' Lives are all in Latin and owe much to Continental models, but were subjected from an early period to increasing influence from secular tradition. . . . A further stage in this assimilation to native patterns was actually to write saints' Lives in Irish rather than in Latin, a process roughly parallel to the gradual drift from Latin to Irish in the annals'; K. McCone, 'An Introduction to Early Irish Saints' Lives', *The Maynooth Review*, 11 (1984), 38.

[74] Kenney, *The Sources*, p. 11, offers a date of 879 × 932 for this 'shift in emphasis from Latin to Irish', arguing from the appearance of *fer léiginn* 'man of reading' to replace *scriba* as the annalistic term for master of the schools.

[75] Kenney, *The Sources*, p. 295 and n. 13, citing H. Zimmer, *Göttingische gelehrte Anzeigen* (1891), pp. 185–6. The *idée fixe* of Zimmer's several articles in 1891 (on which see H. d'Arbois de Jubainville, *Revue celtique*, 12 (1891), 393–7) was the importance of the Vikings' impact on Ireland. He would indulge in any amount of special pleading in this cause, stretching the date of the Book of Armagh to the 840s in one article, 'Keltische Beiträge, III', *Zeitschrift für deutsches Alterthum*, 35 (1891), 1–178, at p. 53 n., but in another, 'Die frühesten Berührungen der Iren mit den Nordgemanen', *Sitzungsberichte der königlich Preussischen Akademie der Wissenschaften zu Berlin* (1891), 279–317, reversing direction and making the Vikings responsible for the death of St Donnan in 617! No argument brought forward constitutes serious evidence for the dating of the Latin saints' Lives.

[76] Kenney, *The Sources*, pp. 397, 400, 404.

during the ninth and tenth centuries, such Latin culture as had
existed in Ireland gave way to the strong literary tradition in the
Irish language.[77] The dominance of the Irish language in this
period makes it seem unlikely that any Latin *uitae* were composed
in Ireland at least between 850 and 1050, and perhaps over a
longer period.

Written literature in Irish had begun before 600, although I
hesitate to say anything about how much survives from that
period, or how much it represents a literary culture rather than the
written survivals of oral verse.[78] During the seventh century, Irish
literary prose came into existence, apparently under the influence
of Latin. In the legal schools, this took the form of didactic prose
modelled on Latin schoolbooks.[79] But religious prose broke away
from the often arcane expressions of the oldest Irish literature,
arguably before the middle of the seventh century, and aimed
instead at direct simplicity.[80] The number of religious texts in Irish
from the seventh century is probably not large, but before the end
of the century the secular prose tales were being written down, and
this developed rapidly as a popular literary vehicle during the
eighth century. The vitality of vernacular literature in this period
may well be judged to exceed that of the Latin learning displayed
in ecclesiastical works of the period.

In the ninth century, we find that the most basic monastic books
were written in Irish, not Latin. A text as linguistically repetitive
and undemanding as a penitential was put into Irish, and all the
writings of the school associated with Maelruain of Tallaght were
in the vernacular, including the Rule of the Céli Dé.[81] The only

[77] This and the related question of what was happening in Irish literature
during the ninth century are discussed by P. Mac Cana, 'The Influence of the
Vikings on Celtic Literature', in *Proceedings of the International Congress of Celtic
Studies, Dublin, 1959*, ed. B. Ó Cuív (Dublin, 1962), pp. 78–118 (at pp. 99–112,
especially p. 110).

[78] On the oldest literary remains in Irish, see J. Carney, 'Three Old Irish
Accentual Poems', *Ériu*, 22 (1971), 23–80; id., 'Aspects of Archaic Irish', *Éigse*, 17
(1977–9), 417–35; id., 'On the Dating of Early Irish Verse', *Éigse*, 19 (1982–3),
177–216. The last provides a list of texts.

[79] T. M. Charles-Edwards, 'The *Corpus Iuris Hibernici*', *Studia Hibernica*, 20
(1980), 141–62.

[80] D. Greene, 'Archaic Irish', in *Indogermanisch und Keltisch*, ed. K. H. Schmidt
(Wiesbaden, 1977), pp. 11–33.

[81] On the Old Irish penitential, see Kenney, *The Sources*, p. 242, and D. A.
Binchy in L. Bieler, *The Irish Penitentials* (Scriptores Latini Hiberniae, 5; Dublin,

known exceptions are liturgical.[82] If the monastic schools no longer used Latin for texts of this elementary kind, it is hardly likely that they were writing the Lives of their patrons—texts directed at a wider and less educated audience if they were to have any value as advertisements—in Latin.

From the Middle Irish period of the ninth to twelfth centuries, there is a considerable quantity of hagiographical material in the vernacular. Little of it has been discussed with regard to its more precise date. The Life of Adomnán has been dated to about 960, but for the rest there are no close dates.[83] A group of saints' Lives— perhaps as many as nine—must have existed in Irish when they were incorporated into a Latin-Irish bilingual *homiliarium*, suitably decked out with homiletic prefaces and perorations. The compilation of this is likely to date from about 1100 or later, and may have extended over a period of time. The texts included were in some cases perhaps as much as a century older, though others were recent compositions.[84] There had also grown up a considerable quantity of disconnected stories or anecdotes. Many of these were copied into the large literary compendia of the later Middle

1963), pp. 258–77. The texts attributed to the school of Maelruain are listed by Kenney, *The Sources*, no. 264 ('The Monastery of Tallaght'), no. 266 ('The Rule of the Céli Dé').

[82] The principal exception is the Stowe Missal, now Dublin, Royal Irish Academy, MS D. II. 3, ff. 12–67 (s. viii/ix). Blume, *Analecta Hymnica*, 51 (1908), 333–5 (no. 249), attributed the hymn, 'Archangelum mirum magnum', following the statement of a collect associated with the hymn; Kenney, *The Sources*, p. 726.

[83] The arguments are summarized by Herbert, *Iona, Kells, and Derry*, pp. 158–71. Full discussion is given in the new edition of the Life by M. Herbert and P. Ó Riain, *Betha Adamnáin* (London, 1988). The argument for a date between 956 and 964, pp. 7–31, depends largely on the encoded use of ancestral names from the seventh century to represent contemporary figures or peoples in the tenth. In particular Congal(ach) mac Fergusa (d. 710), mentioned once in the Life, is seen as surrogate for Congalach mac Maile Mithig (d. 956); both were kings of Tara.

[84] The dating of these homilies, preserved chiefly in the fifteenth-century *Leabhar Breac*, is a vexed question, most recently discussed by K. H. Jackson, 'The Historical Grammar of Irish: Some Actualities and Some Desiderata', in *Proceedings of the Sixth International Congress of Celtic Studies, Galway, 1979*, ed. G. S. Mac Eoin (Dublin, 1983), pp. 1–18 (pp. 6–7), and id., 'The Date of the Tripartite Life', pp. 9–12. The suggestion of F. Mac Donncha, 'Middle Irish Homilies', *Proceedings of the Irish Biblical Association*, 1 (1976), 59–71, that the *homiliarium* was the work of Mael Ísu Ó Brolcháin (d. 1086), is speculative. Herbert, *Iona, Kells, and Derry*, p. 195, speaks of 'a school of homileticists centred on Armagh'.

Ages, particularly the Book of Leinster (s. xii/xiii), the *Leabhar Breac* (*c.* 1410), and the Book of Lismore (s. xv²). Some have been published.[85] Similar stories are sometimes told or alluded to in the tenth- and eleventh-century scholia on the Latin and Irish poetry in the *Liber Hymnorum*, and on the early ninth-century verse martyrology *Félire Oenguso*.[86] The relationship between this anecdotal material and the Lives of saints deserves to be properly investigated. Some stories certainly pass from one tradition to the other. For example, an Irish story about St Ruadán appears to have been translated into Latin (not before the late twelfth century, to judge from the use of the Anglo-Norman name *Odo* to represent *Aed*) and incorporated into the Latin Life.[87]

But during the greater part of three centuries—the ninth, tenth, and eleventh—the literary initiative lay in the vernacular and not in Latin. Where dates have been argued for Latin texts in this period, and not merely advanced as a rough guess, the arguments are very doubtful. Brüning, followed by Kenney, regarded part of the S-text Life of St Columba as older than *Vita S. Brendani* (which Plummer had thought older than the *Nauigatio*). The existence of tenth-century manuscripts of the latter pushed the date of this Life of St Columba back to the ninth century. The *Vita S. Brendani*, however, is known only from the late medieval collections; the recension in question is apparently the fullest text, but it is not the original, whose text and date are extremely uncertain.[88] A fuller understanding of the textual relationship will permit an alternative explanation.[89]

[85] Listed by Plummer, 'A Tentative Catalogue', pp. 198–224. More up-to-date information on publication can be had from the prefaces to the separate volumes of Best *et al.*, *The Book of Leinster*.

[86] The *Liber Hymnorum* and its scholia were edited by J. H. Bernard and R. Atkinson, *The Irish Liber Hymnorum* (2 vols., Henry Bradshaw Society, 13, 14; London, 1898). The *Félire* has been edited twice by W. Stokes, *On the Calendar of Oengus* (Dublin, 1880), which prints several texts separately, and *Félire Oengusso: The Martyrology of Oengus the Culdee* (Henry Bradshaw Society, 29; London, 1905).

[87] *Vita S. Ruadani* S §12, D §§15–18; cf. *Stair ar Aedh Baclámh*, edited from the Book of Lismore, ff. 93ra–95ra, by S. H. O'Grady, *Silva Gadelica* (2 vols.; London, 1892), i. 66–71, ii. 70–4. See below, p. 331.

[88] 'La ricostruzione di questa appare dunque molto problematica' (Orlandi, *Navigatio*, p. 11). He goes on to suggest, p. 53, a date in the eighth century, believing the Life to be earlier than Bili's *Vita S. Machutis*.

[89] Brüning, 'Adamnans Vita Columbae', pp. 281–2, followed by Kenney, *The Sources*, p. 434, meant this to apply to *Vita S. Columbae* (S) §§1–19, which form a

During the late eleventh century, Latin came back into active use. This would seem to be a reflexion of real changes in the Irish church, which, after years of insulation from outside influence, began once again to see itself as part of a wider world. The correspondence of Lanfranc, Anselm, and Ralph d'Escures as archbishop of Canterbury with Irishmen sufficiently indicates the context of the renewed use of Latin.[90] More remarkable perhaps is the letter from St Bernard to Diarmait mac Murchada, king of Leinster.[91] The Latin authors of the late eleventh century were outward-looking prelates, Bishop Patrick of Dublin and Bishop Gilbert of Limerick.[92] Once again books other than liturgical works were written in Latin,[93] though still in Irish script—caroline minuscule was never adopted in Ireland, as far as one can tell.

Two *uitae* have been thought to date from this period. An English manuscript has preserved the Life of St Monenna by Conchubranus, perhaps a Latinization of the Irish name

distinct series within the S-text. *Vita S. Brendani* (O) § 104 has a unique passage specifically derived from a Life of St Columba, which clearly matches § 14 of the S-text of his Life and the equivalent passage in the O-text. The S- and O-texts of this Life were taken from the same exemplar (see below, Chapter 9), which cannot have been older than the thirteenth century. The compiler of the O-collection, whose version of the Life of St Brendan is his own expanded text, was himself responsible for the interpolation of the extract from this particular Life of St Columba; this was probably made not long before or after 1300. Miss Brüning seems to have misunderstood what Plummer says about the date of *Vita S. Brendani*; although he regarded the lost original of the *uita* as early, he himself demonstrated that the O-text was coeval with the work of the collector.

[90] Six letters from Ireland to archbishops of Canterbury survive from the period 1074–1121; see M. Lapidge and R. Sharpe, *A Bibliography of Celtic-Latin Literature 400–1200* (Dublin, 1985), nos. 313, 618, 619, 622, 624, 625.

[91] Edited by J. Leclercq, *Recueil d'études sur Saint Bernard et ses écrits* (3 vols.; Rome, 1962–9), ii. 313–18.

[92] Lapidge and Sharpe, *A Bibliography*, nos. 309–10, 312–13.

[93] For example, fragments of copies of the *Ars Grammatica* of Clemens Scottus and of a treatise *De Abaco*, written s. xi/xii, apparently at Glendalough before 1106, and now London, BL, MS Egerton 3323 ff. 16, 18; see L. Bieler and B. Bischoff, 'Fragmente zweier frühmittelalterlicher Schulbücher aus Glendalough', *Celtica*, 3 (1955), 211–20. Or a copy of Gregory the Great's *Moralia in Job* (now incomplete), written at Armagh, s. xii[1], now Oxford, Bodleian Library, MS Laud misc. 460. Or a collection including Calcidius's translation of Plato's *Timaeus* and an epitome of Eriugena's *Periphyseon*, of similar date, now at Oxford, Bodleian Library, MS Auct. F. 3. 15.

Conchobar.[94] The dating of this text to the eleventh century rests on the fact that it was known to Geoffrey of Burton and used by him in his Life of St Modwenna, written about the second quarter of the twelfth century.[95] One should probably not attempt to push its date back much before 1100. Another text, the Life of St Maedóc, is found in a collection of Lives of Welsh saints from Monmouth. It has been suggested that this Life was translated from Irish into Latin for a Welsh audience in the late eleventh century. The date in this case depends on the supposed use of the text by Rhygyfarch ap Sulien in his Life of St David.[96]

1.4. The Twelfth Century

The twelfth century was a period of great literary activity in Ireland, both in Irish and in Latin. Old materials were being collected on a considerable scale and put into shape during the late eleventh and twelfth centuries.[97] But new material was being composed as well. The Middle Irish *Betha Colmáin maic Luacháin* has been dated to the first half of the twelfth century, when, in 1122, the saint's relics were rediscovered.[98] The Lives of St Flannán, patron of the O'Briens of Killaloe, and St Mochuille

[94] M. Esposito, 'The Sources of Conchubranus' Life', p. 71. The text, first edited by Esposito, 'Conchubrani Vita Sanctae Monennae', *PRIA* 28C (1910), 202–38, has been re-edited by the Ulster Society for Medieval Latin Studies, 'The Life of St Monenna by Conchubranus', *Seanchas Ard Mhacha*, 9 (1978–9), 250–73, and 10 (1980–2), 117–41 and 426–54.

[95] London, BL, MS Add. 57533 (*olim* Mostyn 260) (s. xii), ff. 81–113ᵛ and London, BL, MS Royal 15 B iv (Burton-on-Trent, s. xiii), ff. 76–88.

[96] Plummer, *Vitae*, vol. i, p. lxxvi; the dating rests on C. N. L. Brooke, 'St Peter of Gloucester and St Cadog of Llancarfan', in *Celt and Saxon: Studies in the Early British Border*, ed. N. K. Chadwick (Cambridge, 1963), pp. 294–7 (repr. pp. 78–81). Doherty, 'The Irish hagiographer', p. 18, suggests that Rhygyfarch's father Sulien brought the Life, specially translated into Latin, from Ireland about 1072; he further suggests, from encoded information in the contents, that the Irish original was written between 1042 and 1072. I am not fully convinced by Brooke's argument for Rhygyfarch's knowledge of the Life, but this affects the date of transference to Wales rather than the date of original composition.

[97] The supreme examples are the historical collections in the so-called Book of Glendalough, Oxford, Bodleian Library, MS Rawl. B. 502, and the literary collection in *Lebor na hUidre*, Dublin, Royal Irish Academy, MS 23 E 25.

[98] K. Meyer, *Betha Colmáin maic Lúacháin* (Todd Lecture Series, 17; Dublin, 1911). The discovery of the relics is recorded in AU 1122, and a colophon to the Life mentions the making of a new shrine by a goldsmith.

were written from scratch by a politically committed Munsterman in the 1160s.[99] The unusual aspect of these two works, composed in a ponderous Latin style unlike that of any other Hiberno-Latin *uita*, is that the author was trained in southern Germany, where at that date there was a widespread network of monasteries with Irish personnel and Irish connexions, and where he imbibed imperialist leanings. The oldest manuscripts of both Lives are Continental and date from the late twelfth century; both texts were known in Ireland, perhaps quite soon after they were composed, but the earliest manuscript witness from Ireland is one of our fourteenth-century collections.[100]

The second half of the twelfth century offers several signs of hagiographical exchanges between Ireland and the Continent. The same manuscripts as contain the Life of St Mochuille have other texts of Irish interest. Many, like the Lives of St Patrick, St Brigit, and St Columba, and *Nauigatio S. Brendani*, were well known on the Continent. But the incomplete Life of St Coemgen, in two manuscripts from Bavaria, and the Life of St Íte in others, antedate the related Lives in the Irish collections.[101] The fragment of a Life of St Rónán, in one of the same manuscripts, is even more

---

[99] D. Ó Corráin, 'Foreign Connections and Domestic Politics: Killaloe and the Uí Briain in Twelfth-Century Hagiography', in *Ireland in Early Mediaeval Europe*, ed. D. Whitelock *et al.* (Cambridge, 1982), pp. 213–31.

[100] The Life of St Mochuille is found in manuscripts of the Austrian Great Legendary from the late twelfth century; that of St Flannán once existed in a late twelfth-century copy, of which a fragment survives in Göttweig, Stiftsbibliothek, XII.1, no. 33.

[101] Neither of these Lives has been printed. The Life of St Coemgen is found in Rein, Stiftsbibliothek, MS 51 ff. 28ᵛ–31ʳ and Heiligenkreuz, Stiftsbibliothek, MS 12 ff. 220ᵛ–221ʳ. Its text is a mere fragment distantly related to the Lives in the later collections. It is briefly discussed by P. Grosjean, 'Relations mutuelles des Vies latines de S. Cáemgen de Glenn dá locha', *AB* 63 (1945), 122–9. The Life of St Íte (*BHL* 4498) is found in four out of five manuscripts of the Austrian Great Legendary: Admont, Stiftsbibliothek, MS 25 ff. 186ʳ–189ᵛ; Heiligenkreuz, Stiftsbibliothek, MS 12 ff. 163ʳ–166ᵛ; Lilienfeld, Stiftsbibliothek, MS 59 ff. 34ʳ–37ʳ; and Melk, Stiftsbibliothek, MS 674 ff. 46ᵛ–52ʳ. As Poncelet noted, 'De Magno Legendario Austriaco', *AB* 17 (1898), p. 159, this text may be dated to the middle of the twelfth century from the reference to a recent miracle associated with St Herluca (d. 1127) in Bavaria. It is related to the recension of the Life of St Íte (*BHL* 4497) in the D-collection, but verbal comparisons suggest that the relationship is not direct; it seems probable that the Bavarian version and that in D were edited independently from the same lost Life. This lost Life must have been written, therefore, before the middle of the twelfth century.

surprising; it reads like many of the Hiberno-Latin Lives in the medieval collections, yet it is unknown in any Irish source.[102] The occurrence of Irish saints in the legendaries of Bavaria and Lower Austria may perhaps be put down to the activities of the *Schotten-klöster* in the twelfth century. Although there is no direct manuscript evidence for a connexion, there was considerable coming and going between Ireland and the Irish foundations at Regensburg and elsewhere. Interest in at least one Irish saint, however, spread widely through the Cistercian order: St Malachy of Armagh died in the arms of St Bernard of Clairvaux, who was moved to learn the facts of Malachy's life and to write it up as an example of holiness.[103] St Bernard's Life of St Malachy is the most nearly contemporary Life of any Irish saint. Its nearest rival for this status is probably the Life of St Lawrence of Dublin, who also died abroad, at Eu in Normandy in 1180. Material in support of his canonization was soon collected, including a *liber de miraculis* by Bishop Malachy of Louth and depositions from several Irish contemporaries; but the case was put to the Holy See, not by the clergy of Dublin, as one might have expected, but by the canons of Eu.[104] They turned for information to a successor in the see, Henry of London, archbishop of Dublin (1213–28); his draft account of Lawrence's career has been identified with the 'Arsenal Life'.[105] The final text of the developed *uita* was not completed until after his formal canonization in 1226. The Lives of both Malachy and Lawrence were both copied in Ireland, though how quickly they became available there is not known.

One might guess that it was during the same period that copies came to Ireland of texts such as *Vita I S. Brigitae* and the *Nauigatio S. Brendani*. Although both were composed in Ireland, the textual

[102] Edited by A. Poncelet, *AB* 17 (1898), 161–6.

[103] Edited by J. Leclercq and A. Gwynn in *Opera S. Bernardi*, ed. J. Leclercq, C. H. Talbot, and H. Rochais (8 vols.; Rome, 1957–77), iii. 295–378. The translation by H. J. Lawlor, *St Bernard of Clairvaux's Life of St Malachy of Armagh* (London, 1920), has valuable notes.

[104] Although it is known that the account by Bishop Malachy was in circulation before 1191, this work has not been identified in the dossier assembled at Eu; see M. V. Ronan, 'St Laurentius, Archbishop of Dublin: Original Testimonies for Canonization', *IER*[5] 27 (1926), 347–64 (at pp. 350, 352–3), and ibid. 28 (1926), 247–56, 467–80, and ('Lessons, hymns, litanies, and prayers') 596–612.

[105] M. V. Roche, 'The Latin Lives of St Laurence of Dublin, Edited with a Critical Introduction' (University College, Dublin, Ph.D. thesis, 1981), i. 69–72.

affinities of the copies in manuscripts written in Ireland show that
these descend from Continental branches of the transmission.[106]
We know of no continuous text-tradition in Ireland. The same is
true of *Vita III S. Patricii* and of Adomnán's Life of St Columba.
The Life of St Fursu, found in two of the three medieval
collections, perhaps also arrived in Ireland in the same phase of
importation of texts.

Interest in Ireland on the Continent, and especially in southern
Germany and Austria, shows in the inclusion of Irish saints in the
legendaries, in the dissemination of St Bernard's Life of Malachy,
and in the popularity of texts such as the *Visio cuiusdam Hiberniensis*
(as it is titled in many manuscripts), familarly known as the *Visio
Tnugdali*, and the *Purgatorium S. Patricii*, written in England by H.
of Saltrey. The increasing number of copies, however, of the Lives
of St Patrick, especially *Vita III*, and of St Brigit, especially Cogitosus, is not so much an index of interest in Ireland as of the
multiplication of *legendaria*. I have tended to assume that the
Continental interest in Irish saints may have led to the transmission of texts *to* Ireland as well as *from* Ireland. This is a
minimal assumption. The alternative is that in the late twelfth
century, or perhaps later, there was an upsurge of hagiographical
interest within Ireland, which led to the seeking out of Lives of
Irish interest. I do not think it is possible readily to choose between
the two.

It is, however, certainly true that in the twelfth century there was
a fair amount of hagiographical activity in Ireland. The Bollandist
Daniel Papebroch attributed this to the arrival in Ireland of the
Cistercians and other Continental religious orders.[107] He was
followed by Plummer and Kenney.[108] The incomplete Life of St
Buite in the Oxford collection is one of the few texts to offer any
foundation for this view in that it seeks to associate the saint, who
supposedly died in the sixth century, with the twelfth-century

---

[106] Of the two copies of *Vita I S. Brigitae* from Ireland, that in O is said often to
agree with Saint-Omer, Bibliothèque municipale, MS 715, and Cambrai, Bibliothèque municipale, MS 857 (both used in the Bollandist edition), which exhibit
β-text and 'alternative ending'; S. Connolly, 'The Authorship and Manuscript
Tradition of *Vita I Sanctae Brigitae*', *Manuscripta*, 16 (1972), 67–82 (pp. 78–80). The
copy in D was evidently also a β-text, as I show in Chapter 5. On the copies of
Nauigatio S. Brendani transmitted in Ireland, see above, n. 61.

[107] *Acta Sanctorum*, Mart. I (1668), 390.

[108] Plummer, *Vitae*, vol. i, p. lxxxix n. 2; Kenney, *The Sources*, p. 19.

Cistercian foundation of Mellifont.[109] Kenney, perhaps followed by Heist, sees the impetus from the religious orders as one to collect and revise rather than to write anew.[110] If this is so, the revisers did not make their identity or their reforming aspirations at all clear. The collections seem rather concerned with the literary memorials of the old and unreformed churches. But this does not in itself argue against Papebroch's suggestion. In Wales, for example, the saints of the unreconstructed Welsh church were certainly adopted by the religious orders. Geoffrey of Llandaf and Benedict of Gloucester went so far as to put their names to Lives of St Teilo and St Dyfrig.[111] The history of the arrival and spread of the religious orders in Ireland, however, must surely impose a limit on Papebroch's suggestion. There were very few Benedictine foundations in Ireland in the twelfth century, all at new sites. Rather more Cistercian houses were established, again, all at new sites. But the most widespread manifestation of monastic reform was the adoption of the Augustinian Rule by some, perhaps even many, of the ancient monasteries.[112] This in itself should remind us that Irish 'monasteries' of the early Middle Ages probably had more in common with secular colleges than with houses following the Benedictine Rule. In such cases, one would hardly expect a significant change of outlook to be reflected in the Lives of their founders and patrons. The Lives which do reflect reform—those of the Cistercian St Malachy and the Augustinian St Lawrence—were not composed by Irishmen.

A more important motivation in the late twelfth century came from other organizational developments in the Irish church. Church leaders from Gilbert of Limerick to St Malachy had been concerned to establish a diocesan constitution in Ireland such as existed everywhere else in western Europe.[113] This would involve

[109] *Vita S. Boecii* §§ 2, 26.

[110] Kenney, *The Sources*, p. 294. Heist, *Vitae*, p. xi, adopts the view that 'almost all the Lives seem to have been composed in the eleventh and twelfth centuries', but refers also to 'the materials upon which they were based'.

[111] Both were published, from London, BL, MS Cotton Vespasian A XIV (Monmouth, s. xii/xiii), by H. Wharton, *Anglia Sacra* (2 vols.; London, 1691), ii. 662–6 and 654–61.

[112] J. A. Watt, *The Church in Medieval Ireland* (Dublin, 1972), pp. 42–5.

[113] Commentators have generally treated this movement positively, as marking a major step forward in the development of the Irish church. See, for example, K. Hughes, *The Church in Early Irish Society* (London, 1966), pp. 253–74;

reducing the number of churches with a bishop, and at the same time increasing the administrative role of the bishop at the expense of the largely secular abbots or coarbs of the great communal churches. A series of synods during the twelfth century created an episcopal hierarchy.[114] From the Synod of Rath Breasail in 1111, it was obvious that a diocesan structure would eventually be imposed, but this was not really achieved until the revised plan was drawn up at the Synod of Kells–Mellifont in 1152. At this meeting, four bishops were invested with metropolitan *pallia* by a papal legate, and thirty-two other churches were confirmed as having episcopal status.[115] It is impossible to say how many churches felt the loss of episcopal status. A classic case of this is Ardmore, which was not approved by the Synod of Kells–Mellifont but which none the less claimed the right to a bishopric. Between 1171 and 1210 its episcopal status was generally recognized, and two occupants of the see are known.[116] The

A. Gwynn, *The Twelfth-Century Reform* (Dublin, 1968); J. A. Watt, *The Church and the Two Nations in Medieval Ireland* (Cambridge, 1970), pp. 1–34. These views focus on the establishment of a formal diocesan organization, but outstanding problems are ignored; see, for example, M. P. Sheehy, *When the Normans Came to Ireland* (Cork and Dublin, 1975), pp. 67–8 and 81–3, on the reformers' failure to integrate the *familia* of St Columba, or ibid., pp. 65–6 and Sharpe, 'Some Problems', p. 267, on their failure to deal with coarbial families whose continued existence deprived some of the new dioceses of essential property.

[114] For brief discussion of the First Synod of Cashel (1101), see Watt, *The Church and the Two Nations*, pp. 11–12; on the Synod of Rath Breasail (1111), ibid., pp. 14–19; on the Synod of Kells–Mellifont (1152), ibid., pp. 28–32. The evidence for these synods is poor: brief entries in the various annal-collections, and summaries of their constitutions in vernacular texts of the late sixteenth and early seventeenth century. Only the list of dioceses drawn up by the Synod of Kells–Mellifont is known from twelfth-century sources (see next note).

[115] The dioceses approved at Rath Breasail are listed with some indication of their bounds by Geoffrey Keating, drawing on the now lost Annals of Clonenagh. His list is edited and discussed by J. MacErlean, 'Synod of Rath Breasail: Boundaries of the Dioceses in Ireland', *Archivium Hibernicum*, 3 (1914), 1–33. There are three twelfth-century witnesses to the list of dioceses as determined by the Synod of Kells–Mellifont: the *Prouinciale* of Albinus (dated 1188–9), edited by P. Fabré and L. Duchesne, *Le Liber Censuum de l'Église romaine* (Paris, 1889–1952), ii. 85–137 (at pp. 101–2); the *Liber Censuum* (1192), ibid. i. 232–4; and a list discovered by H. J. Lawlor in Montpellier, École de médecine, MS 92, 'A Fresh Authority for the Synod of Kells, 1152', *PRIA* 36C (1921–4), 16–22.

[116] At the end of the dioceses in the province of Cashel, the lists of Albinus and the Montpellier manuscript add, 'Duo autem ecclesie sunt sub eodem

church was rebuilt as a cathedral, though it did not long retain this status.[117] The patron of Ardmore, St Declán, was the patron saint of the whole district of the Déisi and it is the prevailing argument of his *uita* that, as he brought the Déisi to Christ, so his see should be the seat of the bishop of the Déisi for ever. Although the only surviving version of the Life has been quite heavily revised by the compiler of the collection in which it is found, it is possible that the original was written by an advocate of the episcopal status of Ardmore in this period. A case could perhaps be made out for attributing it to Bishop Eugenius of Ardmore, who is known to have had some hagiographical and historical interests.[118] On the opposite side, the relatively obscure church of Leighlin was recognized as a diocese at Rath Breasail and at Kells–Mellifont. The Life of its patron glories in its episcopal status: 'Sanctus Lasrianus, apostolice sedis legatus et Lethglinnensis ecclesie gloriosus antistes . . .'. Its distinction between *Hibernia* 'Ireland', *Scotia* 'Scotland', *Britannia* 'Wales', and *Anglia* 'England' suggests a date not earlier than the late twelfth century. On internal arguments, its episcopal position and legatine posturing may

archiepiscopo que dicunt se habere debere episcopos, quorum nomina sunt hec. Ardimor et Mungareth' [i.e. Ardmore and Mungret]. A bishop of Ardmore was among those who attended the Second Synod of Cashel in Nov. 1171 (on date, see Watt, *The Church and the Two Nations*, pp. 38–9 n.); the list is given in W. Stubbs (ed.), *Gesta Regis Henrici Secundi Benedicti Abbatis* (2 vols., Rolls Series 49; London, 1867), i. 26–7, being the first draft of Roger of Howden's chronicle, where this list is repeated, W. Stubbs (ed.), *Chronica Magistri Rogeri de Houedene* (4 vols., Rolls Series 51; London 1868–71), ii. 31. This bishop may have been Eugenius, who witnessed a charter datable to 1172 × 1179 (C. A. Webster, *The Diocese of Cork* (Cork, 1920), p. 375), and who visited England in 1184–5 (E. B. Fryde *et al.* (edd.), *Handbook of British Chronology* (3rd edn.; London, 1986), p. 334 n.). In 1203 the Annals of Inisfallen record the death of Mael Étáin Ó Duib Rátha, *uasalsacart* 'archpriest' of Ardmore, who rebuilt the church. The diocese is mentioned in a list of those in the province of Cashel in a *titulus* of protection from Innocent III to the archbishop, dated 6 Apr. 1210 (M. P. Sheehy (ed.), *Pontificia Hibernica: Medieval Papal Chancery Documents Concerning Ireland 640–1261* (2 vols.; Dublin, 1962–5), no. 68). No more is heard thereafter of a bishop of Ardmore.

[117] J. T. Smith, 'Ardmore Cathedral', *JRSAI* 102 (1972), 1–13.

[118] When in England in 1185 he provided the corroboration which induced the author of the *Libellus de ortu S. Cuthberti* (*BHL* 2026) to produce that book; R. Sharpe, 'Were the Irish Annals Known to a Twelfth-Century Northumbrian Writer?', *Peritia*, 2 (1983), 137–9. He was also one of the bishops who wrote in support of the canonization of St Lawrence; Ronan, 'Original Testimonies', pp. 349–50.

suggest more precisely that it was written to celebrate its recognition at the Synod of Kells–Mellifont.[119]

The second half of the twelfth century saw a significant impetus toward hagiographical production, whether in celebration of formal diocesan status or in the demand for such recognition on historic grounds. The style of these Lives is not markedly different from the generality, and I do not think we need to suppose any strong external influence—either from Continental religious orders, or from those Anglo-Norman ecclesiastics, who began to arrive in some Irish dioceses as early as 1181, in the wake of the invasion from England.[120] The two works in the medieval Irish collections that are known to be by writers from England are considerably more ambitious in their literary intention and achievement than most others in the collections. These are the Life of St Brigit, written in the 1130s by Lawrence, prior of Durham, dedicated to St Aelred of Rievaulx, and the Life of St Patrick, commissioned in the 1180s from the professional hagiographer, Jocelin of Furness.[121] The latter is particularly interesting as revealing what a relatively sophisticated, foreign practitioner could do with the variety of Latin and Irish materials made available to him at this date. Among these resources we learn incidentally that there was a Life of St Comgall which must predate any of the surviving recensions.[122]

[119] Arguments from the form of the text and its transmission may rather indicate a date around 1300, when provincial constitutions required the commemoration of the patrons of suffragan sees. See below, Chapter 13.

[120] John Cumin was appointed archbishop of Dublin by Henry II in 1181. The king had already taken a hand in the appointment of Master Augustine to the diocese of Waterford in 1175; Watt, *The Church and the Two Nations*, pp. 43–6.

[121] Lawrence's Life of St Brigit (*BHL* 1461) is conveniently accessible in Heist, *Vitae*, pp. 1–37; the opening of the text is here defective. The prefatory letter is printed by A. Hoste, 'A Survey of the Unedited Work of Laurence of Durham with an Edition of his Letter to Aelred of Rievaulx', *Sacris Erudiri*, 11 (1960), 249–65. The opening chapter of the *uita* has still to be consulted in the manuscripts, Oxford, Bodleian Library, MS Laud misc. 668 (? Rievaulx, s. xii²), f. 106ᵛ, and Oxford, Balliol College, MS 226 (s. xiiiᵉˣ), f. 86ʳ. Jocelin's Life of St Patrick (*BHL* 6513) was last edited by D. Papebroch, *Acta Sanctorum*, Mart. II (1670), 540–80; it is also available in Colgan, *Trias*, pp. 64–108. My references to this work are based on a critical edition by the late Ludwig Bieler and myself which will, I hope, be published in the near future.

[122] Jocelin, *Vita S. Patricii* § 98, gives a short account of St Comgall and the monastery of Bangor. His sources incuded Lives of St Comgall and St Malachy,

Another difference between Irish hagiography and that of Anglo-Norman or Angevin England is the relatively low emphasis on direct contemporary cult-building. The author of the twelfth-century Life of St Flannán, as untypical a *uita* as any from Ireland, gives an account of the translation of the saint's relics to a shrine, where cures were miraculously performed.[123] But generally speaking, posthumous miracles do not engage the writers' attention, and stories of miracles going on in their own and their readers' time are hardly found in Ireland at all.[124] The only clear examples of the *uita et miracula* structure are the Lives of St Fursu and St Lawrence, neither of them native works.

1.5. *Medieval Collectors and their Resources*

Our survey of hagiography in Ireland has now reached a point near the year 1200, and it is time to take stock. It is possible to speak very broadly of four phases of hagiographical activity before that date: the first phase extends from the earliest hagiographical activity we know about, the works of Ultán and Cumméne, to about the end of the eighth century; the second phase runs from the early ninth century to about the middle or late eleventh century, and is a period when all literary initiative seems to have been in the vernacular; the third phase extends from the late eleventh century until about 1150, during which a number of new Lives were written, and an Irish *homiliarium* was perhaps assembled; the fourth phase, the second half of the twelfth century, is in essence a continuation of the third phase but is characterized by a distinctive concern with the diocesan reorganization of the Irish church.

There are many questions one would like to be able to answer at this point. How many Latin Lives were available in 1200, and how

---

the latter by St Bernard; his mention of St Columbanus may derive from a knowledge of Jonas's Life, and a reference to 'ex filiis Benchorensis cenobii Luanus nomine centum monasteriorum solus fundator fuit' suggests an account of St Moluag, founder of Lismore in the Firth of Lorn.

[123] *Vita S. Flannani* S §34.

[124] The most remarkable exception is an early fourteenth-century text in Irish, preserved in O'Clery's transcripts, dealing with manifestations of St Senán's continuing power in and around Scattery Island in the writer's own time. It is edited by C. Plummer, 'The Miracles of St Senán', *ZCP* 10 (1914), 1–35.

widely? How many Irish Lives? To what extent were the Lives of Phase III and Phase IV original compositions or reworkings of Lives composed in Phases I or II? We cannot yet answer any of these questions, but perhaps by the end of this study answers will seem less remote.

A problem which becomes increasingly important from the last years of the twelfth century is the significance of the division between native Irish culture and international Latin culture. In 1150 or in 1200 a man of learning was probably educated in both traditions. During the thirteenth century, in ecclesiastical as well as in political life, the English-dominated area on the east side of Ireland became for a time increasingly assimilated to English and Continental ways. Gaelic Ireland became more and more separate from the English lordship. To what extent this appears in the saints' Lives has still to be established, but the writing of hagiography can hardly fail to reflect the milieu in which it is carried out. How the milieu would affect the transmission of texts is less clear.

The manuscripts of the three large medieval collections in which the Latin Lives are preserved were all written in a gothic hand during the fourteenth century. This would seem to place them in an Anglo-Irish milieu. But in several of the manuscripts, there are additions made in an Irish hand. All three collections include copies or recensions of imported or reimported texts, and all contain one or two Lives of non-Irish saints. But in general they are national collections of the *uitae* of Irish saints, compiled sympathetically. The age of the materials used by collectors, and the manner in which they were used, are the central concerns of this study. The audience for whom the collections were compiled, and by whom they were read, was presumably devoted to the saints of Ireland, but read in the international medium of Latin. It was almost certainly an ecclesiastical audience.

The compilers of the *Leabhar Breac*, the Book of Lismore, and other fifteenth-century codices, were interested in the Lives of Irish saints. These vernacular compilations, however, are much more varied than the Latin legendaries—they contain a wide range of religious literature, although almost exclusively in the Irish language. As with the Latin collections, the texts included date from different periods, and the degree to which the collectors alter their sources is also variable. One may say, however, as a general rule, that these vernacular manuscripts were written for lay patrons.

A considerable quantity of information is available about the production of Irish manuscripts in the fourteenth, fifteenth, and sixteenth centuries. The number of surviving manuscripts is not inconsiderable, though it is doubtless only a fraction of what was produced. It was a frequent habit of Irish scribes to enter their names in colophons, often adding the name of the patron for whom the book was written and the date of writing. Scribal hands, named in one book but not in another, can be identified; dates may be assigned from one dated colophon to undated manuscripts by the same scribe. Although this information has yet to be collected into a history of Irish book-production in the period, the facts are there for the finding. In the case of Latin manuscripts, the evidence is very much poorer. The number of Latin books of known Irish origin in this period is relatively small, and most are liturgical books. While the professional scribes who produced books in Irish for the Irish gentry provide a good deal of information about their own work, we are almost completely in the dark about the production of Latin books in a gothic hand. It is very difficult to form any sense of how many centres had the resources to produce even their own liturgical books, much less literary works. Evidence for the production of scholastic books is non-existent. How many such books were available in Irish libraries and whether they were produced at home or not, are questions we cannot answer. Similarly, it is very hard to know in what quantities the books of earlier centuries remained in the bookcases to be read or copied in the fourteenth or fifteenth century.

Only three collections of Latin Lives of saints survive. A small number of lections are known from liturgical manuscripts, but besides these and a few texts preserved in seventeenth-century copies, there are no uncollected *uitae* from Irish manuscripts. We should assume the loss of all the sources used by the collectors, and probably of other collections too.

The survival of texts in Irish was hardly less precarious, and many are now known only because they were transcribed by Br. Micheál Ó Cléirigh, *alias* Michael O'Clery, in the 1620s and 1630s. The originals have perished, but O'Clery's colophons provide a glimpse of how widespread was the interest in vernacular Lives. Apart from stating where and when he copied each text, he often gives information taken from colophons in his exemplar, showing when, by whom, or for whom the exemplar was written.[125]

It is not yet possible to divide the centuries from 1200 to the sixteenth century into phases. Our study of the three collections will help for the Latin texts, but a thorough analysis of the later vernacular texts will be necessary before the whole picture can be understood. The two traditions were not wholly separate.

Medieval Irish hagiography may reasonably be thought to end with Manus O'Donnell's *Betha Coluim Cille*, a huge Life of St Columba of Iona put together about 1530, for the heir to the ruler of Donegal.[126] The research that went into this composition was wide-ranging, encompassing sources in both Irish and Latin. The main source was a copy of Adomnán's *Vita S. Columbae*, not in the full recension which appears to have been long unknown in Ireland, but from the Continental shorter recension. In fact, there are several indications that O'Donnell's text of Adomnán's Life was the same as the version in our Dublin collection, Colgan's *Codex Kilkenniensis*, agreeing even in errors.[127] Since O'Donnell also cited the Lives of SS. Mochutu, Fintán of Clonenagh, Munnu, and Maedóc, and his citations correspond to the readings of the Dublin recension for these too, we may probably suppose that he used a copy of that collection.[128] The O'Donnell Life is one of the

---

[125] See below, p. 52 n. 57.

[126] The text is edited and translated by A. O'Kelleher and G. Schoepperle (Urbana, Ill., 1918).

[127] In *Betha Coluim Cille* § 237, O'Donnell's reading 'Lughaidh' agrees with the reading of **D** 'lugidus' (cited by Reeves, *The Life of St Columba*, pp. 56–7), where Adomnán's original has 'Lugbeus' (I 28); the explanation of this reading is simple: the shorter recension (of which this is a specimen) has retained the words 'cuius supra mentionem fecimus', but has omitted the previous mention, I 24, along with the whole of I 23–7, yet in I 22—the chapter which precedes I 28 in the shorter recension—there is a story involving Lugaidus, and the compiler of the collection has substituted this name for Lugbeus in the later chapter. In *Betha Coluim Cille* § 238, O'Donnell's reading 'Colmán liath' translates 'Colman canus', the shorter recension, where Adomnán has 'Colman canis' (I 43). At § 289 Adomnán reads 'caupallum' (II 27), but **D** reads 'caballum', which O'Donnell translates *capull* 'horse'. Finally in § 367, Adomnán's reading Hinba has become Hinna in **D** (cited by Reeves, p. 237), Inda in O'Donnell.

[128] *Betha Coluim Cille* § 121 cites the Life of St Mochutu, translating into Irish *Car.* **D** § 42, adding one point from ibid. § 53. At § 160 the Life of St Fintán is cited, translating *FintC.* **D** § 2. At § 161, the Life of St Munnu is cited, translating *Mun.* **D**

last significant compositions in this genre from Ireland, and its manuscripts are unusual: fine books containing this text only, produced for noble readers.[129] Manus O'Donnell has been portrayed as something of a Renaissance prince, and his literary inclination and taste for fine manuscripts are aspects of that role.[130] But there was no large-scale change in the production or use of books in Ireland in the sixteenth century. In particular, few printing-presses were established and there was no incentive to publish ancient Irish texts. So, while Cogitosus's Life of St Brigit was printed as early as 1486 at Milan, and Jocelin's Life of St Patrick in 1514 at Antwerp, manuscripts continued to be used, or to languish unused, in Ireland. Copies of saints' Lives in Latin were in little demand, but the number of manuscript copies of Irish Lives actually written in the sixteenth century suggests that a quite lively interest in the subject continued.[131]

§2, §4 (part), §§5, 7. At §248, O'Donnell appears to elaborate on *Aed* **D** §36. At §249, he cites the Life of St Fintán again, this time translating *FintC.* **D** §21, a passage peculiar to the **D**-text. At §368, he cites the Life of St Maedóc, translating *Maed.* **D** §39.

[129] There are two contemporary copies: Oxford, Bodleian Library, MS Rawl. B. 514 (Clarendon MS 25); Killiney, Franciscan House of Studies, MS A. 8 (on which see P. Walsh, *Irish Men of Learning* (Dublin, 1947), pp. 161–71). These finely written and elaborately bound books are discussed by F. Henry and G. L. Marsh-Micheli, 'Manuscripts and Illuminations 1169–1603', in *A New History of Ireland*, ii: *Medieval Ireland*, ed. A. Cosgrove (Oxford, 1987), pp. 807–8.

[130] B. Bradshaw, 'Manus "the Magnificent": O'Donnell as Renaissance Prince', in *Studies in Irish History presented to R. Dudley Edwards*, ed. A. Cosgrove and D. McCartney (Dublin, 1979), pp. 15–36.

[131] See the list of manuscripts in Plummer, 'A Tentative Catalogue', p. 175. A high proportion of manuscripts copied by O'Clery but now lost were also written in the sixteenth century, as one learns from his colophons.

2

The Background to Acta Sanctorum Hiberniae

THE sixteenth century may have seen something of a boom in the production of manuscripts written in Irish, but one cannot tell whether this had a favourable or an adverse effect on the survival of older copies. The rate of survival of medieval manuscripts written in Ireland has not been very good, either for Latin texts or Irish ones. Not one medieval library from Ireland found its way into safe hands.[1] What manuscripts have survived from before 1500 did so by ones and twos in the hands of individual owners. Some survived for the very reason that they escaped notice, but most perished for want of interest during the late sixteenth and seventeenth centuries, and thereafter. The losses, even of early modern copies, were considerable.[2] The total losses would have been very

---

[1] See L. Gougaud, 'The Remains of Ancient Irish Monastic Libraries', in *Féilsgríbhinn Eóin Mhic Néill*, ed. J. Ryan (Dublin, 1940), pp. 319–34; C. Mooney, 'Irish Franciscan Libraries of the Past', *IER*[5] 60 (1942), 215–28.

[2] The considerable number of eighteenth- and nineteenth-century manuscripts containing Irish Lives, listed by Plummer, 'A Tentative Catalogue', pp. 176–7, may be thought to prove sustained interest. Manuscripts of earlier date, however, do not seem to have survived in any quantity. The great majority of O'Clery's sources perished at some point: in the case of *Beatha Grealláin*, we may say that this happened after 1720. Michael O'Clery's transcript, dated 12 Feb. 1629, was made from the book written by Brian Ó Corcrán for Fr. Donnchadh Maguire (about 1600); Dublin, Royal Irish Academy, MS 23. O. 41, dated 1720, was copied from the same exemplar (so P. Grosjean, 'De Sancto Greallano confessore in Hibernia occidentali', in *Acta Sanctorum*, ed. J. Bolland *et al*, Nov. IV (Brusssels, 1925), p. 484), since lost. An extreme example of the mishaps which might befall a manuscript is presented by the Book of Lismore, from which O'Clery copied the Lives of SS. Mochua of Balla, Baoithín, and Fionnchu of Brigown (Brussels, Bibliothèque royale, MS 2324–2340, ff. 107–122). Subsequently, at Lismore Castle, the volume was put in a wooden box together with a crozier and walled into the masonry when a doorway was blocked. In 1814 it was rediscovered, and the story of its mutilation and recovery thereafter is told by E. O'Curry, *Lectures on the Manuscript Materials of Ancient Irish History* (Dublin, 1861), pp. 196–9.

much more serious for the student of hagiography if it were not for the work of a number of seventeenth-century scholars. All the three major collections of Latin Lives from medieval Ireland and a significant proportion of the Irish Lives survive because of the interest taken in them by a few Irish scholars working in different places in the years between about 1610 and 1650.

Irish Lives rescued from oblivion at this stage were deliberately collected and transcribed for a great hagiographical and historical project undertaken by Fr. Hugh Ward and other Irish Franciscans at Louvain. The same Franciscans also obtained copies of Lives in Latin from the two collections which they called the *Codex Kilkenniensis* and the *Codex Insulensis*; the original codices survived through the intervention of the Protestant primate, Archbishop James Ussher, and his associate in Irish antiquarian research, Sir James Ware.[3] The Franciscans also enjoyed close links with a Jesuit project begun in Antwerp about 1607 by Fr. Heribert Rosweyde, and now famous as the Bollandists and their *Acta Sanctorum*. Rosweyde acquired and his successors preserved the third of our Latin collections, the *Codex Salmanticensis*.[4] To understand how the texts were preserved and what limitations affect the surviving material, it is necessary to know something of these three groups of scholars—the Irish Franciscans of Louvain, Ussher and his associates in Dublin, the early Bollandists in Antwerp. But all three groups were helped by a few isolated scholars who were their forerunners in searching for manuscripts containing Lives of Irish saints. Among these, I would mention Fr. Henry FitzSimon, Fr. Thomas Messingham, and chiefly Fr. Stephen White.

All of these men were concerned to trace and if possible publish the evidence for the Lives and works of all the saints of Ireland, including the *peregrini* in the monasteries of Europe. Their work was timely, in that they were able to achieve much that might have been impossible a generation or two later, and remains in varying degrees important and even useful. Native learning and culture were under no small pressure from English and Anglo-Irish political and cultural domination; under Protestant rule, the Catholic clergy in Ireland could work only in severe difficulties.[5]

[3] See below, pp. 100–1, 262–3.
[4] See below, p. 228.
[5] A brief but trenchant account of the English assaults on Irish culture is given by Kenney, *The Sources*, pp. 26–37.

Yet these seventeenth-century scholars seem to have been motivated less by a desire to salvage the records of ancient Irish Christianity from these destructive forces than by indignation at the work of a Scottish Catholic, Thomas Dempster.[6] He had claimed for Scotland all the saints of ancient *Scotia*, a word which meant Ireland until the twelfth century. These seventeenth-century Irishmen not only wrote treatises to refute him on the name *Scotia* or on the ancient names of Ireland in general, but also sought to vindicate Ireland's claim to be the Island of Saints by amassing the evidence for the lives of those saints, at home and abroad.[7] The treatises of vindication are now of little interest to the medievalist, but the collection of texts was a most important step in the preservation of medieval Irish hagiography.

2.1. *FitzSimon, White, Messingham*

Fr. Henry FitzSimon (1566–1643) was a Dubliner, of Protestant stock, who became a Catholic and a Jesuit.[8] He appears to have left Dublin for Paris in 1587, studied rhetoric and philosophy at Pont-à-Mousson University from 1587 to 1591, and in 1592 was received into the Society of Jesus at Douai. In 1595 he returned to Dublin, where for five years he ministered to a repressed Catholic population before he was imprisoned in Dublin Castle in 1600 and released into exile in 1604. More a controversialist than a scholar, he lived in various places, Tournai, Rome, Liège, Douai, until in 1630 he joined the Jesuit mission in Ireland, working chiefly in

[6] For a fuller account of the motivation of the work, and of Dempster's role, see C. Mooney, 'Father John Colgan', in *Father John Colgan, OFM*, ed. T. O Donnell (Dublin, 1959), pp. 13–21.

[7] For a bibliographical account of the controversy, see P. Grosjean, 'Un soldat de fortune irlandais au service des *Acta Sanctorum*: Philippe O'Sullivan Beare et Jean Bolland (1634)', *AB* 81 (1963), 418–46, appendix, 'Sur quelques pièces, imprimées et manuscrites, de la controverse entre Écossais et Irlandais au début du xviie siècle', pp. 436–46. Among the treatises, I mention only Stephen White's *Vindiciae Scotorum Veterum*, of which there are copies in Brussels, Bibliothèque royale, MS 7658–7661, ff. 1–305, from the library of the Bollandists, and in Dublin, Trinity College, MS 573, from Ussher's library.

[8] E. Hogan published a Life of FitzSimon in several forms: first as 'Sketch of Father Fitzsimon's Life', in *Words of Comfort to Persecuted Catholics by Henry Fitzsimon*, ed. E. Hogan (Dublin, 1881), pp. 200–84; next as a series of articles in the *Month* in 1891; and finally in his *Distinguished Irishmen of the 16th Century* (Dublin, 1894), pp. 198–310.

Dublin until 1641, when, in the wake of the Irish rebellion, the persecution of Catholic priests forced him to leave the city in fear of his life. He died at Kilkenny on 29 November 1643.

Of his various works, we are concerned only with the *Catalogus praecipuorum Sanctorum Hiberniae*. Hogan lists nine editions, but this number is exaggerated.[9] The published texts, in any case, offer only two recensions. Hogan and Grosjean treat the version dated 'Romae, 9 Aprilis 1611' as the first edition or Recension A; this version is first known in the edition by Philip O'Sullivan Beare.[10] At the end of the catalogue in this recension, FitzSimon's colophon continues (in Hogan's translation): 'If anyone should find out any more, let him deign to communicate it in time, and thus contribute towards the Irish History, which I have now on hands.'[11] O'Sullivan treated the catalogue as an original work by FitzSimon, but we know on FitzSimon's own testimony and from a statement of David Rothe, bishop of Ossory (1573–1650), that an original list of 94 names had been drawn up by Fr. Richard Fleming, SJ, who was chancellor of the university at Pont-à-Mousson during FitzSimon's time as a student there.[12] In FitzSimon's Recension A, the list extends to 289 names, but it is not certain that this was published prior to the O'Sullivan edition. An untraced edition of Douai 1615 may have contained this recension. Recension B, as printed at Liège in 1619, contains over 400 names and a great deal of additional matter. The work of adding to it occupied FitzSimon over a long period, but it is not clear how vigorously he pursued the task. Recension B (but not A) contains an entry for 'Salmius vel Solonius Comes Palladii. MS Duac. Vita S. Patricii'; Solonius is known from *Vita II S.*

---

[9] Hogan, 'Sketch of Fitzsimon's Life', pp. 281–2; P. Grosjean, 'Édition du *Catalogus praecipuorum Sanctorum Hiberniae* de Henri FitzSimon', in *Féilsgríbhinn Eóin Mhic Néill*, ed. J. Ryan (Dublin, 1940), pp. 325–93 (at pp. 336–7). For criticism of Hogan's list, see R. Sharpe, 'The Origin and Elaboration of the *Catalogus praecipuorum Sanctorum Hiberniae* Attributed to Henry FitzSimon, SJ', *Bodleian Library Record*, 13/3 (Oct. 1989), 202–30.

[10] 'Catalogus aliquot Sanctorum Iberniæ', in P. O'Sullivan Beare, *Historiæ Catholicæ Iberniæ Compendium* (Lisbon, 1621), ff. 49r–54v.

[11] Hogan, 'Sketch of Fitzsimon's Life', p. 261.

[12] FitzSimon's statement was copied by Ussher in Oxford, Bodleian Library, MS Add. C. 299, f. 124v invers.; compare [D. Rothe], *Hibernia resurgens* ... (Rouen, 1621), p. 21. The matter is discussed in Sharpe, 'The Origin and Elaboration'.

Patricii §24, and it happens that there is a copy of this text in a twelfth-century Marchiennes manuscript, now Douai, Bibliothèque municipale MS 840, which was perhaps FitzSimon's source.[13] He may have first met this manuscript in the early 1590s. Writing in another work, dated 1611, he refers to twenty years of study, during which time he 'ransacked all libraries in [his] way for our countrie's antiquities, and found a hand-written Life of St Patrick in the library of our college at Douay'.[14] This was presumably a fresh discovery, else one would expect to find it in Recension A. Copies of his book were used by other scholars: Ussher's annotated copy of the 1619 edition from Liège is still in the library of Trinity College, Dublin;[15] and one was sent, perhaps by Fr. Stephen White, to Fr. Hugh Ward, about the end of 1634, with annotations.[16] Another expanded version is known, in a copy begun by Rosweyde, and now among the papers of the early Bollandists in Brussels.[17]

How and when this reached Rosweyde, indeed, its connexion with FitzSimon himself, are all uncertain. At some stage, however, probably after Rosweyde's death, FitzSimon was responsible for sending copies of a number of *uitae* to the Bollandists in Antwerp. These included texts not now preserved in any other form, such as

---

[13] This entry is no. 620 in Grosjean's edition, '*Catalogus* de Henri FitzSimon'. The text of *Vita II S. Patricii* and discussion of this manuscript will be found in L. Bieler (ed. and trans.), *Four Latin Lives of St Patrick* (Scriptores Latini Hiberniae, 8; Dublin, 1971), p. 1. Bieler notes that Brussels, Bibliothèque royale, MS 4241 (written *c.*1608), is an apograph 'e libro manu scripto patrum Societatis Iesu Duacensium, collectore Baltazare Bisscot', which agrees closely with the Marchiennes manuscript, and supposes that the Jesuit manuscript was likewise a copy of the Marchiennes volume.

[14] H. FitzSimon, *The Justification and Exposition of the Divine Sacrifice of the Masse* (Douai, 1611), p. 119, quoted by Hogan, 'Sketch of Fitzsimon's Life', p. 205.

[15] Grosjean, '*Catalogus* de Henri FitzSimon', p. 336, notes that this edition, part of *Hiberniae sive Antiquioris Scotiae Vindiciae . . . authore G. F.*, describes the *Catalogus* as 'recognitus et auctus per R. P. Henr. Fitz-Simon'. Ussher's annotation is reported in Grosjean's notes on the text.

[16] The evidence is an undated letter, printed by B. Jennings, 'Documents from the Archives of St Isidore's College, Rome', *Analecta Hibernica*, 6 (1934), 203–47 (at p. 226). Jennings thought the initials were 'B.V.' but I suspect they are 'S.V.' for Stephanus Vitus: the previous letter, dated 14 Nov. 1634, ibid., pp. 224–5, asks Ward whether he knew Fr. White's views on the history of St Ursula; the letter on p. 226 appears to be an answer (? White's) to a query from Ward on this subject.

[17] Brussels, Bibliothèque royale, MS 8530–8534 (Grosjean's Recension C). See below, pp. 97–9.

Vita S. Commani.[18] Some of these texts have been discussed by Grosjean, and in a later chapter we shall try to place their source in its medieval context.

Fr. Stephen White, SJ (1574–1646), was a scholar of much greater stature than FitzSimon.[19] He was born at Clonmel, and may have been one of the first students enrolled at Trinity College, Dublin. But he would not take the Oath of Supremacy and left to pursue his studies at the newly founded Irish college at Salamanca, where he entered the Society of Jesus in 1596. From about 1593 until 1629, his career was spent mostly in Spain and Germany, teaching and studying. He held professorships at Ingolstadt and Dillingen. Of his several treatises, only one has been published.[20] A remark by FitzSimon suggests that White may have read FitzSimon's *Catalogus* before its publication.[21] As early as about 1607 he began to correspond with Rosweyde, and he is said to have compiled 'huit catalogues de saints irlandais et un recueil de courtes notices sur les mêmes'.[22] For many years, the Bollandists leant on White's communications for their articles on Irish saints, but the volume containing this correspondence seems to have gone astray in the nineteenth century.[23] White used his position at Dillingen to search the manuscript collections of

---

[18] P. Grosjean, 'Notes sur quelques sources des Antiquitates de Jacques Ussher', *AB* 77 (1959), 178–85.

[19] E. Hogan, 'Life of Father Stephen White, SJ', *Journal of the Waterford and South-east of Ireland Archaeological Society*, 3 (1897), 55–71, 119–34, describes him (with pardonable exaggeration) as 'one of the three or four most learned men that Ireland has ever produced'. At p. 61, Hogan cites the authority of 'Charles McNeill, of Hazelbrook, Malahide, in his very careful MS memoir of Stephen White'; I have not succeeded in tracing this, but do not doubt that White merits the attentions of a biographer.

[20] *Apologia pro Hibernia adversus Cambri Calumnias*, ed. M. Kelly (Dublin, 1849), from Brussels, Bibliothèque royale, MS 7658–7661, ff. 306–409. Other works are listed by Grosjean, 'Un soldat de fortune', p. 439.

[21] Hogan, 'Life of Father White', p. 66, quotes in translation from the *Catalogus* (citing p. 121 of the 1615 edition, which has not been traced): 'I warn you, gentlemen, that my friend the Rev. Father Stephen White is a most accomplished theologian [*solertissimus theologus*], and very seldom makes a mistake.'

[22] V. De Buck, 'L'archéologie irlandaise au couvent de Saint-Antoine de Padoue à Louvain', *Etudes réligieuses historiques et littéraires de la Compagnie de Jésus*, 4th ser., 3 (1869), p. 590, citing the catalogue of the Museum Bollandianum and various references to *Acta Sanctorum*.

[23] De Buck thought the volume was last known in the hands of Monsignor Ram in Antwerp in the 1840s.

Germany, where he made a number of major discoveries, notably the copy of Adomnán's *Vita S. Columbae* written by Dorbbéne. The manuscript was then at Reichenau, but was lent to White at Dillingen where he copied it.[24] He supplied copies to Ussher, to the Louvain Franciscans, and to the Bollandists.[25] Another important discovery was a text of *Vita I S. Brigitae* in a manuscript of St Magnus in Regensburg, which he also communicated to the same recipients.[26] If one were to collect all the acknowledgements for texts supplied by White, it would perhaps be possible to form a clearer picture of his manuscript researches.[27] In 1629, White was taken from his professorial duties and sent to join the Jesuit mission in Ireland, under very difficult circumstances. He taught and ministered in his native diocese of Lismore, and in nearby

[24] W. Reeves quotes White's account of the manuscript, which he appears to have borrowed from Reichenau in May 1621 (*The Life of St Columba by Adamnan* (Irish Archaeological and Celtic Society, Dublin, 1857; Bannatyne Club, Edinburgh, 1857), p. xxxviii nn.). So far as I know, White's transcript nowhere survives in his own hand, but Reeves was able to borrow the partial copy which had belonged to Ussher, a folio volume 'lately sold by Mr Kerslake of Bristol' (*The Life of St Columba*, p. ix n.). Thomas Kerslake (1812–91) was a bookseller and antiquary. The new owner was John C. Nicholl of Merthyr Mawr. Ussher's copy (partly in his own hand and partly that of a clerk) is still preserved, as part of MS F. 119, in this private library, the property of Mr and Mrs Murray Maclaggan, Merthyr Mawr House, Bridgend. (Esposito tried to trace this volume, but inexplicably failed; 'On the Early Latin Lives of St Brigid', p. 147 and n. 93. He hoped that it contained more of White's transcripts, but he would have been disappointed.)

[25] In his *Veterum Epistolarum Hibernicarum Sylloge* (Dublin, 1632), Ussher knew only the shorter recension (as printed by Canisius), but from the addenda to the 1639 edition of his *Antiquitates*, Grosjean was able to show that White had supplied Ussher with the text of the Reichenau manuscript while the book was in press; Grosjean, 'Notes sur quelques sources', pp. 154–87 (at pp. 163–4). White supplied Colgan with a transcript of the same manuscript; *Trias*, p. 372 n. 1, 'ex peruetusto codice MS monasterii Augie Diuitis'. The edition in *Acta Sanctorum*, Jun. II (1698), 197–236, was based likewise on a transcript supplied by White fifty years before; the editor, F. Baert, was criticized for taking many liberties with the copy by Reeves, *The Life of St Columba*, p. x.

[26] Colgan printed the text from White's copy, *Trias*, pp. 527–42. Bolland initially intended to follow suit, and his copy of White's apograph, now Brussels, Bibliothèque royale, MS 7763, was marked up for the printer; but Bolland changed his mind. Ussher was lent a copy of the apograph by White in the 1630s (see below, p. 62 and n. 90).

[27] See W. Reeves, 'Memoir of Stephen White', *PRIA* 8 (1861–4), 29–38 (at pp. 30–1).

Waterford, but before 1640 was in Dublin. In 1641, circumstances forced White to leave the city, and it is thought that he died in Galway in the early part of 1646.

FitzSimon and White, along with the Catholic primate Peter Lombard, Bishop David Rothe, and the Franciscan Hugh MacCaghwell, are acknowledged for their contribution to the vindication of Ireland's saints in a work called *Florilegium Insulae Sanctorum*, published by Fr. Thomas Messingham, a secular priest and rector of the Irish college in Paris, in 1624.[28] Little is known about Messingham. His *Florilegium* includes a reprint of Jocelin's Life of St Patrick from the Antwerp edition of 1514, of Adomnán's Life of St Columba from Canisius's edition of the shorter recension, and of Cogitosus's Life of St Brigit from the same source. Jonas's Life of St Columbanus was taken from the edition of Surius. Other Lives of *peregrini* were taken from Canisius, and other printed sources. At the end of the volume, the *Regula S. Columbani* was printed from a manuscript at Bobbio, a copy of which, together with hymns and verses, had been communicated by Fr. MacCaghwell.[29] The *Florilegium* was for the most part, therefore, a derivative compilation. The reference to MacCaghwell, however, and the Rule of St Columbanus leads us from these forerunners to the three principal projects which I now wish to discuss.

2.2. *The Irish Franciscans of Louvain*

Fr. Hugh MacCaghwell, OFM (1571–1626), in Latin Hugo Cavellus, was the third Guardian of the Irish college, St Anthony's, at Louvain in 1619.[30] In 1623, as Definitor General of the Order, he travelled to Paris accompanied by another young

---

[28] T. Messingham, *Florilegium Insulae Sanctorum seu Vitae et Acta Sanctorum Hiberniae* (Paris, 1624), sig. d4, towards the end of the 'Tractatus praeambularis de nominibus Hiberniae'.

[29] There is an acknowledgement to MacCaghwell at p. 414.

[30] There is a sketch of his life in [E. Hogan], 'Irish Historical Studies in the Seventeenth Century, III: Patrick Fleming, OSF', *IER*[2] 7 (1870–1), 193–216 (at pp. 201–4). (On the authorship of this anonymous series of articles, see Grosjean, 'Un soldat de fortune', p. 423 n. 1.) For a more detailed treatment, see T. Ó Cléirigh, *Aodh Mac Aingil agus an Scoil Nua-Ghaedhilge i Lobháin* (Dublin, [1935]), pp. 46–99; and C. Giblin, 'Hugh McCaghwell, OFM, Archbishop of Armagh († 1626): Aspects of his Life', *Seanchas Ard Mhacha*, 11 (1984–5), 258–90.

Irish Franciscan, Fr. Patrick Fleming, *en route* for Rome. At the same time, Fr. Hugh Ward, OFM, was on his way to Louvain from Salamanca, where he had entered the order under the influence of the great Irish Franciscan scholar, Fr. Luke Wadding. MacCaghwell, Fleming, and Ward met in Paris, where they also encountered Messingham, about March 1623. The meeting is not directly documented, but the ensuing correspondence between Fleming and Ward shows that they had become filled with enthusiasm for searching out the records of Irish saints, with a view to communicating the fruits to Messingham for publication. Friendship appears to have grown up immediately between the two young Franciscans, though their backgrounds were entirely different. Patrick Fleming (1599–1631) was born in Co. Louth into a family with distinguished Anglo-Norman connexions, but was sent abroad at the age of 13—away from the pressures then trying to suppress the Catholic faith in Ireland.[31] From about 1612 he studied at Douai, and in 1617 was received as a Franciscan at Louvain. Hugh MacCaghwell took Fleming with him as his companion to attend a General Chapter of the Order in Rome; Paris in 1623 was an early stage on their journey. Hugh Ward (1593–1635) met them there on his way to Louvain. He, like MacCaghwell, came from one of the hereditary learned families of Gaelic Ulster, the family of Mac an Bháird, poets to the O'Donnells of Tirconnell.[32] He had been schooled with Irish teachers until in 1612 he became a student at Salamanca.[33] Having completed his studies in philosophy and theology, he was appointed by the General of the Order in 1622 to teach philosophy at Louvain.[34] Both Ward and Fleming were eager to join the search for records of Irish saints with which to rebut Dempster, but it is not known how clear a plan was formed at this early stage.

During 1623, Fleming continued to Rome with MacCaghwell, writing to Ward at intervals to report progress. These letters

[31] There is a family tree in W. Reeves, 'The Irish Library, 2: Fleming's *Collectanea Sacra*', *Ulster Journal of Archaeology*, 2 (1854), 253–61 (at p. 254). For his career, see [Hogan], 'Patrick Fleming, OSF', pp. 193–216.

[32] [E. Hogan], 'Irish Historical Studies in the Seventeenth Century, II: Hugh Ward', *IER*[2] 7 (1870–1), 56–77; F. O'Brien, 'Irish Franciscan Historians of St Anthony's College, Louvain: Father Hugh Ward', *IER*[5] 32 (1928), 113–29.

[33] D. J. O'Doherty, 'Students of the Irish College, Salamanca (1595–1619)', *Archivium Hibernicum*, 2 (1913), 1–36 (at p. 29).

[34] B. Jennings, *Louvain Papers 1606–1827* (Dublin, 1968), no. 26.

survive, but his letters to Messingham do not; nor do the letters from Ward or Messingham to Fleming. From the first of these letters, we learn that Fleming had not time to search the library at Clairvaux, but had set an Irish Cistercian, John Cantwell, to search for and copy such texts as were relevant to Irish saints. These included a Life of St Deicolus, one of St Mansuetus of Toul, the Miracles of St Columbanus (which were already in Messingham's hands), and a commentary on the *Regula S. Benedicti* by an Irish monk.[35] Fleming hoped that Cantwell would find the letters of St Malachy who had died at Clairvaux; when the second letter was written, they had not turned up, but Fleming gives curious notices of St Malachy's mitre and chalice.[36] The next letter is lost, but the fourth was written from Rome on 22 July 1623. Nothing had been found until Bobbio was reached, but here Fleming was delighted to find the Rule of St Columbanus, which he had sent to Messingham.[37] He hoped to have other works copied, including Columbanus's *Homiliae* (now called his *Instructiones*), and thought there might be enough for Messingham to produce a second volume. With the help of Fr. Luke Wadding in Rome, he had found Lives of St Patrick, St Brendan, St Donatus of Fiesole—a ninth-century Irish *peregrinus*—and other texts. He was still concerned with the issue of the name *Scotia*. In the next letter, Fleming scolded Ward, who had written only once though this was Fleming's fifth communication.[38] Messingham had received the Rule of St Columbanus, and was ready for press; he was eager for the Homilies. If Ward had anything, he should send it soon or, if he were unable, he should ask Fr. Gallagher to write. The rebuttal of Dempster was again mentioned.

Meanwhile, Ward had been travelling before making his way to Louvain, which may explain why no answers reached Fleming in Rome until September. He had visited Rouen, Harfleur, and Nantes, before travelling to Louvain. What fruit these travels bore

[35] Fleming to Ward, Clairvaux, 25 Apr. 1623; text in [Hogan], 'Hugh Ward', pp. 60–1 n., translation, pp. 60–3.

[36] Fleming to Ward, Lyons, 8 May 1623; text and translation, [Hogan], 'Hugh Ward', pp. 63–5.

[37] Fleming to Ward, Rome, 22 July 1623; text in Jennings, 'Documents from St Isidore's', pp. 203–7, part translation in [Hogan], 'Patrick Fleming, OSF', pp. 194–6.

[38] Fleming to Ward, Rome, 16 Sept. [1623]; text in Jennings, 'Documents from St Isidore's', pp. 207–9.

is not recorded. By 1624, however, the project was changing direction. In the latter part of 1623 or early 1624, a man arrived from Donegal, in his mid-forties, ignorant of Latin but learned in Irish, who wished to join the Franciscans at Louvain. He was received, took the name of Michael in religion, and over the next twenty years laid the basis of his posthumous fame as Br. Michael O'Clery, chief of the Four Masters. He is first mentioned, though not by name, in another letter from Fleming, dated 1 June 1624—the next letter in sequence, which asks Ward to inquire 'ab ipso laico, germano Fratris Mileri Cleri, si novit ullum fuisse regem in Hybernia nomine Romanum, et reginam nomine Plantulam'.[39]

This letter contains much of interest. Ward's tardy correspondence had evidently irritated Messingham, who had complained to Fleming that when he chid Ward for his lack of response, Ward answered harshly (*durius*). Though Messingham was ready to print, Fleming would send not to him but to Ward the Lives he had collected: Frigidianus, Andreas, Donatus, Peregrinus, Marinus, Silanus, Fuleo. The Palatine library had been opened to him at the Vatican and he hoped for discoveries there. Meanwhile, he had learnt of a Life of St Coemgen—whom he knew to be mentioned in the Life of St Lawrence of Dublin—at Ingolstadt; we may guess that Stephen White had something to do with this information.[40] An associate of Messingham's in Paris, Fr. Eugene

---

[39] Fleming to Ward, Rome, 1 June 1624; text in Jennings, 'Documents from St Isidore's', pp. 209–13, part translation (omitting the reference to O'Clery) in [Hogan], 'Patrick Fleming, OSF', pp. 197–9 (misdated 21 June 1624). Cf. Jennings, *Michael O Cleirigh, Chief of the Four Masters, and his Associates* (Dublin, 1936), p. 36.

[40] The manuscript in question from the Jesuit College at Ingolstadt supplied texts to both Rosweyde and Colgan. It had come to the college on the dissolution of the abbey of Biburg, and is referred to by Colgan and the Bollandists as a *codex Biburgensis*. The volume is now Munich, Universitätsbibliothek, MS 2° 312 (s. xii); see Bieler, *Four Latin Lives*, pp. 14–15. Rosweyde, who had been in correspondence with White since at least 1615, was sent a copy of the Lives of St Patrick and St Coemgen from this manuscript by White; the copy is now divided between Brussels, Bibliothèque royale, MS 3196–3203 ff. 347ʳ–354ᵛ and Bibliothèque des Bollandistes, MS 121, on which see Grosjean, 'Les Vies latines de S. Cáemgen et de S. Patrice du manuscrit 121 des Bollandistes', *AB* 70 (1952), 313–15. White also provided Ussher with readings from the Biburg copy of *Vita III S. Patricii*, when Ussher's *Antiquitates* was in press; c. 22 is quoted in the addenda to the edition of 1639, p. 1093 (*Whole Works*, vi. 514). Colgan, *Trias*, p. 29, acknowledges White for the Biburg text of the same Life, and I presume that White had communicated to the Franciscans copies of both texts.

Sweeney, had written asking for the homilies of Columbanus; these had not yet arrived from Bobbio, but Fleming hesitated over sending them to Paris. This is the first sign of a rift with Messingham, and the letter goes on to say that Fr. Eugene Gallagher, at the time Guardian of the College, was to take charge of this historical enterprise, a man whom Fleming thought unsuitable.[41]

The next letter returns to these themes.[42] Ward had written to Fleming to stop him from sending anything to Messingham, a decision with which Fleming agreed. The decision to appoint Gallagher to the task of publishing the saints' Lives had come from the superiors of the Irish Province in Dublin, and both Ward and Fleming opposed it. This matter was dropped, but in the next and last letter we discover that Ward and Fleming had decided to publish on their own account, and would have nothing more to do with Messingham, who had not acknowledged Fleming's research in supplying the Rule of Columbanus.[43] Researches were continuing: a Fr. Hugo in Rome had promised more texts, the letters of Columbanus had been found, Fr. Edward MacCaghwell reported a Life of Adomnán in Latin though Ward already knew of one in Irish. Ward wished Fleming to search libraries on his route home to Louvain, but Fleming doubted whether this would be practical. More significantly, he urged Ward to proceed with a plan to send Br. Michael to Ireland to collect texts there. Moreover, he earnestly desired Ward to go ahead and publish what he had, and in brief, Latin Lives and Lives translated from Irish, rather than delay publication in order to write elaborate notes. It appears from this letter that Ward had been making more progress than Fleming, whose discoveries in Rome had little bearing on genuinely Irish saints, Columbanus and Donatus excepted. But Ward's opportunities for research must have been

[41] Gallagher's name, in sixth place, precedes Ward's in the list of Guardians (Jennings, *Louvain Papers*, no. 219), but I have not established the date of his election. He contributed a translation from French into Latin of J. Desmay's account of St Fursu to Colgan, *Acta*, pp. 282–99.

[42] Fleming to Ward, Rome, 27 July 1624; text in Jennings, 'Documents from St Isidore's', pp. 213–14.

[43] Fleming to Ward, Rome, 24 Aug. 1624; text in Jennings, 'Documents from St Isidore's', pp. 214–16; also cited by Sheeran in Fleming's *Collectanea Sacra*, sig. *2. On the breakdown of the co-operation with Messingham, compare Mooney, 'Father John Colgan', pp. 15–16.

much reduced when in April 1629 he became the seventh Guardian of the College.

How rapidly the project progressed from there it is difficult to ascertain. A letter from Malachy O'Queely (writing under the false name of David Rice) to Ward at the beginning of 1629 reports that he had met Br. Michael at Cashel, and that he had already collected more than three or four hundred Lives, presumably in Irish.[44] Of these collections, a small part survives.[45] Fleming appears to have met Stephen White at Metz about 1627 or 1628, and was given a complete transcript of White's collection on Irish saints.[46] By 1630, Fleming was working on a book devoted chiefly to St Columbanus, but he had little time to spend on it.[47] It is not known how far from completion it was when Fleming was sent to establish a Franciscan house in Prague, and at Beneschau in Bohemia he was martyred by Protestant fanatics on 7 November 1631.[48]

Fleming's book on St Columbanus was not published until 1667, when it was brought out by Fr. Thomas Sheeran.[49] It contains what was for long regarded as the full canon of the saint's works, copiously annotated.[50] To these are added Aileran's *Interpretatio mystica progenitorum Christi* from St. Gallen MS 433,[51] and the Penitential falsely attributed to Cummean from another St. Gallen manuscript.[52] There follows an edition of Jonas's Life of

---

[44] 'Rice' to Ward, 30 Jan. 1628/9; text in Jennings, 'Documents from St Isidore's', pp. 217–18, and in [Hogan], 'Hugh Ward', pp. 66–7. See Jennings, *Michael O Cleirigh*, pp. 65–6, for the identification of the author.

[45] Notably Brussels, Bibliothèque royale, MSS 2324–2340 and 4190–4200.

[46] White to Colgan, 31 Jan. 1640; text in Reeves, 'Memoir of Stephen White', p. 35, translation in Hogan, 'Life of Father White', p. 126.

[47] Fleming to Br. Robert, 18 Feb. 1630; text in Jennings, 'Documents from St Isidore's', pp. 216–17.

[48] Jennings, *Michael O Cleirigh*, pp. 107–12.

[49] P. Fleming, *Collectanea Sacra, seu S. Columbani hiberni abbatis . . . necnon aliorum . . . sanctorum acta et opuscula*, ed. T. Sirinus (Louvain, 1667), on which see Reeves, 'The Irish Library, 2', pp. 253–61; Jennings, *Michael O Cleirigh*, pp. 112–14.

[50] Fleming's principal sources were two manuscripts in Bobbio, apparently of early date, but not now known; see Bieler *apud* G. S. M. Walker, *Sancti Columbani Opera* (Scriptores Latini Hiberniae, 2; Dublin, 1957), pp. lxxiii–lxxv.

[51] Kenney, *The Sources*, pp. 279–80; M. Lapidge and R. Sharpe (edd.), *A Bibliography of Celtic-Latin Literature 400–1200* (Dublin, 1985), no. 299.

[52] Kenney, *The Sources*, p. 243. Three ninth-century manuscripts from St. Gallen contain this text; they are MSS 150, 550, and 675.

St Columbanus based on a manuscript of St Maximinus, Trier, a copy of which was supplied by Rosweyde.[53] In the long commentary on Jonas, Fleming introduced the Life of St Comgall and excerpts from the Lives of SS. Coemgen, Cainnech, Mochutu, and Munnu, all from a *Codex Ardmachanus seu Dubliniensis* in the possession of Archbishop Ussher.[54] At the end of the commentary he adds from the same source the Lives of St Molua and St Mochoemóc. In the margins of the former he not only marks his own emendations but also notes a reading from a second manuscript, supplied by Rosweyde and possibly the *Salmanticensis*, although the whole contents of this manuscript did not become known to the Franciscans until after 1634.[55] In annotating the Life of St Mochoemóc, he refers to a *Vita Hibernica*, presumably that which still survives in the collections of Br. Michael O'Clery;[56] this suggests that at least part of the volume known as MS O'Clery 1, Brussels, Bibliothèque royale MS 2324–2340, had reached Louvain by 1630.[57]

Evidently the resources for the project were building up. It is interesting to see that the manuscripts of St. Gallen, for instance, had already been quarried. Moreover, for those saints whose cult remained confined to Ireland, the materials available to Fleming appear to have been those on which we still depend. The *Codex Ardmachanus* has been shown to be Dublin, Marsh's Library,

---

[53] Fleming, *Collectanea Sacra*, p. 212. The manuscript is now Trier, Episcopal Seminary, MS 36 (s. xiii); see *Ionae Vitae Sanctorum Columbani, Vedastis, Iohannis*, ed. B. Krusch (Hanover and Leipzig, 1905), pp. 97, 141.

[54] Fleming, *Collectanea Sacra*, p. 431; see below, pp. 99–100.

[55] *Collectanea Sacra*, p. 303, mentions a fragment supplied by Rosweyde, on which see below, p. 228 n. 5. The two sections quoted on the margins may, however, have come from the Oxford text which was also available to Fleming.

[56] The Irish Life in Brussels, Bibliothèque royale, MS 2324–2340, ff. 289ʳ–302ᵛ, is unpublished but is a close translation of the Latin text; Plummer, *Vitae*, vol. i, p. lxxix n. 1, and 'A Tentative Catalogue', p. 192.

[57] The colophons at the end of each Life are said by Plummer, *Bethada Náem nÉrenn* (Oxford, 1922), vol. i, p. xii, to bear dates ranging from 1620 (surely an error?) to 1635, but most frequently 1629. Plummer's method in dealing with the collection is, however, less than helpful. He prints only a selection of texts, giving the colophons in his notes at the end of each one; but he provides no list of contents for the volume as a whole, he does not indicate whether the volume is a unity or a series of booklets bound up at Louvain, and for the unprinted Lives the colophons are inaccessible. The description by V. Tourneur in the manuscript catalogue is not much more helpful.

MS Z3. 1. 5, the principal witness to the Dublin collection.[58]
Fleming also mentions a manuscript which had belonged to
Saints' Island.[59] This manuscript is also cited by Ward and
repeatedly by Colgan.[60] It can be identified with the volume now
Oxford, Bodleian Library, MS Rawlinson B. 505.[61] Fleming says
that copies of both were supplied in 1626–7 by Francis
Matthews.[62]

Fr. Francis Matthews, OFM (d. 1644), whose surname appears
also as Matthaeus, Matthew, and in its Irish form Ó Math-
ghamhna or O'Mahony, and who was also known as Ursulanus,
is an elusive figure.[63] From 1625 to 1629 he was Minister Provincial
in Ireland, and must have been asked to seek out texts useful to the
Louvain scholars. He had copies made of both the Dublin and
Oxford collections, and in this way placed in the hands of Fleming
and Ward the two sources on which they leant most heavily. The
copy of the Oxford collection commissioned by him still exists,
Killiney, Franciscan House of Studies, MS F. 1 (formerly A. 24),
one of the few remnants from the working library at Louvain.[64]
Matthews also commissioned Domhnall Ó Duinnín, alias
Donnell Dinneen, to compile a volume of sixteen Irish Lives; the
transcript was made at Cork in September 1627 and survives
today.[65] About this period, Matthews himself wrote a *Brevis
synopsis provinciae Hiberniae FF. Minorum* which we shall have

---

[58] By Reeves; see below, p. 93.

[59] *Collectanea Sacra*, p. 431, quoted below, pp. 99–100.

[60] H. Ward, *S. Rumoldi . . . Acta*, ed. T. Sirinus (Louvain, 1662), p. 189; Colgan,
Acta, passim.

[61] See below, p. 252.

[62] *Collectanea Sacra*, p. 431, quoted below pp. 99–100.

[63] C. Plummer (ed.), *Miscellanea Hagiographica Hibernica* (Subsidia Hagio-
graphica, 15; Brussels, 1925), p. 157 n. 2, quotes a personal communication from
J. G. O'Keeffe which refers to an article on Matthews in *Franciscan Tertiary*, III ii
(Mar. 1897). Kenney, *The Sources*, p. 40 n. 143, repeats the reference. I have been
unable to see a copy of this journal, but believe the reference should be to
Franciscan Tertiary, VIII (1897), as given by Mooney, 'Colgan's Inquiries', p. 295.
The mistake seems to have arisen from a misreading of minims in the roman
numeral.

[64] See below, pp. 258–9.

[65] Dublin, Royal Irish Academy, MS A. 4. 1 (formerly Stowe MS 9), on which
see Plummer, *Bethada*, vol. i, p. xii. Three Lives in this collection were also copied
by Br. Michael O'Clery; on the relationship between the two copies, see *Bethada*,
vol. i, p. xiii. Dinneen was evidently a much less faithful copyist than O'Clery.

occasion to cite later.[66] In 1629 he left Ireland, and for the next three years he was Guardian of St Anthony's College.

Matthews's appointment as Guardian relieved Hugh Ward of this responsibility and perhaps allowed him more time to work on the Lives of saints. His only published work on this subject, however, is not of material value: *Sancti Rumoldi Acta*, begun in 1631 at the request of the archbishop of Malines and completed in the same year, contains an edition of the Life by Thierry of Saint-Trond, a later Life, and a mass, followed by a long historical dissertation of which the greater part is devoted to showing that *Scotia* and *Hibernia* were one and the same in St Rumold's time. The work was brought out by Thomas Sheeran, with a brief memoir of the author, in 1662.[67] Ward introduced in his dissertation a number of extracts from Lives of Irish saints from both the Dublin and Oxford collections, which he presumably used in the transcripts supplied by Matthews. The range of reading deployed in this work is considerable, and shows the extent of Ward's researches in early Irish history. It is often said that Ward worked indefatigably at his task.[68] But he was kept busy too with teaching and the business of his Order,[69] and he suffered much from ill heath;[70] the fact is that we do not know how much else Ward had accomplished before his death on 8 November 1635.

The great endeavour was continued by Fr. John Colgan, OFM (1592–1658), who successfully published two large volumes of *Acta Sanctorum Hiberniae*.[71] Colgan appears to have been collaborating in the work as early as 1628; a letter from him to Ward discusses

[66] Edited by B. Jennings, *Analecta Hibernica*, 6 (1934), 139–91; on its date and authorship, see pp. 139–42.

[67] Hugo Vardaeus, *Sancti Rumoldi Martyris Inclyti . . . Acta, Martyrium, Liturgia Antiqua, & Patria*, ed. T. Sirinus (Louvain, 1662).

[68] For example, by Fleming, *Collectanea Sacra*, p. 84: 'R. P. Hugo Vardeus, qui in rebus nostrae gentis erudiendis & illustrandis cum magno ut speramus fructu indefesse laborat'

[69] A letter (Jennings, *Louvain Papers*, no. 127) asks Ward to take over Fr. John Barnewall's teaching in addition to his own; others (ibid., nos. 143, 148, 152) show him assisting the Commissary General.

[70] Ward to Wadding, Louvain, 9 Aug. 1630: 'La poca salud y la ética y tisis que padesco, con la falta de ayuda, me desmayan mucho para acabar cosa, que los médicos me dicen que no puedo ya vivir mucho tiempo'; B. Jennings (ed.), *Wadding Papers 1614–38* (Dublin, 1953), no. 221.

[71] For a survey of Colgan's career, see Mooney, 'Father John Colgan', pp. 7–13, 21–7.

two catalogues of saints which Colgan had used.[72] He may perhaps have done some searching out of manuscripts in the early stages of the project, but we know very little of his role until after Ward's death.[73] Thereafter, we have what survives of Colgan's correspondence to show him at work, and the handsome acknowledgements he makes in his two published volumes. In the preface to the *Acta*, which contains articles on saints commemorated in January, February, and March, published in 1645, Colgan pays warm tribute to the work of Ward, Fleming, and O'Clery, and acknowledges his debts to Stephen White and Brendan O'Conor.[74] He gives one to believe that Ward had already drawn up the greater part of the volume:[75]

Almost all the complete Lives in this and the following volumes, except for a few that are translated from the Irish and from other languages, and some which I received from elsewhere, have been collected and prepared by the Reverend Father Hugh Ward; to him those whom I have mentioned contributed also some documents which have been turned to account for the present edition. I myself did no more than add the chapter numbers, marginals, explanations or notes to each Life, and appendices to some of them; my original contribution is merely a few brief texts which I have compiled from these and other documents.

This may have been so for the first volume; but if much of the transcription of texts had been done by Ward, Colgan was still responsible for the greater part of the editorial work. His notes especially are full of learning, and pay particular attention to the names of Irish saints, rulers, and places mentioned in the Lives. In preparing these notes, he used many of the Irish texts, including

[72] Colgan to Ward, no address [but evidently from Germany], 26 Dec. 1628; Killiney, MS A. 30, no. 6. Cf. Mooney, 'Father John Colgan', p. 12.

[73] L. Bieler has so interpreted a letter, dated 29 Aug. 1629, from Dom Benedict Lessing of Saint-Hubert to Ward. The letter, printed by [Hogan], 'Hugh Ward', p. 67, merely reports that two members of Ward's community had visited Saint-Hubert and requested copies of the Lives of SS. Fursey, Brigit, and Cadroe, and a fragment on St Patrick. When Colgan took over Ward's work, he naturally used the transcript from Saint-Hubert, and Bieler's inference that he was one of the two who visited that monastery seems to me speculative; L. Bieler, 'John Colgan as Editor', *Franciscan Studies*, 8 (1948), 1–24, (at p. 5).

[74] Colgan, *Acta*, sigs. b2ᵛ–b3ᵛ. On his debt to Fr. Brendan O'Conor, OFM, see A. Gwynn, 'Archbishop Ussher and Father Brendan O Conor', in *Father Luke Wadding Commemorative Volume* [ed. B. Millett] (Dublin, 1957), pp. 263–5.

[75] Colgan, *Acta*, sig. b4; translated by Bieler, 'John Colgan as Editor', p. 3.

annals and genealogies, collected by O'Clery, and he sent inquiries to Ireland, concerning sites, antiquities, and place-names.[76] The second volume, *Trias Thaumaturga* (1647), was primarily Colgan's work, though it is likely that some at least of the texts were printed from copies made by Ward. A third volume was ready for press soon after, and attempts to get it printed lasted until about 1670.[77] But nothing came of it. Funds to pay the printer could not be found, Colgan's health broke down, and no more was accomplished. An outline of Colgan's scheme remains to show what *Acta Sanctorum Hiberniae* might have contained when complete.[78]

Several appreciations of Colgan's books have appeared over the years, showing from where he drew his texts and considering his merits and shortcomings as an editor.[79] Without doubt, Ward, Fleming, and Colgan all deserve considerable credit for their achievement. They, like Stephen White, saw the importance of publishing authentic texts without alteration, and the value in publishing more than one Life of the same saint. This latter approach was systematically applied in *Trias Thaumaturga*, though in the *Acta* one text was usually selected. This fact is the chief reason why the *Trias* is still a more useful book than the *Acta*. But three hundred years on, what we should most appreciate is Ward's policy of collecting and publishing the original texts. It was this policy that motivated him to send Br. Michael O'Clery to Ireland, so helping to save from oblivion a number of valuable manuscripts and a considerable quantity of texts. O'Clery was

[76] Two letters of reply to queries concerning the dioceses of Limerick and Kildare are printed by Jennings, 'Documents from St Isidore's', pp. 229–30. Cf. C. Mooney, 'Colgan's Inquiries about Irish Place-Names', *Celtica*, 1 (1946–50), 294–6.

[77] Jennings, *Michael O Cleirigh*, pp. 181–2; Mooney, 'Father John Colgan', pp. 26–7.

[78] This outline of the scheme is found in Oxford, Bodleian Library, MS Rawl. B. 487, f. 68, and a list of saints to be included in the three remaining volumes, those for Apr.–Dec., is preserved at Killiney. The latter was printed by C. MacDonnell, 'Notice of Some of the Lives which seem to have been Ready, or in Preparation, for the Continuation of the "Acta Sanctorum Hiberniae", at the Death of Colgan', *PRIA* 7 (1857–61), 371–5.

[79] Jennings, *Michael O Cleirigh*, pp. 175–83; Bieler, 'John Colgan as Editor', pp. 1–16, with a survey of his textual sources, pp. 17–24; id., 'Trias Thaumaturga', in *Father John Colgan, OFM, 1592–1658*, ed. T. O Donnell (Dublin, 1959), pp. 41–9; Mooney, 'Father John Colgan', pp. 28–38.

required to copy with exact fidelity what he found, though he found this irksome.[80] But it was the right approach. Colgan's numerous essays on saints for whom no Latin or Irish Life was available are of much less value than his editions. The usefulness of these is diminished by the fact that the manuscripts have in most cases—fortunately—survived. But in those cases where the manuscript has not survived, we must be grateful to Ward and Colgan. It was, for example, they who preserved *Vita IV S. Brigitae* which, as I shall show, is a key text in understanding the Dublin collection. It is all the more to be regretted, therefore, that so much of the collections built up by Ward, Fleming, Colgan, O'Clery, and others of the Four Masters has been lost without trace.

2.3. *White's Letter to Colgan (1640)*

By way of illustrating the attitudes and working environment of these scholars, I can do no better than quote, in English translation, the long letter which Stephen White wrote to Colgan from Dublin at the end of January 1640:[81]

I.H.S.

Reverend Father in Christ, John Colgan. *Pax Christi*

I have received your three letters, though later than I should have wished. That of 4 October 1638, after long delays and hiding, reached me at the end of August 1639; that of 4 September 1639 came to hand at the end of November; the third written on 9 October I got on 2 December. You see, my Father, that it was not for want of good will or courtesy that I

---

[80] O'Clery on a number of occasions reflects on the tediousness or tastelessness of the texts he copied, but sometimes adds as his excuse that he was required 'to follow the track of the old books'; no revision was to be undertaken until after the texts were collected. See Plummer, *Bethada*, vol. i, pp. xiii, 182, and id., 'On the Colophons and Marginalia of Irish Scribes', *PBA* 12 (1926) 21 n. 5; B. Ó Bua-challa, '*Annála Ríoghachta Éireann* agus *Foras Feasa ar Éirinn*: An Comhaim-seartha', *Studia Hibernica*, 22/23 (1982–3) 90–2.

[81] Killiney, Franciscan House of Studies, MS s.n. The text was edited by Count MacDonnell, who found the letter 'on a mouldering and nearly decayed half-sheet of paper' at St Isidore's College in Rome; Reeves, 'Memoir of Stephen White', pp. 33–8. With other manuscripts from St Isidore's it was repatriated to the Franciscan Convent, Merchant's Quay, Dublin, in the 1870s, from where it moved with the greater part of the library to Killiney. Hogan translated long extracts from the letter, 'Life of Father White', pp. 125–9.

have not answered your three letters, which were most welcome to me as coming from one who is most dear to me and to our whole nation. I congratulate our country on having found one, so gifted by God as you are, to watch over, promote, and proclaim her glory. Be of good courage, persevere as you have begun and go on cheerfully; for God is the exceeding great reward of your labour, which the sweet love of homeland will much lighten; all else shall be added unto you, your memory shall live in eternal benediction amongst all the good men of our nation as long as our people shall survive.

I am present with you in spirit, I would I were with you in body also, in order that putting our heads and shoulders together we might, both of us, with joyful and untiring labour, advance first the glory of God and, next, the glory of our most beloved Ireland. Meanwhile, since we cannot be and work together, let us, though separated, labour as best we can, setting our sights on that noble target. I indeed do not cease working to the best of my power, although not as much as I should wish, being old, and in want of a good library.

In truth from day to day for the last twenty-nine years there have grown in me a desire and evermore ardent endeavour, according as places, times and business permitted, to draw forth from a few and widely separated dark caverns of antiquity, and place in the light of day, the *Gesta Dei per Ibernos*, that is, the history of the ancient Scots or natives of Ireland, the Island of Saints, who were once so celebrated at home and abroad for holiness of life, literary culture, and bright deeds in war and peace.

The reason that some of these, my historical writings, have not been published is chiefly the lack of funds to pay the printers, something of which you too complain. I had two good-sized volumes prepared for press: one with the title *Scoto-Caledonica Cornix deplumanda ab auibus orbis*;[82] the other, of equal or larger size, and to my mind greater value, has the title *Commentarii et defensio historiarum Venerabilis Bedae. . .*[83] In the former volume, a work in five books, I refute the false histories and interpretation of names by the Scots of Alba from start to finish, methodically, by plain arguments, and in addition I lay before any reader who is not blind proof that through the first nine Christian centuries and more the name *Scotia*, whether used by Christians or pagans, Irish or foreigners, applied only to Ireland. Only later, perhaps from the early eleventh century, was the name used of both our Ireland

---

[82] For the full fifteen-line title, see Grosjean, 'Un soldat de fortune', p. 437 n. 2. The work survives in Poitiers, Bibliothèque de la ville, MS 258, a volume which passed through the hands of another controversialist, John Lynch.

[83] I have shortened the six-line title. The work is not known to survive.

and of Alba or Caledonia ... This use of the name for both kingdoms lasted until the fourteenth or fifteenth century ...

In your letters you ask me to forward to you at least a summary of my *Selecta* (as you kindly call them) which I had put together in Germany and elsewhere. To the best of my recollection, there was hardly anything of those *Selecta* that I did not give to two of our countrymen, O.S.F.; one of whom was Patrick Fleming, who, as I believe, was martyred by heretics in Bohemia, and who, with his companion, spent many days and weeks in the same town with me, at Metz, in the year 1627 or 1628. They were all copied, and the transcripts were taken by him to Louvain, where your Reverence, I think, may find them, if they have not been found already.

Secondly you ask me to send you a catalogue of such Lives of our saints as you say I had seen in the library of Mr. James Ussher, Archbishop Primate of the Protestants of Ireland. Well, I was invited by him, and three times I spent many hours with that Mr. Ussher. He recieved me with the greatest affability and treated me with candour and unaffectedness, and bade me good-bye with the greatest politeness. Moreover, in person and by letter, he often invited me to his house, not only to dine, which I modestly declined, but to everything of his house, even to his most choice library, which is really of very great value. In that library I saw that catalogue and those Latin Lives of our Irish Saints written at length in manuscript. Outside Mr. Ussher's library, I saw elsewhere in Ireland not only other catalogues of Irish Saints, but many manuscript copies of the Lives of our Saints at still greater length. But you will be astonished to hear it, and yet it is true, as I have found from examination, in those manuscripts. I have not seen one life (or not one of any worth or reliability) unless of those saints contained by name and in alphabetical order in your catalogue, which you sent me, and in which I read the names of saints and some of their Lives mentioned that I had never seen before.

Thirdly, you ask me to endeavour by myself or through friends to have copied out and transmitted to you a list of each and every one of the dioceses, churches, old sanctuaries, etc., of Ireland. I have done my best, in order that the catalogue of the two Dioceses of Waterford and Lismore (in the latter of which I was born), which the Most Rev. Patrick [Comerford], Bishop of Waterford and Lismore, sends to you, should reach you in a more correct and faultless form, in certain details about which I was consulted by that Bishop, who is a very dear and intimate friend of mine. I had scarcely finished correcting some mistakes of that catalogue, when I met my most dear and familiar friend, Father John Barnewall, Provincial of your Order in Ireland. I told him of your letter to me and of the catalogue of the churches, etc. He said that he had urgently and often charged many of his Religious, who had an aptitude for such investigations, to make out those lists everywhere in Ireland, by their own exertion and that of their friends, and to send them to you. Having heard this I ceased to prosecute any further inquiries in that direction, as I considered it unnecessary.

I hope I have now given answers on the more important matters contained in your letters. I cannot in words express to you the joy I felt at your endeavours, diligence, progress (in your work), etc., at the real glory that redounds therefrom to our nation and its saints; and I am especially delighted with your *Féiliride*. How I wish that that book and your other works were not only printed at once, but in the hands and under the eyes of all Europeans!

Before this happens, as a friend, I warn you of a few things. One is that the Lives of SS. Ailbe, Declan, and Gerald of Mayo, who are mentioned in the catalogue you sent me, are swarming (if the Lives you have are the same as those I have read here) with improbable fables, and contain things opposed not only to all that has been written, delivered by tradition, and believed about St Patrick, our Apostle, and about his legation to Rome and thence to Ireland, but contrary to the old and modern Roman Martyrologies, and clearly conflicting with the undoubted statements of St Prosper of Aquitaine, and the Venerable Bede, etc., as I at one time proved to demonstration.

I warn you again of a matter, which I deem of great importance, as affording a very expeditious way of diminishing the credit of our adversaries, Dempster, Chambers, Boece, Major, Buchanan, etc. This is to urge at once each and every single writer known to you, at home or abroad, present or absent, secular or religious, Dominicans, Augustinians, etc., never to allow to be printed anything, whether on a grammatical, philosophical, theological, historical, or other subject, unless it bears on the title page these or similar words—"By the Rev. Father N.N., an Irishman or Old Scot". The constant commemoration of *Scotus Vetus* will not merely irritate our adversaries, though in truth it ought not, but it will awaken in foreign readers at least a curiosity to inquire about the Old Scots and the more recent Scots of Alba and who seeks shall find. Those foreigners will find out the enormous and manifold injustice done to us by those modern Scoto-Albans, Dempster *et al.*, who deny, against the manifest truth, that our Irish were formerly everywhere known by the name of Scots, and that our Ireland was formerly, and everywhere in Europe, known under the name of *Scotia*, *Scotia Insula*, *Scotia Major*, *Scotia Ulterior*, etc.

Finally I beg of you to send copies to me of what I remember I read at Metz, when Patrick Fleming, Martyr, was with me, and had it then in his keeping; also some epistles of our St Columbanus to Pope Boniface and, as an Apologia, to the Bishops of the Council of Mâcon in France, when they reprehend him and ordered him to account for his peculiar observance of the date of Easter, which differed from the canonical Rite of the Roman Church. Patrick, the Martyr, told me also that he had certain *selecta* about Irish history from a remarkable manuscript, seen and copied by him while he was at Regensburg. How I wish I had read these *selecta*!

Here I must perforce end this letter, as in truth during these days and for many months past I am occupied in solving tangled cases of conscience, which are constantly occurring, and in reconciling people who are at variance, etc. Farewell, dear Father, and command my service, as I shall be always ready, as far as my power and opportunities allow, to gratify you, whom, together with all your Fathers, I lovingly greet, and commend to God, whom that He may ever be propitious to me I pray, and I beg you to pray.

Your Reverence's Servant in Christ,
STEPHEN WHITE, S.J.
Dublin, 31 January 1640 (Roman style).

2.4. *Archbishop Ussher and Sir James Ware*

Ussher's career had been spectacular from the outset.[84] He was born in 1581 to a notable Protestant family in Dublin, and his intellectual talents were soon recognized. A scholar at Trinity College from 1594, a fellow from 1599, he gained a reputation as a controversialist.[85] In 1601 he began to receive religious appointments in the college, and was ordained in the same year by his uncle, Henry Ussher, archbishop of Armagh. Preferment soon followed: in 1605 the chancellorship of St Patrick's cathedral, in 1607 the professorship of divinity at Trinity; in 1609 Ussher turned down the provostship. In 1621 he became bishop of Meath and in 1625 archbishop of Armagh, an office which he held until his death in 1656.

Throughout his primatial career, Ussher remained first and foremost a scholar, concerned with all aspects of biblical and

---

[84] Outline by A. Gordon, *DNB*, s.n. See also P. Styles, 'James Ussher and his Times', *Hermathena*, no. 88 (1956), 12–33, and R. Buick Knox, *James Ussher, Archbishop of Armagh* (Cardiff, 1967).

[85] Hogan, 'Sketch of Fr. Fitzsimon's Life', pp. 221–4, gives a very condescending account of Ussher's supposed debate in 1599 with his kinsman, Henry FitzSimon. Elrington, in Ussher, *Whole Works*, i. 11–14, offers a very different account.

patristic studies, doctrine, and ecclesiastical history.[86] His writings were voluminous, his reading prodigious. He had a lifelong interest in the collection of books and manuscripts.[87] As early as 1602 he had made contact with Thomas Bodley, and from 1606 was a friend of Sir Robert Cotton. Ussher's own library, especially his manuscripts, which were acquired mostly in England but with an important Irish element, was famous and attracted many visiting scholars. Among them we have already mentioned Matthews, Strange, and White. Unlike some collectors, however, Ussher studied his books, and in his writings he deployed a great range of information from texts which he had read in manuscript.[88] When a text commanded his serious attention, he was not content to read whatever copy he owned but often sought to borrow or to have transcribed for his own use further copies of the same or related texts for purposes of comparison. An interesting example of this can be found in Dublin, Trinity College, MS 179: ff. 1–21 here contain a copy of the incomplete *Vita I S. Brigitae* from Sir Robert Cotton's MS Otho D. VIII, which lacks eleven sections of the text; the copyist sought to shorten his task by omitting about thirty sections present in the exemplar; he was found out, and ff. 21–25 have the missing chapters, written by a different scribe.[89] The version of *Vita I* in this manuscript is considerably altered from the original, as Ussher was to discover when he later compared this transcript against a copy of the Regensburg text lent to him by Stephen White.[90] He also knew a

---

[86] J. E. L. Oulton, 'Ussher's Work as a Patristic Scholar and Church Historian', *Hermathena*, no. 88 (1956), 3–11, offers only a thin sketch; Buick Knox, *James Ussher*, pp. 98–112, does little justice to Ussher as a scholar.

[87] W. O'Sullivan, 'Ussher as a Collector of Manuscripts', *Hermathena*, no. 88 (1956), 34–58.

[88] O'Sullivan, ibid., p. 35, notes that Ussher's correpondence shows that as early as 1606 he had 'visited many of the best manuscript collections in England'.

[89] The sections missing from the Cottonian manuscript were later copied from White's transcript of the Regensburg manuscript at ff. ii^v–iv (see next note). P. Grosjean, 'Catalogus Codicum Hagiographicorum Latinorum Dubliniensium', *AB* 46 (1928), 100, fails to distinguish the two series of additional sections.

[90] Dublin, Trinity College, MS 179, f. ii^v. Ussher wrote: 'Descripta est uita haec Brigidae ex antiquo ms° Bibliothecae Cottonianae, cui consimilis est sed aliquanto plenior habetur in uetustissimo codice coenobii S. Magni, Canonicorum Regularium B. Augustini, ad pedem Pontis Ratisbonae in Bauaria. Ad cuius finem habetur Hymnus in laudem Brigidae cuius initium "Christus in nostra insula, que uocatur Hibernia" etc., quem in aliis codicibus Ultano

different version of the same Life, from a manuscript in his own possession, as well as another in a manuscript to which he had ready access, in addition to the quite different Life by Cogitosus, published by Canisius.[91]

It is of particular relevance here to know that Ussher owned both copies of our Dublin collection of *uitae* of Irish saints. This is made explicit in the *Antiquitates*, where he says of the Life of St Mochutu 'in uita Carthagi cujus penes me duo sunt exemplaria'.[92] He used both of them extensively, though it is often impossible to determine where he is citing from one rather than the other. Besides these, he was familiar with a considerable number of other Lives of Irish saints. We have mentioned those of St Brigit, but he also knew several Lives of St Patrick, including the Book of Armagh texts.[93] At what stage he came to know or acquire these various Lives, it is not easy to say.

His first relevant publication dates from 1622. This was *An Epistle . . . Concerning the Religion Anciently Professed by the Irish and Scottish*, published as an appendix to a work by Sir Christopher Sibthorp. Among the numerous texts, both printed and unprinted, which he cites here, are: Adomnán's Life of St Columba, of which he had compared Canisius's edition with a manuscript;[94] Cogitosus's Life of St Brigit, which he knew from Canisius and from Cotton's manuscript, Nero E. 1;[95] the references in Marianus Scottus and Jocelin of Furness to Ireland's fame as *insula sanctorum*.[96] He cites here the letter of Cummian on the Irish

Ardbraccanensi attributum inuenimus, uirtutum S. Brigidae scriptori, quem huius Vitae auctorem fuisse omnino existimamus. Unde ex Stephani Viti apographo, uariantes lectiones ad marginem apposuimus, additis hic capitibus illis que a codice Cottoniano aberant.'

[91] The Life of St Brigit in the Dublin collection, then in his possession, is quoted on several occasions; see below, Chapter 5. The Life in the Oxford collection was presumably known to him, since he cites other Lives from it frequently.

[92] *Whole Works*, vi. 475.

[93] See above, p. 12.

[94] *An Epistle*, p. 37, cites Adomnán 1 16 (of the shorter recension, published by Canisius), which he says was 1 20 in his manuscript. (In the manuscript M, this chapter is numbered 30; could 20 be Ussher's misprint?)

[95] Ibid., p. 54. He mentions the omission by Canisius (or his exemplar) of the story of a pregnant nun.

[96] Ibid., p. 58.

calculation of Easter and its defects, a text which he was himself to publish in 1632 from Cotton MS Vitellius A. XII. In discussing the Easter controversy, he cites the account of the synod of Mag nAilbe from a Life of St Munnu in manuscript, almost certainly the version in the Dublin collection.[97] A further indication that he already knew one of our two copies of this collection is his reference to a book belonging to the Friars Minor of Kilkenny which contained the Life of St Brendan; the coincidence of this provenance with the term *Codex Kilkenniensis* suggests that Ussher already knew the copy now in Marsh's Library.[98] That the entire collection was known to him we may perhaps infer from a letter, dated 26 March 1622, from Sir Robert Cotton to Ussher, in which Cotton says, 'I cannot forget your lordship's promise to get me a copy of the Irish saints' Lives'.[99]

Ussher's serious interest in the Irish saints was then perhaps two or three years old: the earliest evidence of systematic work on the subject is his annotation of FitzSimon's *Catalogus*, a book which he owned in the edition of 1619.[100] Besides his study of the 'Religion anciently professed', first published in 1622 and reissued independently in 1631, two of Ussher's works are particularly relevant here, *Veterum Epistolarum Hibernicarum Sylloge* (1632) and *Britannicarum Ecclesiarum Antiquitates* (1639).[101] The former, a slim volume, printed forty-five original texts concerned with the church in Ireland, but without discussion. The *Antiquitates*, on the other hand, was a lengthy study, meticulously researched, of the origins and early history of the Christian church throughout the British Isles; the two chapters devoted to Ireland were by far the most original parts of the work. For the greater part of twenty years, therefore, Ussher gave at least some of his study-time to the religious history of Ireland in the early Middle Ages. The Lives of the saints were the evidence to which he most frequently referred.

---

[97] Ibid., pp. 72–3; cf. *Mun.* **D** §§ 26–7. He cites the same passage from M at *Antiquitates*, pp. 936–7 (*Whole Works*, vi. 503–5).

[98] Ibid., p. 21; see also below, pp. 100–1.

[99] Ussher, *Whole Works*, xv. 171–2; O'Sullivan, 'Ussher as a Collector', p. 37.

[100] Grosjean, '*Catalogus* de Henri FitzSimon', p. 336.

[101] Ussher's *Antiquitates* (as the work is now usually known) is often referred to by contemporary writers as his *Primordia*; this may have been the intended title, since the running-heads of the first edition read 'De Britannicarum Ecclesiarum Primordiis'.

It is, perhaps, unfortunate that he did not publish any of these texts entire.

During these twenty years, he cultivated contacts with a wide range of scholars, freely exchanging information, borrowing or obtaining copies of texts, and allowing copies to be taken from his own manuscripts. In the study of the saints' Lives, almost all of these contacts were with Roman Catholic religious.

David Rothe, bishop of Ossory, and vicar-general for the absent Papist archbishop of Armagh, actually approached Ussher in 1621, very tentatively, since Ussher was already a bishop and had called for the strict enforcement of legislation against Catholic clergy. Contact between the two men was dangerous for both; it was conducted under pseudonyms, Rothe writing as Nicholas Laffan, Ussher as Jacobus de Turrecremata.[102] Their scholarly friendship was inevitably hedged with reservations, and towards the end of 1622 was interrupted, following a sermon in which Ussher demanded firm action to suppress the Catholic clergy.[103] It was later resumed, but already Rothe had acted as intermediary to obtain copies for Ussher of texts in the collections of Fr. Heribert Rosweyde. These texts are specified in a letter from Rothe: the Office and the Life of S. Dympna, the verse epistle supposedly addressed by St Livinus to St Florbert, and the Rules of St Columbanus.[104] In some cases Rothe passed on Rosweyde's marginal comments. The poem of St Livinus was published by Ussher in his *Sylloge*.[105] I have not discovered further evidence for

[102] The earliest letters between Rothe and Ussher survive in Dublin, Trinity College, MS 568, and are listed by Gwynn, 'Archbishop Ussher and Father Brendan O Conor', p. 265 n. 8. Mr William O'Sullivan is preparing an edition for publication.

[103] The sermon is published in *Whole Works*, i. 58–60. Rothe, in a letter dated 4 Feb. 1623, to Dr Christopher Talbot, mentions the discontinuing of his contact with 'the Paedagogus'; P. Grosjean, 'Les Vies de S. Finnbarr de Cork, de S. Finnbarr d'Écosse et de S. Mac Cuilinn de Lusk', *AB* 69 (1951), 344 n. 2. The autograph of the letter was preserved between the leaves of Dublin, Trinity College, MS 580 (E. 3. 8), a collection of transcripts made for Ussher.

[104] Grosjean, 'Les Vies de S. Finnbarr', p. 344 n. 2. The texts on St Dympna survive among Ussher's papers, Dublin, Trinity College, MS 580 (E. 3. 8), ff. 53–56.

[105] 'Hos autem S. Liuini elegos, ex manuscripto Corssendonckiano ab Heriberto Rosweydo descriptos, communicauit mihi D. Rothaeus, patriarum antiquitatum indagator diligentissimus'; *Sylloge*, no. VIII, pp. 19–22, and n. at p. 125

direct or indirect contact between Ussher and Rosweyde, and there is no sign of exchanges between Ussher and Bollandus in the years following Rosweyde's death.[106] Rothe also mentions on two occasions the collection of Irish saints' Lives 'in manuscripto Salamantino', referring specifically to the Lives of St Mochta and St Fursu; I am not certain when or where Rothe may have seen this manuscript.[107]

In the *Antiquitates*, Ussher handsomely acknowledges the help he had received from Rothe, both from his published works and private correspondence.[108] Where he actually quotes from such a letter, it was from one written fifteen years earlier, about 1623.[109] It is possible therefore that further exchanges did not flourish, though in 1631 Rothe still speaks of the possibility of borrowing texts from the primate.[110]

Between December 1623 and the beginning of 1626, Ussher was in England, working on the book which was eventually to become his *Antiquitates*, the 'period of [his] greatest commerce with Sir Robert [Cotton]'s library'.[111] In 1626, when he was at home in Drogheda, he permitted his volume of saints' Lives to be copied for Fr. Francis Matthews to send to the Irish Franciscans in Louvain; this was his major contribution to the Franciscan enterprise. Fr. Thomas Strange, however, was the Franciscan most familiar to Ussher, acting over a period of years as an intermediary between Ussher and Wadding.[112]

During the 1630s, there are no letters indicating the cultivation of such exchanges with Catholic scholars other than Wadding. One should not necessarily imagine that the controversial climate

[106] When he first published this letter of Rothe, Grosjean assumed that 'Laffan' (whom he had not then identified) was merely acting as an intermediary; 'Les Vies de S. Finnbarr', p. 343. Later, 'Notes sur quelques sources', p. 161, he says that Rothe may have had the texts for some time himself and have passed them to Ussher without the intention of facilitating exchanges between the two scholars.

[107] Dublin, Trinity College, MS 568, pp. 139, 142. I owe these references to Mr O'Sullivan (see n. 102). It is possible that Rothe had studied at Salamanca before 1609, when he returned to Ireland, but his name is not given in O'Doherty, 'Students of the Irish College'.

[108] *Whole Works*, vi. 284. Ussher refers to Rothe in complimentary terms elsewhere, ibid., iv. 425; v. 309; vi. 286 and 377.

[109] Ibid., p. 377.

[110] Letter to Wadding, dated 20 July 1631; *Wadding Papers*, no. 227, p. 551.

[111] O'Sullivan, 'Ussher as a Collector', p. 37.

[112] Gwynn, 'Archbishop Ussher and Father Brendan O Conor', pp. 270–2.

made them more difficult, but perhaps that Ussher was by this stage engrossed in writing. About 1638 or 1639, Ussher met Stephen White, whose account of the relationship has been quoted. From Ussher's point of view, one can say that he is generous in his praise of White's learning. As Grosjean has shown, Ussher had reason to be grateful, since White had made available to him (at the last moment) the most important witness to monastic life in early medieval Ireland.[113]

With the publication of the *Antiquitates*, Ussher's interests moved on, so that we have no evidence that he derived the full benefit from White's copy of the longer text of Adomnán's Life of St Columba. We need not follow Ussher's career in England in the 1640s and 1650s. Gwynn, however, discovered a letter of interest as a footnote to this phase of the archbishop's career. It was written in 1641, addressed to Ussher, by Colgan's assistant, Brendan O'Conor.[114] In it, we see Ussher still pursuing manuscripts: Colgan had agreed to send him the letters of St Columbanus from Fleming's papers; O'Conor had been copying annals and other texts from books belonging to Finghin Mac Carthaigh Mór in London. But O'Conor was much exercised by the prospect of imminent conflagration in Ireland, and urged the collection of manuscripts into the hands of such men as James Ware, through whom copies could be communicated. The text is difficult, and the background obscure, but in the year of the Catholic Revolt he was probably right.

Ware, who had been using Ussher's manuscripts for twenty years, was building up a major collection of his own. Several books once owned by him have been or will be referred to in this study, but chiefly the two manuscripts of the Oxford collection. Ware himself was born in 1594, in Dublin, the son of another Sir James Ware, auditor-general of Ireland. Having graduated from Trinity College in 1616, he took up antiquarian pursuits, encouraged by Ussher and assisted by the Gaelic scholar Dubhaltach Mac Firbhisigh. He was knighted in 1629, and followed his father as auditor-general in 1632, but his scholarly interests did not decline and he remained productive of antiquarian works until his death in 1666. He was responsible for the *editio princeps* of St Patrick's

[113] See above, p. 45.
[114] Gwynn, 'Archbishop Ussher and Father Brendan O Conor', pp. 281–2, with comments at pp. 279–81.

writings, which he printed from Cotton MS Nero E. I.[115] Few of his works now command attention, but the collection of manuscripts which he assembled is of the first importance, and it is in that connexion that I mention him here.[116]

2.5. *Heribert Rosweyde and the Bollandists*

The name of Heribert Roswey or Rosweyde has already come up often in this chapter. He was born at Utrecht in 1569 and died at Antwerp in 1629, a Jesuit, who spent his entire life in teaching and study. In 1607 he proposed the publication, in twelve folio volumes according to the calendar, of the *uitae* of saints known from manuscripts in Belgian libraries.[117] With the encouragement of the Society, he embarked on collecting the materials, on a wider scale than merely Belgian sources. The only major publications achieved in his lifetime, however, were an expanded edition of the *Martyrologium Romanum*, and a monumental edition of *Vitae*

[115] *S. Patricio Adscripta Opuscula* (Dublin, 1656).

[116] The earliest catalogue of Ware's library is his own, *Librorum Manuscriptorum in Bibliotheca Jacobi Waræi, Equitis Aur., Catalogus* (Dublin, 1648). A later and fuller catalogue exists in BL, MS Add. 38693 (s. xvii), ff. 74–88. The entire library, including his working notebooks as well as the older manuscripts acquired by him, was sold by his heir in about 1686 to Henry Hyde, 2nd Earl of Clarendon, the historian of the Great Rebellion. In the 1690s the books were deposited in the Bibliotheca Tenisoniana, Leicester Square, where they were catalogued in some detail; this catalogue was published in E. Bernard, *Catalogi Librorum Manuscriptorum Angliae et Hiberniae* (Oxford, 1697), part 2, pp. 3–15. Clarendon's library was acquired (after various discreet offers of sale) in 1709 by James Brydges, 1st Duke of Chandos, who resisted Dean Swift's efforts to persuade him to return the manuscripts to Dublin. When his collection was sold in 1747, Dr Richard Rawlinson (1690–1755) bought many of the older books but not the notebooks. Some of these were bought by Dr Jeremiah Milles (1714–84), dean of Exeter. The large library of Rawlinson was bequeathed to the Bodleian in 1756; Milles's volumes were presented to the British Museum in 1766, where they are now MSS Add. 4783–4801, 4821–2. Not all of Ware's manuscripts reached these havens; some are safe in the library of Trinity College, Dublin, but some have disappeared. The enormous interest of many of Ware's manuscripts makes a study of his collections something much to be desired. Cf. R. Flower, 'Manuscripts of Irish Interest in the British Museum', *Analecta Hibernica*, 2 (1931), 292–340 (pp. 300–3).

[117] *Fasti Sanctorum Quorum Vitae in Belgicis Bibliothecis Manuscriptae . . .* (Antwerp, 1607). I have not seen a copy of this essay. The scope of the proposed work, including its additional volumes, is discussed by H. Delehaye, *L'Œuvre des Bollandistes à travers trois siècles* (2nd edn., Brussels, 1959), pp. 13–15.

Patrum.[118] After his death, the superiors of the Society chose Jean Bolland (1596–1665) to continue the task, and from him the work of the Bollandists takes its name. There are several accounts of this, the longest lived of Knowles's 'Great historical enterprises', and I shall not re-cover that ground here.[119]

In the early years, Rosweyde and Bolland were in close contact with the Irish Franciscans at Louvain. Many texts came to them from Ward and Colgan; in return Rosweyde sent extracts from the third of the major collections, *Codex Salmanticensis*. It is perhaps surprising, however, that, though Rosweyde had this manuscript in the 1620s, the entire text was not made available to Ward or Colgan until after October 1634.[120] The first volumes of *Acta Sanctorum*, representing the saints commemorated in January, were published in 1643, two years before the same section of Colgan's *Acta*. The printing of the latter had probably begun before 1643. Bolland acknowledges Colgan's edition as his principal source for the Life of St Íte, which he had compared with a copy of the text from the Saints' Island manuscript supplied by Ward. In the same volumes, Ward had supplied texts for the Lives of SS. Mochua, Maedóc, and Fechin; O'Sullivan Beare had provided several texts, including that of another St Mochua translated from Irish; the *Codex Salmanticensis* was used for several Lives; and a copy of the Life of St Fechin, differing a little from that supplied by Ward, came from FitzSimon. The same individuals, and also Stephen White, had provided help with the interpretation of the texts. Bolland had been advised by FitzSimon that there was considerable influence from Irish secular literature, and that anyone not versed in this should tread carefully when using these texts.[121] He deliberately abdicated any concern with the dispute between the Irish and the Scots.[122]

The principle, from the outset, was to present a carefully chosen text of each Life, representing as nearly as possible the original

[118] *Martyrologium Romanum* (Antwerp, 1613); *Vitae Patrum. De Vita et Verbis Seniorum Libri X Historiam Eremiticam Complectentes, Auctoribus suis et Nitori Pristino Restituti* (Antwerp, 1617).

[119] Delehaye, *L'Œuvre*, *passim*; M. D. Knowles, *Great Historical Enterprises* (London, [1962]), pp. 1–32.

[120] See below, pp. 228–9.

[121] *Acta Sanctorum*, Jan. I (1643), p. 45.

[122] Ibid., p. xxx.

words of the author. With Lives in the three collections, however, only one recension was generally given. For saints of whom no Life was known, Bolland, like Colgan, would give extracts from martyrologies and from the Lives of other saints where their deeds were mentioned. Although these simple principles had been set out by Rosweyde, and are reiterated by Bolland in the preface to the volumes for January, we are nowhere told how they and their assistants and successors worked. It may seem unnecessarily remote from our present needs to inquire into such matters, but this is not the case.

The collection of transcripts began straightaway after 1607, and by the time of Rosweyde's death, there were many volumes of them. The volumes we know now contain transcripts arranged roughly according to the calendar. These *collectanea* (as they are termed by the catalogue of what remains) have not survived intact. Much is preserved, in no apparent order and without published index, in the Bibliothèque royale in Brussels.[123] Other volumes survive elsewhere, especially in the Bollandists' present library in the Collège St-Michel, but much has been lost. A survey of these *collectanea* could be of considerable interest, but the historians of the enterprise have never discussed them. So far as their Irish interest is concerned, Grosjean was able to uncover several texts, not previously known to survive, lying unpublished in the *collectanea*, while Plummer drew attention to the fact that the published volumes of *Acta* used, for a number of Irish saints, copies no longer known to us. Both categories of text are potentially of great importance to our study of the transmission of Hiberno-Latin *uitae*. It would, therefore, be of some help to know how and from what sources the collections were assembled, and how they were organized and used. This task is a large one, for which at this juncture I have neither the opportunity nor the space. A few observations must suffice.

Most volumes of the *collectanea* contain the Lives of saints commemorated in the same month or even on the same day or two days of the month. All were copied out by Rosweyde or Bolland or, in most cases, one of their assistants. Each text was then marked with its source; in the volumes we are concerned

---

[123] J. Van den Gheyn, *Catalogue des manuscrits de la Bibliothèque Royale de Belgique*, v (Brussels, 1905), pp. 406–675 (catalogue nos. 3439–560).

with, this was done by Bolland. Thus, in Brussels, Bibliothèque royale, MS 3196–3203 (cat. 3439), for example, among the saints of March, we find: St David, ff. 112–117 'ex manuscripto R. P. Hugonis Vardei minoritae Hiberniensis'; St Énda, ff. 120–130 'ex manuscripto insulae omnium sanctorum in Hibernia'; St Fridolin, ff. 169–203 'ex manuscripto R. P. Hug. Vardei'; St Patrick, ff. 347–354, with a note in the hand of Daniel Papebroch, 'eruta ex antiquo ms. a Petro Vito Soc. Iesu';[124] St Patrick's Purgatory, ff. 364–367 'ex manuscripto minoritarum Hibernorum Lovanii'; and St Senán, ff. 415–430 'ex ms. Hibernico Seminarii Salmanticensis Soc. Iesu collato cum ms. R. P. Vardaei'. The occurrence of Papebroch in this miscellany shows that the present volumes are the result of binding at least two generations later than the origin of the collection. Elsewhere varying sequences of folio-numbers and divided or displaced texts confirm that these volumes are not original compilations, but result from the subdivision and rearrangement of earlier volumes. Unfortunately, the catalogue provides no help on this aspect of the manuscripts. Already, from the case of St Senán, we see evidence from the *collectanea* of the collation of different texts.

These *collectanea* provided the foundation of later work, but editors were not bound by the original collections. When February was published, under the editorship of Bolland, in 1658, for the Life of St Fintán of Clonenagh Henskens reprinted from Colgan the text of the Dublin collection, collated with those of Oxford and *Salmanticensis*.[125] Yet in the *collectanea* there is a copy of the fullest text, that of *Salmanticensis*, on which Bolland has written, 'Ex manuscripto Hibernico seminarii Salmanticensis Hibernorum Soc. Iesu et collatum cum ms. Kilkenniensi ut puto R. P. Hugonis Vardei'.[126] Another volume, MS 7773 (cat. 3444), which now contains material on the saints of April, includes at ff. 550^r–551^v (previously ff. 276^r–277^v) a Life of St Ibar 'ex ms. P. Fitzimon'. This text was not published in the notice of St Ibar by Henskens at 23 April, which appeared in 1675. Some work, however, had been done on it. Papebroch, still Henskens's assistant at that date, had written to Fr. Sheeran at Louvain,

---

[124] For which read Stephen White; see above, n. 40.
[125] *Acta Sanctorum*, Feb. III (1658), pp. 17–21. The errors of Colgan's text are repeated.
[126] Brussels, Bibliothèque royale, MS 7763 (cat. 3443), ff. 191–200.

sending him the text of this Life. Sheeran had returned it on 10 April 1671, together with a text and translation of the fragment on St Ibar in the Book of Leinster.[127] Sheeran had not seen FitzSimon's text elsewhere. There was no Life of St Ibar in the copies, which he and the Bollandists had, of the manuscripts in the possession of Ussher and Ware. (Here he incidentally shows that, though both men were by then dead, the ownership of both the Dublin and Oxford collections was known to him.) He directs Papebroch to the mention of Ibar in other Lives in these collections.[128] It is not apparent why Papebroch and Henskens decided not to publish the texts. For our immediate purpose, it is more to be regretted that there is so little information about the manuscript of Father FitzSimon, from which this and other texts were copied but which was unknown to the Louvain Franciscans.

Lying behind these miscellaneous collections, there were presumably copies of the sources. With the Lives from *Salmanticensis*, we know the Bollandists had the original, which survives. If, however, they possessed complete or near complete copies of Francis Matthews's transcript of the Dublin collection, or John Goolde's of the Oxford collection, or FitzSimon's manuscript, no trace of them remains. An interesting volume in Dublin, Trinity College, MS 1140, appears to be a compilation from calendars of Irish saints for February and March, put together by Ward and Colgan for Bolland. Other such volumes lying behind the *collectanea* are presumably lost.

Whilst Rosweyde and Bolland were able to consult White, FitzSimon, Ward, and Colgan, and Papebroch could write to Sheeran, their successors were without such Irish assistance and so depended on their existing files. Thus in 1753 a letter written by Ward in 1634 is cited in the discussion of St Ailbe.[129] De Buck informs us that White's letters continued to be used for guidance,[130] but for the most part the Bollandists were without expertise in Irish hagiography until almost the moment when the

---

[127] Sheeran's letter is printed by P. Grosjean, 'Deux textes inédits sur S. Ibar', *AB* 77 (1959), 427–9, regrettably omitting the text, translation, and comments on the fragment from the Book of Leinster.

[128] The Lives he mentions are Patrick, Brigit, Ailbe, Declán, Abbán, Ciarán of Saigir, Moninna, 'etc.'

[129] *Acta Sanctorum*, Sept. IV (1753), pp. 26–7.

[130] 'L'archéologie irlandaise', p. 590.

Acta were finally (?) suspended. Grosjean contributed to one volume only. During these years, however, many Irish saints were dealt with, but Lives were printed for a declining proportion. Bolland had found Irish Lives rather excessive in their taste for fantastic miracles, but his successors often found them unacceptable.[131] There are long runs where no notice of any importance appeared for an Irish saint. As late as 1867, when St Abbán's Life was published, the old *collectanea* were still the only source. De Buck's comments are both informative and, inasmuch as he arrived at the correct decision, judicious, but he might as well have written in 1650:[132]

Colganus in Actis sanctorum Hiberniae, ad diem 16 Martii, edidit hanc vitam, ex hibernico latine versam, ex codice ms. membraneo Kill-Canigensi; eamque contulit cum tribus aliis vitis ejusdem sancti, duabus hibernicis, atque una latina, codicis Salmanticensis. Qui codex Salmanticensis, olim Bollandianus, nunc in bibliotheca publica Bruxellensi conservatur, notatus num. 7672 et 7673. Editionem Colgani contulit P. Fitzsimon, in republica literaria Hibernica non incognitus, cum codice hibernico Dubliniensi, seu potius versionem Colgani correxit ex codice Dubliniensi eamque cum codice conformavit. In Colgani versione centones aliquot insunt, alii ad ethicam pertinentes, alii explanatorii; nulli historici: plerosque uncinis [ ] inclusimus. Maluimus autem versionem Colgani et Fitzimonii edere, quam codicis Salmanticensis textum latinum; quoniam hic nonnisi versio latina est, saeculo forte xv facta, proculdubio multo minori labore et diligentia quam Colganus et Fitzsimonius adhibuerunt.

One may well wonder how De Buck came to think that the text of the *Codex Kilkenniensis* (for such it is) was a seventeenth-century

---

[131] Bolland remarked of the Lives of Irish, British, and Breton saints, 'Plane portentosae sunt Sanctorum Vitae atque miraculis fere incredibilibus contextae'; *Acta Sanctorum*, Jan. I, p. xxxiv. Cf. passages quoted from the volumes for Mar. and Apr., Plummer, *Vitae*, vol. i, p. xcii n. 9. Later editors took a more hostile view; for example, Suyskens on the Life of St Ailbe: 'Porro Acta illa in omnibus memoratis exemplaribus satis ampla sunt; sed, quod in aliis etiam Sanctorum Hiberniae Vitis crebro contingit, quo ampliora sunt, eo plures fabulas continent, eoque pluribus fabellis et enormibus anachronismis vera sancti Antistitis gesta obscurant. Verbo, non sunt, nisi quaedam figmentorum farrago, quae risum pariter ac stomachum lectori moveant; ideoque nullam ex memoratis vitis S. Evino, quiscumque demum is Sanctus fuerit, sine injuria possum adscribere'; ibid., Sept. IV, p. 27.

[132] De Buck, 'De SS. Abbanis Kill-Abbaniensi et Magharnuidhiensi', *Acta Sanctorum*, Oct. XII (1867), p. 277 n. (a).

translation from Irish. It is, however, the fullest and most original Life of St Abbán still extant.[133] It is of special interest to learn that FitzSimon, presumably in the 1630s, verified Colgan's copy of the Dublin collection against the manuscript. Here, in following Colgan, one might suppose that De Buck was persuaded by the latter's reverence for his *Kilkenniensis*, as Henskens was in treating of St Fintán of Clonenagh. Yet De Buck appears to have formed his own opinion about the differences between the two texts. The passages which he brackets are absent from the *Salmanticensis* text, and he took them for translator's interpolations; they were, as we shall come to see, passages characteristic of the scholarly compiler of the Dublin collection. De Buck does not mention that in Brussels, Bibliothèque royale, MS 8922–8924 (cat. 3488), the text of the *Salmanticensis* Life was prepared for publication with introductory notes by Rosweyde, and a commentary was added later by Papebroch.[134]

It would be easy to criticize the work of some Bollandist editors after Papebroch and before De Buck, but it serves no purpose. When using the *Acta*, however, it would be advantageous to have to hand some information on the sources available to the editors, and on what survives in the *collectanea*; perhaps one day the modern Bollandists will supply a companion to the *Acta*, which relates the published text to its sources, to the *collectanea*, and to the evidence which might be drawn on by an editor today. Such a companion would insure that the *Acta*, which can hardly now be revised and replaced when the resources are not there even to complete them, could remain a valuable source and could be consulted with greater security than is now the case.

The long era when the Bollandists alone, however inadequately, persisted in the publication of these *uitae*, brings us from the period of endeavour—to preserve and explain—to the period when scholarship turned the tools of research and criticism to the study of saints' Lives. Bollandists have played a notable part in this, but in Ireland a renewal of interest began when De Buck was still following the track of Colgan and FitzSimon.

---

[133] See below, p. 350.

[134] The notes occupy ff. 21–22, the text ff. 23^r–45^v, and Papebroch's commentary ff. 46–51. I have not read these.

3

Modern Scholars and their Methods

A NEW era in the study of Irish saints' Lives begins with the work of the Revd William Reeves (1813–91), a learned curate to whom preferment in the Church of Ireland came only late in life: in 1875 he became dean of Armagh, and eventually in 1886 bishop of Down and Connor.[1] But already in 1857 he had published his finest book, the edition of Adomnán's *Vita S. Columbae*.[2] In the notes to that edition, Reeves frequently cites from the Lives of other Irish saints from the medieval collections, and he had published notes on Colgan's *Acta Sanctorum Hiberniae* and Fleming's *Collectanea Sacra*.[3] His study of the Lives was kept up over a number of years, but the only notable result was a study of the collection till then known as the *Codex Kilkenniensis*.[4] Reeves tried to replace this title with *Codex Armachanus*, presumably an act of local patriotism by the dean and librarian of Armagh; in the matter of provenance, this name is worthless since it means no more than that the book belonged to Archbishop Ussher.[5] Reeves's papers in the library of Trinity College include a number of transcripts of Lives, often made from the Bollandist edition, collated with the two Dublin manuscripts. Occasionally, as in the case of St Cainnech's Life, Reeves also collated the *Salmanticensis* text and began to form critical opinions as to which copy of a Life was the most valuable:[6]

---

[1] M. C. Ferguson, *Life of the Right Rev. William Reeves, DD* (Dublin, 1893), pp. 112, 132.

[2] *The Life of St Columba by Adamnan*; for the rapturous reception of this book, see letters quoted by Ferguson, *Life of Reeves*, pp. 47–51.

[3] W. Reeves, 'The Irish Library, 1: Colgan's Works', *UJA* 1 (1853), 295–302; 2 (1854), 253–61.

[4] 'On a Manuscript Volume of Lives of Saints (Chiefly Irish), now in Primate Marsh's Library, Dublin, Commonly Called the Codex Kilkenniensis', *PRIA*[2] 1 (1870–9), 339–50.

[5] See below, pp. 100–1.

[6] Dublin, Trinity College, MS 1059, p. 611.

The Life as given in the Cod. Salmant. is much superior to that in Cod. Armach. as fuller & more archaic, both in the Latin expression & in the forms of the Irish names. The latter is evidently doctored, softened, and expurgated for ordinary or devotional purposes, and is greatly deficient in the antiquarian smack which in a marked manner characterizes the former. I regard the former as a most curious & valuable composition. Though not accurately represented in Lord Ormonde's text, it is better done than most of the Lives printed in the Bollandists, in whom as in most such editors the religious or moral impulse is ever at work to disfigure the archaeological verity.

Colgan had not reached St Cainnech in his liturgical arrangement, and the Bollandists, when they did so, did not print a Life. But the same critical observations could be made of the Life of St Fintán of Clonenagh, of which Colgan, followed by the Bollandists, preferred to publish the Dublin text rather than the 'fuller & more archaic' version in the *Salmanticensis*, a mistake Colgan repeated with the Life of St Aed mac Bricc.[7] It appears that Reeves was the first to form a correct opinion as to the inferiority in some cases of the Dublin text as against the *Salmanticensis*.

He had perhaps been helped towards this by the fact that John Butler, second Marquess of Ormonde, had printed the *Salmanticensis* version of the Life of St Cainnech in full, noting only the additions made by the Dublin text. But Ormonde's edition makes little attempt to assess the value or interest of the Life. A little later, Richard Caulfield published the Life of St Finnbarr, usefully juxtaposing the texts of the Dublin and Oxford collections, but again forming no critical opinion as to the priority or worth of either text.[8]

The year 1882 marks a turning-point in the history of hagiography. In that year, publication of *Analecta Bollandiana* began, a major indicator of the reorganization achieved by Fr. Charles De Smedt (1831–1911) in the work of the Bollandists. His new methods included the systematic cataloguing of hagiographical manuscripts in European libraries, the beginnings of *Bibliotheca Hagiographica Latina*, and an increase in the linguistic range and detail of the *Acta Sanctorum* from the first volume of November.[9]

---

[7] The superiority of the S-text was in this case first remarked on by Plummer, *Vitae*, vol. i, p. xxvii.   [8] *The Life of St Fin Barre* (London, 1864).

[9] H. Delehaye, *L'Œuvre des Bollandistes à travers trois siècles* (2nd edn., Brussels, 1959), pp. 149–57.

The first two issues of the *Analecta* included the greater part of the Patrician dossier from the Book of Armagh, edited by Fr. Edmund Hogan (1831–1917), who made use for the first time of the Brussels manuscript of Muirchú. In the same year, Whitley Stokes (1830–1909) gave up his position as Legal Member of the Viceroy's Council in the government of India and returned to England. He had already published at Calcutta in 1877 the Middle Irish Lives of Patrick, Brigit, and Columba from the fifteenth-century *Leabhar Breac*. In 1887, these were followed by the Tripartite Life of Patrick, and a large number of other texts about the saint, including those from the Book of Armagh. In 1890, the Lives of saints from the Book of Lismore were also published in an edition by Stokes. With the exception of the Tripartite Life and three Lives copied by O'Clery from the Book of Lismore, these texts were all unknown to Ward and Colgan.

Even as Stokes laboured to publish scholarly printed texts, manuscript copies of Irish Lives were still being produced in the 1890s. By this date the copies were derived from the collections of Michael O'Clery.[10]

The first significant step towards superseding the Franciscans' work was made in 1887 when the Bollandists De Smedt and De Backer published the whole text of the *Codex Salmanticensis*, the fullest and most varied of the three Latin collections used by the seventeenth-century editors. This work was financed by John Patrick Crichton-Stuart, third Marquess of Bute (1847–1900), who had become a Roman Catholic as a youth, and who in 1882 edited the poem *Altus prosator* attributed to St Columba. How much further his interest in Hiberno-Latin saints went, his biographer does not say.[11] The method of printing the entire collection was

---

[10] For example, between 1893 and 1897 Patrick Stanton of Cork is known to have made twenty-one copies of the Irish Life of St Finnbarr, patron of Cork, from O'Clery's transcript, adding an English translation. Notwithstanding their inaccuracy, and the fact that Stanton also published text and translation in the *Journal of the Cork Historical and Archaeological Society*, 2 (1893), 61–9, 87–94, these manuscript copies came to be highly valued according to C. J. F. MacCarthy, 'St Finbar and His Monastery', *Journal of the Cork Historical and Archaeological Society*, 40 (1935), 57–61 (p. 60). Two of Stanton's copies survive at Killiney, Franciscan House of Studies, MSS A. 42 and A. 44.

[11] His life was written by the Benedictine baronet D. O. Hunter Blair, *John Patrick Third Marquess of Bute, KT: A Memoir* (London, 1921), but this work makes no reference to the edition of *Salmanticensis*.

surely a sound one. It made it possible to see the collector's work as a whole for the first time. The need to compare different versions of Lives in the different collections was already apparent from the work of Ormonde and Caulfield, if not from Colgan. One might have hoped, therefore, that the edition of the *Salmanticensis* would have been followed by similar editions of the collections in Dublin (on which Reeves had worked extensively) and in Oxford (to which attention had been drawn by Caulfield). But nothing was done.

The next landmark is the work of the Revd Charles Plummer (1857–1927), the great editor of Fortescue, Bede, and the Anglo-Saxon Chronicle, who in 1902 turned his attention to Irish hagiography. He began by reading the *Salmanticensis*,[12] and went on to collate the edition with the Lives of the Oxford collection in two Bodleian manuscripts. He published the results as a study of the Oxford collection and a separate study of the Life of St Brendan contained in it.[13] Some Lives in the two collections were identical, others were closely related, and for these he regarded the published text of the *Salmanticensis* as serviceable, notwithstanding the disfigurement of Irish names. He next studied the two manuscripts of the Dublin collection; though he recognized that in many cases this presented a version inferior to the published *Salmanticensis* Life, he none the less regarded the Dublin texts as of interest and transcribed them for publication in the two volumes of his *Vitae Sanctorum Hiberniae*. In making his selection, he only once duplicated a text published by De Smedt and De Backer, the Life of St Tigernach, which is incomplete in the *Salmanticensis*, and which Plummer printed from the Oxford collection. Otherwise Plummer printed most of the Dublin collection, twenty-two Lives, while from the Oxford collection he printed nine unique texts, but omitted all that he thought adequately covered by the recensions published elsewhere.[14] He did, however, conscientiously note

---

[12] A note in his copy of De Smedt and De Backer, *Acta*, col. 946, records that he finished reading the collection on 18 Aug. 1902, and in the same month of 1903 he reread most of the book (omitting items 1–3, 9, 28, 30, 39).

[13] 'Some New Light on the Brendan Legend', *ZCP* 5 (1904–5), 124–41.

[14] Plummer's omissions from **D** were: the Lives of St Patrick and St Brigit no longer extant in the manuscripts (see below, pp. 121–2, 217–20); the foreign saints Louis and Anthony; the Life of St Columba, shorter recension of Adomnán; the Life and *Nauigatio* of St Brendan already published by Moran; the

where other recensions deviated from the one he had chosen to print, and in March and April 1906 he recollated a number of Lives in the *Salmanticensis* against the manuscript for this purpose. Having selected what he thought worth publishing, Plummer seems to have worked through these *uitae* one by one in the order of the alphabet, preparing his text and notes, and drafting the textual section of the introduction.[15] These sections on the individual Lives must surely have been written at intervals, for it is otherwise hard to understand how Plummer could have made the same observations time after time without ever connecting them up. The introduction was completed while the texts were in proof, and the two chapters on the manuscripts and on the composition and character of the Lives are brief and perfunctory.[16] Plummer's interests had by that stage strayed into mythology, an area fashionable at the time, thanks largely to Sir James Frazer; but Plummer's speculations on this front incurred immediate censure from reviewers when the book was published in 1910.[17]

In discussing the Latin Lives, Plummer had made careful comparisons with Irish Lives, most of them unpublished. He followed this by editing with an English translation seventeen texts, chiefly from two surviving volumes of Michael O'Clery's collections, adding two Lives from the manuscript written by Dinneen for Francis Matthews. He chose not to print Irish Lives which were already published or which were little more than a

verse Life of St Senán; the fragment on St Flannán and the Lives of the twelfth-century saints Malachy and Lawrence.

[15] He justifies the alphabetical arrangement as appropriate to a work of reference, *Vitae*, vol. i, p. xvi n.

[16] Plummer, *Vitae*, vol. i, pp. ix–xxiii, lxxxix–xcv.

[17] I place on record here a note of the reviews which I have been able to trace. Among the magazines, reviews were published in July 1910 or soon after by *The Athenaeum*, no. 4314 (2 July 1910), 6–7; *Dublin Review*, 147 (1910), 179–83 (B. A. C. W.); *The Guardian*, 65 (1910), 946–7; *Oxford Magazine*, 29 (1910–11), 256; *The Nation* (New York), 91 (1910), 368; and *Deutsche Literaturzeitung*, 31 (1910), 2785–6 (R. Thurneysen). In the learned journals I have found ten reviews: *Analecta Bollandiana*, 29 (1910), 326–9 (A. Poncelet); *English Historical Review*, 24 (1910), 562–3 (N. Moore); *Folklore*, 21 (1910), 401–8 (E. Hull); *Irish Theological Quarterly*, 5 (1910), 334–47 (J. MacCaffrey); *Journal of Theological Studies*, 12 (1910–11), 490–2 (E. C. Butler); *Revue Bénédictine*, 27 (1910), 418–20 (L. Gougaud); *Revue celtique*, 32 (1911), 104–6 (J. Vendryes); *Revue critique d'histoire et de littérature*, 71 (1911), 250–1 (A. Dufourcq); *Revue d'histoire ecclésiastique*, 12 (1911), 526–8 (L. Van der Essen); 'Some Saints of Ireland', *Church Quarterly Review*, 74 (1912), 62–81 (E. J. Gwynn).

translation from a Latin Life included in *Vitae Sanctorum Hiberniae*. His concern was with content, not with hagiographical activity *per se*.[18] Although ready for press at the outbreak of the Great War, the two volumes of *Bethada Náem nÉrenn* did not appear until 1922. By this date, Plummer had moved on to the study of Old Irish legal texts, and had collected a personal slip-index of Irish words which, after his death, materially increased the files of the Royal Irish Academy's Dictionary. Finally, in 1925 the Bollandists published three more Lives from the O'Clery collections, edited and translated by Plummer, along with what he called 'A Tentative Catalogue of Irish Hagiography'.

These five volumes form what is without question a most impressive edifice. Within the limits of his selection, Plummer was unsparing in his attention to detail, so that in addition to recording significant textual variants, he would note the particular importance of specially interesting readings or of marginal notes from the manuscripts.[19] To find these one has always to read his notes; much valuable information can be got by doing so. The strengths of the work in detail, however, are not matched by any broad understanding of the texts edited. Indeed, a great many central questions are left not merely unanswered but with barely a word. For example, in the matter of dating the Lives, one is told, 'In their present shape none of them are very ancient.'[20] The question was one which Plummer felt unable to answer more clearly, and so he did not discuss it.

There is, moreover, a deep-seated confusion in Plummer's editorial methods in these volumes. Repeatedly, in his introduction, he notes that the Dublin texts add little to the recension in *Salmanticensis* but are interesting for purposes of comparison. His

---

[18] 'To print Irish lives which are mere late translations of existing Latin lives can add nothing to our knowledge, except possibly as regards the Irish vocabulary of the last two and a half centuries' (*Vitae*, vol. i, pp. iii–iv). Here 'late' appears to mean after 1650, yet Plummer also excluded late medieval translations of known Latin texts.

[19] The accuracy of Plummer's transcription or his proof-reading, however, cannot be taken for granted; see the errors in the Life of St Brendan from MS e Musaeo 3, *Vitae*, ii. 270–92, listed by Plummer in *Bethada Náem nÉrenn* (Oxford, 1922), vol. i, pp. xxii–xxiii; or the list of errors and omissions in the Life of St Ciarán of Clonmacnoise given by R. A. S. Macalister, *The Latin and Irish Lives of Ciaran* (London, 1921), p. 6.

[20] Plummer, *Vitae*, vol. i, p. lxxxix.

notes constantly attempt to compare recensions. But to what end? Presumably the point of comparisons is to establish which version of any particular Life is the most valuable, and how the other versions differ. By exercising selection both in what Lives he printed and in the comparisons drawn in the notes, Plummer has interposed his judgement between the user and the several versions. He has, of course, made the comparisons for himself, and presumably decided which versions of a Life should command our most serious attention. But if so, the reader is never told on what basis these decisions were made and rarely to what effect. In fact nowhere in the two volumes are parallel passages in the different versions compared and discussed. When it is clearly stated that one version is most nearly original, this is oftenest said of the versions in *Salmanticensis* not printed by Plummer. Did he perhaps see his work as one of sweeping up what remained after De Smedt and De Backer? No attempt is made to consider how versions differ, or what the differences signify. The only comparisons drawn are those affecting a study of the documents concerning one saint at a time, and the fact that almost all the Latin texts survive in collections is passed over as though it had no bearing on the interest or use of the separate texts. Texts from the collections which did not meet Plummer's requirements for selection, such as the Lives of St Finnian or St Columba of Terryglass in the *Salmanticensis* and Oxford collections, are given no discussion whatever. If Plummer believed that it was for the reader of his volumes to draw comparisons, why did he publish a selection which impedes comparison, for example, by entirely excluding comparative material from the Oxford collection? If, however, he believed he had formed the necessary critical judgements which enabled him to select texts, why did he not say what the differences between versions amounted to?

Essentially, Plummer ignored the importance of the collections in which the Latin texts survive, and presented thirty-two individual texts, each studied in isolation from the other texts in the same collections. I suspect he assumed a reader such as Reeves, who might be interested in all or most of the saints but who would expect to read the Lives saint by saint and, so long as he believed he was reading a version chosen for its particular interest, would not spare too much thought for comparisons, either between versions or among the Lives in one collection.

Paul Grosjean, the first Bollandist to give serious attention to Irish saints since the early days of co-operation between Antwerp and Louvain, also worked on individual Lives. He printed all available versions in an order of critical value, added a full introduction, and left the reader to get on with comparisons. Unfortunately, he edited only one text in this way for the *Acta Sanctorum*, the Life of St Aed mac Bricc. When he discussed other Lives in *Analecta Bollandiana*, he was not so helpful. Yet even if every dossier had been treated like the Life of St Aed, it is possible that no one would have examined to what degree the characteristics of the versions are determined by the collections.

When James Kenney endeavoured to write a brief introductory note to the dossier on each saint, intending to provide the historian with some critical guidance, he found that the work of Plummer and the small amount of Grosjean's then available provided him with very little guidance. Plummer's 'Tentative Catalogue' had put the versions of each saint's Life in an order of preference—apart from the most complex ones, for which Plummer gave only a reference to *Bibliotheca Hagiographica Latina*. But the basis of his order is never stated. What Kenney has to say about dates or places of composition in most cases rests on no foundation whatever, but is generally said as though it might apply to one or all versions, or to some conjectured archetype.

In short no critical basis yet exists for the study of the Lives preserved in collections from the later Middle Ages, and editorial selectivity has probably directly interfered with the formation of one. Plummer more than anyone else has determined what texts we read, and how we read them. We should therefore try to discover what critical views he held, and how they influenced his methods.

After his Life by Life comparison of the different versions, Plummer writes:[21]

The foregoing analysis has already thrown some light on the character and mode of composition of the lives. In their present shape none of them are very ancient. But they contain earlier, sometimes primitive materials.

The reference to the 'foregoing analysis' is probably misleading, for in it nothing has been said about how earlier materials were

[21] Plummer, *Vitae*, vol. i, pp. lxxxix–xc.

moulded into their present shape. For the most part, the discussion had considered what version of each Life was closest to the 'original', which those responsible for the later versions had altered:[22]

The three recensions M T, S, and R are often very close together showing that they all come from some common original. And S is clearly nearest to this original, which R and M T have edited independently. R is of the two much nearer to the common source than M T; . . . the M T text is therefore of little independent value, but is interesting for purposes of comparison as a specimen of the way in which earlier lives were treated by later scribes.

So Plummer on the three versions of the Life of St Aed mac Bricc. The idea of three independent versions of a common original we may call 'parallel redaction'. But he goes on:

The S text itself shows signs of compilation from various sources. Thus the story of Aed's chariot flying through the air is repeated in different forms no less than four times over (§§ 11, 19, 36, 42); and in all four cases the story is retained by R and omitted by M T.

There is some muddle here. The second quotation suggests that the S-text is compiled from various sources, and that the later versions R and M T are scribal revisions of the S-text. But according to the first quotation, the S-version merely comes closer to the original than the others, presumably meaning that it was subjected to less scribal revision. In that case, what had been compiled from various sources would have to be the putative common original. Plummer gives a fuller account of this 'process of composition' when speaking in general:[23]

We have seen in many cases the process of composition going on under our eyes: the conflation of two different recensions of the same or closely analogous series of incidents as in the combination of the Vita Brendani and the Nauigatio Brendani in our R life of Brendan; the harking back to include another version of the saint's youth, as in the life of Boecius, §§ 19–20; the insertion of an 'aliter' version of certain transactions, as in the life of Enda; the incorporation of separate documents or stories, as in the R lives of Finnian of Clonard, Bairre, Ciaran of Saigir; the 'farcing' of an earlier life with scriptural references and religious commonplaces for purposes of edification, as in our life of Abban, and many of the lives in

[22] Ibid., p. xxvii.   [23] Ibid., p. xc.

the R recension; the abbreviation of an earlier life to make it more suitable for use as Lections in Choir or Refectory; the translation of an Irish life into Latin. The uncritical amalgamation of materials drawn from different sources is shown by the way in which doublets, triplets, and even quadruplets occur in some lives, a very slight difference in form being often enough to conceal from the compiler the fact that they are only varying versions of the same incident. One very obvious way of expanding the life of a saint was to incorporate incidents relating to the saint from the lives of other saints; or again, whether intentionally or not, stories belonging to one saint are transferred to another saint of the same name.

Much of this catalogue belongs to the level of revision by later scribes working on an existing text; most of the examples derive from Plummer's understanding of the work of the compilers of the Oxford collection (his R).[24] This has nothing to do with original composition. The question of doublets, triplets, or quadruplets is out of place; hagiographical texts often multiply examples of saints' characteristic actions. These can be found in the work of a single and original author.[25]

Plummer here does not draw a sufficiently clear distinction between the process of composition whereby an author composes a *uita*, and the process of redaction whereby an existing text may be added to, abbreviated, or otherwise revised. Nor is it clear whether he attributes the latter process to the incidental activity of 'later scribes' or to a redactor with a definite purpose such as preparing a homiletic lectionary. He does however relate some of the process to the work of the redactor of the R collection. Elsewhere he sums up the features of each of the three collections:[26]

It remains to say a few words as to the character of the three collections, S, M T, and R. The Lives in S are curiously disparate in character; for whereas some contain extremely primitive, not to say savage elements, others are late and meagre epitomes, while others again show the degenerate verbiage of the professional hagiologist. The primitive character of some of the materials used by the compiler of S is further illustrated by the early form in which many of the Irish names of persons

---

[24] Ibid., p. xxiii, quoted below.
[25] For example, Adomnán, *Vita S. Columbae*, II 12, 13; and cf. I 4.
[26] Plummer, *Vitae*, vol. i, pp. xxii–xxiii.

and places appear; and by the retention of Irish words and phrases which the other recensions, as a rule, have obliterated.

M T represents a literary recension of earlier materials fairly evenly carried out. Things likely to cause difficulty or scandal are toned down or omitted, and style and matter are more homogeneous than in S.

R represents a still later stage. The object of the compiler is homiletic, 'to the use of edifying'. His sources are nearer akin to S than to M T. Often he retains the S text practically unaltered. In other cases lives already evidently abbreviated in S are still further shortened, especially by the omission of names of places and persons. The process of expurgation is carried further than in M T. The additions of R are sometimes explanations of things which might seem obscure, but by far the greater number of R's insertions are due to the homiletic purposes of the compiler, and consist of pious or moral reflexions, scripture quotations and parallels, especially parallels to those miracles which might cause difficulty or incur disbelief. But the compiler of R not only abbreviates, expurgates, and 'farces' his materials, he also conflates them.

These observations have a real point, trying to describe how preservation in one of the three collections may have influenced the form of the different versions. But nowhere are these observations applied in the comparison of several versions of a particular Life, nor are they sufficiently detailed to be of much help in understanding the results of such comparison.

The lesson to be learnt is that before one can make any critical headway in the evaluation of the Lives in these collections, it is necessary to arrive at the closest possible understanding of the work of the collectors. When the work of the collectors is understood, the results of comparing their different versions will make sense. The difficulty is knowing how to arrive at an understanding of the collectors except by comparing their different versions. As long as one admits the possibility that all three have revised their lost 'common originals', such comparisons lack *terra firma*. The only way out of this difficulty is to begin with texts in one or other collection which are based on a source preserved elsewhere. The fact that Plummer restricted his discussion to his limited selection prevented him from establishing a secure basis on which to work, a basis outside the collections. None the less, his assessments of the *Salmanticensis* and of the Oxford collection (R) are not far off the mark, while his characterization of the Dublin collection is valid as far as it goes, but is too brief to be illuminating.

Kenney was not much troubled by the difference between the versions in the later medieval collections:[27]

The collections give us fairly faithful reproductions of the individual *uitae* on which they were based. Some of the Latin Lives were abridged for lectionary purposes, and almost all were in some degree edited. The methods of compilers differed, but it is clear that certain of them deliberately suppressed details considered irrelevant or unedifying, and interpolated explanatory or devotional padding ... nevertheless, it is broadly true that there is available the substance of the individual Latin Lives as they were known in the thirteenth century, and of the Irish as they were known in the fourteenth, fifteenth, or sixteenth.

Kenney goes on to say that these *uitae* 'were themselves late compositions', the product of generations of reworking the materials:[28]

The historical student, then, has before him, in the main, Lives of the saints of the fifth, sixth, and seventh centuries as, with a few exceptions, they were written in the eleventh, twelfth, thirteenth—perhaps in a few cases the tenth. Some of these—as the Life of Colmán mac Lúacháin— were compositions then written down for the first time. But more frequently the available text is the last of a series of redactions. For Patrick so many of these have been saved that it is possible to trace the genealogical tree of the latest biography with considerable precision. Though other saints were not so fortunate, traces of dependence on, or actual survivals from, older Lives of the ninth, eighth, even seventh, century, are not infrequent. For some—as for Brendan of Clonfert—late versions are available in sufficient numbers to invite the restoration, by the methods of comparative criticism, of a *uita*, perhaps not the earliest, but certainly early in date and dominating in influence. In other Lives the workmanship has been crude to such a degree that a serviceable distribution of the contents into their principal *strata* should be possible. Nevertheless it remains 'very difficult to distinguish in a saint's Life that which belongs to the first text and that which has been added one hundred or two hundred years later,' [Fustel de Coulanges] and, although critical analysis of the *acta* should still yield important results for Irish history, there obviously is much we would like it to do which the nature of the materials makes impossible.

This is more clearly expressed than Plummer's views: Kenney does not allow any confusion between the process of composition

[27] Kenney, *The Sources*, p. 294.
[28] Ibid., p. 295.

and the changes introduced by a late medieval collector. Kenney's view would appear to be that Plummer's method of comparing versions may establish, for example, in the case of St Aed, that S has most nearly preserved the basic text of the Life, but he assumes that this text is itself the end-product of a series of revisions. In other words, he assumed that what happened in the case of a large and complex dossier, such as Patrick's, happened in every case, but for most saints the intermediate texts are lost. Kenney's model could be called 'serial redaction'. This view takes us out of the reach of help from textual comparisons, and demands the invention of a kind of *Formkritik*. I am sure that Kenney's final thought is correct: the kind of analysis he hoped for is impossible. Possessing as we do *Vita II S. Patricii*, *Vita III S. Patricii*, and the Tripartite Life of Patrick, it would not be possible to reconstruct the works of Muirchú and Tírechán, on which they were based, if these had perished.

Perhaps Plummer too had in mind some such chain of successive revisions when he spoke of primitive materials used by a later compiler. Alternatively, he may have imagined that a late medieval compiler had access to little batches of stories which he could work up into a *uita*, something more in the nature of composition than redaction. I do not know what he meant by his term 'materials', an amorphous mass of traditions or a written *uita*. But both Plummer and Kenney thought that the Lives which underlay the different versions in the collections were, relatively speaking, 'late'. Kenney puts a date of eleventh- to thirteenth-century on these texts, Plummer merely says that 'in their present shape none of them are very ancient'. Neither offers any reason why they believed that a textual study of the versions in our fourteenth-century manuscripts could not be expected to lead one to a text more than one or two hundred years older than the manuscript. Both reiterate the view first expressed by Papebroch that the majority of the Lives as we have them resulted from the interests of the religious orders introduced to Ireland in the twelfth century.[29] I have already indicated that most of the Lives in the collections are far removed in character from the few which can be associated with the introduction of the Continental religious orders.

[29] Plummer, *Vitae*, vol. i, p. lxxxix n. 2; Kenney, *The Sources*, p. 19. See above, p. 29.

I suspect that Plummer and Kenney were unduly pessimistic in assuming that, even after one made allowance for the final revisions of the collectors, the Lives in the late medieval collections were no earlier than the eleventh or twelfth century. Neither seems to have attempted to test the assumption by trying to put a date on a text like the Life of St Aed in the *Salmanticensis*, which Plummer regarded as close to the base text underlying the other versions. Kenney takes a guess, suggesting that the Life was 'compiled at a late date, probably the twelfth century, and not in Aed's own community'.[30] But without argument, such random speculation is best disregarded. Any estimate of the value of the Lives resting on such guesswork, has no foundation.

Since the time of Plummer and Kenney, no one has attempted to view the Lives of Irish saints as a whole. Indeed, for the best part of sixty years there has been no evident sense of purpose in the study of these *uitae*. Only Grosjean has worked on a wide range of problems in the *uitae* of the late medieval collections, but his papers, valuable though they are, tackle individual problems without showing any overall perspective.

From the 1930s onwards, most work on Hiberno-Latin and Irish hagiography has been concerned with texts preserved outside the three collections. Esposito, Grosjean, and Ó Briain all contributed to the study of the Lives of St Brigit. Bieler single-handedly re-edited almost the whole of the hagiographical dossier on St Patrick. Adomnán's Life of St Columba was re-edited in the 1950s.[31] Inevitably, perhaps, critical and historical studies have followed where textual work showed the way, and close attention has been paid to the Lives of all three, Patrick, Brigit, and Columba, in recent years.

It has become normal for any study of saints' Lives to start from the dossier, by comparing the different versions of the Lives of the same saint. With the Lives of St Patrick this has been productive in that we have a much clearer view of the growth of the Patrician

---

[30] Kenney, *The Sources*, p. 393.

[31] The edition by Dr and Mrs Anderson, completed in 1957, did not appear until 1961. During the 1950s, Professor Bieler had himself worked towards an edition, and some of his results show in his review of the Andersons' text, *IHS* 13 (1962–3), 175–84. It is one of many kindnesses I have received from Mrs Eva Bieler that she placed in my hands her late husband's photographs of the manuscripts of Adomnán and his typescript copy of the Schaffhausen text.

legend than previously, and this has much enhanced our historical assessment of the role of St Patrick's church, Armagh, in Irish ecclęsiastical development. Students of the Patrician legend have never had to give attention to the problems of the collections, which were thought to contain only Jocelin's Life of St Patrick.

This method has been applied to Lives in the collections: St Ciarán's Lives were studied by Macalister, St Finnian's by Kathleen Hughes, St Abbán's by Heist and Ó Riain, St Flannán's by Ó Corráin, and St Maedóc's by Doherty. In the most recent studies there is a particular emphasis on the search for encoded information, in which the contemporary interests and connexions of the writer are worked into the events of the saint's career. When dealing with Lives in the collections, such studies can lead only to very uncertain conclusions. Unless one understands the work of the collectors, it may be difficult to say whether a passage present in one version and not in another represents interpolation or abbreviation. If it be interpolation, a theory founded on this as regards one version of a particular Life would be undermined if similar interpolations were found in other Lives of the same collection. Dossier-studies, therefore, cannot confidently be made of Lives in the collections until the groundwork has been carried out.

A further problem in dossier-studies is that there is often an underlying assumption that each recension in the dossier represents a deliberately different statement, encoding clues to changing interests and circumstances as they relate to the promoter of a particular saint's cult. While this is sometimes true of a large dossier, it is more often the case that revisions reflect nothing more deliberate than changing tastes in hagiographical material and style. Students of individual dossiers on Irish saints, having assumed that each recension was a revised version of an individual Life, have in my view been blind to the role of the collectors in transmitting texts. If the purpose of the compiler was to *transmit* texts in a form acceptable to their contemporaries, rather than to revise the substance in support of any particular stance or argument, their changes will have interfered less with the intention of the underlying text. Before attempting to apply historical criticism to the different recensions of one Life, it is necessary first to assess the differences textully. Before this can be done with individual Lives, it is essential to establish the methods of the collectors and the extent to which their work, so briefly sketched by Plummer, has determined the form of the texts now surviving.

In attempting to do this, I am essentially going over again the work done by Plummer, but with three major differences in approach. First, where Plummer worked Life by Life within the collections, I shall present discussion of one collection at a time, working by comparing collected texts with witnesses from outside the collections, and only thereafter extend the discussion to comparisons of collected versions without independent guidance. Secondly, where Plummer discussed only selected saints, I consider it necessary to treat each collection as a whole, and not to exclude the Lives of St Malachy and St Lawrence 'on chronological grounds'[32] without assessing their place in the collections. Thirdly, where Plummer summarizes his comparisons but does not support them with quotation, and often writes in terms of 'covering the same ground' as though a comparison of content were adequate, I shall maintain that comparison of wording is essential, and that it must be illustrated. Versions having nothing in common but 'covering the same ground' are not easily compared and interpreted; where the wording can be compared, it is possible to analyse how texts were handed on and revised, so that in this way the writing and rewriting of *uitae* can be critically assessed. A textual comparison can show which texts a redactor used, and how, in a way that a comparison of content cannot. It should be possible by this means to break away from models of 'parallel redaction' or 'serial redaction', and instead to study the redactors at work.

---

[32] Plummer *Vitae*, vol. i, p. xiii. The dates which mattered were those of the saint, not of the Lives.

PART II

THE TEXTUAL EVIDENCE

4

Manuscripts of the Dublin Collection

THE best-known Irish collection of *uitae*, commonly referred to as
the *Codex Kilkenniensis*, survives in two parchment manuscripts,
both now in Dublin libraries. I have for this reason chosen to refer
to their contents as the Dublin collection.

This deliberately avoids the term *Kilkenniensis*, which was used
by Colgan to describe the manuscript from which he derived his
texts of this collection and which belonged, as he says, to the Friars
Minor at Kilkenny.[1] This manuscript was probably that now in
Marsh's Library which we shall shortly consider in detail.[2] Reeves
denied this connexion, identifying the Marsh's Library manuscript with the volume Patrick Fleming referred to as the *Codex
Ardmachanus*. The latter identification he sufficiently proved, but
he failed to establish that this was different from Colgan's
Kilkenniensis.[3] One is left with a state of affairs in which the same

[1] For example, Colgan, *Acta*, p. 215 n. 1, 'ex vetustis membranis conventus
Fratrum Minorum Kill Canniae'; ibid., p. 596 n. 1, 'ex pervetusto illo codice
bibliothecae Fratrum Min. Kilkeniae'.

[2] The connexion between Colgan's *Kilkenniensis* and the manuscript in
Marsh's Library was first made by a Mr Downes, according to W. Reeves, *The
Life of St Columba by Adamnan* (Irish Archaeological and Celtic Society, Dublin,
1857; Bannatyne Club, Edinburgh, 1857), pp. xxv–xxvi n. Plummer, *Vitae*, vol. i,
p. xiii, 'M is almostly certainly the MS. which Colgan used'; ibid. ii. 96 n. 3, 100
n. 5 regards the evidence as 'conclusive'. Cf. ibid, ii. 161 n. 2, 177 n. 2.

[3] Reeves, *The Life of St Columba*, pp. xxv–xxvi n., claimed that 'a slight
comparison shows that [M] is *not* Colgan's original. *Codex Armachanus* is more
likely to be its correct designation.' He demonstrates the connexion with
Fleming's *Codex Ardmachanus*, 'On a Manuscript Volume of Lives of Saints
(Chiefly Irish), now in Primate Marsh's Library, Dublin, Commonly called the
Codex Kilkenniensis', *PRIA*[2] 1 (1870–9), 339–50 (pp. 339–41), but in claiming the
manuscript for Armagh, he plays down the point that Fleming calls the volume a
codex Ardmachanus seu Dubliniensis (see below, pp. 99–101), and that its Armagh
association is merely that it belonged to the archbishop of Armagh, Ussher.
Reeves supposed Ussher to have obtained it from Armagh. Plummer, 'On Two
Collections of Latin Lives of Irish Saints in the Bodleian Library, Rawl. B. 485 and
Rawl. B. 505', *ZCP* 5 (1904–5), 429–54 (p. 454 n.), challenged Reeves's denial that

manuscript has two different labels in seventeenth-century authors, and where one of these names has been transferred from that manuscript to the whole collection of texts. Add to this the fact that the connexion with Kilkenny rests only on report, and one has more than sufficient reason to discard the term *Kilkenniensis*.

Colgan had an extremely high opinion of the Lives of this collection, assigning some of them to the late sixth century, and others to dates in the seventh century.[4] He does not apparently seek to reconcile these observations with his expressed opinion that all the Lives which he gives from this collection were the work of one author.[5] The merits which he perceived are nowhere set out. It is not even clear whether he based the early date on any consciousness of the historical detail, or whether the high valuation issued from the supposed early date. Time and time again, however, Colgan uses this manuscript as his principal and (in cases where there was a choice) his preferred authority.[6]

For the two manuscripts I have retained Plummer's symbols M and T, but I introduce the symbol **D** to represent the recension common to both.

4.1. *Dublin, Primate Marsh's Library, MS Z3. 1. 5*

This is the manuscript most extensively used by Ussher, Colgan, and Reeves, and for the texts printed in *Vitae Sanctorum Hiberniae* by Plummer.[7] It has already been briefly described by Reeves and by Grosjean, but I shall present a fuller account.[8]

M was Colgan's *Kilkenniensis*. Reeves had completely overlooked the fact that Colgan used a transcript supplied by Matthews, and that he might take certain liberties in his own editing.

---

[4] Colgan, *Acta*, p. 353, notes that the author of the Life of St Fintán of Clonenagh 'floruit circa finem sexti saeculi' and was a contemporary of the events he recounted; ibid., p. 71, he dates the Life of St Íte to c.640 (see above, Chapter 1 n. 53); and again, p. 215, the Life of St Maedóc, which mentions St Moling, must therefore be later than 690.

[5] Ibid., p. 596 n. 1. See below, p. 117.

[6] Its primacy is indicated not only by the frequency of citation but also by the way in which Colgan explicitly refers to it as 'often cited' (*sæpius laudatus*).

[7] For Ussher's use, see below, n. 35. Colgan printed nine texts from this collection: Íte (*Acta*, pp. 66–71), Maedóc (pp. 208–15), Fintán of Clonenagh (pp. 349–53), Aed mac Bricc (pp. 418–22), Ciarán of Saigir (pp. 458–63), Senán (pp. 512–28), Mochoemóc (pp. 589–96), Abbán (pp. 610–21), and as I shall show

[*See opposite page 95 for n. 7 cont. and n. 8*]

M   Dublin, Primate Marsh's Library, MS Z3. 1. 5 (formerly V. 3. 4),
    variously known as the *Codex Kilkenniensis* or *Codex Ardmachanus*, was
    written in the fifteenth century,[9] by more than one scribe, on
    membrane now approx. 350 × 240 mm. but originally somewhat
    wider. When the MS was bound, the margins were cropped by at
    least 10 mm.; many marginal notes were retained but were cut
    around, leaving tabs, but some chapter numbers in the outer
    margins were lost. The present binding is of of the late seventeenth
    century and is broken. The writing is in two columns of 44 lines,
    rising to 49 or 50 lines in the latter part. The manuscript contained
    159 leaves when foliated in the early seventeenth century from f. 1 to
    f. 158 (a leaf was overlooked between f. 135 and f. 136). There may
    originally have been 160 or 168 leaves, but in its present state the
    manuscript has lost ff. 1–32, 36–38, and individual leaves removed
    elsewhere, ff. 100, 137, 153. We may tentatively reconstruct the
    collation of the manuscript:

Original	*Extant*
[i⁸ ff. 1–8]	
[ii⁸ (lacked two leaves at time of foliation) ff. 9–14][10]	
[iii⁸ ff. 15–22]	
[iv⁸ (lost before foliation)][11]	
[v⁸ ff. 23–30]	
vi⁸ ff. 31–38 (now lacks 1–2, 6–8)	f. 33, ff. 34–35
vii⁸ ff. 39–46	ff. 39–46

below, Brigit (*Trias*, pp. 546–67). Reeves cites this MS as D in his *Life of St
Columba*, quoting from other Lives in his notes; his papers in the library of Trinity
College, Dublin, include many Lives transcribed from M. Plummer based 19 of
the 22 Lives which he printed from **D** on the text of M.

  [8] W. Reeves, 'On a Manuscript Volume', 339–50; P. Grosjean, 'Catalogus
Codicum Hagiographicorum Latinorum Dubliniensium', *AB* 46 (1928), 81–148
(at pp. 109–11). There is also a brief description in Plummer, *Vitae*, vol. i, pp. xi–
xiv, but no more than a cross-reference in J. R. Scott and N. J. D. White (edd.),
Catalogue of Manuscripts Remaining in Marsh's Library, Dublin (Dublin, [1913]),
p. 35.

  [9] Macray and Madan, *apud* Plummer, *Vitae*, vol. i, p. xii n. 1, agreed on
c.1400. This date has long enjoyed general acceptance, but in 1986 Dr A. I. Doyle
examined the manuscript (at the request of Mr O'Sullivan) and proposed a date
in the second half of the fifteenth century.

  [10] The two missing leaves would account for the lacuna (1 13–33) in the Life of
St Brigit; see below, p. 149.

  [11] See below, p. 105.

viii⁸ ff. 47–54	ff. 47–54
ix⁶ ff. 55–60	ff. 55–60
x⁸ ff. 61–68	ff. 61–68
xi⁸ ff. 69–76	ff. 69–76
xii⁸ ff. 77–84	ff. 77–84
xiii⁸ ff. 85–92	ff. 85–92
xiv⁸ ff. 93–100 (now lacks 8, f. 100 cut out)	ff. 93–99
xv⁶ ff. 101–106	ff. 101–106
xvi⁸ ff. 107–114	ff. 107–114
xvii⁸ ff. 115–122	ff. 115–122
xviii⁸ ff. 123–130	ff. 123–130
xix⁸ ff. 131–137 (now lacks 8, f. 137 cut out)	ff. 131–135, 135bis–136
xx⁸ ff. 138–145	ff. 138–145
xxi⁸ ff. 146–153 (now lacks 8, f. 153 cut out)	ff. 146–152
xxii⁶ ff. 154–158 (6 canc.)	ff. 154–158

Although much is known about the use made of this manuscript during the seventeenth century, its full history remains obscure. It was given to Marsh's Library in 1763 by the archbishop of Dublin, according to a note in a handwritten catalogue in the library.[12] No other provenance is known. But citations traceable to this manuscript, texts edited from it, and annotations made in it have suggested that the book passed through the hands of various seventeenth-century scholars: Archbishop Ussher certainly, and Francis Matthews or his agent, also Dr Thomas Arthur and Sir James Ware; probably Stephen White and Henry FitzSimon; it has also been thought that Hugh Ward and perhaps John Colgan handled the manuscript. Some of the evidence is difficult to unravel, and I have not been entirely successful with it.

The earliest information comes from a version of FitzSimon's *Catalogus*.[13] This work was printed several times in the seventeenth century; its editions are divided into two recensions, termed A and B, by the modern editor, Grosjean.[14] A third recension, Grosjean's C, was discovered by Esposito in Brussels,

---

[12] *BB* f. 5.

[13] On FitzSimon, see above, pp. 41–2.

[14] P. Grosjean, 'Édition du *Catalogus praecipuorum Sanctorum Hiberniae* de Henri FitzSimon', in *Féilsgríbhinn Eóin Mhic Néill*, ed. J. Ryan (Dublin, 1940), pp. 335–93 (at pp. 335–7).

Bibliothèque royale, MS 8530–8534, and was used by Grosjean in his edition.[15] This Recension C is in the handwriting of Fr. Heribert Rosweyde and an amanuensis, and was made for the use of the early Bollandists. There are added to the catalogue in Recension C the names of many Irish saints taken from a book referred to as *Anonyma SS. Hib. Legenda Manuscripta* and similar expressions. Folio numbers are often given, and from these Grosjean was able to prove that the manuscript was none other than M. The book was then known as *Lour Darg*, in Irish spelling *Leabhar Dearg* ('Red Book'), and belonged to an Englishman called Wulverston who lived at Stillorgan, near Dublin.[16] This evidence is extremely important: it is the earliest indication of the name and provenance of the book, it shows that the manuscript was already foliated when an index was made, which later came into the hands of the compiler of Recension C (the foliation may have been done by the indexer), and it proves that the manuscript had not then suffered any serious mutilation. We shall be able to use Recension C in seeking to identify texts now missing from the codex.

I do not share Grosjean's confidence that the compiler of Recension C was FitzSimon.[17] Rosweyde died on 5 October 1629, so the recension must have been put together before that date incorporating an earlier index made from the manuscript at Stillorgan. FitzSimon left Ireland to go into exile in 1604 and did not return until 1630. If he had had access to the manuscript when in Dublin between 1595 and 1604, he would surely have included its information in his expanded text of 1619, Grosjean's Recension B. Thereafter he could not have seen the manuscript until after the

---

[15] M. Esposito, '*Lour Darg*', *Hermathena*, no. 45 (1930), 259–60; Grosjean, '*Catalogus* de Henri FitzSimon', pp. 337–41.

[16] The compiler of Recension C says in a note at f. 12ʳ: 'Manuscriptam Legendam Hibernicam, quae obiter citatur, seu Latinum codicem perantiquum et amplum, qui *lour darg* appellatur, et reperitur apud Wulverstonum Anglum Stalorgani iuxta Dubliniam, in quo de solis sanctis Ibernis agitur'. Esposito, '*Lour Darg*', p. 260; Grosjean, '*Catalogus* de Henri FitzSimon', pp. 337–8, 341; L. Bieler, 'Recent Research in Irish Hagiography', *Studies*, 33 (1946), 230–38, 536–44 (at p. 231 n.) identifies a James Wolverstone living at Stillorgan in 1604.

[17] Grosjean, '*Catalogus* de Henri FitzSimon', p. 340. In his later article, 'Notes sur quelques sources des Antiquitates de Jacques Ussher', *AB* 77 (1959), 154–87 (p. 180), he continued to maintain that FitzSimon himself had used M in compiling Recension C.

death of Rosweyde.[18] Who, then, indexed the volume to supply
the additions of Recension C? The assiduous Stephen White, a
frequent correspondent of the early Bollandists, had scarcely set
out for Ireland when Rosweyde died, so he cannot be the source;
the fruits of his use of the manuscript, in this context at least,
appear elsewhere.[19] James Ussher owned a copy of the Liège
edition dated 1619, Grosjean's Recension B, which he had used
with care, correcting it against his own books.[20] He may have
indexed Wulverston's manuscript and sent the information to
Rosweyde. This would, however, go far beyond any evidence we
have for the contact between them; further, the corrections and
additions in Ussher's printed copy are not incorporated in
Recension C, which in any case uses Recension A, not Recension
B, as its base. Ussher is therefore a most unlikely source. The
available evidence does not allow us to identify the indexer; it was
surely not Rosweyde, though the other sources used in Recension
C suggest that this was compiled in his study at Antwerp.

The hand which foliated the manuscript also compiled a table
of contents, now bound in as f. 159, which will be found printed
below. Grosjean thought the hand to be that of John Colgan who,
if he ever saw the book at all, did not use it until after the
compilation of Recension C of the *Catalogus*, so that even as a
guess this seems unlikely. Grosjean also thought that Ward was

[18] Plummer, *Vitae*, vol. i, p. lxxxi, noted that the Bollandists printed extracts
from a Life of St Moling supplied by FitzSimon, and commented that the extracts
'belong to the M recension, and are very inaccurate'. FitzSimon supplied a
number of Lives to the Bollandists which are demonstrably not from M or any
other manuscript of **D**. In view of this, one cannot exclude the possiblity that his
Life of St Moling came from a different source; these extracts, therefore, do not
show that FitzSimon used M.

[19] Oxford, Bodleian Library, MS Add. C. 299, ff. 124ᵛ–122ᵛ *invers.*, contains
FitzSimon's own 'Auctuarium' to the *Catalogus*, compiled with White's help,
about 1641, on which see R. Sharpe, 'The Origin and Elaboration of the *Catalogus
Praecipuorum Sanctorum Hiberniae*, Attributed to Henry FitzSimon, SJ', *Bodleian
Library Record*, 13/3 (1989), 202–30. In this FitzSimon adds many names
mentioned in this collection, and it is likely that he or White, or both, used the
Lour Darg in Ussher's library. V. De Buck, 'De SS. Abbanis Kill-Abbaniensi et
Magharnuidhiensi', in *Acta Sanctorum*, Oct. XII (Brussels, 1867), p. 277 n. (a),
also tells us that FitzSimon recollated for Bolland Colgan's text of the Life of St
Abbán derived from his *Codex Kilkenniensis*; see above, p. 73.

[20] Ussher's copy is in the library of Trinity College, Dublin (shelf-mark A. 1. 34,
formerly A. 2. 8), and was used by Grosjean in his edition. He also owned a copy
of Recension A as published at Lisbon in 1621 by Philip O'Sullivan Beare.

responsible for much marginal annotation.[21] Both suggestions can be ruled out with some confidence: first, because the two men did not return to Ireland; secondly, by comparison with known examples of their handwriting. Further, Ussher added a note on the table, so that it must predate his use of the manuscript.[22] Perhaps the unidentified compiler of Rosweyde's source was himself responsible for the foliation and the table of contents. Both would obviously have been a help in the indexing of the manuscript.

At what date Wulverston's *Lour Darg* was indexed it is difficult to say: before Rosweyde's death in 1629, obviously, and presumably before the manuscript came into Ussher's possession. The archbishop certainly knew the manuscript as early as 1622, and probably already owned it. In this case, the index used by Rosweyde may date from before then, perhaps even from before the publication of Recension B in 1619. The genesis of Recension C is much more interesting than Grosjean realized.

Our next information about M comes from the Irish Franciscans of Louvain. Francis Matthews, Minister Provincial in Ireland, supplied them with texts from Ireland shortly before he became Guardian of the college. The detailed information comes from Patrick Fleming, who prints the anonymous *Catalogus Sanctorum Hiberniae secundum diuersa tempora* (from the *Codex Salmanticensis*),[23] and then comments:[24]

Haec ibi, quae totidem fere verbis, regum tamen et Sanctorum praetermissis vocabulis, leguntur in antiqua et fideli S. Finniani vita, quae cum aliis plurium Sanctorum Hiberniae Legendis, quas R. P. Franciscus Matthaeus, nunc collegii nostri Guardianus, & nuper Provincialis Minister nostrae Provinciae, circa annum 1626, summo studio ac diligentia, ex duobus MSS. voluminibus pergamineis, (quorum unum

---

[21] Grosjean, 'Catalogus Codicum Dubliniensium', p. 109, identifies Colgan as the writer of the contents list, though this does not seem to me to resemble Colgan's hand as represented in Dublin, Trinity College, MS 1140 (a list of Irish saints for Jan. and Feb. put together from calendars by Ward and Colgan for the use of the Bollandists). It is certainly not the hand of Hugh Ward, as Felim Ó Briain thought, and as Grosjean allowed to be possible.

[22] See below, p. 105 n. 48.

[23] Fleming does not specify the source of his text but it was established by Grosjean, 'Édition et commentaire du *Catalogus Sanctorum Hiberniae*', p. 202.

[24] Fleming, *Collectanea Sacra*, p. 431.

ad Ecclesiam Ardmachanam vel Dubliniensem spectat, & in Bibliotheca
Iacobi Usserii, ex ordinatione Regis Angliae, Primatis Ardmachani,
asservatur; alterum ad Insulam quae omnium Sanctorum dicitur
pertinet) transumi curavit ac ad Collegium nostrum transmitti.

We shall discuss the Saints' Island manuscript in Chapter 8. Here
we are concerned with the *Codex Ardmachanus*, from which
Fleming prints in whole or part the Lives of SS. Comgall, Molua,
Mochoemóc, Coemgen, Cainnech, Mochutu, and Munnu.[25]
Reeves was able to establish that the manuscript in question was
our M.[26] Hugh Ward, a colleague of Fleming's in the Irish College
at Louvain, and from 1623 a close associate in his hagiographical
researches, had access to the same source. In his *Sancti Rumoldi
Acta*, a work begun and finished in 1631, he quotes from several
Lives 'in . . . Codice Ardmachano seu Dubliniensi'.[27] It is entirely
clear from Fleming's statement that the actual manuscript, M,
belonged to Ussher by 1626. He had presumably acquired it from
Wulverston. M is presumably the same old parchment manuscript belonging to Ussher which was used by Dr Thomas Arthur
in 1627 as the chief source for his collection of *uitae*.[28] It is also clear
that Fleming worked, not on the manuscript itself, but on a
transcript commissioned by Francis Matthews. One of the Lives
printed by Fleming, that of St Mochoemóc, was also printed by
Colgan in *Acta Sanctorum Hiberniae* 'ex pervetusto illo Codice
Bibliothecæ Fratrum Min. Kilkeniæ'.[29] The Bollandists also
printed this Life 'ex Codice Kilkenniensi', from a copy supplied to
them by Hugh Ward.[30] The fact, noted by Plummer, that there are
points in the text where all three editions agree on a reading
different from that of M does not undermine Reeves's identifica-

[25] The Lives of Comgall (pp. 303–13), Molua (pp. 368–79), Mochoemóc
(pp. 380–91) are included from M, ibid. Extracts are quoted from the others
mentioned.

[26] Reeves, 'On a Manuscript Volume', p. 341; Plummer, *Vitae*, vol. i, p. xiv
and ii, 9n.

[27] H. Ward, *S. Rumoldi Acta*, ed. T. Sirinus (Louvain, 1662), p. 189: 'ex ipsorum
Actis manuscriptis, in utroque Codice, Ardmachano seu Dubliniensi, & Loch-
rivensi'.

[28] Arthur's copy, in which he altered the texts a good deal, is now in Maynooth,
St Patrick's College, MS 3 G 1; see Plummer, 'A Tentative Catalogue', p. 178;
Grosjean, 'Catalogus Codicum Dubliniensium', pp. 116–18.

[29] Colgan, *Acta*, pp. 589, 596.

[30] *Acta Sanctorum*, Mart. II (1668), 280.

tion of the *Codex Ardmachanus* with M but demonstrates that Fleming, Ward, Colgan, and the Bollandists all worked on the transcript originally supplied by Matthews.[31]

One may puzzle over why Fleming and Ward at an early date, around 1630–1, refer to the manuscript as *Ardmachanus seu Dubliniensis*, when Ward before 1635 and Colgan thereafter associate it with the Friars Minor of Kilkenny. The first title I take to mean no more than that it belonged to Ussher, the archbishop of Armagh,[32] but was kept or used in Dublin.[33] The first indication of the other title, *Codex Kilkenniensis*, came some years before in 1622, from Ussher himself. When discussing the Life of St Brendan, he mentions 'the manuscript books which I have met withal here, in St Brendan's own country, (one whereof was transcribed for the use of the friars minors of Kilkenny, about the year of our Lord one thousand three hundred and fifty).'[34] The sentence from which this is quoted is very obscure, but I infer that he is referring to the text of the *Vita S. Brendani* in M which he regards as less far-fetched than the *Nauigatio*. In his *Antiquitates*, published in 1639, he quotes frequently from texts in M, not specifying a provenance but referring sometimes to the manuscript as being in his possession.[35] There are also several notes in his hand in the manuscript, though he was not the writer (as Plummer thought) of the extensive marginal annotation.[36]

These marginal notes present another thorny problem. We have already questioned Grosjean's suggestion that the table of contents was written by John Colgan. By the same token we must doubt Grosjean's identification of the hand which has left

---

[31] Plummer, *Vitae*, vol. i, p. lxxix.

[32] Reeves appears to claim the manuscript for Armagh, but this perhaps results from partiality; in 1877 he was both dean and librarian of Armagh.

[33] Arthur, however, in his colophon, indicates that in 1627 Ussher's library was at Drogheda.

[34] Ussher, *An Epistle Concerning the Religion Anciently Professed by the Irish and Scottish* (1622), p. 21; rev. ed., *A Discourse of the Religion Anciently Professed by the Irish and British* (1631), pp. 26–7; *Whole Works*, iv. 268. J. Ware, *De Scriptoribus Hiberniae* (Dublin, 1639), p. 13, interpreted this as a reference to the *uita* of St Brendan in M.

[35] An extensive (though incomplete) list of Ussher's references is given by Plummer, *Vitae*, vol. i, p. xiv n. 4.

[36] Grosjean, 'Catalogus Codicum Dubliniensium', p. 109. Mr William O'Sullivan kindly confirmed the identification of Ussher's hand.

extensive notes in the margins, drawing attention to the content, with that of Hugh Ward.[37] There is certainly a similarity of appearance.[38] But there is a real problem here which Grosjean has overlooked. Between 1623, when Ward took up the study of hagiography, and his death in 1635, he did not return to Ireland. Nor did Colgan ever return to Ireland after he had left as a youth. How, therefore, could either of them have used the manuscript directly, whether at Wulverston's house in Stillorgan, or in Ussher's library? One must either reconsider the identification of the handwriting or postulate that for a time the manuscript itself was lent to the Louvain Franciscans and safely returned to Ireland. If the latter were the case, one of them would surely have mentioned the fact, which must be deemed extremely unlikely. The handwriting, therefore, must be reconsidered.

The problem of the marginalia goes deeper than this. There are, it seems to me, perhaps as many as five different hands responsible for these notes. That most commonly found, supposedly Ward's, marks points of historical or moral interest, notes references to minor saints, and occasionally adds cross-references. In the lower margin of f. 103[r], this hand has written 'Forsan Seachnallus hic episcopus est idem cum Senacho episcopo apud Jocelinum cap. 130'. A second hand has corrected the reference, '131 (impress.), 132 (MS.)', and added the different opinion, 'Idem est cum Secundino episcopo apud Jocelinum cap. 177 (codicis impress.) vel 179 (MS.)'.[39] Marginalia at ff. 121[r], 129[v] (left margin), and 147[r] (right margin) appear to be written by three further users of the manuscript. The first of these, f. 121[r], has marked the false date given in the Life of St Lawrence O'Toole for the saint's death, 'm°c°xxiiij'.[40] 'Forsitan verius,' the note reads, 'fertur ipsum fuisse

[37] Grosjean, 'Catalogus Codicum Dubliniensium', p. 109.

[38] I have compared the hand with the examples of Ward's writing in Dublin, Trinity College, MS 1140 (see above, n. 21).

[39] The second hand is probably Ussher's. In Ussher's copy of FitzSimon's *Catalogus*, he regularly amended chapter references to Jocelin's Life of St Patrick.

[40] Cf. C. Plummer, 'Vie et miracles de S. Laurent, archevêque de Dublin', *AB* 33 (1914), 121–86 (at p. 155). The true date is 1180 (mciiij[xx]).

[41] The first of these is reported by Plummer, *Vitae*, ii. 35 n. 15: 'S. Declanus fuit de Fiachaid Suidge fratris Conn Cedcathach filii Fedlimid Rechtmar et in hoc libro et in lib. Sligunte de Genealogiis SS. Hybernie fol. 48B'; compare P. Ó Riain (ed.), *Corpus Genealogiarum Sanctorum Hiberniae* (Dublin, 1985), §107.6, where the reading of the Great Book of Lecan (the modern name for the Book of

mortuum an. dom. 1142 ut in Ultorum ⟨...⟩ reperitur ibi-
demque Lorcan o Tuaithail appellatur.' The missing word is
surely 'annalibus'; both Ussher and the Louvain Franciscans were
acquainted with the Annals of Ulster, although these give the true
date of 1180. At two places in the Life of St Declán, one of the
annotators draws attention to the genealogies of the saints in
another manuscript, the Book of Sligo.[41] Who these readers were I
do not know; the laborious task of identification may illuminate
the question of who was allowed the freedom of Ussher's library,
but it will probably not shed much light on how knowledge of
these *uitae* was transmitted.

I have not disproven the possibility that the manuscript was lent
to the Louvain scholars, but such a loan is certainly not necessary.
Francis Matthews had supplied the texts by 1626, and it was his
copy used by Fleming that still supplied Colgan and the
Bollandists with their texts. In any case, Ussher was generous in
allowing scholars the use of his library, and almost any of them
may have made his mark.[42] Among the scholars who used the
manuscript was Ussher's associate, Sir James Ware, though in his
published works this does not show as much as might have been
expected.[43]

What happened to the manuscript thereafter is not known.
Ussher left Ireland in 1640, and his books followed him. After his
death in England in 1656, his library was shipped to Dublin and
stored in Dublin Castle from 1657 until it was transferred to
Trinity College in 1661.[44] Reeves suggested that the manuscript
might have been removed at this stage, but it might equally well
have been lent by Ussher to an interested person associated with
St Patrick's Cathedral in Dublin, where we may suppose it to have
stayed until placed in Marsh's Library.

At this point, one may well ask when the codex could have been

---

Sligo) agrees. The second is mentioned by Plummer, *Vitae*, ii. 55 n. 8: 'Albeus fuit
episcopus Imlechensis et inde uocatur in Genealogiis SS Hybernorum ex lib.
Sligunte *Ailbhe Imleacha* Albeus Imlacensis'; cf. Ó Riain, *Corpus*, §135.

[42] Apart from Matthews and Arthur already noted, in 1629 Thomas Strange,
OFM, was allowed access (letter to Luke Wadding, dated 20 Nov. 1629, in
B. Jennings (ed.), *Wadding Papers 1614–38* (Dublin, 1953), p. 15). For Stephen
White's use of Ussher's library, see above, pp. 59, 98 n. 19.

[43] Plummer, *Vitae*, vol. i, p. xiv n. 5.

[44] Reeves, 'On a Manuscript Volume', p. 342.

at Kilkenny. Between its being at Stillorgan around 1620 and in Ussher's possession by 1622, there is little room to suppose it was in Kilkenny in the same period. We must deduce therefore that, if the term has any basis, it reflects an earlier provenance reported to Ussher and to the copyist whom Matthews engaged to prepare a transcript.

I have devoted so much space to the history of the book because it will be highly relevant to my discussion of the original contents of the collection, and the identification of works now missing from the manuscript. To this end, the fragment of parchment, 240 × 115 mm., now bound as f. 159, is of special interest. The list of contents was made before the manuscript was seriously mutilated, and enables us to see what has been lost. The leaf is badly worn and stained with reagent on both sides, a feature of which Reeves already complained in 1877. He drew attention to the recto, of which very little can be read, though there is a mention of *ego ffr. Anthonius de Clane* and a date 'anno domini .MDXX[.].' (?), written in a sixteenth-century hand.[45] The Franciscan house at Clane seems to have been destroyed in the 1540s, and we may hardly build anything on these words.[46] The verso, which Reeves and Plummer both overlooked, contains the list of contents.[47] This was made in the early seventeenth century by the person who foliated the manuscript. It is very difficult to read, and the following copy is partly guesswork.

> Vita incipit nec non [
> [De uita] S. Patricii   in fronte libri huius
>   obit 17 Martii anno dni 528
> De [uita san]ctae Brigidae uirginis incipit foll. 11
>   obit Febr. 548

---

[45] Reeves, 'On a Manuscript Volume', p. 342. He read the date as .MDXV. Mr William O'Sullivan has drawn my attention to notes made by James Ware in Dublin, Trinity College Library, MS 6404 ff. 55–56; these are excerpts from the Lives of St Ailbe and St Declán, taken from a manuscript belonging to James, bishop of Meath, that is Ussher between 1621 and 1626. That it was M is shown by Ware's note that the manuscript was written by Anthony of Clane in 1520. I think Ware was mistaken in treating this as a colophon, but he shows that it was already hard to decipher.

[46] A. O. Gwynn and R. N. Hadcock, *Medieval Religious Houses: Ireland* (London, 1970), p. 245.

[47] It was first noted by Grosjean, 'Catalogus Codicum Dubliniensium', p. 109.

S. Ludouici	foll. 23[48]	
S. Anthonii	foll. 25 cuius obitus est 13 [ ] 1232	
S. Flannani	foll. 35	
S. Columbe	foll. 39	
[S. Aedani] Maedog	foll. 51	
[S. Brendani]	foll. 57	
S. Coemgeni	foll. 64	3 Junii
S. Mol[ing	foll.] 70	[17 Junii]
S. F[intani	foll.] 74	17 Feb.
S. Senani	[foll.] 76	[8] Mart.
S. Mocoeuog	[foll.] 80	13 Martii
S. Finani	[foll.] 84	7 Aprilis
S. Ruadani	foll. 86	17 Apr.
S. Cronani	foll. 88	27 Apr.
S. Comgalli	foll. 90	10 Maii
S. Mochtu	foll. 94	14 Maii
S. Declani	foll. 101	24 Julii
S. Kyarani	foll. 106	5 Martii
[S. Ite	foll. 109]	15 Januar.
S. Mollue	foll. 112	4 August
S. Laurentii	foll. 116	15 Octob.
S. Caynichi	foll. 124	11 Octob.
[S. Munnu]	foll. 127	21 Octob.
S. Col[man Elo]	foll. 129	30 Octob.
S. B[airre]	foll. 132	25 Sept.
[S. Aidi	foll. 134]	15 Nov.
[S. Albei	foll. 135*bis*]	12 Sept.
[S. Abbani	foll. 138]	15 Mart.[49]
[S. Cyarani	foll. 144]	9 Sept.
[S. Malachiae	foll. 148]	

From this list of the original contents, it is apparent that Lives of St Patrick and St Brigit have been lost. So has the Life of St Louis of Toulouse, though the very short space allowed for it (ff. 23–25) makes one suspect that a quire had been lost before the leaves were numbered: a comparison with the sister manuscript, Plummer's T, where the text is complete, allows one to estimate the length of missing text at about eight leaves. In the recon-structed collation above, I have supposed that the Life of St Brigit

---

[48] Against St Louis's name Ussher wrote 'minoritae Caroli II regis Siciliae'.

[49] Calendar date, not the date of his death. See Plummer *Vitae*, vol. i, p. xxiii n. 9.

may have ended on f. 22, and that the first eight leaves of the Life of St Louis may have been lost between there and the fragment on ff. 23–25 recorded in the table of contents. Most of the Life of St Anthony of Padua is now lost too, only the end being preserved. The Life of St Flannán is a fragment: it begins at f. 35vb but the text is acephalous, though columns 34vb, 35ra, 35rb, and 35va are blank. Only one column of text survives, since ff. 36–38 are lost.

From f. 39 we are on better ground, for the remainder of the book is largely intact. Of the missing leaves, f. 100 contained from §64 of the Life of St Mochutu to near the end of the long §1 of the Life of St Declán. Plummer plausibly suggested that it was removed because of the scandalous nature of the conception of St Declán.[50] It is possible that the compiler of Recension C of the *Catalogus* read this leaf, but the evidence in his Catalogue is uncertain.[51] F. 137, part way through the Life of St Ailbe, §§22–37, was still in place when Francis Matthews had this Life transcribed for Ward, Colgan, and the Bollandists.[52] The third missing leaf, f. 153, contained a portion of St Bernard's Life of St Malachy.

4.2. *Dublin, Trinity College MS 175*

The text of the few single leaves missing from M may for the most part be supplied from the sister manuscript:

T Dublin, Trinity College MS 175 (formerly E. 3. 11), a codex containing three distinct manuscripts. We are concerned with the second part, numbered in the latest hand (M. L. Colker, 1968) ff. 14–71.

[50] Plummer, *Vitae*, ii. 32 n. 2.

[51] Grosjean, '*Catalogus* de Henri FitzSimon', p. 378 n. 516, guessed that 'Molronus monachus' mentioned in what he took to be the Life of St Mochutu was a corruption for St Molua, one of two saints accompanying St Mochutu, in a passage in S §17 which would correspond to the missing part of M; at this point there is also a lacuna in T so that any reconstructed **D**-text (such as that in brackets in *Vitae*, §64) must be uncertain. Less speculatively, I notice that St Coemell, the virgin mentioned in **D** §65 (where T is available) is not indexed in the *Catalogus*. Negative evidence one way against speculation the other is no basis for assertion.

[52] Brussels, Bibliothèque des Bollandistes, MS 141, ff. 265–80; cf. Grosjean, 'Catalogus Codicum Dubliniensium', p. 109. The Bollandists chose not to print a Life of St Ailbe, though they had several recensions available to them, and Plummer did not know of this copy derived from M; Plummer, *Vitae*, vol. i, p. xxix and n. 2, and 'A Tentative Catalogue', p. 235. For the text of the missing leaf he depended on the sister manuscript T.

Written in the fifteenth century on membrane, 300 × 240 mm., 2 columns, 44 lines.[53] The leaves bear the original foliation so that, notwithstanding several chasms, the collation of the manuscript can be established up to the point where it is mutilated at the end.

	Original	*Extant*
	[i^8 ff. 1–8]	
	[ii^8 ff. 9–16]	
	[iii^8 ff. 17–24]	
Fr.1	iv^8 ff. 25–32 (now lacks 1–3, 6–8)	ff. 28–29 now ff. 14–15
	[v^8 ff. 33–40]	
	[vi^8 ff. 41–48]	
Fr.2	vii^8 ff. 49–56	ff. 49–56 now ff. 16–23
	viii^8 ff. 57–64	ff. 57–64 now ff. 24–31
Fr.3	ix^8 ff. 65–72 (now lacks 1, 8)	ff. 66–71 now ff. 32–37
	[x^8 ff. 73–80]	
	[xi^8 ff. 81–88]	
Fr.4	xii^8 ff. 89–96 (now lacks 1–3, 6–8)	ff. 92–93 now ff. 38–39
	[xiii^8 ff. 97–104]	
Fr.5	xiv^8 ff. 105–112	ff. 105–112 now ff. 40–47
	xv^8 ff. 113–120	ff. 113–120 now ff. 48–55
	xvi^8 ff. 121–128	ff. 121–128 now ff. 56–63
	xvii^8 ff. 129–136	ff. 129–136 now ff. 64–71
	Codex mutilus; deest finis	

[53] This manuscript has been generally recognized as more or less contemporary with M, but its greater neatness has encouraged the view that it is a little earlier than the other, which need not be so. In 1986 Dr A. I. Doyle dated the writing to the second half of the fifteenth century, and this view is now incorporated in M. L. Colker's catalogue of manuscripts at Trinity.

Plummer suggested that 'about 19' leaves were lost at the end.[54] Up to this point, the quires are regular, and a comparison with M suggests that T originally contained 152 or 160 leaves, having lost two or three quires.

The history of T is largely unknown. In the sixteenth century, John Dillon signed his name in it in two places.[55] On this basis Mr O'Sullivan has suggested that we may suppose a provenance in Meath.[56] By the 1630s it was available to Archibishop Ussher, and it may have come to Trinity College as part of his library.[57]

4.3. The Relationship of M and T

All evidence points to the identical nature of the contents of M and T in their original, unmutilated condition. In script, the two manuscripts are more or less contemporary, though Reeves thought T was a little older than M.[58] He was certainly mistaken in dating both manuscripts to the early thirteenth century.[59]

Both manuscripts are written in a fluent gothic *textura*, indistinguishable from what might be written in England. One might perhaps infer from this that both were produced in religious houses *inter Anglos* in eastern or south-eastern Ireland. It is, however, a feature noticeable in M that the names of places and persons are sometimes written in Irish script or using some Irish letter forms. An Irish hand of the fifteenth century has added a

[54] *Vitae*, vol. i, p. xiii n. 1.

[55] Ibid., vol. i, p. xiv n. 5 notes the entry on f. 109ʳ. At f. 124ᵛ 'John Dillone' signed twice. See below, pp. 257–8, for the Dillon family's connexion with the manuscripts of the Oxford collection.

[56] W. O'Sullivan, 'Medieval Meath Manuscripts', *Ríocht na Midhe*, 7 (1980–6), 3–21, and 8 (1987–), 68–70 (at p. 10).

[57] *Vitae*, vol. i, p. xiv n. 4; cf. Grosjean, 'Catalogus Codicum Dubliniensium', p. 98, for Ussher's marginalia in T.

[58] Dublin, Trinity College, MS 1100, f. 4ᵛ, a copy of the Life of St Mochutu taken from T, 'which is older & more exact than the other [M], tho' more difficult to read off-handedly; and is in fact, if not the exemplar from which the other was copied, at least an early transcript of the same materials'. This was written on 27 May 1880; compare his note of 24 May 1880 in MS 1098, f. 4ᵛ, on the Life of St Declán: 'With the exception of a few unimportant varieties in the orthography of proper names, the two MSS. are identical in matter, though the T.C.D. MS. is better & more archaic.'

[59] R. Caulfield (ed.), *Life of St Fin Barre* (London, 1864), p. iv, cites Reeves's opinion that both manuscripts were written c. 1200. Reeves himself, *The Life of St Columba*, p. xxv, less specifically dated M to the thirteenth century.

genealogy in the lower margin at the opening of twenty-two Lives.[60]

Plummer has proved beyond question that M and T were copied from the same original (which I call Δ), and not one from another. In those Lives which are wholly or partly preserved in both manuscripts (Brendan, Mochoemóc, Fínán, Ruadán, Crónán, Comgall, Mochutu, Declán, Molua, Munnu, Colmán Élo, Bairre, Aed, Ailbe, and Abbán), we find many shared errors and omissions, and even some shared orthographical variants:

Common errors and omissions

Mchg. §17 inde speratus *Plummer* in speratus *Colgan*] indesperatus MT
      §22 frater *Colgan*] pater MT
      §27 ac M *corr.*] an M*T
      §30 profundissimi M *corr. Colgan*] profundiosi M*T

FinC. §17 creditoribus *Plummer*] debitoribus MT
      §24 eum M *corr.*] *om.* M*T

Rua. §15 habitum sanctum accipientes *Plummer*] habentes sanctum acceperunt MT
      §17 dari *Plummer*] dare MT
      §17 perfodiet *Plummer*] perfodit MT
      §18 iacintini **SO**] iachincti M iacinti T

Cron. §17 ⟨uestes⟩ *Plummer*] *om.* MT
      §27 isset *Plummer*] esset MT

Com. § 7 ⟨construxit⟩ *Plummer*] *om.* MT
      §21 da *Plummer*] et da MT
      §23 molestie M *corr.*] moleste M*T
      §24 quoddam *Plummer*] quodam MT
      §34 temeritate *Plummer*] demeritate MT
      §44 in quadam ualle *Plummer*] in quodam ualle MT
      §44 ⟨cum esset⟩ *Plummer*] *om.* MT
      §56 acres *Plummer*] acros MT

Car. §16 loca et parrochiam suam *Sharpe*] loca et parrochia sua T loca et parrochias suas M
      §21 et ait *Boll.*] *om.* MT
      §32 stridentem *Boll.*] se ridentem MT

---

[60] Printed by Grosjean, 'Catalogus Codicum Dubliniensium', pp. 119–22. Fifteen of the twenty-two pedigrees agree with those of the Book of Glendalough recension in the Bodleian Library, MS Rawlinson B. 502; Ó Riain, *Corpus*, pp. xlviii, l.

§ 36 ⟨exposuit⟩ *Boll.*] *om.* MT
§ 51 scatentes *Plummer*] scandentes MT
§ 55 dolebant *Boll.*] dicebant MT

Decl. § 1 ueneniferam *Plummer*] ueniferam MT
§ 3 ⟨tempore uero⟩ *Plummer*] *om.* MT
§ 3 ⟨edidit⟩ *Plummer*] *om.* MT
§ 3 multorum locorum de gentilitate *Plummer*] multorum de gentilitate locorum MT
§ 4 illi iam gentiles T illi iam gentes M* ille iam gentes M *corr.*
§ 16 paciemur *Plummer*] pacientur MT
§ 16 ut . . . deseras *Plummer*] ut . . . deseres MT
§ 16 apparent *Plummer*] apparet MT
§ 16 Fertach Declain *Plummer*] Fertach Declani T Feartach Declani M
§ 16 cepit *Plummer*] et cepit MT
§ 19 consensit *Plummer*] conscensciit T consenciit M
§ 23 in spiritu cognoscens *Boll.*] *om.* MT
§ 25 frusta *Plummer*] frustra MT
§ 33 anilem *Plummer*] anualem T annalem M
§ 36 *blank space, nothing wanting* MT

Lug. § 52 paratam *Plummer*] paratum MT
§ 54 cui M *corr.*] qui M*T (quem *Fleming*)

Mun. § 26 ultra **S O**] intra MT

ColE. § 1 ⟨nutritur⟩ *Plummer*] *om.* MT
§ 4 at *Plummer*] ut MT
§ 10 ⟨cumque reuerterentur uiri illi a sancto uiro, ut irent in domo suo⟩ *Plummer based on* **S**] *om.* MT
§ 13 illi *Plummer*] ille MT
§ 17 capellano *Plummer*] capło MT (i.e. capitulo)
§ 26 mergatur *Plummer*] mergetur MT
§ 28 scandalizetur *Plummer*] scandalizatur MT
§ 29 dies ille . . . festivus *Plummer*] dies illa . . . festivus MT
§ 33 in uia *Plummer from* Ps. 118.1] *om.* MT

Ba. § 2 Echach *Plummer*] Exhach MT (Echact T *Caulfield*)
§ 4 coma *Plummer*] comma MT (coma T *Caulfield*)
§ 4 tondetur *Plummer*] tondeatur MT
§ 7 Roma *Plummer* cf. de Roma **O**] Romam MT *twice*
§ 14 uisu carnali *Plummer*] uisus carnalis MT
§ 14 soluantur *Plummer*] soluentur MT

Aed. § 9 orauit *Plummer* cf. **S**] orans MT
§ 16 casula *Plummer*] casulam MT

§ 27 Dei M *corr.*] *om.* M*T
§ 28 presenti M *corr.*] presente M*T
§ 29 contigit M *corr.*] contingit M*T
§ 35 per hiatum terre *Plummer*] pariatum terre MT

Ail.   § 6 auferret *Plummer*] afferet MT
§ 7 ad M *corr.*] *om.* M*T
§ 9 totam *Plummer*] totum MT
§ 42 *Irish verses corrupt* MT

Abb.   § 10 stilum *Plummer*] stilam MT
§ 10 ⟨aemulatores⟩ *Plummer from* 1 Pet. 3.13] *om.* MT
§ 10 ⟨fecit⟩ *Plummer*] *om.* MT

A brief look at the notes to any of these Lives in Plummer's *Vitae Sanctorum Hiberniae* will demonstrate how many errors and omissions are peculiar to M or T, so proving that neither can have been copied from the other.

The extent to which T is mutilated led Plummer to print his texts of the **D**-collection from M; he gave only three Lives from T—Mochutu, Declán, Ailbe—all because of missing leaves in M. While M is at times less careless than T, the latter is in some respects the more conservative manuscript, and one could wish that Plummer had more consistently attempted to ascertain the reading of the parent copy. Reeves, though wildly inaccurate in dating both manuscripts to the thirteenth century, judged T to be the 'better & more archaic' copy of the exemplum, an observation which applies particularly to the treatment of Irish names, where M is more given to modernizing orthography than T.

4.4. *The Original Extent of the* **D**-*collection*

Plummer observed that the two manuscripts, M and T, not merely contained the same collection, but that the arrangement of the Lives was also the same, excepting the fact that the Lives of the two foreign saints, Louis and Anthony, are differently placed.[61] But his comparison took no account of the Lives completely lost from both manuscripts. What follows is an extended form of Plummer's table of comparison, substituting folio numbers for Plummer's serial numbers, and adding the date of liturgical commemoration.

[61] *Vitae*, vol. i, pp. xii–xiii.

Δ		M	T	
1.	Patrick	1	–	17 March
2.	Brigit	11	–	1 February
	Louis	23‡	[see	
	Anthony	25†	below]	
	Flannán	35vb‡	–	18 December
3.	Columba	39ra	–	9 June
4.	Maedóc	51va	–	31 January
5.	Brendan	57	28–29‡	16 May
			[= 58rb–60va in M]	
6.	Coemgen	64vb	–	3 June
7.	Moling	70va	–	17 June
8.	Fintán of Clonenagh	74ra	–	17 February
9.	Senán	76	–	8 March
10.	Mochoemóc	80va	49†	13 March
11.	Fínán	84vb	51rb	7 April
12.	Ruadán	86vb	53ra	15 April
13.	Crónán	88vb	55va	28 April
14.	Comgall	90va	57rb	10 May
15.	Carthach/ Mochutu	94rb†	60vb†	14 May
16.	Declán	100†	66rb	24 July
17.	Ciarán of Saigir	106va	–	5 March
18.	Íte	109va	–	15 January
19.	Lugidus/ Molua	112va	92–93‡	4 August
			[= 115va–116rb in M]	
20.	Lawrence	116	–	
21.	Cainnech	124ra	–	11 October
22.	Fintán of Taghmon/ Munnu	127rb	105ra†	21 October
23.	Colmán Élo	129va	106rb	26 September
24.	Bairre	132ra	109ra	25 September
25.	Aed mac Bricc	134rb	110vb	10 November
	Louis	[see		
	Anthony	above]		
26.	Ailbe	135bis^{rb}†	132rb	12 September
27.	Abbán	138va	135rb†	27 October
28.	Ciarán of Clonmacnoise	144vb	–	9 September
29.	Malachy	148	–	

Some superficial inferences immediately present themselves. The Lives of St Louis of Toulouse and St Anthony of Padua appear to have had a floating position in the exemplar from which M and T were copied. In T they occur in a position toward the end of the volume, but in M the quires v and vi may have been intruded between the end of the Life of St Brigit and the beginning of the Life of St Columba. The Lives of St Louis and St Anthony would therefore appear not to have belonged to the original D-collection. As foreign saints, they have no place in it. Reeves suggested that their presence in these manuscripts indicates that the exemplar Δ belonged to a Franciscan house. This is certainly plausible. But the lack of fixed position suggests that they may have been a loose insert. If it was in a Franciscan house that these Lives were added to Δ, it does not follow that the original D has any Franciscan connexion. I have therefore left these Lives without a number in the Δ list. Their exclusion leaves the Life of St Lawrence O'Toole, finished about 1226–7, as the latest datable text in the collection.

I have also left the Life of St Flannán without a number. This is because of the fragmentary nature of the text in M.[62] Though what survives has perhaps lost some text on ff. 36–38, it is nevertheless the case that the text is acephalous though preceded by four blank columns. The absence of any confirmation of its place from T proves nothing. But if Flannán is excluded from Δ, it is an attractive result that the order of Lives appears to begin with Colgan's *Trias thaumaturga*, St Patrick, St Brigit, and St Columba; an appropriate beginning for a national collection.

When one considers that in the Life of St Brendan ff. 28–29 in T correspond to ff. 61–62 in M, it is obvious that some 33 or 34 folios of text in the early part of M were absent from T. Most of this is easily accounted for, with the Lives of St Louis and St Anthony (approximately 20 folios), and perhaps a few folios of the Life of St Flannán. But it is still apparent that f. 28ra in T corresponds to f. 58va in M, f. 49ra to f. 81vb, f. 60vb to f. 94rb. Of this gap of 33 or 34 leaves, only about 20 to 24 are accounted for. With the fourth fragment of T, this situation has changed. F. 92ra corresponds to f. 115va in M. In other words between the Life of St

---

[62] The fragment is printed by Grosjean, 'Catalogus Codicum Dubliniensium', pp. 122–3.

Declán and the Life of St Molua there must have been a text of about 10 folios in T which was not in M. The probability is that it was one of those early in M, before the Life of St Brendan. Since T fits about 5 per cent more words per folio than M, these 10 or so folios might be accounted for by any one of the Lives of St Patrick, St Brigit, or St Columba. But that will destroy our inference that Δ may have begun with these three, and weakens the supposition that M and T reflect the order of the original collection as closely as their textual agreement leads one to expect. In the absence of more information about the contents of T before its mutilation, one can hardly do more than speculate as to the differences between the arrangement of the two manuscripts. But for reasons which will be made clear later I suspect that the Life of St Columba is the text most likely to have changed its position, disrupting the parallel arrangement of M and T.[63] This aberration is somewhat surprising for the two manuscripts otherwise appear to run *pari passu*.

As to their arrangement, there is no intelligible pattern. If we suppose that Patrick, Brigit, and Columba were intended to come first, it may be significant that St Maedóc comes next after those three. In the Irish treatise on the genealogies of the saints, the name which follows those of Patrick and Brigit in each manuscript often indicates where the copy was composed.[64] There is also a long section in the order of the liturgical calendar: items 8–16. The sequence is then interrupted by St Ciarán of Saigir and St Íte, and seemingly by another text in T, but may be thought to resume with St Molua. The latter part of the book contains the latter part of the year, but the order is very jumbled. Nor can we offer any reason why items 5, 6, and 7 do not occur between 15 and 16 in the liturgical sequence. It appears that we have an arrangement with more liturgical order than can be accidental, but which was not carried out fully, or which has been corrupted between the original arrangement of the collection and the writing of the exemplar Δ from which our witnesses derive. I am tempted to speculate that the original liturgical arrangement ran thus: items 8, 9, 10, 11, 12, 13, 14, 15, 5, 6, 7, 16, 19; that items 5, 6, and 7 were at some point transposed into their present forward position; and

[63] See below, p. 118.
[64] Ó Riain, *Corpus*, pp. xx, xxvii–xxviii, xxxii, xxxv.

that items 20–9 were never in sequence. But the placing of items 17 and 18 defies such attempts to tidy up the arrangement.

4.5. *The Unity of the* **D**-*Collection*

Plummer briefly noted:[65] 'MT represents a literary recension of materials fairly evenly carried out. Things likely to cause difficulty or scandal are toned down or omitted, and style and matter are more homogeneous than in S[almanticensis].' 'Fairly evenly carried out' is a remarkable understatement. Almost every Life in the collection betrays the interests, the idiosyncrasies, and the linguistic stamp of one redactor. This may be briefly illustrated by a single motif—the redactor's understanding of how Ireland was converted to the Christian faith, and his habitual manner of expressing this.

Four saints whose Lives are included in **D** were credited with a missionary role in Ireland before St Patrick: St Declán of Ardmore, St Ailbe of Emly, St Ciarán of Saigir, and St Abbán of Moyarney. A fifth early saint, St Ibar of Beggery Island, is represented as the maternal uncle of St Abbán.[66] They were regarded as 'elder contemporaries of St Patrick, who preceded him in the work of converting the south of Ireland; and . . . on St Patrick's arrival in Munster, they acknowledged, but only after some controversy, his superior authority.'[67] Kenney in this way states the views of **D**, the only authority for this view.[68] In the Life of St Declán **D** §3 we read, 'Declanus . . . qui habitatores multorum locorum de gentilitate ad Christum . . . conuertit' and 'tunc iam Hibernia gentilitati dedita erat'. In §21 St Patrick, 'archipontifex et patronus tocius Hibernie', assigned to St Declán

[65] Plummer, *Vitae*, vol. i, p. xxii.

[66] A brief Life of St Ibar survives among the Collectanea Bollandiana from a text supplied by Henry FitzSimon, and there is a fragment from a Life in the Book of Leinster. Both are edited by Grosjean, 'Deux textes inédits sur S. Ibar', *AB* 77 (1959), 426–50; the Book of Leinster text is also edited in R. I. Best *et al.*, *The Book of Leinster formerly Lebar na Núachongbál* (Dublin, 1954–83), vi. 1690–1, and in Ó Riain, *Corpus*, §721. Neither of these sources gives him a pre-Patrician role.

[67] Kenney, *The Sources*, pp. 309–19 (quotation from p. 310).

[68] I have discussed how the compiler worked out his own interpretation, and how it has been subsequently received, in an essay, '*Quatuor sanctissimi episcopi*: Irish Saints Before St Patrick', in *Sages, Saints, and Storytellers: Celtic Studies in Honour of Professor James Carney* (Maynooth, 1989).

the people of Déisi 'quos de gentilitate ad fidem conuertit'. In the Life of St Ciarán of Saigir **D** we find very similar passages: 'in tempore quo ipse natus est, omnes Hybernenses gentiles erant' (§1); 'quia gentiles tunc erant Hybernenses' (§3); St Patrick sent Ciarán to Ireland before him (§3), and he 'suam gentem, id est Osraighi, et plurimos alios de errore gentilitatis ad Christi fidem conuertit' (§37). St Abbán was a pupil of St Ibar who was 'unus . . . de prioribus predicatoribus, quos elegit Deus, ut Hibernienses de gentilitate ad fidem Christi conuerterent' (*Abb.* **D** §9). Abbán and Ibar encountered St Patrick (§18), and eventually Abbán died 'post ydola et simulacra destructa, post multos conuersos de gentilitate ad fidem' (§53), which we may compare with the reference to St Declán's death, 'delubris et ydolis destructis, gentilibus ad fidem conuersis' (*Decl.* **D** §39). St Ailbe arrived in Ireland, 'missus a sede apostolica ad Hiberniam insulam multis annis ante Patricium, ut fidem Christi ibi seminaret. Hibernienses autem tunc fuerunt gentiles' (*Ail.* **D** §2, cf. ibid., §14). He converted many of the Irish to the faith, but not all—that was St Patrick's role. 'Nam Patricius episcopus totam Hiberniam a gentilitate ad fidem et baptismum conuertit' (§22). In this Life, St Ailbe and St Ibar meet St Patrick at Cashel (§24). The role of Ailbe, Ibar, Declán, and Ciarán of Saigir before St Patrick is summed up in the Life of St Ciarán of Saigir **D** §7. In the **D**-text of the *Nauigatio S. Brendani*, this interest shows in what is *demonstrably* an addition by the redactor of **D**: where the *Nauigatio* has the words 'a tempore sancti Patricii et sancti Ailbei patrum nostrorum', **D** adds, 'Sanctissimus Patricius archipontifex tocius Hybernie erat qui eam de gentilitate ad fidem conuertit; beatissimus uero Ailbeus archiepiscopus prouinchie Mumenie erat que est Hybernie quinta pars'.[69]

In no sense is the language here particularly unusual, nor is it necessary to suppose a single redactor to explain the consistency of view. But the degree of sameness in these passages is impressive, and examples could be multiplied almost *ad infinitum*.

The evenness of this literary recension is so striking that Hugh Ward thought that all the Lives in M were the work of a single

[69] P. F. Moran, *Acta Sancti Brendani* (Dublin, 1872), p. 104n. Moran's manuscript F is our M. For the phrase 'que est quinta pars Hibernie' as a favourite in **D** see notes on *Vita IV S. Brigitae* 1. 8, and for *archipontifex* the notes on 1. 34.

author. Once on his own account he identified the author of the Life of St Ailbe as 'sanctus Euinus Abbas monasterii Sancti Abbani in Laginia', that is St Éimíne of Ross.[70] Although Colgan did not consistently endorse the attribution—we have seen he assigned various dates to Lives from the one collection—yet he repeated Ward's view on more than one occasion, even extending St Evin's authorship to the collection as a whole.[71]

[70] Letter, dated at Louvain, 7 Oct. 1634, to Bolland; the original is now bound as Brussels, Bibliothèque des Bollandistes, MS 141, ff. 335–336ᵛ. The text is quoted in *Acta Sanctorum*, Sept. VII (1760), 27, and by Grosjean, 'Un soldat de fortune irlandais au service des *Acta Sanctorum*: Phillipe O'Sullivan Beare et Jean Bolland (1634)', *AB* 8 (1963), pp. 424–7.

[71] Annotating his edition of the D-text of the Life of St Ciarán of Saigir, Colgan writes: 'Hanc damus ex Codice Kill-kenniensi, saepius laudato. Et in schedis P. Hugonis Vardei, qui annis multis in his vitis sanctorum colligendis pie laboravit, reperio quod S. Euinus scriptor actorum sancti Patricij juxta dicta supra tomo 1. sit author earum communiter vitarum, quae in isto codice habentur' (*Acta*, p. 463 n. 1). He goes on to endorse Ward's opinion of the common authorship of all the Lives in D on the basis of a similarity of style, and even to accept the attribution to St Euinus, supposed author of the vernacular Tripartite Life (discussed at *Trias*, pp. 170–1): 'Porro et stylus hujus authoris est subsimilis ejus stylo, et tempus quo scripsit optime in ipsum quadrat.' There is no comment on the difference of language. Elsewhere Colgan reiterates the view that all or most of the D-texts had a single author: 'Hanc [uitam S. Mochoemoci] damus ex peruetusto illo Codice Bibliothecae Fratrum Min. Kilkeniae, ex quo dedimus [uitas SS Itae, Maidoci, Fintani] et daturi sumus postea plures alias; quarum plerumque author videtur mihi idem ac praesentis' (*Acta*, p. 596 n. 1). Colgan infers that this author was a contemporary of St Mochoemóc and St Cainnech.

Elsewhere Colgan deviates from Ward's attribution: 'Reperio in diuersis schedis nostri P. fratris Hugonis Vardei, qui ex magna parte, eas quas damus in hoc opere vitas sanctorum Hiberniae, ex diuersis Bibliothecis sedulo collegit, . . . quod S. Euinus fuerit author huius, quam hic damus, vitae [S. Maidoci], et aliquot aliorum uitarum, quae in laudato Codice Kilkenniensi habentur' (*Acta*, p. 215 n. 1). He refers to Jocelin's attribution to St Euinus of a Life of St Patrick, but goes on to say, 'Si sermo sit de S. Euino Abbate de Ros-mic-treoin in Lagenia, non potuit esse author huius vitae, vel aliquot aliarum ex illis, quae in praedicto Codice Kill Keniensi habentur, si vera sint alia quae de ipso scribuntur.' He goes on to show that St Euinus of Ross died about AD 600, and for that reason 'non videtur esse author huius vitae, cum in hac fiat mentio S. Munnae anno 634 et S. Molingi post annum 690 mortui'. He admits the possibility that the author was a different St Euinus.

The author of the Life of St Íte, from the same manuscript, is said by Colgan 'floruisse circa annum 640' (*Acta*, p. 71 n. 1). It is not obvious whether Colgan was conscious of the contradictions, whether he thought the author was an unidentified but later Euinus, or whether he excluded some Lives from the common authorship.

There are many and cogent reasons why one cannot say that all the Lives in **D** were the original work of one author, nor even just those which exhibit the greatest degree of homogeneity. But it is demonstrable that nearly all the Lives known from **D** were subjected to editorial revision which imposed on them a high degree of similarity of expression and outlook. It is demonstrable because of examples such as the passage quoted from the **D**-text of the *Nauigatio*: where we can see the redactor of **D** adding in more than one place phrases, or motifs, which exactly match one another, we may be sure that this is an editorial feature liable to turn up anywhere in the collection. It is significant, therefore, to note that the phrases quoted above from the Lives of St Ailbe and St Ciarán of Saigir are not found in the other recensions of those texts. In the case of the Life of St Declán we have no other version for comparison.

Comparisons are essential if one is to build up a coherent picture of how the redactor of **D** worked. But comparisons across the three collections lack firm ground. It is much more desirable to compare the **D**-version with an independently preserved copy of its basic source text. The case of the *Nauigatio S. Brendani* regrettably does not provide very much to go on; the **D**-text is a reasonably faithful copy of the *Nauigatio* incorporated into a *uita* which we cannot see to be independent of the *uitae* of St Brendan in the other two collections. The *Vita S. Columbae* is the other obvious case of a version of an early *uita* which is independently preserved. But here too the redactor of **D** has altered the text very little: this text is a copy of the shorter recension of Adomnán with only minor rearrangement of chapters and very little to show the hand of the redactor at work.[72] So little, in fact, that I am prepared if necessary to believe that the Life of St Columba was not originally a part of **D**, and that it was added as an afterthought. Hence the guess above that if one of the Lives at the beginning of M appeared at a later position in T, it was most likely that of Columba.

---

[72] Finding next to nothing in collating several columns, I gave up. From the citations of this manuscript (called D) in Reeves, *The Life of St Columba*, I note the following: p. 6 n. 25 Patricii episcopi] Patricii archiepiscopi D (f. 39ra); p. 121 nn. 9–11 achad bó] .i. ager uaccarum *adds* D (f. 45ra); p. 207 nn. 2–4 in mediterranea Scotiae habitabat parte] in media parte Hybernie que uocatur Midi habitabat D (f. 49ra).

By a stroke of good fortune, however, the dossier of St Brigit has preserved an external text for comparison which will serve as a key to the **D**-collection. This is *Vita IV S. Brigitae*, which we shall now discuss in detail.

5

A Paradigm of the Dublin Collection
Vita IV S. Brigitae

ALTHOUGH we know from the table of contents in M that **D**
originally contained a Life of St Brigit, it is now lacking from both
manuscripts. I shall show here that it survives as the anonymous
Vita IV in two seventeenth-century editions.[1]

The Life was attributed by Ward to Ultán of Ardbraccan and by
Colgan to an unknown author, Animosus, both mentioned as
writers on St Brigit in the prologue to the metrical Life of St Brigit,
probably written by Donatus of Fiesole in the ninth century.[2]
Colgan equated this Animosus with the Irish name Anmchad,
and pointed to a bishop of St Brigit's church, Kildare, who died in
980.[3] But since Colgan thought the metrical Life to have been
written in the eighth century, it was obvious that this Anmchad
could not be the Animosus there referred to.[4] Whatever the value

---

[1] *BHL* 1460. Edited by Colgan, *Trias*, pp. 546–57, and in *Acta Sanctorum*, Feb.
I (1658), 155–71.

[2] Ward, *Sancti Rumoldi Acta*, p. 154; Colgan, *Trias*, p. 563 n. 1, 582, 596–8 nn. 1
and 7. Cf. D. N. Kissane (ed.), '*Vita Metrica Sanctae Brigidae*: A Critical Edition',
PRIA 77 (1977), 84. Ussher, *Whole Works*, vi. 534–5, preferred not to speculate on
whether Animosus might be the author of this text or of another, or even whether
he might be the same as Cogitosus.

[3] J. O'Donovan (ed. and trans.), *Annals of the Kingdom of Ireland by the Four
Masters* (7 vols.; Dublin, 1851), ii. 712–13.

[4] *Acta Sanctorum*, Feb. I, 102 § 14, has Bolland agreeing that Animosus may be
Anmchad, but denying that he could have written *Vita IV*, which he dated to after
1152. He says that if Colgan had not wished to attribute the metrical Life to
Coelán of Inis Cealtra before 750, he might have attributed that text to Anmchad.
The absurdity of fathering a text on a tenth-century author on the basis of a
supposedly eight-century witness is attacked by M. Esposito, 'On the Early Latin
Lives of St Brigid of Kildare', *Hermathena* no. 49 (1935), 129 n. 39. It had not
escaped Colgan, who appears to suppose that, though the Animosus mentioned
in the metrical Life must have lived no later than the date of that text, he might
still apply the name, albeit a different individual, to a text written later; *Trias*,
p. 563 n. 1.

of Donatus's reference to Animosus, there is no reason to continue Colgan's arbitrary association of his name with *Vita IV*.

Kenney thought highly of *Vita IV*, saying that it 'is extensive, containing much of detail, and is of value for the study of Irish social conditions'.[5] This is surprising, since it is derived from *Vita I*, a much earlier text which he described as 'a loose and prolix document'.[6] Its value is greatest as an index to the changes in style and content between seventh-century hagiography and the works of the age of the **D**-redactor, and especially as a paradigm of the latter's editorial activity.

5.1. M *the Manuscript from which* Vita IV *was Printed*

Colgan, who first printed the Life, gave no indication of his source, but his text is almost identical to that of the Bollandists: it is almost certain that they used the same source, specified by Bolland as 'ex MS. Hugonis Wardaei Ord. Minor.'[7] Ward had, after all, supplied the Bollandists with copies of many texts used by himself and Colgan. Unfortunately, there is no indication of where Ward found the text of *Vita IV*.[8]

This Life was also known, probably independently, to Archbishop Ussher, who quotes from it in his *Britannicarum Ecclesiarum Antiquitates*.[9] He specifically describes it as a Life in two books. There are many references to a Life of Brigit in two books

[5] Kenney, *The Sources*, p. 362.

[6] Ibid.

[7] *Acta Sanctorum*, Feb. I, 102 §14: 'aliam subnectimus uitam ab Hugone Wardaeo olim nobis communicatam, quam & Colganus ex illius collectaneis edidit'. The divergences are noted occasionally in the apparatus criticus of the Bollandist text.

[8] Esposito refers to *Vita IV* as 'a modern forgery', 'On the Early Latin Lives of St Brigid', p. 165; and as 'the patched up Life of Brigid, which has imposed even on modern scholars' (ibid., p. 145 n. 84). It seems he thought it to be Ward's own reworking of *Vita I S. Brigitae*, using the copy of that text made by Stephen White from the Regensburg manuscript, for he speaks of 'the curious use made of this transcript by Ward' (ibid., p. 146 n. 88). This is inference from Bolland's remark that White's transcript was communicated to him by Ward, *Acta Sanctorum*, Feb. I, 102 §14. But it is unwarranted guesswork and contrary to all probability that Ward revised that work and passed off his revision as a different *uita* to Colgan and Bolland; Ussher's knowledge of it, however, proves Esposito to have been mistaken.

[9] *Whole Works*, vi. 162–3, 347, 436, 446, 450, 451, 535.

in the additions made in Recension C of FitzSimon's *Catalogus praecipuorum Sanctorum Hiberniae*. Grosjean has shown that these additions, including the references to a Life of Brigit, cited from a volume described as 'Anonyma SS. Hib. Legenda manuscripta', derive from our manuscript M.[10]

Although this manuscript no longer contains a Life of St Brigit, we know from the table of contents that it originally followed the Life of St Patrick, at ff. 11–22. It is impractical to hope that one could work out what portions of *Vita IV* might occupy which folios, and then to correlate with the references in the *Catalogus*.[11] But it is possible to prove by other means that the Life of Brigit in question was *Vita IV*: in *Vita IV* II 19, a person called Cellanus in the source, *Vita I* §51, has been confounded with Conlaed or Conlae, the first bishop of Kildare, and the name is written 'Conlianus'. This spelling lies behind the entry in the *Catalogus* misprinted or misread as 'Conhanus'.[12]

The chain is now complete: Ward provided a copy of *Vita IV* in two books; Recension C of the *Catalogus* cited a Life of Brigit in two books from an anonymous manuscript; that manuscript is demonstrably Marsh's Library MS Z3. 1. 5; this codex, now mutilated, originally contained a Life of Brigit; a form drawn from it by the compiler of Recension C, but misread or misprinted, tallies with *Vita IV* in a peculiar reading. If any doubt remains, it is surely dispelled when we remember that the two other writers whom we know to have used *Vita IV*, Ward and Ussher, were both familiar with the contents of the manuscript now in Marsh's Library.

Vita IV is thus the **D**-text of the Life of St Brigit.

This discovery is of some importance for the study of the redaction of the *uitae* of Irish saints in the three later medieval

---

[10] P. Grosjean, 'Édition du *Catalogus Praecipuorum Sanctorum Hiberniae* de Henri FitzSimon', in *Féilsgríbhinn Eóin Mhic Néill*, ed. J. Ryan (Dublin, 1940), nos. 37, 89, 163, 240, 284, 287, 382, 513–14, 539, all derive from this Life of St Brigit. Nos. 89, 382, and 539 are cited by book and chapter.

[11] In one case, this seems possible: Grosjean's no. 240, Darlugdacha, was mentioned on f. 202 of the manuscript source according to Grosjean's edition. She appears in what is almost the last section of *Vita IV*, II 97, and we know from the table of contents that the text in the Marsh manuscript ended at f. 22. Is 202 Grosjean's misprint for 22?

[12] No. 163.

collections, for it provides us with a paradigm which enables us to understand in some detail the work of the redactor of **D**. He depended closely on *Vita I S. Brigitae*, a text preserved in more than thirty manuscripts, including one of the ninth and several of the tenth century. An exact comparison of *Vita IV* against *Vita I* will show up in what way the redactor manipulated his source text, what interests he imposed, and what are the characteristics of his editorial and literary style. A comparison of these changes in the Life of Brigit with any similar passages elsewhere in the **D**-collection may be expected to show up the unity of the editorial characteristics of **D**.

These comparisons can most practically be made by presenting a text of *Vita IV*. In the edition which follows, I use italics to make obvious the deviations of *Vita IV* from the wording of *Vita I*. The footnotes then compare these deviations with similar passages from other Lives in the **D**-collection.

5.2. *The Dependence of* Vita IV *on* Vita I

The dependence of *Vita IV* on *Vita I* is very close indeed. In fact, the two are often identical in wording. One may see from the concordance of sections that the writer of *Vita IV* took over *Vita I* almost entire, adding only here and there a passage of his own.[13] The following passage at the beginning of the text indicates the general tenor of the relationship:

Vita I, § 2: Quadam *autem* die sederunt *ambo* in curru *uir ille* et ancilla, *et exierunt secus*	*Vita IV*, 1 2: Quadam *postea* die sedentes in curru *dux Dubtachus* et sua ancilla *Broseach, sequentesque eos comites sui, peruenerunt prope*
domum cuiusdam magi. Audiens autem magus sonitum currus, dixit seruis suis, 'Videte quis sedit in curru; currus enim sub rege sonat.' Tunc serui dixerunt. '*Neminem* cernimus	domum cuiusdam magi. Audiens autem *ille* magus sonitum currus, dixit seruis suis, 'Videte quis sedet in curru; sonat enim currus sub rege.' Tunc serui dixerunt *ei, 'Nullum uirum* cernimus

---

[13] See below, pp. 210–12.

nisi Dubthacum in curru.'   in curru nisi *dominum*
Dubtachum.'

Magus dixit, 'Vocate illum   Magus dixit *eis*, 'Vocate illum
ad me.'   ad me.'

This illustrates the degree of change normal throughout the text, verbal changes amounting to no more than clarification of the rather concise expression of *Vita I*. This short passage also includes one of the most readily identifiable aspects of the language of the redactor of **D**, the attributive use of the word *dux* applied to Dubthach.[14]

If this normal level of comparison were universal, one would readily conclude that the compiler of **D** had simply taken a copy of *Vita I* and revised it with only trivial verbal alterations of a kind which he habitually applied in his compilation. There are more difficult comparisons. In the next example, **D** takes over all of *Vita I* but elaborates somewhat:

Vita I, § 10: Sancta puella
cibos *fastidiebat* magi

atque uomebat cotidie.

Haec magus considerans.
scrutabatur causam nausiae
eamque *inuenit et* dicit,
'Immundus
sum ego: puella autem ista
plena est *de spiritu sancto.*
Cibum *autem* meum non
*acc*ipit.'

Deinde elegit uaccam
albam et destinauit

Vita IV, 1 7: Sancta *iam* puella
cibos *communes* magi, *domini
matris sue, respuebat*
et uomebat quotidie.
Ille enim homo poeta et magus erat.
Hec magus *ipse* considerans.
*per*scrutabatur caussam nausee;

eamque *sciens* dixit, 'Immundus
ego sum; puella autem illa est
plena *gratia omnipotentis Dei,
ideoque* cibum meum non capit.'
*Ille enim tunc erat gentilis et
incredulus cum domo sua, quia
nuper antea fides Christi peruenit
ad Hiberniam; et tunc statim ipse
non credidit sed post tempus,
sicuti audietis.* Deinde *magus
ille* elegit uaccam albam *sine
macula*

---

[14] See below, on II 41 n. 149.

eam puellae;

et mulgebat *eam* uaccam
aliqua femina Christiana.
uirgo ualde religiosa, *et*
bibebat lac illius uaccae *sanoque*
uentre non uomuit illud, et illa
femina Christiana nutriebat
puellam.

et destinauit eam *sancte* puelle,
uidens dei gratia albedinem in ea;
contigitque unam feminam
Christianam
ibi esse que erat multum religiosa
et fertur uirginem *fuisse eam,*
quam
fecit magus ille ut nutriret sanctam
Brigidam. Et *ipsa* mulgebat
predictam uaccam *et de lacte*
eius nutriuit sanctam Brigidam.
quia beata infans libenter
istius uacce lac *recepit, et*
diligenter ancillam Christi
nutriuit Christiana femina,
ualde amans illam.

For the most part, the elaboration is of a purely literary sort. But the allusion to the paganism of the *magus*, its explanation, and the reference ahead to his conversion represent alteration of a more sophisticated sort, the logical tidying up of the narrative.[15] This is less obviously a matter of editorial revision made when *Vita I* was rewritten for **D**, but it is of a piece with the view of the early conversion period which we have already suggested the redactor held. There is no reason why this cannot belong to the editorial stage. The same could be said of the reordering of chapters between *Vita I* and *Vita IV*, done to smooth out the geographical movement of the narrative.[16] But it should be borne in mind that such changes may belong to an intermediate stage of revision of this particular Life, unless they can be paralleled elsewhere in the collection.

Some features of *Vita IV* not derived from *Vita I* are without parallel in **D**, and so might have been added to the text at a stage prior to the compilation of the collection. The most obvious passage which falls into this category is the prologue, written with personal reference to the author but unfortunately not naming

[15] Elsewhere, the redactor of *Vita IV* shows an awareness that Brigit lived in the early days of Irish Christianity: at I 3, he observes that Patrick was only just then preaching in Ireland, and at II 23, adds of Bishop Ibar 'qui seminator fidei multis in locis fuit ante beatissimum Patricium'.

[16] See the concordance of chapters preceding the text, and I 49 n. 84.

him.[17] The other Lives which begin with prefaces—Adomnán's Life of St Columba, St Bernard's Life of St Malachy, and the Life of St Lawrence O'Toole—were so equipped by their original authors, and were scarcely tampered with by the redactor. *Vita I*, on the other hand, was extensively rewritten in the **D**-collection, and in such a way as to suggest that this was the compiler's work. One must wonder, therefore, whether the prologue too was written by the redactor or whether it was taken over from an already slightly revised and rearranged version of *Vita I*.

This question can only be answered by an examination *membratim et particulatim* of *Vita IV* in relation to *Vita I*, and by a comparison of every word and sentence in which the two texts differ with the style of **D** and especially with those features of **D** which distinguish its recension of a text from the equivalent in **S** or **O**. My findings in doing this are presented in the form of notes on the edition which follows. In these notes, an asterisk against a reference (such as *Aed* § 5*) indicates that a parallel passage exists in **S** or **O** which does not have the feature under·consideration, and that the feature is thus verifiably a part of the editorial work in **D**. Conversely, an obelus is used to indicate where such a feature is paralleled in another recension. In later chapters I shall argue that the sources of **D** still survive in many cases.

5.3. *Method of Editing* Vita IV

The primary evidence for the text of *Vita IV* (V[4]) consists of the editions of Colgan (C) and the Bollandists (B; 3rd edition, b), the quotations given by Ussher (U), and a very few citations from Ward's manuscript in the critical notes of the Bollandist edition or in the margin of Colgan's. It is also implicit that where the Bollandist edition cites the reading of Colgan in its notes (c), Colgan's text differs from the manuscript and is to be rejected. On the face of it, therefore, the Bollandist text appears more critical and supposedly better founded than Colgan's. This leaves unweighed the question of how faithful either edition really attempts to be: Colgan is known to have been an editor indifferent to minutiae;[18] the fact that the Bollandists' critical notes record

---

[17] A suggested identification was proposed by Felim Ó Briain; see below, p. 209.

[18] L. Bieler, 'John Colgan as Editor', *Franciscan Studies*, 8 (1948), 14–16.

only a small fraction of the divergences suggests that they too set no great store by fidelity in points of detail.

There is a third witness to the reading of Ward's transcript of M, from which both editions derive, in the form of marginal annotations in Brussels, Bibliothèque royale, MS 7763. This is an early Bollandist manuscript, some of it written by Bolland himself, containing 'AA. SS. Februarii rejecta et reservata'. At ff. 112–133 (in the red foliation, ff. 131–152 in the original numbering) is a copy of *Vita I S. Brigitae* as supplied by Stephen White 'ex vetustissimo Codice Coenobii S. Magni ad pedem Pontis Ratisbonae', the same text from which Colgan printed *Vita I*.[19] Bolland has made various marginal notes, noting where he preferred to deviate from 'MS. Ratisp.'; it appears, therefore, that he may have intended to print *Vita I* from this copy. But he changed his mind, and based his text on Saint-Omer, Bibliothèque municipale, MS 715.[20] For our present purpose, we are concerned with those marginal readings marked 'MS. War.' which are obviously derived from Ward's copy of *Vita IV*. For example, at 1 5 of our text, the reading of *Vita I* §4 is 'uenit ancilla magi ad domum, portans uas plenum lacte'; the reading of *Vita IV* is 'uenit ancilla illa mater sancte Brigide deforis ad domum proximi domini sui, portans uas plenum de lacte'. In the margin of his transcript of *Vita I*, Bolland here notes 'addit MS. War *proximi domini sui*'. These words represent a change of meaning, and are found only in *Vita IV*. Incidentally, it should be noted that Colgan omitted the word *proximi*, whether deliberately or accidentally. But the agreement of B with these marginalia (which I shall call Q^w) against C is not generally maintained. In *Vita IV* 11 27, B and Q^w agree on 'aquae turbatae' against C 'quae turbatae', but this is surely a typographical error in C. In the same chapter the reading 'ad aquilonalem plagam' in C is changed to 'ad aquilonarem plagam' by B; compare at 11 37 'aquilonis pars' C, 'aquilonaris pars' B, and 'aquilonalis pars' Q^w, where Q^w has the true reading, C has a typographical error and B has made a substitution.

The agreement of Q^wCB represents in substance (one can hardly speak for accidentals) the reading of Ward's transcript (W), which is not guaranteed to be a faithful copy of M. The quotations

---

[19] Colgan, *Trias*, pp. 527, 542n.
[20] *Acta Sanctorum*, Feb. I, 101 §7.

in Ussher's *Antiquitates* were taken from M directly, and therefore have independent authority. But these tend further to diminish one's confidence in the accuracy of the text preserved by B and C. Occasionally U will support C against B:

ɪɪ 89 absentior UC　absentius B
　　　praesentior UC　praesentius B
ɪɪ 99 cum gloria UC　in gloria B

This is slender support for C. Unfortunately Ussher's text all too often diverges from CB and, in one passage where this is particularly conspicuous, Ussher seems to be right:

ɪɪ 89 quodam tempore U　quodam die CB
　　　sanctissima U　beata CB
　　　sancta uirgo U　uirgo CB
　　　sol justitiae Christus U　sol justitiae CB
　　　sancta Brigida U　sancta CB
　　　iterum mater U　*om.* CB

The judgement that Ussher here has the true reading is not based on internal evidence since in each case either reading is acceptable on face value. But in each case Ussher is supported by the witness of *Vita I* against CB. Where Q^w is available, this view is reinforced:

ɪɪ 99 ei U　*om.* Q^wCB
　　　adveniens U　veniens Q^wCB

Where U is available, this level of divergence is common, and leaves one hesitant over many readings where CB are in agreement in the absence of the third witness. Fortunately, these are not generally differences of substance. But we may have to accept that our edition may well represent the text of W rather than the text of M.

　　Whereas U and Q^w are only occasionally available, the close relationship throughout the text between V^4 and *Vita I* (V^1) makes it possible to use V^1 as a secondary witness to the text of V^4, one without which many textual decisions between C and B would be arbitrary. (In making such comparisons, I have disregarded those accidentals where the divergence in the age of the witnesses makes variation inevitable.) This comparison shows time and time again that B has introduced trivial changes, always preserving the sense, sometimes clarifying it:

I   1 quidam dux CV¹ dux quidam B
     meam progeniem CV¹ progeniem meam B
I   2 ambo CV¹ *om.* B
     poterit nocere CV¹ nocere poterit B
I   5 alterum pedem foris CV¹ alter pes foris stans B
I   7 plena est CV¹ est plena B
I   9 domui CV¹ domum B
I 12 patriam CV¹ prouinciam B
I 37 ut ego CV¹ ego ut B
I 39 carris C *cf.* carras V¹ curribus B
I 42 per illam solui posset CV¹β solui per eam possit B
I 44 fuerat CV¹β (fuit V¹α) erat B
I 48 recipere CV¹ accipere B
     et auferent CV¹ qui auferent B
     plurimos CV¹ multos B
I 52 nocte fecit CV¹ fecit nocte B

The reverse agreement of B with V¹ against C is also frequently found, but in a higher proportion of these cases C has not fiddled with the text but has corrupted it:

I   7 de lacte eius B (illius V¹) de lacte eo C
I 12 habitatores BV¹ habitores C
I 34 tunc BV¹ *om.* C
     illorum BV¹β *om.* C
I 37 regione BV¹ regine C
     die BV¹ *om.* C
I 42 tunc BV¹ tum C
I 43 ut tu BV¹ *om.* C
I 45 egit BV¹ agit C
II 2 custodiat te BV¹β te custodiat C
II 4 media . . . Brigidam (*14 words*) BV¹ *om.* C
     et de medio . . . capita sua (*15 words*) BV¹ *om.* C
II 7 mihi praestat BV¹ sentio C

Where possible, I have chosen the reading which is supported by V¹. In circumstances where this is not available, I have more often followed C than B, where the difference might result from B's editorial interference.

All too often CB agree on a reading which is inadequate. These occasions fall into two classes. First, occasions when CB does not give adequate sense; in these instances I have corrected the text, usually by reference to V^1, occasionally by conjecture:

I   3 intrauerunt V^1 *om.* CB
I   4 poeta V^1 postea CB
I   12 qua V^1 quod CB
II   4 uero remanebo V^1 uero B redire C
    primo V^1 primi CB
II   10 ut V^1 et CB
    magnis V^1 magis CB
II   17 honorem V^1 honore CB
II   20 et V^1 at CB
II   32 et V^1 at CB
II   39 ipsi] illi V^1 ipse CB
II   56 uti V^1 *om.* CB

False readings in this class are likely to be errors of copying, whether when W was copied from M or when M was copied from Δ. Their correction is a simple matter.

The second class is made up of those occasions when the redactor of V^4 was following an already corrupt text of V^1 and did not necessarily reword to avoid the corruption:

I   50 ipsum CB   *cf.* altare V^1
II   4 habuerunt CB   *cf.* inuenerunt V^1
    cum suis CB   *cf.* cum bobis suis V^1
II   17 egit CB   *cf.* fecit V^1
II   29 quibus rapta sunt CB   *cf.* a quibus grana rapta sunt V^1
II   50 modulanter CB   *cf.* modulantur V^1
II   52 medium CB   *cf.* dimidium V^1
II   53 praeparantem CB   *cf.* saepientem V^1

In all these cases, the reading of V^4 could result from an error in the text of V^1 used by the redactor, a misreading or an omission which the redactor did not detect and paraphrase his way round. In these cases, I have not corrected the text of V^4 but have marked the reading with *ita* in the apparatus and have given there a better reading of V^1.

In the examples cited above, the errors in the copy of V^1 used by the redactor of V^4 could be individual. In the absence of a complete recension of the text of V^1 it is impossible to know. But it is possible to detect some readings preserved in V^4 from the underlying text of V^1 which give some clues to the text-type of V^1 which was used. The textual history of V^1 divided at an early date between two broad families, α and β. As it happens, α is reflected in Colgan's edition, β in the Bollandist text, though neither edition is at all accurate. In comparing V^4 with text-types of V^1 I have consulted the earliest manuscript of each type: London, British Library, MS Add. 34124 (A; s. ix^1) for α, and Munich, Staatsbibliothek, Clm. 2531 (M; s. x) for β.[21] It is quickly apparent that V^4 followed a copy of V^1 of the β type:

I   1 qui emit ancillam V^4 $V^1M\beta$ ille emit V^1A
      erat perfecta V^4 $V^1M\beta$ fuit perfecta V^1A
I   2 uocatoque eo V^4 $V^1M\beta$ uocatoque V^1A
      magus dixit: 'Uxoris . . .' V^4 $V^1M\beta$ magus ait: 'Uxoris . . .' V^1A
      seruiet usque in finem seculi V^4 $V^1M\beta$ seruiet usque ad finem
         seculi V^1A
      que sicut sol in uertice celi ⟨sic V^4⟩ lucebit in mundo V^4 $V^1M\beta$
         que lucebit in mundo sicut sol in uertice celi V^1A
      tantum filior V^4 $V^1M\beta$ filios tantum V^1A
I   3 in domum V^4 $V^1M\beta$ domum V^1A
      famule uestre partus V^4 $V^1M\beta$ partus famule tue V^1A
I 11 ordinemque baptismatis V^4 V^1M ordinem baptismatis $V^1\beta A$
I 34 miserta illorum V^4 $V^1\beta$ miserta erat illis V^1A
      uos esse uenturos V^4 $V^1\beta$ uos futuros esse V^1A
I 35 benigne suscepit V^4 $V^1\beta$ benigne accepit V^1A
I 37 V^4 $V^1\beta$ *omit the last words of section* leprosa mundata est,
         demens sanata est V^1A
I 39 subrogauit eos V^4 $V^1\beta$ rogauit eos V^1A
      comederunt et dormierunt V^4 $V^1\beta$ comederunt et biberunt V^1A
I 42 in fornicationem V^4 V^1M in peccatum $V^1\beta A$

This does not exhaust the examples of this pattern, even in Book I, but the basic inference is clear. However, where M disagrees with the Bollandist text of β, V^4 will sometimes agree with one, sometimes the other. The agreement of V^4 $V^1\beta$ against V^1M is a relatively simple matter: either M has introduced a peculiar reading or $V^4\beta$ represents a β reading later than the tenth century. The consensus of V^4 and V^1M against $V^1\beta$ raises the question of where V^4 branches off the stemma of $V^1\beta$, or whether the Bollandist text deviates from $V^1\beta$: these questions cannot be answered without a full investigation of the textual history of V^1.

[21] In the notes on the text a reading attributed to β is taken from the Bollandist edition unless M or another manuscript is specified.

As a rule, when confronted with an unintelligible reading in V¹, the redactor of V⁴ produced a paraphrase. For example:

V¹α §117: Quodam die alius reus perductus est ad iugulandum ab alio rege. In hora autem iugulationis eius sancta Brigita orans argentum a Deo in sinum accepit et regi pro eo reddidit.

V¹β has corrupted *in hora* into *mora*. The redactor of V⁴ therefore recast the second sentence:

V⁴ II 83: Moram autem iugulationis eius piissima uirgo Brigida faciebat, petens uitam eius. Tunc desuper purum argentum in sinum uirginis a Deo directum est, et regi pro misero ipsa reddidit.

Medieval students were accustomed to the problem of reading a defective text, and this one has used his intelligence to overcome such difficulties in his exemplar.

An editor of V⁴ has no business attempting to restore a reading from V¹ where it is reasonably certain that the redactor of V⁴ had a different, albeit corrupt, reading in front of him. In some cases, it is hard to know whether a reading is likely to have come from the redactor's copy of V¹ or not. In V⁴ I 4 the reading 'Ut uenderet aemulam' makes sense, for Dubtach's wife regarded the slave-girl as a rival. The text of V¹ has 'ancillam', a more obvious reading. It is possible that the redactor altered 'ancillam' to 'emulam', but such a change, imposing a psychological interpretation, is not easy to accept. I think it likelier that 'æmulam' is a misreading of 'ancillam' (bearing in mind that the digraph æ belongs to Ward's orthography, not to that of his medieval exemplar). In this case, I have taken the risk of restoring the reading from V¹.

As a general policy I have been cautious about introducing readings from V¹. Decisions between U on the one hand and QʷCB on the other must be based on the merits of a particular reading. In the absence of other witnesses, many decisions between C and B are somewhat arbitrary. I have preferred to follow C except where the reading of C is clearly corrupt, where the Bollandists specifically set aside the reading of Cc, or where B has the positive support of V¹. This preference has to be borne in mind even on certain occasions where B yields the smoother or easier text, for the occasions where C has the support of V¹ against B show that the latter was more likely to correct than to corrupt.

Finally, there are two areas of accidentals demanding editor's decisions but where the textual witnesses fail to provide a reasonable basis for his guidance.

First, there is the question of the division of the text into sections: this was provided by the original text in M, which was followed by Recension C of the *Catalogus* and by Ussher. But the two editions have each provided their own. It is possible to reconstruct the chapter-numbering of M only in part, so this cannot be followed and another must be chosen.[22] Notwithstanding the wider accessibility of the Bollandist *Acta Sanctorum*, I have preferred to follow Colgan's numbering (correcting one or two misprints). This is partly because Colgan's divisions have more support from the chapters cited in the *Catalogus* and by Ussher than the Bollandist text has, and partly because they adhere more closely to the paragraphing formulae ('Alia autem die', etc.) in the

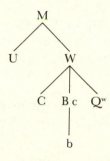

M = Marsh's Library, MS Z3. 1. 5
U = Ussher's quotations from M
W = lost transcript of M made for Ward
Q^w = collations against W in Brussels, MS 7763
C = Colgan's edition of W
B = Bollandist edition of W
c = a reading in C denied by B's reading of W
b = Paris reprint of B

FIG. 1 *Vita IV S. Brigitae*: Textual Relationships

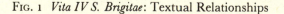

[22] On the basis of chapter references in FitzSimon's Recension C (here called H) and Ussher's *Antiquates* (U), I have reconstructed the numbering of Book II in M and print this in parallel with those of Bolland and Colgan (see Concordance 1, p. 135).

text. But these divisions are in some measure arbitrary, and where sense seems to me to demand different paragraphing, I have marked paragraphs by indentation independently of the section numbers.

Secondly, the textual witnesses have on the whole made the spelling of the text conform to seventeenth-century practice. I have decided to abandon this and to attempt instead to restore spelling in general agreement with that of M. In doing this, I have limited alterations to a few basic points: the diphthongs *æ* and *œ* are not used but are levelled to *e*; *j* is not used but always *i*. The orthography of M presents its own problems where fifteenth-century usage is variable, and under these circumstances I have adopted usage consonant with the likely date of the text. M uses *u* and *v* at random, so no restoration could be attempted, and I have used *u* in all cases; likewise M is indiscriminate on forms in -*tio* and -*cio*, whereas I avoid -*cio*, a form which became widespread only in the late thirteenth century; M's frequent use of *y* for *i* I have not attempted to follow. Seventeenth-century printers were much more generous with capital letters and marks of punctuation than we are now; I have treated this as a matter of conscience and followed my own inclination. In reporting the readings of the printed editions, it is unnecessary to mention mere printers' errors, so that I have silently corrected inverted type and such like except where a reading is reported for other reasons.[23]

5.4. *Annotated Text of* Vita *IV*

In the text which follows, roman type indicates that the wording is taken directly from V^1, nine-point is used for wording which represents the reading of $V^1\beta$, and *italic* is used where the redactor of V^4 has paraphrased or added to his source.

---

[23] One misprint occurs with remarkable frequency in the Paris 'third edition' of the Bollandist text, *r* for *t*: I 45 *ducetis* (*duceris* b), I 46 *habetis* (*haberis* b twice), II 29 *caeletis* (*celeris* b), II 33 *sedetis* (*sederis* b), II 55 *ito* (*iro* b), II 72 *astutiam* (*asturiam* b).

Concordance 1

Chapter-references from M are given by Ussher (U) and FitzSimon (H), and these provide fixed points in the table; the second and third columns give section-numbers from the Bollandists and Colgan. Chapter-numbers not marked U or H are my conjecture. Long stories in M may be divided up differently in B and C, but from II 55 onwards it is noticeable that M and C run in parallel where B often joins stories together. I have therefore preferred the numbering of C to that of B.

BOOK I

H no. 89   I c.38   (= *Colgan* I 42–3)

BOOK II

U p. 347	II c.14	(=II 23)
U p. 450	II c.20	(=II 30)
H no. 284	II c. 31	(=II 41–5)
H no. 37	c.32	(=II 47)
H no. 89	II c.43	(=II 58–9)

H no. 593	c.55	(=II 76)
U p. 436	II c.60	(=II 81)
H no. 382	II c.61	(=II 82)
U pp. 162–3	II c.68	(=II 89)
U pp. 446, 451	II c.77	(=II 99)

BOOK TWO

	M	B	C	H	M	B	C
	1–2	1–4	1–4		29	34	39
	3	5	5		30	35	40
	4	6	6	H	31	34–9	41–4
	5	7	8–9	H	32	40–1	45–7
	6	8–10	10–13		33	42	48
	7	11	14		34	43	49
	8	12	15–16		35	44	50
	9	13	17		36	45	51
	10	14	18		37	46	52
	11	15	19–20		38	47	53
	12	16	21		39	48	54
	13	17	22		40	49	55
U	14	18–19	23–4		41	50	56
	15	20	25		42	51	57
	16	21	26	H	43	52	58–9
	17	22	27		44	53	60
	18	23	28		45	54–5	61–3
	19	24	29		46	56	64
U	20	25	30		47	57	65–6
	21	26	31		48	58	67
	22	27	32		49	59	68–70
	23	28	33		50	60	71
	24	29	34		51	61	72
	25	30	35		52	62	73
	26	31	36		53	63	74
	27	32	37		54	64	75
	28	33	38	H	55	65	76

	M	B	C			M	B	C
	56	66	77		U	68	73	89
	57		78			69	74	90
	58	67	79			70	75	91
	59	68	80			71		92
U	60	69	81			72	76	93
H	61		82			73	77	94
	62	70	83			74	78	95–6
	63		84			75	79	97
	64	71	85			76	80	98
	65		86		U	77	81	99–100
	66	72	87					
	67		88					

Concordance 2

This table allows readers to find the section of V¹ corresponding to any chapter of
V⁴. I cite both by Colgan's numbering (middle columns). For readers with access
only to the Bollandist edition, I give its numbering here (outer columns). The one
table allows comparison of the two *uitae* in either edition and conversion from one
edition to the other for any reference.

VITA IV		*VITA I*	
Boll.	Colg.	Colg.	Boll.
BOOK I			
1	Prol.	—	—
2	1a	—	—
3	1b	1	1
4	2	2a	2a
5	3	3a	3a
6	4	2b, 3b	2b, 3b
7	5a	4	4
8	5b, 6	5, cf. 9	5a, cf. 7
9	7	10	8
10	8	5b	5b
11	9	5c	5c
12	10	6	5d
13	11	7, 8	6
14, 15	12	9	7
37	34	32	29
38	35	33	30
39	36	34	31
40	37	35	32
41	38	36	33
42	39	37	34
43	40	38	35
44, 45	41, 42	39	36

VITA IV		VITA I	
Boll.	Colg.	Colg.	Boll.
46, 47	43	40, 41	37, 38a
48	44	42	38b
48*bis*	45	43	39
49	46	44	40
50	47	45	41
51	48	46	42
52	49	94a	91a
53	50	94b	91b
54	51	95	92
55	52	96	93

BOOK II			
1, 2	1, 2	97	94
3	3	98a	95a
4	4	47	43
5	5	48	44
6	6	87	86
7	7, 8, 9	88, 89	87
8, 9, 10	10, 11, 12, 13	90	88
11	14	91	89
12	15, 16	92, 93	90
13	17	49	45
14	18	50	46
15	19, 20	51	47
16	21	52	48
17	22	53	49
18, 19	23, 24	54	50
20	25	55	51
21	26	56	52
22	27	57	53
23	28	58	54
24	29	59	55
25	30	60	56
26	31	61	57
27	32	62	58
28	33	63	59
29	34	64	60
30	35	65	61
31	36	66	62
32, 33	37, 38	67	63, 64
34	39	68	65
35	40	69	66
36	41	70	67
37, 38	42, 43	71	68, 69
39	44	72	70

VITA IV		*VITA I*	
Boll.	Colg.	Colg.	Boll.
40, 41	45, 46, 47	73	71, 72
42	48	74	73
43	49	75	74
44	50	76	75
45	51	77	76
46	52	79	78
47	53	80	79
48	54	81	80
49	55	82	81
50	56	83	82
51	57	84	83
52	58, 59a	85	84
53	59b, 60	86	85
54, 55	61, 62, 63	78	77
56	64	98b	95b
57	65, 66	99	96
58	67	100	97
59	68, 69, 70	101	98
60	71	102	99
61	72	103	100a
62	73	104	100b
63	74	109	102a
64	75	110	102b
65	76	111, 112	103
66	77, 78	108, 107	101b, 101a
67	79	113	104a
68	80	114	104b
69	81, 82	115, 116	105
70	83, 84	117	106a
71a	85	119	*om*
71b	86	121	107a
72	87, 88	122, 123	107b
73	89	124	108
74	90	125	109a
75	91, 92	126, 127	109b
76	93	128	110
77	94	129	111
78	95, 96	130, 131	112, 113
79	97	132a	114
80	98	—	—
81	99	—	—
82	100	—	—

VITA IV S. BRIGITAE

Prologus

Tribus[24] *iam, fratres mei,* ᵃ*mens mea*ᵃ *impugnatur, uidelicet amore, pudore et timore.* *Amor enim scribendi me cogit commendare uitam preclarissime Brigide in chartis ne magna charismata uirtutum, que Dei gratia ei contulit, uel plurima miracula, que eadem per eam patrauit, abscondita uel inaudita essent.* *Pudore autem prohibeor ne, ut reor, meus sermo ualde incultus aut sententia insubtilitatis mee sapientibus legentibus seu audientibus displiceret.* *Timore uero magis trudor quia periculum est imbecillitati mee hoc opus dictare, quoniam obtrectatorum iniquorumque sugillationes timeo ingeniolum meum tamquam dapes probantes.*

Sed quia, cum Dominus iussit pauperibus populi res offerre uiles ad construendum tabernaculum, nonne nos debemus ad edificandam ecclesiam offerre? *Quid est*ᵇ *ecclesia nisi collectio iustorum?* *Quomodo uita prudentium edificatur nisi documentis et exemplis prudentium?* *Igitur amori cursum dimittam, pudorem calcabo, et susurronibus indulgeo.* *Sed te, lector prudens et auditor intelligens, adiuro ut non positionem uel textum uerborum*ᶜ *curans miraculis Dei et beatitudini*ᵈ *famule ejus intendas.* *Omnis enimuero*ᵉ *agricola uesci debet fructibus sulcorum agri sui.*

Prol. ᵃ⁻ᵃ mea mens B   ᵇ est] *om.* B   ᶜ versorum B   ᵈ beatitudini *conjecit* B] beatitudine *a* beatissimae Cc   ᵉ iamvero C

[24] **Prologus.** The rhetorical but conventional prologue is peculiar to V⁴: there is no prologue to V¹. Although it is written in the first person, there is no indication of the identity of the author. Where prologues exist elsewhere in **D**, they are taken over from the source text (see above, p. 125–6). This raises the possibility that V⁴ may have been a text already revised from V¹ when it came to the hands of the redactor of **D**; see below, pp. 210–12.

Liber Primus

1 *Fuit*[25] *gloriosus*[26] *rex in Hibernia nomine Feidlimidh qui dicebatur Feidli-*
   midh Reachtmar eo quod magnas in suo regno in Hibernia leges fecit;[27]
   'reacht' enim Scotice Latine sonat 'legem'.[28] *Ipse rex habuit tres filios quo-*
   rum nomina dicuntur Fiacha Suighe, Eochaid[a] *Fionn, Cond Keudcha-*
   thach, qui in summa et maxima fertilitate Hiberniam in Temoria
   regnauit.[29] *Defuncto patre*[b] *suo, Fiacha Suighe habuit tres filios, scilicet*

---

1 [a] Eochaidh C   [b] fratre Cc

[25] The long genealogical preamble, not derived from V[1], uses information from
the Irish tract on the Expulsion of the Déisi, and is probably an addition in **D**,
which has similar passages elsewhere. In *Ita* **D** §1, the same legendary genealogy
is given, but instead of following Brigit's line from Eochaid Find in Leinster, the
career of Fiachu Suidge in Munster is recounted, from whose line Ita was born.
Decl. **D** §1 offers the longest and most elaborate narrative of this kind in Hiberno-
Latin hagiography. Once again, it is the same dynasty but told with more detail of
earlier generations and of brothers here merely mentioned. Although no comparative texts exist for *Ita* and *Decl.*, the number of phrases shared with V[4] is
enough to attest their common authorship. See below, nn. 27, 29, and 30. The
same Irish text treats of Eithne Uathach, on whom V[4] has a digression at II 12.

[26] *Gloriosus* is a favourite word in V[4], frequently applied to Brigit (see below, I 34
n. 61). It is frequent in **D** as a whole, occurring 27 times in the **D** texts printed by
Plummer. Unfortunately few of these are verifiable as **D** additions, but note *Aed* **D**
§14* 'qui erit rex gloriosus' (= S §18 'et ipse erit magnus'; *Mol.* **D** §19 'gloriosus
rex Temorie'; *CiS.* **D** §7 (a substantial passage, characteristic of **D**; cf. above,
p. 116) 'gloriosus archiepiscopus Patricius'.

[27] Cf. *Decl.* **D** §1 'Feidlimmid Reacthmar qui leges magnas in regno suo fecit'.
Feidlimid Rechtmar 'the lawgiver' (in older texts called Feidlimid Rechtaid) is
correctly glossed as from OIr. *recht* 'law', though the use of *magnus* here and in
Decl. §1 may indicate a false interpretation of the second element as OIr. *már, mór*
'great'.

[28] This form of gloss, also found in V[4] at II 3, 63, is one of the most recognizable
features of the redactor of **D**: cf. *Abb.* **D** §§9, 22, 27, 33, 40, 41, 43, 47, *Aed* **D** §§5*,
33*, *Car.* **D** §§55, 58, 64, 65, *Coem.* **D** §§1, 6*, 16*, 29, *Com.* **D** §§21, 52, *Decl.* **D**
§§6, 15, 16, 17, *FintC.* **D** §17*, *Maed.* **D** §§8*, 25*, *Mchg.* **D** §§6, 11, 14, 15, *Mol.* **D**
§§2*, 28, *Mun.* **D** §§5*, 18*, *Rua.* **D** §3*.

[29] Cf. *Ita* **D** §1 'Conn autem totam Hyberniam . . . in maxima fertilitate
regnauit', *Decl.* **D** §1 'Cond uiginti annis regnauit, set fama fertilitatis et pacis
atque bonitatis eius erit ad finem mundi'; cf. also *Aed* §1* where the simple words
'de nepotibus Neill' in S are elaborated thus in **D**: 'de nobiliori, Hybernie genere,
id est de semine Cuind Cetcathaidh, qui in summa pace et maxima fertilitate
Hyberniam in Temoria uiginti annis regnauit'.

ᶜ*Rossa, Ængus, Eogan,* ᶜ *qui expulsi ab Arthuro*ᵈ *predicti Connii filio a Temoria regionem magnam in confinio Lageniensium et Momoniensium gladiis suis apprehenderunt;*[30] *sed ipsi Momonienses uocantur. Eochaid*ᵉ *Fionn autem perrexit ad Lagenienses*ᶠ *et in multis locis rex Lageniensium*ᵍ *dedit ei terras, et ibi habitant nepotes ejus usque huc*ʰ*; iam ipsi inter Lagenienses*ᶠ *numerantur et Lagenienses*ᶠ *uocantur. De quibus* fuit ⁱquidam *dux*ⁱ[31] *magnus et potens,* nomine Dubtachus, qui emit ancillam *que uocabatur* Broseach.ʲ *Ipsa* erat *multum* formosa et moribus *honesta. Amans eam dominus Dubtachus fecit eam concubinam suam* et dormiuit cum ea et concepit illa ab eo. Hoc sciens propria uxor Dubtachi contristata est ualde et dixit uiro suo: 'Vende ancillam *tuam Broseach*ʲ *quam fecisti concubinam tuam; timeo enim si* progenies ipsius superauerit ᵏmeam progeniemᵏ.' Sed *dominus Dubtachus* noluit *hoc facere* ualde amans eam; in omnibus enim moribus *illa femina* erat perfecta.

Quadam *postea* die sedentes amboᵃ in curru, *dux*[32] *Dubtachus* et *sua* ancilla Broseach, *sequentesque eos comites*ᵇ *sui, peruenerunt prope* domum cuiusdam magi. Audiens autem *ille* magus sonitum currus dixit seruis suis: 'Videte quis sedet in curru; sonat enim currus sub rege.' Tunc serui dixerunt *ei:* '*Nullum uirum*[33] cernimus

---

ᶜ⁻ᶜ *Here* B *notes:* 'Hi Wardaeo dicuntur Rossaeus, Æneas, Eugenius.'   ᵈ Arthurio C   ᵉ Eochaidh C   ᶠ Lagenenses C   ᵍ Lagenensium C   ʰ hoc C   ⁱ⁻ⁱ quidam dux C dux quidam B   ʲ Broschach C *but the heading in Colgan's notes is* Brosoach   ᵏ⁻ᵏ progeniem meam B   2   ᵃ ambo] *om.* B   ᵇ communiter C

---

³⁰ Cf. *Ita* D §1 'ad terram Mumenensium ... uenerunt et ibi maximam regionem nobiliter et fortiter gladiis suis apprehenderunt'; *Decl.* D §2 'nolebant enim aliam regionem ... accipere nisi quam in quodam confinio gladiis suis causa liberalitatis acciperent'.

³¹ Here the opening of V¹, 'Fuit quidam uir', is taken up by V⁴. The substitution of *dux* is characteristic of D (see I 2 n. 32).

³² This use of *dux* attributively is found in V⁴ at I 2, 4, II 10, and to replace another noun at I 1. Cf. *FinC.* §21 'et noluit rex', D §16 'set dux Nechtayn noluit'; *Lug.* S¹ §33 'tunc Berachus dixit Lugido', D §28 'hoc uidens dux Berachus ... ait sancto Molue'; *Mun.* S §20 'Dimma filius Aidi', D §18 'dux Dimma filius Aedha'. There are numerous examples of this attributive use in D where no comparison with another version is possible: *Ba.* §§2, 8, *Car.* §§9, 40, *CiS.* §§8, 9. *Com.* §58, *Decl.* §§19, 22, 35, *Mchg.* §§17, 31. Overall, the word *dux* is remarkably frequent in D, 369 times in the 22 texts printed by Plummer as against 14 times in his nine O-texts. For its particular use in D to substitute for *rex*, see II 41 n. 149.

³³ 'Nullum uirum' is substituted for V¹ 'neminem' for clarity of sense: obviously there was the woman Broicsech in the chariot with Dubtach.

in curru nisi *dominum* Dubtachum.' Magus dixit *eis*: 'Vocate illum
ad me.' Vocatoque eo ait *ei*[c] magus: 'Mulier que post tergum
tuum sedet in curru, an *est pregnans*?' Dubtachus respondens ait:
'*Iam ita est*.' Magus dixit: 'O mulier, de quo uiro concepisti?' Illa
respondit: 'De domino meo Dubtacho.' Magus dixit *ad Dubtachum*: 'Hanc mulierem ualde custodi; mirabilis enim erit
conceptus eius.' Dubtachus ait: 'Compellit me uxor mea ut hanc
uendam; timet enim semen huius.' Magus dixit: 'Uxoris tue
semen semini famule huius seruiet usque in finem seculi.' Ad
ancillam uero ait: 'Constans esto animo, quia nullus tibi [d]poterit
nocere[d]; gratia enim infantule te liberabit. Claram namque filiam
paries que sicut sol in uertice celi *sic* lucebit in mundo *usque in finem
seculi*.' *Tunc* Dubtachus ait: 'Deo gratias ago quia hucusque filiam
non habui sed tantum filios.' Deinde reuersi sunt Dubtachus et
concubina sua *cum comitibus suis* in domum suam; Dubtachus
uero multum dilexit illam propter sermones magi.

3 In diebus iam illis Deo instigante duo sancti episcopi ex Britannia
⟨intrauerunt⟩[a34] in domum Dubtachi uenientes, quorum alter
uocabatur Maol at alius Maolchu; [b]*ipsi erant discipuli sancti Patricii
archiepiscopi qui tunc predicabat uerbum Dei in Hibernia*.[b35] *Videns
episcopus* Maol[c] uxor*em* Dubtachi *tristem esse*,[36] ait ei: 'Quare tristis

---

[c] illi B   [d-d] nocere poterit B   3 [a] ⟨intraverunt⟩ V[1]   [b-b] ipsi . . .
Hibernia] Q[w] f. 112[r]   [c] Mael C

[34] In CB this sentence lacks a main verb; V[1] §3 has 'duo sancti episcopi ex
Pretannia uenientes intrauerunt domum Dubthaci', but *intrauerunt* is awkward in
the revised text because of the change in position of *uenientes*.

[35] Maol and Maolchu (Mel and Melchu in the older spelling of V[1]) are always
regarded as disciples of St Patrick, cf. V[1] §18, 'Mel et Melchu qui discipuli sancti
Patricii fuerant et in oppidis Medi illi habitauerunt'. V[4] has brought the
explanation forward to their first mention. Two other aspects of this interpolation
are noteworthy: first, the use of *archiepiscopus* for St Patrick is normal in V[4] (cf. I 34,
41, II 27, 34, 42, 99); and secondly the addition 'qui tunc predicabat uerbum Dei
in Hibernia' falls in line with several other additions in V[4], cf. I 7 'quia nuper antea
fides Christi peruenit in Hiberniam'; I 41 'sanctum Patricium predicatorem
Hibernie'; II 12 'Patricius predicator Hibernie'; II 23 'Hybarus qui seminator fidei
multis in locis fuit ante beatissimum Patricium'. Both features can be paralleled
elsewhere in **D** (see below, I 34 n. 64, and notes on other passages here).

[36] Here V[1] §3 reads 'dixitque Mel ad uxorem Dubthaci, "Quare tristis es?"' but
V[4] has characteristically anticipated the question.

es?' *Et addidit, sciens causam eius prophetice*:[37] '[d]Famule *uestre* partus[d] precellet te et *omne* semen tuum. Sed tamen illam sicut filiam tuam ama quia progenies illius tuis proficiet multum.' Sed tamen illa adhuc in furore mansit.

Ipsa iam irata cum fratribus suis, *qui erant uiri fortes et potentes*, urgebant[a] ualde Dubtachum ut uenderet ancillam[b] suam in regionem longinquam. Tunc quidam poeta *de aquilone Hibernie*[38] *nutu Dei*[39] uenit, *et timens dux Dubtachus iram uxoris sue que erat nobilis et fratrum eius furorem consensit uendere illam. Et ipse dux inde erat multum mestus*.

[d-d] *cf.* famulae tuae partus V¹(M), partus famulae tuae V¹(A)   4 [a] urgebant CB] urgebat V¹   [b] ancillam V¹] aemulam CB

---

[37] The adverb *prophetice* (cf. below I 43, II 63) seems to be inserted sufficiently often by **D** to be regarded as another mark of its editorial style: cf. *Ba.* §4, *Car.* §§6, 35, 37, 40, *CiC.* §12, *Coem.* §§25, 30, 43, *ColE.* §§15*, 26*, *Cron.* §§5, 11, 27, *Decl.* §§5, 8, *Ita* §§20, 27, *Mchg.* §27, *Lug.* §§28*, 50*, *Rua.* §29*. In the nine O-Lives printed by Plummer it is used once only, *Bren.* §61.

[38] In this sentence V⁴ appears to conflate two passages in some texts of V¹. Here, V¹α has 'quidam poeta de nepotibus Neill Deo inspiratus' (where V¹β has *magus*), but at the end of §3 V¹α adds a duplicate of this, in which the *poeta* is said to sell Broicsech on to a *magus*, 'uenit quidam magus aquilonali parte ad domum huius poetae'. The latter passage is not found in V¹β, as represented by Boll, but appears to have been in the text used by the redactor of V⁴. The text is evidently confused, and the redactor has tried to clarify the use of *poeta* and *magus*; see below, I 7 n. 51. In the Middle Irish Life (edited by W. Stokes, *Three Middle-Irish Homilies on the Lives of Saints Patrick, Brigit, and Columba* (Calcutta, 1877), pp. 50–87, and id. (ed. and trans.), *Lives of the Saints from the Book of Lismore* (Oxford, 1890), pp. 34–53, 182–200), §6, the two are separate, and the *file* is said to come from Uí Meic Cuais, the *drui* from *crich Conaill*, i.e. Conaille Muirthemne.

[39] The adverbial phrases *nutu Dei* and *nutu diuino* are added on several occasions in V⁴ (e.g. I 34, II 24 (= V¹), 29, 48, 63, 86, 94). Both phrases are very common in **D**; *nutu diuino* or *diuino nutu*: *Aed* §§5*, 12†, 28*, *Ba.* §3, *Car.* §§ 27, 62, *CiC.* §§4, 6, 11, *CiS.* §18*, *ColE.* §§5*, 34*, *Com.* §§2, 7, 40, *Cron.* §§23, 26, *Decl.* §§15, 16, 32, *FintC.* §4†, *Maed.* §8†, *Mchg.* §§1, 23, *Mol.* §§10, 17*, 27; *nutu Dei* or *Dei nutu*: *Alb.* §41*, *Ba.* §12, *Car.* §27, *CiC.* §23, *CiS.* §8*, *Coem.* §§2*, 9, 27*, 33, 34, 43, *ColE.* §§12*, 20*, 21*, 31*, *Com.* §§31, 45, *Decl.* §§5, 7, 11, 25, *FintC.* §§3* 11*, *Mchg.* §§11, *Mol.* §4*, *Lug.* §§4*, 10*, 20*, 21*, 52*, *Rua.* §12*. In two cases here (*Aed* **D** §12, *FintC.* **D** §4) the phrase was taken from the corresponding passage in **S**; in the case of *Maed.* **D** §8 the absence of the phrase from **V** but its presence in **S** is probably because **S** derives directly or indirectly from **D** (cf. *Vitae*, vol. i, p. lxxvii). The occurrence of one or other phrase occasionally in **S** and several times in **O** hardly outweighs the evidence of some score of examples where it is verifiably an interpolation in **D**. But in unverifiable cases, it cannot be assumed that the phrase is an addition of **D**.

Et *poeta predictus* emit *illam feminam in* ancillam. Sed *Dubtachus* non uendidit partem *illius, perhibens quod illa haberet filiam mirabilem in utero.* Perrexit ille poeta[c] cum ancilla in regionem suam. Venit quidam hospes sanctus qui orabat Deum per totam illam noctem uidebatque in illa nocte sepe globum igneum in loco in quo ancilla *mater sancte Brigide* dormiebat; et hoc mane poete *domino eius* narrauit, *et ille inde gauisus est.*

5 *Ipso tempore ille poeta parauit cenam magnam regi suo,*[40] *et ipse* rex *cum* regina *uenit* ad cenam, sed regina erat partui *proxima.* Tunc amici et serui regis interrogabant quemdam prophetam *quando bona* hora *esset ut* regina pareret *prolem suam.* Ille ait: 'Si die crastino orto sole nasceretur, neminem in terris haberet equalem.' Sed regina ante *illam* horam *contra uoluntatem suam* genuit filium. Mane autem facto et orto sole, uenit ancilla *illa mater sancte Brigide deforis* ad domum *proximi*[a] *domini sui*[41] portans uas plenum *de* lacte nuper mulso; et cum posuisset unum pedem trans limen domus et [b]alterum pedem foris[b], cecidit super limen sedens et *repentissime sine ui doloris parturiendi Dei gratia* filiam *pulcherrimam* facie genuit. Sic enim ille propheta dixit quod nec in domo nec extra domum ipsa femina *prolem* pareret. Et de lacte illo calido quod portabat illa corpus *bone* infant*ule*[42] *lotum* est.

Signa iam maxima illico[43] *secuta sunt dono Dei sanctam Brigidam, quorum hoc unum est.*

---

[c] poeta V¹ postea CB   5 [a] proximi] *om.* C   [b-b] alter pes foris stans B

[40] Cf. *Lug.* **D** §42 'cenam magnam regi Laginensium parauit' where **S** §50 has 'fecit cenam magnam regi Lagensium'. *parare cenam* is used elsewhere in **D** but sometimes is taken from its source: *Aed* §15†, *ColE.* §31*, *Mun.* §4†.

[41] According to V¹ §4 'orto sole uenit ancilla magi ad domum', implying that she did not sleep in the house, because she was a servant. But V⁴ appears to imagine that she slept *in* the house, and in the morning came *out*, taking milk to a neighbour's house; this is surely confused.

[42] There appears to be a preference for the diminutive in V⁴, here and at 16, 12; cf. *ColE.* §1*, *FintC.* §1*.

[43] The adverb *illico* occurs 20 times in V⁴, 4 times derived from V¹, II 25, 43, 49, 76, and 16 times interpolated, I 5, 10, 34, 38, 40, 42, 47, II 3, 11, 13, 31, 73, 77, 92, 93, 99. If this does not in itself indicate that **D** had a penchant for the word, note that *ilico* is attested 196 times, *illico* 15 times, from the 22 **D**-Lives edited by Plummer, as against one example in the 9 **O**-Lives in Plummer's *Vitae.*

Ipso[44] *iam die natiuitatis sue, quidam infantulus preterita nocte natus subita morte preuentus fuit.*[a] *Et aliquo euentu, cum esset sancta Dei prope illum, tetigit corpus eius extinctum; et subito sanctissime infantule tactu ille infans uiuus surrexit. Hoc omnes uidentes dicebant quod merito illa filia predicata esset a prophetis. Villa illa in qua sancta Brigida nata est Fochart Muirthemne uocatur que est in prouincia Ultorum, scilicet in regione que dicitur Conaille Muirthemne.*[b] *Ipsam uillam modo habet sancta Brigida in cuius honore monasterium canonicorum in ea est.*[45] *Ibi illa ecclesia et cemiterium eius est ubi fuit domus et curia*[46] *in quibus nata*[c] *est beata Brigida. Lapis*[47] *uero super quem genita*[d] *est sanctissima Christi sponsa*[48] *post tergum ipsius sanctuarii constat et ab incolis istius terre colitur*

---

6 [a] est B   [b] Muirtemne B   [c] nota C   [d] nata B

[44] According to V^1 §3, St Brigit was born in the house of the *magus* from some *pars aquilonalis* who bought her mother. In the OIr. Life of Brigit, this portion of the text is lost due to mutilation of the manuscript, but when the text begins St Brigit and her mother are with the *druí*. The earliest surviving text to identify the district is the MIr. Life which specifies that she was born in Conaille Muirthemne at Fochart Muirthemne, now Faughard, Co. Louth. V^4 appears to be following MIr. in this chapter. In one particular, however, V^4 departs from MIr. which told how the queen's child was a son, born dead before sunrise, and that he was the child revivified by the infant Brigit. The stone on which Brigit was born remained at Fochart according to both texts; MIr. specifically says 'to the south-east of the church', while V^4 mentions the founding of the church.

[45] This reference places the passages in a context not earlier than the late twelfth century. A similar reference is found at *Decl.* §26, and one might compare the allusion to a modern 'monasterium sanctimonialium' in *Car.* §65, cf. below, 1 37 n. 65.

[46] *Curia* refers to a simple enclosure around the house, here likened to the cemetery around the church. Cf. *Mol.* D §17 'frangere curiam et extrema domus'.

[47] While V^1 §4, MIr. and V^4 1 5 merely say that Brigit was born on the threshold of the house, here a feature is added from stories where the mother delays birth by sitting astride a stone which thereafter bore the mark of the child's head and was venerated; cf. *Aed* S §1, D §1, *Decl.* §3, *Mun.* S §1, D §1, and contrast the story of the birth of Fiacha Mullethan, whose head is flattened by the stone, M. O Daly (ed. and trans.), *Cath Maige Mucrama* ([London], 1975), §§42–3 and n. p. 112. Cf. H. Zimmer, *Göttingische gelehrte Anzeigen* (1891), 168–70. This is only one of several story-types to explain the aetiology of the bullaun-stones frequently kept in medieval Irish churches; cf. *Decl.* §§25, 32, *Rua.* D §14. Cf. Plummer, *Vitae*, vol. i, p. cxxxii (and nn. 5–6), cxxxix–xl (and nn. 1–2); P. Grosjean, 'De Sancto Aido, episcopo Killariensi in Hibernia', in *Acta Sanctorum*, Nov. IV (Brussels, 1925), p. 505 n. 3.

[48] See below, 1 34 n. 61.

honorifice[49] *eo quod multa signa super eum per merita sancte Brigide patrantur.*

7 Sancta[50] *iam* puella cibos *communes* magi *domini matris sue respuebat* atque uomebat quotidie. *Ille enim homo poeta et magus erat.*[51] Hec magus ipse considerans, *per*scrutabatur causam nausee eamque *sciens* dixit: 'Immundus ego sum; puella autem illa ᵃplena estᵃ *gratia omnipotentis Dei ideoque* cibum meum non capit.' *Ille enim tunc erat gentilis et*ᵇ *incredulus cum domo sua, quia nuper antea fides Christi peruenit ad Hiberniam,*[52] *et tum*ᶜ *statim non credidit sed post tempus, sicuti audietis.*[53] Deinde *magus ipse* elegit uaccam albam *sine macula* et destinauit eam *sancte* puelle, *uidens Dei gratia albedinem in ea. Contigitque* unam feminam Christianam *ibi esse que erat* multum religiosa, *et fertur* uirginem *fuisse eam, quam fecit magus ille ut nutriret sanctam Brigidam.* Et ipsa mulgebat predictam uaccam et de lacte eiusᵈ nutriuit sanctam Brigidam *quia beata infans libenter* illiusᵉ uacce lac *recepit,* et *diligenter* ᶠ*ancillam Christi* nutriuitᶠ Christiana femina *ualde amans illam.*

7 ᵃ⁻ᵃ est plena B   ᵇ et] *om.* C   ᶜ tunc B   ᵈ eo C   ᵉ istius B
ᶠ⁻ᶠ ancilla Christi nutrita est a C

---

[49] The adverb *honorifice* occurs regularly in **D**: *Abb.* §§9*, 27*, 32*, 37*, 52*, *Aed* §31*, *Alb.* §46*, *Ba.* §§13, 14, 15, *Cain.* §§23†, 32*, *CiC.* §15*, *CiS.* §32, *Coem.* §28*, *Com.* §§52, 58, *Cron.* §26*, *Decl.* §§10, 15, 19, 34, *Lug.* §38*, *Mol.* §§19, 30. Its unverifiable occurrence in **D**-texts is probably but not certainly the result of the redactor's work.

[50] This story, V¹ §10, is told after St Brigit and the *magus* go to Munster (see below, I 12) in both V¹ and the Irish Lives. It is perhaps brought forward because it makes most sense when the infant is very young.

[51] At this point the redactor of V⁴ has felt it necessary to explain that the *poeta* of I 4–5 is the *magus* of I 7–12. On the frequent use of the two terms for the same individual, see Plummer, *Vitae*, vol. i, pp. clxi–clxii and nn. But it will be remembered (see above, I 4 n. 38) that the text of V¹ is confused as to whether there are two separate individuals or one involved in the story.

[52] Cf. above, p. 115–16 and I 3 n. 35 for the redactor's interest in the period of conversion. Presumably the interpolation indicates that the redactor believed that paganism disappeared soon after St Patrick's arrival, and therefore that these events must belong to the very early days of Christianity in Ireland.

[53] The second part of this interpolation presumably anticipates the story of the conversion of a *magus* on his death-bed at II 88, though neither there nor in V¹ §123 is any connexion made with the *magus* who brought up St Brigit.

Post hec iam ipse magus cum *omni domo sua* perrexit ad regionem Connachtorum[a], *que est pars quinta Hibernie*,[54] et habitauit ibi. Fuit enim mater eius de Connachtis, pater uero de Momoniensibus. *Causa iam magice artis sue circuibat totam prouinciam illam aliasque prouincias et habebat magnum honorem in eis.*[55]

Quadam quoque die *dimissa est beatissima Brigida* sola in domo dormiens. Tunc domus illa accensa igne apparebat, et circumuenerunt omnes ut extinguerent ignem. Et cum appropinquassent [a]domui[b], ignis non apparuit *sed domus incolumis inuenta est.* Viderunt, *excitantes illam*, puellam pulchra facie[a] et genis rubicundis et dixerunt omnes: 'Hec puella uere plena est spiritu sancto.'

Die autem alio magus et *mater sancte Brigide* cum *nutrice sua et* ceteris *foris* in quodam loco sedentes subito uiderunt pannum contingentem caput puelle *iuxta se sedentis* flamme incendio ardere et, porrigentibus illis manus suas uelociter, *illico* ignem non uiderunt *sed pannum intactum. Et ex hoc significatur gratia spiritus sancti ardens in sancta Dei.*[56]

[a]Quadam *deinde*[a] die idem magus dormiens uidit duos clericos uestibus albis indutos effundere oleum super caput puelle ordinemque baptismatis complentes consueto more. Unus autem ex illis dixit *ad magum*: 'Hanc uirginem uocate Brigidam. *Ipsa*

---

8 [a] Connaghtorum B 9 [a-a] *two lines reversed* C [b] domum B
11 [a-a] Qadam diende C Quadam denique B

---

[54] The phrase *quinta pars* is a regular calque on OIr. *cóiced* 'fifth', meaning one of the five provinces of Ireland. Here Connacht is so glossed; cf. *Bren.* D quoted above, p. 116 (Munster), *Abb.* D §9* (Ulster), and *Coem.* D §1* (Leinster). (On the problem of the fifth 'fifth', see T. F. O'Rahilly, *Early Irish History and Mythology* (Dublin, 1946), pp. 172–83). Such additions in D belong to the common class of added geographical information. Cf. below V⁴ II 1, 49.

[55] Asides of this kind alluding to aspects of Irish custom are found elsewhere; cf. below, I 38.

[56] Such concluding remarks are often added to chapters in V⁴; cf. I 11 (end of paragraph), 35, 39, 40, 43, 44, 50, 52, II 5, 9, 10, 11, 27, 29, 30, 39, 42, 56, 59 (end of paragraph), 60, 87, 95.

autem erit plena gratia coram Deo et hominibus, et nomen eius cele-
berrimum erit per totum orbem. ' *Hisque dictis discesserunt angeli.*[57]

Nocte *iam* quadam idem magus erat uigilans suo*que* more astra
celi considerans, et per totam illam noctem uidit columnam ignis
ardentem consurgentem*que altius ea* domuncula in qua beata
Brigida dormiebat, et uocauit ad se alium[58] uirum *in testimonium*
qui et ipse similiter uidit. *Hoc uero mane omnibus narrabant.*

12 Quadam quoque die, *cum adhuc* infant*ula tenerrima beata Brigida*
esset, orauit *intente* ad Deum, expandens manus *suas* ad celum.
Tunc quidam uir *ad illam uenit* salutauit*que* eam. *Ita ei beata puella*
respondit: 'Meum erit hoc.' *Mirans uir ille inde narrauit mago.*
Respondens magus dixit: 'Vere[59] prophetia est qua[a] respondit
infans, quia hec loca erunt illius in eternum.' Quod postea
completum est, nam parrochia[b] magna est hodie sancte Brigide in
istis regionibus. Hoc audientes habitatores[c] illius regionis congre-
gauerunt se ad magum dicentes ei: 'Tu mane *cum domo tua* nobiscum; puella uero hec que prophetat quod regiones nostre sue
erunt recedat a nobis.' Magus ait: '*Non ita fiat.*[d] Sed potius terram
uestram deseram *propter eam. Ipsa enim magna* [e]*erit in celo*[e] *et quod*
ipsa prophetauit post tempus ita erit.'[60] Tunc magus cum suis omnibus
deseruit prouinciam Connachtorum et uenit ad patriam[f] suam que est
in regionibus Momoniensium, ubi habebat hereditatem patris
sui.

---

12 [a] qua V¹ (quae A)] quod C B   [b] parochia B   [c] habitores C   [d] fiet B
[e-e] in caelo est B   [f] provinciam B

[57] V⁴ evidently found the version in V¹ §7 too terse and has added that the white
figures who performed Brigit's baptism were angels, and enunciates the significance of their ministration.

[58] Here V¹ §8 has 'aliquem uirum', probably an example of the reversal of *alius*
and *aliquis* common in Hiberno-Latin, though *alius* for standard *aliquis* is more
common. I take the sense to be 'he called over to him a second man to act as
witness'; V⁴ has the grammatically more correct 'alium'.

[59] It is tempting to emend 'uere' CB to 'uera' with V¹α, but it is apparently
taken over from V¹β. The adverb *uere* was in any case popular with V⁴ and **D** as a
whole, see below, II 14 n. 102.

[60] As at I 11, V⁴ explains the significance of the prophecy, whose fulfilment is
noticed at I 49.

Cum iam creuisset *quidem corpore sed plus fide, spe, et caritate*, sancta puella *fideliter* ministrabat [. . .

[*The equivalent of* Vita I §§11–31 *is lost*; see above, p. 95.]

Alio *autem* tempore sancta Brigida iter agebat per campum Theba sedens[a] in curru. Tunc illa uidit quendam *uirum* cum sua familia et uxore et cum multis pecoribus laborantes et portantes onera grauia, qui in ardore solis lassi *tunc* fuerunt.[b] *Christi uirgo*[61] tunc[c] miserta illorum[d] dedit eis equos currus sui ad onera portanda. Sancta autem in uia cum suis *comitibus*[62] sedens mansit, dixitque *ministris suis sancta uirgo*: 'Fodite *in illo loco*, et erumpet inde *fons;*' *(aqua enim ibi antea non fuerat)*[63] 'uenient enim *citius* ad nos, *quibus necesse erit potum habere.*' Tunc illi foderunt et *illico fons* erupit. Post paullulum[e] uenit per illam uiam dux cum turba multa equitum. Ipse audiens quod sancta Brigida de equis suis fecit, obtulit ei duos equos indomitos *dicens:* '*Sanctitas bone uirginis faciat* [f]*eos mites sibi*[f].' Et statim ita *diuino nutu* [g]domiti facti sunt[g], quasi unquam essent[h] sub curru. Post hec [i]per eandem uiam[i] discipuli sancti

---

34 [a] sedens] *om.* C   [b] fuerant B   [c] tunc] *om.* C   [d] illorum] *om.* C [e] paullulum C   [f-f] sibi eos mites B   [g-g] facti sunt domiti B   [h] issent B   [i-i] *post* venerunt B

[61] Where V[1] is normally content with *Brigita* or *sancta Brigita*, V[4] regularly makes substitutions or elaborations. Favourite formulae are: *uirgo Christi*, cf. 1 36, 42, 47, 11 10, 81; *uirgo Dei*, 11 10, 31, 93; *gloriosa uirgo*, 1 34, 40, 50, 52, 11 1, 4, 6, 15, 23; *Christi sponsa*, 1 6, 37, 39, 40, 45, 11 1, 2, 5, 7, 10, 41, 44, and *gloriosa Christi sponsa*, 11 75, 96; *Christi amica*, 11 4, 50; *Christi ancilla* or *famula*, 1 7, 11 73, 97; also very frequently added is the phrase *sancta* or *beata uirgo*, 1 34, 39, 40, 43, 48, 11 2, 6, 10, 11, 15, 18, 20, 24–7, 29, 30, 41, 50, 52–4, 57, 58, 67, 76, 80. It will be noticed how often these formulae are italicized in the remainder of the text. The formulae *uirgo Christi, sponsa Christi, ancilla* or *famula Christi* are also common in the Life of St Ita, D's only other female saint; cf. *Bren.* D §3 'gloriosa uirgo Yta'. Only *ancilla* or *famula Christi* is used in the O-text Life of St Samthann. Among masculine saints, *miles Christi* and *famulus Christi* are commonly added by D.

[62] In V[1] §32 'cum puellis suis'; the change to 'comitibus' may indicate that the redactor thought it unlikely that the *puellae* would dig for water, or even that it was unfitting for Brigit and her nuns to travel without escort. But the alteration of *puellae* to *comites* happens more than once: cf. 11 1, and note that at 1 39, 40, 11 35, 43, her *comites* are mentioned in V[4] though not in V[1]. But in many places, V[4] retains *puellae*, and twice (1 43, 11 23) changes V[1] *comites* to *puellae*.

[63] The redactor adds what is an obvious inference from the text of V[1], a common feature of his editorial work.

Patricii *archiepiscopi totius Hibernie*[64] uenerunt et dixerunt ad beatam Brigidam: *'Nos ualde sitientes sumus et comedere non possumus.'* Tunc comites *gloriose uirginis* dixerunt eis: 'Nos *iubente domina nostra* potum uobis preparauimus; ipsa enim nobis predixit uos esse uenturos.' Postea omnes *de uiatico suo* comedebant et gratias Deo in communi agentes et suam sanctam ancillam glorificantes bibebant.

35 *Inde* duo leprosi secuti sunt sanctam Brigidam euntem cum turba multa quos *sancta uirgo* benigne suscepit. *Contigit eis ante sanctam Dei* rixari, et miseri se inuicem percutiebant. *Sed* manus illius qui prius percutiebat *socium* incuruata *semel*, non potuit iterum erig*ere eam*; alterius quoque dextera ad percutiendum sursum erecta recuruari *arefacta* non potuit. Riguerunt itaque manus miserorum manentes immobiles donec sancta Brigida ueniens *pacem fecit inter eos*. Tunc illi leprosi penitentiam agentes, *sancta Dei* manus eorum *pristine* sanitati *restituit. Postea accipientes elemosinam leti redierunt.*

36 Alio quoque die currus sancte Brigide conductus est ut in eo quidam infirmus ueheretur qui in extremo uite confinio anhelabat. Cumque positus esset in curru, *melius habuit* et ueniens ad sanctam Brigidam *hoc ei indicauit*. Et crastino die, benedicente eum *Christi uirgine, bene ualens* ambulauit. *Hoc uidentes quidam* leprosi postulauerunt currum illum, et eis *Christi uirgo* donauit eum cum equis suis.

37 Beatissima Brigida rogata ad *quoddam monasterium*[65] *sanctimonialium* in regione[a] Theba exiuit ut celebraret pascha. Et *beata abbatissa*[66] illius *loci* in die cene Domini dixit *ad omnes uirgines*:

37 [a] regine C

---

[64] Cf. 13 n. 35, for the title *archiepiscopus totius Hiberniae*, cf. *CiS.* **D** §3*, *Decl.* §9; ibid. §19 'archipatronum tocius Hiberniae', §21 'archipontifex et patronus tocius Hibernie'; *Bren.* **D** quoted above, p. 116, 'archipontifex tocius Hybernie'; and for the *archiepiscopatus*, *CiS.* **D** §3*, *Decl.* §12.

[65] V[1] §35 'ad aliam ecclesiam'. This change was so common that Bolland noted at II 26 (Q[w] f. 120) 'MS. W. semper monasterium habet, ubi hic' (i.e. in V[1]) 'est ecclesia'.

[66] V[1] §35 'domina aecclesiae illius'. *Abbatissa* is rare in all three collections, and may have been substituted in order to avoid *domina* (used in the Annals of Ulster for the head of a women's community), which in V[4] is always Brigit's title. See below II 5 n. 92.

'Que ex uobis hoc die[b] lauacrum faciet infirmis nostris?' *Ceteris omnibus nolentibus* sancta Brigida dixit: 'Volo [c]ut ego[c] miseras et infirmas *sorores* abluam.' *Et hoc placuit illi abbatisse scienti fuisse a Deo.* Erant autem ibi quatuor egrote in una domo, una paralitica que iacebat immobilis, alia uero energumena demonio plena, tertia ceca, quarta leprosa. Tunc sancta Brigida prius cepit lauare paraliticam, et ait ei: 'O beata mater, roga Christum pro me ut me sanet.' Et orante *Christi sponsa pro ea*, statim *in ista hora* sanata est.[67]

Manens beata Brigida in eadem regione in *quadam cellula* aliquibus diebus, casu *remansit illa sola* cum uno puero in domo, et ille puer mutus et paraliticus erat; nesciebat uero ancilla Dei quod mutus et paraliticus esset. In eadem iam hora uenerunt *uiatores*[68] querentes *comestionem*. Tunc sancta uirgo ad puerum iacentem ait: 'Nosti ubi est clauis *cellarii?*' Ille *aperta lingua illico* ait: '*Bene* scio.' Cui ait: 'Surge et *affer* mihi eam.' *Ad hanc uocem paraliticus* surrexit *sanus* et dedit ei clauem et ipse ministrabat cum *sancta uirgine* cibos hospitibus [a]*largiter secundum morem Scotorum.*[a] Deinde *familiares* [b]uenientes *deforis*[b] domum uidentesque puerum loquentem et ambulantem ualde mirabantur. Tunc ipse narrauit *eis* quomodo sanatus est. *Hoc illi scientes* omnes gratias Deo egerunt, *benedicentes ancillam eius.*

Aliquando sancti episcopi Maol et Maolchu *uenientes* ad sanctam Brigidam dixerunt ei: 'Vis ut nobiscum pergas in campum Breagh ad *uisitandum patronum nostrum*[69] sanctum Patricium *ibi manentem?*'

---

[b] die] *om.* c   [c-c] ego ut B   **38** [a-a] Q[w] f. 117[r]   [b-b] deforis venientes C

[67] In V[1]α §35, this sentence continues, 'leprosa mundata est, demens puella sanata est'. We should presumably insert in third position '⟨caeca illuminata est⟩' or some such phrase; cf. *Bethu Brigte* §36. The omission of all except the paralytic in V[4] follows V[1]β.

[68] V[1] §36 'laici quaerentes cibum'. Here and elsewhere V[4] avoids the word *laicus*: I 44 'homo' (V[1] §42 'laicus'), II 47 'homo' (V[1] §73 'laicus'). This is probably because the redactor was conscious of the ambiguity with *laicus* in its most pejorative sense; see R. Sharpe, 'Hiberno-Latin *laicus*, Irish *láech*, and the Devil's Men', *Ériu*, 30 (1979), 75–92. But D permits both *laicus* 'layman' and *laicus* 'brigand' where the context is not ambiguous.

[69] Patrick is described as *patronus noster* on several occasions. Here *noster* refers to Mael and Maelchú; at II 30 the phrase is used by Brigit herself. At II 99 Patrick is described as *her* patron. Cf. *ColE.* D §25* 'beatissimus noster patronus Patricius'.

Que respondit: 'Ego *multum* uolo ipsum alloqui ut me benedicat.'
Tunc perrexerunt in uiam *sancti* episcopi et beata *uirgo cum suis
comitibus*. Subrogauit eos quidam clericus, qui habebat multam
familiam et pecora et *duos* currus, uolens ire cum sanctis *ne quid
paterentur in uia*. Sed nolebant episcopi ne iter eorum propter
multitudinem pecorum et onerum eius tardum esset. Dixitque ad
eos *sancta uirgo*: '*Precedite* ante nos; ego iam manebo et compatiar
cum istis.' Tunc *euntibus episcopis sancta Dei* remansit *cum illis* et ait
illis: 'Cur non ponitis *omnia*[a] *uestra* in carris[b]?' Illi aiunt: 'Quia
unus paraliticus et *femina* ceca in carris[c] iacent egroti.' Nocte illa
ueniente, comederunt et dormierunt; sola *uirgo sancta* Brigida
ieiunauit et uigilauit. Mane autem facto, *Christi sponsa benedicens
aquam* effudit super paraliticum, et statim ipse surrexit sanus, et
similiter ceca femina illuminata est. Tunc *sancta uirgine iubente*,
onera imponunt in[d] carris et ceptum iter agebant gratias Deo
agentes. *Deinde sancta uirgo, accepta licentia et benedictione ab illis, cum
suis in uiam suam exiuit.*[70]

40   Et[71] uidentes quemdam plebeium *iuxta domum suam circa pecora sua
ualde tristem*, beata Brigida dixit *suis*: 'Interrogate eum cur *tam
tristis sit*.' Ille dixit: 'Quia tota familia mea in dolore est, *et nulla
mulier mulgere uaccas potest*.' In illius enim domo duodecem[a] *in
infirmitate* iacebant. Tunc dixit *gloriosa uirgo* puellis suis ut mul-
gerent uaccas illius. *Cum mulgerentur uacce ille*, ille homo rogauit ut
post laborem prandium acciperent, et ibi comedebant *comites
sancte uirginis*; ipsa autem ieiunabat. *Pransis illis omnibus* sancta *Dei*
aquam benedixit et aspersit domum illius *et omnes qui* [b]*in infirmitate iacebant illic*[b], *et illico presente Christi sponsa omnes ualentes surrexerunt et gratias Deo egerunt benedicentes ancillam suam*.

---

39 [a] *but* V[1] onera *as here below*   [b] curribus B   [c] curribus B   [d] in] *om.* C
40 [a] duodecim B   [b-b] in ea infirmitate iacebant C

---

[70] For the phrase *accepta licentia et benedictione*, especially in an added conclusion
of this kind, cf. 143 'accepta licentia a sancto Patricio'. It is common elsewhere in
D: *Abb.* §§7, 16, 33, *Ba.* §7, *CiC.* §15, *CiS.* §31, *Coem.* §10, *Decl.* §§9, 15, *FinC.*
§8*, *FintC.* §§3*, 4*, 21*, 22*, *Ita* §31, *Mchg.* §§8, 33, *Lug.* §24*.
[71] There is a marked change in the story between V[1] §38 and V[4]: in V[1] the man
is overburdened by the effort of milking the cows alone, but in V[4] he makes no
effort to milk them, merely grieving that there is no woman available to do this
task.

Postea[72] sancta Brigida *cum suis* uia *prospera* uenerunt ad locum qui dicitur Tailten ubi erat sanctus *Patricius archiepiscopus* cum *sanctorum* episcoporum *et aliorum sanctorum* conuentu, *et cum honore debito beata Brigida ab eis*[a] *suscepta est. Beata iam Brigida accepit sanctum Patricium predicatorem Hibernie in patrem, et ipse accepit eam in filiam. Inuenitur enim quod ibi prius uiderunt se inuicem. Ab illo scilicet die maior sanctorum Hibernie mirabilis uirgo post sanctum Patricium omnium iudicio habetur.*

In illo quoque concilio maxima questio orta est. Quedam enim *mulier*[73] que in fornicationem *incidit* dicebat infantem quem genuit cuiusdam episcopi nomine Broon[a] fuisse qui fuit *alumnus*[74] sancti Patricii. Ille autem negabat *coram omnibus.*[75] Tunc[b] omnes in concilio audientes mirabilia et opera *que Deus per* sanctam Brigidam *ostendit* dixerunt quod hec questio [c]per illam solui posset[c]. *Tunc rogata sancta Brigida ab omnibus*, illa mulier extra concilium[d] cum suo infante adducta est ad eam. Cui ait *Christi uirgo*: 'De quo *uiro* concepisti hunc infantem?' Illa respondit: 'De episcopo Bron.' *Ad hoc suasione diabolica illa falsum testimonium perhibente* beata Brigida humilis ad sanctum Patricium *ueniens* dixit: 'Pater *mi*, tuum est hanc questionem soluere.' Respondens *sanctus*

---

41 [a] illis B   **42** [a] Broon C (*cf.* V[1])   [b] Tum C   [c-c] solvi per eam possit B   [d] consilium C

---

[72] The first sentence and a half of V[1] §39 is here expanded to a full chapter, telling how Patrick and Brigit adopt each other as father and daughter, an inference from *pater* and *filia* in the conversation between them in V[1] §39, Cf. V[4] I 42, II 27, 30. The final sentence is one of the most direct statements of the status of Patrick and Brigit as leading saints, and gives colour to the suggestion (above, p. 113) that the order of their Lives at the head of the collection was the redactor's own intention.

[73] An interpretative change in V[4] from V[1] §39 'uirgo'—a pregnant virgin was clearly unacceptable. The story was too good to be cut altogether, but it could not be told of a nun.

[74] The syntax of V[1] §39 has been slightly altered, and *alumnus* is a substitution for *discipulus*; D adds *alumnus* elsewhere, e.g. *Aed* D §4*, *Rua.* D §14*, *ColE.* D §3*.

[75] The phrase *coram omnibus* is added to V[1] here and at the end of the chapter; in I 11 ('coram Deo') and II 94 ('coram Dei famula') we find *coram*-phrases added by V[4]. While phrases such as *coram omnibus* or *coram Deo* are not uncommon in O (36 times in Plummer's *Vitae*), they seem to be especially common in D (148 times in Plummer's *Vitae*).

Patricius ait ei: 'Mea filia carissima, *tu* reuelare dignare.' *Hoc audiens* sancta Brigida illius femine os signo sancte crucis signauit, et statim, *illa nolens uerum dicere*, totum caput eius cum lingua intumuit. *Illico* sancta Brigida *conuersa* linguam infantis benedixit, dicens ei: 'Quis est pater tuus?' Ille *infantulus ante tempus loquendi*[76] *ait clara uoce*: 'Non *est utique* episcopus Bron pater meus sed uilis ille qui sedet ultimus concilii huius est pater meus.' Tunc omnes *illum hominem cognoscentes* gratias egerunt Deo *pro liberatione innocentis episcopi*, et beata Brigida *digne* magnificata est, et illa mulier penitentiam egit *coram omnibus*.

43 *Die illa*[a] *uesperascente quidam homo*[77] *uidens uirtutes quas fecit sancta Brigida ipsa*[b] *die rogauit* eam dicens: 'Habeo domum nouam. Volo [c]ut tu[c] cum tuis prima introeas in eam consecrandam.' Exiit *ergo* sancta *Dei* cum eo, et *ipse* ministrabat cum gaudio magno. Ipso cibum *largiter* apponente, sancta Brigida *prophetice* dixit suis: 'Ostendit mihi Dominus modo quod iste[d] *homo* gentilis sit, *et non debemus cibum eius sumere, cum non uult ipse baptizari*.' Respondit ei *una* de *puellis*[78] suis dicens: 'Verum est quod dicis. Nam *audiui quod* ille pre cunctis sancto Patricio resistebat ualde et baptizari renuit.' Tunc *beata* Brigida dixit ad illum: 'Non possumus cibos tuos comedere nisi prius baptizatus fueris.' Tunc a Deo ille compunctus credidit *toto corde* cum omni domo sua et ab episcopo Bron baptizatus est discipulo sancti Patricii *qui tunc erat cum sancta Brigida*.

Sequenti autem die *audiens* sanctus Patricius dixit ad *beatam uirginem*: 'Ex hac die non licebit tibi sine sacerdote ambulare. *Sit tibi* sacerdos semper in *comitatu tuo*.'[79] Ordinauit *tunc sanctus*

---

43 [a] illo B   [b] ipso B   [c-c] *om.* C   [d] ille B

[76] Elsewhere in **D**, cf. *Ba.* §2 'usque ad tempus congruum infantibus loquendi' (**O** has 'donec consueta adloquendi tempora aduenerint'); ibid. §15* 'loqucionem apertam ante congruum tempus loquendi'.

[77] Here and a few lines below, V[4] replaces V[1] §40 'plebeus' with the more neutral *homo*. The special sense of *plebeus* 'layman' in seventh-century texts had been lost, but V[4] is cautious with the word *laicus* (see above I 38 n. 68). *Plebeus* is rare in **D**: *Aed* §3 (cf. *S* §3 'plebiles'), *Ba.* §12, *Coem.* §13, *Maed.* §27 (where it appears to have been added by **D** to **V** §26).

[78] Cf. above, I 34 n. 62.

[79] Cf. V[1] §41 'auriga tuus semper sacerdos fiat', where the intended meaning was probably 'driver', as in V[1] §52 which depended on the fact that Brigit's *auriga*

Patricius sacerdotem nomine Natfroich[f] qui in tota uita sua *feliciter in comitatu* sancte Brigide *uixit. Deinde accepta licentia a sancto Patricio beata Brigida cum suis remeauit.*

In diebus illis ueniebat ad sanctam Brigidam quidam *homo* portans matrem suam paraliticam in suis humeris et, cum ille ad locum ubi sancta uirgo erat uenisset, deposuit matrem suam in terra *in* umbra sancte uirginis. Et cum illa tetigisset umbram sancte surrexit dicens: 'Gratias ago Deo quod quando umbram tuam, o sancta, tetigi statim sanata sum, nihil dolens.' *Tunc clamor omnium in laudem Dei ortus est.*

Deinde transacto temporis interuallo quidam uiri hominem demoniacum *fortibus* uinculis alligatum ad sanctam Brigidam deduxerunt[a], qui cum cognouisset[b] quod ad *sanctam Dei* deduceretur cecidit in terram *semper* dicens: 'Non me *ducetis*[c] ad Brigidam.' *Illi* dixerunt ei: 'Numquid[d] *scis quo duceris? aut* locum in quo sancta Brigida *est?*' Ille respondit: 'Scio et *bene* noui et ad illum non ibo.' Dixitque illis nomen loci in quo fuerat[e] *sancta* Brigida, et *nullo modo* potuerunt mouere illum de terra. Con-silioque facto *miserunt* ad sanctam Brigidam rogantes eam ut *pro Christi nomine dignaretur*[f] uenire ad illum. *Christi iam sponsa humiliter* cum eis *exiuit*, et, cum uidisset *sanctam* Brigidam demon ad se uenientem, longe antequam ueniret[g], effugit ab homine. Demones enim quando sanctam Brigidam ad loca eorum aliunde uenire *sentiebant* timebant et fugiebant. Et sanus factus est ille homo *illa hora* et gratias Deo egit[h].

[f] Natfroich V[1]C] Natfrohc BQ[w] f. 117[v].   45 [a] adduxerunt C
[b] agnovisset C   [c] duceris b   [d] nunquit C   [e] fuerat CV[1]β] erat B fuit V[1]α
[f] dignetur B   [g] ipsa veniret B   [h] agit C

'driver' was a priest. At that point V[4] II 21 makes this an exceptional chance (*euentu*). Here V[4] goes further and removes the *auriga* altogether. In so doing he is rejecting (wrongly, in the present case) the Hiberno-Latin usage *auriga* 'attendant'. At II 22, V[4] changes the *auriga* (who was there cooking) into a *minister*. The redactor has no objection to the word in its proper place (II 20, 53), but seems not to accept the older usage 'attendant, servant', cf. OIr. *arae* 'driver, servant' (*Dictionary of the Irish Language*, ed. E. G. Quinn *et al.* (Dublin, 1913–76), s.v. *3 ara*). An example of a similar change occurs at *FinC.* S §32 'auriga', which becomes 'unus de discipulis' in D §24.

46 *Postea* sancta Brigida peruenit ad *monasterium* sancte uirginis Lasre[a] *et manebat ibi aliquibus diebus.* Quadam autem die ad uesperam uenit sanctus Patricius cum magno *populo predicans in illa regione* ad idem *monasterium* ut hospitaretur ibi *illa nocte.* Tunc familia illius[b] loci commota dixit ad sanctam Brigidam: '*Pia mater*,[80] quid faciemus? quia non *est in promptu* nobis tantam *reficere multitudinem.*' Dixit eis sancta *uirgo*: 'Quantum habetis[c]?' Illis dicentibus *quantum habebant*[81] ait sancta Brigida: 'Sufficienter *habetis*[d] iam nobis plurimis; *gratia enim Dei hec augebit.*' *Postea benedicente sancta Brigida illa cibaria administrata sunt* duobus populis, id est Patricii et sancte Brigide, et ipsi saturati sunt et dimiserunt maiores reliquias quam que fuerant ante *in illo apparatu* quem sancta Lasra[e] *sanctis preparauit*, et suum locum *Deo et* sancte Brigide in eternum obtulit.

47 Ibidem quoque quidam *uir quem uxor sua ualde odio habuit*[82] uenit ad sanctam Brigidam rogans *in Dei amore eam* ut *inuocato Christi nomine uxor sua eum amaret.* Tunc *Christi uirgo* benedixit aquam *et iussit domum illius aspergi ea in Christi nomine.* Et aspersa domus illius est et cibus et potus et lectus uxore absente illa aqua. *Veniens illa mulier domum et uidens* maritum suum *illico* nimio amore dilexit *eum et* quamdiu uixit *in eodem amore mansit.*

48 Quedam *femina* de nepotibus Gayssii[a] *per regiones*[b] elemosinam querens uenit ad sanctam Brigidam, cui ait sancta Dei: '*Do tibi* sagum meum uel uaccam *que mihi nuper data est.*' Illa dixit: 'Non prosunt mihi hec recipere[c]; uenient enim latrones in uia et[d] auferent ea[e] a me.' Dixitque[f] *sancta uirgo*: '*Visne* zonam meam? Dixisti enim mihi multos *dolores* esse in regione uestra, et per

---

46 [a] Lasarae C [b] istius B [c] haberis b [d] haberis b [e] Lasara C Lafra b
48 [a] Gayssii B Guassii Cc *cf.* Gais V[1]. *The Irish form is correctly Uí Guassai* [b] regionem b [c] accipere B [d] qui B [e] eam C [f] -que] *om.* B

---

[80] The formula *pia mater* is also added at II 22, 92.

[81] Here V[4] suppresses the details given in V[1] §44, twelve loaves, a little milk, and one sheep.

[82] In V[1] §45 the request precedes the reason for it; V[4] (with its general tendency to anticipate explanations) prefers to make clear at once the reason for the request.

zonam meam intinctam in aquam in nomine *filii sui, Deus*[83] sanabit eos, et dabunt tibi homines uictum et uestitum.' Tulit ergo *illa femina sancte uirginis* zonam *secum*, et primum abiit ad quemdam puerum egrum quem *multum* parentes *eius* diligebant, et *statim* eum sanauit *Dei gratia per zonam sancte Brigide*[g]. Et sic illa faciebat per omnes annos uite sue sanans plurimos[h] languores et accipiens multa lucra, et de illis lucris emit agros, et diues fuit; [i]*que custodiens castitatem suam puram et* tribuens *omnia sua Christi* pauperibus *sancta effecta est.*[i]

Post[84] hec exiit sancta Brigida *cum suis*[85] ut peregrinaretur in *prouincia* Conachtorum[a], *nolens*[b] *habitare in propria terra, id est in regione Lageniensium.* Et habitauit ibi in campo [c]Hay[d] *edificans*[e] *cellas et monasteria per circuitum*[c].[86] *Tunc acceptauit parrochiam*[f] *quam prophetauit in sua infantia, dicens: 'Meum erit hoc. Meum erit hoc.'*[87]

[a]Quadam ergo die[a] accessit ad *ipsum*[b] beata Brigida ut eucharistiam sumeret de manu *cuiusdam* episcopi, et calicem desuper

---

[g] virginis B   [h] multos B   [i-i] Q[w] f. 118[r]   49 [a] Q[w] f. 128[v]   [b] nollens C
[c-c] Q[w] f. 128[v]   [d] Haij C   [e] aedifficans C   [f] porrochiam C parochiam B
50 [a-a] *om.* B   [b] *ita* CB] *evidently an error in exemplum for* V[1] altare

---

[83] In V[1] §46, the virgin says to Brigit 'in nomine Iesu Christi sanabis eos', but V[4] changes the active part to God. Cf. *FinC.* D §2 where D adds 'gratia Dei' after the words of S §2 'saliua eius omnem langorem sanabat'; the intervention of God's grace is added by D in the following cases: *ColE.* D §§12*, 26*, *FintC.* D §§2*, 15*, *Maed.* D §§10*, 54*, *Lug.* D §8*, *Mun.* D §§20*, 22*, 24*, 30*, *Rua.* D §27*.

[84] I 49–II 3 are here brought forward from their late position in V[1] §§94–8. These stories are set in Connacht, while §98 tells of Brigit's return to Leinster from Connacht. By bringing these stories forward, V[4] has tidied up the geographical sequence, describing her return before mentioning Kildare, her principal church in Leinster.

[85] V[1] §94 makes Brigit's companions two bishops, which presumably seemed unlikely to the redactor. Their removal forced him to change 'de manu episcopi' to 'de manu *cuiusdam* episcopi' (I 50).

[86] Both *per circuitum* and *in circuitu* are quite common in D: the former is found 3 times in V[4] (here, II 53, 81) and 16 times elsewhere in the D texts of Plummer's *Vitae*, the latter 12 times in the D texts. For comparison with this passage, note especially *Abb.* §28 'cellas et monasteria per circuitum . . . construxit', *Maed.* §24* 'multa monasteria per circuitum regionis . . . construxit', *Decl.* §8 'septem claras construxerunt Deo cellas in circuitu predicti campi'.

[87] This addition demonstrates how Brigit's prophecy of I 12 was fulfilled, showing the redactor's regular desire to tie up loose ends.

intuens uidit prodigium, id est *formam* hirci. Unus *tunc de ministris Christi* tenebat calicem. Tunc *sancta* Brigida noluit ex illo bibere, dixitque ei episcopus: 'Cur non bibis ex hoc calice?' Brigida *autem* manifestauit episcopo quod uidit. Tunc episcopus *illi ministro* dixit: 'Quid *tu* fecisti? Da gloriam Deo *confitendo peccatum tuum.*' Ille *iam* confessus est se comedisse carnes[c] hirci *furtiui.* Dixitque ei episcopus: 'Penitentiam age et funde lacrymas.' Et *ille* iussis obediens penitentiam egit. *Deinde beata* Brigida uocata[d] uenit ad calicem et non uidit in eo *monstrum*; lacryme enim illius *hominis* culpam soluerunt. *Postea corpore et sanguine Christi refecti sanctus episcopus et gloriosa uirgo Brigida leti de ecclesia redierunt.*

51 Alio tempore quedam *uetula ibi* infirmabatur *usque* ad mortem, ueneruntque ad illam omnes *sorores* loci illius ut uigilarent et orarent *apud eam*; et sancta *mater* Brigida uenit cum illis. *Et cum illa esset in agone mortis, uolebant uirgines meliora*[a] uestimenta *sua* de ea tollere ne sub ipsis moreretur. Hoc beata Brigida prohibuit dicens: 'Paruo tempore uobiscum erit; facite *ergo* misericordiam *ne uideamini rapinam facere.*' Caritas[b] *et humanitas beate Brigide nolebat uestimenta tolli de ea, timens si ipsa frigus pateretur.* Omnes *uidentes tantam beatitudinem religionis* Deum *glorificabant.*

52 Cum *gloriosa uirgo* beata Brigida ibidem *adhuc* habitaret, stagnum aque *gelide quod erat iuxta monasterium* frequentabat. Quadam[a] autem nocte, in qua erat nix et *frigus multum*, omnibus ⟨dormienti-bus⟩[b], uenit *ipsa mater* ad stagnum cum una puella, et erat illa nocte in stagno[c] *usque ad gallorum cantus* orans et flens; et quod in illa [d]nocte fecit[d], hoc semper omnibus noctibus *statuit* facere et in consuetudinem *habere.* Sed Christi *pietas et* misericordia hoc fieri diutius non est passa, *sciens hoc esse supra uires Brigide uirginis.* Nocte enim *sequenti euntes simili modo sancta Brigida cum socia ad stagnum, non* inuenerunt *in eo* nisi arenam siccam sine *ulla* aqua, *et mirantes reuerse sunt.* Prima uero hora diei stagnum *impletum est aquis suis.* Similiter et in *tertia* nocte aruit stagnum *in aduentu sancte Brigide, et in crastino die repletum est eadem hora. Ideo*[e] *hoc fecit* Deus ut mani-festaret *qualem affectionem*[f] *habuit circa sponsam suam sanctam*

[c] carnem C   [d] *om.* B   **51** [a] Q[w] f. 129[r]   [b] Charitas C   **52** [a] C *begins a new chapter without a number*   [b] ⟨dormientibus⟩ V[1]   [c] illo stagno B   [d-d] fecit nocte B   [e] idem B   [f] dilectionem C

Brigidam, sicuti circa Ioannem euangelistam dilectorem suum ceteris liberans plagis penarum et dolore corporis. Omnes illud scientes magnificabant *uirtutem Dei in uirgine sua, rogantibusque eam ne hac re plus esset contra uoluntatem Dei, et ipsa sciens illud fuisse factum causa sui cessauit ab hoc uoto semper.*

Liber Secundus

Orta est iam magna *controuersia* apud Lagenienses de absentia sancte Brigide. *Ipsi enim scientes cursum totius Hibernie esse ad beatam Brigidam, et plures uirtutes et maxima miracula que Deus per ipsam agebat, uolebant* ᵃ*ut tanta*ᵃ *Dei gratia in sua regione esset; inde enim sancta Brigida nata est.* Inito iam consilio miserunt *honorabiles personas et fideles* nuntiosᵇ, ᶜ*quos ipsa negare non possit*ᶜ*, rogantes eam* ut *dignaretur* redire ad gentemᵈ suam. *Gloriosissima autem uirgo sciens hoc esse a Deo, ordinatis locis in quibus tunc habitabat,* uenit cum illis. Cumque ad flumen Sionnaᵉ *sancta Brigida et sui comites* uenirent, ibi duos populos sedentes ᶠ*in contentione*ᶠ ex utraque parte uadi Luain, id est nepotes Neill et Connachtorum gentes inuenerunt. *Flumen enim Sionna*ᵍ*, quod est egregius fluuius Hibernie, diuidit*ʰ *regiones nepotum Neill et Connachtorum.*[88] Tunc *comites* sancte Brigide ab omnibus *nauigatoribus* postulaueruntⁱ et non impetraueruntʲ ut trans flumen portarentur; *ipsi autem postulabant naulum super flumen*ᵏ. *Comites autem gloriose uirginis* dixerunt: 'Non,[89] sed nos nunc ibimus per flumen *pedibus nostris,* et benedictio sancte Brigide *domine nostre* nos custodiet *per gratiam Dei qui mare Rubrum et flumen Iordanis seruis suis diuisit.' Postea* dixerunt adˡ sanctam Brigidam: 'Signa *fluuium, mater,* in nomine Domini nostri Iesu Christi, ut mitior et *minor* efficiatur nobis.' Tunc sancta uirgo

---

1 ᵃ⁻ᵃ ut tanta CB] 'ut tam MS.' *notat* C ᵇ amicos C ᶜ⁻ᶜ *om.* C ᵈ regionem B ᵉ Syonna BQʷ f. 129 ᶠ⁻ᶠ *om.* B ᵍ Sionna] Syonnan B Sionann C *noting* 'Sionan MS.' ʰ dividit CB] 'defluit MS.' *notes* C ⁱ postularunt B ʲ impetrarunt B ᵏ fluvium B ˡ a b

[88] Cf. *CiC.* **D** §28* 'Flumen enim Synna, quod est fructiferum ualde in diuersis piscibus, regiones Neill, id est Midhi, et prouinchiam Connactorum diuidit'.

[89] 'Non' has been retained from V¹ §97, though the *oratio recta* request for a cloak as passage-money, which it answers, has been paraphrased without reporting the words of the request.

flumen signo sancte crucis benedixit, et duobus populis ᵐut diximus
circa flumen astantibusᵐ *Christi sponsa* cum puellis suis flumen
intrauit *et sui omnes secum*; et usque adⁿ genua alueus ingentis
fluminis non peruenit quod et fortissimi *milites* sine naueᵒ non
poterant transire. Omnes itaque uidentes sanctam Brigidam
laudauerunt.

2   Et priusquam beata Brigida flumenª intraret cum suis, alii clerici
ementes paruam ratemᵇ ingressi sunt *in ea*, qui dixerunt ad
sanctam Brigidam: 'Potest *illa nauis* unam puellarum tuarum
nobiscum portare.' Tunc *beata mater* uni *tenerrime* puelle ᶜ*que
multum timebat aquam*ᶜ precepit ut ante se iret *in illa nauicula* trans
flumen, dixitqueᵈ *ei illa* puella: 'Benedic me diligenter, *mater mea*,
quia timeo a te separari in flumine.' Dixitᵉ ei *sancta uirgo*: 'Vade in
pace, Deus ᶠcustodiat teᶠ.' Deinde nauigantes in medio fluminis
mersa est nauis sub aqua cunctis uidentibus; puella uero *ista* in
magno posita periculo clamauit nomen sancte Brigide in auxilium,
benedicensque eam *de terra Christi sponsa*, super aquas sedens illa
puella ducta est in sua sede ad portum, et uesti*menta sua erant* sicca
quasi ab aqua intacta. Tunc omnes *laudantes Deum mirabiliter confisi
sunt* in sanctissima uirgine Brigida.

3   Dum⁹⁰ autem uenisset *gloriosissima uirgo* Brigida ad patriam suam,
cum magno honore et totius *prouincie* gaudio suscepta est. *Et cella
assignata est illico ei in qua ipsa Dei sancta mirabilem uitam deinde duxit.
Ibi magnum monasterium plurimarum construxit uirginum, ibique
maxima postea ciuitas in honorem beate Brigide creuit, que est hodie metropolis Lageniensium.*⁹¹ *Illa iam cella scotice dicitur Killdara, latine uero*

ᵐ⁻ᵐ ut diximus circa flumen astantibus B] astantibus circa flumen ut praedix-
imus C adstantibus ut diximus V¹   ⁿ *om.* C   ᵒ navi C   **2** ª fluvium C
ᵇ navem B   ᶜ⁻ᶜ Qʷ f. 129ᵛ   ᵈ -que *om.* C   ᵉ -que C   ᶠ⁻ᶠ te custodiat C

⁹⁰ This whole chapter, hung on the opening sentence of V¹ §98, leads us back
(after the transposed Connacht passages) to where we left V¹ (see above, n. 84). In
V¹ §47 *Cella Roboris* 'the cell of the oak tree', Ir. *Cell dara*, Kildare, is mentioned,
but ahead of this V⁴ introduces an explanatory chapter. The redactor did not like
the casual introduction of the name, without even a reference to the establishment
of the church, so here he says how Brigit founded her monastery there, explains
the name, and provides an aetiological story.
⁹¹ The word *metropolis* is not used elsewhere in **D**. This sentence is particularly
puzzling: Kildare claimed metropolitan status in the seventh century, but not

sonat cella quercus. *Quercus enim altissima ibi erat quam multum* ᵃ*sancta Brigida diligebat*ᵃ*, et benedixit eam: cuius stipes adhuc manet, et nemo ferro abscindere audet, et pro magno munere habet qui potest frangere manibus aliquid inde, sperans per illud Dei auxilium, quia multa patrata sunt miracula per illud lignum per benedictionem beate Brigide. Et quo nomine cella dicebatur eo et ciuitas uocatur.*

Ante diem cuiusdam solemnitatis uenit ad sanctam Brigidam *manentem* in predicta cella *quedam iuuencula* portans *uirgini* elemosinam. Cumque assignasset donum, dixit: '*Debeo cito reuerti* ad domum meam, *quia* parentes *mei uolunt* uenire *et pernoctare* tecum per istam sanctam noctem; ego uero ⟨remanebo⟩ᵃ ad custodiendum domum et pecora.' *Cui ait Christi amica*: 'Non sic *erit*, sed tu mane hic et parentes tui uenient *post te* huc; substantiam autem uestram et domum Dominus seruabit.' Veneruntque parentes sicut sancta dixit et simul omnes celebrabant festum istud apud sanctam Brigidam. ᵇMedia uero nocte fures uenerunt ad domum eorum, scientes habitatores exiisse ad sanctam Brigidamᵇ, et furati sunt boues. Cumque uenissent ad amnem Liffiiᶜ, *habuerunt*ᵈ fluuium repletum abundantia aque et non poterant minare boues trans flumen. Cumque laborarent *per* partem maximam noctis, consilio facto, alligauerunt omnia uestimenta et arma super capita pecorum, *uolentes ipsi natare post ea*; ᵉet de medio flumine retrouersa *animalia illa* portauerunt secum spolia inimicorum suorum super capita suaᵉ, currentiaque per campum Liffii uiri nudi *sequebantur* ea. Non *quidem* ad propriam domum boues reuersi sunt sed recto cursu ad *monasterium* sancte Brigide. Primoᶠ igitur diluculo *peruenientes illuc boues cum persecutoribus*ᵍ, homines cognouerunt eos ambos. Tunc fures laudes Deo dederunt et *confitentes peccata* penitentiam *egerunt secundum iussionem gloriose uirginis Brigide. Ille* uero *homo* exsultans cum suisʰ ad domum suam exiit et *inueniens omnia sua integra secundum uaticinium sancte Brigide* gratias egit Domino.

---

3 ᵃ⁻ᵃ amabat sancta Brigida B   4 ᵃ vero remanebo V¹] vero B redire C
ᵇ⁻ᵇ *om.* C   ᶜ Lyffii C   ᵈ *ita* CB] invenerunt V¹   ᵉ⁻ᵉ *om.* C   ᶠ primo V¹]
primi b   ᵍ prosequutoribus C   ʰ *cf.* bobus suis V¹

---

later. Since this recension can hardly be older than the twelfth century (see above 1 6 and n. 45), one may wonder whether the redactor preferred to advance this statement against the interests of Dublin, which became the metropolitan see of Leinster in 1152.

5 Alia quoque puella ante alium diem festum pari cum elemosina ad sanctam Brigidam uenit[a]; et[b] accepto eius munere dixit: 'Vadam ad domum meam, *domina*,[92] quia non *est* ibi *mecum* nisi nutritor meus, qui est senex ualde et paraliticus, et non est qui mulgeat uaccas uel domum custodiat.' *Christi autem sponsa* dixit ei: 'Mane hic hac nocte sancta. Deus iam custodiet domum tuam, et uacce erunt immulse, *et non nocebit eis*.' Tunc illa mansit *ibi* et crastina die sumpta eucharistia rediit. Vaccas et uitulos separatim in agris comedentes sana mente et sine tedio inuenit. *Et puella dicente quod illa nocte mansit apud sanctam Brigidam, fatebatur* ei senex *quia erant*[c] *pecora hucusque*[d] *in pascuis et* quod ipse non dormiuit neque *ullum* interuallum temporis sensit nisi acsi illa hora qua puella ab eo exiisset. *Mysterium huius rei Deus qui fecit ipse scit.*

6 Post[93] hec *gloriosa uirgo* Brigida ad domum patris suis Dubtachi[a] *exiuit*, uolens post longum tempus uisitare parentes suos. Et pater suus *et omnes cognati sui* gauisi sunt ualde in aduentu ipsius, et rogauit eam *pater suus* ut *saltem* illa nocte in [b]domo sua[b] maneret, *et impetrauit*. In illa autem nocte angelus *Domini* uenit et suscitauit beatam Brigidam *dormientem*,[94] dicens: 'Surge cito et suscita patrem tuum *dormientem* et suam *totam* familiam et tuas puellas, nam hostes appropinquant qui uolunt occidere patrem tuum cum suis. Sed propter te hoc non uult Deus. Exite hinc citius, nam domum[c] istam *inimici uenientes* statim comburent.' Et cum omnes *de domo* exirent, hostes statim uenientes succenderunt domum; *dolebant enim quod inimicus euaderet ab eis*. Tunc *uidentes rogum* pater *et alii sancte uirgini* dixerunt: 'Tua benedictio, sancta Brigida, nos[d] in hac nocte custodiuit a morte presenti. *Modo scimus omnia que*

---

5 [a] *post* alium C   [b] *om.* CV[1](a)   [c] essent C   [d] hinc usque C
6 [a] Dubhtachi C   [b-b] sua domo B   [c] domam b   [d] *post* nocte C

[92] Brigit is often referred to as *domina*, especially in the vocative (I 34, II 5, 10, 15, 20, 25, 29, 34, 50, 55, 56, 64, 71, 89, 94, 97). In the only chapter where the word is taken over from V[1], II 49 (= V[1] §75), it is used (not of Brigit) in its strict sense of 'mistress' in relation to her *ancilla*. Elsewhere, it is not taken over from V[1] but a substitution is made; see above, I 37 n. 66. Cf. *Maed.* D §57* 'Brigida, domina Hybernie'.

[93] Here V[4] has again rearranged the order of V[1], II 6–16 being brought forward from V[1] §§87–93.

[94] V[4] omits the detail from V[1] §87 that Brigit awoke only at the third call from the angel.

predicta sunt de te.' Dixitque illi Brigida: 'Non solum in hac nocte *sed quamdiu uixeris*, sanguis non effundetur in habitaculo tuo.' Quod *ita postea probatum* est. Nam cum quidam quandam ibi feminam percutere uolebat, riguit manus eius quam extenderat et non potuit eam retrahere donec *feminam liberam* dimisit.

7 Crastina autem die una puellarum suarum ad sanctam[a] Brigidam dixit: 'Utinam angelus *Domini* te semper adiuuaret, sicut fecit in nocte transacta, *liberans te et patrem tuum cum suis!*' Cui ait *sponsa Christi*: 'Non in ista nocte tantum sed *etiam*[b] per omnem etatem meam auxilium *Dei mei per angelos* habeo in omnibus. Nam quotidie letitiam *cordis* [c]mihi prestat[c], dum per ipsum sonos et spirituales cantus *carminum et* organorum celestium quotidie audio. Sanctas[d] quoque missas, que[e] Domino procul in terris celebrantur[f], quasi prope per ipsum *Dominum* essent quotidie audire possum, et meas orationes nocte ac die offerunt *angeli* Domino, et in presentia et in absentia [g]semper *ipse*[g][95] audit me. Quod duobus exemplis nunc tibi *ostendam*.

8 'Quodam autem tempore rogauit me quedam mulier leprosa et infirma ut ei aquam deferrem et ut in ceteris necessariis misericorditer ministrarem. Vas itaque *plenum* aqua benedixi et dedi ei dicens: "Pone istud inter te et parietem ne aliquis preter te solam tangat illud donec reuertar." Angelus uero benedixit illam aquam in presentia mea et conuersa est in quemcumque saporem leprosa uolebat. Nam quando *uolebat uel* concupiscebat *illa* mel, saporem[a] mellis, quando *iam* uinum siue cereuisiam uel lac uel alios liquores, *in* eadem aqua habebat, *et per* eius uoluntatem uicissim uertebatur.

---

7 [a] beatam B   [b] iam B   [c-c] mihi prestat BV[1]] sentio C   [d] *ita* CB] sanctorum V[1]   [e] *ita* CB] qui V[1]   [f] *ita* CB] celebrabant V[1]   [g-g] ipse semper B
8 [a] sapore C

---

[95] Two changes here from V[1] §89 misinterpret the text there: the subject of 'offert' and 'audiuit' in V[1] is 'angelus', earlier in the chapter. V[4] has changed this personal angel into a general plural, and transferred the help of her angel to the Lord. Here 'ipse' presumably refers to the Lord, but the two stories which illustrate the point (II 8–9) have as the helper St Brigit's personal angel.

9 'Item cum ego parua puella essem, feci altare lapideum ludo
puellari *Domino*, uenitque angelus *Domini me presente* et perforauit
lapidem in quattuor angulis et supposuit quattuor pedes ligneos.
'Hec duo de angelo meo tibi, o puella, demonstraui ut Dominum nostrum *Iesum Christum* glorifices. *Et ita gratia eius semper
mecum permanet.*'

10 Eodem tempore *dux Dubtachus*[a] pater *sancte Brigide dixit ad eam*:
'Rogo *te*[b], *sancta uirgo, uade* ad regem nostrum ut[c] gladium, quem
ipse *ad* tempus mihi *concessit*, in perpetuum *donet*; *ualde enim
pretiosum munus est.*' *Obediuit ergo Christi uirgo patri suo et* exiit ad
regem *Lageniensium* in campum Liffii *manentem*. Cumque *uirgo Dei
cum suis* ad portam[d] ciuitatis *regis* sedisset, unus seruorum regis
uenit ad eam dicens: 'Si me [e]absolueris, *domina*, a iugo *Domini mei
regis*[e], seruus tuus ero in perpetuum cum omnibus meis *et semen
meum post me*, et ego et cognati mei erimus Christiani.' Dixitque ei
uirgo: 'Petam pro te.' Tunc *beata uirgo* uocata est ad regem.
Dixitque ei rex: '*Virgo beata* Brigida, quid uis a me?' Cui ait *sancta
uirgo*: 'Ut gladium tuum *quem pater meus habet* sibi dones *in
eternum*, et *illum* seruum tuum *cum suis* mihi *liberum offeras.*'
Dixit*que ei* rex: '*O sancta, pretiosissimus est gladius quem tu petis, sed*
quid mihi pro his duabus petitionibus magnis[f] dabis?' Ait ei *sancta
uirgo*: 'Si uis[g], uitam eternam *inueniam* tibi, et *de* semine tuo reges
erunt usque *in finem* seculi.' Dixit*que ei* rex: 'Vitam quam non
uideo non quero. De filiis *etiam* qui post me erunt non procuro.
Alia uero duo da mihi, *id est* ut longeuus fiam in presenti uita
quam diligo et in omni bello uictor existam[h]; iugem enim[96] *nos
Lagenienses* pugnam habemus contra *semen Cuind*[j].[97] Dixit*que*[k] *ergo*

10 [a] Dubhtachus C   [b] *om.* C   [c] ut V[1]] et CB   [d] portum C
[e-e] absolueris de manu mei regis C   [f] magnis V[1]] magis Cb   [g] *om.* C   [h] ut
existam B   [i] iugem enim CBV[1]β jugem enim Q[w] f. 128[r] ingentem V[1]α   [j] Q[w]
f. 128[r]   [k] -que] *om.* B

[96] The reading 'iugem enim' is found in many copies of V[1] §90, though the
oldest manuscript reads 'ingemenin' (A). Colgan's source had 'ingentem enim'.
Since *enim* is desirable for the syntax, and 'ingentem' appears to be a guess at
'ingemenin', I prefer to think that 'iugem enim' is the correct reading: 'for we
have a continual battle against the Uí Néill'.

[97] Rendering Ir. *Síl Chuind*, as in Rawlinson B. 502, f. 139b30 (M. A. O'Brien,
Corpus Genealogiarum Hiberniae, i (Dublin, 1962), 133), the seed of Conn
Cétchathach. The term includes all the peoples of *Leth Cuind*, the northern half of

beata[1] Brigida *regi*: 'Hec duo dabuntur tibi, *id est* longa uita et uictoria in omni bello.' *Deinde gloriosa Christi sponsa benedicens uictoriam regis cum suis donis ad sua reuersa est.*

Nec multo post ille rex cum paucis *militibus in terram inimicorum, id est nepotum Cuind, scilicet* in campum Breagh, *perrexit. Occurrit ei ibi turba parata hostium.* Cumque uidisset[a] multitudinem hostium, dixit ad suos: '*Estote fortes et* uocate sanctam Brigidam in auxilium; *ipsa enim* sua promissa adimplebit.' Et *clamantes* in celum clamauerunt *nomen sancte uirginis.* Et tunc *illis inuicem irruentibus,* rex uidit *quasi* sanctam Brigidam preire ante se *ad bellum* cum baculo in dextra et columna ignis ardebat de capite eius usque ad celum. *Et illico plures* hostes in fugam conuersi sunt. *Rex uero et sui peracta uictoria gratias Deo et beate Brigide egerunt.*

Post hec rex triginta bella *in Hibernia* gessit et uicit omnia, *octo*que[98] certamina in Britannia prospere egit, et multi reges *donis* datis *amicitiam eius rogabant scientes* eum inuictum esse. *Ipse rex uocatur Iolland*[a] *mac Dunluing, id est, qui fuit filius Dunluing; quique Engusum*[b] *filium Nadfraich regem Momoniensium, quem baptizauit Patricius predicator Hibernie,*[99] *occidit cum uxore sua Ethne hUathach*[c] *filia regis Criomhthain*[d] *regis Hikenselach et Lageniensium; quique Olill Molt regem Hibernie iuxta Temoriam interfecit et regnauit post eum; et ipse moriens sepultus est apud sanctam Brigidam in suo monasterio.*[100]

---

[1] beatissima B   11 [a] rex vidisset B   12 [a] Q[w] f. 128[r] 'MS. W. huius regis nomen fuisse Iolland'   [b] Æingussium C   [c] Huachach CB   [d] Criôh-thain C Crionhthain B

Ireland, but here signifies the Uí Néill. Cf. below, II 11 ('nepotum Cuind'), and *Aed* D §1* (quoted above, I 1 n. 29).

[98] V[1] §90 has 'nouemque certamina in Britannia', but the number was presumably expressed in figures and open to misreading.

[99] For both phrase and context, cf. *CiS.* D §13, 'Interea sanctus Patricius, predicator Hybernie, in regionem Mumenensium uenit; et credidit ei Aengus filius Nafraich, rex Mumenie, in ciuitate regali Cassel, et baptizatus est'. Cf. also above, I 3 n. 35.

[100] The whole of this interpolated passage can be paralleled in *CiS.* D §13 (see previous note) and §16, 'Ipse enim rex Aengus in bello, quod commissum est in campo Fea, in prouinchia Laginensium, iuxta grandem uillam, Ceall Osnadh, cum sua uxore regina occissus est a rege aquilonalium Laginensium, Illand filio Dunlainge, .uiii. idus Octobris. Et hec cedes maxima abusio erat. Et ipsa regina

13 Factum est autem post mortem *Iolland*[a] *qui uixit* [b]*cxx annis*[b], *congregantes* nepotes Neill *exercitum fines deuastare* Lageniensium, inierunt Lagenienses consilium, dicentes: 'Ponamus corpus mortuum regis nostri *ante*[c] nos in curru [d]contra hostes, et pugnemus contra circa cadauer eius.[d] Et illis sic facientibus, *illico* nepotes Neill in fugam uersi sunt, *et cedes facta est in eis*; donum enim *uictorie* per sanctam Brigidam adhuc in [e]*corpore* regis[e] mansit.

14 Alio quoque die quidam uir sanctus ad *locum* in quo sancta Brigida sola orabat uenit et inuenit eam stantem[a] et manus in oratione tendentem *ad* celum. Eadem hora clamor magnus *mulierum et iuuenum*[101] *in illa uilla factus est*, nam ad uaccas ipsa[b] hora uituli foras irruerunt, *et cum homines separarent eos a matribus inde ortus est clamor.* Sed hec sancta non audiuit in mentis excessu Deo intenta. Vir *sanctus uidens Brigidam non audientem clamorem* reliquit eam ne turbaret orationem eius. *Et post* horam reuersus ad eam dixit: 'O sancta Dei[c] *nonne audiuisti* clamorem *magnum qui fuit in uilla?*' At ait illa: '*Vere*[102] clamorem istum non audiui.' Dixit ei

---

13 [a] Illānd C   [b-b] annis cxx C   [c] conditum ante C   [d-d] *cf.* V[1] et pugnemus circa cadaver eius contra hostes   [e-e] corpore regis C] corpore B rege V[1]
14 [a] orantem C   [b] illa B   [c] Brigida B

Ethne hUathach uocabatur, que erat filia Crymthain filii Endai Kennselaygh, qui Crymthann multum subiugauit aquilonales Laginenses, accepto regno magno Hybernie postquam ipse in graui bello Oche in regione Midhi occidit Aillill Molt regem Hybernie.' A particular similarity between the two passages is the fact that Ailill Molt is said to have been killed by Crimthann, son of Énda Cennselach, the founder of the Uí Chennselaig kings of south Leinster: according to AU 482 Ailill Molt was killed at the battle of Ochae by his Uí Néill cousins and rivals Lugaid mac Loegaire and Muirchertach mac Ercae, and according to an addition to AU 483 by Fergus Cerrbél of the Southern Uí Néill and Fiachra Lon of Dál nAraide in the same battle. Cf. F. J. Byrne, *Irish Kings and High Kings* (London, 1973), p. 85. The annals seem here to have an Uí Néill version of events, whereas D has an Uí Chennselaig version. The battle of Cenn Losnada or Cell Losnaig (AU 490) is mentioned in the Uí Chennselaig genealogies, LL. 316c25–31 (O'Brien, *Corpus Genealogiarum Hiberniae*, i. 345; R. I. Best *et al.* (edd.), *The Book of Leinster, formerly Lebar na Núachongbála* (Dublin, 1954–83), vi, lines 40636–40).

[101] Here V[1] §91 has 'clamor magnus habitatorum loci illius'; this change seems intended to parallel the cows and their (male) calves.

[102] The adverb *uere*, taken over from V[1] at I 9 is added by V[4] here and at II 15, 21, 31, 33 and in a longer passage in II 62. It occurs 55 times in the 22 D-Lives in Plummer's *Vitae*, including *Aed* §§1*, 2*, 25*, *ColE.* §§2*, 4*, 16*, 24*, 25*, *FintC.* §21*, *Lug.* §§11*, 28*, 30*, 35*, 37*, 52*, etc.

ille *sanctus*: '*Ubi fuit auditus* tuus?' Respondit ᵈ*beata* Brigidaᵈ: '*Deo teste* in urbe Romana iuxta sanctos Petrum et Paulum *tum*ᵉ missas audiui, et nimis desidero ut ille ordo et uniuersa regula Roma ad me deferatur.' Tunc *beata* Brigida uiros sapientes *Romam* misit *ut ipsi* inde missas et regulam *ecclesiasticam* ferrent.¹⁰³

Quadam autem die pluuiali *uirgo gloriosa* Brigida ad *cellam* suam *de uia* uenit, et cum *post pluuiam sol luceret*, radius solis domum per parietem *domus intrauit*, et posuit sancta Brigida uestimenta sua *humida* super illum radium, putans quod funis esset. Tunc in domo illa *quidam sapiens* uerbum Dei predicabat, et beata Brigida multum diuinis uerbis intendebat, et usque ad magnam partem noctis mens *uirginis* inebriata *diuina doctrina* oblita est *secularia* presentia. Radius uero ille super quem posuit *uirgo* uestimenta sua usque ad mediam noctem permansit. Tunc unus illorum qui in illa domo erant dixit ad *uirginem sanctam*: 'Vestimentum, *o domina*, tolle de radio solis.' *Dei uirgo* ait: '*Vere* putabam quod funis esset *et* non radius.'

Eodem *die* quidam ueneruntᵃ per campum Liffii ad sanctam Brigidam, *et nox cecidit super eos in campo, sed radius ille solis illustrabat illis uiam*. Et *ipsi* dixerunt se uidisse radium illum illustrantem *sibi* campum donec media nocte ad sanctam Brigidam uenirent. Tunc omnes *qui ibi erant in Dei laudibus uoces erexerunt, et insuper* sanctam Brigidam *per quam Deus*ᵇ *talia egit* laudauerunt.

Sanctissima *uirgo* Brigida cenam magnamᵃ in honoremᵇ *cuiusdam* solennitatis *dominice egit*ᶜ, sed hancᵈ cenam *ante festum*ᵉ pauperibus *aduenientibus* diuisit. De hoc iam familia *uirginis* contristata est; *multi enim uocati de* plebe *a sancta Brigida* ad diem festum *illum* uenerunt.¹⁰⁴ *Hoc uidens sancta Dei* orauit *ad Dominum illa nocte, et*

ᵈ⁻ᵈ *om.* B   ᵉ tunc B   16 ᵃ *post* Liffii C   ᵇ Dominus C   17 ᵃ *om.*
B   ᵇ honorem V¹] honore Cb   ᶜ *ita* CB] fecit V¹   ᵈomnem C   ᵉ factam C

---

¹⁰³ The redactor has omitted one of the most interesting features of this story as told in V¹ §91, to wit, that when the messengers returned, Brigit explained to them that the Roman mass had been changed during the period of their homeward journey and that they would therefore have to make a second journey. Such a change in the Roman liturgy was presumably no longer credible.

¹⁰⁴ In V¹ §49 we are told that the *plebs* was in the habit of coming for the feast; here custom is replaced by Brigit's summons—a sign of changing attitudes to the lay population?

ecce in eadem regione *quidam uillicus*, homo diues ualde, cenam regi uehebat in plaustris ad diem festum *eundem*, errauitque[f] ille in uiis suis *notissimis*[105] donec recto cursu ad ianuam *monasterii* sancte Brigide peruenit. Hoc sciens sancta *Dei diuinitus*[106] exiit obuiam illi et interrogauit uiam eius. Ille autem a Deo admonitus obtulit *totum suum apparatum* sancte Brigide, dicens: 'Ob hanc causam fecit me Deus errare in propria mea *regione*; aliam uero cenam *domino meo* regi faciam.' Hoc cum audisset[g] rex illum *uillicum* cum suis omnibus *obtulit Deo et sancte Brigide* ut seruiret *loco eius* in eternum. Plaustra quoque altera plena ad supplementum sancte solemnitatis idem rex *iterum* ad sanctam Brigidam misit. *Tunc sancta Brigida euangelicum promissum inuenit quo dicitur 'centuplum accipiet.'* Quibus conuentus *apud sanctam Brigidam solemniter refectus est.*

18 Regina quedam cum magnis donis ad beatam Brigidam uenit, in quibus erat argentea catena que habebat in summitate formam hominis. *Quibus assignatis regina cum benedictione ad sua remeauit.*[107] Illam *iam* catenam puelle *tollentes*[a] *de manibus sancte Brigide* posuerunt in thesauro *ecclesie*[b]. Beata uero *mater cetera* omnia [c]pauperibus diuisit[c] *statim*.[108] Quadem uero[d] die pauper ad sanctam Brigidam uenit, et[e] *beata uirgo* nihil[f] *aliud* habens tunc exiuit ad thesaurum *communem* et predictam catenam *tollens* dedit eam pauperi. Hoc autem agnoscentes puelle *locute sunt* ad beatam Brigidam: 'Perdidimus, o mater, per te que Deus *per bonos Christianos* nobis mittit; omnia enim das pauperibus et nos inopes relinquis.' Tunc beata Brigida *uolens solari*[g] eas dixit illis: '*Ite, filie,*

---

[f] -que]   *om.*   B   [g] audivisset   B   **18** [a] tolentes   b   [b] Q[w]
f. 119[r]   [c-c] divisit pauperibus C   [d] iam B   [e] *om.* C   [f] nil B   [g] sedare B

[105] This addition anticipates the point made later that the man was in his own district, and so clarifies the miraculous element in his losing the way on familiar ground.

[106] For *diuinitus* as an addition, cf. II 39, 58. Elsewhere in **D**, it occurs 20 times in the 22 **D** Lives in Plummer's *Vitae*, against 3 times in the 9 Lives from **O**. Note *FintC.* §4*, *Lug.* §§28*, 38*, 53*, *Maed.* §§13*, 30*, *Rua.* §17*, etc.

[107] The redactor's aversion to loose ends here demanded that we be told of the queen's departure; V[1] §50 leaves her visit hanging open-ended.

[108] This *statim* and the change below from 'ad thesaurum puellarum' to 'ad thesaurum communem' diminishes the point of the story: Brigit invariably gave away to the poor whatever came to her, but in this case the nuns tried to retain the silver chain by storing it in their own safekeeping.

et querite catenam ubi ego oro[h] in ecclesia; forsitan ibi inuenietis.' Cumque *exirent*, inuenerunt illic catenam *simillimam per omnia illi catene* et *obtulerunt* eam sancte Brigide *petentes ueniam*. Tunc sancta uirgo dixit: '*Terrena date Deo; terrena et celestia dabit uobis Deus.*' Et puelle illam catenam semper seruauerunt[i] in testimonium uirtutis.

Conlianus[a][109] episcopus sanctus et propheta Dei qui habebat cellam in *australi*[110] parte campi Liffii uenit in curru ad sanctam Brigidam et moratus est apud eam aliquot diebus. *Quem beata Brigida primum episcopum elegit in ciuitate sua Killdara*[b].[111]

Die autem quadam[a] rediens episcopus ad [b]locum suum[b] dixit ad *sanctam uirginem*: 'Benedic, *domina*, currum *et nostrum iter.*' Et[c] sancta benedixit. Auriga uero episcopi iungens currum rosetos[d] oblitus est ponere contra rotas. *Postea* currus ipse uelox pertransiit campum. Cumque post magnum spatium diei episcopus currum conspexisset, uidit illum non habere rosetos[d]. Tunc ipse *descendens* de curru [e]in terram[e][112] gratias egit Deo et[f] benedixit sanctam Brigidam, *magnificans miraculum* benedictionis eius.

[h] oro V[1]] ero C eo B   [i] servarunt C   **19** [a] Q[w] f. 119[r]   [b] Q[w] f. 119[r]
20 [a] alia C   [b-b] sua C   [c] et C] at B   [d] rosetas Cc   [e-e] *om.* B   [f] *om.* C

[109] In V[1]*a* §51, the bishop in this story is called *Cellanus*, but the name was corrupted in the course of Continental transmission: Munich, Clm. 2531 (s. x) has *Gallanus*, Zürich, Zentralbibliothek, MS Rheinau 81 (s. x/xi) has *Gollanus*, but a widespread reading is *Coalianus* or sim., found also in the developed β-text of St-Omer, Bibliothèque municipale, MS 715 (used by the Bollandists) and Cambrai, Bibliothèque communale, MS 857. I suggest that some such reading was in the exemplum used by V[4] and that *Conlianus* adds confusion to corruption by association with Conlae, a form of Conlaed, the name of Brigit's first bishop at Kildare, on whom see below, n. 111.

[110] Cf. V[1] §51 'in dextera parte', a usage obsolete by the redactor's time?

[111] Conlaed, first bishop of Kildare according to the Life by Cogitosus, and later regarded as Brigit's craftsman. Stories about him are found in the scholia on *Félire Oengusso*, ed. W. Stokes, Henry Bradshaw Society, 29 (London, 1905), p. 186, and in those on the poem *Ní car Brigit* in W. Stokes and J. Strachan (edd. and trans.), *Thesaurus Palaeohibernicus* (Cambridge, 1901–10), ii. 346–7.

[112] Perhaps the copy of V[1] used by the redactor lacked the words *et corruens* from the reading of V[1] §52, 'Tunc ille desiliuit de curru et corruens in terram gratias egit Deo'.

21 Quadam quoque die sancta Brigida per campum Liffii et alia
    sancta uirgo simul sedens in curru uno[a] uenit. Auriga *iam uirginis
    euentu*[113] *sanctus*[b] *presbyter erat qui* predicabat *uirginibus* uerbum
    Dei. *Plures non erant in uia.* Dixitque illi sancta Brigida: 'Noli uerso
    uultu nobis predicare[c]. Habenas tuas post tergum tuum pone.
    Equi nostri recto itinere ibunt *Deo ducente* ad *monasterium*
    nostrum.' Et ita factum est. Exierunt enim equi [d]rectam uiam[d] per
    campum. Cumque *sanctus presbyter* predicaret uirginibus, et ille
    intentis auribus et curioso animo audirent, unus equus abstulit
    caput suum et collum a iugo et ambulauit liber post currum, illis
    nescientibus. Tunc rex *Lageniensium*[e], sedens *prope* uiam in *colle*
    sublimi, dixit omnibus circumstantibus et illud admirantibus:
    '*Dico uobis uere quia* sancta Brigida in isto curru sedet, *non curans* de
    equis dum de sola anima[114] intendit.' *Alter iam equus fortiter et apte
    currum trahebat. Sed ille* equus audiens clamorem turbe admirantis
    et currentis uenit ad currum et imposuit collum sub iugo suo solus.
    Tunc *uoces* regis et *exercitus sui in celum* attolluntur, et admiranda
    uirtus per totam regionem diuulgata est, et glorificarunt Deum et
    beatam Brigidam.

22 Leprosus quidam de nepotibus Neill uenit ad sanctam Brigidam,
    querens ab ea uaccam. Dixit sancta armentario suo: 'Da illi
    uaccam.' Ait armentarius: 'Qualem uaccam dabo ei?' Sancta ait:
    '*Mihi placet ut sit omnium* optima.' Tunc elegerunt uitulum
    elegantem, et dimittentes eum *ad armentum* occurrit *magno* cum
    mugitu optima uaccarum, et in tantum se inuicem dilexerunt ut
    nullus posset[a] separare eos; uitulus autem ipse non erat illius
    uacce sed alterius, *tamen* dilexit eum magno *amore ut suum propter
    uoluntatem sancte Brigide, quia ipsa uoluit ut optimum pecorum suorum
    pauper Christi tolleret. Deinde* ille leprosus dixit ad *sanctam Dei*: 'Non
    possum *ego* solus uaccam *cum uitulo* minare ad prouinciam
    meam.' Dixitque *pia mater* ad *quendam ministrum*[115] tunc coquen-

---

21 [a] una C   [b] sancto B   [c] praedicares C; V¹α *add.* verbum Dei   [d-d] *ita*
CBV¹β] recta via V¹α   [e] Qʷ f. 119ᵛ   22 [a] possit C

---

[113] Here the addition 'euentu' compensates for the change made in V⁴ at 1 43
(see n. *ad loc.*), because this story demands a priest as *auriga*.

[114] Here 'intendit' has no object: we should perhaps add 'Dominum', following
V¹ §52, supposing the word to have been missing from the exemplum.

[115] See 1 43 n. 79.

tem carnes in cacabo: 'Vade *et pecora usque ad terram suam* cum leproso *mina.*' Ille ait: 'Quis coquet carnes?' *Sancta* inquit: 'Tu ipse [b]ad eas uelociter[b] ueni.' Et ita completum est sicut sancta dixit. Exiit enim ille cum leproso iter duorum dierum in una *hora* et in eadem confestim reuersus est inuenitque carnes in cacabo necdum coctas. Miratique sunt omnes *de hac re*, sed Dominus *omnipotens* donauit hoc uoluntati *fidelis ancille sue*.

Alio tempore beata Brigida [a]rogata est a familia[a] ut ad sanctum Hybarum[b] episcopum in campo Gesill[c] *manentem* iret et peteret ab eo frumenta[d]. Suis obediens beata Brigida *iter arripuit*. Sanctus autem Hybarus[e] *qui seminator fidei multis in locis fuit ante beatissimum Patricium*[116] gauisus est gaudio magno in aduentu *gloriose uirginis* Brigide. *Cenantibus sancto Hybaro[f] episcopo et sancta Brigida cum suis et sumentibus carnes*, due uirgines de *puellis* beate Brigide duas partes *lardi que contingebant sibi respexerant[g], nolentes carnem comedere.*[117] Et ille partes uerse sunt in duos serpentes. Hoc *uidens* beata Brigida illas uirgines grauiter coram Hybaro episcopo increpauit et iussit eas[h] manere foris et *penitentiam agere* cum lacrymis[i]. Dixitque[j] *sancta* ad suas: 'Oremus et nos Dominum pro eis.' *Et data a Deo uenia*, uersi sunt illi serpentes [k]in duos panes *quos sancti consecratos comederunt[k]*.

[b-b] ad eas velociter V[1]] ad eos velociter C velociter ad eas B   23 [a-a] rogata a familia C a familia rogata est B   [b] Hibarum C Hybarum Q[w] f. 119[v]   [c] Q[w] f. 119[v]   [d] frumentum C   [e] Hibarus C   [f] Hibario C   [g] *ita* CB] *? l.* despexerant   [h] eos C   [i] lachrymis C   [j] -que] *om.* B   [k-k] Q[w] f. 120[r]

[116] In V[1] §54, this St Ibar—dwelling in Mag Gesilli in Offaly—is clearly distinct from St Ibar of Beggery Island, but V[4] has confounded them, giving rein to his interest in pre-Patrician saints. The Leinster saint appears in the Loígse genealogies, Rawlinson B. 502, f. 127a20–26 (O'Brien, *Corpus Genealogiarum Hiberniae*, i. 90). On the Munster saint, St Ibar of Beggery Island, see above, p. 115. Ussher, *Whole Works*, vi. 347–8, does not detect the confusion in V[4], though he notes that other Lives do not locate Ibar in Mag Gesilli.

[117] In V[1] §54 we are told that this happened in Lent, which was why the two nuns refused to eat the bacon. The point of the story is that St Ibar relaxed the Lenten fast for the reception of St Brigit as a guest (cf. Plummer, *Vitae*, vol. i, p. cxiv n. 4, for other examples of this practice), which was right and proper. The nuns' attitude was holier-than-thou. In V[1] Brigit bids them 'foras manere et ieiunare cum lacrimis', but here V[4] replaces *ieiunare* with 'penitentiam agere'— after all, the story says they should break the fast.

24 *Deinde* sanctus episcopus ait ad sanctam *uirginem*: 'Qua causa, *mater*, ad me uenisti?' Respondit *uirgo*: '*Mei dicunt quod frumenta sibi desunt.*' Episcopus subridens ait: 'O beata *uirgo, non multum modo nobis abundat.*' *Sancta Dei* ait: 'Non sic est[a], sed[b] uiginti quatuor plaustra *ibi* in horreo tuo[c] consistunt.' Et ita nutu Dei *euenit quod erant in illo horreo*; *non enim multum antea ibi erat. Iubente episcopo id probari*, inuenta sunt uiginti quatuor plaustra ibi *secundum uaticinium* sancte Brigide, et *gratias Deo agentes* diuiserunt id inter se: duodecem[d] iam plaustra *dimissa sunt* episcopo, et beata Brigida cum duodecem[d] reuersa est ad sua.

25 Rex quidam ad solemnitatem[a] Pentecostes[b] celebrandam apud sanctam uirginem uenit et, cum celebraret noctem illam, *mane post missarum solemnia*, cucurrit cum suis in curribus et equis ad *castrum* suum. Sancta *uirgo* post expleta diei solemnia uenit ad mensam. *Sedentibus ante se communiter diuitibus et pauperibus*, largus iam *apparatus* apponebatur cunctis. Tunc quidam leprosus superbissimus diaboli magisterio cibum respuit comedere nisi beata Brigida sibi daret hastam supradicti regis. Dixerunt omnes rogantes eum comedere: 'Leprose[c], uidisti hastam heri. Cur *tunc*[d] non postulasti tibi dari?' Ille dixit: 'Quia hodie concupiui eam.' Tunc sancta Brigida et omnes rogauerunt eum comedere et non impetrauerunt. Beata iam Brigida abrenuit cibum sumere, *paupere iam ieiunante ante se*.[118] Illico beata Brigida misit equites post regem ut *peterent* hastam suam. Illi currentes inuenerunt regem transeuntem uadum cuiusdam *fluuioli* et ei indicarunt suam questionem[e]. Et inde letatus est rex et dedit eis hastam suam[f] dicens: 'Si *domina mea*[g] Brigida [h]omnia arma mea[h] *postularet, ego* statim *darem ei.*' Tunc *nuntii* sancte Brigide interrogauerunt[i] ubi [j]moratus esset rex[j] *tamdiu quod non peruenit longius*. Dixerunt illis comites regis:

24 [a] est secundum vaticinium B   [b] sed modo C   [c] uestro C   [d] duodecim B
25 [a] solennitatem B *passim*   [b] Penthecostes C   [c] Leproso C   [d] tunc C *only, perhaps compensating for loss of* statim V[1]   [e] quaesitionem B   [f] *om.* B
[g] nostra B   [h-h] nostra arma omnia B   [i] interrogarunt B   [j-j] rex moratus esset B

---

[118] Cf. V[1] §55 'Brigita abnuit cibum sumere donec leprosus proteruus comederet', because the situation was one of distraint by fasting, Ir. *troscad*. It is perhaps interesting that V[4] accepts the situation; for other examples of the retention of such occasions in **D**, see D. A. Binchy, 'A Pre-Christian Survival in Mediaeval Irish Hagiography', in *Ireland in Early Mediaeval Europe*, ed. D. Whitelock *et al.* (Cambridge, 1982), pp. 165–78 (at pp. 171–4).

'Non sumus morati *alicubi* sed uelociter *equitauimus*; scimus tandem quod *potestas Dei* per beatam Brigidam nos retinuit ut cito solueretur *sancta Dei ab improbitate* leprosi.' Tunc omnes laudauerunt Deum et sanctam Brigidam, et rex *gaudens* citius peruenit ad *castrum* suum. *Nuntiis autem monstrantibus hastam regis sancte uirgini, ipsa iussit dari leproso. Et* gratias agentes Deo *omnes cum ea refecti sunt solemniter.*

Cum esset *aliquando* Brigida in *monasterio*[a]119 et sedisset iuxta ianuam loci illius, uidit ad ripam fluminis *proximi* hominem ambulantem ualde curuum, et ipse onus portabat. Miserta illius sancta Dei dixit: 'Eamus ad hominem illum et onus eius portemus.' Cui ait sancta ueniens ad eum: 'Da nobis onus tuum; te enim ualde incuruat.' [b]Respondens ille dixit: 'Non onus me incuruat, sed dolor antiquus a iuuentute mea[b].' Illi iam interroganti *que esset uirgo*, dictum est quod sancta Brigida erat. Ipse homo dixit: 'Deo gratias ago quia quesitam inueni.' *Et ait ad sanctam uirginem*: '*Rogo te, sancta mater*, ut Deum ores *pro me* ut erigatur corpus meum.' Dixitque ei[c] beata uirgo: '*Intra* hospitium et requiesce in eo hac nocte, et faciam quod uis.' Et illa nocte sancta orabat[d] Dominum pro eo. Mane autem facto, dixit ad eum hominem: 'Vade ad flumen et laua te in nomine saluatoris ibi et roga Deum, [e]*et dico tibi quod* eriges ceruicem, et ne *discedas* donec ego dicam tibi quod eriges ceruicem[e].' *Et agens secundum iussionem sancte uirginis*, sanatus est et *benedicens medicam suam* gratias egit Deo qui se incuruatum annis octodecim erexit.

Post hec cum Patricio *archi*episcopo ad aquilonalem[a] *plagam*120 Hibernie exiuit. Quadam quoque die sanctus Patricius uerbum

---

26 [a] Q[w] f. 120[r] 'MS. W. semper monasterium habet, ubi hic est ecclesia' [b-b] Ille respondit: 'Non ita est, sed dolor antiquus a iuuentute mea me incuruat.' C   [c] *om.* B   [d] rogavit C   [e-e] *ita* B, *perhaps repeating words*] et dico tibi quod eriges ceruicem C, *omitting words*; *cf.* V[1] §56 erigesque ceruicem et ne descendas donec dicam tibi   **27** [a] aquilonarem B

---

119 Cf. I 37 n. 65.
120 Cf. V[1] §57 'partem'. The word *plaga*, used of the quarters of the compass, is introduced by the redactor of V[4] here and at II 61, 81, 99. At II 64 it is taken over from V[1]. The word is extremely common in **D** as a whole, 73 times in those Lives in Plummer's *Vitae*, against 16 in the **O**-texts (of which 14 belong to the Life of Brendan). In almost all cases it is an addition in **D**.

Dei predicabat *ibi populo*, sed sancta Brigida obdormiuit illa hora. Et post *predicationem* dixit sanctus Patricius ad beatam Brigidam: 'O *sancta uirgo*, cur *dormiuisti*[b] in uerbo Dei?' Hec ut audiuit uirgo, ueniam petens genua flectit, dicens: 'Parce mihi, pater, parce mihi, domine sancte. Ego in illa hora somnium uidi.' Ait ei *sanctus pontifex*: 'Narra nobis illud, *filia*.' *Sancta uirgo* ait: 'Ego ancilla tua uidi quatuor aratra arantia totam *Hiberniam*, et seminatores seminarunt semen, et statim illud creuit et maturescere cepit, et riui lactis noui impleuerunt sulcos, et seminatores illi [c]induti fuerant[c] uestibus albis. Post hec uidi alia aratra et arantes erant nigri qui bonam messem euerterunt et scinderunt uomere et zizania seminauerunt, et [d]*aque turbate*[d] impleuerunt sulcos.' Dixitque *episcopus uirgini*: 'Beata uirgo, ueram et mirificam uisionem uidisti. *Hec est interpretatio eius*. Nos sumus [e]boni aratores[e] qui quatuor euangeliorum aratris corda humana scindimus et seminamus uerbum Dei, et lactis *fidei Christiane riui a nobis fluunt*. In fine uero seculi mali doctores malis hominibus consentientes uenient qui nostram doctrinam euertent[f] et pene omnes homines seducent.' *Deinde autem qui ibi erant cum sancto Patricio et sancta Brigida Deum benedixerunt.*

28 Alio quoque die quidam pauper leprosus ad Brigidam uenit, rogans ut apud sanctam Brigidam uestimenta sua lauarentur. Dixitque ei uirgo: '*Fiet tibi* quod *uis*.' Ait leprosus: '*Necesse est mihi nudus esse quamdiu uestimenta mea humida erunt*.' Sancta Brigida ait ad unam puellarum suarum: 'Da uestimenta tua leproso, *quia alia*[a] *habes*,[121] donec uestimenta eius mundentur.' Sed illa puella *renuit dare et statim* illa inobediens lepra percussa est, *sed post* spatium unius hore *penitentiam agens et orante sancta Brigida pro ea munda facta est*. Alia uero puella dedit segnum[b122] [c]suum leproso[c]; *omnes enim*[d] *timor accepit*.[123] Deinde leprosus postquam exuit se uestimentis suis *ante sanctam Brigidam* mundatus est a lepra sua. Et omnes uidentes talia Deo laudes dederunt.

---

[b] obdormiuisti B   [c-c] erant induti B   [d-d] *ita* BQ[w] f. 120[v]] quae turbatae C   [e-e] aratores boni B   [f] vertent C   **28** [a] alias C   [b] segnum BV[1]β] sagum CcV[1]α   [c-c] leproso suum   [d] vero C

[121] V[4] adds the obvious to complete the sense.

[122] V[4] has accepted this ghost word from V[1]β. Colgan corrected the reading to *sagum*.

[123] That is, her fear of Brigit overcame her fear of contact with the leper.

Illa in regione[124] tempore quadragesime sancta Brigida cum puellis suis *in quadam cellula mansit*. Quadam autem nocte octo fures, uiri *fortes*, uenerunt ut *tollerent* quatuor equos quos *beata* Brigida cum suis habebat. Tunc una que erat sine somno dixit ad *sanctam* Brigidam: '*O mater*, equi nostri furto tolluntur.' Cui sancta ait: 'Sine, *filia*[a], ego *iam* sentio, sed fortiores nobis sunt qui auferunt eos.' Tunc latrones, ablatis quatuor equis, exierunt ad domum cuiusdam plebei[b] et furati sunt inde xl modios frumenti, ponentes in quatuor equis et in humeris suis, et putantes se ad propriam domum ire *reducti sunt Dei nutu ad cellam uirginum, et deponentes onera de equis post laborem*[125] graui somno dormierunt in angulo *atro*[c]. Facto autem mane, ecce uiri, [d]quibus rapta sunt[d] preterita nocte, uenerunt ad cellam Brigide acceptis armis sequentes uestigia furum et equorum [e]usque ad cellam. Et ueniente ad eos sancta Brigida dixerunt ad eam[e]: 'Grana nostra rapta sunt preterita nocte, sed uestigia furum et equorum usque ad ianuam *loci huius* secuti[f] *sumus*. Oramus uos ne nobis [g]celetis *quidquam huius rei*[g].' Tunc reuersa uirgo beata *uidit latrones dormientes* et suscitauit eos dicens: 'Cur attulistis furtum ad nos?' Illi iam expauescentes et mirantes dixerunt: 'Quia putabamus, *domina*, nos ad nostram domum uenisse.' Tunc sancta Brigida misit ad sanctum Patricium in proximo manentem *ut ueniens liberaret latrones*. Venitque statim sanctus Patricius ad *sanctam uirginem*, et fures liberati sunt et penitentiam egerunt. Et *illi homines* suum *frumentum* beate Brigide cum suis uirginibus obtulerunt, scientes quod a Deo donatum esset eis. *Et per hec nomen sancte Brigide in istis regionibus diuulgatum est*.

Sanctus Patricius quadam die [a]*in terra Ultorum*[a][126] uerbum Dei predicabat turbis et beate Brigide. Tunc uidit populus nubem

29 [a] *om.* C   [b] plebeii B   [c] atro B] *cf.* secreto V[1] horrei Cc   [d-d]*ita* CB] a quibus grana rapta sunt V[1]   [e-e] et venientes dixerunt C   [f]sequuti C [g-g] celetis quidquam hujus rei C] quid huius rei celetis B (celeris b)
30 [a-a] Q[w] f. 121[r]

[124] V[1]α §59 specifies that these events happened in Mag nInis, but V[1]β lacks the place-name.

[125] In V[1] we are merely told that they entered 'in paruum tugurium', but V[4] anticipates the denouement that they have been unwittingly brought back to the scene of their crime.

[126] The events of II 27–9 have all happened in the territory of the Ulaid though V[4] has not said so. But in this chapter, the place-name of Dún Lethglaisse has

magne claritatis descendentem de celo in terram et coruscantem[b] fulgure[c] immenso, et stetit modico temporis spatio iuxta populum in propinquo et postea *nubes illa surgens* [d]ad arcem Leathglasse, ubi sepultus est ipse sanctus Patricius *et beata Brigida et reliquie beatissimi abbatis Columbe post multos annos collocate in uno sepulchro*[d],[127] exiit et diutius ibi morata illic euanuit. Et non audebant turbe interrogare sanctum Patricium quid significaret illa uisio mirabilis sed *mitem uirginem* Brigidam interrogauerunt. Dixitque eis sancta: 'Interrogate *patrem nostrum* Patricium.' Audiens *hoc sanctus* Patricius ait: 'Tu et ego [e]equales sumus[e]; reuela ergo eis hoc mysterium.' Tunc dixit *sancta uirgo*[f] *ad turbas*: '*In illa* ⟨nube⟩[g] *angelus*[128] patris nostri sancti Patricii erat qui uenit ad uisitanda loca ubi corpus ipsius requiesceret et sepeliretur post obitum eius. Nam ubi stetit nubes prius prope nos, ibi erit corpus *patroni nostri* post obitum *inhumatum per aliquot*[h] *dies*,[129] sed deinde ducetur et sepelietur in arce Leathghlaisse, et ibi manebit usque in diem iudicii.' Tunc *sanctus* Patricius ad *sanctam*[i] Brigidam dixit ut ipsa suis manibus linteamen faceret quo corpus eius post obitum tegeretur, optans ut in illo linteamine ad uitam eternam migraret. *Et sic fecit sancta uirgo. Et dixit ad sanctum Patricium: 'De uno sepulchro ego et tu, pater, et dilectus Dei sanctus*[j] *Columba' (qui natus non fuit) 'resurrecturi sumus'.* Et in illo *linteamine* corpus *beatissimi patris nostri* Patricii inuolutum est. *Et his dictis turbe dederunt Deo laudes*.

31 Fuit quidam homo nobilis et diues atque bonus in campo Macha[a] qui *patiebatur* dolorem grauissimum et pestem, et non potuit curari a medicis. Misitque *ipse* ad sanctam Brigidam ut *dignaretur ipsa* uenire ad se. Cum ergo *uirgo Dei* domum illius uidisset a longo dixit: 'A quacumque *iam* parte uentus uenerit ad domum illam, infert secum maledictionem et morbum ad *dominum domus*.'

---

[b] corruscantem C [c] fulgore B [d-d] in arce Leath-laidhi sepultus est sanctus pater Patricius et beata Brigida et reliquiae beatissimi abbatis Columbae post multos annos collatae in uno sepulchro U [c-c] *ita* CBV¹β] equaliter scimus V¹α, *Vita IV S. Patricii* §91 [f] *om.* C [g] in illa CB ista nubes V¹ [h] *om.* B [i] beatam C [j] *om.* C 31 [a] Qʷ f. 121ᵛ

---

provided the redactor with the information, which he uses at the beginning of the chapter.

[127] See below, pp. 210–11.
[128] Cf. V¹ §60, 'nubes ista ut puto spiritus est patris nostri'.
[129] Cf. Jocelin of Furness, *Vita S. Patricii*, §190–1.

Cum hoc nuntiatum[b] *esset homini illi,* ait: '*Videtur mihi quod* nulli hominum feci malum.'[130] Tunc *stans ante se* armentarius suus dixit ei: 'Audiui, *domine,* omnes *uiatores*[131] quasi uno ore maledicentes te eo quod agricole *tui* agros tuos sepibus munientes omnes uias planas et rectas commutauerunt in asperas et spinosas.' Audiens hoc sancta Brigida ait: '*Vere* hec est causa dolorum tuorum.' Tunc *illo iubente* tote uie conuerse sunt in *uestigia pristina* et omnes uiatores benedicebant illi et *illico* homo ille, *sancta Brigida orante pro eo,* sanatus est *ab omni dolore,* et Deo et sancte Brigide gratias egit.

Quadam quoque die sancta Brigida sedente cum puellis suis in latere oppidi Macha[a], *uenerunt* duo uiri ad eam portantes uas *ligneum apertum*[132] plenum *aqua,* et cum uenissent rogauerunt *sanctam Dei ut* aquam benediceret. Et[b] illa benedixit aquam et uiros. Euntibus autem illis contigit ut caderet in terram uas *ab eis* super latus suum et non est fractum neque aqua effusa est *de eo quamuis aperto* gratia benedictionis sancte Brigide custodiente illam. *Audiens* sanctus Patricius *illud miraculum,* iussit aquam illam ecclesiis regionis illius diuidi[c] ut ad eucharistiam sanguinis Christi mitteretur, et ut aspergerentur egri ipsa[d] in sanitatem. Et sic factum est. Et *qui sanabantur ista aqua* laudabant Deum et suam *famulam* sanctam Brigidam.

Deinde *cum conuenirent in unum locum sanctus pater*[a] *et sancta Brigida cum suis,* beatus *pontifex*[b] Patricius per tres dies [c]*et noctes*[c] non cessauit predicare uerbum Dei *populo, et* nec sol occidit eis sed omnes putabant esse unam horam. Quidam autem homo, *sciens*[d]

---

[b] nunciatum C   32 [a] Q[w] f. 121[v]   [b] et V[1]] at CB   [c] divide C   [d] ipsi C   33 [a] Pater CB] *? l.* Patricius   [b] *om.* C   [c-c] *om.* C   [d] videns C

[130] Cf. V[1] §61, 'nulli hominum feci malum, nec clericis lesi nec fabris'. The notion that clergy or *áes dána* would be probable sources of the curse was apparently outdated or unacceptable in the redactor's period.

[131] At this point in V[1] the source of the curse is 'omnes in circuitu tuo', presumably his neighbours, though at the end of the chapter it is *uiatores* who bless him. V[4] has omitted the neighbours and any possible implication for local agricultural co-operation or want of it, retaining only these passers-by.

[132] Both adjectives anticipate the development of the story, in which it is implied that the vessel might have been broken in its fall or the water spilt. The vessel could not therefore have been iron, nor could it have had a secured lid.

eos esse ibi tamdiu,[133] superuenit et dixit: 'Cur tanto tempore, *o sancti*, sedetis*[e]* hic?' Dixit ei episcopus: 'Que est hora nunc diei?' Ille respondit: '*Vere* per tres dies et noctes hic estis.' Tunc dixit pater Patricius: 'Per xl dies et noctes ita fuissemus nisi aliquis extrinsecus indicasset nobis, et nullam lassitudinem uel esuriem sentiremus, diuina *hec nobis* donante gratia.' Tunc *sancti* ad sua reuersi sunt.

34 Post hec *accepit*[a] *beatissima Brigida a sancto Patricio archiepiscopo licentiam ueniendi ad suam patriam* et uenit ad campum [b]Breagh *in regione Midie*[b]. Et cum ibi habitaret in *quadam cellula*, uenit ad eam uxor filii Conalli *filii Neilli* regis *Hibernie* ut rogaret pro se quia *ipsa* sterilis erat, et habebat phialam argenteam *in elemosinam sancte Brigide*. Nolens iam *sancta Dei* exire ad eam, unam de puellis suis ad salutandam illam foris *manentem* misit. *Rediens illa uirgo*[134] ad sanctam Brigidam dixit: 'Cur, *domina, non uis uenire* ad reginam ut ores pro ea Deum ut[c] filium habeat, cum sepe roges[d] pro uxoribus *rusticorum?*' Cui respondit *sancta Dei*: '*Ideo* quia *rustici et pauperes* seruiunt Deo *nisi pauci*[135] et Deum poscunt. Filii uero regum serpentes sunt et filii sanguinum et *fornicationum*,[136] exceptis paucis electis a Deo. Sed tamen quia ipsa adiurauit nos, uade *ad eam* et dic ei: "Habebis semen quod sanguineum et maledicte stirpis erit, sed tamen multos annos regnum tenebit." ' Et sic[e] *euentus probauit*.

35 Quadam quoque die occurrit sancte Brigide quidam insanus de loco in locum transcurrens furore agitatus qui affligebat omnes occurrentes per loca ista. *Videns eum* sancta *uirgo* dixit ei: 'Predica mihi, *o homo*, uerbum Domini mei Iesu[a] Christi.' *Comites autem*

[e] sederis b   34 [a] petit C   [b-b] Q[w] f. 122[r]   [c] et B   [d] rogas C   [e] sit B
35 [a] Jesus C

---

[133] Here again V[4] tries to anticipate and make clear the briefer wording of V[1] §63. This man is 'quidam homo ignarus' there, but though simple, he was clearly not unknowing, for he asked, 'Quid tanto hic tempore sedetis?' V[4] has therefore removed *ignarus* and told us in advance what could be inferred from his question.

[134] Added because V[4] realized the nun could not speak to Brigit unless she had returned from meeting the queen at the gate.

[135] Cf. V[1] §64, 'quia plebei cuncti seruiunt Deo omnesque patrem poscunt'. V[4] has lost the earlier confidence in the goodness of the poor.

[136] Cf. V[1] 'filii sanguinis filiique mortis'. V[4] appears to have misunderstood the phrase, which surely means that kings live by murder and will not have eternal life.

sancte Dei ualde timentes confidebant in sanctitate domine sue. Insanus
iam factus mitis ait *uirgini*:[137] 'O beata Brigida, tua iussa implebo.
Ama Deum et amabunt te omnes boni, honora Deum et honora-
bunt te omnes, time Deum et timebunt[b] te omnes.' Et cum hec
dixisset, cum clamore fugit.

5 Eodem tempore Conallus[a] Neilli filius ad sanctam Brigidam in uia
ambulantem uenit et dixit ad eam: 'O sancta uirgo, benedic me
diligenter ne me occidat frater meus Carbreus[b] qui me multum
odit *propter regnum.*'[138] Ait ad eum *sancta Dei:* 'Tui *milites* ante me
precedant, et benedicam te *sequentem eos*; non enim oportet nos ire
cum eis.' Tunc illi precesserunt, et cum accederent omnes per
collem, una ex uirginibus dixit ad sanctam Brigidam: 'Heu, *mater*,
quid faciemus? Ecce Carbreus post nos, *frater istius domini*,
aduenit, et ipsi fratres se mutuo *^cnunc interficient^c.*'[139] Ait eis sancta:
'Non sic faciet nobis Deus noster.' Et cum aduenisset ille, dixit ad
sanctam Brigidam: 'O sancta *uirgo*, benedic me quia in his locis
timeo fratrem meum Conallum.' Tunc simul *omnes cum sancta Dei*
ibant, *et* nec se agnoscebant; excecauit[d] enim Deus oculos illorum
ne se agnoscerent propter sanctam Brigidam. Et separantes in
diuersis uiis ^eConallus et Carbreus^e osculabantur se inuicem, *alter*

---

^b timebant C   36 ^a Q^w f. 122^r   ^b Q^w f. 122^r   ^{c-c} ferient C   ^d caecauit
B   ^{e-e} Carbraeus et Conallus B

[137] The addition in V[4] attempts imperfectly to imply a healing, where V[1] simply
shows that obedience to Brigit pierces even lunacy, so that in the midst of his
afflictions the *insanus* obeys her command to preach. It is tempting, however, to
emend the text of V[1] in the last sentence of the chapter, inserting some word such
as *daemon* as the subject of 'fugit'.

[138] V[4] alone gives this reason for the hatred between the brothers, though
without apparent justification. Neither was regarded as king of the Southern Uí
Néill by the genealogists and historians (though Coirpre is mentioned as king in
the only ancient king-list, *Baile Chuind*, ed. G. Murphy, *Ériu*, 16 (1952), 146–9). V[4]
appears to imply that Conall had the kingdom. The reason behind this may be
that Tírechán, writing of St Patrick, portrays Coirpre as hostile to the saint where-
fore his line was cursed while Conall (Cremthainne) received Patrick and was
baptized; Tírechán §§9, 10. But an attitude favourable to Conall is not
maintained in V[1] or V[4]: cf. above, II 34, and below, II 37, 38.

[139] It is hardly possible to choose between the two readings 'nunc interficient' B
and 'ferient' C, but the word in V[1] is 'iugulabunt', a word common in texts of the
seventh and eighth centuries, meaning 'kill'. I have preferred the reading closer in
meaning.

alterum tamquam[f] *suum amicum putans. Et postea hoc scientes*[140] *multum* Dei nomen et sancte Brigide magnificabant.

37   Iterum alio tempore idem Conallus cum suis satellitibus circumdatus sub stigmatibus malignis uenit ad sanctam Brigidam, dicens: 'Tua benedictione, *o sancta Dei*, indigemus: nam uolumus ire ad regiones longinquas *terrarum*[141] *deuastare* et interficere inimicos.' Respondit sancta: 'Deum meum [a]rogo omnipotentem[a] ut ista uice a nullo ledamini et nullus sit Iesus a uobis, et ista signa diabolica *deinde*[142] deponatis.' Et hec *uota* uirginis Christus uelociter compleuit. Illi enim *his auditis* in regionem Cruthuniorum[b], [c]*que est aquilonalis*[d143] *pars Britannie, nauigarunt*[c144] et expugnauerunt quoddam castrum, et uisum est eis quod incenderunt illud, et putarunt multos inimicorum se interfecisse et decollasse[e]. Et reuersi sunt ad patriam suam cum sonitu et *letitia*[145] grandi, portantes capita inimicorum *principum*. Et cum *uenissent ad portum*, capita uel sanguinem non uiderunt, et nec in uestimentis nec in armis ullus cruor apparuit, et stupuerunt et dixerunt ad inuicem: 'Quid nobis contigit? Ubi sunt que cernimus?' Tunc

---

[f] quemdam B   37 [a-a] rogabo B   [b] Cutheniorum Cc   [c-c] Q[w] f. 122[v]
[d] aquilonalis Q[w]] aquilonis C aquilonaris B   [e] decolasse B

---

[140] By adding 'hoc scientes' here and omitting V[1] 'omnes' as the subject of the verb, V[4] alters the story from one of 'ships passing in the night' to one in which the antagonists acknowledge what has happened.

[141] Conall's words in V[1] §67 are, 'Tua benedictione indigemus, nam uolumus ire in regiones longinquas ut ista uincula nostra soluamus; est enim solutio eorum inimicos iugulare et interficere', on the significance of which see Sharpe, 'Hiberno-Latin *laicus*, Irish *láech*, and the Devil's Men', pp. 80–5.

[142] The prayer in V[1] is 'ut ista signa diaboli deponatis ut uultis et a nullo ledamini et nullum offendatis'. It is not clear to me why V[4] has reversed the elements.

[143] I take it that C's reading is a misprint and that B here as elsewhere has changed *aquilonalis* into *aquilonaris*, a form never used in **D**.

[144] V[1] refers to the *regio Cruthiniorum*, the territory of the Cruithin, that is Dál nAraide. The identical name was, however, sometimes applied to the Picts of northern Scotland and the redactor of V[4] has followed that sense in this geographical gloss, though the distances involved make a nonsense of it (as Bolland observed, *Acta Sanctorum*, Feb. I, 127 n. e). The changes 'nauigarunt' and 'ad portum' issue from this misunderstanding.

[145] Cf. V[1] 'iubilatione' (v.l. 'iugulatione' is an error), a word which **D** uses in similar contexts elsewhere, e.g. *ColE*. §8, *Cron*. §18, *FintC*. §13.

inito consilio[f] remiserunt legatos ad castellum quod succenderant ut interrogarent si quid eis accidisset. Legati uero interrogauerunt habitatores istius loci dicentes: 'Utrum aliquid nouum uobis accidit?' At illi dixerunt: 'Non, nisi stipulas [g]incensas hodie[g] inuenimus, destructosque *de capite*[146] lapides undique reperimus. Neminem autem uidimus neque sensimus quis hoc fecit.' Legati iam reuertentes hec Conallo nuntiauerunt[h]. Tunc Conallus *magnificans* [i]*nomen Dei cum suis tendit*[i] *ad patriam suam, ueniensque ubi erat sancta Brigida narransque omnia hec ei*, posuit ipse et sui stigmata sua *secundum iussionem uirginis*. Que dixit ad Conallum: 'Quia stigmata tua *respuisti* propter me, in quocumque periculo inuocabis me defendet te Deus per me et *incolumis* euades.'

Et hoc promissum *aliquando sic* completum est. Nam *post tempus* exiit ipse Conallus cum exercitu suo multo in regionem inimicorum suorum, et ibi magnam cedem fecit et *post uictoriam gloriose* reuersus est ad terram suam. *Cum non longe uenissent a terra illa, cadebat super eos nox, et uidens Conallus quoddam* castellum *desertum*, intrauit *illud*. Tunc *milites* sui dixerunt ei: 'Si hic *prope terram inimicorum* manserimus, *morti trademur*; inimici enim *nostri latenter nos sequentur et irruentes*[a] interficient nos *dormientes*.' Dixit eis dominus suus: '*Nox iam cadit, et* lassus ego sum. *Scitote quia* beatissima Brigida promisit mihi quia me defenderet[b] in omni periculo *se inuocantem*, et credo quia quod ipsa promisit uerum foret. In manus Dei per eam me cum comitibus meis in hac nocte commendo.' Statimque inimici in illa nocte post eos uenerunt, sequentes eorum uestigia, et cum uenissent prope castellum ubi erat Conaldus, tres uiros ad considerandum castellum miserunt. [c]Et illi castellum[c] *ubi erat Conaldus* intrantes[d], uiderunt magnum populum sedentem in habitu clericali, et ignem in medio eorum, et libros apertos coram eis; sic enim posuerunt milites capita inimicorum suorum ante se, et uisi[e] sunt quasi libros apertos scrutantes. Reuersique exploratores talia *dominis suis* narrauerunt.

[f] concilio C   [g-g] hodie incensas B   [h] renuntiauerunt B   [i-i] nomen Dei cum suis, tendit C nomen Dei, cum suis tendit B   **38** [a] venientes C [b] defendet C   [c-c] *om.* C   [d] et intrantes C   [e] visi V¹] visa CB (*? attracted to* capita)

---

[146] I do not know what this is intended to mean. V¹ reads 'distructum castellum et lapides grandes undique comparatos reperimus'. Perhaps again V⁴ had a corrupt reading in its source copy.

Et iterum alios tres uiros sagaciores miserunt, et ipsi uiderunt similiter clericos cum suis libris apertis, sicut priores uiderunt. Tunc exercitus inimicorum reuersus est ad regionem suam. *Crastina autem die ipsi* legatos post Conaldum miserunt ut peterent ab eo capita, *ut cum corporibus sepelirentur*; qui legati hoc Conaldo nuntiauerunt, *et acceptis capitibus reuersi sunt, nuntiantes dominis suis quod Conaldus cum exercitu suo illic erat. Utrique talia scientes*, Deum et sanctam Brigidam *glorificabant*.

39 Alio tempore beata Brigida, rogata *a quibusdam*, adiuit regem in campo Breagh manentem ut liberaret quendam uirum qui erat in uinculis apud regem, et *promisit sancta uirgo* precium[a] pro illo dare regi. Sed rex nullo modo uoluit dimittere eum, *promittens quod* ipse illo die *occidendus esset*. Et uix obtinuit sancta Brigida ut concederetur illi *spatium istius*[b] noctis. Deinde sancta Brigida illa nocte *perrexit ad* proximum locum cum cognatis et amicis illius uincti; *omnibus dormientibus, sola* Brigida uigilabat. Dixerunt sui ad regem: 'Nisi in hac nocte ille captus occidatur, *domine rex*, nemo poterit eum cras occidere *quia* sancta Brigida eum liberabit. Statuimus [c]ergo nos[c] consilium[d] ut per uim rapiamus eum et sine tuo consilio occidamus, et tu eris inculpabilis.' Et hunc dolum *sancta Dei diuinitus* cognouit, et in *prima uigilia* noctis uisio apparuit uiro qui erat in uinculis; uidit iam ipse[e] sanctam Brigidam ei astantem[f] et dicentem sibi: 'Ecce mali homines cogitant te[g] occidere in hac nocte. Sed cum traheris ab eis ad iugulandum, uocabis nomen meum sepius; et cum catena de collo tua ablata fuerit ut *occiderent te*, declina[h] ad dextram tuam[i] partem et *incolumis euades* ad nos ab eis.' Postea ipso euigilante, uenerunt illi et rapuerunt eum de *palatio* regis, et *ducentes eum foras* soluerunt catenam[j] de illo. Ipse autem absolutus statim *euasit ab eis, et incolumis* uenit ad sanctam Brigidam. Ipsi se putabant interficere eum et amputasse caput eius. Crastino autem die nec corpus nec caput apparuit quippe quia phantasma uidebant; etiam omnes admirabantur stupidi. Orto iam sole misit beata Brigida *nuntium ad narrandum regi que gesta fuerant*.[147] Rex

39 [a]precem B   [b]illius C   [c-c]inter nos ergo nos C   [d]concilium C   [e]*om.* C   [f]adstantem B   [g]se C   [h]declina ab eis C   [i]*om.* C   [j]cathenam C catenas B

[147] Cf. V[1] §68, 'misit Brigita ad regem ut dimitteretur ei uinctus'; but V[4] has realized that the prisoner was by this stage already released, and so has paraphrased.

uero hec audiens penitentiam egit, et dimisit *illi homini propter sanctissimam Brigidam omnem inimicitiam suam*.

Quadam die ad beatam Brigidam quidam uiri *fatui* uenerunt, habentes stigmata[a] diabolica in capitibus suis, qui querebant *sanguinem fundere*. Et cum postularent se benedici a sancta Brigida, illa rogauit eos uicissim ut *his uanis uti cessarent*. At illi dixerunt: 'Non possumus *ita* stigmata[a] nostra dimittere.' Et uidens uirgo signorum formas multum mirabatur, et signauit ea signaculo Christi, *non causa benedicendi sed ne homines per ea perirent*.[148] Illi autem abierunt querentes sanguinem effundere; et reperientes *in uia uirum* plebeium, uisum est eis quod eum iugulauerunt et decollauerunt. *Vir* uero ille per medium illorum incolumis exiuit in domum suam, apparens eis phantasma. Illi postea querentes caput eius uel corpus uel sanguinem, nihil inuenerunt, dicebantque ad inuicem: '*Miraculum nobis contigit a Deo factum* sancte Brigide causa *putantibus occidisse uirum* et non interfecimus.' Et diuulgatum[b] est factum *ab eis* per omnem regionem, ipsique postea sua stigmata, glorificantes Deum et sanctam Brigidam magnificantes, reliquerunt.

Dux[a149] quidam in campo Liffii ad sanctam Brigidam uenit[b] ut [c]benediceretur ab ea[c]. Et sancta benedixit eum diligenter. *Dux*

40 [a] stygmata C   [b] diu vulgatum C   41 [a] Q^w f. 123^v   [b] accesit B
[c-c] ab ea benediceretur B

[148] V[4] adds this to explain the otherwise surprising action of the saint in signing the *stigmata diabolica*.

[149] Cf. V[1] §70, 'rex' throughout the chapter. The redactor of V[4] is sparing in the use of *rex*, applying it to the kings of Ireland (ii 12, 34), Leinster (i 1, ii 10, 21, etc.) and on one occasion *rex Hikenselach et Lageniensium* (ii 12), Munster (ii 12), the old Ulster of the heroic age (ii 99), and of the Uí Néill overlord (ii 34); though it quite often stands unqualified, context generally shows that it refers to a king of at least provincial status. The petty king of the early Middle Ages is not recognized (cf. below ii 50 n. 158), and *dux* is here substituted. The same substitution is common elsewhere in **D**: for example, *Aed* S §29 'rex Thethbe', **D** §21 'dux Tedbe', **O** 'princeps Tedphe'; *Aed* S §34 'regem Baiethene', **D** §25 'ducem Baithenum'; *Aed* §37 'rex quidam', **D** §27 'quidam dux'; *Cain.* S §§8–10 *rex* passim, **D** §§6–7 *dux*; *Cain.* S §46 'rex Ossirgi', **D** §39 'dux regionis Osraidhe', **O** 'regulus in Osrigia'; *Lug.* S[1] §10 'Felanus rex', **D** §10 'dux Faolanus'; *Lug.* S[1] §50 'rex Luigse', **D** §42 'dux Laighys'; *Mun.* S[1] §24 'rex Fothartorum', **D** §21 'dux Fothartorum'.

uero *gaudens* reuersus est ad *castellum*[150] suum. Quidam uir *audax*, qui inimicus *ducis* erat, intrauit illa nocte castellum occulte, *omnibus dormientibus*, et tenens candelam de candelabro, quesiuit *ducem* dormientem et inueniens eum *uidit* gladium super ceruical iuxta se et arripiens[d] *ipsum* gladium *ducis* in cor *ducis* tribus uicibus *fortiter* fixit et statim in fugam perrexit. Tunc omnes *scientes* effusionem sanguinis surrexerunt et fecerunt planctum putantes *ducem* esse mortuum. *Dux* uero de graui somno euigilans et pusillum uulneratus sospes remansit, et consolatus est eos, dicens: '*Ponite planctum uestrum, quia* benedictio sancte Brigide que hodie me benedixit custodiuit me *de hoc magno periculo.*' Crastina quoque[e] die cum magnis muneribus[151] uenit ipse *dux* ad sanctam Brigidam *agens ei gratias. Deinde gloriosa* Brigida pacem inter *ipsum ducem* et inimicum qui eum iugulauit et inter genera eorum in sempiternum fecit, per merita eiusdem uirginis Deo donante.

42   Post hec beata Brigida in prouinciam Momoniensium, uolens *loca sancta et sanctos qui ibi erant uisitare*, exiuit simul et episcopus Ercus qui fuit discipulus sancti Patricii *archiepiscopi* quique natus de Momonia erat. Cum *quodam die ambularent*[a] in uia, sancta Brigida dixit ad episcopum Ercum: 'Demonstra, uenerabilis pater, sub qua parte celi gens tua *in Momonia* consistit.' Et cum *episcopus indicasset, sancta uirgo* dixit ei: 'Nunc ibi bellum geritur inter unam gentem et aliam.' Dixitque ei *episcopus*: 'Credo quod dicis, *sancta mater*, uerum esse. Nam quando ab eis ad te ueni dimisi eos[b][152] discordes.' Dixitque ei *sancta uirgo*: 'Gens tua, *pater*, nunc in fugam conuertitur.' Tunc unus de *discipulis sancti episcopi, hoc non credens, proterue* dixit ad sanctam Brigidam: 'Quomodo potes uidere bellum per magnum spatium terrarum?' Arguitque eum *episcopus*

---

[d] accipiens B   [e] *om.* C   42 [a] ambubarent C   [b] eas B

[150] Cf. V[1] §70 'in uiam suam'; there, the king set off homewards, grew tired, and rested, and the enemy entered 'in castellum et in domum'. This need not be his own cashel, but V[4] has so interpreted the story, and shortened the account here.

[151] Here V[4] follows V[1], but in the V[1] story this is the second lot of gifts the king brought to Brigit, for there he had brought gifts with him when he first came to seek blessing.

[152] The masculine 'eos' in V[1] and V[4] interprets *gentes* in terms of people, rather than agreeing with the feminine noun; the reading of B is a grammarian's correction.

ne blasphemaret spiritum sanctum *qui illuminabat*[c] *sanctam uirginem corpore et anima.* Dixitque ad *sanctam*[d] *uirginem*: 'Oro te, *sancta Dei*, signa oculos meos et *huius fratris* ut uideamus que uides.' Tunc signauit oculos eorum *Christi sponsa*, et uiderunt bellum *lucide.* Et ait *ille discipulus Erco* episcopo uoce lacrymabili[e]: 'Heu, heu, domine mi, ecce iam modo uidentibus oculis meis duo fratres mei decollantur.' *Et omnia euentus rei probauit.*

Deinde in quodam loco iuxta montem[153] sanctus episcopus Ercus et *beatissima uirgo* Brigida *cum suis comitibus*, itinere fatigati, *esurientes sederunt.* Tunc unus puerorum dixit: '*Ille* magnam misericordiam fecisset qui nobis modo *comestionem* dedisset.' Respondit *ei sancta* Brigida: 'Ego uobis *predico.* Si uultis cibo et potu satiari, expectate hic *parumper* adiutorium saluatoris. Video domum in qua elemosina hodie cuidam ecclesie offerenda parata est, que huc uenit hac hora. Ecce modo in sarcinis est.' Adhuc *sancta* loquente, *ecce* uenerunt qui elemosinam portabant. Et illi cognoscentes quod sancta Brigida et beatus Ercus episcopus *cum suis esurientes* sedissent illic, letati sunt ualde et obtulerunt eis suam elemosinam dicentes: 'Accipite[a] elemosinam quam uobis misit Deus. Non enim inuenimus ecclesiam meliorem quam uos.' Tunc gratias Deo agentes, comederunt illic, sed tamen potum non habebant. Dixit eis sancta Brigida: 'Fodite terram illic.' Et illis fodientibus terram, [b]illico fons lucida[b] erupit qui usque hodie manet, et *fons* sancte Brigide *uocatur.*

Deinde campum Femyn[a] *intrantes*, inuenerunt ibi magnam synodum *sanctorum*, et detenti sunt in synodo. Narrauit autem *sanctus* episcopus *Ercus* synodo uirtutes *quas ipse uidit factas per* sanctam Brigidam. *Audientes habitatores illius regionis sanctam Brigidam ibi esse*, adduxerunt multos infirmos ad eam ut curaret eos, inter quos erant claudi, leprosi, demoniaci. *Et orante Christi sponsa pro eis, statim illos diuina potestas languoribus suis* sanauit.

---

[c] illiminabat C   [d] beatam B   [e] sacrymabili C   43 [a] aspicite B
[b-b] fons lucidus illic B   44 [a] Q[w] f. 124[r]

---

[153] So V[1]β but V[1]α §71 'ad montem Ere' (in London, BL, MS Add. 34124; vv. ll. Aere in Paris, BN lat. 10864 (s. x), Emere or Imere in Zürich, Zentralbibliothek, MS Rheinau 81). The place-name was presumably omitted because of confusion with Erc, the name of the bishop; I have not identified the place.

45 Postea exiuit sancta Brigida ad *locum*[154] qui erat prope mare, haud
procul a loco in quo tunc sanctus episcopus Ercus manebat, et
mansit illic cum puellis suis longo tempore. Non longe ab eis
quidam anachorita[a] habitabat. Ipse Deo deuotus et perfectus erat
et, *uolens* uitare facies mulierum, [b]*deseruit locum suum*[b] *et direxit iter*
ad quamdam insulam *uallatam aqua*. Et ingrediens uiam, uenit
prope cellam in qua sancta Brigida *habitabat*, suique[c] discipuli dixerunt ei: 'Eamus, *domine*, ad sanctam Brigidam ut nos benedicat.'
Respondit anachorita[a]: 'Scitis, *filii*, uotum meum quod nullam
uolo uidere feminam.' *Postea surgentes* obliti sunt *aliqua necessaria de
rebus suis*. Facto autem uespere steterunt in quodam hospitio et
iterum recordati sunt *rerum* suarum, dicentes: 'Ideo *res* nostras
perdidimus quia non declinauimus ad *sanctam Dei* ut benedicat
nobis. Et pro hac culpa *orantes Deum* in hac nocte ieiunabimus.'
Mane autem facto reuersi sunt ad sanctam Brigidam et inuenerunt apud eam *res* suas. *Cum enim obliuiscerentur fratres res suas, sancta
uirgo sedens in cella* dixit suis: 'Ite, et adducite res seruorum Dei que
relicte in uia proxima nobis[d] sunt.' *Sanctus anachorita et sui apud*
sanctam Brigidam tres dies et noctes *manserunt* in Dei laudibus et in
predicatione uerbi Domini.

46 Deinde *reuersi sunt illi*, et *beata* Brigida, *uolens satisfacere eis, iter illius
diei* exiuit cum eis. Videns autem sancta *Dei* onera *discipulorum
anachorite* grauia *fuisse*, miserta est eis.[155] Tunc uiderunt duos
equos de monte *propinquo* descendentes ad se, et *iubente sancta
Brigida* imposuerunt super eos onera; et cum uenirent ad finem
itineris, dixit eis sancta Brigida: 'Dimitte equos *ad sua reuerti*.'
Tunc *soluti* equi *reuersi sunt*, et nemo illorum nouit unde essent uel
cuius fuissent. Et ibi beata uirgo Brigida, *data benedictione ad
inuicem*, reuersa est ad *cellam* suam.

---

45 [a] anachoreta C   [b-b] desertum quaerebat locum sibi C   [c] -que] *om*. B
[d] *om*. B

[154] Cf. V[1]α §73, 'ad alium hominem qui erat secretus et solitarius et
propinquus mari', but several early MSS have 'ad alium hominem qui et
propinquus mari', a reading which presumably led to that underlying V[4]. The
omission of the first solitary, before the anchorite enters the story, may therefore
be accidental, and not represent a simplification in the narrative.

[155] Usually V[4] makes *misereri* take the genitive, as in Classical Latin: I 34
illorum (V[1] illis), II 26 illius (V[1] illum), II 71 mulieris (V[1] mulieri). But here the
dative is retained from V[1] §73. As a whole, **D** presents a mixed picture.

Anachorita autem *perueniens* ad insulam *intrauit eam*. Sed *homo cuius possessio erat insula illa exiuit cum pecoribus suis et hominibus in eam, uolens pecora sua per estatem ibi pascere*.[156] Sanctus autem uir, deuitans uidere mulieres, rogauit *illum hominem* ut exiret de insula, sed non impetrauit. Dicebat enim *ille homo* quod habebat illam terram in hereditate paterna. Tunc misit anachorita ad sanctam Brigidam ut ueniret adiuuare eum. At sancta perueniens, rogauit *illum hominem* et non potuit impetrare. Crastina autem die uenit ingens aquila et rapuit *filiolum illius sursum in aere*. At uxor eius, *mater infantuli*, plorans et flens uenit ad sanctam Brigidam, *petens adiutorium*. Cui ait sancta: 'Noli flere, quia uiuit infans, et dimisit eum aquila in littore super terram[a].' Et sic infans inuentus est *incolumis*. Sed adhuc *homo ille* durus permansit, *et in littore nolens discedere habitauit*. Crastino autem die subito, *diuina potentia*, uentus ualidissimus uenit et illum cum suis trans fretum in proximum portum leuiter uexit. Tunc *homo* ille compunctus corde penitentiam egit et deuouit se Deo et sancte Brigide.

Alio quoque die hospites religiosi uenerunt *ibi* ad sanctam Brigidam. Tunc dixit *sancta Dei* piscatori suo, qui solebat tauros marinos, *id est phocas, occidere*: 'Vade ad mare, si possis adferre aliquid hospitibus.' Tunc ille *nauigans* assumpsit hastam *qua iugulauit belluas marinas*. Et statim occurrit ei *phoca*, et *eleuans ille hastam*, infixit eam in taurum. Sed funis pendebat circa manum uiri *innixus*[a] *haste, hasta uero in capite phoce fixa erat*. Taurus autem grauiter uulneratus traxit secum uirum in sua *nauicula in pelago*, et non cessauit donec peruenit [b]ad littus *cuiusdam insule in mari posite longe*[b].[157] Et tunc funis scissus est, ubi uir mansit in sua *nauicula* in littore. *Phoca* uero, *pendente* hasta *in suo capite*, reuersus est in mare et uenit recto cursu ad littus loci illius in quo sancta Brigida erat, et ibi mortuus est. Vir autem ille *confidens in Deo per sanctitatem domine*

---

47 [a] terras B   48 [a] *ita* CB] *? l.* innexus   [b-b] Q[w] f. 125[r]

[156] In V[1] §73 the man (*laicus*, cf. 1 38 n. 68) simply arrives, claiming 'quod habebat agrum in illa insula' (to which V[1]β adds 'ex paterna hereditate'). V[4] has made up some context, and changed the man's wife and children into his flocks and labourers. The omission of wives and daughters makes a nonsense of the story, removing the anchorite's grounds for hostility, and leaving the part later played by wife and child dangling.

[157] V[1] §74 says 'ad Brittaniae littora', but evidently this strained the credulity of the redactor of V[4].

su̯e tentauit nauigare, et prospera nauigatione, *Dei nutu*, uenit sexta
hora ad suum portum, et inuenit recto cursu ibi *phocam* mortuum
cum hasta in littore, et ingressus domum narrauit omnibus illam
suam nauigationem.

49   *Deinde* sancta Brigida cum suis in campum Cliach, ᵃ*in Momonia
positum*ᵃ, exiuit et habitauit illic in quodam loco *ad tempus. Ibi* ad
sanctam Dei quedam ancilla uenit, fugiens dominam suam, *quia
non poterat mores eius sufferre.* Domina autem eius secutaᵇ est eam,
uolens reducere eam. Sancta uero Brigida, *uolens liberare miseram*,
rogauit dominam suam ut dimitteret ancillam *Deo liberam*, sed illa
mulier noluit; ancilla enim *pretiosas* uestes texebat. Et tunc illa
domina manum ancille sue tenuit et traxit eam uiolenter de latere
sancte Brigide. Et hoc sancte Dei displicuit. Et cum per*transisset*
paullum ancilla sanctam Brigidam, manus dextra domine aruit
qua tenuit manum ancille. Videns autem illa quia non poterat
mouere manum suam, fleuit et rediens egit penitentiam et dimisit
ancillam liberam sancte Brigide. Et illico manus eius sanata est.

50   *Alio tempore* beata Brigida rogata est ut iret ad regem *illius regionis
qui tum erat*¹⁵⁸ in campo Cliach ad liberandum uirum qui erat in
uinculis apud regem. Et perueniens *Christi amica* ad domum regis,
non inuenit regem ibi, sed nutritor eius cum suis amicis erat in
domo. Et uidens *beata uirgo* citharasᵃ in domo, dixit: 'Citharizate
nobis.' Responderunt ei homines: '*Domina*, non sunt modo cithariste in domo.' Tunc quidam de comitibus sancte Brigide ioculari
uerbo illis dixit: 'Benedicat sancta uirgo manus uestras ut possitis
complere que ipsa precipit uobis, et obedite uoci eius.' Tunc
nutritor regis *cum suis filiis* dixit: 'Benedicat nos *sancta Dei ut cithar-
izemus ei.*' *Et benedicente eos sancta*, acceperunt citharas et modulan-
terᵇ rudes *quasi periti* chithariste *et dulciter citharizabant.* Tunc rex

---

49   ᵃ⁻ᵃ Qʷ f. 125ʳ   ᵇ sequuta C   **50** ᵃ cytharas *etc.* C   ᵇ *ita* CB] modulantur V¹

---

¹⁵⁸ Like the change from *rex* to *dux* at II 41, the alteration here from V¹ §76 'ad
quendam regem in campo Clioch' rests on the rejection of the term *rex* for a petty
ruler. The redactor does not accept '*a* king in the plain of Cliach', but makes him
'*the* king of that region (? province), who *at that time* was in the plain of Cliach'.
This makes the plain a part of the kingdom, instead of the king's being one of
several on the plain. It is the reverse of substituting *dux*.

uenit ad domum suam et audiens sonum carminis dixit: 'Quis facit hoc carmen?' *Occurrensque*^c unus ei dixit: '*Nutritor* tuus, *domine*, et filii sui, iubente *illis sancta* Brigida.' Intrauit rex domum, *mirans de hac re*, et postulauit statim benedictionem sibi a sancta uirgine. Dixitque sancta: 'Tu *pro benedictione* uirum illum quem tenes in uinculis dimitte liberum mihi.' Tunc rex *benedictione accepta* a sancta Brigida gratis et benigne donauit ei captum. *Nutritor* uero regis *et filii sui probi* cithariste usque ad diem mortis sue fuerunt et *nepotes* eorum regibus uenerabiles *cithariste* erant.

Alio uero die duo leprosi ad sanctam Brigidam uenerunt, rogantes ut salui fierent. Tunc *Deum* orauit sancta et benedixit^a aquam et dixit eis ut alterutrum se lauarent in aqua sancta. Et *cum alter alterum lauaret*, unus statim mundatus est et uestibus lotis induitur. Dixitque illi uirgo: 'Laua et tu socium tuum.' Ille autem uidens quia mundatus est et uestes haberet lotas,¹⁵⁹ noluit lepram alterius tangere sed de sua salute gloriabatur. Ait ei sancta: 'Quod uoluisti ut ille faceret tibi, te decet similiter ei facere.' Ille uero negauit et contradixit. Tunc beata Brigida surrexit et *lauans leprosum* mundatus est *inter manus eius* et uestibus lotis induit eum. Qui uero prius sanatus fuerat ait: 'Modo sentio scintillas ignis super humeros meos.' Et statim totum corpus eius lepra percussum est propter superbiam suam. Alter uero humilis mundatus est *sicut legitur: 'Qui arrogat deiicietur et qui se inclinat altus fiet.'*¹⁶⁰ Et gratulabatur ille, gratias agens Deo qui se per merita sancte Brigide sanauit.

Duo *alii* leprosi ad sanctam Brigidam uenerunt querentes elemosinam. *Sancta* autem nihil aliud habens^a quod daret eis, unam uaccam quam habebat dedit eis, quorum unus gratias egit Deo; alter uero superbus et ingratus extitit dicens: 'Nisi mihi soli detur uacca, medium^b eius non *habebo*.' Dixit tunc *sancta* ad humilem leprosum: 'Tu *ergo* hic mecum expecta paullisper, *donec* nobis Dominus aliquid mittat; ille autem uaccam *solus* habeat.' Exiit

---

^c Occurensque B   51 ^a benedicens C   52 ^a tunc habens C   ^b *ita* CB] dimidium V¹

---

¹⁵⁹ The clash of moods is here taken from V¹β, while V¹α has 'quia mundatus est et uestimenta lauata (*sc.* sunt)'. One might have expected V⁴ to have smoothed this awkwardness away.

¹⁶⁰ Source not identified.

deinde cum uacca sua sed solus non potuit eam minare. Tandem labore fatigatus reuersus est ad *sanctam* Brigidam et multis con-uiciis *insultabat in eam*, dicens: 'Ideo non potui eam minare quoniam non ex corde donasti eam. Dura es^c nimium et immitis.' Sancta autem consolabatur eum et non potuit eum lenire. Et hoc displicente *beate uirgini*, ait ad eum: 'Filius perditionis *iam* es. *Vacca modo tibi mitis erit*, sed tum^{161} non tibi proderit.' Tunc uero uir quidam ad sanctam Brigidam uenit, habens uaccam in oblatione, *quam sancta Dei alteri leproso dedit*. Deinde duo leprosi minauerunt duas uaccas suas, et cum uenirent ad quoddam flumen, *mersus est ibi proteruus leprosus* et absorptus est in profun-dum, neque unquam inuentum est corpus eius. Humilis uero euasit incolumis cum sua uacca.

53 *Multa alia beata Brigida in regionibus Momoniensium fecit et plura loca et monasteria*^{162} *ibi signauit.*^{163} *Post hec iter arripuit* uenire ad *ciuitatem suam in* terram Lageniensium.^{164} *Cumque uenisset in curru suo per campum Femhin*^{a}, inuenerunt quemdam *agricolam preparantem*^{b}

---

^{c} *om.* B   53 ^{a} Feamhire B *? l.* Feamhin ^{b} *ita* CB] saepientem V^1

---

^{161} 'Tum' here represents V$^1\beta$ 'tamen', perhaps from reading *tn* as *tu*; there is no corresponding word in V$^1\alpha$.

^{162} This somewhat perfunctory allusion to a saintly career of church founding is perhaps characteristic of the redactor of **D**. In *Maed.* V §24, we read, 'Alio in tempore, cum esset sanctus Aidus in loco illo qui dicitur Cluain Mar', **D** §24 reads, 'Multa monasteria per circuitum regionis Cennselach santus Moedhog construxit. Et cum esset in uno eorum quod dicitur Cluain Mor Dicholla Gairbh' (for the change from *locus* to *monasterium*, cf. above, I 37 n. 65). Compare the opening of *Aed* **D** §6* as far as 'cellas et monasteria in utraque regione edificauit' for which there is no parallel in S §10 or O §6. Cf. *Abb.* §§28, 51, *Bren.* §§8*, 11*, 12*, *Cain.* §39*, *Car.* §11, *Coem.* §16, *Com.* §13, *Decl.* §17, *FinC.* §8*, *Lug.* §§5*, 29*, 52*.

^{163} This use of *signare* with reference to the foundation of a church or monastery appears to be a feature of **D**. It issues from the common usage, to sign with the cross in token of blessing, as is clear from *Ba.* **D** §§6*, 7* (in both, **O** uses *bene-dicere*), 13* (treated as equivalent to *consecrare*); other examples are found at *Car.* §§29, 30, 35, *Ita* §36. In *ColE.* **D** §21 (taken over from S §29) the meaning is to mark or designate.

^{164} Brigit's departure for Leinster is taken from V^1 §80, where she is simply said to have moved 'a campo Clioch ad fines Laginensium'. In V^1 §81 she is said to be in Uí Labraithe (cf. II 54), in the border region, but her arrival at home is not clearly mentioned. Only at V^1 §87 (transposed in V^4) has she reached her home territory. V^4 has articulated this journey more clearly, saying here that she left

agrum suum. Dixit ei auriga *sancte uirginis*: 'Concede nobis ut sancta Brigida curru suo transeat agrum tuum, et postea circumdabis sepe agrum tuum.' Respondit ille uir: 'Non, sed ite per circuitum agri.' Tunc dixit *sancta uirgo*: 'Faciamus quod ipse dicit ne aliquid offendat nos causa illius uiri.' Sed tum auriga cogebat equos transire *agrum*. Videns hoc uir ille furibundus fuste[c] cedebat nares equorum, equisque calcitrantibus beata Brigida de curru cecidit et lesa[d] est et *de equis* auriga *cadens* lesus est,[165] et steterunt equi *postea*. Tunc ait *sancta*: 'Nonne dixi uobis ut uitaremus hunc hominem, quia eum uirum pestilentie et mortis esse uidi?' Et uir ille inceptum opus aggreditur, paruipendens scelus quod fecit *contra Dei famulam*. *Et uindicans Deus iniuriam ancille sue, ille uir* statim corruit in terram et *ibi* mortuus est.

Deinde sancta Brigida ueniens ad fines Lageniensium, intrauit regionem Labrathi[a], ibique quedam femina ad eam cum filia sua leprosa uenit ut sanaretur illa. Tunc *sancta uirgo* ieiunans orauit et benedixit aquam et iussit leprosam aspergi ea. Et statim, *aqua benedicta aspersa*, mundata est a lepra sua et gratias egit Deo *cum matre sua* et *sancte* Brigide.

Postquam sancta Brigida ad suam ciuitatem peruenit, quidam religiosi *uiri ad eam uisitandam* uenerunt et predicauerunt ei uerba diuina. Post hec dixit sancta Brigida ad *cellariam*[a] suam: 'Prepara prandium pro sanctis hospitibus' Respondit *cellaria*: 'Quale prandium?' Ait ei *sancta*: 'Multa fercula *dentur eis*.' Respondit *cellaria*: '*Fiet* sic, sed tu, *domina*, ito[b] prius ad ecclesiam *et ora ibi*.'

---

[c] *om.* B [d] laeta C 54 [a] Labrathi] Labraithi Cc Labrachy BQ[w] f. 126[v]
55 [a] Q[w] f. 126[v] [b] iro b

Munster to return to Leinster and at II 55 (= V[1] §82) that she reached Kildare. Here, at II 53, Colgan wrote in the margin, 'Videtur hoc initium libri tertii', but Bolland rightly observes, 'Ast Usserius, qui saepissime hanc uitam citat, diserte asserit, libris duobus ab auctore ueteri descriptam.'

[165] V[1] §80 was here corrupt at an early date. Without a critical edition, it is difficult to know what is the true reading, but I suspect that MS Paris, BN lat. 10864 (s. x) has the best, 'equis calcitrantibus sancta Brigita et auriga ceciderunt de curru, sed nihil eis lesit, et equi steterunt in uno loco'. The other earliest manuscripts, BL Add. 34124 and Zürich, Rheinau 81, omit 'nihil eis', while later manuscripts have 'et lesi sunt', the reading of V[1]β which was presumably in front of the redactor here.

Nihil enim eorum que sancta dixit[166] habuit *cellaria tunc*; *nimia enim largitas caritatis beate Brigide diuidebat citius quicquid donauerat ei Deus*. Et dixit *sancta* ad *cellariam, sciens causam eius*: 'Vade modo ad *cellarium tuum et signa illud*[167] et claude ipsum et *rediens* ora, atque ego ibo ad ecclesiam.' Hora autem sexta uocabat sancta Brigida *cellariam suam* et dixit ei: 'Adest tempus ut reficiantur serui Dei. Vade modo ad *cellarium* et quecumque inueneris ibi da illis largiter.' Aperiens iam illa *cellarium*, omnes escas quas nominauit sancta Brigida mater inuenit ibi. Et non defecerunt ᶜipsi esceᶜ per septem dies et *tamdiu* erant sufficientes tam hospitibus quam omni familie *et pauperibus*. Nemo tunc nouerat *hanc rem* preter ipsam Brigidam et piam cellariam suam; unde ille esce erant aut quis illas attulit, *scientia Dei nouit*.

56 *Alio tempore cum esset beata Brigida in quodam loco ubi erant riuuli sine aquaticis*ᵃ *oleribus que nascuntur in riuulis fontium sine humano labore, quibus uescuntur multi in occiduis partibus sancti qui crucifigunt se in ieiuniis*,[168] chorus illius loci uirginum uenit ad eam habentes questionem et dixerunt ad eam: 'Cur, *domina mater*, olera aquatica in ˌhis aquis non nascuntur quibus sancti homines ⟨uti⟩ᵇ assuescunt?' *Sciens pia uirgo quod uellent illa olera habere*, sequenti nocte uigilans Deum rogauit. Mane autem surgentes puelle uiderunt *riuulos* supra modumᶜ illis oleribus *plenos*, ᵈid est, brisia et sampsia,[169] *et ceteris*ᵈ *oleribus* abundantes; et transeuntes per longa

ᶜ⁻ᶜ ipsi escae C] ei escae B illae escae V¹ *⸮ l.* ipse esce   56 ᵃ aquatilibus B
ᵇ ⟨uti⟩ V¹   ᶜ undam B   ᵈ⁻ᵈ Qʷ f. 126ᵛ] et sampsia *om.* C *in text, but quoted in notes*

---

[166] In V¹ §82 Brigit had specified 'panem et butyrum et cepas et fercula multa', which V⁴ represented as 'multa fercula dentur eis', leaving this relative clause somewhat pointless.

[167] This replaces V¹ 'scopa pauimentum cocinae', which the redactor perhaps thought too undignified.

[168] All this anticipates what is said later in V¹ §83.

[169] I cannot explain these words, apparently referring to something like watercress. Classical Latin *brisa* 'grape skins' and *sampsa* 'pulp of olives' are scarcely appropriate. Colgan, *Trias*, p. 566 n. 16, writes: 'per *Brisia* videtur intelligere genus aquatici oleris, quod Hibernice dicitur *Biorar* et latine anasturtium aquaticum, quo passim Eremitae istius temporis et Patriae vescebantur; per *Sampsia*, quid intelligat, nescio, nisi forte herbam quam latini vocant Sampsychum, & aliis nominibus vocatur *amarucus* et *maiorana*; vel aliam, quam Hiberni vocant *Samhadh*, latini vero *accetosam*.'

spatia locorum inuenerunt in illis locis magnam multitudinem olerum que ante ibi inuisa erant donata a Deo sicut rogauit *famula sua*. *Et ibi adhuc olera eiusdem generis Dei dono sancte Brigide non deficiunt*.

Quidam homines de longinquis *locis* uenerunt ad Brigidam, *uolentes se commendare ei*,[170] et ducebant secum munera multa in plaustris et[a] equis. *Sed die quo putabant peruenire ad sanctam Dei*, nox[b] in silua densa super eos cecidit, et errantes non poterant plaustra *pre tenebrositate* ducere. Beata autem Brigida laborem eorum *spiritu prophetie*[c] sciens, Deum rogauit pro eis, et dixit suis: 'Accendite ignem et calefacite aquam *ut lauentur pedes*[171] hospitum *uenientium ad nos*.' *Et mirabantur quod dixit homines ambulare in tenebrositate densa illius noctis*. Tunc apparuit illis lampas ingens illuminans eis [d]lucide uiam[d] usque dum uenerunt ad *monasterium sancte Brigide*, et *sanctissima uirgo* obuiam illis[e] exiuit. Deoque omnes gratias egerunt et *soluentes sua uota* post tres dies reuersi sunt per eandem uiam, et uix maximo cum labore in die uacua plaustra duxerunt[f] *pro austeritate* uie. Sed Christus in nocte illa loca plana et lucida fecit eis propter sanctam Brigidam se rogantem.

Simili modo sanctus episcopus Broon, cuius mentionem fecimus, cum curribus et equis et cum multo populo *ad sanctam Brigidam uisitandam* uenit et accidit sicut supra diximus eis. Nox enim hiemalis[a] *longe a monasterio sancte Brigide* foris in densa silua[b] cecidit super eos. *Sancta uirgo* uero hoc[c] *diuinitus* sciens dixit puellis: 'Oremus, *filie*, pro hospitibus *sanctis* qui laborant uenientes ad nos ut misereatur Deus laborum eorum.' Mira multum, *fratres carissimi*[d], dicturus sum uobis. Tunc *episcopus Broon et sui comites* prope se quasi *monasterium* sancte Brigide conspexerunt; et sanctam Brigidam letam cum suis puellis in occursum uiderunt, que subito in magnam *aulam* paratam eos deduxit et,

57 [a] in C   [b] mox C   [c] prophetico B   [d-d] viam lucide B   [e] *om.* B
[f] dixerunt b   58 [a] hyemalis C   [b] sylva C   [c] haec B   [d] charissimi C

[170] The use of *commendare* or *offerre* in this form of personal commendation is potentially of considerable interest, but may belong to the redactor's period; cf. *Lug.* D §15*, *Mun.* D §14*, *Rua.* D §5*.
[171] V⁴ spells out the purpose of heating water for the visitors; cf. Plummer, *Vitae*, vol. i, p. cxiv and n. 2.

detractis calceamentis, abluit pedes eorum abundantiaque ciborum *et potuum* refecit eos *et currus eorum bene curauit*, stratisque lectis collocauit eos et omnia que necessaria sibi erant *prebuit* eis *ᵉsancta uirgo* cum *filiabus* suis sicut *uisum est eisᵉ*.

59   Mane autem facto sancta Brigida *in suo monasterio* dixit puellis suis: 'Properemus obuiam *episcopo Broon cum comitibus suis* qui errabant preterita nocte in siluaᵃ.' Tunc *sancta cum suis* festinauit, et inuenerunt hospites in siluaᵃ sedentes. *Et scientes quod Deus fecit miraculum in eis propter sanctam Brigidam et narrantes que fuerunt gesta erga se, quasi nesciret uirgo, glorificantesque Deum* cum ingenti letitia illi uenerunt cum *sancta Dei* ad *monasterium* suum. *Ideo iam sancta Brigida ad eos in siluamᵇ exiuit quia sciebat quod illi putabant se esse in monasterio suo.*

   Manensqueᶜ ibi per aliquot dies episcopus Broon, reuersus est *cum suis* ad regionem suam, et *donauit ei* sancta Brigida uasculum chrismatis *quod pro magno munere episcopus accepit ab ea. Sancta enim Dei suas magnas res peregrinis et pauperibus Christi donabat.*

60   Quodam quoque die ipse episcopus transiens per littus maris, *frater* qui habebat illud uasculum *oblitus est* in littore et recordans uenit *et indicauit episcopo* flens. Cui ait sanctus episcopus: 'Noli flere, *frater*, quia credo quod donauit nobis beatissima Brigida non poterit *diabolus perdere*.' Sed mare ad plenitudinem ante suam uenerat. *Rediens autem frater*, non mutatum fluctibus maris, crescente et decrescente mari, *a quo ibi dimissum est*, et ibi *uiatoribus transeuntibus*, uasculum inuenit *et gratias Deo egit. Et cum ostenderat sancto episcopo, similiter ipse Deo et beate Brigide gratias retulit.*

61   Quodam¹⁷² die cum *gloriosa* Brigida *paullulum a monasterio* in campo *Liffii ad orientem plagam esset*, quidam iuuenis scholasticus *per propinquam uiam uenit et uidens ille sanctam Brigidam eleuauit uesti-*

ᵉ⁻ᵉ *om.* C   59 ᵃ sylva C   ᵇ sylvam C   ᶜ *new chapter here* B

¹⁷² Here V¹ §78 has been transposed out of a sequence of miracles set in Mag Cliach into a run of stories apparently set at a time when Brigit was at home in Leinster. It now comes at the end of this run, but where V¹ would continue (§§87–97) with miracles elsewhere, these have already been fitted in the narrative earlier in V⁴. The story of Ninnid, therefore, now occupies a bridge position as V⁴ returns to the order of V¹.

menta et cepit ᵃ*uelociter et scurriliter*ᵃ *currere. Et ait sancta Brigida uni de uirginibus suis: 'Voca illum ad me.' Et uix ille declinauit ad eam; cumque ueniret ille,* ait ei sancta mater: 'Quo tu curris tam cito?' Ille respondit dicens: '*Hodie oportet me intrare* regnum Dei *et* ad illud curro.' Ait *sancta*: 'Utinam mererer currere tecum *hodie* ad regnum Dei! Ora pro me, *frater*, ut perueniam ad regnum Dei.' Respondit scholasticus: 'Et tu roga Deum, *sancta*, ut cursus meus *sit assiduus in regnum Dei* et ego pro te uicissim rogabo ut tu et plurimi tecum ad regnum Dei uadant.' Et tunc orante sancta Brigida pro eo *repletus est ipse gratia spiritus sancti et conuersus* egit penitentiam et factus est religiosissimus uir usque ad mortem suam, *qui uocabatur Ninnidius filius Eathach*ᵇ*, de partibus Muli, et inter maiores sanctos Hibernie nominatur.*¹⁷³

*Cui ait sancta Brigida: 'In die obitus mei de manu tua communionem corporis et sanguinis Domini nostri Iesu Christi accipiam.' Et ait sanctus Ninnidius: 'Utinam tu uiueres donec de manu mea eucharistiam acciperes!' Ideo iam dixit*ᵃ *hoc uolens ipse diu peregrinari et non uidere iterum sanctam Dei ut ipsa maneret ad finem mundi. Sed sancta affirmauit quod foret uere et acciperet ab eo communionem in die obitus sui. Post hec benedicentes se salutaribus dictis et commendantes se inuicem Deo ad sua separatim recesserunt.*

*Sanctus*ᵃ *Ninnidius, uolens ab illa die manum suam mundissimam seruare de qua beatissima Brigida predixit ut in die exitus sui diuinum uiaticum sumeret, fecit circa eam eream arctam manicam cum sera et claui ne illa corpus suum tangeret neque de aliquo immundo tangeretur. Inde agnomen ipse habet; nam* ᵇ*Scotice uocatur*ᵇ *Ninidh Lamghlan*ᶜ*, quod sonat Latine Ninidius manus munde. Deinde sancti seniores contra suam uoluntatem ordinari eum curarunt, ut poterat de eo dici quod sermo diuinus ait: 'Ecce sacerdos magnus'. Deinde transnauigauit ad Britonum regiones, uolens semper Hiberniam deserere, sciens ipse quod uerum esset quod ait sancta Brigida, dicens se non migraturam de hoc seculo donec de manu eius communionem acciperet. Et intrans nauem proiecit clauem manus sue in pelagus ne semper aperiretur. Sed contigit quod dixit scriptura sancta, 'Non est sapientia, non est prudentia, non est consilium contra Deum.' Cum*

61 ᵃ⁻ᵃ velociter Cc   ᵇ Ethac Cc   62 ᵃ ipse dixit C   63 ᵃ *om.* C
ᵇ⁻ᵇ vocatur Scotice B   ᶜ Lamghlan B Lamglan C

¹⁷³ See below, p. 211.

enim dies remunerationis sanctissime uirginis Brigide post multum tempus
appropinquaret, nauigans tunc sanctus Ninnidius in Britannico mari, nutu
Dei, uis uentorum ad Hibernicas partes eum compulit, et collatus est ei
piscis magnus, et inuenta est in eo cum esset partitus[d] *clauis sere manus*
sancti Ninnidi[e]. *Et beatus Ninnidius hec omnia uidens de predestinatione*[f]
diuina euenisse, compunctus corde[g], *ait: 'Non oportet me* [h]*mortalem am-*
plius[h] *esse contra Dei uiuentis et omnipotentis nutum.' Et audiens ipse*
beatam Brigidam infirmam esse, adiuit eam, et in hora dormitionis sue
corpus et sanguinem Domini nostri Iesu Christi Filii Dei uiui, de mundis-
sima sancti Ninnidi[i] *manu, sicut ipsa prophetice predixit, accepit. Reliqua*
autem [j]*series uite sancti Ninnidi*[j] *et miracula que Dei gratia per eum egit in*
uita sua habentur.

64   Alio[174] tempore quidam homo qui habitabat in orientali plaga
campi Liffii qui erat uir bonus et largus uenit ad beatam Brigidam
et dixit ad eam: 'Veniant mecum *nuntii*[a] tui, *domina*, et afferant
uobis aliquantos modios *frumenti*.'[175] Cumque rediissent[b] ab eo
cum oneribus, inuenerunt amnem Liffii ultra ripas *lue*[176] plenum,
et non potuerunt transire aquis tumescentibus; *pons enim uel nauis*
non erat prope in locis illis. Vadum nimirum[c] *illius amnis, cum non sit*
lues, transeunt homines et[d] *animalia.*[177] Tunc *sederunt* super ripam
inuocantes beatam Brigidam sibi in auxilium. Continuoque
omnes simul trans amnem in alteram ripam cum omnibus suis
Dei potestas gratia sancte Brigide conduxit. Quomodo aut qualiter
translati essent ignorabant. Deinde uenientes ad sanctam Brigidam, narrauerunt ei miraculum quod factum est in eis. Beata

---

[d] partibus b   [e] Ninnidii B   [f] praedemonstratione B   [g] corne b
[h-h] amplius mortalem B   [i] Ninnidii B   [j-j] series vitae S. Ninnidii B] senis vitae
S. Ninnidi C *? l.* uite sancti   **64** [a] nuncii C   [b] redissent B   [c] enim C
[d] ei b

---

[174] After the rearrangements in the sequence of V¹, we have now reached §98
again, picking up after the first sentence, which has already been incorporated
above at II 3.

[175] V⁴ 'frumenti' I take to represent V¹β 'farine'; V¹α appears not to specify the
commodity.

[176] Cf. *ColE.* S §29 'Inundatione fluminum facta, periclitabatur cella ipsorum',
becoming in **D** §21, 'hyemali tempore facta inundacione pluuiali, periclitabatur
cella ab aquis. Monachi uero timentes impetum luei fluminum . . .'.

[177] A detail from V⁴, probably to tidy up the open-endedness of V¹, which does
not make it clear how they had intended to cross, by ford, bridge, or boat.

autem precepit eis ut nemini diceret, ^esed tamen celari non potuit *quia ante alii audiuerunt*^e.[178]

5 Quodam die *una de uirginibus que dicebatur* alumna sancte^a Brigide, Darlughdacha^b nomine, non bene custodiens oculos suos, uidit *aliquem militem* et *in amore eius capta est*, et ipse similiter amauit eam. Quadam nocte, *manente sancta Brigida in quodam uico in plebe, erat inter ceteras cum ea illa uirgo Darlughdacha*^b, *et ille miles ad eandem domum in qua sancta Brigida cum suis erat uenit. Et iacebant in uno stratu*^c *separatim beata Brigida et uirgo Darlughdacha*^b, *et fecerunt inter se conuentionem miles et uirgo Darlughdacha*^d.[179] Cum ergo paullisper sancta Brigida dormiret, surrexit illa uirgo *ire ad conuentionem suam*. Et procedens de lecto, irruit in eam mira perturbatio^e cogitationum, et magnum et inenarrabile^f certamen habebat in corde inter amorem et timorem; timebat enim Deum et *nutricem*[180] sanctam Brigidam et uehementissimo igne amoris uiri urebatur. *Et conuersa ad se*, orabat Dominum ut adiuuaret eam in magna angustia. Et inspirans in ea gratia Dei, impleuit duos ficones suos uiuis carbonibus ignis et intinxit duos pedes suos in eos. Et sic factum est ut ignis ignem extingueret et dolor dolorem uinceret; atque ita in suum lectulum *pedibus combustis* reuersa est.

Hec autem *euigilans* beata Brigida uidit sed tamen tacuit ut puella tentatione probaretur. Crastina autem die beata puella suum peccatum confessa est. Cui sancta mater Brigida ait: '*Ego uidi, filia, certamen tuum, sed* quia uiriliter dimicasti et pedes tuos in presenti combussisti, ignis carnalis iterum non tentabit te, et ignis in futuro gehenne non ^ate tanget^a.' Deinde *accipiens* beata Brigida beate uirginis pedes combustos *et signans eos signo sancte crucis*, sanauit

---

e–e *om.* B   65 ^a beate C   ^b Darlughacha C   ^c statu CB   ^d Darlu-
chacha C   ^e turbatio C   ^f inexecrabile C   66 ^{a–a} tanget te B

[178] Again V¹ is ambiguous. Did 'sed tamen celari non potuit' mean that it was already too late to conceal the miracle, or might it perhaps have meant the nuns could not keep a secret? V⁴ leaves no doubt.

[179] As told in V¹ §99, Darlugdacha brought the man into the house; V⁴ prefers simply to say that he came in, perhaps implying that the proximity of temptation was not deliberate. The reference to a *conuentio*, however, anticipates Darlugdacha's action, and implies some forward planning.

[180] Darlugdacha was Brigit's *alumna*; the corollary therefore is that Brigit was her *nutrix*.

eos ita ut nec uestigium quidem combustionis appareret in eis *et quasi ignis non tetigisset eos*.

67 Quodam[a] die beata Brigida messores suos in messem misit. Sed *incipiente hora tertia* per totam prouinciam *pluuia densa apparuit et inde* tota die effluxit, et cum omnes messores totius regionis illius illa[b] die pluuiali prohibiti essent, *sola messis beatissime Brigide sine intermissione* et sine ulla[c] umbra caliginis tota die, potestate Dei, *agente gratia sancte uirginis* cum serenitate incessabiliter *metebatur*.

68 Alio[181] die *quidam episcopus cum turba multa comitum uisitauit sanctam Brigidam, et uolens beata uirgo reficere eum, non habebat in promptu quod uolebat illi ministrare. Sed multiplex Dei uirtus uolens adiuuare eam donauit ei repente unde omnes sufficienter reficeret.*

69 *Similiter duobus aliis episcopis ad sanctam Dei non simul aduenientibus refectio inuenta est.*

70 *Quamdam uaccam iam habebat sancta uirgo que ualde incredibiliter copiam lactis dabat.* Hoc sciens quidam *auarus*[a] rogauit sanctam Dei *illam proximo sibi dari. Et donauit ei caritatiua*[b] mater illam uaccam. Sed *priusquam ad suam possessionem duxit*, similis aliis uaccis effecta est. *Deinde quidam homo donauit aliam uaccam sancte Brigide que in copia lactis Dei dono* talis facta est qualis supradicta fuerat.

71 Alio quoque die uenit[a] quedam mulier ad sanctam Brigidam, dicens: '*Domina*, de hoc filio meo quid faciam? Nam pene abortiuus est et cecus a natiuitate, habens tabulatam faciem; et ideo pater eius uolebat occidere eum [b]ne uiuat[b]. Tunc beata Brigida mulieris miserta iussit faciem pueruli in aqua propinqua lauari, et statim

---

67 [a] *Quadam* B   [b] ita B   [c] *om.* B   70[a] Q[w] f. 130[r]   [b] charitativa C
71 [a] venit *post* mulier B   [b-b] *om.* B

---

[181] In V[1] §101, the story was that three bishops visited Brigit, when she had nothing with which to feed them. The deficiency was supplied by the miracle of the triple milking. Perhaps V[4] could not believe that the bishops would be fed on milk or butter, and therefore divided one story into these three very brief stories, II 68–70. The triple milking in II 70 is reduced to no more than an incredible abundance.

factus est sanus, *Domino donante salutem propter sanctam Brigidam.*
Ille uocabatur Crimthannus[c], *qui uixit multum tempus.*[182]

2   *Dum esset quodam die sancta Brigida foris in ericeto*[183] *iuxta gregem*
ouium monasterii sui, quidam *iocularis homo* sciens eam miseri-
cordissimam esse in pauperes, causa ludi et ioculari aliorum *sua-*
sione,[184] uenit in forma pauperis ad eam et ueruecem *pro caritate*[a]
postulauit. Et sancta Dei iussit ueruecem illi dari. Et ipse *eodem*[b] *die*
mutato habitu[185] septem uicibus uenit[c] et septem uerueces in
nomine Domini *a sancta* postulans per astutiam[d] in forma
pauperis, ut uoluit, impetrauit. Sed facto uespere certus numerus
gregis inuentus est, additis septem ueruecibus a Deo *abscondite*
innocenti[e] gregi, *quia quamuis non pauperes primos uerueces tulerunt,*
tamen in Christi caritate[f] *quasi mendico donati sunt.*[186]

3   *Quodam*[a] *die quidam* leprosi *sitientes de uia* ceruisiam[b] *anxie* a beata
Brigida postulauerunt. *Christi autem ancilla,* uidens quia *tunc illico*
non poterat inuenire ceruisiam[b], aquam ad balneum portatam
benedixit, et in optimam ceruisiam conuersa est a Deo et abun-
danter sitientibus *propinata est.*

---

[c] Q[w] f. 130[v]   72 [a] charitate C   [b] eadem B   [c] nenit b   [d] asturiam b
[e] *ita* CB] in nocte V¹(A); *other MSS read* innocenti *or omit*   [f] charitate C
73 [a] Quadam C   [b] cerevisiam B

[182] The child's name in V¹ is Cretanus.

[183] This word, *ericetum,* 'a place where heather grows, heath' < *erica,* is
extremely rare.

[184] V¹ §103 reads 'causa ludi et ioculari uerbo aliorum postulauit ab eo
berbicem de grege in forma pauperis ueniens'. But how is one to construe
'aliorum'? V⁴ has tried to complete the sense.

[185] The man had assumed the role of beggar, and this is regarded as *astutia* in
V¹; the redactor obviously thought that a change of garments would be needed,
especially if the trick were to work seven times.

[186] As told in V¹ the story is more complicated: at the end of the day, the flock
was counted and 'certus numerus inuentus est', i.e. there was no deficiency,
though seven sheep had been given away. Then, 'item additis berbicibus .uii.
gregi in nocte [v.l. innocente] qua causa erat ludi, nihil superfluum erat', which I
take to mean that by night the trickster returned the seven sheep to the flock but
miraculously by morning the number of sheep was still unchanged. V⁴ seems to
have missed the point, perhaps misled by the false reading 'innocente' or
'innocenti'.

74   Alio[187] die cum aper ferox *multis canibus et uenatoribus* fugatus esset,
     ad gregem porcorum felicissime *uirginis lassus* uenit, quem sancta
     inter suos sues cernens *precepit ei manere domitus cum eis*. Ac deinde
     ferus in grege porcorum sancte Dei impauidus et familiaris
     permansit, quia bruta animalia et bestie sermonibus et uoluntati
     eius obediebant, et subiecta *ac*[188] placida sibi seruitute famula-
     bantur.

75   Quodam tempore *gloriosa Christi sponsa* Brigida uirum *ferocissimum
     et* fortissimum nomine Luguidum a nimia estione curauit, quem
     asserunt in uno prandio bouem manducasse et porcum cum pane
     sufficienti et potu. Quanto enim uirtute eminebat, tanto estione
     precellebat. Hunc ergo similem ceteris hominibus estione *gratia
     Dei per sanctam Brigidam* effecit, nulla uirtute priuatum.

76   *Vir quidam* cum sua uxore quadam nocte in uno hospitio cum
     sancta Brigida pernoctabat, et ille rogauit sanctam Dei ut signaret
     sancto signo uuluam uxoris sue, *que non habuit filium*, ut filium
     haberet. Et *beata uirgo* signo Dei benedexit uuluam illius[a] femine.
     In illa iam nocte uir ille cum sua uxore dormiens, conceptus est
     sanctus precipuus.[189] In illa nocte lunulam argenteam mulieris
     illius *uiri* quedam ancilla furata est, *et hoc displicuit sancte Brigide,
     timens si illa dixisset quod a suis esset decepta*. Et in crastino ancilla fugit,
     et multi secuti[b] sunt eam, *et non potens euadere*, lunulam illam in

     76 [a] istius B   [b] sequti C

     ---

     [187] Here V[4] II 74–8 has rearranged the order of V[1] §§107–12, to no apparent
     purpose, and §§105–6 have been omitted entirely. The story of V[1] §105, of a
     woman who, having taken a vow of virginity, lapsed and became pregnant but
     whose pregnancy miraculously vanished, was perhaps considered unedifying.
     (The equivalent story in Cogitosus's *Vita S. Brigitae*, c. 9, is omitted by some
     copies.) Cf. *Aed.* S §15, *Cain.* S §56, both of which are omitted by **D**. The same
     miracle is allowed to remain in *CiS.* **D** §8, though there are there extenuating
     circumstances, and more surprisingly in *Ita* §16. There is, however, no apparent
     reason for the omission of §106; perhaps the redactor merely felt that some of
     these very brief stories could be dispensed with.

     [188] In V[1] §109, the animals, 'domita et subiecta placidā seruitute sibi ut uolebat
     famulabantur'. V[4] has added *ac*, presumably taking 'placida' as neuter plural.

     [189] Cf. V[1] §111, 'inde natus est Etchenus sanctus praecipuus'. The name has
     dropped out. The compiler of Recension C of FitzSimon's *Catalogus*, using V[4],
     made Precipuus the name of a saint; Grosjean, '*Catalogus* de Henri FitzSimon',
     p. 385, no. 593.

amnem proiecit. Sed piscis mire magnitudinis eam statim *deglutiuit*. Piscatores quoque in illa hora piscem illum in rete suo[c] apprehenderunt, et illico ad sanctam Brigidam illum in oblationem portauerunt. Et[d] lunula illa pisce inscisso inuenta est in uentre eius, et iussit sancta dari domine sue. Tunc uir ille cum uxore pregnante gratias egit Deo, *benedicens* sanctam uirginem.

Alio die *erat sancta Brigida ueste candida induta*[190] et uenit quidam *mendicus* petens aliquid carnis ab ea. Et *illico sancta Dei* ad *coquum* exiuit, et ille stulte *crudam* partem carnis in sinu *sancte matris* proiecit, *et portans ipsam in sinu suo mitis* tribuit *mendico*. Sed in *signum caritatis*[a] *uirginis*, uestis *gratia Dei* candida mansit *quasi fuisset sanguine intacta*.

Quodam die beata Brigida in quodam loco frustum carnis posuit, uolens conseruare pauperibus. Sed canis ueniens ad illud sedit nulloque modo tetigit;[191] non enim ausus est canis comedere depositum sancte uirginis sed custos parcens carni et idoneus contra suum solitum morem diuina refrenatus uirtute extitit edomitus.

Alio tempore sancta Brigida quandam uirginem religiosam *uisitauit que uirgo uitam solitariam cum paucis ducebat*,[192] habens unam uaccam cum uitulo. Illa uero uirgo uolens parare cenam beate Brigide *et non potens aliter carnes inuenire*, fecit uitulum uacce sue occidi, et inde parari. Et *cum non essent ligna satis* ad coquendum, ligna tele sue fecit comburi. Audiens hec omnia beata Brigida *illa nocte ad Dominum orauit, et Dominus per orationem eius sua magna potentia* omnia mane renouabat. Vitulus *eiusdem magnitudinis et forme ludens et mugiens* ad matrem suam uenit et ligna tele inuenta sunt integra sicuti ante fuerant.

<hr/>

[c] *om.* B   [d] at C   77   [a] charitatis C

<hr/>

[190] Anticipating the words 'in sinum ipsius proiecit candidae uestis' in V[1] §108, V[4] tells the reader from the start that St Brigit wore white.

[191] In V[1] §107 the bacon (*larda*) is dropped accidentally while Brigit's mind was on heavenly matters, and it fell where the dog used to sit. This version in V[4] is very weak but perhaps arose from a corrupt exemplum: the text of V[1] should read, 'partem grandem lardae cum cane dimisit', but many MSS read 'cum carne', which makes the story impossible to follow.

[192] This addition perhaps suggests that to the redactor of V[4] a religious virgin living in her own home, as in V[1] §113, was unlikely; she is therefore changed into a small group of eremitic nuns.

80 *Venientes aliquando pauperes ad sanctam Brigidam petebant elemosinam,
et Sancta Dei tunc*[a] non aliud habens uestimenta missalia Conlaidi
episcopi *que habebat in custodia* tradidit illis. Veniensque sanctus
episcopus hora sacrificii quesiuit sua uestimenta, dicens: 'Corpus
et sanguinem Christi sine meis uestimentis *conficere non ualeo.*'
Tunc orante *ex corde* beata Brigida *manifestauit Deus ibi suam clemen-
tiam propter caritatem*[b] *sancte uirginis.* *Etenim in eodem loco* simillima
uestimenta *Dei dono* apparuerunt; *que sanctus episcopus accipiens,*
omnes uidentes glorificabant Deum.

81 Alio quoque tempore beata Brigida *missalia indumenta parauit
sancto episcopo Senano, et cum ab inuicem longa uia ualde essent,
manensque tunc iuxta mare sancta Dei,*[193] et dedit illa in scrinio et
iussit scrinium in mare mitti, *confidens in corde quod Deus duceret id ad
sanctum Senanum.* [a]Sanctus Senanus habitabat in quadam insula *in
ostio pelagi posita, freto septa lato, in occidentali plaga Hibernie*[a].[194] *Et
diuina conductione illud scrinium per circuitum Hibernie ad predicte insule
portum ad sanctum episcopum per multa maris spatia nauigabat.* Quo
iam periti naute in magnis nauibus sine maximo labore *nauigare* non
possunt, scrinium *duorum sanctorum* solo Deo gubernante *nauigauit.* Et sanctus pater Senanus quodam die reuelante sibi spiritu
sancto fratribus suis ait: 'Ite quantocius[b] ad mare et quicquid[c]
inuenietis huc uobiscum ducite.' Illi inuenientes ibi scrinium *ad
suum senem duxerunt.* Senanus autem *episcopus enarrans fratribus
donum sancte Brigide esse,* gratulabatur[d] Deo et benedixit *Christi
uirginem.*

82 Sancta iam Brigida massam argenti *donauit beate uirgini Hymne*[a], *sed
non recepit uirgo.*[195] *Hoc uidens sancta mater* proiecit *illam* in quod-

---

80 [a] tum C *post* habens   [b] charitatem C   81   [a-a] = U in occ. plaga Hib.
Q[w] f. 131[r]   [b] quantocyus B   [c] quidquid C   [d] gratulatur B   82   [a] Q[w]
f. 131[v]

[193] As so often, facts relevant to the development of the story are brought
forward in anticipation.

[194] A geographical gloss, characteristic of the redactor.

[195] Again, the order of the story in V[1] §116 has been changed, so that relevant
facts are stated in order. The original runs, 'Alio quoque die sancta Brigita
proiecit massam argenti in flumen ut ueniret per illud ad alium uirginem nomine
Hinna, quae paulo ante respuit eam massam portare; et sic postea Deo deducente
accepit'.

dam flumen et ueniens per flumen massa ad cellam beate uirginis Hymne, sic postea Deo ducente et concedente accepit.

Homo quidam ad occidendum reus perductus est, rege iubente. Moram[a][196] autem iugulationis eius *piissima uirgo* Brigida *faciebat, petens uitam eius. Tunc desuper purum* argentum in sinum *uirginis* a Deo *directum*[b] est, et regi pro *misero ipsa* reddidit. Et sic reus a morte *per sanctam Dei* liberatus est.

Die quoque alia sancta Brigida tunicam *suam unam* diuisit duobus pauperibus et unusquisque dimidium tunice accepit[a], *sed Dei gratia efficiente secundum uelle cordis sancte matris*, illa hora plena tunica apud unumquemque eorum facta est.

In[197] alio die beata Brigida digitis suis petram durissimam perforauit, maximam necessitatem habens, quam nunc tacemus breuitatis causa.

Quidam[198] rex quemdam principem *de ciuitate sua repulit qui fuit amicus beate Brigide. Rogauitque sancta Dei regem pro eo ut concederet ei rex esse in suo principatu, et rex respuit et non audiuit eam. Et ipso die, diuino nutu*, de curru suo rex cecidit et capite colliso mortuus est.

Alio tempore *cum multitudo hospitum conueniret et minimus apparatus esset*, beata Brigida urticam in butyrum et corticem arborum in lardum pinguissimum et dulcissimum commutauit, *Dei gratia cooperante*.

---

83 [a] *ita* CB] mora V¹β *cf.* V¹ in hora autem jugulationis   [b] dejectum B
84 [a] accesit b

---

[196] The redactor has paraphrased around an awkward misreading in V¹β; see above, p. 132.

[197] V¹ §118, one sentence, has been omitted.

[198] V¹ §120 has been entirely omitted, perhaps surprisingly. It tells a virtuous tale of the daughter of a *princeps* avoiding marriage in order to serve God and St Brigit as a nun.

88 Cuidam[199] mago sancta Brigida qui suam hereditatem *Deo obtulit*,[200] obuiare ei[a] in hora mortis sue promisit. Quod ita factum est. Cum scilicet ille magus iacuisset in lecto expectans mortem, dixit familie sue: 'Disponite cito omnia que necessaria sunt, nam sanctam Brigidam in ueste candida cum multis obuiare mihi uideo.' Et tunc demum baptizatus est in Christo et defunctus est credulus in Deo.

89 [a]Quodam tempore[b] sanctissima[c] Brigida et alia sancta[d] *uirgo* nomine Daria colloquentes inuicem de Christo *sed*[e] non senserunt noctem. Ubi enim sol iustitie Christus[f] presens fuit, nihil tenebrosum erat. Sed sancta Daria oculis a natiuitate orbata erat, que ait ad sanctam Brigidam: '*Domina*, benedic oculos meos ut ualeam mundum uidere sicut desidero.' Tunc sancta Brigida[g] oculos eius benedixit et statim aperti sunt, et respexit mundum, et ait sancta Daria *ad beatam*[h] *Brigidam*: '[i]Iterum, *mater*[i], reclude oculos meos; quanto enim mundo absentior[j] fuerit homo, tanto presentior[k] Deo erit.' Et *signans* sancta Brigida oculos eius, reclusi sunt sicut ipsa rogauit.[a]

90 Nocte quadam sancta Brigida sola, Dei adiutorio adiuta, immobile *pene* lignum mire magnitudinis [a]*ex* loco suo[a] transmutauit quod in die plurimi homines mouere non poterant. Angelus enim Domini cum *beata* Brigida *illud lignum* ad locum ad quem sancta uolebat perduxit.

91 Quedam mulier aliquando cum filia muta ad ecclesiam sancte Brigide perrexit, et *ueniens illuc* uocauit ad se quandam uirginem

---

88 [a] *om.* C   **89** [a-a] = U   [b] die CB   [c] beata CB   [d] *om.* CB   [e] sed CB] *om.* U *cf.* V[1]α simul V[1]β   [f] Christus U *cf.* V[1]] Christus *add.* U *om.* CB   [g] *om.* CB   [h] sanctam CB   [i-i] *om.* CB   [j] absentius B   [k] praesentius B
90 [a-a] ex loco suo B] de loco suo C *cf.* V[1]β a loco suo V[1]α *om.*

---

[199] In V[1] §123 there is nothing to connect this *magus* with Brigit's childhood foster-father, nor is any such connexion made here. But above, 17, it is said that he did not give up his pagan beliefs at once, but that he was later baptized 'sicuti audietis', which I take to refer to this story. It is a sign that the redactor had read through his entire text beforehand, and had planned his changes as a whole, not merely changing chapters as he came to them.

[200] Cf. above, II 57 n. 170.

Darlughdacham[a] nomine *cuius supra mentionem fecimus*, dicens ei: 'Dispone, *bona*[b] *uirgo*, ut filia mea sanetur *per sanctam Brigidam*.' Tunc ducens *uirgo* filiam *rogantis secum, statuit eam* ante conspectum beate Brigide *et non indicauit ei quod ita esset muta. Et uidens eam sancta mater, putans quod loquelam habuit*, ait ei: 'Utrum uis, *filia*, permanere *in uirginitate Deo* an nuptiis copulari?' Statimque illa soluta respondit: 'Quodcumque dixeris mihi, *mater*, hoc uolo facere.' Et postea in uirginitate usque ad mortem suam permansit [c]*sub cura sancte Brigide*[c] et eloquens multum erat.

Alia die uidens sancta Brigida anates in quodam amne natantes et aliquando per aera uolantes, accersiuit eas ad se. *Illico*[a] *collecta* multitudine, anates[b] uoci *sanctissime uirginis* obedientes sine ulla formidine *mansuetissime* ad eam uolando uenerunt, quas *pia mater* per aliquantulum temporis nunc manu sua tergebat[c], nunc amplectebatur, deinde eas ad sua redire permisit.

Quodam die rusticus quidam *magna* suffultus[a] *stultitia de uico* ad palatium regis perrexit, et uidit ibi uulpem *familiarem discurrentem*, et putans quod non mansueta neque familiaris esset, uidente multitudine, occidit eam in palatio. Et illa uulpes docta *et astuta* uariis artibus *ludendi* erat et spectaculum *ludificum* regi et suis comitibus prestabat. Tunc ille alligatus est et perductus ad regem. Iussit eum rex *tradi ad carcerem ut in tempore apto* occideretur et uxorem et prolem eius et omnia que habebat in seruitutem regi dari. *Et interpellantibus quibusdam pro eo, rex iratus ait*: 'Nisi uulpes alia in omnibus calliditatibus illius similis restituta fuerit, *ita erit sicut ego dixi*.' Cum autem sancta Brigida hec audiuisset[b] et pro eo misero precibus ad Deum oraret, [c]arripuit uiam[c] ad palatium regis. Et sine mora Dominus eius unam de siluestribus[d] *mansuetam* uulpem ad eam transmisit que *illico* in currum ascendens *mitissima* ad sanctam Brigidam et sub ueste eius se constituens, sobrie in curru cum ea sedebat. Cum uero *sancta Dei* ad regem uenisset, cepit eum precari ut miser improuidus uinculis solueretur ad uitam. Sed rex nolens ait ei quod non dimissurus esset illum nisi uulpem simillimam in omnibus calliditatibus alterius *sancta* pro

---

91 [a] Darlughacham C   [b] *om.* C   [c-c] Q[w] f. 132[r]   92 [a] *om.* B   [b] anatum C   [c] *ita* CB] *cf.* V[1]α tangens V[1]β tergens   93 [a] *om.* B   [b] audisset C [c-c] arripuit currum et ivit C   [d] sylvestribus C

eo restituisset. Tunc *uirgo Dei* uulpem suam protulit in medium, que omnes mores et calliditates alterius agens coram *rege et populo*[e] artibus lusit uariis. Et placatus inde rex dimisit ei reum abire. Sed cum *sancta Dei* ad *cellam* suam properaret, uulpes illa dolosa in turbas callide *se immiscens*, *foras in plateis* ad loca deserta et ad suam speluncam fugit et equitibus et canibus insequentibus se[f] longe incolumis euasit. Et omnes uidentes hec mirati sunt uirtutem Dei per beatam uirginem.

94 Vir *diues aliunde ueniens* ad sanctam Brigidam ait ei: 'Veniant [a]nuntii tui,[201] *domina*, mecum[a] ad uillam meam ut tibi pingues sues perducant.' *Vir ille* longe a *ciuitate* sancte Brigide *habitabat*, spatio itineris *uiantibus* quatuor dierum, *uidelicet in Momonia in terra na nDesi in campo Femhin*.[202] Sed *euntes* [b]*nuntii sancte Dei*[b] cum illo, *suos porcos in primo die inuenerunt incolumes nutu Dei* a lupis *fugatos*. Pro reuerentia enim beate uirginis Brigide per siluas[c] maximas sues illesos a lupis rapacibus *fecit Deus* minari. Et agnoscens uir ille sues[d] proprias esse, miratus est ualde cum omnibus *et*[c] *assignauit eas nuntiis sancte Brigide* dans gloriam Deo. Et sic crastina die illi cum porcis *oblatis* ad sanctam Brigidam ueniunt et narrantes miraculum *auditum*[f] *coram Dei famula sciente* gratias Deo egerunt.

95 Alio quoque die *cum beata uirgo* Brigida cogeretur necessitate et quereret mel, adiutorium Dei postulans, apparuit ei mel in pauimento domus sue *multum purum et dulce*. *Deus enim, quem uirgo semper in corde tenebat, citius audiuit eam. Hoc uirgo Dei uidens pro uiribus suis gratias suo conditori retulit.*

96 Quadam die *gloriosa Christi sponsa* Brigida quoddam flumen in alterum locum *aptiorem* de loco suo, *Deo concedente*, mutauit, et

---

[e] populis B [f] illam B 94 [a-a] mecum nuntii tui, Domina B [b-b] nuntii S. Brigidae B S. Dei C [c] sylvas C [d] suos C [e] *om.* C [f] auditentes C *? l.* inauditum

[201] The reading here is V[1]β, against V[1]α 'ueniant a te comites mecum'; but it is not the reading of the so-called alternative ending as found in the Bollandist edition.

[202] The place-name has been brought forward in V[4] from its position in V[1] §130, where the α text reads 'campo Feae', the β text 'campo Femini'. V[4] has added some geographical explanation.

prima uestigia istius fluminis usque in hodiernum[a] diem omni-bus[b] *sicca* apparent.

Cum iam *beatissima Christi famula* Brigida *senectute uenerabili pre-meretur*, alumna sua *uirgo probata* Darlughdacha[a] quadam die *ait ei: 'Mea mater et domina, ad regnum Dei tecum statim migrare uolo.'* Cui respondit *sancta* mater dicens: *'Non ita fièt*, sed successeris[b] mihi uno anno et *finito eo anno* in die mei obitus morieris, et [c]*sub* una *celebratione* solennitas tua et mea coletur[c].'*

[a]*Hic, fratres carissimi, miraculis et uirtutibus beatissime matris Brigide scribendi uel narrandi terminum ponimus, quia dignum aliquid poni in chartis quotidie nouum semper de ea sola iam inuenissemus. Non enim modo cessant neque cessabunt usque ad finem seculi talia miracula per eam a Deo qualia audistis per eam in uita sua. Per hec autem pauca que scripta sunt lecturi et audituri qui sitis qualis et quanti meriti apud Deum omni-potentem gloriosissima uirgo fuerit scire potestis.*

Ipsa[203] *iam siquidem sciens quod tempus et dies remunerationis sue instabat et prenoscens spiritu prophetico locum resurrectionis sue, constituit suam ciuitatem et monasterium et loca*[a] *que erant sub cura eius per Hiberniam et dicebat suis quod uellet sepulchrum et reliquias patroni sui sancti Patricii archiepiscopi uisitare ante mortem suam. Ipsa autem sciebat se non reuersuram quidem corpore, et* [b]*iter faciens benedicebat totam*[c] *Hiberniam ex omni parte, sicut precepit ei*[d] *sanctus Patricius episcopus moriens, et dicens: 'Per triginta annos beata Brigida post mortem meam benedic Hiber-niam.' Et adueniens*[e] *sanctissima in aquilonalem plagam Hibernie, uide-licet in prouinciam*[f] *Ultorum, Brigida illico doloribus correpta est, et post breue spatium temporis inter multitudinem sanctorum, etatis sue anno lxxx*[g]*, anno uero xxx post obitum sancti Patricii archiepiscopi, regnante in Themoria regnum Hibernie* [h]*Murchiartach mac Erc*[h]*,* [i]*cui successit in regno Tuathal Moelgarbh*[ij]*, primo autem anno regni Iustiniani imperatoris,*

96 [a] hodiernam C   [b] hominibus V[1]α   97 [a] Darluagdacha C   [b] *ita* CB] *cf.* V[1]α successor mea eris *? l.* successor eris   [c-c] Q[w] f. 133[r]
98 [a] *Chaps. 98–100: in* Q *the last § of* V[1] *has been deleted, the* V[1]β *version substituted in the hand of* JB's *amanuensis (?), followed by ch. 98–100 of* V[4], f. 133[r-v].
99 [a] loco b   [b-b] = U   [c] *om.* U   [d] *ita* U] *om.* CBQ   [e] *ita* U] veniens CBQ
[f] provincia U   [g] lxxxi Q   [h-h] Murchiártach MacErc B Murchiarta mac Erc C Moriartus mac Erc Q Murchertach filio Earc U   [i-i] *om.* Q   [j] Maelgarbha U

[203] See below, pp. 210–12.

sedente in sede apostolica papa Hormisda, anno quoque ab incarnatione Domini dxluiii, uisitantibus eam angelis Dei, felicissime obiit. [b] *Et* [k]*sepulta est cum*[l] *gloria et honore in uno sepulchro cum beatissimo* [m]*Patricio archiepiscopo*[m] *secundum uoluntatem eorum in ciuitate posita in regione Ultorum*[n] *prope mare, nomine Dundalethglas,*[o] [p]*que priscis temporibus* [q]*Aras Kealtuir*[q] *filii Cuitheachair*[r] *comitis regis Ultorum*[s] *Conchubhair filii Nessa*[t] *uocabatur.* [kp] *Tamen gratia et honor et sedes sancte Brigide in ciuitate Kildara*[u] *in terra Lageniensium per seculum manet.*

100 *Igitur sanctissima et gloriosissima uirgo* Brigida migrauit de hac *uita Calendis Februarii* post uictoriam *perfectam* inter choros patriarcharum et prophetarum atque apostolorum et martyrum [a]sanctarumque uirginum[a] et inter angelorum et archangelorum[b] agmina ad coronas eternas *regis*[c] celestis in Ierusalem celestem et ad regnum sine fine ubi sibi prestarentur eterna premia a Domino nostro Iesu Christo, qui cum Deo patre et spiritu sancto [d]*uiuit* dominator[d] et regnat Deus per omnia secula seculorum.

[k-k] = U   [l] cum UC] in BQ   [m-m] archiepiscopo Patricio U   [n] Ultonum U   [o] Dun-dà-lethglas C Dun-dale-thglas B Dun dale thglas Q Dun-Leath-glaysse U   [p-p] *om.* Q   [q-q] Aras Kealtuir C Aras Kealtuic B Arascealltair U   [r] Cuitheachyr CB   [s] Ultonum U   [t] Neassa U   [u] Killdaria C Kildara BQ   100 [a-a] sanctorumque C *cf.* V[1]α omniumque sanctorum ac   [b] C *breaks off here*   [c] V[1]α regni   [d] V[1]α dominatur

5.5. *The Redactor of* Vita IV

The great number of points where *Vita IV* shows change from *Vita I* which can be paralleled elsewhere in the **D**-collection adds up to a persuasive case that all the differences between *Vita I* and *Vita IV* can be explained in this way, that is, as the work of the redactor of **D**. But the case is not conclusive. The possibility has been raised that the text on which the redactor of **D** based *Vita IV* might have been an already modified text of *Vita I*.[204] The rhetorical prologue, for example, has no parallel in **D** but was not taken over from *Vita I*. Similarly the synchronisms of II 99 at the end of the Life do not come from *Vita I* and yet have no obvious parallel in **D**.[205]

[204] See above, p. 125.
[205] In the next chapter, I shall suggest that the dossier of St Patrick provides a parallel for the synchronizing of dates with Irish rulers and Roman emperors; see below, pp. 220, 222.

The late Fr. Felim Ó Briain compared the passages with the rhetorical prologue and the synchronistic ending of the Life of St Patrick written about 1185 by the English Cistercian Jocelin of Furness, and guessed that both works were written by Jocelin.[206] The circumstances of Jocelin's visit to Ireland were that John de Courcy brought him to his new Cistercian foundation at Down in south-east Ulster; there the triple grave of St Patrick, St Brigit, and St Columba was discovered, and there Jocelin was commissioned to write his Life of St Patrick. The triple burial is referred to in *Vita IV*, though the discovery and translation of the relics is not.[207] None the less, Ó Briain inferred that de Courcy had commissioned new Lives of all three national patrons, and that *Vita IV* was Jocelin's Life of St Brigit.

Against Ó Briain's suggestion stands the evident fact that *Vita IV* corresponds closely to the language of the other Lives in **D** and shows no trace of the rhetorical style which marks Jocelin's Lives of St Patrick and St Waltheof.[208] It is hard to believe that in re-fashioning *Vita I* Jocelin would not have imposed his own ornamental style, with his passion for *paronomasia*. Admittedly the prologue to *Vita IV* is rhetorical, with its tripartite organization around *amor*, *pudor*, and *timor*, whereas elsewhere in *Vita IV* there is no trace of such cultured embellishment. But here, too, if Jocelin were the writer, and if he wrote to commission, paving the way for

---

[206] F. Ó Briain, 'St Brigid of Ireland', unpublished typescript in the library of the Franciscan House of Studies, Killiney (n.d. [1930s]), pp. 282–3. His suggestion is referred to by L. Bieler, *The Life and Legend of St Patrick* (Dublin, 1949), p. 142 n. 32; id., 'Trias Thaumaturga', in *Father John Colgan, OFM*, ed. T. O Donnell (Dublin, 1959), pp. 41–7 (at p. 47 n. 16); id., 'The Celtic Hagiographer', *Studia Patristica*, 5 (1959), 243–65 (at p. 262); and id., 'Jocelin von Furness als Hagiograph', in *Geschichtsschreibung und geistiges Leben im Mittelalter: Festschrift für Heinz Löwe* (Cologne, 1978), pp. 410–15 (at pp. 410–11). Bieler had himself earlier commented on the possibility that the Life lost from M might have been Jocelin's; *Codices Patriciani Latini* (Dublin, 1942), p. 47 no. 65. He had also suggested that *Vita IV S. Brigitae* ('Animosus') might date from the twelfth century, 'Recent Research in Irish Hagiography', *Studies*, 33 (1946), 538.

[207] *Vita IV* II. 30.

[208] The Life of St Waltheof (*BHL* 8783) was printed in *Acta Sanctorum*, Aug. I (1733), 248–76. This text is inaccurate. Notwithstanding the inexplicable reference in T. D. Hardy, *Descriptive Catalogue of Materials Relating to the History of Great Britain and Ireland* (London, 1862–71), ii. 285, to a Gale manuscript at Trinity College, Cambridge, the only witness to the text is Madrid, Biblioteca del Palacio Real, MS II 2097 (Dunfermline, s. xiii[1]), ff. 47[v]–68[r].

de Courcy's invention and translation of the relics of the national patrons, it is likely that he would have made this clear.

Although Ó Briain's case is untenable, one must none the less enquire also what can be learnt about the redactor of *Vita IV* from those passages which represent significant additions to the text of *Vita I*. These are: the prologue, the genealogical preamble (i 1), the Faughard details of the birth-tale (i 6), the paragraph about Kildare (ii 3), the digression on Iolland mac Dúnlainge (ii 12), the prophecy of the triple burial at Down (ii 30), the story of Ninnid Lámidan (ii 62–3), and the Ulster death-narrative with synchronisms (ii 98–9).

This bald summary is enough to indicate that there is no strong local sympathy showing which might distinguish the interest of *Vita IV* and set it apart from the rest of D. There is some prominent interest in south-east Ulster, but in the case of the birth-tale the essentials were established in the early Lives and what *Vita IV* adds appears to have been taken from the twelfth-century Irish Life.[209] The story of the prophecy that Brigit would make Patrick's shroud is found in *Vita I* and in some of the Lives of St Patrick, but the addition that Brigit travelled to Ulster to die near him is novel.[210] It was presumably prompted by a desire to accommodate the story, twice mentioned by the redactor, of the triple burial of SS. Patrick, Brigit, and Columba at Down. The remains of the three patrons were discovered and translated by Jocelin's Irish patron, John de Courcy, in 1185.[211] Reference to the triple burial can hardly have been made before the grave was discovered. From this, therefore, we may infer a *terminus post quem* for the redaction of *Vita IV*. The *inventio et translatio* were commemorated chiefly, perhaps exclusively, in the churches of the

---

[209] See above, i 4, 6 nn. 38, 44.

[210] *Vita IV S. Patricii* §§91, 96; Jocelin of Furness, §191. At *Vita IV S. Patricii* §93 and Jocelin §192, St Brigit travels to Brega at the time of Patrick's death.

[211] The primary witness to this event is Gerald of Wales who was in Ireland at the time; he gives a brief account in *Topographia Hibernie*, ii 18 (ed. Dimock, pp. 163–4), attributing the principal role to John de Courcy. A sixteenth-century English version, by George Dowdall, of a Life of de Courcy, translated from Latin, in London, BL, MS Add. 4791 (Clarendon MS 44), ff. 41ʳ–61ᵛ, similarly makes de Courcy responsible for the event (f. 57). The story was taken up by several English and Anglo-Irish chroniclers. Ussher, *Whole Works*, vi. 450–5 and 457, mentions Roger of Howden, Ranulph Higden, John Brompton, Henry of Marlborough, and Thomas Case.

English lordship.[212] The redactor, however, shows no Anglo-Norman sympathies, and we may perhaps assume that the supposed triple burial was widely publicized, even if it was not generally given liturgical commemoration.

The reference to the founding of Kildare shows no partisan interest; any biographer of St Brigit might be expected to mention it. The fact that other Lives take it for granted, and that *Vita IV* finds a specific place for it, shows rather that the redactor did not like loose ends. The story of Ninnid Lámidan, set in Uí Labraithi territory on the borders of Leinster and Munster, is no more than an elaboration of a story already found in *Vita I*; most of this fuller version is found in the Middle Irish Life.[213] The details of his metal sleeve and his avoidance of Brigit are peculiar to *Vita IV*. The reference, however, to the Life of St Ninnid, not now known in either Latin or Irish, presumably indicates that the redactor of *Vita IV* was acquainted with the Lives of other saints.

Although the redactor of **D** has clearly imposed his style on these passages, it is hard to be sure whether he was responsible for composing the additions to *Vita I*. The birth-tale, the Kildare passage, and the Ninnid story, are all long enough to show the wording of the redactor of **D**, but their content cannot be shown specifically to conform to his interests. Has he imposed his style on additions by an earlier redactor of *Vita IV*? On a balance of probabilities, I think this is unlikely. Other major additions, such as the genealogical preamble and the digression about Iolland mac Dúnlainge, have exact parallels in other Lives in

---

[212] The celebration of the *inuentio et translatio* appears at 10 June in the *Kalendaria* of liturgical books from the English lordship; W. Hawkes, 'The Liturgy in Dublin, 1200–1500: Manuscript Sources', *Reportorium Novum: Dublin Diocesan Historical Record*, 2 (1958–60), 45, 48, 50, 53. It is also one of the feasts required to be kept in the Constitutions of Archbishop Bicknor; A. Gwynn (ed.), 'Provincial and Diocesan Decrees of the Diocese of Dublin During the Anglo-Norman Period', *Archivium Hibernicum*, 11 (1944), 83. By contrast, it is ignored and even contradicted by the Gaelic annalists. The Four Masters actually record the invention and translation of the three national patrons as happening at Saul in 1293 under the auspices of Archbishop Nicholas Mac Mael Ísu. Saul had otherwise been abandoned for over a century, according to H. J. Lawlor (ed.), *The Rosslyn Missal* (London, 1899), p. xvii and nn. pp. xxii–xxiii n. 2.

[213] Stokes, *Three Middle-Irish Homilies*, p. 76; id., *Lives of Saints*, lines 1554–69. The latter, lines 1759–65, also has a version found much earlier in the *Liber Hymnorum*.

the **D**-collection, and are without doubt the work of the redactor. In the account of St Brigit's death, verbal changes identify the hand of the redactor of **D**, who was, I suggest, also responsible for the synchronisms which arise out of one of his genealogical digressions.[214]

There seems to me insufficient particularity in any of the additions to permit the distinction of two phases of redaction, and I think we must conclude that *Vita IV* is entirely the work of the redactor of **D**, using *Vita I* and his own independent store of information. The supposition that he was responsible only for the last stratum of linguistic changes to a text already revised from *Vita I* cannot easily be maintained. The identifiable additions and alterations made by the redactor of **D** are so extensive and so significant—including the opening and closing of the Life so as to provide an elaborately worked out historical context—that we must regard the major changes as his. The fact that a short addition such as the reference to the triple burial cannot be pinned down and proved to belong to this redactor is not sufficient grounds to conjecture an intermediate hand.

The knowledge which the redactor brought to his task was extensive, but his method of work appears to have been fairly straightforward. Although he knew the Middle Irish Life of St Brigit, he did not attempt to integrate this with *Vita I*. Rather, he kept his copy of *Vita I* in front of him the whole time. Having first read right through it, he decided to reorganize the order of events in Book II, amalgamating her Connacht miracles into one group, before the founding of Kildare, and tidying up the edges of the group of Munster stories. At the same stage, he picked up the cross-references about the conversion of the *magus* and about the *parrochia* in Connacht. He presumably also planned his major additions which for the most part derive from his wide knowledge of Irish genealogies. The additions about Faughard and Ninnid were the only episodes taken over from another version of the Life.

For the rest, he simply revised to his own taste as he worked chapter by chapter through the text. We may here attempt to summarize his editorial habits:

---

[214] Such synchronisms can be paralleled in what I shall show is the **D**-text Life of St Patrick, below, pp. 220, 222.

1. He made an overall attempt to smoothe the chronological narrative.

See nn. 50, 84 90, 93, 164, 172, 174.

2. Story by story, he aimed at a logical tidiness. He made sure that essential elements of the story were spelt out, and not left to be inferred or merely mentioned in an illogical order. He added words to anticipate the development of the narrative. Aspects of a story which he regarded as particularly improbable were done away with, either by omission or revision; apparent contradictions were removed. But sometimes he did not succeed in overlaying his own approach to a story on the original text of *Vita I*, which may show through.

See nn. 33, 36, 41, 51, 53, 60, 63, 73, 82, 85, 87, 105, 107, 113, 117, 121, 125, 133, 190, 195.

3. He had his own ecclesiastical perspective, an awareness of the period of conversion to Christianity, and of the monastic character of the Irish church. The apostolic role of St Patrick in the conversion is implicit, and so is his hierarchical position as *archiepiscopus*—a term anachronistically applied since Ireland had no formal archbishops until the twelfth century—and patron of all Ireland. Widespread use of the word *patronus* reflects the redactor's devotion to the saints of Ireland.

See nn. 35, 52, 64, 65, 72, 99, 116.

4. His interpretation of miraculous events is more pious than that of his source, and he repeatedly attributed the outcome of stories to the grace of God. Often at the end of a chapter he added a sentence to show that witnesses to miracles recognized their significance and glorified the saint.

See nn. 56, 57, 83.

5. Passages of a remotely scandalous nature were likely to be toned down or removed.

See nn. 73, 131, 179, 187.

6. He was familiar with the genealogical and historical learning of his day and regularly added little digressions on such matters. He would also note aspects of Irish customs, as though his

audience might not know such things. But his political perspective did not recognize the plethora of petty kingdoms of the time when *Vita I* was written; hence the change of *rex* to *dux* where it did not apply to a major territorial unit such as a province. He subscribed wholeheartedly to the view that from remote antiquity there was a national monarchy with its seat at Tara.

See nn. 25, 29, 30, 47, 97, 100.

7. He shows an interest in and a knowledge of Irish topography, and a constant desire to share this with his audience.

See nn. 88, 126, 194, 202.

8. The provision of a Latin explanation for many place-names indicates that he was aware of their meaning as Irish words, and presumably that he thought his audience would not know and would be helped by being told.

See n. 28.

9. His vocabulary is quite wide, but his use of it is often determined by habit, such that the same word or phrase may occur again and again.

On some habitual words or phrases noted see nn. 26 (*gloriosus*), 29 (*in maxima fertilitate*), 32, 149 (*dux*), 37 (*prophetice*), 39 (*nutu Dei, nutu diuino*), 43 (*illico*), 49 (*honorifice*), 54 (*quinta pars*), 61 (periphrasis for saint's name), 69 (*patronus*), 70 (*accepta licentia*), 75 (*coram omnibus*), 76 (*tempus loquendi*), 86 (*per circuitum*), 102 (*uere*), 106 (*diuinitus*), 120 (*plaga*), 162 (*cellas et monasteria edificauit*), 170 (*commendare, offerre*). On the avoidance of dated expressions see nn. 58, 68, 77, 79, 110.

10. While in general his revisions lengthen the text considerably, he from time to time omitted whole chapters, in most cases for no discernible reason beyond that of mere economy.

See nn. 197, 198.

All of these features apply to the **D**-collection in general, though there are some Lives in which the hand of the editor is more conspicuous than elsewhere, and some where it is hardly evident at all. They are the main characteristics of the homogeneous style which Plummer remarked on but did not analyse. Our study of *Vita IV S. Brigitae* has established a framework of information about the habits of the redactor which is indispensable when reading other Lives. Having learnt to recognize the signs of his revision, we are in a better position to read the collection as a whole.

6

Applying the Paradigm: St Patrick and St Maedóc

In the previous chapter, I used *Vita IV S. Brigitae* as a paradigm to show how the redactor of **D** worked up an individual text in his own way. The comparison of this text with other Lives in **D** shows that the habits of the redactor are for the most part consistent. Not only does he draw repeatedly on the same subjects or ideas, he uses the same words. His larger additions and alterations reflect his interests, but it is the trivial changes—such as the use of phrases like *nutu diuino*, or words like *honorifice* and *plaga*, which are very widespread—that provide the most convincing proof that the unity of the **D**-collection is the result of a single individual's habits of mind and preferences of style.

We know that he had some familiarity with the genealogical and historical learning of his own time, and his references to a *monasterium canonicorum* at Faughard and to the triple burial at Down both suggest that he lived no earlier than the late twelfth century, and probably after 1185. He applied his learning on a broad scale. Thus information drawn from the origin-legends of the Forthuatha Laigin is worked into several Lives; it dominates in the preamble to both the Life of St Brigit and of St Declán, and reappears also in the Lives of SS. Íte, Ciarán of Saigir, and others.[1] From this we can infer that the redactor of the collection used his knowledge without any very dominant partiality for one saint over another. His collection appears to take a national view.

So far, what we have learnt about his methods, from one text and the comparisons made with it, is not sufficient to allow a systematic account of his interests, his knowledge, or his experience; still less is it possible yet to try and answer the questions when or where the redactor was at work. There is much more to be learnt from a comparison of the **D**-texts with the other texts in **S**

---

[1] See above, p. 140 nn. 25, 27, 29, 30.

and **O**, but until we have examined the other collections in isolation, such comparisons are premature. When we have studied the **O**-collection and more importantly the **S**-collection, there will be a much greater body of information showing up the individual features of **D**. But in order to establish the relationship between the collections, it is necessary first to know as much as possible about each. For **D**, the Life of St Brigit has given us an important insight because our essential comparisons were made against *Vita I*, a text lying outside the three collections. This therefore provides a starting-point, and I should like now to continue by investigating another text whose source lies outside the closed group, though, as with *Vita IV S. Brigitae*, its own connexion with **D** has yet to be demonstrated. In this way, it is hoped both to put to the test our understanding of the editing of that collection, and to extend it in readiness for making comparisons with **O** and **S**.

6.1. *The Life of St Patrick*

The table of contents in **M** shows that **D** began with a Life of St Patrick, now lost from both **M** and **T**. The Life of St Brigit is also lost from both manuscripts, but with the help of Ussher and Recension C of FitzSimon's *Catalogus*, it proved possible to recover the text. It may not be a waste of effort to try and identify among the many Lives of St Patrick one which contains those features that we know to be the habits and style of the redactor of **D**.

Long ago, Ó Briain suggested that **D** contained the Life of St Patrick by Jocelin of Furness, but this was a mere guess.[2] His Life is much too long to have fitted in **M**, where the contents-page proves that the **D**-Life occupied only eleven folios; Jocelin's Life would take nearly fifty folios. Ó Briain thought that Jocelin was responsible for the Life of St Brigit in **D**, and attributed the whole collection to him. But the style of the **D**-redactor is quite unlike that of Jocelin's work. This road leads nowhere, but Ó Briain did not have the awareness we now have of the verbal habits of the redactor.

One could read through all the extant Lives of St Patrick bearing in mind the style of the collection. If the **D**-text survives

---

[2] F. Ó Briain, 'St Brigid of Ireland', unpublished typescript in the library of the Franciscan House of Studies, Killiney (n.d. [1930s]).

anywhere, one should find it, eventually. But one can shorten the search by first considering what Lives of St Patrick were known to those who had access to the **D**-collection. Colgan printed seven Lives of St Patrick. Since he and Ward both held their *Codex Kilkenniensis* in high esteem, we may be sure that if they had a copy of its Life of St Patrick, it would figure prominently in *Trias Thaumaturga*. But I have not found in Colgan any reference to a Life from this source. In Ussher's *Antiquitates*, however, there are frequent quotations from an anonymous Life in three books which he commonly refers to as an *Opus Tripartitum*. Colgan collected most of these quotations in his appendices to the Lives of St Patrick, and Bieler has completed this task, arranging the excerpts in an order according to their place in the narrative of the other Patrician Lives.[3] Bieler was unable to identify among Ussher's sources the text from which these passages came. He was, however, able to determine that Ussher's *Opus Tripartitum* was more closely related to *Vita III S. Patricii* than to any other known text, and in particular to the Continental text-type (Γ) of *Vita III*.[4] Let us compare a passage:

Vita III S. Patricii Γ §80: Fuit quidam homo diues et honorabilis in regionibus aquilonis Hyberniae nomine Daire.	*Opus Tripartitum* fr. 26: Fuit quidam homo diues *multum* et honorabilis *in aquilonali Hibernie plaga*, nomine Dare; *in regione scilicet que modo dicitur Airthir. Gloriosus presul*
Hunc autem rogauit sanctus Patricius ut aliquem locum daret ei, ubi habitaret cum suis, deditque illi Daire locum quendam paruum ubi nunc est Ferta iuxta	Patricius ipsum diuitem rogauit ut aliquem locum daret sibi, ubi habitaret cum suis, deditque ei Dare locum quendam paruum, nomine Fearta, *qui est in orientali plaga ciuitatis*
Ardmacha,	Ardmache, *in quo iacet soror sancti Patricii Lupita, sicut superius diximus,*
et ibi habitauit Patricius.	et ibi habitauit sanctus Patricius *aliquo tempore.*

---

[3] Colgan, *Trias*, pp. 197–8; L. Bieler, *Four Latin Lives of St Patrick* (Scriptores Latini Hiberniae, 8; Dublin, 1971), pp. 235–44.

[4] Bieler, *Four Latin Lives*, pp. 244–5.

It certainly looks as though the author of Ussher's *Opus Tripartitum* had a copy of *Vita III S. Patricii* in front of him, and simply copied or revised *ad libitum*. The phrases 'in aquilonali Hibernie plaga' and 'in orientali plaga ciuitatis' have a familiar ring to them; the redactor of **D** uses *plaga* very frequently, whereas other Hiberno-Latin *uitae* use it hardly at all. 'Gloriosus presul' likewise recalls the style of the redactor, and in two places here the reviser has added a brief topographical identification, another habit of the redactor of **D**. Ussher, of course, owned both M and T, and he was able to use the Life of St Brigit before M was mutilated. Neither he nor Colgan explicitly associated that Life with the *Codex Kilkenniensis*, but there is no doubt that this was their source. I suggest that Ussher made the same use of the Life of St Patrick, and that the fragments of his *Opus Tripartitum* are remnants of that **D**-text.[5]

A comparison of *Vita III S. Patricii* with these fragments will therefore provide another witness to the habits of **D**, independently of the other collections. Here is a second example:

Vita III S. Patricii Γ §38:	*Opus Tripartitum* fr. 19: Unus
. . . sed unus ex illis Erc	ex *iuuenibus regis* Ercus
nomine filius Dego, qui	nomine filius Dego, *uidens sancti*
nunc adoratur in ciuitate	*Patricii uultum, diuino nutu*
Slane, surrexit,	surrexit *ante sanctum, et dedit*
	ei honorifice locum suum ad
	sedendum, contra precepta
	regis et magorum.
et benedixit illum	Et benedixit illum *sanctus*
Patricius et	Patricius *archiepiscopus*, et
uitam aeternam	*sedem coram omnibus*
promisit ei,	promisit ei eternam *in celo.*
	Et *beatus iuuenis Ercus ibi*
et ille credidit Deo.	Deo credidit, *et effectus est*
	uir sanctus et mirabilis;
	cuius uita miraculis fulget.
	Quem ipse Patricius post tempus
	episcopum consecrauit, qui uitam
	felicissimam in sua ciuitate
	Slane *in regione Breg*
	prope fluuium pulcherrimum
	et fertilem Boyn duxit.

[5] I first made this suggestion in M. Lapidge and R. Sharpe, *A Bibliography of Celtic-Latin Literature 400–1200* (Dublin, 1985), p. 124.

One sentence of *Vita III* is thus elaborated to introduce Erc Sláine mac Dego as one of the saintly bishops consecrated by St Patrick. The incidental words reveal the hand of the redactor of **D**: *diuino nutu, honorifice, archiepiscopus, coram omnibus*. The desire to explain everything leads to the clarification of the connexions between St Patrick and St Erc, and between St Erc and his church at Slane, and to the topographical gloss.[6] Further illustration is hardly necessary to establish the point that Ussher's *Opus Tripartitum* bears all the hallmarks of a text edited by the redactor of **D**.

Ussher himself presumably read the Life in M, but it is puzzling that Colgan seems to have had no knowledge of it apart from what he gleaned from Ussher. This must, I suppose, indicate that the Life of St Patrick was not included in the transcript supplied to him by Fr. Francis Matthews, else he would surely have included the entire text in his *Trias Thaumaturga*. One cannot, however, go further and determine whether this means that M had been divided into parts before 1626 or whether Matthews decided that his colleagues in Louvain would have little use for yet another Life of St Patrick. The former possibility seems more likely than the latter, but cannot alter the fact that the whole book was accessible to Ussher, even if it was no longer in one piece.

I add here a concise description of how the fragments of the **D**-text correspond to the narrative of *Vita III S. Patricii*, noting also points which are revealing about the editorial work of the redactor, or about the text-type of his source, the Continental recension (Γ).

Fr. 1 cf. V^3 §1.

Fr. 2 cf. V^3 §12. Ussher himself, *Whole Works*, vi. 379, draws a comparison here between his *Opus Tripartitum* and his two witnesses to the text of V^3, both belonging to the Γ family.

Fr. 3 cf. V^3 §13. This passage is largely the work of the redactor, leading up to 'ductus est ad Hiberniam', where the parallel with §13 begins. The mention of two sisters of the saint appears to be an innovation of the redactor. The synchronisms with Niall Noigiallach and with Roman emperors are comparable with those in his version of the Life of St Brigit. The use of the term *Anglia* for England suggests a date no earlier than the twelfth century. Other possibly significant details are the use of the word *plaga* ('aquilonalem plagam Britanniae') and the reference to the taking of captives as an Irish custom.

---

[6] The comment on the River Boyne may perhaps be compared with those on the River Shannon in the Life of St Brigit, **D** ii 1 and in *CiC*. **D** §28.

Fr. 4 cf. V³ §13. The name 'Miliucc filius Buain' appears in the spelling of Γ.

Fr. 5 cf. V³ §13. The redactor ignores the etymology for the name 'Cothirge' given by V³, that Patrick served four houses, and advances his own. The rejected etymology is found as early as Tírechán ('quia seruiuit iiii domibus magorum') and led to the form of the name Cothirthiacus (*cethir* 'four', *tech* 'house'). On the forms of the name, and its meaning, see A. J. R. Harvey, 'The Significance of *Cothraige*', *Ériu*, 36 (1985), 1–10.

Fr. 6 cf. V³ §21.

Fr. 7 cf. V³ §22. The phrase 'cum honore debito', though not peculiar to **D** (cf. *Ber.* **O** §15, *Bren.* **O** §105), is relatively frequent: *Abb.* **D** §52, *Ba.* **D** §15, *Brig.* **D** I 41, *CiC.* **D** §30, *Cron.* §29, *Mchg.* §35, *Lug.* **D** §52*.

Fr. 8 cf. V³ §22. Ussher notes that the *Opus Tripartitum* differs from Jocelin as to who, Patrick or Martin, withdrew 'ad Tamerensem insulam'. As Bieler, *Four Latin Lives*, p. 238, has noted, the former agrees with V³Γ, the latter follows V³Π.

Fr. 9 cf. V³ §24. A largely rewritten account of Patrick's episcopal consecration while on his way to Rome. The phrase *diuino nutu* occurs. The reference to a *sanctus senior episcopus* is more likely to derive from the frequent use of *senior* or *senex* in **D** than to have any connexion (*pace* Bieler) with the reading in Probus's Life of St Patrick, I 17.

Fr. 10 cf. V³ §§24–5.

Fr. 11 cf. V³ §26, V² §24. After mentioning Celestine's commission to Palladius, here dated to 430, the redactor adds what Bieler calls a 'geographical excursus' on Ireland, including an allusion to the absence of snakes and frogs. This excursus is mostly taken from Bede, *Historia Ecclesiastica*, I 1, though a reference is added to 'miranda loca que uidit sanctus Brendanus in Oceano'. The passage on Palladius's foundations, introduced from V² and expanded, includes two 'Scotice' explanations of Irish place-names and other touches indicative of the redactor.

Fr. 12 cf. V³ §27. A detail peculiar to V³.

Fr. 13 cf. V³ §28. The redactor adds 'Scotice' to the place-name.

Fr. 14 cf. V³ §29. Another detail peculiar to V³.

Fr. 15–16 cf. V³ §31. These two fragments appear to read consecutively. After describing the conversion of Dichu and the founding of Saul, the redactor adds a digression on this church. Patrick is referred to as 'sanctus pontifex'. The spelling *zabulum* for *stabulum* is also used in **D** at *CiC.* §12, *Decl.* §28.

Fr. 17 cf. V³ §36. The word *honorifice* occurs in the redactor's addition.

Fr. 18 cf. V³ §37. The redactor adds to the account of the *Feis Temrach*, 'maxima festiuitas ritu gentili'.

Fr. 19 cf. V³ §38. Discussed above, p. 219.

Fr. 20 cf. V³ §40. The word *diuinitus* identifies the redactor. His use of *comes*, instead of *poeta*, is probably (as Bieler suggested) a guess necessitated by the reading of V³Γ 'postea' where V³Π has 'poeta'.

Fr. 21. Two passages written by the redactor, on the chronology of St Patrick's mission, which have no certain place in relation to V³. There is again an imperial synchronism; Patrick is called 'beatissimus archiepiscopus' twice, and the phrases 'predicando et baptizando' and 'in suis cellis et in monasteriis' are in character for the redactor.

Fr. 22 cf. V³ §§43–4. Patrick is here characteristically called 'gloriosus pontifex'. The words *castellum* and *monasterium* also reflect the usage of the redactor. The term *agon regalis* is used elsewhere by him at *Mol.* D §19, 'in regali agone qui dicitur Ænach Tailtean'.

Fr. 23–4 cf. V³ §58. Two consecutive fragments, showing much elaboration by the redactor. Favourite phrases include 'gloriosus pontifex', 'que est quinta pars Hibernie', 'ad fidem conuertit et baptizauit'. Explanations are given concerning Uí Dúnlainge, Uí Chennselaig, the church of Sleaty and its founder Fiacc.

Fr. 25 cf. V³ §60. An expanded treatment full of characteristic explanations and phrases, 'gloriosus presul', 'plaga', etc.

Fr. 26 cf. V³ §80. Two minor topographical glosses added, including an interesting one on the location of *Fearta* at Armagh. 'Gloriosus presul' again. Textual agreement with V³Γ again. See above, p. 218.

Fr. 27. A digression on Armagh, its primatial position ('omnis archiepiscopatus Hibernie') and its school ('summum studium literale'), perhaps added to §80 or §82; cf. *Mchg.* §4 on Ros Ailithir.

Fr. 28. Probably about §84 of V³. Refers to Patrick's *pallium*.

Fr. 29 cf. V³ §87. Agrees with V³Γ.

Fr. 30, Fr. 31. Unplaceable allusions.

Fr. 32 cf. V³ about §91. Another reference added by the redactor to 'summa ciuitas Patricii Ardmacha'.

Bieler noticed the high incidence of topographical asides, giving the impression that the redactor wrote for non-Irish readers, but he did not connect this with the marked frequency of such references in the D-collection. He inferred a date after the middle of the twelfth century from the mention of a *pallium* in Fr. 28.[7]

---

[7] Bieler, *Four Latin Lives*, p. 245.

As a witness to the work of our redactor, these fragments are reassuring rather than illuminating. They confirm the impression of a redactor who works closely with a single text in front of him, paraphrasing and expanding according to personal inclination. His interests are somewhat antiquarian, and seek to present Irish places, people, and customs to an unfamiliar audience. Seeing, however, they are the work of a redactor who revised many *uitae*, any impression of local enthusiasm for Armagh must be discounted. Bieler thought the description of the Boyne as *pulcherrimus et fertilis* (Fr. 19) voiced 'a feeling of local patriotism', but the Boyne is one of the most significant rivers of Ireland. Perhaps the most surprising and interesting point to emerge is the writer's use of Bede (or something derived from Bede) as his source for a brief description of Ireland in Fr. 11, introduced when Patrick's story shifts across the water.

6.2. *The Life of St Maedóc*

St Maedóc was bishop and patron of Ferns, Co. Wexford, one of the principal churches of south Leinster. He died in 626, according to the Annals of Ulster, and is commemorated on 31 January. All three collections contain a version of his *uita*, and there are two Lives in Irish.[8]

If that were all, the dossier of St Maedóc would present much the same kind of problems as those of other saints represented by our collections. For whatever reason, however, a version of his Latin Life was known in Wales and was included in a collection of the Lives chiefly of Welsh saints, assembled around the end of the twelfth or the beginning of the thirteenth century. This collection survives as London, British Library, MS Cotton Vespasian A. xiv, which is thought to have been put together at Monmouth.[9]

---

[8] The Life from D has been printed by the Bollandists, *Acta Sanctorum*, Jan. II (1643), pp. 1112–20; by Colgan, *Acta*, pp. 208–15; and by Plummer, *Vitae*, ii. 141–63; the S-text by De Smedt and De Backer, *Acta*, cols. 463–88, and by Heist, *Vitae*, pp. 234–47. See C. Plummer (ed. and trans.), *Bethada Náem nÉrenn* (Oxford, 1922), i. 183–9 for the short Life and i. 190–290 for the long Life.

[9] S. Harris, 'The Kalendar of the *Vitae Sanctorum Wallensium*', in *Journal of the Historical Society of the Church in Wales*, 3 (1953), 3–53 (pp. 10–12, 20–1); K. W. Hughes, 'British Museum MS Cotton Vespasian A. xiv ("Vitae Sanctorum Wallensium"): Its Purpose and Provenance', in *Studies in the Early British Church*, ed. N. K. Chadwick (Cambridge, 1958), pp. 183–200.

Written about 1200, this manuscript is older than any of the Irish versions of the Latin Life, and provides an independent witness to the text. Plummer established that the Life of St Maedóc in this manuscript, which he calls V, was closely related to the **D**-text of the Life, and that the redactor of the latter text had used a copy which closely resembled V.[10] The two texts certainly run *pari passu* almost right through the Life, and there are places where the resemblance is so striking that one text has to have been copied from the other. For example:

V § 49 Quidam fur	D § 50 Quidam fur
coronam de peccoribus	coronam de peccoribus
sancti Aidi furatus est,	sancti Moedhog furatus est,
et comedit. Cumque fur ille	et commedit. Cumque fur ille
coram sancto Aido iurare	coram sancto Moedhog iurare
uoluisset quod animal illud	uoluisset quod animal illud
non comedisset,	non *furaretur nec* commedisset
auris corone in labiis	*eum*, auris corone *ex* labiis
illius uisa est. Et omnes	illius uisa est, et omnes
circumstantes deriserunt	circum astantes deriserunt
eum.	eum, *glorificantes Christum*
	in sancto suo. Et ille
	confussus reuersus est.

The peculiar use of *corona* to mean some kind of domestic animal is especially unusual; it seems to have defeated the redactor, who might have been expected to try and interpret the word.[11]

Plummer founded his argument for the dependence of the **D**-version on V, not on this remarkable verbal proximity, but on textual evidence. His proof rested on this passage:

V § 31 Subito autem ex propinquo mari bouem ad se uenire conspiciunt, qui suam uocem exaltans, *tribus uicibus* clamauit, suumque collum in iugum alterius bouis humiliter posuit, et *tribus mensibus* ueris apud illos arauit.

D § 31 Subito, mirabile dictu, de mari bouem conspiciunt uenientem, qui exaltans mugitum *ter* clamauit, suumque collum apcius in iugum alterius bouis humiliter possuit. Et *tribus uicibus* ueris ibi ipse bos arrauit.

---

[10] Plummer, *Vitae*, vol. i, p. lxxv.

[11] The short Irish text has *caora* 'sheep' (§ 36), the long one has *damh* 'ox, stag' (§ 166).

Although the text here reads 'ter', the erroneous reading 'tribus uicibus' for 'tribus mensibus' is evidence that in place of 'ter' 'tribus uicibus' was the reading of the source of **D**. Plummer concluded, therefore, that the source closely resembled V. It could not have been V itself, however, for in § 33 of that text the second of four petitions has been omitted by homoeoteleuton; it is not missing from the **D**-text.[12] One should therefore distinguish between the earlier recension (**V**) and the manuscript V which has preserved it. I would add further that in **V** §8 there is another lacuna in the reading of V:

Statim ista duo ligna ceciderunt in terram, unum ad aquilona⟨l⟩em partem, et aliud ad australem; ut per hoc intellegerent quod unus eorum, id est Molassus, ad aquilonalem ⟨. . .⟩ insulam Boum, Aidus autem ad dexteram, id est in fines Laginensium pergeret.

I presume one should supply words such as 'partem Hibernie, id est ad'. The **D**-text reads:

. . . beatissimus Lasreanus ad aquilonalem plagam Hybernie exiuit, et construxit clarissimum monasterium in stangno hErne, nomine Daim Inis, quod sonat Latine bouis insula. Sanctus autem Moedhog ad australem plagam Hybernie perrexit.

Already, in this brief example, one can recognize that the relationship between the two versions must be that between the redactor of **D** and his source. The use of words like the superlative *beatissimus* and his favourite *plaga*, and the explanation of the place-name in Irish and Latin all show the style of this redactor. The greatest difference, the mention of Devenish as a famous monastery in Lough Erne, is probably a topographical explanation added by the redactor. Our understanding of his method, therefore, is sufficient to explain all the minor differences between the two versions of these passages.

It will be found that this is so for the entire Life. Plummer describes the two versions as 'nearly coincident in matter and arrangement', and considered **V** to have been the earlier recension out of which the **D**-text was developed. He formed this opinion solely on the basis of a comparison of the two versions of the Life of St Maedóc. When this is understood in the light of our knowledge

---

[12] Plummer, *Vitae*, vol. i, p. lxxxvi.

of the redactor of **D**, it is clear that all the changes made between **V** and **D** are explained by his methods.

Continuing now with our comparison between this text and the **D**-text dependent on it, I give two more extensive examples of the redactor's treatment of his source:

V §55 Quidam homo uenit a Roma paraliticus, qui per totum mundum sanitatem sui doloris quesiuit et non inuenit. Cui omnes dicebant: 'Nullus potest te sanare nisi sanctus Aidus in Hibernia.' Cumque uenisset trans mare, inuenit sanctum Aidum mortuum. Set saliua, quam in ore sancti Aidi inuenit, illum sanauit ab omnibus doloribus suis.

D §56 Quidam homo paraliticus erat Rome *qui fuit potens*, et per multa loca sanitatem quesiuit et non inuenit. Cui *quidam uiri sancti* dixerunt: '*Est quidam episcopus sanctus, nomine* Moedhog, in Hybernie insula; *et scimus dono Dei, si peruenires tu ad eum*, ipse prestaret tibi sanitatem. Et non habebis unquam sanitatem donec peruenies ad eum.' Cumque ille ueniret in Hyberniam, inuenit *uirum Dei* Moedhog mortuum *in campulo*. Set ipse paraliticus *confidens in sanctitate famuli Dei* accessit et tetigit corpus. Et *ilico coram omnibus* sanatus est ab omnibus doloribus suis. *Gratias Deo et suo sancto Moedhog agens, sospes et ualidus cum suis nauigauit de Hybernia.*

In every way this recalls the pattern of change from *Vita I S. Brigitae* to *Vita IV*, the work of the **D**-redactor: the fuller phrasing, the favourite words and phrases (*dono Dei, uir Dei, famulus Dei, ilico, coram omnibus*), the omission of *saliua* as perhaps too coarse, and the characteristic coda. But there is otherwise nothing specially significant here.

V §19 Post hec autem sanctus Aidus cum benedictione beati Dauid ad Hiberniam insulam nauigauit, uenitque ad regiones Fothart campi Itha. Et cum appropinquasset ad terram, uidit de mari occisionem quorundam peregrinorum, qui cum barcis in istam regionem uenerunt, et a rege gentis illius occisi sunt. Tunc sanctus Aidus dixit familie sue: 'Cito eamus ut ipsos miseros qui nunc iugulantur adiuuemus.' Percussitque Aidus suum cimbalum de mari. Audiens rex uocem cimbali dixit: 'Ista uox cimbali hominis cum gratia.' Et dimiserunt occidere peregrinos. Cum uero Aidus ad portum uenisset, misit rex unum de suis, nomine Dimma filium Cainre, et sanctum Aidum suis humeris de naui accepit. Statimque rex obtulit ei regionem nomine Brentrocht; ipse quoque dimittens suam regionem cum suo genere sancto Aido optulit in eternum.

D §19 Postea *iussione et* benedictione sancti Dauid *episcopi, magistri sui*, sanctus Moedhog, *acceptis discipulis*, nauigauit ad Hyberniam. Et cum appropinquasset ad litus Hybernie, uidit *latrones rapientes et uulnerantes* *peregrinos.* Dixit sanctus Moedhog suis: 'Eamus propere ad miseros peregrinos qui iugulantur adiuuandos.' Tunc percussit cymbalum de mari. Et audiens *dux latronum* sonum cymbali a longe dixit: 'Hec est uox cimbali hominis Dei, *et ideo pulsat ne nos ageremus tale scelus.*' Et cessauerunt *rapere et uulnerare* peregrinos. *Ille dux latronum uir potens et diues erat, habens opulentos milites sub se.* Cumque uenisset sanctus Moedhog ad portum, *dux* ille *compunctus corde* misit unum *militem*, nomine Dymma, in occursum *uiri Dei*. Et ipse *miles* Dymma accepit sanctum Moedhog in humeris suis de naui. Statimque *dux* ille, *agens penitentiam*, agrum in oblacionem *Deo et sancto Moedhog* obtulit. Et ipse *miles Dymma* se ipsum et suam regionem cum suo genere beato Moedhog in eternum obtulit. *Ipsa loca sunt in australi parte Hybernie que dicitur Cynnselach, et in ipsis locis uir Dei ecclesias fecit edificari.*

Once again, the parallel with the Lives of St Brigit is very close. The redactor has read through the chapter, decided to remove the King of Fothairt Maige Itha from the episode and replaced him not merely with a *dux*, but with a *dux latronum* who might with less prejudice attack pilgrims. Their fate is eased, from death to assault. In order to explain the donation of land, the *dux latronum* has to be made into a 'uir potens et diues'. As he responds to the saint, he is made to do penance.[13] At the end, as often in this collection, we are told that the saint founded churches, this time in Uí Chennselaig, the area of south Leinster where Maedóc's churches were mostly situated.

From external sources, we now have three Lives where it is possible directly to compare the redactor's text with his source and so to observe him at work. It is imprudent, however, to speculate further at this stage as to what manner of scholar the redactor was, or when and where he worked. Once the other collections have been examined, it will be possible more safely to embark on the comparison of the work of the collectors. This will add to the number of Lives where it is possible to see exactly what the redactor of **D** contributed to the texts which passed through his revising hands, and so increase the basis on which to assess his role and to discover the context in which he worked.

---

[13] The cliché *compunctus corde* is perhaps used with disproportionate frequency by the redactor; cf. *Cain.* §44*, *Coem.* §§4, 29, *ColE.* §2*, *Lug.* §30*, *Mun.* §18†, and equivalent phrases, *Abb.* §33, *Car.* §44, *ColE.* §29*. The phrase is used twice in Plummer's Lives from **O**.

7

The Collection in the Codex Salmanticensis

THE *Codex Salmanticensis* is so called from the title on the spine of its seventeenth-century binding. It is explained by a note in the handwriting of the Bollandist, Fr. Daniel Papebroch (1628–1714), written on a loose sheet once pasted at the front of the volume:[1]

Codicem hunc Rector Collegii Salmanticensis Hibernici Societatis Iesu dono dedit nostro Patri Aegidio de Smidt, qui eundem donavit P. Heriberto Rosweydo.

It is not known how the manuscript came from Ireland to Salamanca, where the Irish College was established about 1592.[2] The earliest writer to show any acquaintance with it was David Rothe.[3] It was presumably sent to Rosweyde between 1607 and his death in 1629.[4] According to Grosjean, a leaf from the Life of St Comgall was removed by Rosweyde for the use of Patrick Fleming at Louvain, whose active interest in Irish hagiography (as we have seen) belongs to the period 1623–31.[5] Folio *88 (in the original foliation) went the same way, as a note records: 'Deest fol. 88. Habetur Lo⟨vanii⟩ apud PP. H⟨ibernos⟩'.[6] These leaves are lost.

---

[1] J. Butler, 2nd Marquess of Ormonde, *Vita Sancti Kannechi a Codice in Bibliotheca Burgundia Transcripta*, Kilkenny Archaeological Society extra volume, Kilkenny, 1853), p. v.

[2] Heist, *Vitae*, p. xxix.

[3] See above, p. 66 and n. 107.

[4] Grosjean has suggested that it was sent after 1613; 'Un soldat de fortune irlandais au service des *Acta Sanctorum*: Phillipe O'Sullivan Beare et Jean Bolland (1634)', *AB* 81 (1963), p. 434.

[5] Heist, *Vitae*, p. xxxv, citing oral information from Grosjean. (Fleming, *Collectanea Sacra*, p. 303, refers to a fragment supplied by Rosweyde, but the two sections he quotes from it (S §§ 1, 6, in the margins against his §§ 5, 31) are not from the missing leaf: perhaps Grosjean jumped to an unwarranted conclusion.) The leaf, f. 195 of the original foliation, belonged between f. 191 and f. 192 of the standard numbering. Hereafter, I shall prefix an asterisk to numbers of the original foliation.

[6] Heist, *Vitae*, p. xxxv.

Grosjean also showed that Fleming's text of the *Catalogus Sanctorum Hiberniae secundum diuersa tempora* was derived from *Salmanticensis*.[7]

Other interesting details about the manuscript in the hands of the early Bollandists are noted by Heist.[8] It passed thence into the Burgundian Library in Brussels in 1827, now part of Bibiothèque royale Albert I, where it is MS 7672–7674.[9]

The Bollandists published a number of texts from this volume, and continued to use it into the eighteenth century. The habit of removing leaves for the benefit of the Irish Fathers at Louvain was fortunately given up. Although as late as October 1634 Ward seems not to have been apprised of the full contents of this volume, Colgan must have had a copy of the manuscript as a whole, or at least as much of it as still exists.[10] From it, he published several Lives, most of them unique to this collection, and he refers to it repeatedly in other contexts, though not as often as one might have expected.[11]

In 1853, John Butler, second Marquess of Ormonde, edited the Life of St Cainnech from S for the Kilkenny Archaeological Society.[12] This text was used by Reeves in his own work on the

---

[7] Grosjean, 'Édition et commentaire du *Catalogus Sanctorum Hiberniae*', p. 202.

[8] Heist, *Vitae*, pp. xxxi–xxxviii.

[9] Listed in J. Van den Gheyn, *Catalogue des manuscrits de la Bibliothèque royale de Belgique*, v (Brussels, 1905), pp. 146–7 (catalogue no. 3179).

[10] In corresponding with Bolland about St Ailbe, Ward says that he knew only two Latin Lives, which would have been D and O. It is not clear when Bolland made the whole collection available, nor why he had not done so sooner. See Grosjean, 'Un soldat de fortune irlandais', p. 427.

[11] Colgan printed the Lives of Fintán of Dún Bléisci, *Acta*, pp. 11–12; Cuanna, pp. 250–1; Finnian of Clonard, pp. 393–7; Ciarán of Saigir, pp. 467–9; Mochta, pp. 729–31; Mac Cairthinn, pp. 738–9; and that of St Brigit by Lawrence of Durham, *Trias*, pp. 567–82. He used S and D for the Life of Senán, preferring the text of D, his *Codex Kilkenniensis*. For the Life of St Fintán of Clonenagh, *Acta*, pp. 349–55, he prints D, comparing the versions in S ('iisdem paene verbis') and O ('paulo latinior et stylo recentior'). He might have said the same of the Life of Aed mac Bricc, *Acta*, pp. 418–22, but here he mentions only D and O, ignoring the longer text in S. Single chapters from S are quoted incidentally on many of the minor saints.

[12] *Vita Sancti Kannechi a Codice in Bibliotheca Burgundiana Transcripta*, Kilkenny Archaeological Society extra volume (Kilkenny, 1853). Plummer, *Vitae*, vol. i, p. xliii n. 2, reports the British Museum catalogue in his day as saying that only 25 copies were printed. Later, 'A Tentative Catalogue', p. 238, notes that this was the

Lives of Irish saints, largely unpublished, and he was perhaps the first scholar to realize that here S contained an early and valuable text.[13] Then in 1887 the entire text of the manuscript was published in an edition, executed by Charles De Smedt, the founder of modern 'Bollandisme', and his colleague Joseph De Backer. It was paid for by the noble coal and shipping millionaire, the builder of gothic fantasies at Mountstuart, Cardiff Castle, and Castell Goch, John Patrick Crichton-Stuart, third Marquess of Bute, who had as a young man chosen to become a Roman Catholic; printed at Bruges; and published with varying title-pages by Blackwoods in Edinburgh and Desclée, De Brouwer in Bruges.[14] The learned editors, experts in Latin hagiography, were ignorant of Irish, and seem not to have consulted (as they might have done) their colleague Edmund Hogan.[15] The names in the text are often corruptly treated: Heinrich Zimmer published a frenzied review in 1891,[16] though Plummer more charitably observed, 'still, it is not difficult for an Irish scholar to correct the mistakes of the editors'.[17] In transcribing the Latin, and in correcting their proofs, it is worth noting that De Smedt and De Backer were more accurate than either Plummer in *Vitae Sanctorum Hiberniae*, or W. W. Heist whose edition of S has now generally superseded theirs. Moreover theirs is the only edition of any of the three collections to be based on sound editorial principles: they did not judge the Lives before the basis for judgement had been established, so they printed the collection entire. Zimmer's harsh words should not be allowed to obscure their achievement.

number of copies with red-letter titles. A note in the Bodleian Library copy says that 100 copies (with black titles) were printed 'for the first hundred members who have paid their subscriptions to the Annual Volume . . . for the year 1853'.

[13] See above, p. 76.

[14] *Acta Sanctorum Hiberniae ex Codice Salmanticensi nunc primum integre edita*, opera Caroli De Smedt et Josephi De Backer e Soc. Jesu, hagiographorum Bollandianorum; auctore et sumptus largiente Joanne Patricio marchione Bothae (Edinburgh and London, Bruges and Lille, 1887–8). Cf. Heist, *Vitae*, p. xi n. 1.

[15] Hogan had worked with the Bollandists in the publication of the Patrician texts from the Book of Armagh in *AB* 1 (1882), 531–83; 2 (1883), 35–68, 213–38; and as a two-part separate including the *Liber Angeli* (from *IER*[3] 7 (1886), 846–53), *Documenta de S. Patricio* (Brussels, 1882–9).

[16] Zimmer, *Göttingische gelehrte Anzeigen* (1891), 153–200. The review itself was severely criticized by d'Arbois, *RC* 12 (1891), 393–7.

[17] Plummer, *Vitae*, vpl. i, p. ix n. 3.

7.1. *Description and Contents of the* Codex Salmanticensis

The description of the manuscript by Heist is long but far from complete.[18] We are told much about the foliation of the manuscript, though the table comparing the different systems in the codex itself is too concise to be of practical use, and for reasons not specified Heist found it impractical to reconstruct the original foliation, though this can easily be done.[19] The separability of the gathering containing the Life of St Cuanna is noted, and other implications of the relationship of texts to gatherings are used in argument about the compilation of the collection.[20] But the only information Heist gives as to the collation is that it is generally in twelves.[21]

Heist was entirely correct in realizing that *Salmanticensis* can be divided into a number of parts, and he was also right to interpret this as a legacy of the actual process of compilation. But to appreciate properly the information to be derived in this way, we must set out in full the relationship between the collation of the codex and the texts contained in it. The prevailing messiness in the foliation makes the presentation of this somewhat laborious, so I shall deal with it section by section.

S Brussels, Bibliothèque royale MS 7672–7674, was written in the late fourteenth century by two or three scribes on membrane of varying quality now measuring 330 × 235 mm., but cropped by the seventeenth-century binder. There are now 175 folios, though there were originally about 230. The writing is in two columns, 38–40 lines per column.

i[2] ff. *48–49 = 48–49
Brigit

Two separate leaves pasted together with cuts from a MS of s. xiv and sewn in as bifolium.

ii[10] ff. *50–59 = 50–59
Brigit

Quinion, complete.

---

[18] Heist, *Vitae*, pp. xiii–xvi.
[19] Ibid., pp. xiv–xv. The reason for his following the second (seventeenth-century) foliation seems to be that some numbers of the original foliation have been lost by cropping as well as by the loss of leaves. But it is only by using the original foliation that one can conveniently refer to any portion of the codex, including missing or misbound leaves.
[20] Ibid., pp. xxiii, xli–xlii.
[21] Ibid., p. xv.

iii¹⁴ (14 canc.) ff. *60–72 = 60–72

Brigit	–62d
Fursu	62a–69b
Brendan	69b–

13 leaves. After cancellation, catchword 'erit illud' entered in lower margin, f. 72d.

iv¹² ff. *73–84 = 73–84

Brendan	–77c
Ciarán C.	77c–78c
Catalogus	78c–79a
Darerca	79a–82d
Finnian	83a–

12 leaves. Complete, catchword f. 84d.

v¹² (lacks 4) ff. *85–96 = 85–95

Finnian	–86c
Tigernach	86c–Ø
Columba¹	Ø–88b
Fintán of Dún Blesci	88c–90a
Ailbe	90a–94c
Lugidus¹	94c–

12 leaves, f. *88 sent to Louvain and lost before second (standard) foliation. F. 92 (*93) pasted in with paper tabs. Catchword, f. 95d.

vi¹² ff. *97–108 = 96–108

Lugidus	–99c
Fintán of Clonenagh	99c–103b
Finán	103b–105d
Ruadán	105d–108b
Aed	108b–

12 leaves, complete, catchword f. 108d. The second foliation has f. 99 followed by f. 101, presumably to keep in line with original, still visible; the foliator added catchword to show that there was no lacuna between f. 99 and what he called f. 101 (*101).

vii¹² ff. *109–120 = 109–120 (misbound)

Aed	–*112b (114b)
Cainnech	*112b (114b)–*119c (110c)
Munnu¹	*119c (110c)–

12 leaves, complete, but now bound out of order.

viii¹² ff. *121–132 = 121–132

Munnu¹	–123d
Colmán Élo	123d–129c
Columba of Terryglass	129c–132d

12 leaves, complete.

After the end of the Life of St Columba of Terryglass, the remaining sixteen lines of f. 132d are left blank to the end of the gathering. The new gathering, from f. 133, begins with a different scribe and a slight change in page layout: the space between the columns is reduced from 19 mm. to 14 mm., and the writing is more compressed, 18–20 characters per 50 mm. instead of 15–16 characters.

ix¹² ff. *133–144 = 133–144

Maedóc	133a–137d
Munnu²	137d–140c

12 leaves. The fifth bifolium (137/140) was misbound at some stage

Abbán	140c–	as notes in lower margin show. Now two separate leaves, joined by tab and sewn in correct order. Catchword f. 144d.

x¹² ff. *145–156 = 145–156   12 leaves, complete,

Abbán	–147b	catchword, f. 156d.
Crónán	147b–149a	
Malachias	149a–	

xi¹² (12 canc.) ff. *157–167 = 157–167   11 leaves. 12 canc.

Malachias	–167b
Laurentius	167b

The verso of f. 167 is blank. The last leaf of the gathering, f. *168, was cancelled, though it had already been numbered. The cancellation was presumably later, saving a blank leaf at the end of the section. The compressed writing comes to an end, and the new gathering returns to the less compressed hand.

xii¹² (9 canc.) ff. *169–179 = 168–177   11 leaves. At end of St

Flannán	168a–174d	Flannán, 29 lines of
Catherine	175a–	f. 174d are blank, and the following (? blank) leaf was cancelled.

xiii¹² ff. *180–191 = 178–188*bis*   12 leaves, complete.

Catherine	–186b
Senán	186b–188*bis*

Where the Life of Senán ended, 15 lines down f. *191a (now 188*bis*), the lower half of the leaf and the outer column were left blank at the end of the section. The blank has now been cut away leaving only part of the inner column. In the next section, the number of lines written on the page has changed from 40 to 38.

xiv¹² (lacks 4, 9) ff. *192–203 = 189–198   12 leaves originally, but

Brendan²	189a–191c	f. *195 (sent to Louvain)
Comgall	191c–Ø–192b	and *200 now lost.
Mochutu	192b–194d	
Lasrén of Leighlin	194d–Ø	
Mac Cairthinn	Ø–197a	
Ciarán of Saigir	197a–	

xv¹²⁺² (lacks 8) ff. *204–217 = 199–211 (misbound)   13 leaves, and one (*211)

Ciarán of Saigir	–*204d (199d)	missing; but original
Moling	*204d (199d)–*206a (201)	order much disturbed.
Colmán of Dromore	*206a (201)–*207b (203)	Ff. *216–17 is now a
Coemgen	*207b (203)–*209a (205)	bifolium ff. 202/208 in
Columba²	*209a (205)–Ø–*214d (210)	quire xv¹⁴ (lacks 9).
Baithéne	*214d (210)–*216a (202)	
Molua²	*216a (202)–	

xvi[6] ff. *218–223 = 212–217   6 leaves.

Molua[2]	−*218a (212)
Daig	212a–213d
Mochta	213d–215d
Eogan	215d–217b
Mac Nisse	217b–

xvii[?] ff. *227–? = 218–220   3 leaves. F. 227 (*218)

| Cuana | Ø–*227 (219)–Ø–219 |
| Mochuille | Ø–220–Ø |

joined by tab to f. 220 (*???); f. 219 (*228) now glued between. Text discontinuous.

xviii[?] ff. *224, ??? = 221–222   2 leaves, pasted to tab

| Mac Nisse | −221a |
| Brendan[3] | Ø–222 |

and sewn in. F. 221 (*224) continues from f. 217 (*223) to end. F. 222 part of column only, containing last few sentences.

These last few leaves defy sorting out. But since all of ff. 218–22 have been disjointed and then glued to tabs, and include f. *224, f. *227, it would seem on the face of it that the present separableness of the Life of St Cuanna, regarded by Heist as a booklet, may not in fact reflect the original arrangement.

From the beginning of the volume, it appears that four gatherings are now largely gone; ff. 48–9 may be the remaining vestiges of the original fourth. In what remains, it is apparent that the manuscript could be divided into parts. As far as the eighth gathering, the writing is uniform, though quires ii and iii are irregular in size. Some fifteen lines are left blank at the end of quire viii with no effort to begin the next text. Gatherings ix–xi have a slightly different appearance in the size of handwriting and the ruling of the page. The fact that, at the end of the Life of St Lawrence O'Toole, what remained of f. 167 and the next leaf were left blank suggests that a group was completed: no attempt was made to continue with the next text. Perhaps no more *uitae* were intended, perhaps no more were available, or perhaps quire xii was already begun and the blank leaf removed when the sections were brought together. Quires xii–xiii present a similar case: three *uitae* filling two gatherings, at the end of which there remained most of a leaf unused. The following text begins a new gathering. But there is the extra problem of why the remainder of f. 174 was left blank at the end of the Life of Flannán, and why the next leaf was cancelled in the middle of the quire. The cancellation may have been done because of a serious error in beginning the next text; but this will not explain why no attempt was made to use the remaining 29 lines of f. 174d.[22] From gathering xiv there is again a minor change in the ruling, but there is no further obvious dividing-point. In the case of ff. 218–22, the disjointed state of the bifolia makes it impossible to speculate with any confidence. Quire xviii must obviously have begun with f. *224 (221), which completes the Life of Mac Nisse in one column; the verso is blank and the outer half of the leaf is cut away. Of ff. *225–6 we have nothing, but f. *227 is now f. 218, beginning part way into the Life of St Cuanna. After this leaf, there is a lacuna before the end of the text on f. 219. Folio 220, a fragment of the Life of Mochuille, and f. 222 with the tail end of the Life of a saint called Brendan cannot be related to the rest. But this part of the manuscript is so mutilated that to identify as Heist does separate booklets for the Lives of Cuanna and Mochuille goes beyond the evidence of the collation.[23]

We have noted that gaps were left in several places at the end of gatherings, and even at the end of Lives within gatherings. More surprising are the several gaps in the middle of texts: nearly three lines at the foot of f. 55a in §45 of the Life of St Brigit filled with wavy lines; in the next column, f. 55b, four lines in §46 are treated in this way in the middle and eleven lines at the foot of the column; at f. 58c the last seven lines of the column are filled with coloured wavy lines in §59 of the same text; at f. 60c four lines in the middle of the column are indented and the space filled with wavy lines. Gaps of this kind also occur in the Life of St Maedóc, six lines at the foot of f. 137a, twenty-two lines at the foot of f. 137b.[24] These aberrations are local, and I have no explanation to offer for them.

The merely physical evidence of the codex, curious though it seems, does not lead to any very secure conclusions. One may guess that S is not a copy of an existing manuscript of the same collection, but shows a collection being assembled for the first time. But one cannot tell whether the physical breaks represent progressive stages of the compilation, or whether a group such as quires ix–xi had not been intruded between quires viii and xii. It is

---

[22] Heist, *Vitae*, p. xliii, attributes this to a desire of 'giving the Life of Catherine more prominence, by starting it on a fresh page, than is accorded most of the Lives'.

[23] Ibid., pp. xxiii, xxvii, xli.

[24] Ibid., notes *ad loc*.

possible that different copyists worked concurrently on the different parts. The handwriting shows no major variations, so it
appears that the collection is the product of a single effort of
finding and copying *uitae*, not the work of successive collectors
over many years, and certainly not the result of binding together
small collections which came to hand from different sources.

Fortunately, there is other internal evidence which allows us to
infer rather more about the process of compilation: a number of
colophons indicating that texts had been borrowed by the
compilers.

7.2. *The Compilation of the* Codex Salmanticensis

The most informative of these colophons comes at the end of the
Life of St Cuanna, on the remnant of f. 219:[25]

Bennac⟨h⟩t Cuanna agus noem daroni a cattach fris ar animain inti tuc a
gaedailch ˋi lladin´ in bethusa .i. fratris Iohannis mac Kerñ de Ergallia.

'The blessing of Cuanna and the saints who made their covenant with
him on the soul of the man who translated this Life from Irish (into
Latin), to wit, Brother John mac Tighernáin of Oriel.'

After this a second hand, not significantly later in date, has added
these words:[26]

Anima quoque fratris Dermicii Í Dhunchadha requiescat in pace. Amen.

Although Plummer described these colophons as 'the only scribal
note which throws any light on the history of the MS', he made no
attempt to say what kind of light. Heist, however, derived several
pieces of information: Br. John Mac Tighearnáin who translated
the Life knew both Irish and Latin; he was apparently dead when
the colophon was written, since it calls for blessings on his soul; he

---

[25] S. H. Bindon, ['MSS of Irish Interest in Brussels'], *PRIA* 3 (1845–7), 477–502
(pp. 496–8, with facsimile); De Smedt and De Backer, *Acta*, cols. 937–8;
Plummer, *Vitae*, vol. i, p. xi; Heist, *Vitae*, p. xxii. It was Plummer who noted that
'Mac Kerñ' probably represented phonetically the genitive 'Meic
Thighearn⟨áin⟩', alias Mac Tiernan.

[26] Printed in the same works. Heist, *Vitae*, p. xxiii n. 1, disposes of the interpretation proposed by N. Moore, [review of Plummer, *Vitae*], *EHR* 24 (1911),
562–3, to turn Diarmait Ó Donnchadha (Dermot O'Donohue) into Dermicius o
Theaghlach Dhonnchadha (Dermot of Tallyhunco).

did not himself write the colophon, therefore. He goes on to guess from the second colophon that Diarmait Ó Donnchadha, for whom this prayer is added, was the scribe of the text who had also penned the prayer for the translator. An associate of his, or the compilers themselves, then added the prayer for the deceased scribe.[27]

Combining these inferences with the physical evidence of the codex, Heist inferred further that the few leaves of the Life of St Cuanna, of which only two survive, formed a booklet written by Diarmait Ó Donnchadha and donated to the compilers, who simply bound it in towards the end.[28] The scribe of the surviving leaves of this Life is not the scribe of the adjacent texts, but his handwriting is of the same type. The evidence of script alone, therefore, will not support the inference of a different occasion of writing for this supposed booklet. I suspect that the colophons were what led Heist to this reading of the physical evidence, which seems to me less certain than his interpretation implies. But if one has to weaken the interpretation, one might guess that Ó Donnchadha supplied the text which was copied, with the prayer for the translator, by the compilers. After Ó Donnchadha's death, a second prayer was added in an appropriate place. But it may be said in support of Heist's interpretation that where mention is made elsewhere of texts borrowed from Ó Donnchadha, wording is explicit on this point.

These other references were first discussed by Heist.[29] The first occurs at the foot of f. 58^r: 'Isti quaterniones sunt fratris Derm⟨icii⟩ i Dunch⟨adha⟩'. Heist suggested that this explained the gaps filled in with wavy lines on ff. 55 and 58. He inferred that the compilers possessed a defective copy of Lawrence of Durham's Life of St Brigit, that they left a gap in copying this into S, and that the gap was filled by borrowing a full text from Ó Donnchadha. This does not explain the *three* short gaps, and Heist himself was hesitant about associating text of less than three folios with *isti quaterniones* which means several gatherings. He supposes that Ó Donnchadha's copy may have been a manuscript of much smaller format. But it is surely possible that the marginal note on the recto of f. 58 has nothing to do with the short gap on the verso, and may

---

[27] Heist, *Vitae*, pp. xxii–xxiii.

[28] Ibid., p. xiii; cf. ibid. xliv.

[29] Ibid., pp. xxiii–xxvi.

rather indicate that the whole text of Lawrence's Life of Brigit—
and perhaps more—came from a manuscript lent by Ó Donnchadha.

Another marginal note to the same effect presents some
problems of interpretation. On f. 96ʳ, that is, on the first recto of
quire vi, we read, '3ᵃ qᵃtᵃ Isti fuere accommodati mihi a fratre
Dermicio Ó Dunchade'. Reading the first two words as *tertia*,
quarta, one must wonder to what these refer. Heist took *Isti* in the
masculine as referring to *quaterniones*, but could not establish what
the ordinals referred to. Perhaps the note should be read as 'tres
quaterniones isti . . .'. The gatherings involved in this loan Heist
took to be a small volume of several Lives. Starting with the
reasonable assumption that the loan included the first Life of St
Lugidus or Molua (where the note appears), he attempted to guess
the extent of the loan from physical evidence—suggesting a group
commencing with the first Life of Molua and extending to that of
St Maedóc where there was a part column left blank on f. 137, or
to that of St Columba of Terryglass at the end of quire viii.[30] In this
inference, he came close to being right. But the physical structure
of the codex is not in itself sufficient to decide this point. In
Chapter 10, below, I shall try to define this group on textual and
linguistic evidence.

Meanwhile, we may take it as certain that the compilers—or
perhaps compiler, to judge by the use of *mihi* in the note on
f. 96ʳ—put together the collection in part by borrowing. Diarmait
Ó Donnchadha is mentioned in association with three different
sections, *very* different sections: (i) the Life of St Brigit by Lawrence
of Durham (d. 1154), (ii) the Lives of Molua and others, which (we
shall argue) form a group already collected in one manuscript by
about 800, and (iii) the Life of St Cuanna, translated from Irish
perhaps for the compilers' use. Ó Donnchadha, if he was not a
text-broker, appears to have had a very varied library.

Heist also made deductions about the milieu in which the
compilers worked, and especially about their knowledge or
ignorance of Irish.[31] Certain misspelt Irish names led him to suggest that the compilers did not themselves know Irish and that
they were unfamiliar with Irish names.[32] The evidence is not over-

---

[30] Ibid., p. xxvi (Molua¹–Maedóc); cf. p. xli (Molua¹–Columba of Terryglass).
[31] Ibid., p. xxviii.   [32] Ibid., pp. xix–xxi.

whelming: the spelling *Cluain Sid*, which the corrector altered (on what basis?) to *Cluain Asid*, in § 17 of the Life of St Abbán does not necessarily show that they did not know the name *Cluain Aird* but rather that it was unrecognizable in their exemplar.[33] In the same passage, the corrector's alteration of *Fer Muige* to *Fer Muege* is more serious: the letters *ue* cannot form a diphthong in Irish. Likewise the alteration of *Lochano* to *Lochurano* in the Life of Coemgen, § 2, suggests misinterpretation of the mark of lenition (*h*) as the abbreviation for *ur*. The corrector's familiarity with the Irish language was presumably slight, but the main scribes did not perpetrate the kind of wholesale corruption of names that we find in the edition of De Smedt and De Backer. I suspect that we should allow them some knowledge of Irish, perhaps only passive knowledge. This would suggest that the compiler worked in a religious community *inter Anglos*, in which Irish was not generally used.

None the less, the compiler was able to collaborate with Irish clerics. Br. Diarmait Ó Donnchadha was clearly an Irishman, and so was Br. John Mac Tighearnáin. The latter, so the colophon says, came from *Ergallia*, the ancient territory of *Airgialla* in southern Ulster—conventionally Anglicized as Oriel in the later Middle Ages. This area, roughly what is now Co. Armagh, remained a thoroughly Gaelic area, ruled by the MacMahons, even after the primatial see of Armagh, in their territory, had passed into Anglo-Irish control from 1303. How far from this district the house was in which the compiler worked it is impossible to guess, but the reference to Oriel is likely to mean that it was not here.[34] At the time we are concerned with, the late fourteenth century, many English colonists had adopted Irish speech and ways. If our compiler knew only English or French (besides Latin), we should probably be looking towards one of the towns, where this Gaelicization was not going on.

---

[33] There is reason to think that the S-Life of St Abbán is actually based on the D-text; see below, p. 350. I note that in the corresponding passage to S § 17, the only manuscript of the D-text, M, has *Cluain Aird* at one point and *Cluain Aid* with the *r* added above the line at another. Perhaps *aid* in the exemplar gave rise to *sid* in S.

[34] *Pace* F. Henry and G. L. Marsh-Micheli, 'Manuscripts and Illuminations 1169–1603', in *A New History of Ireland,* ii: *Medieval Ireland*, ed. A. Cosgrove (Oxford, 1987), p. 788: 'It was written in Oirghialla by Brother John MacKern'.

There is a group of Lives from Ulster in S but not in the other collections: the Lives of St Mochta of Louth, St Eogan of Ardstraw, St Mac Nisse of Connor. These immediately precede the Life of St Cuanna and may have been obtained through the link with John Mac Tighearnáin. Otherwise, there is no marked local interest shown in the collection, and Heist rightly regarded it as an essentially national collection.[35]

In considering the contents of the D-collection, I allowed myself some room for speculation as to the original plan of the collection. Heist attempts to take such speculation much further with the *Salmanticensis*. His supposition that the collection began with a Life of St Patrick, now lost, seems very likely.[36] Heist thought forty-seven folios too much for just a Life of St Patrick and the missing portion of Lawrence's Life of Brigit—the prefatory epistle and little more than one column of text.[37] Accordingly, following Kenney, he guessed that there had been a Life of St Columba between those of Patrick and Brigit, so making the collection begin with the three national patrons. This guess is unnecessary: if the twelfth-century Anglo-Latin Life of St Brigit were preceded by Jocelin's Life of St Patrick, this would take up about the right amount of space, and is a less unlikely conjecture than that a Life of St Columba has been lost.[38] The collection does contain a Life of St Columba, related to the O-text, at f. 205a. Some saints are duplicated in S, so this is not a decisive argument. But our study of D leads us to expect Brigit to follow Patrick, with Columba in third place, if at all. So Heist's conjecture is both unlikely and unnecessary.

After Patrick and Brigit come the Life and Miracles of St Fursu, a Continental work about an Irish saint in Francia, and the Life and Voyage of St Brendan. These texts were well known outside Ireland, except for the *uita* in which the *Nauigatio* is incorporated. They might be expected to appeal to an Anglo-Irish compiler. But

---

[35] Heist, *Vitae*, p. xxxviii.

[36] Ibid., pp. xxxix–xl.

[37] All four printed editions of this Life are based on *Salmanticensis* and lack the beginning of the text; the prefatory letter (but not the opening chapter of the Life) has been printed by A. Hoste, 'A Survey of the Unedited Work of Laurence of Durham with an Edition of his Letter to Aelred of Rievaulx', *Sacris Erudiri*, 11 (1960), 249–65.

[38] In MS R of the O-collection, Jocelin's Life occupies pp. 1–92, 46 folios.

thereafter there is certainly no obvious plan. Heist conjectured that the Lives as far as the *Nauigatio* formed one group, borrowed and copied as a unit, and that the Lives from St Ciarán of Clonmacnois to St Ailbe formed a second group.[39] But such groupings need to be supported by more argument than he advanced if they are to be credible. The Lives of SS. Flannán, Catherine of Alexandria, and Senán may form another group, occupying quires xii–xiii.[40] The Life of St Flannán was written at Killaloe by an Irishman who had lived abroad.[41] The Life of St Catherine reflects the Anglo-Norman cult of that saint.[42] The verse Life of Senán—the only text found in all three collections, S, D, and O—appears to be an Anglo-Norman composition.[43] So all three texts in this group are uncharacteristic of Hiberno-Latin hagiography. The Life of St Mochuille, however, was written by the same author as the Life of St Flannán, and one might have expected them to have been found together.[44] But the fragment which survives here of Mochuille's Life is right at the end of the codex.

To speak of planning this collection, if one means more than the ambition to assemble a major repertory of Lives of Irish saints, seems to me misplaced.[45] An assessment of grouping in the

---

[39] Heist, *Vitae*, p. xli.

[40] Ibid., pp. 42–3.

[41] D. Ó Corráin, 'Foreign Connections and Domestic Politics: Killaloe and the Uí Briain in Twelfth-Century Hagiography', in *Ireland in Early Mediaeval Europe*, ed. D. Whitelock *et al.* (Cambridge, 1982), pp. 222–3.

[42] G. J. Hand, *The Church in the English Lordship 1216–1307* (Dublin, 1968), p. 35; A. O. Gwynn, *Anglo-Irish Church Life: Fourteenth and Fifteenth Centuries* (Dublin, 1968), pp. 44–5.

[43] The use of octosyllabic Latin verse sets this text apart from any known Hiberno-Latin composition, and Heist has noted that the author treats Irish diphthongs as two syllables on occasion, something a speaker of Irish would be unlikely to do, even in syllabic verse; Heist, *Vitae*, p. xliii.

[44] Plummer, *Vitae*, vol. i, p. xxii n. 3, regards them as similar in style. Kenney, *The Sources*, p. 467, compared the Life of Mochuille with that of Cuanna, but Heist, *Vitae*, pp. xliv–xlv, rightly challenged this and established certain common features of the Lives of Flannán and Mochuille. Ó Corráin has shown that these are the work of the same author, 'Foreign Connections and Domestic Politics', pp. 219–22.

[45] Cf. Heist, *Vitae*, p. xxxviii: 'It seems to have been intended as essentially a national collection of Lives of saints. The Lives are of many and very different styles, but all the material is hagiographical. The volume is a planned one and in

collection is likely to reflect the manner in which texts were acquired rather than to show the compilers' deliberate arrangement. Groupings cannot be based purely on physical evidence and a general appraisal of the character or form of the various Lives. But the insights afforded both by the physical features of the codex and by the scribal memoranda have shown that texts might be obtained piecemeal or in small groups. It appears from one note that the compilers might have had access to more than one copy of some texts. At f. 147c, §4 of the Life of St Crónán, the text has 'Sanctus Moban' and the corrector has added in the margin '⟨ali⟩us liber habet Mobhi'.[46] Heist argued from this that the compilers were in a position to exercise 'editorial selection' rather than 'completely indiscriminate copying', but this is not a valid inference. The second copy may have become available only after the text was written, or the note may refer to a mention of St Mobí in a another Life or in a quite different source.[47] One can hardly judge without a careful analysis of the correcting hands, a subject on which Heist's edition is somewhat negligent.

The picture which emerges from a study of the work of S is precisely what Heist denies, 'completely indiscriminate copying'. The compilers appear to have copied what came to hand as it came to hand, regardless of whether a text was a developed literary production such as the Life of St Brigit, a homily like the Life of St Fintán of Dún Blésci, a short anecdote such as the story of St Columba at f. 88, a long 'primitive' Life like the Life of St Aed mac Bricc, a brief summary such as the paragraph *De miraculis beati Laurentii Dubliniensis archiepiscopi* at f. 167, or short Lives like those of Eogan or Mac Nisse. More surprisingly, they included two

no sense a miscellany. According to Kenney, the Lives in the codex exhibit no particular plan, the compiler seeming to have copied the different *uitae* as they came to hand. There is perhaps some truth in this view, but it seems an odd way to prepare a volume planned for so definite an aim, and I do not think it is the whole truth.' At pp. xiv–xvi, Heist says: 'Although I have repeatedly spoken of a "plan" of the Codex Salmanticensis, the description that I have given so far may seem rather to justify Kenney's view that none existed.' On pp. xlvi–xlix he attempts (unsuccessfully, to my mind) to demonstrate the plan.

[46] Heist, *Vitae*, p. xxxix, draws attention to this, though in his text, p. 275, he follows Plummer, *Vitae*, ii. 23 n. 8, in giving the form of the main text as 'Molan'. The sister-text in **D**, §S, has the form 'Mobai'.

[47] For example, *FintC.* **S** §3, in the form 'Mobi'.

Lives of several saints, and in three cases—Molua, Munnu, Brendan—the second Life is much briefer than the first, and covers much the same ground. This suggests a catholic taste, preserving whatever was to hand, rather than any editorial selection.

This indiscriminate collecting is one of the most valuable aspects of the S-collection. It is also strikingly apparent that the compiler of S took no trouble to even out or harmonize what he collected. This conservatism allows us to use S as a critical key for understanding the circulation of *uitae* in medieval Ireland and assessing more thoroughly the work of the other collections.

7.3. *The Conservatism of the* Codex Salmanticensis

This conservatism was noted by Plummer:[48]

The lives in S are curiously disparate in character; for whereas some contain extremely primitive, not to say savage elements, others are late and meagre epitomes, while others again show the degenerate verbiage of the professional hagiologist. The primitive character of some of the materials used by the compiler of S is further illustrated by the early form in which many of the Irish names of persons and places appear; and by the retention of Irish words and phrases which the other recensions, as a rule, have obliterated.

Heist's observations are very similar:[49]

Of all the collections, that of the Codex Salmanticensis has on the whole undergone the least editorial revision by the fourteenth-century compilers. Hence, although almost all of the Lives seem to have been composed in the eleventh or twelfth centuries, and thus have eliminated most of such truly primitive details as may have occurred in the materials upon which they were based, the present collection preserves more of whatever primitive material escaped the censorship of these earlier centuries than do the other collections.

In both statements, the factual observations are entirely valid, though Heist's more interpretative formulations ('the Lives seem to have been composed . . .', 'the censorship of these earlier centuries') are without foundation. What both lack is any sense of textual understanding.

---

[48] Plummer, *Vitae*, vol. i, p. xxii.   [49] Heist, *Vitae*, p. xi.

Heist devotes some space to describing the 'primitive' nature of the contents of some Lives in **S**, drawing his examples from the Lives of Aed, Colmán Élo, Cainnech, Ailbe, and Molua (the first Life).[50] Plummer's examples of 'savage elements' or the retention of Irish expressions come from the Lives of Aed, Comgall, Fínán, Ailbe, and Cainnech.[51] With the exception of the Life of St Comgall, whose inclusion in Plummer's group seems to me unjustified,[52] recensions of these saints' Lives exist in all three collections. Plummer's comments on the recensions of individual Lives are evidently based on a comparison of the texts in the three collections, but these comparisons seem always to have been made with the assumption that a comparison of recensions could not be made on the same basis as a textual comparison. Working through his selected texts in alphabetical order, he seems not to have asked whether texts exhibiting similar features of content might have common recensional or textual relationships to the versions in the other collections. Having observed that some Lives in **S** preserve early forms of personal and place-names, he did not ask whether those which do so are consistent in their treatment of names, nor did he try to list which Lives have these early names. Early spellings of names imply a text in written form at an early date. If these forms were found in Lives which also preserved 'primitive' elements in the stories, as one might have expected, this would constitute at least prima-facie evidence for the uncontaminated survival of an early text.

The possibility of finding unrevised Lives of a date substantially earlier than that of the collection as a whole will be investigated in detail in a later chapter. For the moment, I want only to emphasize the extreme disparity in the contents of the collection. Any compiler who will copy side by side texts as varied as those in **S** can have had no inclination to impose on his texts even the slightest editorial veneer of uniformity. In this respect, the compilers of **D** and **S** are about as different as they could be. While the former devoted a good deal of effort to evening out the style and content of his collection, the latter must simply have copied what he had in front of him. If this is really so, it is of the greatest

---

[50] Ibid., pp. xii–xiii.

[51] Plummer, *Vitae*, vol. i, p. xxii nn. 1, 4.

[52] It belongs to a quite different group among the textual sources of the collection; see below, pp. 276–7.

importance, for it enables us to use any text from the S-collection as a fixed point against which to test Lives in the other two collections. But certainty is hard to attain when one is looking for the absence of something.

The evidence of textual comparisons, however, strengthens the inference. The Life of St Brigit by Lawrence of Durham can be compared with the two English copies of this work; all three manuscripts are textually in general agreement, and there is no room to allow for editorial interference in S.[53] The Life of St Mochuille, mutilated at start and finish in S, is otherwise textually in agreement with the three manuscripts of the Austrian Great Legendary which contain the complete Life.[54] The same can be said in reverse of the Life of St Flannán, but the evidence is small: the text is complete in S except for one missing leaf, and nine lines preserved in a twelfth-century Göttweig fragment are in exact agreement with it.[55]

These texts, preserved independently of the three Irish collections, provide an external check on the compiler. Their evidence confirms that his methods were conservative to the extent that he copied his texts as he found them, preserving their textual integrity. Internal comparisons among the three collections reinforce this impression, and it will not seriously anticipate what I have to say in Chapter 9 to mention something which Plummer observed, namely that S and O contain a number of Lives in identical form, not merely within the limits of scribal accuracy but actually exhibiting common errors.[56] This can only result from the faithful preservation of their exemplar by the scribes of S.

Heist's discussion of the conservatism of S focused on the fact that certain texts in S had preserved primitive features of a kind that a later compiler might have been expected to remove. Such

---

[53] The best witness is Oxford, Bodleian Library, MS Laud misc. 668 (? Rievaulx, s. xii²), ff. 106ᵛ–134ᵛ; a second complete text is found in Oxford, Balliol College, MS 226 (s. xiiiᵉˣ), ff. 86ʳ–94ʳ (ends imperfect).

[54] Printed by Poncelet, 'De Magno Legendario Austriaco', *AB* 17 (1893), 135–54, from the copies at Admont, Heiligenkreuz, and Melk.

[55] The leaf is numbered 33 in a collection of miscellaneous fragments, Göttweig, Stiftsbibliothek, XII.1. L. Bieler, 'An Austrian Fragment of a Life of St Patrick', *IER*⁵ 95 (1961), 176–81 (p. 176).

[56] Plummer, 'On Two Collections', pp. 433–4. See at length in Chapter 9, below.

textual evidence as can readily be used shows that the con-servatism of S goes much deeper, and may be better described as textual fidelity to the sources used. The disparity of the texts in the collection, therefore, has to reflect the variety of the sources.

This fact gives *Salmanticensis* its unique importance as a critical key to the collections as a whole, over and above the possibility that it may have preserved some texts of much earlier date. It was feasible to analyse the work of the redactor of D without help from S, but to do the same for the O-collection would be difficult; the contents of the two collections show a great degree of interdepend-ence. Using S, therefore, as a fixed point, we will now examine the O-collection before attempting to work out the relationship between them.

8

Manuscripts of the Oxford Collection

WHAT I shall call the Oxford collection is preserved in two parchment manuscripts in the Bodleian Library, MS Rawlinson B. 485 (R) and MS Rawlinson B. 505 (I).

Plummer has proven beyond reasonable doubt that the latter is a copy of the former. The two manuscripts contained (before the mutilation of R) the same collection of saints' Lives in exactly the same recension, though in a different order.[1] More importantly Plummer noted that the agreement of the two manuscripts extended to 'the most minute peculiarities of reading', which he briefly illustrated in places where S offered a parallel and more accurate text.[2] All this might show only that both were conscientiously copied from the same exemplar, but the decisive argument is this: R uses a large number of capricious contractions, which the scribe of I tried to expand, but frequently his expansions are incorrect. These false expansions prove that I was copied from a text which used peculiar abbreviations—at the meaning of which the copyist had to guess—and all can be explained from R.[3]

Were it not the case that several texts are now missing from R, that manuscript alone would have primary value for the texts of the O collection. Mutilation, however, has meant that seven texts now survive only in I.[4]

Plummer was also able conclusively to prove that I was the manuscript from which were derived those texts edited or used by Colgan from a collection which he variously called the *Codex Insulae Sanctorum*, *Codex Lochriuensis*, *Codex Inisensis*, *Codex Insulae*

---

[1] C. Plummer, 'On Two Collections of Latin Lives of Irish Saints in the Bodleian Library, Rawl. B. 485 and Rawl. B. 505', *ZCP* 5 (1904–5), 429–54 (pp. 430–7).

[2] Ibid., pp. 437–8. He added further examples at *Vitae*, vol. i, p. xvii n. 5.

[3] Plummer, 'On Two Collections', pp. 438–9.

[4] Ibid., p. 432.

Omnium Sanctorum, and most frequently *Codex Insulensis*.[5] The term *Codex Insulensis* has since enjoyed the same conventional status as *Codex Kilkenniensis*. Though better founded than that term, I still prefer to avoid it since it properly applies only to the later manuscript I and does not designate the origin of the collection as a whole. I shall refer to the common materials of R and I as the Oxford collection (**O**) on the basis of the present location of the manuscripts.

This is paradoxically the best studied and the least known of the three medieval collections. Plummer devoted to it much more thorough discussion than to **D** or **S**, and printed nine texts from it.[6] But he edited only those *uitae* peculiar to **O** and ignored those where **O** merely had a text related to ones he preferred to print from **D** or which were already in print from **S**. In so doing he disregarded the interest these texts have for the relationship of the three collections. However, where **O** has a Life parallel to one which he was printing from **D**, its readings were selectively cited in the apparatus criticus of his *Vitae Sanctorum Hiberniae*, so the reader is able to make limited comparisons without recourse to the manuscripts. Plummer's discussion of the 'house style' of the **O** collection is much more informative than his brief remarks on this aspect of **D**.[7] In this way, a much better introduction is available for **O** than for either of the other collections, but very few texts are in print to enable one to appreciate the significance of that discussion.[8]

This state of affairs need not be too greatly deplored, however, for the **O**-collection is certainly the least interesting in its contents.[9] Because of its relationship to the other collections, though, it does

---

[5] Ibid., pp. 448–54; cf. *Vitae*, vol. i, p. xx and nn. 5–8.

[6] Plummer, 'On two collections', *passim*, cf. *Vitae*, vol. i, pp. xv–xxii. The nine Lives are those of SS. Berach, Brendan, Molaisse of Devenish, Énda, Gerald, Fechin, Mochua, Tigernach, and Samthann.

[7] Plummer, 'On Two Collections', pp. 439–43, supplemented by *Vitae*, vol. i, pp. xxii–xxiii.

[8] These are notably the Lives of Finnbarr (ed. R. Caulfield, 1864), Ciarán of Clonmacnoise (ed. R. A. S. Macalister, 1921), Aed mac Bricc (ed. P. Grosjean, 1925), and Comgall (ed. P. Grosjean, 1934).

[9] Grosjean planned to print the collection as a whole, but before his death the task had been handed on to Heist. In 1965, Heist reported that his student Mrs Mary Laurence hoped to edit all the **O**-texts omitted by Plummer; Heist, *Vitae*, p. vii n. 2. So far as I know, no one now contemplates this task.

have considerable importance as a witness to the circulation of copies of Latin saints' Lives in medieval Ireland and to their milieu.

Since Plummer's work, the two manuscripts have generally been regarded as a pair, related not only by textual dependence but by a supposed common history and common provenance. Both manuscripts belonged to Sir James Ware, and came to the Bodleian among other survivors from his library. Before that, Plummer had the testimony of Colgan and of his source, John Goolde, that I had belonged to the priory of Saints' Island in Lough Ree. Both manuscripts contain numerous marginal entries—signatures, obituaries, and the like.[10] Two families, the Dillons of Co. Westmeath and the O'Farrells of Co. Longford, are represented in both. These facts led him into several suppositions. He presumed that I was associated with R, not just at its point of origin but 'during a great part of their subsequent history'.[11] He knew that I was connected with Saints' Island and thought 'it is possible that R[1] [our R] belonged there also'.[12] The two manuscripts have generally been discussed together as though they had no separate history.[13]

Yet it has never been established that R had any connexion with Saints' Island, nor that the two books ever belonged to the same religious house or lay family until they came into the possession of Sir James Ware. In dealing with the history of these manuscripts, therefore, we must guard against falling into these common suppositions.

8.1. *Description and History of the Manuscripts*

I begin with summary descriptions of the two manuscripts:

R   Oxford, Bodleian Library MS Rawlinson B. 485 (Clarendon MS 41) was written in the early fourteenth century by one scribe on

---

[10] See below, pp. 256–8, 259–61.

[11] Plummer, 'On Two Collections', p. 443.

[12] Ibid., p. 444; cf. *Vitae*, vol. i, p. xx, where he says 'it is probable that R[1] belonged there also'.

[13] *Vitae*, vol. i, pp. xv–xxii; C. McNeill, 'Reports on the Rawlinson Collection of Manuscripts', *Analecta Hibernica*, 1 (1930), 12–178 (pp. 139–41); L. Bieler, *Codices Patriciani Latini* (Dublin, 1942), pp. 38–9.

membrane now approx. 230 × 140 mm., in two columns, of about 37 lines. The present binding dates from s. xvii and bears the arms of Sir James Ware on both boards. The MS now contains 160 leaves, though more than forty leaves have been lost. Each leaf bears an original page or folio number (pp. 1–92, ff. 94–234) and a nineteenth-century folio number. The collation of the MS is as follows:

	Old	New
flyleaf (once f. 93), with list of contents, s. xv		f. 1
i¹² pp. 1–24	pp. 1–24	ff. 2–13
ii¹² pp. 25–48 (lacks 1–11)	pp. 47–48	f. 14
iii¹² pp. 49–72	pp. 49–72	ff. 15–26
iv¹⁰ pp. 73–92	pp. 73–92	ff. 27–36
(NOTE: f. 93 now flyleaf)		
v¹⁰ ff. 94–103	ff. 94–103	ff. 37–46
vi¹² ff. 104–125 (lacks 4, 5, 9, 11)	ff. 104–106,	ff. 47–54
(NOTE: f. 120 follows f. 109)	109–121,	
	123, 125	
vii¹² ff. 126–137	ff. 126–137	ff. 55–66
viii¹² ff. 138–149	ff. 138–149	ff. 67–78
ix¹² ff. 150–161	ff. 150–161	ff. 79–90
x¹² ff. 162–173	ff. 162–173	ff. 91–102
xi⁸ ff. 174–181	ff. 174–181	ff. 103–110
xii¹² ff. 182–193	ff. 182–193	ff. 110–122
xiii¹² ff. 194–205	ff. 194–205	ff. 123–134
xiv¹² ff. 206–217	ff. 207–217	ff. 135–145
xv⁶ ff. 218–223	ff. 218–223	ff. 146–151
xvi¹² ff. 224–235 (lacks 6, 7, 11)	ff. 224–228,	
	231–233,	ff. 152–160
	235	

xvii–xviii ? ff. 236–247, 248–259
  (lost)
Most gatherings end with a
  catchword.

The manuscript appears to have been kept without covers, and it began to suffer damage in the fourteenth century. Thanks to a list of contents made in the fifteenth century, it is known what texts were originally in the collection:

]tabula super vitas sanctorum

Sci Patrici archipiscopi et confessoris atque primatis Hybernie
Sci Columbe ab.
[*St Baithéne*]
Sci Furcei ab.   102
[*St Moling*]
Sci Colmani Drumorensis ep.   120
Sci David ep. et conf.   121
Sci Finniani ab. de Cloynard   125
Sci Berachi conf. et ab.   130
Sce Brigide virginis   134
Sci Brandani ab. de Clonferta   144
Sci Kerani ab. de Clonmacnoys   162
Sci Molassi Damynsi   165
Sci Aidi ep. qui dicitur Aed mac Bric   169
Sci Endei ab. de Arann   174
Sci Geraldi ab.   179
Sci Fechini ab.   182
Sci Mochua Ballu   185
Sci Tyernachi ep. et conf.   187
Sci Barri ep. et conf.   190
Sci Munnu qui Fintanus dicitur   193
Sci Laurencii Dubl[in]iensis archiep.   196
Sci Kynneci ab.   [199]
Sci Colmani Ela   [   ]
Sci Columbe de Tyraglas   211
Sci Finani ab.   214
Sci Ruadani ab. de Lochra   217
Sci Fintani Cluana Edneach   220
Sci Samthane virginis de Cluayn Broni   222
Sci Congalli ab.   225
Sci Maedochi ep. de Ferna   227
Sci Flannani ep. et conf.   232
Sci Elvei ep. et conf.   237
Sci Kerani ep. de Saygir   242
Sci Senani ep.   245
Sce Ite virginis   248
Sci Caingini ab.   252
Sci Molua Droma Snecta   254
Sci Boecii ep. et conf.   256

The last leaf of this manuscript was either so badly abraded that it
could not be read or (more likely) it was already detached and lost

when MS Rawlinson B. 505 was copied, for the text there breaks off in mid-sentence.[14] Since this copy was made less than one century later, this negligence is surprising. The table of contents has two omissions: the Life of St Baithéne which comes between St Columba and St Fursu, and the Life of St Moling between St Fursu and St Colmán of Dromore. The former is the result of an oversight, but the latter suggested to Plummer that ff. 107–108 were lost after the copying of I but before the compiling of this contents list.

I   Oxford, Bodleian Library MS Rawlinson B. 505 (Clarendon MS 53), ff. 1–210,[15] was written in the late fourteenth century by one scribe on membrane now 370 × 255 mm.[16] The scribe has given his name as Matthew O'Dwyer in an Irish note at f. 5 and in his prayer appended to the Life of St Fursu at f. 178.[17] Ff. 1–89 are written in a very large, square *textura*, in two columns, 26 lines to the page; ff. 90–210 are written in a normal size, in a less formal hand, two columns, 51 lines per page. The manuscript now contains 211 leaves, including f. 85*bis*; three leaves are lost. The collation is in regular quires of eight leaves, with a catchword at the end of every quire: i⁶ (1–6), ii⁸–xi⁸ (ff. 7–85*bis*), xii⁸ (ff. 86–93; writing changes style at f. 90), xiii⁸–xviii⁸ (ff. 94–141), xix⁸ (lacks 1, 8) (ff. 142–147), xx⁸–xxvi⁸ (ff. 148–203), xxvii⁸ (lacks 8) (ff. 204–210). From f. 90 a second pagination runs from 1 to 245, skipping 36–39, and missing a verso between 227 and 228.

I have replaced Plummer's symbols R[1] and R[2] for the two manuscripts in order to avoid the misleading parallel with his use of S[1] and S[2] for different Lives of the same saint in S.[18]

---

[14]   Plummer, 'On Two Collections', pp. 430 n. 1, 436–7.

[15]   Folios 211–220 are a different manuscript, a fine copy in Irish script of the *Félire Oenguso* but lacking the prologue and epilogue; W. Stokes, *Félire Oengusso: The Martyrology of Oengus the Culdee* (Henry Bradshaw Society, 29; London, 1905), pp. xxi–xxii. It was already associated with the *uitae* when both parts belonged to Cormac Óg Moriarty in the 1610s and 1620s.

[16]   A marginal note of the seventeenth century on f. 47 shows cropping by the binder.

[17]   Printed by Plummer, 'On Two Collections', pp. 446–7. Cf. F. J. Byrne, *1000 Years of Irish Script* (Oxford, 1979), p. 20, who notes that O'Dwyer, a scribe at home in both Irish script and the gothic *textura*, uses the *punctum delens* to represent lenition in writing his name *Mathei ẏ duiḃẏr* (in Gothic script), a practice current from the fourteenth century.

[18]   *Vitae*, vol. i, p. ix, cf. lxxxiii, lxxxv. Plummer's symbols are used by Macalister, Grosjean, and others. J. W. James, *Rhigyfarch's Life of St David*

An unusual feature which the two manuscripts share is the distinction made between the Life of St Patrick and the other Lives in the collection. The Life is that by Jocelin of Furness, which occupies pp. 1–92 of R, ff. 1ʳ–89ᵛ of I.[19] In the first case, R is paginated whereas the rest of the manuscript is foliated; in the second, the script is quite different—an exceptionally large *textura formata*, of the kind one might find in liturgical books, for the Life of St Patrick, after which it reverts to ordinary size and a second pagination begins. In R, the collation of the manuscript would allow Jocelin's Life to be used as a separate booklet, but the continuity of foliation from the end of it suggests that this was not intended. In I, the change of script occurs at the mid-point of the twelfth quire, so that no separate use was possible here.[20]

Various dates appear in the literature for these two manuscripts. Macray in his catalogue of the Rawlinson manuscripts regarded both as having been written at the beginning of the fifteenth century.[21] He later changed his mind, dating R to *c*.1350, I to the early fifteenth century.[22] T. D. Hardy regarded R as fourteenth century and I as fourteenth or fifteenth century.[23] Falconer Madan, at Plummer's request, examined both manuscripts and dated R to the first half of the thirteenth century and I to the first half of the fourteenth century, considerably earlier than had been thought.[24] His view appears to have been accepted on trust by Plummer, McNeill, Grosjean, and others. Bieler, using a facsimile of I, concurred with Madan in dating this manuscript to the first half of the fourteenth century, and so took on trust Madan's date

(Cardiff, 1967), pp. xxvi–xxvii, used I1 and I2 for the two manuscripts (witnessing to his 'Irish' recension); S. Connolly, 'The Authorship and Manuscript Tradition of *Vita I Sanctae Brigitae*', *Manuscripta*, 16 (1972), 67–82 (pp. 78–80) uses O and I.

[19] On this Life, see Bieler, *Codices Patriciani Latini*, pp. 37–41.

[20] *Pace* Byrne, *1000 Years of Irish Script*, p. 20, who regards ff. 90–210 as the second of three originally independent manuscripts now bound together. On the third, see above n. 15.

[21] [W. D. Macray], *Catalogus Codicum Manuscriptorum Bibl. Bodl.*, v. 1 (1862), cols. 705, 723.

[22] So Plummer, *Vitae*, vol. i, p. xxi.

[23] T. D. Hardy, *Descriptive Catalogue of Materials relating to the History of Great Britain and Ireland* (3 vols. in 4; London, 1862), i. 64–5, offers these dates for Jocelin's Life of St Patrick. For the rest of the collection, he gives both manuscripts a fourteenth-century date; pp. 86, 105–6, 125–6, etc.

[24] Plummer, *Vitae*, vol. i, p. xxi.

for R which he had not seen.[25] Kathleen Hughes asked Francis Wormald to express an opinion, and he tended to agree with Macray's revised dating, *c*.1350 for R and *c*.1400 for I.[26] Since then, most writers have followed either this 'late' view or Madan's 'early' view, whether by choice or indifference. Françoise Henry preferred a compromise date for R as late thirteenth century, leaving I as late fourteenth.[27]

The dating of gothic *textura* is established with some confidence for English manuscripts, but the adoption of this hand in Ireland was uneven and variable, and one may suspect that developments in its use came later in Ireland than in England. Henry described both manuscripts as being in an English type of script, and regarded this as an imitation of imported books. This avoids the issue of how closely the development of the gothic *textura* as used in Ireland paralleled that in England, and seems to play down the significance of book-production in this script in Ireland. Commenting on the figure of St Berach in I f. 191ᵛ, she described this as 'a figure of a saint, crosier in hand, under an arcade, which is obviously adapted from an English manuscript'.[28] To portray these books as essentially imitative is to underestimate the adoption of this hand in Ireland. The scribe, Matthew O'Dwyer, was perfectly at home in both the gothic hand and the Irish hand. At the start of some Lives, there is a genealogy entered in Irish script. These genealogies were not necessarily by O'Dwyer, but the space left for them shows they were not added as an afterthought. In this scribal *mélange*, a date on strictly palaeographical grounds must be very uncertain.

F. J. Byrne, in a discussion of these manuscripts, has looked for other criteria. He associates I with Aughuistín Magraidhin, canon of Saints' Island (1350–1405), whose obituary in the Annals of Saints' Island refers to his work on the Lives of saints.[29] This provides a date at the end of the fourteenth century for I. In the

---

[25] Bieler, *Codices Patriciani Latini*, p. 39.

[26] K. Hughes, 'A Manuscript of Sir James Ware: British Museum Additional 4788', *PRIA* 55C (1952–3), 111–16 (p. 116).

[27] F. Henry and G. L. Marsh-Micheli, 'Manuscripts and Illumination, 1169–1603', in *A New History of Ireland*, ii: *Medieval Ireland*, ed. A. Cosgrove (Oxford, 1987), pp. 787–8.

[28] Ibid., p. 788 and plate 26c.

[29] See below, p. 264.

margins of R are notes in Irish which he compared with the hand of a Galway scribe of 1340s, Lúcás Ó Dalláin; this led him to date R to the first half of the fourteenth century.[30]

From the character of the main script, one must say that both manuscripts were made by scribes accustomed to writing the gothic *textura*. This extends from the highly abbreviated writing of R to the formality of the *textura formata* in which the Life of St Patrick is written in I. One may suppose that the scribal milieu was a religious house *inter Anglos*, but on the borders of Connacht. The prominence given in I to the Life of St Berach, the only Life in either manuscript to have a miniature portrait attached to the initial, may seem to point to *Cell Bearaigh*, Kilbarry, Co. Roscommon, on the west side of Lough Forbes. It may be doubted, though, whether a small church like this was able to produce or could have afforded to commission a manuscript such as I in the late fourteenth century. Kilbarry is little more than thirteen miles north of Saints' Island in Lough Ree, with which the provenance of both manuscripts has generally been associated. To find out how well founded this association may be, we must work backwards from the evidence for the later history of the manuscripts.

Evidence for the vicissitudes of both manuscripts between the time of writing and their reaching the shelves of Sir James Ware takes two forms: the internal evidence of the marginal annotations and the external evidence of statements made by students who used the books in the seventeenth century.

In the case of R, the external evidence appears conclusive. Ware, whose working library included many volumes of his own notes, compiled some excerpts from R on 6 August 1639. These still exist in one of Ware's notebooks, now London, British Library, MS Add. 4788 (Clarendon MS 39), ff. 49–70. These excerpts are headed:[31]

'Ex vetusto codice scripto circa tempora Ed. II olim pertinente ad Conventum Ord. Minorum de ⟨   ⟩yn.'

---

[30] Byrne, *1000 Years of Irish Script*, pp. 19–20. Lúcás Ó Dalláin wrote a part of Dublin, Trinity College, MS 1298 (H. 2. 7); R. I. Best, 'The Oldest Fragments of the Senchas Már: Addenda and Corrigenda', *Analecta Hibernica*, 10 (1941), 301–3.

[31] Hughes, 'A Manuscript of Sir James Ware', p. 112.

Another hand has filled in the reading *Athloyn*, that is, Athlone in Co. Westmeath, which Kathleen Hughes was willing to accept. She was unaware, however, of other excerpts in Ware's notebooks where the heading is quite clearly 'Ex lib. conv. fratrum minorum de Dublin script. sub temp. Ed. 2 vel Ed. 3'.[32] Moreover Ware reports that the basis for this statement was an inscription in the volume: '93b Iste est liber communitatis fratrum minorum Dubl.' Internal evidence confirms the reading. This folio is now the fly-leaf, and at the top of the verso one can still read the lower part of 'Iste e*st*' and the compendium for *com*-; the hand appears to be late medieval rather than seventeenth-century.

Apart from this, the internal evidence only creates confusion. Some of the marginalia in R were printed by Plummer.[33] They present no coherent picture. Apart from the genealogical notes already referred to, the earliest addition appears to be the annal for 1504 in the lower margin of f. 97ʳ (now f. 40ʳ):[34]

Bellum apud Cnoc Thua in festo Sci Ludowici episcopi, feria 2a. Anno Domini m°ccccc°iiii. Frater Dermicius O Bragan, ego fui pro tu⟨n⟩c scolaris

The battle of Knockdoe, near Galway, took place on Monday, 19 August 1504, but the words 'pro tunc' indicate that Br. Dermot O Bragan only made this entry some years after, when he was no longer *scolaris*. O Bragan, presumably the same, appears as a witness to a deed dated 1550, on the verso of the flyleaf of R:[35]

Notum sit omnibus quod ego. Hobertus Mc Karruna filius Haneri consceci [*sic*] potestatem meam domino Jacubo Dillon, priori Gillikanie, luendi sive solvendi omnia feuda a me et a patre meo pignorata, cum parte castri Meteratte [?]; et fesi [*sic*] eum esse meum eredem, et

---

[32] London, Victoria and Albert Museum, Clements Heraldic Collection of Bindings, MS 1, part 2, f. 80ᵛ. The folio references given in what follows prove that R was Ware's source.

[33] Plummer, 'On Two Collections', pp. 444–6.

[34] Ibid., p. 445.

[35] Plummer's text, ibid., p. 446, corrupts the name to Robertus McKarrinia and omits the dating clause, though both were correctly given by Macray, *Catalogue*, col. 705 (though I do not know why he thought the date to be a manifest error for 1450). Hobert McKarruna is identified by C. McNeill, 'Reports', p. 139, with Hobbert McCarron of Killenefaghna, Co. Westmeath, who became chief serjeant of his nation in 1578.

ten⟨ebitur⟩ me Hobertum defendere in quantum potest [*sic*], nec aliquis preter me vel meum heredem abeat potestatem luendi predictum feudum et partem castri a domino priore nisse [*sic*] ego vel meus heres, et hoc de rebus nostris propriis et non alliter acquisitetur. Coram his testibus, domino Dermicio O Bragan, et domino Cormaco Magu⟨iro⟩ [?], ac froco [?] Dillon filio Emdi [sc. Edmundi] iuvenis. Peregrino ⟨filio⟩ Edemdi [*sic*] Dillon. Anno domini m ccccc l.

The priory of St John the Baptist, Kilkenny West, Co. Westmeath, was of the order of Crouched Friars, and from its foundation (perhaps in the thirteenth century) to its dissolution it remained closely associated with the Dillon family. James Dillon here mentioned was the last prior of the house, whose property was surrendered to the king in 1544 and granted to Robert Dillon in 1569.[36] Lucas Dillon, presumably Sir Lucas Dillon of Moymet, Co. Meath, 'seneschal of the barony of Kilkenny West',[37] signs his name in the volume in several places (f. 145ʳ twice, f. 167ʳ; now ff. 74ʳ, 96ʳ). His son James Dillon was created Lord Dillon, Baron of Kilkenny West, in 1620.[38] Charles McNeill was firmly of the opinion that the book belonged to the friars of Kilkenny West, and passed from them to the Dillon family, who took possession of the friary on its dissolution.[39]

At a later date the supposed provenance of Athlone, accepted by Hughes, had some plausibility. The Dillons were traditionally buried at the Franciscan friary there, and enjoyed a close connexion with that house too.[40] And among the signatures in the margins of the manuscript is this one: 'per me Thomas Mulldoone de Athlone' (p. 47, now f. 14ʳ in a hand of s. xvii). One might have supposed that the book originally belonged to the priory of Kilkenny West; that it passed into the hands of the Dillons; and

---

[36] A. Gwynn and R. N. Hadcock, *Medieval Religious Houses: Ireland* (London, 1972), p. 213; McNeill, 'Reports', p. 139, re James Dillon's surrender of 1544, not mentioned by Gwynn and Hadcock.

[37] GEC, *The Complete Peerage*, ed. V. Gibbs *et al.* (13 vols; London, 1910–59), xi. 124.

[38] Ibid., iv. 363.

[39] McNeill, 'Reports', p. 139. He allowed himself here to introduce a note of confusion over the term *Kilkenniensis*, and was taken to task by P. Grosjean, [review], *AB* 48 (1930), 361–8 (pp. 363–4).

[40] According to Francis Matthews, 'Brevis Synopsis Provinciae Hiberniae FF. Minorum' (written about 1628), ed. B. Jennings, *Analecta Hibernica*, 6 (1934), 139–91 (pp. 145–6).

that after the days of Lucas Dillon they kept it at the friary of Athlone. This had been dissolved in 1568, but a house of friars kept up an informal existence for twenty years, before their friary came together again.[41] In 1630, the guardian of the house was George Dillon. Ware's direct evidence, however, confirmed by what remains of the *ex libris*, makes such supposition void. The book had belonged to the Franciscans of Dublin. How it came into other hands during the sixteenth and seventeenth century is unexplained. The quantity of names and other scribblings in the margins shows that the book was treated with little respect. Unfortunately, these notes provide no further clue to the history of the manuscript. How, where, or when James Ware acquired it remains unproven.

The external evidence for the provenance of I is of the same kind as that for R. We have Colgan's testimony that his *Codex Insulensis* belonged to Saints' Island in Lough Ree, an island close to the eastern shore and lying in Co. Longford. Better still, we have the testimony on which Colgan relied. For he never used I directly, but only in the form of a transcript. This copy was found among his papers after his death and has by a happy chance survived. It is now at Killiney, Franciscan House of Studies, MS F. 1 (formerly A. 24).[42] At the end of this volume is an instructive colophon:[43]

Ego frater Joannes Goolde ordinis minorum regularis observantiae Provinciae Hyberniae, religiosus Corcagiensis, et conventus Cassellensis humilis Guardianus, ex mandato R. P. fratris Francisci Matthaei, ministri provincialis, diligenter et veraciter, anno 1627, propria manu exscripsi praescriptas omnes triginta tres vitas sanctorum Hyberniae, ex authentico transumpto vetustissimi manuscripti pertinentis ad Inis na Naom super Loch Rij, qui quidem vetustus liber originalis in custodia cuiusdam nobilis viri G.E. fideliter conservatur. In cuius rei fidem et testimonium praesentibus subscripsi rogans lectoris preces et orationes ut sanctorum meritis et intercessione ad gaudia eterna pervenire valeam, prestante Domino nostro Jhesu Christo, cui sit laus et gloria in saecula saeculorum. Amen. Frater Joannes Goolde qui supra.

---

[41] Ibid.

[42] J. T. Gilbert, 'The Manuscripts of the Former College of Irish Franciscans, Louvain', *HMC 4th Rept.* (1874), 599–613, item xxxiii (p. 605a), cf. ibid., p. 612a; Plummer, 'On Two Collections', pp. 451–3; P. Grosjean, 'Catalogus Codicum Hagiographicorum Latinorum Dubliniensium', *AB* 46 (1928), 112–14.

[43] Plummer, 'On Two Collections', pp. 452–3.

Here is direct confirmation of Patrick Fleming's statement that Francis Matthews had commissioned a copy of the manuscript from Saints' Island.[44] John Goolde, as Guardian of the Franciscan convent at Cashel, played host to Br. Michael O'Clery in 1629 when he was collecting copies of Irish Lives.[45] It appears from his wording, 'ex authentico transumpto vetustissimi manuscripti', that Goolde's copy was at two removes from I itself. 'Inis na Naom super Loch Rij' is, of course, that Saints' Island in Lough Ree to which Colgan invariably refers his texts from O. Goolde says that the manuscript belonged here but in 1627 was in the custody of a 'nobleman', G.E. By this date the priory itself was decayed, and its ownership of the book can hardly have counted for much. But who was G.E.? No one has offered an identification.[46] Moreover, the internal evidence appears to be in conflict with Goolde's detailed statement.

Some of the marginalia of I have been printed at various times.[47] That Plummer described as 'the entry of greatest interest for the history of the MS.' is one of a series of obits at f. 89[vb]:

Obitus domini Luce barrone Dillon De moiemehalle qui ingressus erat viam universe carnis in Ciuitate Dublinie xiii Februarii Anno Dni 1592.

Obitus Fanttussi y Fergaill boy qui erat Dominus Analye in occidentali parte. qui universse carnis viam erat ingressus in Palis, xxvi° Die decembris Anno Dni 1592.

Obitus Thadeii Flawy qui erat Dominus de Cloynnchnochair In comitatu longffordie qui viam ultimam diem claucit in Tyerlickin xxvii° Julii A° 1591.

Obitus Cormaci Junioris mycmoirtay qui Fuit prior in manesteryo deryck ac etiam viccarius ecclicia de Killilacam In predicto comytatu qui Diem ultimam claucit xxix Die Septembris Anno Dni 15lx et qui sepultus fuit in Killdacamog agus tabra⟨dh⟩ gach aon leabhfis sin bennacht air ⟨a⟩ anmuin agus do in ti do scribhadh.

Obitus Jacobi Filii Cormaci Juvenis mc Moirertai qui ocsissus erat in Mothar in comitatu predicto 4° nonas Junii Anno dni 15xxxv.

Obitus Seffaredii filii Cormaci mc Moirertai qui sumersus Fuit apud snaw rayim in predicto comitatu. Obitus Flerdij Filij Nimee y Fergaill qui Fuit prior in insula sanctorum Anno Dni 15iiii°.

[44] Fleming, *Collectanea Sacra*, p. 431; see above, p. 99–100.
[45] B. Jennings, *Michael O Cleirigh, Chief of the Four Masters, and his Associates* (Dublin, 1936), pp. 66, 195–6.
[46] Indeed, the manuscript could be taken to read 'G.F.'.
[47] Plummer, 'On Two Collections', pp. 447–8; McNeill, 'Reports', pp. 140–1.

All were written at the same time, therefore, after February 1592/ 3. Further obits were entered at the foot of the same page:

Obitus Fantussi fili Thadeii Flawy yFergail qui Diem ultimam claucit in castro nowo vi Januarii anno Dni 16⟨0⟩7.

Obitus Geralldii Filii Heberti y Fergail qui ocsisus fuit in Darog per excercitum Donatii bhraday' Iagain ductum de Wltania ad patria de Cloinncnochyr xvi die mensis Maii Anno Dni 1595.

The latest obits were entered in the lower margins of f. 88ᵛ and f. 89ʳ:

Obitus Congallii Ferrall filii fergusii Ferrall qui demigrauit Tynilicke die Lunae post Dominicam palmarum mensis Martii Anᵒ Dni 1621. Ego Thadeus Mortagh qui scripci.

Obitus Cormacii iuuenis Moriartii fratris Edmondi Moriartii qui demigrauit Killdacamaog die martis post natiuitatem domini 29 die decembris 1629.

Obitus Antonii Moriartii fratris praedicatorum ordinis de Longfordiensi conuentu filii supradicti Cormacii Moriartii qui diem ultimum clausit in Leclunagh et sepultus fuit in praedicto Monesterio 1631.

The key entry is that relating to 'Flerdij filij Nimee y Fergaill', or Flaithbheartach mac Conmidhe Uí Fhearghaill, prior of Saints' Island. The O'Farrell family may have had earlier links with the priory.[48] Plummer conjectured that Flaithbheartach kept the manuscript and that after his death it passed into his family's hands. In this way, the internal and external evidence agree in pointing to Saints' Island as the medieval home of the manuscript.

This was challenged by Charles McNeill, who, looking at the evidence of the obituaries, placed I in Co. Longford, 'with much probability in the monastery of Abbeyderg'.[49] These other obituaries relate to members of the O'Farrell family, lords of Annaly, Co. Longford, between 1591 and 1621, and to members of the Moriarty family, their kinsmen, between 1535 and 1631. One of these obits, that of Comgall O'Farrell (*ob.* 1621), was entered by 'Thaddeus Mortagh'. This man's hand and name appear elsewhere in the volume as 'Taodhg Mac Muriartaid' and 'Teige

---

[48] Gwynn and Hadcock, *Medieval Religious Houses: Ireland*, p. 194, mention Kianan O'Farrell, O. Cist., as intended prior of this Augustinian house in 1410, citing the Papal Registers.

[49] McNeill, 'Reports', p. 140.

Mortagh' (f. 49ᵛ), 'Teigue Murtagh' (f. 104ʳ), and 'Thadeus Moriartus' (f. 181ᵛ). Tadhg is evidently a contemporary, perhaps a brother, of Cormac Óg Moriarty who owned the manuscript. His name appears very often: 'Misi lebhur Chormaik oig mhic Muirithich' (f. 53ᵛ), 'Misi Cormaic og' (f. 54ᵛ); at f. 89ᵛ he adds his *explicit* to the Life of St Patrick, saying 'Mise Cormac Og do scrib so', and copies the original scribe's prayer, 'cuius meritis deleatur culpa scriptoris. Amen. Cormac Og'; 'Cormacus Moriartus' (f. 112ᵛ, in a very clear hand), 'Misi Cormack Og 1623' (f. 117ᵛ), 'CM' (f. 133ᵛ) next to an effaced note 'Amy Farrell his book'; the copy of *Félire Oenguso* bound with I also belonged to Cormac Óg, and his name appears here at ff. 212ʳ, 215ᵛ, 217ᵛ ('Hic liber pertinet ad me Cormacum Moriartum, Anno domini 1617'),[50] 219ᵛ, 220ᵛ. Cormac was a meddler: we have seen how at f. 89ᵛ he appropriated the original colophon of the scribe Matthew O'Dwyer; likewise at f. 117ᵛ he copies the catchword 'Venerabilis' and there are other similar examples of such imitation unsigned. Most misleadingly, he added his name to the note entered by Donnchadh Ó Cobhthaigh at f. 89ᵛ, who had written into the book, somewhere on Lough Derg, some Latin elegiacs with his own translation into Irish verse in 1584.[51] This led Plummer to suppose that the book was already in Cormac's possession at that date, which it almost certainly was not. The only dated references are 1617 and 1623.

Other marginalia include the names of Thomas Morghue, who adds his name to an elegiac couplet on the triple burial at Down (f. 33ʳ; cf. f. 48ʳ, a first attempt?); Bernardus (?) (f. 70ᵛ); Sean Comaghan (?) (f. 127ʳ); Conell Geoghegan, 1 Apl. 1641 (f. 144ʳ); Fergallus Comaghan (f. 198ʳ); Thomas Fitz—— (f. 203ʳ); and curiously, 'Jhon Monny his booke. God make him an old blinde thiefe as hee is' (f. 161ᵛ).

We have some slender chronological data. The last Moriarty obits are 1629 (Cormac Óg) and 1631 (his brother Anthony). So

---

[50] The date 1617 was misread as 1621 by Plummer, 'On Two Collections', p. 447.
[51] Ibid., p. 448; id., 'On the Colophons and Marginalia of Irish Scribes', *PBA* 12 (1926), 11–44 (p. 25); cf. D. I. Ó Cróinín, 'A Poem to Toirdhealbhach Luimnech O Néill', *Éigse*, 16 (1975–6), 50–66 (pp. 53–4, 66). Ó Cobhthaigh's verses are now edited (with a facsimile) by Ó Cróinín, 'A Poet in Penitential Mood', *Celtica*, 16 (1984), 169–74, with corrections by D. R. Howlett, 'Penance for an Editor', *Celtica*, 18 (1986), 150.

the manuscript was presumably still in the hands of the family in 1627 when Goolde copied it for the Louvain scholars. 'G.E.' remains a puzzle. Conell Geoghegan is a noteworthy name, handling the volume in 1641. This is presumably the antiquary Conall Mac Eochagáin, a man from Co. Westmeath, who in 1627 translated the Annals of Clonmacnoise into English. He had some connexion with the Franciscan enterprise: in 1630 he joined George Dillon, OFM, Guardian of the convent of Athlone, in attesting the authority of the Four Masters' Genealogies of the Saints on 4 November 1630.[52] On 11 October 1636, he performed a similar service for O'Clery's copy of the metrical *Naemsenchas*.[53] Who owned the book in 1641 when Mac Eochagáin handled it? When did it come into the possession of Sir James Ware? These are questions to which only rather uncertain answers can be given. But we have reached the point when R and I were reunited.

The extracts which James Ware himself made from R were dated 6 August 1639. In the same manuscript are extracts from I, begun by a secretary and completed by Ware himself; these are undated, but follow the excerpts from R in the manuscript.[54] Conall Mac Eochagáin's signature in I is dated 1641. Now, it is possible that Ware had lent him the manuscript at this date; it is more likely that Ware's extracts from I date from after 1641.

It is difficult to determine when Ware acquired either book. Although he used R in his *De Scriptoribus* of 1639, neither it nor I appears in the 1648 catalogue of his library.[55] Before 1639, one or both were known to Ussher when he was preparing his *Antiquitates*.[56] If either manuscript had belonged to Ussher himself, it is most unlikely that Ware would have kept hold of it, whereas Ware freely lent his manuscripts to the archbishop, his mentor in antiquarian researches.[57] It would appear probable, therefore, that

---

[52] *Genealogiae Regum et Sanctorum Hiberniae by the Four Masters*, ed. P. Walsh (Maynooth, 1918), pp. 9, 145.

[53] Brussels, Bibliothèque royale MS 5100–5104 f. 232; P. Grosjean, [review], *AB* 48 (1930), p. 365.

[54] BL, MS Add. 4788, ff. 71–90.

[55] See above, 68 n. 116.

[56] Plummer, *Vitae*, vol. i, p. xxi n. 1.

[57] Plummer, ibid., cites a letter from Ware to Ussher, dated 21 Sept. 1627, from Ussher, *Whole Works*, xvi. 461. This letter notably refers to Ussher's returning to Ware the latter's copies of the Annals of Ulster and Inisfallen, now in the

Ware acquired R before 1639, perhaps from a member of the Dillon family. It is not established whether he acquired I in the same period or after 1641. But all the evidence of ownership points rather to the two manuscripts, R and I, having had separate histories until they reached Ware's library.

The occurrence in I of an obituary notice of Lucas Dillon of Moymet, sometime owner of R, does not argue against this. He was a man of importance, well known beyond Co. Westmeath, as Chief Baron of the Exchequer. The entry of his death among the family obits of the O'Farrells and Moriartys suggests that friendly relations existed between them, not that both books were in the same ownership. Arguably stronger evidence for a connexion between R and I is some verses found in the margins of both:

> Cum pater est Adam cunctorum, mater et Eva,
> cur non sunt homines nobilitate pares⟨?⟩
> R f. 151ᵛ

> Si pater est Adam cunctorum, mater et Eva,
> cur non sunt homines nobilitate pares⟨?⟩
> ⟨signature cropped⟩ I f. 136

There are other examples of sententious verses in one manuscript or the other, but this is the only one in both. There is no common hand at work in any case. While I cannot offer an explanation for an interest in such verses in different owners leading to these entries, I do not think this is evidence for common ownership outweighing the contrary evidence we have already discussed.

It is desirable that we should have a study of how and where James Ware obtained his Irish manuscripts as a whole, for this would at least show up whether other books came from similar sources.

Also among the manuscripts once owned by Sir James Ware was Bodleian Library, MS Rawlinson B. 488 (Clarendon MS 3). The first item in this manuscript is a fragment of the Annals of Tigernach; this is followed by two fragments of Connacht annals (1237–49; 1303–14); third is the fragment known as the Annals of

---

Bodleian, as Rawlinson B. 489 and B. 503 respectively; cf. S. Mac Airt, *The Annals of Inisfallen* (Dublin, 1951), pp. x–xi.

Saints' Island (1392–1407).[58] The several fragments were perhaps bound together by Ware, who recognized that these annals were written by Magraidhin.[59]

Aughuistín Magraidhin wrote the annals from where the fragment begins in 1392 to 1404, ff. 29ra–33va. At 1405 a second hand took over, and under 1405.22 entered this obituary:[60]

Aughuistín Magraidhin, one of the canons of Saints' Island, an undisputed master of sacred and secular wisdom, including Latin learning (*léghend*), history, and many other sciences, *ollamh* of eloquence for Western Europe, compiler of this book and of many other books, including Lives of Saints and histories, died on the Wednesday before the first of November in his fifty-sixth year, on the sixth day of the moon. May the Saviour Jesus Christ have mercy on his soul.

Colgan appears to have put together this information that Magraidhin had compiled Lives of Saints with the fact that manuscript I was a compilation of *uitae* from Saints' Island, and inferred that Magraidhin was the compiler of the collection. He himself, however, prefers to credit this suggestion to Ware.[61]

---

[58] The relevant portions of the Annals of Tigernach were published by W. Stokes. The other two sets of annals are printed in S. Ó hInnse, *Miscellaneous Irish Annals (AD 1114–1437)* (Dublin, 1947), pp. 116–42 and pp. 142–84.

[59] Ó hInnse thought that leaves had been lost since Ware's time, citing the fact that, in one of Ware's notebooks, now Dublin, Trinity College, MS 804 (F. 1. 18), pp. 327–30, there is a series of excerpts from the Annals of Saints' Island, covering the years 1004–1441; Ó hInnse, *Miscellaneous Irish Annals*, p. xvi. It is, however, clearly stated in Ware's *Librorum Manuscriptorum . . . Catalogus* (Dublin, 1648), p. 4, that the volume consisted of the same fragments as now, including 'Fragmentum Annalium Prioratus Insulae omnium Sanctor. . . . ab an. 1392 usque ad annum 1407. Horum partem aliquam scripsit Augustinus Magraidin illius coenobij canonicus Augustinianus, qui obiit anno 1405.'

[60] O'Curry, *Manuscript Materials*, pp. 74–5, 529; Ó hInnse, *Miscellaneous Irish Annals*, pp. 176–7.

[61] Colgan, *Acta*, p. 139 n. 1, credits the attribution to Ware: 'Hanc vitam [S. Fechini] damus ex Cod. Inissensi, seu Monasterii Insulae omnium sanctorum in occiduo limite comitatus Longfordensis, authore Augustino Magraidin eiusdem Coenobij Canonico regulari, ut scribit Eruditus, atque animo & genere nobilis vir, Jacobus Varaeus de scriptoribus Hiberniae l. 1 c. 11. Author est satis recens, utpote ipse floruerit post adventum Anglorum in Hiberniam, ut ipse indicat in hac vita, c. 8.' This appears to be Colgan's own inference from the obituary notice for Magraidhin as given by Ware, *De Scriptoribus Hiberniae* (Dublin, 1639), p. 75, which Colgan goes on to quote. Elsewhere, discussing the anonymous Life of St David, Colgan again writes: 'Cum autem hanc [vitam] acceperimus ex Codice

The suggestion has not much to recommend it. The date of writing of R is earlier that the date of Magraidhin's birth, so that he must be ruled out as a possible compiler. If one may judge by palaeographical impressions, the rather crude character of the parchment of the Saints' Island annals, and the exclusive use of the Irish script, may even suggest that the priory there would not be equipped to produce a manuscript such as I. Yet this is where Goolde says the manuscript came from. The other well-known reference to Magraidhin may allow us the possibility of an explanation. As a colophon to the Life of St John the Evangelist in the *Liber Flauus Fergusiorum*, we read:[62]

And it was Aughuistín Magraidhin, canon of Saints' Island, who translated this Life of Eoin Brunni ['John of the breast', i.e. the Evangelist] from Latin into Irish, and let everyone who reads it give a blessing on the soul of the said canon.

Magraidhin lived in a period when a good many texts were being translated from Latin into Irish, and it is possible, but beyond knowing, that he borrowed I for the sake of preparing an Irish translation and never returned it to its original home.

It is frustratingly the fact that this quantity of evidence, some of it to all appearances authoritative, does not pin down the original place of writing or even the medieval repository of either manuscript. One may be sure, however, that both belonged from the start somewhere in the district of Longford or Westmeath.

8.2. *The Style of the* O-*collection*

The collection contains thirty-nine Lives. With one exception, they are the Lives of Irish saints, and the exception, St David, is

---

Insulae Sanctorum in lacu Riensi , & iuxta Vareum de Scriptoribus Hiberniae lib. 1 c. 11 Augustinus Magraidin Monachus ejusdem monasterii composuerit vitas illius codicis, videtur & huius author' (*Acta*, p. 430 n. 1). Of the O-text of St Ciarán of Saigir, he writes, 'authore, ut putatur, Augustino Magraidin' (ibid., p. 463 n. 1), and similarly of the Lives of St Gerald and St Énda (ibid., pp. 602 n. 1 and 710 n. 1).

[62] MS Dublin, Royal Irish Academy, MS 23. O. 48, vol. i, part iv, f. 1ᶜ: quoted by Plummer, 'Colophons and Marginalia', p. 16 n. 4. The text is edited by G. Mac Niocaill, 'Beatha Eoin Bruinne', *Éigse*, 7 (1953–5), 248–53, 8 (1955–7), 222–30; the colophon is given at p. 253.

portrayed as having close ties with Ireland. Eight of the saints included in this collection have no other known Latin life; these are SS. Berach, Molaisse of Devenish, Énda, Gerald, Fechin, Mochua, Samthann, and Buite, and their *uitae* were printed by Plummer. In the absence of any comparative material, one is not well placed to judge these texts. All of them are quite brief, and several could not have been written in their present form before the thirteenth century. Five texts represent Lives widely known outside the three collections—the Lives of SS. Patrick (by Jocelin), Fursu, David, Brigit, and Lawrence O'Toole. These texts may provide guidance in studying the work of the collector. Of the remainder, there are more than twenty Lives related to texts in S which I propose to discuss in later chapters, and five—those of SS. Brendan, Ciarán of Clonmacnoise, Finnbarr, Flannan, and Íte—which present questions yet to be resolved concerning their relationship to texts in the other collections.

Plummer surveyed the collection and established common features running through it, which he considered to show that **O** 'represents as a rule a later literary tradition' than either **D** or **S**.[63] His remarks depend largely on comparisons made with texts in these other collections, though he had not sought to establish any exact literary or textual relationship between the texts concerned. His method, for that reason, does not carry the same weight that our analysis of the editorial features of **D** can carry, since that is based on a comparison of redactor against his undoubted source. The observations Plummer makes, however, are entirely valid, and I propose first to present a summary of these, and then to test them, as well as one may, by comparing readings of **O** against their textual sources.

Plummer in 1905 noted that the redactor of **O** tended to omit the names of places and persons where these are found in comparable *uitae* in the other collections. 'A sure mark of lateness', he says, for 'such details grow less interesting as time goes on; they do not conduce specially to edification; and they tend to embarrass the reader who has to read the text aloud.'[64] The redactor also omits 'things and phrases characteristically Irish, which might be unintelligible to ordinary readers', and also 'omits or tones down

---

[63] Plummer, 'On Two Collections', p. 439.
[64] Ibid., p. 440.

things likely to cause difficulty or scandal'. The insertions on which Plummer remarks correspond to these omissions, that is, Irish names which are retained are sometimes explained, as are some obvious facts of Irish history and topography. Plummer in the same article drew attention to three cases where the redactor of O has conflated two texts available to him or restructured his source.[65] He noted only briefly the insertion of long moral reflexions, but five years later, in *Vitae Sanctorum Hiberniae*, the emphasis of his remarks had shifted. He there recognized the purpose of the compiler as homiletic, and his additions to consist of 'pious or moral reflexions, scripture quotations and parallels, especially parallels to those miracles which might cause difficulty or incur disbelief'.[66]

It is much less easy to demonstrate points of this type than it was with the D-collection, the reason being that the compiler of O seems sometimes to have copied a text almost verbatim and sometimes to have paraphrased systematically. Here are two examples, both from texts where a witness outside the three collections was the model. First, following on from our treatment of the Life of St Brigit in D, it must be noted that here too *Vita I S. Brigitae* was the compiler's source:

Vita I S. Brigitae § 53: Dixitque leprosus ille ad Brigitam: 'Non possum solus uaccam minare ad prouinciam meam.' Dixitque Brigita ad aurigam suum: 'Vade cum leproso.' Erat autem in illa hora auriga coquens carnes in caccabo. Dixit auriga: 'Quis coquet carnes istas?' Brigita dixit: 'Tu ipse ad eas uelociter ueni.' Et ita completum est sicut illa dixit. Exiit auriga cum leproso iter duorum dierum in uno puncto temporis, et in eodem puncto confestim reuersus est, et inuenit carnes istas in caccabo necdum coctas esse. Et omnes mirati sunt quod auriga potuit iter duorum dierum in unius horae puncto transcurrere, sed Deus donauit uoluntati sanctae Brigitae.

Vita S. Brigitae O § 46 (R f. 137[vb]): Dixitque leprosus ad Brigidam: 'Non possum solus uaccam minare.' Dixitque Brigida ad aurigam suum: 'Vade cum leproso.' Erat autem in illa hora auriga coquens carnes ad opus eorum in cacabo. Dixit auriga: 'Quis coquet carnes istas?' Brigida dixit: 'Tu ipse uelociter uenias ad coquend⟨as⟩ eas.' Et completum est

---

[65] Ibid., pp. 435–6; these three—Columba, Finnian, and Brendan—are discussed in Chapter 9. Compare *Vitae*, vol. i, p. xc, where he remarks on the insertion of additional stories in other Lives in O.

[66] *Vitae*, vol. i, p. xxiii; cf. above, p. 85.

uerbum eius, nam auriga iussa eius complens iuit cum leproso iter duorum dierum in unius hore spacio et, confestim reuersus, inuenit carnes in cacabo nec adhuc in toto coctas. Omnes admirabantur quo⟨d⟩ auriga potuit iter duorum dierum in unius hore spacio sic pertransire, sed Deus hoc uoluntati sancte ancille condonauit qui quondam Abacuc ad Danielem perduxit.

In the Life of St Brigit there are few places where **O** differs even so much from *Vita I*, to which it provides a serviceable witness, though not one of textual value. Part or all of more than thirty chapters of *Vita I* are omitted, especially in the latter part of the text where the chapters are very short, so there is clearly a marked desire to abbreviate. Otherwise, the changes here are trivial and of a strictly cosmetic nature, apart from the biblical allusion at the end, 'qui quondam Abacuc ad Danielem perduxit'.[67]

The same biblical comparison appears in the Life of St Berach, §20, only known from **O**: 'per aera uirtute orationis sanctorum ad eos uolitabat, tanquam alter Abacuc ad lacum leonum ubi Daniel orabat'; and in the **O**-text of the Life of St Brendan, §92: 'ueluti alter Abacuc propheta, ab angelo subleuata et sursum per aera et . . . ad Cluayn Ferta mirabiliter deducta' (the parallel passage to this, **D** §22, reads 'eleuata est uirgo Dei ab angelo ad monasterium suum').[68]

My second example is taken from *Vita S. Flannani*, a text for which we rely on the copy in **S** supported by the witness of the Göttweig fragment:

S §18: Vir autem sanctus, Christi pauper factus, frater Theodricus, post oscula sancti patris, uniuersis fratribus ualefaciens, cum paucis comitibus iter arripiens, eodem die taurus furiens, seuis cornibus truculentus ac multos, spiritu diabolico stimulatus, uulnificans, uirum sanctum Theodricum fratrem cum sociis suis inuasit. Quem taurum homo Dei manu forti tamquam edum caprarum diserpsit ac sociis suis distribuit.

This, 'the degenerate verbiage of the professional hagiologist',[69] was penned in the 1160s, probably at Killaloe. Compare the parallel passage:

---

[67] See Dan. 14: 32–8.
[68] P. F. Moran, *Acta Sancti Brendani* (Dublin, 1872), p. 20.
[69] Plummer, *Vitae*, vol. i, p. xxii.

O §13: *Postquam uero humilis discipulus* Theodoricus *paternam susceperat benedictionem*, patri ac fratribus uniuersis ualefaciens, cum paucis commitibus iter arripiens, accurrit in itinere taurus quidam, ut puto spiritu satanico instigatus, qui uirum Dei inuadere temptauit; quem ipse *in Domino confidens* manu forti, tanquam *Dauid leonem*, discerpens occidit ac suis comitibus distribuit.

Plummer and Kenney hinted, and Ó Corráin has argued, that **S** is an extended reworking of **O**. There is certainly enough verbal similarity to be sure that one writer had the other in front of him, but it is more in line with the work of the two compilers to suppose that **O** has got rid of the verbiage of the original Life.[70] Humility in saints is a quality the redactor admires and emphasizes, and the pious phrases in the last sentence are also his work. The parallel 'tanquam Dauid leonem' is of a type very commonly added in **O**. In another passage, fully conformable with my interpretation of the relationship, we read:

S §26: . . . At ille perfidissimus, maligno spiritu repletus menteque obstinata amore predarum, respondebat, 'Si prepete fugacis equi cursu te antecedere ualeam, non te exspectabo . . .'.

O §17: . . . At ille, tanquam alter Pharao in malicia obstinatus, respondebat: 'Si cursu equi ualeam te antecedere, non te expectabo . . .'.

Again, the redactor of **O** has taken over the words of the original but added what can almost be regarded as his signature, 'tanquam alter Pharao . . .', the biblical parallel. In the Life of St

---

[70] Ibid., vol. i, p. xvii, thought that **O** was 'a shorter and possibly earlier recension' than **S**, which, he says, 'is in the very worst hagiological manner'. In 'A Tentative Catalogue', p. 246, he calls **O** 'a shorter and, in some respects, better recension'. These statements are both very non-committal as to the priority of **O**. Kenney, *The Sources*, p. 405, merely echoes Plummer. Ó Corráin, 'Foreign Connections and Domestic Politics', pp. 224–5, writes: 'A close and detailed textual comparison shows that S is an extended and elaborate reworking of R in a much more florid style . . . R is itself based on earlier written materials . . . In many ways R reflects a culture similar to that indicated by S and indeed need not be placed much anterior to S itself.' This comparison is not presented to the reader, but the last sentence gives the game away: the relationship is exactly the reverse. **O** reflects its source, **S**, and the reference to earlier writings is copied from that source, **S** §2, **O** §1. The redactor of **O** has generally abbreviated and toned down the verbiage of **S**, and occasionally he adds a pious elaboration. The Latin style of the author of the *uita* is very personal and extremely unusual in these texts; a good deal of his wording has survived in the work of the redactor.

Énda, unique to **O** so that there is no control, the same phrase occurs, 'Hic, tanquam alter Pharao, obduratus in malicia, . . .'. Compare again:

S § 17: '. . . Tres enim tui filii ab inimicis crudelibus interempti sunt.' At frater Theodricus, misera ac flebili uoce suspirans, 'Quid,' inquit . . .

O § 12: '. . . Tres enim filii tui ab inimicis interfecti sunt.' Tunc Theodricus, tanquam alter Iob prole orbatus, suspirans ait, 'Quid . . .?'

Again:

S § 30: Sicque per aliquot menses et annos eiusdem uiri facies, ante admodum reuerenda, terribilis atque uitanda apparuit.

O § 20: In hoc quoque infirmitatis statu homo Dei tamquam alter Iob per aliquot annos et menses cum omni paciencia permansit, licet ab hominibus semotus, Deo autem propinquus.

These are perfunctory allusions, quite different in tone from the parallels with the widow's cruse, the release of Isaac, and the fate of Lot's wife, in **S** §§ 28–9, taken over in **O** § 19, and the type is very widely distributed in the **O**-collection.

The formulation is not in itself remarkable, and could probably be found quite widely. I note, for example, in the Eu Life of St Lawrence O'Toole:[71]

Corpora etiam pereuntium pastor pius inter manus hostium adhuc palpitancia capiebat et, uelut alter Thobias, festinabat christiane tradere sepulture.

This might easily have been written by the redactor of **O**, not only because of the *uelut alter* . . . formula, but because *pastor pius* is another expression unusually common in his work.[72] However, this is the reading of the original Eu Life. The chapter in which it occurs is drastically abbreviated in the **O**-version. Another

---

[71] The passage is found in both *Vita I* and *Vita II*; M. F. Roche, 'The Latin Lives of St Laurence of Dublin Edited with a Critical Introduction' (University College, Dublin, Ph.D. thesis, 1981), ii. 103 (*Vita I*, 1. 7) and 204 (*Vita II*, Plummer's § 11).

[72] Within the limited sample of Plummer's nine **O**-texts, 'pastor pius' is very common in *Bren.* §§ 6, 17, 19, 20, 22, 24, 29, 36, and is also found at *Énda* § 3, *Fech.* §§ 17, 21 (with 'bonus pastor' at § 7), *Ger.* § 13. 'Pius pater' is still more common: *Ber.* § 25, *Boe.* §§ 13, 16, 24, *Bren.* §§ 5, 38, 45, 46, 51, 53, 55, 68, 71, 90, 96, 100, 102, *Fech.* §§ 11, 15, *Las.* § 19, *Tig.* §§ 5, 16.

example of the type outside the **O**-collection is in the Life of St Moling, **D** §17:

Set sanctus senior intra fumum et flammas gratia Spiritus Sancti protectus, quasi quondam pueri in fornace, illesus permansit.

None the less, it is used with marked frequency in the **O**-collection, and can often be shown to be an addition by the redactor. Several formulae are used to introduce the biblical parallel, *tanquam alter* . . . or *uelut alter* . . . being the most common.[73] I have noted a similar use in a liturgical context.[74] A frequent alternative is *sicut quondam* . . . or *quasi quondam* . . ., or if the sentence refers to the work of the deity, *qui quondam* . . .[75]

A likely source from which the compiler may have picked up this habitual form of allusion is Jocelin's Life of St Patrick, the long text with which the **O**-collection begins. The comparison with Habakkuk, miraculously transported to bring food to Daniel in the lions' den at Babylon, is made several times in Lives of the **O**-collection and more than once by Jocelin: in §38 'per aeris uasta sicut olim Abacuc prophetam illos transportans' and again in §55 'ille . . . cuius nutu de Iudea in Caldeam transuectus est Abacuc propheta'. The hardening of Pharaoh's heart (Exod. 10: 27), referred to twice by the compiler of **O**, is also used as a comparison

---

[73] In the **O**-texts printed by Plummer, I note: 'tanquam alter Abacuc . . .' (*Ber.* §20), 'tanquam alter Helyas' (*Boe.* §17), 'tanquam alter Simeon iustus' (*Bren.* §2), 'ut alter Iacob' (ibid. §5), 'tamquam esset alter Moyses' (ibid.), 'uelut alter Moyses . . .' (ibid. 6), 'tanquam alter Thobias' (ibid. 18), 'ueluti alter Abacuc . . .' (ibid. 92), 'tanquam alter Martinus' (*Énda* §1), 'tanquam alter pharao . . .' (ibid. 15), 'tanquam alter Balaam' (*Fech.* §4), 'tanquam alter Daniel' (*Ger.* §16), 'cum esset quasi alter Daniel . . .' (*Las.* §32), 'tanquam alter Martinus' (*Sam.* §3), 'tanquam alter rubus Moysi apparens' (*Tig.* §3). This list, and those hereafter, are drawn from only a quarter of the collection (though the Life of St Brendan is particularly long); a count based on the entire collection would be much larger. Likewise, because Plummer did not print from **O** those Lives for which comparisons can be made, it is the examples not recorded here which most clearly demonstrate that these formulae were the redactor's own additions in most cases.

[74] In the office for St Finnian, datable to around 1300, we read: 'R. Iob ut alter patitur, Abel ut fidus graditur, ut Enoch exorabat, | ut archa Noe regitur, ut Salomon sic loquitur, ut Paulus predicabat. V. Ut Tobias compatitur, ut Helias sic rapitur, ut Moyses minabat'; Hughes, 'The Offices', p. 361.

[75] In Plummer's *Vitae*, I note: 'sicut enim quondam terra deglutiuit Dathan et Abiron' (*Ber.* §10), 'sicut quondam Dathan et Abiron . . .' (ibid. 23), 'sicut Moyses quondam . . .' (*Boe.* §16), 'sicut quondam Moysi . . .' (*Bren.* §81), 'sicut quondam inter discipulos Christi . . .' (*Énda* §19).

by Jocelin: 'induratum est cor regis Leogarii sicut quondam pharaonis coram Moyse' (§49 and cf. §135). The earth's swallowing up of Dathan and Abiron is mentioned several times in the collection, and this too is also in Jocelin's Life of St Patrick: 'terra terribili hiatu aperiens os suum sicut quondam Dathan et Abyron deglutiuit magum illum' (§33). Jocelin was not completely fixated on such comparisons, and on two occasions (§§49, 60) he refers to the earth's swallowing of someone without drawing the parallel. Yet he does make comparisons of this kind very frequently, though his form of words is much more flexible than the formulaic expressions which predominate in the work of our redactor.[76] While there is evidence to indicate that this pattern of reference was widespread and that it could have been known to the compiler from more than one source, the simple facts that Jocelin does this frequently and that his Life of St Patrick accounts for a large part of the O-collection must suggest that he was in this respect a significant influence.

---

[76] Other examples are: 'sicut quondam in tribus pueris camino Caldaico iniectis' (§48), 'instar regis Achab coram Deo meo te humiliasti' (§49), 'ipse . . . qui quondam fluenta Iordanis conuertens retrorsum in aluei proprii fontem retrorsit curru retrogrado' (§51), 'sicut etiam Iambres et Mambres secundum apostolum restituerunt Moysi, sic . . .' (§60), 'sicut non potest ciuitas abscondi super monte posita nec lucerna super candelabrum eleuata' (§64), 'ac si fuisset alter Petrus . . .' (§68), 'eodem modo quo quondam per uirgam operari dignatus est in manu Moysi' (§70), 'sicut quondam Dagon stare non potuit secus archam testamenti' (§73), 'qui de quinque panibus et duobus piscibus quatuor milia hominum satiauit' (§76), 'eiusdem Domini uirtute instar radiantis sideris Patricii deus illuxit qua de molari dente mandibuli asini ad precem Sampsonis' (§86) 'instar Symonis magi' (§92), 'more Pauli' (§103), 'qui quondam fecit in mari uiam et in profundo semitam posuit' (§106), 'huc egit . . . aqua in isto quinquagenario conspirante in necem sancti Patricii quod ignis celestis in duobus superbis quinquagenariis a rege Achab missis ad Helyam prophetam Dei' (§121), 'modo quo quondam in pharaonem et eius exercitum . . .' (§135), 'hoc factum nullus discredere iure poterit qui uxorem Loth in calcem mutatum aut historiam de Nabugodonosor rege legerit' (§152), 'de illis equis quibus Dominus iuxta Abachuc prophetam uiam fecit in mare' (§155), 'sicut quondam in fornace Caldaica' (§157), 'quod quondam in uellere Gedeonis apparuit' (§158), 'imitari ieiunio mystico Moysen adhuc naturali tantum lege constrictum vel pocius Heliam prophetam sub lege constitutum, sed potissimum placere gliscens conditori nature, legis largitori et gracie Christo Iesu, qui in se sacrauit tale ieiunium' (§173) 'uidetur signum istud insigne illud antiquo miraculo sub Iosue in die Gabaon patrato assimulari' (§196), 'qui quondam arcam federis Accaron usque Bethsames perducebat' (§198).

Apart from such easily identifiable formulae, the style of the redactor is neutral and therefore difficult to characterize in the way that I was able to pin down the idiosyncrasies of the redactor of **D**. One particular usage which seems characteristic is a liking for the term *regulus*, used in place of *rex* much as the redactor of **D** used *dux*.[77] It is possible that there are such turns of phrase which characterize the redactor of **O** and that I have failed to detect them with confidence, because reading the texts in manuscript does not permit the same level of familiarity as is possible with texts in print and because it is not practical to scan the folios again and again in search of individual phrases. If there are such characteristic expressions, I can affirm with some assurance that they reflect only a bland, pious Latin, less likely to attract notice than the often interesting usage of the redactor of **D**. In the next two chapters, however, more examples will be given which illustrate the style of the **O**-collection and, in Chapter 10, others which allow the compiler to be studied as he worked.

[77] *Fech.* §§4, 6, *Ger.* §4, *Las.* §§14, 16, 17, *Sam.* §§21, 22.

9

A Group of Texts Shared by S and O

In his discussion of the O-collection, Plummer refers to ten texts
where the recension of S is identical with that in O. Characteristically, he lists them in alphabetical order: Baithéne, Ciarán of
Saigir, Coemgen, Colmán of Dromore, Comgall, Fintán alias
Munnu, Moling, Molua, Senán, and Tigernach.[1] He further notes
that: 'In some instances the relation of CS [our S] and R [our O] is
very close indeed, and they agree sometimes in the most curious
mistakes.'[2] Seven examples of common errors are given. No
inference is drawn from this observation, and Plummer goes on to
list texts where S and O 'cover much the same ground . . . but
show another recension'.[3] The Lives he mentions in this
connexion are those of SS. Aed mac Bricc, Ailbe, Cainnech,
Ciarán of Clonmacnoise, Colmán Élo, Columba of Terryglas,
Fínán, Finnian of Clonard, Fintán of Clonenagh, Flannán, Fursu,
Maedóc, and Ruadán. The qualifications added in the footnotes
remove the impression that this second list consists of texts which
all exhibit a similar relationship to one another. The Life of St
Ciarán in O, for example, is much longer than the 'mere epitome'
in S. In the case of St Finnian, he suggests that O and S may
represent 'an independent recension of the same original, and the
same theory would explain the relation of R to CS in other lives of
this group'.[4] Some of the Lives in this second group are also
represented in the D-collection, and these will be discussed in
Chapter 10. In this chapter we shall deal only with those found just
in S and O.

It is easy to see that the sources of these two collections were not

---

[1] Plummer, 'On Two Collections of Latin Lives of Irish Saints in the Bodleian
Library, Rawl. B. 485 and Rawl. B. 505', *ZCP* 5 (1904–5), p. 433.

[2] Ibid., p. 434 n. 9.

[3] Ibid., p. 434.

[4] Ibid., p. 434 and nn.

independent, but it is less easy to define groups where, for all members, one theory will more tightly explain the relationship between the collections, and in such a way that one may suppose a common exemplar. Where the texts are identical, as in Plummer's first group, agreeing even in error, one can infer the existence of a common textual archetype. It is much harder to show that there was a single archetype from which both **O** and **S** derived a whole group of Lives, when the textual argument alone would allow a separate exemplar for each Life available to the compilers of both collections.

For Plummer's second group, texts which 'cover much the same ground' but in a different recension, this problem is compounded. A common source for each Life may amount to a common exemplar which was revised, rather than copied, by one or both compilers. Again, it is hard to see how one can differentiate between a collective source and individual sources. Furthermore, the difference in the compilers' treatment of the text does not rule out the possibility of a single collective exemplar from which some texts were copied by both compilers, errors and all, while other texts were revised. Members of Plummer's two groups could, therefore, derive from the same source.

In attempting to understand the overlap of texts between the two collections, **O** and **S**, we must be alert at all times to the problem of defining both the extent of any common source and its nature. I propose to begin by considering those texts where a textual comparison can be made without worrying over differences in recension. When we come to consider the second group, it will be necessary to bear in mind what we understand about the methods of the two compilers.

9.1. *Evidence for a Common Textual Archetype*

Where textual comparisons can be made, the limits of speculation as to source or archetype are more clearly defined than in recensional comparisons. Those Lives where the two collections have identical texts are therefore surer territory as a starting-point. Of the ten Lives in Plummer's first group, seven are briefly discussed in his introduction to *Vitae Sanctorum Hiberniae*. For five of these, there appears to be an open-and-shut case for supposing a common textual source. We may start with Plummer's comments. On the Life of St Ciarán of Saigir, he writes:[5]

The text of R is identical with that of S, agreeing sometimes even in obvious blunders. Occasionally R yields a better reading than S; but it also has mistakes of its own. The only important point in which R differs from S is that at the very end of the Life, after the final *Amen*, it adds a section corresponding to M §15 which is not in S.

Discussing the Lives of St Coemgen, Plummer writes:[6]

S and R are identical, agreeing sometimes even in obvious mistakes; sometimes S has the better reading, sometimes R. The SR recension is very much shorter than M.

On the Life of St Comgall:[7]

The text of R is practically identical with that of S. The latter is, however, imperfect, owing to the loss of a leaf in the middle. The SR recension is very much shorter than the text of MT.

On the Life of St Moling:[8]

S and R present an identical text, agreeing sometimes even in obvious mistakes. The SR recension is very much shorter than the M text.

Finally, on the Life of St Tigernach, he writes:[9]

S and R must have some common source, as they agree occasionally in obvious blunders. On the whole the text of S is superior to that of R.

So far as I have detected, the only use Plummer made of these observations was to justify the exclusion from his edition of the R- or (as I call them) **O**-versions: the printed text of **S** adequately served the purposes of study.[10] To these five we may readily add the Lives of St Colmán of Dromore and St Baithéne, where again the two collections have practically identical texts. The textual relationship in all seven cases is so close that for each Life there must have been a common textual source:[11]

---

[5] *Vitae*, vol. i, p. lii; cf. i. 223 n. 4, 233 n. 4.   [6] Ibid. vol. i, p. lv.
[7] Ibid. vol. i, p. lviii.   [8] Ibid. vol. i, p. lxxxi.
[9] Ibid. vol. i, p. lxxxviii.   [10] Ibid. vol. i, p. xvii.
[11] In this list, the section numbers are taken from the published editions of S. The reading of **O** is given from R where it is available and from I where R is defective. An asterisk indicates a primary reading, S^c the reading of the corrector in S.

Tig. S	§4 =	**O** §4 = *Boll.* §3
		disciplinis *Boll.*] discipulis SR
		tertio ⟨flauo⟩ colore *Boll.*] tertio colore SR
	§12 =	**O** §10 = *Boll.* §8
		iungerent *Boll.*] ingerent SR
Com. S	§2	letificatus *De Smedt & De Backer*] letifictus SR
	§3	qui est legitimum matrimonium coniugum *De Smedt & De Backer*] quod est legitimum matrimonium coniugium S*R
	§5	locionis S^c] locucionis S*R
		sciens quod S^c quod S*R
		comparentem S^c]
CiS.	§1	hoc S^c] hunc S*I
	§3	sublimetur S^c] sublimaretur S* sullimaretur I
	§4	que prius sterilis S^c] que prius filis S* que prius filiis I
	§5	⟨nix⟩ attingebat S^c] attingebat S*I
	§6	cumque ⟨. . .⟩ *De Smedt & De Backer*] cumque S tunc I
		⟨qui⟩ eius animam S^c] eius animam S*I
	§7	abscessit *Heist*] abcessit SI
	§8	temporum currente curriculo S^c] temporum currente circulo S*I
		compeditum S^c] competitum S*I
		properare S^c] properat S*I
		Carthacho S^c] Carthaco S*I
	§10	nemphe SI
		Engussum S^c] Engistum S* Engustum I
	§12	properantibus S^c] properatis S*I
	§16	locuples S^c] locuplex S*I
		adduci suis ⟨aspectibus⟩ S^c] adduci suis S*I
Mol.	§2	mouere non poterat *Heist*] moueri non poterat SI
	§8	in lecto S^c] in loco S*R
	§12	locum in quo *Heist*] locus in quo SR
ColD.	§7	unumquodque *De Smedt & De Backer*] unumquoque SR
		uituli *De Smedt & De Backer*] uitulos SR
	§8	⟨erat⟩ *De Smedt & De Backer*] om. SR
	§15	obstinatus S^c] obstius SR
	§18	lingue S^c] ligue S lig^e R
	§20	olei unctione S^c] olim S* olim unctione R
Coem.	§5	releuabant *De Smedt & De Backer*] reuelabant SI

This is not at all an exhaustive comparison of S with the O texts, but establishes the extent of the agreement between the two in trivial errors. Some of the readings supplied by S^c may be right or wrong, but they can hardly be anything but conjectures.

I note here that in printing these Lives, neither De Smedt and De Backer nor Heist made any use of the O-texts to correct the readings of S, nor to supply the missing text where S has lost leaves in the Lives of St Tigernach and St Comgall.[12] Worse still, Heist regularly adopts the reading of the corrector of S even where the textual reading removed as erroneous is found in the corresponding O-text, and was presumably the reading of the archetype.

How can we answer the question whether there was one textual archetype or seven for these seven *uitae*? Simple economy makes a single archetype the more probable explanation, and this derives some support from the placing of the texts in the collections:

	S	R
Tigernach	8	19
Comgall	31	30
Ciarán of Saigir	35	34
Moling	36	5
Colmán of Dromore	37	6
Coemgen	38	37
Columba	39	2
Baithéne	40	3

The sequence in S from Ciarán of Saigir to Baithéne is suggestive: it would be a remarkable chance for six texts, independently obtained, to form a series which exhibits the same textual pattern. We may perhaps infer these Lives occupied consecutive positions in a single common archetype. In copying the archetype, the conservative compiler of S has retained the original order for this sizeable block, while the compiler of O had other ideas of arrangement. I propose to posit the existence of a lost manuscript from which these Lives were copied by the scribes at work on S and by the original compiler of O. Let Θ represent the lost manuscript which served as the exemplar of S; if R is the first copy of the O-

---

[12] Plummer's edition of the Life of St Tigernach from O makes good this defect, and for the Life of St Comgall, Grosjean has published a collation of the two texts, including the ten chapters missing from S, which he numbers 3b–3l; 'S. Comgalli Vita Latina', *AB* 52 (1934), 343–56 (pp. 348–53).

collection, then Θ was the exemplar for this too, but R may rather
be a fair copy of the original O-collection.

It will be noticed that I have introduced the Life of St Columba
to the list. In both collections it is paired with its natural sequel,
the Life of St Baithéne, disciple and successor of St Columba. In
both collections, the wording of the text shows the kind of agreement even in error which admits it to membership of this group.
But the order of chapters in the two versions is different. As
Plummer observed, the S-text divides oddly into two parts:[13] §§ 1–
19 form a highly abbreviated Life, ending with the death of the
saint; §§ 20–40 stand as an appendix to this brief Life and derive
almost verbatim from Adomnán.[14] The compiler of O was
dissatisfied with this arrangement. On the one hand, he inserted
the second series, §§ 20–40, into the middle of § 18, so that they no
longer followed the death of the saint. This presents no problem: S
has preserved the arrangement of Θ while O has improved on it.
But the O-text has two other insertions, one incorrectly placed
between §§ 5 and 6 (when it ought to have been inserted at § 2, as a
marginal note makes clear), the other at § 18, immediately before
the block of transposed chapters. The first of these insertions tells
how St Columba got the name Colum Cille; how an angel named
Axal, 'quia ad auxiliandum te missus sum', gave him the choice of
certain virtues; and how when remonstrated with for his extreme
asceticism, Columba replied, 'Nemo dormiens coronabitur, et
nemo securus possidebit regnum celorum'.[15] The compiler of O
has introduced this from an unknown source. The second
insertion is more problematical, for it is the story *De causa
peregrinacionis S. Columbe* found in S at ff. *88–*89, of which only
f. *89 (now f. 88) remains.[16] The alarming possibility appears to be

---

[13] Colgan, *Trias*, p. 327; Plummer, 'On Two Collections', pp. 435–6.

[14] Once again, there is a gap in S between §§ 20 and 21 where a leaf is missing,
which the editors have made no attempt to supply from O.

[15] Plummer, 'On Two Collections', p. 435.

[16] The fragment in S is printed by De Smedt and De Backer, *Acta*, 221–4;
Heist, *Vitae*, pp. 112–14. Ussher, *Whole Works*, vi. 466–8, printed the opening
part of the story from O; Colgan reprinted this, *Trias*, pp. 462–3, as an appendix
to the second Life. Ironically, Colgan depended on Ussher for this, even though
the relevant leaf (f. *88) of S was lost owing to its removal from the manuscript for
the benefit of the Louvain scholars. The full text of the anecdote is given from O
by H. J. Lawlor, 'The Cathach of St Columba', *PRIA* 33C (1916–17), 241–443
(pp. 408–12).

raised that the compilers of O may have had access to the whole S-collection. It is alarming because we have supposed that R is itself older than S, and that S represents its collection in process of compilation, not a fair copy. If O could have had access to a pre-existing copy of S, we have no need to conjecture the existence of Θ but must open up to wider discussion the relationship between the O- and S-collections.

It is confusingly the case that the Life of St Columba both raises this question and provides the best evidence to answer it negatively. In so doing, it raises the alternative possibility that the redactor of O had already worked on these texts before they reached the compiler of S. The text in S contains a number of features which we had thought to be characteristic of O: in §1, 'sicut quondam Iacob patriarcha quando Effraym et Manasem, suos nepotes, benedixit'; in §3, 'quod quondam per se ipsum in Chana Galilee operatus est, hoc in suo iterum seruo renouare dignatus est' (though this paraphrases Adomnán);[17] §7, 'sicut quondam parum olei in Helysei uerbo pululauit'; §14, 'sicut Christus Lazari dormitionem predixit apostolis'; these all suggest the habit in O of biblical farcing. The use of headings, especially in *qualiter* . . ., is more frequent in O than elsewhere, and is found here. The omission of insignificant names is certainly a feature of §§1–19 of the SO-Life of St Columba, though §§20–40 are much closer to the usage of Adomnán.[18]

So, the rearrangement of chapters and the insertion of the separate anecdote suggest that O depended on S. The occurrence of features associated with the redactor of O in the S-text is incompatible with this, and suggests the reverse relationship. But in that case, the compiler of S must have transferred the second series of stories from their position before the saint's death in O to their present position as an appendix; the less abridged nature of this second series joins with common sense in making this improbable. The way out of the difficulty is this: the anecdote *De causa peregrinacionis* inserted into the O-text, which also occurs in an early position in S, must have belonged to Θ, and Θ must also have had those stylistic features which we have hitherto associated

---

[17] *Vita S. Columbae*, II 1.

[18] Shown briefly by G. Brüning, 'Adamnans Vita Columbae und ihre Ableitungen', *ZCP* 11 (1916–17), pp. 277–8 and n. 6.

with **O**. The first of these points is easily conceded, since the anecdote in question immediately follows the Life of St Tigernach in **S**, a text which we have already supposed to come from Θ. The second point poses a large question as to the correctness of our understanding of the redactor's methods in **O**.

It is certainly true that the biblical parallels which we have associated with the redactor of **O** are also found in these **SO**-texts derived from the lost Θ. In the **SO**-Life of St Colmán of Dromore, §15, we read:[19]

Illos uero poetas, in infidelitate induratos, tamquam alterum Dathan et Abiron, terra absorbuit.

Compare the **O**-text Life of St Berach, §10:

Sicut enim quondam terra deglutiuit Dathan et Abiron propter malitiam suam, sic simili pena has magicas concionatrices cum regina terra absorbuit.

Or in §23 of the same text:

Terra enim sub pedibus eorum se aperiens uiuos eos transglutiuit, sicut quondam Dathan et Abiron absorbuit.

The parallel in the Life of St Colmán is of a type with those introduced by **O**, though it lacks the formula *sicut quondam* . . . On the other hand, **O** had no monopoly on such parallels. The comparison with Dathan and Abiron is found in the **S**-text Life of Molaisse of Leighlin and elsewhere. Other examples we may point to in the **SO**-group of Lives are in the Life of St Tigernach, §3 ('sed tamquam alter rubus Moysi apparens'), the Life of St Colmán of Dromore, §13 ('tanquam alter Moyses'), and the Life of St Coemgen, §3 ('Sed frustra Ioseph temptator . . .' and 'tamquam alter Antonius'); or the use of the word *regulus* in the Life of St Ciarán of Saigir **SO** §§6, 7, where **D** §9 has *dux*. Yet the arrangement of the Life of St Columba prevents us from accepting that Θ is made up of texts already edited *more suo* by the redactor of **O**. We must accept that these features were already in Θ, and that most of these Lives were adopted without editorial interference by the compilers of both collections. This necessitates a modest revision to our view of the redaction of **O**. We already know that

[19] Compare Num. 16: 30.

the compiler of that collection did not edit consistently, and that the most identifiable feature of his editorial style was not peculiar to him. The dominant influence, I have suggested, was Jocelin's use of biblical parallels in his Life of St Patrick. Jocelin's influence may have worked first on the compiler of Θ; the compiler of O would then receive the same stimulus from two sources. We should perhaps consider Θ to represent a stage on the way towards the more comprehensively edited O-collection. The compiler of O did, however, allow himself to merge the disjointed material on St Columba, but otherwise the texts in Θ already suited, if they did not actually help to form, his tastes.

We may have to allow the possibility, further, that with other texts in Θ the redactor of O took greater liberties than he did with St Columba's Life. Before going on to discuss such a possibility, I want first briefly to deal with the other Lives on Plummer's first list which we have not admitted to a place in Θ.

The verse Life of St Senán was regarded by Plummer as identical in S and O. Certainly, the occurrence of a large gap in the text of SO against that of D, a gap amounting to lines 261–671 of Heist's conflate text, establishes them as a textual pair. But apart from this, the agreement of SO is not strikingly more common than SD. Although the text of S is certainly closer to that of O than it is to D, I hesitate to find room for it in Θ. It is possible that all three collectors acquired the text independently; or this Life may be one for which we should admit that, though there are textual grounds for saying that a common textual archetype underlies S and O, there is nothing to connect it with the Θ-group.

The Life of St Molua is problematical, chiefly because S has two texts.[20] We can, however, follow Plummer in accepting that the shorter of the two S-texts, his S^2, agrees minutely with O in such a way as to permit us to assign it to Θ. This can be demonstrated textually:

§3   ouile S^c] obuile S^*I
§9   perseueris S^* frueris S^c perfrueris I
§19   ⟨est⟩ ingressus S^c] ingressus S^*I
§20   ⟨non⟩ confitebatur S^c] confitebatur S^*I
§36   Brannubus SI

---

[20] For more detailed discussion, see Chapter 10, pp. 337–9.

It can even be added to the series which we have already identified, preserved in the order of **S**. The relationship of this **SO**-text to the fuller **S**-text (S[1]) and the **D**-text is too complex to discuss at this stage.

The Life of St Munnu, included by Plummer in his first group, presents similar problems. Here too there are four recensions, but once again the shorter of the two texts in **S**, Plummer's S[2], is very like the **O**-text, though not identical, as he realized: 'The R recension is nearly identical with S[2] but is still further abbreviated in certain parts, and has not been padded with moral and religious commonplaces as is the case with many of the lives in R.'[21] Once again, discussion of the relationship between the **SO**-text and the other versions in **S** and **D** must be postponed, but we may admit this Life to membership of Θ with the qualification that the redactor of **O** has introduced some changes to the Θ-text which served as his exemplar. The expanded tally of Lives with a common source now looks like this:

	S	R
Tigernach	8	19
De causa peregrinacionis fr.	9	[in 2]
Munnu[2]	22	21
? Senán	29	35
Comgall	31	30
Ciarán of Saigir	35	34
Moling	36	5
Colmán of Dromore	37	6
Coemgen	38	37
Columba	39	2
Baithéne	40	3
Molua[2]	41	38

The Life of St Tigernach and the anecdote on St Columba now occur in Heist's second group (**S** items 4–11), that of Munnu in his fourth group (items 21–6) in quires ix–xi, that of Senán in his fifth group, consisting of Lives with an alien character (items 27–9). The rest are in the large ungrouped sequence towards the end, but why, one asks, is Comgall separated from the Ciarán-to-Molua block? Is it perhaps possible that items 32–4 (Mochutu, Lasrén, Mac Cairthind) in **S** were also in Θ, joining Comgall to the larger

[21] Plummer, *Vitae*, vol. i, pp. lxxxv.

group, but were omitted by **O** for want of interest? We shall never know, but this would be an economical though highly speculative explanation for items 31–41 of **S**. Since the very existence of Θ is conjectural, one can hardly press the point. It is reassuring, however, that the anecdote *De causa peregrinacionis*, linked in **O** with the Life of St Columba, now provides a bridge which ties the Life of St Tigernach with the larger series.

9.2. *Other Parallel Texts in* S *and* O

The Life of St Columba belongs textually in Plummer's first group of Lives identical in both **S** and **O**, so close is the verbal agreement between the two copies. The rearrangement of chapters, however, and the transposition of the anecdote *De causa peregrinacionis* are changes of a recensional character, putting St Columba in his second group. Yet we have found a plausible textual explanation which allows us to suppose that both **S** and **O** derived their Columban texts from Θ. This proves the possibility of linking Plummer's first group of shared *uitae* in **SO** with his second group.

Turning now to that second group, we may begin with *Vita S. Finniani*, which Plummer characterized as 'another case of conflation'.[22] The relationship between the versions in **S** and **O** has been considered in detail by Kathleen Hughes:[23]

With the exception of two long passages, which the scribe of the Rawlinson Life inserts from other sources, the CS and R recensions cover exactly the same ground. . . . CS and R make identical blunders on two separate occasions, where the sense is dislocated by omissions. . . . The Life of Finnian in R is considerably longer than in CS, and contains homiletic material which makes it suitable for public reading. It adds nothing to the CS account, and omits many of the place and personal names found in CS. Many primitive elements found in CS have been excluded from R. The *Vita Finniani* of R is therefore of value only in so far as it sheds light on the common exemplar.

The particular passages on which these statements are based are cited in footnotes, to which reference may be made. The 'identical blunders' cited are unfortunately neither of them *textual* errors in

²² 'On Two Collections', p. 436.
²³ 'The Historical Value of the Lives of St Finnian of Clonard', *EHR* 69 (1954), pp. 354–5.

the common exemplar, but result from their common source's abridgement of its model: S preserves while O has modified the common source, which was an already abbreviated recension of the Life; the person responsible for the abridgement has twice omitted parts of the stories without also omitting later allusions which depend on the omitted portion. Even without easily identifiable textual errors, however, there can be little doubt that S and O have a common source:

S §7 Quodam alio tempore uenit Finnianus ad uiros sanctos qui habitabant in insula que Echni uocatur, ut consolationem de uita et doctrina eorum haberet. Cumque illi in aduentu eius gauderent, et nocumenta que passi sunt de passeribus et serpentibus et pulicibus ei intimarent, uir Dei compassus est afflictioni eorum et omnia nocumenta orando penitus amouit. Aquam etiam de petra durissima eis impetrauit.

O §7 (R f. 125ᵛᵃ) Alio quoque tempore uenit Finnianus ad uiros Dei qui habitabant in insula qui Ethni uocabatur, ut consolationem de uita eorum atque doctrina haberet. Cumque illi in aduentu eius multum gauderent, et nocumenta que passi sunt de †passionibus et serpentibus et pulicibus ei intimarent, uir Dei compassus eorum uexationi Deum deuote orauit atque omnia illa nocumenta amouit et aquam dulcem de petra durissima ad solacium eorum impetrauit.

O has modified the source only slightly; elsewhere in the text the variation is sometimes greater, but it is always evident that the two texts represent the same Life. This is not sufficient on its own to justify our enrolling St Finnian among the saints in Θ. I shall offer two grounds which will permit his enrolment.

First, we have noticed that the use of biblical comparisons, so popular with the redactor of O, was probably already found in Θ. In the Life of St Finnian, we read:

S §22 Respondit Finnianus: 'Ille qui huc eam deportauit ad suam reducat patriam.' Quod et factum est. Nam angelus eam sursum tanquam alterum Abacuc leuauit atque ad suam perduxit regionem.

O §20 (R f. 127ᵛᵇ) Sanctus Finnianus respondit: 'Ille qui huc eam transuexerat, ad suam patriam sic reducat.' Quod et factum est. Nam angelus eam uelut alterum Abacuc sursum in aera leuauit atque sic ad suam perduxit regionem.

The redactor of O has introduced a minimal variation in the popular formula, but the parallel itself is one frequently used.

Secondly, as Hughes mentioned, the redactor of O has

conflated with the major exemplar 'two long passages . . . from other sources'. One of these is the *Catalogus sanctorum Hiberniae secundum diuersa tempora*, which is inserted bodily into the Life:

S §§ 12–13 . . . Tunc homo Dei uterum eius benedixit, signans eum cum baculo suo, et ex hac benedictione meruit habere filium sue gentis nominatissimum, Echu nomine, ex quo natus est Brandub rex et multi alii.

Hec de primo libro uite eius excerpta sunt.

`Secundus liber´

Igitur Finnianus, optimus sanctorum secundi ordinis, abbas, uolens multiplicare cultum Dei altissimi, plures monachos in prefato loco, qui Achad Abla dicitur, relinquens, ad regionem Barche perrexit.

O §§ 11–13 . . . Videns igitur uir Dei illius deuocionem, eius uterum benedixit, atque ut eius posteritatem prosperitatem in agendis haberet, Deum suppliciter rogauit. Et ex hac uiri Dei benedictione mulier filium nominatissimum promeruit, viz. Euchodium nomine, ex quo natus est ille famosissimus Branduuus mac Echach qui in multis uictoriam de inimicis optinuit.

Hec de primo uite eius libro extracta sunt.

Igitur sanctus Finnianus erat precipuus inter sanctos secundi ordinis sanctorum in Hibernia. Erant enim tres ordines sanctorum in Hibernia secundum diuersa tempora. [*The* Catalogus *follows here.*]

Volens igitur sanctus Finnianus cultum Dei in diuersis locis plantare, relinquens quosdam de suis in loco qui Achad Abla dicitur, peruenit in regionem que Ybarchi nominatur.

The insertion, prompted by the reference to the second *ordo*, is made in a perfunctory way. The text of the *Catalogus* inserted here closely agrees with the copy of it in **S**, but is abbreviated to a small degree. Grosjean suggested that the **O**-text of the *uita* used a model which included a text of the *Catalogus* very close to that in **S**, and that the redactor abbreviated both *uita* and the inset *Catalogus* as he worked.[24] It is more probable that the redactor of **O** has inserted the *Catalogus* into the *uita* in the same way that he conflated the separate texts on St Columba. Again, both components are preserved separately in **S**. The second addition in the **O**-text occurs at the end of **S** § 20, where **O** has linked into the narrative a passage from the Life of St Columba of Terryglass, SO

---

[24] Grosjean, 'Édition et commentaire du *Catalogus Sanctorum Hiberniae secundum Diversa Tempora* ou *De Tribus Ordinibus Sanctorum Hiberniae*', *AB* 73 (1955), 211.

§§ 26–7.[25] Since this passage tells of the death of both saints, it is distinctly out of place where it has been inserted in **O**. Yet we must note once more that the source of the addition was an **SO**-text. It begins to look increasingly likely that here too the redactor of **O** is conflating material from **Θ** which **S** has simply copied.

There is a third argument possible. We have already observed that the Life of St Tigernach and the anecdote *De causa peregrinacionis S. Columbe* occur side by side in **S**. The Life of St Finnian immediately precedes this pair, and so extends to three this series of texts potentially derived from **Θ**.

Two other Lives from Plummer's second group can easily be shown to have common sources. First, there is the Life of St Fursu, for which the relationship between the texts of **S** and **O** is very close. Here is a short passage from the critical text of Krusch:[26]

Conpletis uero duodecim annis quos angelus praedixerat, sanctus quadam[a] infirmitate correptus, angelica fruitur uisione, ubi etiam praedicationis instantiam admonitur,[b] nullum uiuendi finem audiuit; certam diem tacendo euangelicum[c] praeceptum admonens:[d] 'Vigilate et orate, quia nescitis diem neque horam.' Quod uir Deo plenus intellegens, loco monasterii a praedicto sibi rege[e] traditum adcelerauit[f] construere. Quod monasterium[g] in quodam castro constructum, siluarum et maris uicinitate amoenum rex gentis illius Anna ac nubiles quique tectis et muneribus adornarunt.

B = Brussels, Bibliothèque royale, MS 7984 (s. x, Weissenberg, then Molsheim, then Bollandists in Antwerp), ff. 24–33ᵛ (Krusch's B1a).

L = London, British Library, MS Cotton Nero E. i, part 1 (Worcester, s. x/xi), ff. 93ʳ–97ᵛ (Krusch's B2a′)

[a] quadam] quidam L [b] admonitur] ammonitur B ammonitus L [c] euangelicum praeceptum] euangelico praecepto BL [d] admonens] ammonet B admones L [e] sibi rege] rege Sigiberto sibi BL [f] adcelerauit] adcelebrauit L [g] ⟨uocabatur Cnoberesburg⟩ B ⟨uocabatur Cnoheresburh⟩ L

[25] The addition occurs at R ff. 127ʳᵇ⁻ᵛᵃ.

[26] MGH *Scr. rerum Merov.*, iv. 437–8 (§7, but the section-numbers in this edition are more than ordinarily meaningless, owing to the omission of the visions). Early spellings, such as *nubiles* (for *nobiles*), come from London, BL, MS Harl. 5041 (s. ix), ff. 79ʳ–98ᵛ. The manuscripts are discussed by B. Krusch, MGH *Scr. rerum Merov.* iv (1902), pp. 429–33. Krusch, who appears not to have collated S with much care, thought that the text of S resembled that of an inferior group of British manuscripts, such as London, BL, MS Royal 5 A. vii (s. xii), but

The *uariae lectiones* have been chosen to show the part of the textual tradition of the *uita* from which the common source of the **SO**-text derived:

S §27 Completis autem .xii. annis quos angelus predixerat, sanctus, quadam infirmitate correptus, angelica fruitur uisione. Ubi etiam predicationi instare ammonitus, nullum uiuendi finem audiuit, certum diem *tacitum* euuangelico precepto *cognoscens*, 'Vigilate et orate, quia nescitis diem neque horam'. Quod uir *Dei plenius* intelligens, locum monasterii a predicto sibi rege traditum accelerauit construere. Quod monasterium *uocabatur Cnocberesbruch*, in quodam castro constructum, siluarum et maris uicinitate amenum. Rex autem gentis illius Anna, *religiosus* ualde, ac nobiles quique tectis et muneribus adornarunt *illud monasterium*.

O (R f. 105vb) Completis autem .xii. annis quos angelus predixerat, infirmitate quadam correptus angelica fruitur uisione. Ab angelo quoque qui ei apparuit, ammonitus est ut adhuc predicacioni uerbi Dei insisteret. Cumque nullum uiuendi finem ab eo audiret, certum diem *tacitum* ewangelico precepto *cognoscens* ubi dicitur, 'Vigilate et orate, quia nescitis diem neque horam'. Hic uir *Dei plenius* intelligens, locum monasterii a predicto rege sibi traditum construere accelerauit. Quod monasterium *uocabatur Cnoc beresbruc*, in quodam campo constructum siluarum et maris uicinitate amenum. Rex autem gentis illius animo *religiosus* ac nobiles quique de terra multis muneribus *illud monasterium* adornauerunt.

It is obvious from the italicized words that **S** and **O** agree on readings which distinguish them as a textual pair and demonstrate the existence of a common source. The spelling *cnoc* shows that it was written in Ireland—the copyist has introduced this Irish word for 'hillock' into the place-name. It cannot be proven that the source was Θ, but the possibility is worth keeping in mind. There are, however, clear differences of recension between these two witnesses. In the second sentence, for example, the redactor of **O** appears to have paraphrased the opaque wording of the source as preserved in **S**, which, though corrupt, is closer to the critical text.

Another text where the two collections differ in recension but almost certainly depend on a common source is the Life of St

the **S**-copy was 'adeo immutatum et decurtatum . . . ut operam et oleum perdidisse uideantur uiri reuerendissimi [De Smedt et De Backer]' (p. 433). Krusch was unaware of the **O**-text, since he wrote before Plummer drew attention to that collection.

Maedóc. As we saw in Chapter 6, the primary version of this Life is
V, which was the source of the D-text. There are also versions in
both S and O, which bear a marked similarity:

S § 22 Et incepit referre uisionem memoratam et adiecit: 'Nunc me Deo
et tibi offero et semen meum post me, ut per te in uita dirigar et mortuus
in ecclesia tua cum posteritate mea tradar sepulture.' Et dedit fundum
cum necessariis ad monasterium construendum in loco qui dicitur Ferna
ubi, tempore succedente, ciuitas famosa edificatur et sepultura regum
Lagenie habetur. Deinde, facta synodo et conuenientibus principibus et
maioribus terre, ex consilio regis Brandub et omnium aliorum, decretum
est ut sedes archiepiscopatus totius Lagenie esset in ciuitate Fernie,
sicque sanctus Moedoc a uicinis episcopis cum magna exultatione
archiepiscopus est consecratus.

O (R f. 228vb) Et incepit referre uisionem memoratam et adiecit: 'Nunc
me offero Deo et tibi et semen meum post me, ut per te in uita dirigar et
mortuus in ecclesia tua cum posteritate mea sepulture tradar.' Et dedit
rex fundum cum necessariis ad monasterium construendum in loco qui
dicitur Ferna, ubi tempore succedente ciuitas in Fernia est edificata. Ibi
enim reges Lagnensis gentis consueuerunt sepeliri. Ibi etiam sedes tocius
archiepiscopatus terre pro tempore illo fuit. Ibi enim sanctus Moedocus
a uicinis episcopis cum magna exultatione archiepiscopus est consecratus.

The first half of the passage, very close in the two versions, clearly
indicates a common source, from which one or the other has
deviated somewhat more in the second part. What we know of the
collections suggests that O has diverged from the source, as
happened in the Life of St Finnian, while S has kept to it more
closely. Elsewhere, other changes characteristic of the redactor of
O confirm this impression. It is, however, difficult to find anything
which will tie this Life into the conjectured Θ.

9.3. *The Status of the Supposed Archetype* Θ

There is now a difficult question to be faced. For a number of Lives
we have established the probability of a common source used by
the compilers of S and O. To go on from there and determine
whether these were individual sources, a single collective source,
or a partial collective source plus one or more individual sources is
very hard. It is made harder by the uncertainties over the Lives of
SS. Senán, Molua, and Munnu. There appear to be only two

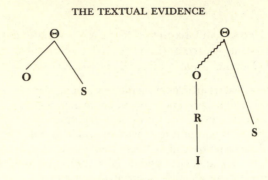

FIG. 2 Lives of the SO-group

possible arguments for grouping texts into a collective source. We have already seen that some of the texts in question form two series in the S-collection. In view of the unplanned arrangement of that collection, in which texts seem to have been copied in the order in which they came to hand, the possibility of the series of texts representing a collective archetype is not implausible. Better evidence for a collective source might come from shared editorial features if any could be shown to occur consistently. The use of biblical parallels of the '*tamquam alter* . . .' type may be such a feature; its presence would certainly be evidence of a connexion, but its absence may not be enough reason to dissociate a text from the collective source.

First, let us go back to the table of Lives for which we can conjecture a common source used by both collections. We can extend it hypothetically and then consider its implications for Θ.

		S	O
Fursu	X	2	4
Nauigatio S. Brendani	?	3	[cf. 11]
Ciarán of Clon-macnoise	?	4	12
Catalogus	X	5	[in 8]
Darerca	—	6	—
Finnian	X	7	8
Tigernach	X	8	19
De causa peregrinacionis	X	9	[in 2]
Columba of Terryglass	X	20	25 [and cf. 8]
Maedóc	X	21	31
Munnu[2]	X	22	21

		S	O
? Senán	ʾ?	29	35
Brendan	?	30	11
Comgall	X	31	30
Mochutu	—	32	—
Lasrén	—	33	—
Mac Cairthinn	—	34	—
Ciarán of Saigir	X	35	34
Moling	X	36	5
Colmán of Dromore	X	37	6
Coemgen	X	38	37
Columba	X	39	2
Baithéne	X	40	3
Molua[2]	X	41	38

I have here arranged the list to show three series of texts as they are found in the sequence of S. In the extra column, the sign X indicates that both S and O derive from a common source, arguably Θ. A dash indicates that no comparison is possible because O lacks these Lives. There is a question-mark against the Life of St Senán, where we have already found the question of a common source difficult. The other question-marks are in places where the sequence leads one to expect to find further common-source texts. If all of these question-marks would resolve into Xs, the sequential argument for a single collective archetype would be overwhelming.

At first sight, the Life of St Brendan seems promising. The S-collection has two distinct texts, *Vita S. Brendani* (item 30) and *Nauigatio S. Brendani* (item 3); the O-collection has only one, a copy of the *uita* into which the *Nauigatio* has been inserted. One might hope to find that this conflation follows the pattern we have seen with St Columba and St Finnian. Unfortunately, it is not so. Textually, the copy of *Nauigatio S. Brendani* used by the redactor of O was closer to the original text (or rather, the critical text of Selmer) than that copied by the compiler of S, while the *uita* as preserved in S is much too abbreviated to have served as the source of the conflated text in O. These texts can have no part in a common collective archetype.

In the case of the Life of St Ciarán of Clonmacnoise, the S-text is truncated at the end, notwithstanding the scribe's 'Finit. Amen'. Presumably the exemplar was incomplete. The O-text does not share this defect, and differs substantially in content, arrange-ment, and wording from the S-text. There is no question here of a common source.

The extended sequence begins to look very shaky. If we accept that the Lives of SS. Brendan, Ciarán, and Senán reached S independently of the main sequence of SO-Lives, can we con-jecture any collective archetype? This is a question which can be seen two ways. Is our Θ, a text conjectured to explain common errors in S and O, a real collection or a text-historical ghost? Does the evidence for its existence override the evidence which tends to undermine its existence?

The sequential argument does, I think, still work in some measure. In the case of items 35–41 in S, it looks very convincing; the series 7–9, joined to the later series by the transposition in the O-text of *De causa peregrinacionis*, is equally plausible. But to extend these series to include the Lives of St Fursu and St Comgall inevitably leads to breaks. The middle series, SS. Columba of Terryglass, Maedóc, and Munnu, appears to be linked only by the use of the Life of St Columba of Terryglass in the O-text of the Life of St Finnian; another explanation may be found for this.

We must turn therefore to the argument from editorial habits. How many of those Lives marked with an X in the table show stylistic features which might credibly indicate a common redactor?

For the long sequence (items 35–41), we have already seen evidence for the habit of inserting biblical parallels. The same habit occurs in the Life of St Comgall,[27] and in the Lives of St Finnian and St Tigernach. The story *De causa peregrinacionis* and the *Catalogus Sanctorum Hiberniae* are connected to the series by the use made of them by the redactor of O. For all these texts it seems likely that one collective source Θ can reasonably be accepted. Other texts on our list of Lives where S and O had a common source may stand outside that collective archetype. This does not undermine the evidence for its existence, though it destroys our hypothetical construction of an orderly table of contents for the lost collection.

Judging by the texts which we can most confidently suppose to derive from it, this was a collection of Lives abbreviated and

---

[27] SO §3 'ut quondam Anna Samuelem'.

'farced' by a compiler whose intentions did not differ greatly from those of the compiler of the **O**-collection. Indeed, one could consider Θ to represent an unfinished form of the **O**-collection, not fully edited and certainly far from complete. A copy of this imperfect collection, closely related to **O**, seems to have been kept and to have reached the compilers of **S**. Just how closely Θ is related to the genesis of the **O**-collection we cannot say; the evidence is insufficient. We may be sure, however, that they were compiled on very similar principles.

9.4. *The Relative Dates of* **D**, **O**, **S**, *and* Θ: *the Lives of St Ciarán of Saigir and St Maedóc*

Any attempt to date and locate the compiler of Θ is doomed to fail for lack of evidence. There is, however, enough information to be got from a comparison of all the collections to allow the working out of an order of compilation. This can be shown by a few examples from the Lives of St Ciarán of Saigir and St Maedóc.

The identification offered earlier for the Life of St Patrick was made possible by the capacity to recognize the editorial style of the redactor of **D**. The Life of St Ciarán of Saigir is one where the redactor of **D** had an active interest, which shows in his treatment of the saint's role as a missionary in Ireland before St Patrick, and in his account of significant battles in the history of Leinster.[28] Where these interests reappear in the **SO**- or Θ-text of the Life, this is highly significant. Plummer could not have recognized this, because his approach would have interpreted the similarities between **D** and **SO** as deriving from a common source.[29] Yet where a feature characteristic of the redactor's work on **D** turns up in another recension, it must be an indication that the latter is derived from the former.

In several places in the early part of the Life, the redactor of **D** expatiates on the theme of how the saints who worked in Ireland before St Patrick in due course accepted his superior position over

[28] See above, pp. 115–16, 165–6 nn. 99–100.
[29] In fact, all Plummer has to say on the comparison of these two texts is that 'the SR text is much shorter than that in M, omitting much that is interesting and adding hardly anything'; *Vitae*, vol. i, p. lii.

them.[30] At § 13, following a story of how St Ciarán had revived the dead son, Loegaire, of a man called Fintán, the **D**-text continues:

Interea sanctus Patricius, predicator Hibernie, in regionem Mumenensium uenit, et credidit ei Aengus filius Nafraich, rex Mumenie, in ciuitate regali Cassel, et baptizatus est.

Tunc quidam homo, filius Erch, de nepotibus Duach de terra Osraighi, equum sancti Patricii euentu ⟨non⟩ sponte occidit.

The story which follows in no way demands any reference to the conversion of Oengus mac Nadfroich by St Patrick, but the latter was a topic of great interest to the redactor of **D**.[31] The source from which the redactor worked does not survive, but there are two other witnesses to it. One is an Irish text in the O'Clery collections, which very likely depends on the same source as **D**. Though the surviving text, published by Plummer as the second Irish Life, did not take its present form until after the Reformation, it depends on a Latin text very like that used by John of Tynemouth in the early fourteenth century as the basis for his abbreviated Life.[32] It appears that at different stages the lost Latin Life was used successively by the redactor of **D**, by John of Tynemouth (or his source), and by the sixteenth-century Irish translator. In this latter Life, although Oengus mac Nadfroich had been previously mentioned, at this point the paragraph begins:[33]

Duine úasal, darbh ainm Mac Eirce, dá shíol Ó nDuach, do marbh each carpait Patraicc . . .

'There was a certain nobleman, named Mac Eirce, of the race of the Uí Duach, who killed a chariot-horse belonging to St Patrick . . .'

There is no reference here to the conversion of Oengus; there was almost certainly none in the source. Its occurrence as an addition in **D** reflects the interest of the redactor of **D**. Yet it appears in the **SO**-recension, joined up with a further passage from **D** § 7:[34]

---

[30] *CiS.* **D** §§ 3, 7.

[31] See below, pp. 303–5.

[32] Plummer, *Bethada Náem nÉrenn* (2 vols.; Oxford, 1922), vol. i, pp. xxv–xxvii.

[33] *Betha Ciaráin Saighre* (II) § 30 (Plummer, *Bethada*, i. 117; ii. 113).

[34] Another Irish Life, this one evidently derived from the **D**-text, though probably written before the O'Clery Life, is found in the manuscript of Donnell Dinneen, *Betha Ciaráin Saighre* (I), in Plummer, *Bethada*, i. 103–12, where at § 19, the Irish text closely parallels the **D**-text.

Cumque [beatus Patricius] terram predicando, baptizando, atque
sanitates uariis languoribus conferendo perlustraret, ad regionem
Mumoniensium perueniens, regem terre Engussum baptizauit. Casu
post hec contigit equm sancti Patricii seruicio necessarium a quodam
Osrigensi genere interfici.

Again at §36 of the O'Clery Life there is a story in which Oengus
and his wife visit the ruler of Ossory, and the saint averts trouble
caused by the queen. The **D**-text concludes with an added
prophecy, briefly told, and a detailed account of its fulfilment,
together with a note on the queen's Uí Chennselaig kinsmen
which is an exact parallel to an addition made by the redactor in
Vita IV S. Brigitae.[35] The **SO**-text, §10, incorporates the fulfilment
into the account of the prophecy, though it omits the note on the
queen's kin.[36]

Turning now, once again, to the Life of St Maedóc, we have
already shown that a comparison of the texts in **V** and **D** reveals
precisely where the latter has revised the text. At the end of **D** §26,
the redactor has added an extensive passage on the status of the

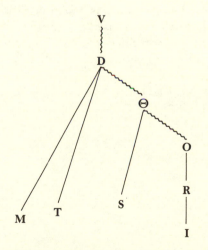

Fig. 3 Life of St Maedóc: Textual Relationship

[35] II 12; see above, p. 165 and n. 100.
[36] The Dinneen Life, §30, also follows the **D**-text, but omits the Uí Chennselaig
reference; Plummer, *Bethada*, i. 108; ii. 104.

church of Ferns.[37] The equivalent passage in the S- and O-texts has been quoted earlier in the present chapter.[38] These latter both derive from Θ, which S represents exactly. A comparison of this with D proves that the addition to the chapter in D was present in the source of Θ, so confirming what we have inferred from the Life of St Ciarán of Saigir, that D was available to the compiler of Θ. The availability of V to clarify the redactor's contribution in D means that in this case we have a clear-cut sequence through four recensions, V, D, Θ, and SO.

The redactor of Θ, the source of the SO-text, did not follow his source as closely as we have seen that the redactors of D or O followed their sources, but the fact that his version has signs of the special interests of the redactor of D must surely lead us to suppose that the D-text was his source. If that is so, and the evidence of other Lives will support it, this is a point of significance, for it allows us to say that the redactor of D had finished his work before the compilation of the abbreviated legendary which I have called Θ, and whose texts survive in SO. Since Θ was available to the compilers of both O and S, it must be older than both of them. It is already established that one of the extant manuscripts of O was written before the S-collection was assembled. So we have now a sequence of collections: D was used as a source by Θ, which was in turn used first by the compilers of O and later in the fourteenth century by the compilers of S.

[37] Quoted below, in Chapter 12, p. 359.
[38] See above, p. 289.

10

The O'Donohue Group of Texts in SDO

N o w we turn to a group of nine Lives preserved in all three collections, together with a possible tenth, the Life of St Columba of Terryglass, in S and O. This group corresponds to Heist's third series in S, which he defined as items 12 to 20 or 21.[1] It includes the memorandum '3ª qᵃtᵃ Isti fuerunt accommodati mihi a fratre Dermicio Ó Dunchade' at f. 96ʳ, which like him I take to refer to the loan of a group of texts which I shall call the O'Donohue group, putting the name Ó Donnchadha into English dress. This does not exhaust Br. Diarmait's contribution to the compilation of S. He is also named in connexion with Lawrence's Life of St Brigit and the Life of St Cuanna, but these cannot be grouped.

The definition of this group rests on formal, textual, and linguistic arguments. In brief, this group consists of texts which are long and detailed in form in S and were available to both D and O, the compilers of which edited the texts according to their habits; the evidence of a number of textual errors detectable even in the different recensions establishes the existence of a common archetype; the forms of Irish names, whose antiquity Plummer noticed in passing, consistently adhere to Old Irish orthography while the Latin vocabulary includes words which had become obsolete or had changed their meaning by the time the later recensions in D and O were made. We shall in due course examine in detail each of these arguments, and provide illustrative examples.

The group as defined by these arguments extends from the Life of St Ailbe to the Life of St Colmán Élo, or perhaps that of St Columba of Terryglass, nine or ten consecutive texts in S (items 11–20). The physical evidence which Heist used to define the group still applies. The memorandum of the loan occurs on the first recto of the first new gathering in the group; Heist presumed

---

[1] Heist, *Vitae*, p. xxvi (items 12–21, Molua¹–Maedóc), cf. p. xli (items 12–20, Molua¹–Columba of Terryglass).

this must be in the first Life of the group, but it is not; it is in the second. There were six leaves of quire v available when the copyist began on this group, which must have been ready to hand. He did not waste those leaves, but started at f. 90 with the Life of Ailbe. The compiler's memorandum, as Heist noted, is at the front of the next new quire. At the end of the group, on f. 132, the half column left at the end of the Life of St Columba of Terryglass is blank, and quire viii ends. Prima facie, therefore, this last belongs to the group, but the close agreement between **S** and **O**, and the absence of a **D**-text, combine to suggest that it should perhaps be regarded as a Life for which **S** and **O** had a common source, not necessarily Θ, and not as one of the O'Donohue group.[2]

10.1. *Recensional Relationships in the O'Donohue Group*

Of the nine texts definitely in the O'Donohue group, the **S**-texts are printed in the editions of De Smedt and De Backer and of Heist, the **D**-texts by Plummer. Only one of them, the Life of St Aed, has been published from **O**.[3] The dossiers of the nine saints from which Plummer edited the **D**-texts are discussed by him, but as with the **SO**-group each Life was studied separately, and he made no attempt to combine his observations on the individual Lives.

At the risk of labouring this point, I shall again quote from his introductions to the individual Lives. On the Lives of St Ailbe, he writes:[4]

The three recensions M T, S, R all clearly go back to a common original. S is certainly nearest to that original, which M T and R have independently edited, R being of the two much the nearer to S. R, however, omits many interesting details, names of places and persons, and also whole sections (S §§ 35, 37, 40, 44, 50). R also makes additions to the text of S,

---

[2] The evidence appears to be equivocal as to whether this Life should be treated as an **SO**-Life, probably from Θ, or as one of the O'Donohue group. The textual argument suggests the former; the linguistic argument, the division of the codex, and certain correspondences with other Lives of the O'Donohue group suggest the latter.

[3] P. Grosjean, 'De Sancto Aido Episcopo Killariensi in Hibernia', in *Acta Sanctorum*', Nov. IV (1925), pp. 517–24.

[4] Plummer, *Vitae*, vol. i, p. xxix.

but they are usually of the nature of ecclesiastical padding, scriptural parallels, and the like, and seldom increase our knowledge. M T also omits whole sections of S (§§ 23, 26, 28, 38, 41, 44), and it should be noted that, except in one instance, these omissions do not coincide with those of R. M T also omits many interesting points in S; and both of the later recensions show a tendency to tone down or omit points in their original which were likely to give offence or not to be understood. But M T, like R, also makes additions of its own, sometimes of doubtful value.

These points are illustrated in footnotes, which are omitted here and in what follows. Next in order within the group comes the Life of St Lugidus or Molua, where the relationship of the recensions is complicated by the presence of two texts in S, the fuller of which belongs here among the O'Donohue Lives. Because of the special complexity of these four recensions, I shall defer discussion of this saint until later in the chapter. On the Lives of St Fintán of Clonenagh Plummer says:[5]

M and S cover much the same ground, S being perhaps nearer to the common source. M has, however, points of interest peculiar to itself. R is nearer to S than to M, and follows S rather closely, though it omits and abbreviates according to its wont.

On the Lives of St Fínán:[6]

The three recensions S, R, and M all go back to some common original. S is certainly the nearest to that common original, which R and M have independently edited and abbreviated, R being much the nearer to S of the two. R omits many interesting details which S has preserved, especially names of places, &c., and leaves out wholly §§6, 16, 19, 33 of S. On the other hand R 'farces' the text, *more suo*, with much ecclesiastical padding, biblical parallels, and such like. The omissions of M are more numerous, §§3, 12, 15, 17, 19, 22, 25, 31 of the S text being all excised, while for § 35 a different incident is substituted. The greater originality of S may be seen by comparing S §§ 16, 21, 35 with M §§ 13, 16, 26 respectively. The comparison affords an interesting study of the way in which primitive ideas or customs which gave offence, or were not understood in later times, were gradually obliterated in successive editions of these lives.

---

[5] Ibid., vol. i, p. lxx.
[6] Ibid., vol. i, p. lxviii.

On the Lives of St Ruadán:[7]

M and S have clearly a common source, S being in some cases nearer to that source. The M text has, however, points of interest of its own, and as it has never been printed before, it is given here . . . The R text is a shorter recension of S.

On the Lives of St Aed mac Bricc:[8]

The three recensions M T, S, and R are often very close together, showing that they all come from some common original. And S is clearly nearest to this original, which R and M T have edited independently. R is of the two much nearer to the common source than M T; there are the usual omissions of proper names, &c., and the usual insertion of ecclesiastical padding, but the only section of the S text which is omitted wholly by R is §18. The M T editor has gone to work much more drastically. He omits the most characteristic parts of S, §§11, 13; and the whole of §§19, 21, 22, 33, 36, 39, 42–4, 49, 51. He also tones down passages in his original which might be likely to cause difficulty or scandal. The only positive addition made by M T is in §6 (consecration of Aed as bishop). The M T text is therefore of little independent value, but is interesting for purposes of comparison as a specimen of the way in which earlier lives were treated by later scribes.

On the Lives of St Cainnech:[9]

The three recensions, S, R, and M, clearly go back to a common original. It is no less clear that S is nearest to that common original, which R and M have edited, each in its own way. Of the two R is much nearer than M to S. But R omits much which S has preserved, names of places and persons, and also two whole sections, S §§38, 41, while inserting, *more suo*, moral reflexions and biblical parallels. M, while retaining more than R in the way of details of place and person, omits a much greater number of sections, viz. S §§15, 23, 34, 52, 55–9; S §§36, 40 (= M §§29, 32), are also very much shortened. . . . M has, moreover, one or two points of interest peculiar to itself.

The Life of St Fintán of Taghmon, alias Munnu, is known from four recensions: a long S-text which is next in order within the O'Donohue group, a revised version in **D**, a short text in **S** which Plummer regarded as 'closely allied' to the **D**-text, and finally an **O**-text which was very closely connected with the shorter **S**-text.

---

[7] Ibid., vol. i, pp. lxxxvi–lxxxvii.   [8] Ibid., vol. i, p. xxvii.

[9] Ibid., vol. i, pp. xliii–xliv.

Plummer's comments on these, however, are misleading, and I have reserved St Munnu for later treatment along with St Molua. Finally, Plummer writes this about the Lives of St Colmán Élo:[10]

All three recensions are sufficiently alike to make it certain that they have some common source or sources. S is the fullest, and, on the whole, the most original; but it is possible that some of the sections peculiar to S have been transferred from lives of other saints to whom they refer. R is much nearer to S than to M T, but is shorter. Its omissions as compared with S sometimes coincide with those of M T, and sometimes not. M T has, however, some original points, and as this text has never been printed, it seemed worth while to give it for purposes of comparison.

Plummer consistently refers to a 'common original' or 'common source', to which the extant recensions were judged to be more or less close. The S-texts, with the same degree of consistency, emerge as being closest to that original, and are in fact those Lives which caused Plummer to remark on the 'primitive' nature of some of the S-Lives, though he did not attempt to list them.[11] In most cases the O-text is considered to be next closest to the original, and also to be very close to the text of S. In the case of Ruadán, Plummer recognized that the O-text is derived from the S-text. Since Plummer was also aware that all the additions made to these Lives in O conformed to a pattern of what he called biblical farcing, for which the compilers were responsible, it would have been a very short step to realize that in all these cases the O-texts were based on the S-texts.

The 'common original', however, seems to have been demanded to explain that S and D often each contain material absent from the other. This supposes that a redactor is incapable of adding but can only omit. Anything which is in either text is presumed to have been in the original which the two recensions have edited independently. But if this is the reason why in all these cases Plummer hypothesized a common original, it is nowhere spelt out. The clearest statement of this is made of the Life of St Fínán: 'S is certainly the nearest to the common original, which R and M have independently edited and abbreviated'. It is perhaps also implied that this is the relationship when he says of Colmán Élo's Life that 'M T has . . . some original points'. In saying that

---

[10] Ibid., vol. i p. lvii.
[11] Compare above, pp. 243–4.

the Lives of SS. Fintán of Clonenagh, Cainnech, and Ruadán in **D** have 'points of interest' of their own, it is not explicit that these are preserved from the original. But this 'common original' theory begins to crack when Plummer admits of the Life of St Ailbe that 'M T . . . makes additions of its own, sometimes of doubtful value', or that in the Life of St Aed 'the only positive addition made by M T is in §6 . . . The M T text is therefore of little independent value.'[12]

If **D** could add as well as omit, the need to hypothesize a common original vanishes. If 'the M T text is of little independent value' in the case of Aed, on what did it depend? Answer: the S-text. Indeed, Grosjean in his discussion of the three recensions of the Life of Aed admits that he can see little reason to conjecture a common original and that everything in **D** or **O** that was not taken over from **S** could have been the work of the redactor.[13] Plummer himself was perhaps unconsciously aware of this, for, though he talks of how **D** and **O** have independently edited the common original, he never alludes to the editorial differences between that supposed original and **S**.

In all nine cases, therefore, where these Lives are found in the three recensions we may replace Plummer's view of the general relationship (Fig. 4*a*) with the one that is not open-ended (Fig. 4*b*). Plummer himself had virtually arrived at this conclusion in the case of the Life of St Cainnech, but he did so on textual evidence, which we shall consider shortly, and did not go further than saying that **O** and **D** depended on a text 'akin' to **S**.

Meanwhile, I wish to show that the treatment of **S** by **D** and **O** conforms in all cases to what we have learnt to expect. Examples

---

[12] The 'positive addition' in *Aed* **D** §6, to §10 of the S-text, reads: 'Post hec sanctissimus Edus uocatus est ad regionem Midi, patriam suam, et ordinatus est episcopus, et aliquando in Mumenia adhuc conuersabatur, et cellas et monasteria in utraque regione edificauit.' This is entirely the work of the redactor of **D**. The reference to 'cellas et monasteria' is of a common type in **D**. The rest merely shows the redactor tidying the narrative, as he did with the Life of St Brigit. The previous story told how he was sent to Munster as an envoy by the Uí Néill king, but his return is not mentioned, while **S** §12 refers to the saint as 'episcopus Aidus', so the redactor has added a mention of his consecration. He might have done better to place his addition a little later for **S** §11, **D** §7, is still set in Munster.

[13] Grosjean, 'De Sancto Aido', p. 496 n. 5: 'Nihil tamen perspicimus cur non a Vita I [i.e. **S**] fluxerint Vitae II [**O**] et III [**D**]. Sed peracutus sit qui litem diremerit.'

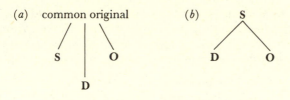

FIG. 4 Lives of the O'Donohue group

will be taken from some of the nine Lives of this group available in all three recensions.

First, a passage from the Life of St Ailbe, which draws on a theme which we have already shown to be one of the interests of the redactor of **D**, the role of the pre-Patrician saints in the conversion of Ireland:

Ail. **S** §29: Post hec sanctus Albeus circumibat Hyberniam. Cumque uenisset ad Casselum, inuenit ibi Patricium et regem Engussum. Tunc Patricius obtulit Albeo omnes uiros Munnensium, ut esset eorum pater, et regem Engussum in manum Albei.

The redactor of **O** found nothing here of special interest, but added that Patrick had received his missionary commission from the Pope, according to a well-established tradition:

Ail. **O** (I f. 133ra): Post hec sanctus Helueus peruenit ad locum qui Casselum dicitur et ibi inuenit sanctum Patricium *Hibernie primatem* una cum rege terre qui Engus dictus est. Tunc sanctus Patricius tradidit potestatem suam Helueo super Momonienses *sicut ipse recepit a papa super omnes Hibernienses. Specialiter quoque predictum* regem ei commisit, *eo quod uir iustus et bonus esset.*

This very slight expansion on the text of **S** certainly does not require us to suppose that the two are independently derived from a common original. The redactor of **D**, who found this passage particularly interesting, revises and elaborates to a large extent:

Ail. **D** §22: Sanctus uero Albeus circuibat totam Hiberniam, *predicans baptismum, et multos ibi conuertit ad fidem, set non omnes; quia uoluit Dominus omnipotens ut beatus Patricius episcopus, qui post Albeum in Hiberniam uenit, conuerteret omnes ad fidem Hibernences. Et ita factum est. Nam Patricius episcopus totam Hiberniam a gentilitate ad fidem et baptismum conuertit.* Cum *beatus Albeus audisset quod* Patricius regem *Memonensium,* Engussum *filium Nefrich, conuerteret ad Christum ac esset cum eo in ciuitate regali* Cassel, uenit *ut eos salutaret. Rex autem et Patricius gauisi sunt in aduentu Albei, et ille est gauisus eos uidens. Ibi uero accepit Patricium magistrum suum sanctus Albeus, quia ualde erat humilis. Tunc rex Engus et Patricius ordinauerunt ut in ciuitate et cathedra sancti Albei esset arciepiscopatus omnium Memonensium semper.*

The student working on this Life in isolation might easily imagine that here was evidence for supposing that the **D**-text was produced at Cashel, at a time when the Eoganacht rulers of Cashel were busily emphasizing the religious status of the kingdom of Cashel. The story of St Patrick's role in this episode appears also in his own *uitae*:

Vita III S. Patricii Γ §60 (part): Tunc uenit Patricius per Beluch Gubroin ad reges [*? l.* regiones] Mumunentium, et	**D** fr. 25: *Gloriosus presul* Patricius, *seminata in regionibus Laginensium fide, uiam suam*
	ad fines Muminensium *direxit: transiensque terram Ossargy, que est orientalis Laginensium plaga, intrauit in terram na nDesi, que est orientalis Mumonie pars.*
	Et audiens rex Mumoniensium filius Nafroich *nomine* Engus *aduentum sancti Patricii,*
occurrit illi in campo Femin Oengus filius Nafroich rex Mumunentium, et ille gauisus est in aduentu sancti Patricii et adduxit eum secum ad habitaculum suum quod dicitur Caissel,	occurrit illi in campo Femyn, *qui est in terra na nDesi.* Et gauisus est *rex* in aduentu sancti Patricii, *multum desiderans credere et baptizari.* Adduxitque *sanctum pontificem* secum *cum honore et letitia* ad suam *ciuitatem regalem nomine* Casseal, *que est in regione Eoghanacht.*
et ibi credidit ei et baptizatus est.	Et ibi credidit Deo *rex* Engus, et baptizatus est.

The redactor of **D** also mentions the episode briefly in the Life of St Ciarán of Saigir, another pre-Patrician saint, §13, and more importantly in his Life of another, St Declán, §18. Here the arrival of St Ailbe is integrated into the story, along with Declán, Ciarán, and Ibar:

Decl. **D** §18: Ailbeus autem, uidens maiores Hibernie post Patricium concurrere, uenit ad sanctum Patricium in ciuitate Caissell, et accepit eum ibi cum omni humilitate magistrum suum coram rege Enguso, quod prius non habuit in mente.

It is clear enough from this that the points added by the redactor of **D** to the passage in the Life of St Ailbe draw on his personal interests, and again do not demand the existence of any common source used by **S** and **D**. The text of **S** is itself the source.

For our second example showing that it is not necessary to look beyond **S** for the source of the later redactions, here is a passage from the Life of St Ruadán:

Rua. **S** § 19: Alio autem tempore, cum sanctus Ruodanus et sui monachi habitare⟨n⟩t in loco illo qui dicitur Dare Ethnech, misit ad eum Filius Darane Daire Moir corticem magnum plenum butiro. Cumque cortex iste super duos boues immites mane impositus esset, perrexerunt boues per grunnam a Dairi Moir, et in ista grunna ualde uiam durissimam et planam inuenerunt, quam nullus ante ⟨nec⟩ post ibi inuenit. Cortex autem iste apud Ruodanum diuidebatur quinquaginta ter uiris ab inicio uernalis tempore, et in die Pe⟨n⟩tecostes plenus sine diminutione cortex inuentus est.

The redactor of **O** has altered a fair amount, but to little effect:

Rua. **O** (R f. 219va): Cum uir Dei Ruadanus habitaret in loco qui Dayri Ednech dicitur, misit ad eum *quidam uir pietate permotus* quoddam *uas* magnum plenum butiro, ponens id super duos boues immites. Hii boues perrexerunt per *moram* illam grandem atque profundam *que mora de Hely dicitur* ubi uiam planam *nutu Dei* inuenerunt atque rectam quam nullus hominum nec ante nec post inuenire potuit. Hoc uero butirum miraculose missum, miraculosius translatum fratribus ad pastum a principio uernalis temporis usque ad pentecostem sine sui diminutione durauit.

The elimination of *cortex* 'bark', used here in the sense 'vessel', suggests that this had become obsolete. The same substitution is made by the redactor of **D**, who also takes the opportunity to add two pieces of local interest:

Rua. **D** § 25: Alio tempore, cum sanctus Ruadhanus in *monasterio* quod *olim* dicebatur Dayre Ethnech (*modo autem Daire na Fland dicitur, in quo semper uiri religiosissimi habitant, et est positum in confinio regionum Eile et Eoganacht*) cum monachis suis habitaret, *sanctus episcopus Columbanus* filius Darane, *qui habitabat in loco qui dicitur* Daire Mor, *uas* plenum misit butyro sancto Ruadhano et monachis suis in carro per duos boues. *Grunna maxima et humidissima est inter loca predicta que dicitur gronna stagni Lurgan. Stagnum enim olim ibi erat, in quo bestia ualde uenenosa erat, que multos* *occidit. Et ipsam quidam heros fortissimus nomine Ferdomuyn gladio in duas partes uno ictu diuisit; set postrema pars bestie, natans ad eum per aquam, abscidit eum per uentrem iuxta terram, et mortuus est ibi. De quo fertur quod ipse in uno bello sexcentos occidit milites. Ipse iam de genere Laginensium erat.* Et cum uenissent boues ad gronnam illam, inuenerunt uiam planam ac durissimam in gronnam usque ad cellam sancti Ruadani, quam uiam nullus ante uel post ibi inuenit. Ab inicio iam ueris usque Pentecosten diuidebatur illud uas apud sanctum Ruadhanum centum quinquaginta monachis cum hospitibus suis, et in die Pentecostes illud uas *Deo dono* butyro plenum inuentum est.

The name Derrynavlan, which has recently been made famous by the discovery of a hoard of precious goods including a chalice, had evidently replaced the original name of Daire Ethnech between the time of the writer of the Life and the redaction of **D**. Of its monastery little is known.[14] St Colmán mac Oengusa[15] (his father was Oengus mac Nadfroich, king of Cashel), whose name is given in full, so to speak, in **D**, was well known by the nickname Mac Daráine.[16] The reading shared by **S** and **O** is not incomplete, but the redactor of **D** has preferred to fill in the detail. In each case, the redactor is exhibiting his interest in topography and in minor saints. His longer interpolation is more surprising, since it seems quite irrelevant—so irrelevant that it must seem rash to suppose that this passage could belong to a common source and was omitted by both **S** and **O**; interpolation by the redactor of **D**, surely, it must be.

In both of these examples, the differences between **S** and **O** amount to no more than a change of wording, and the addition of some generally known allusions. The redactor of **D** in both cases has moved a good way from **S**, but in neither do we need to suppose that he had any text other than **S** in front of him. As with the Life of St Brigit or that of St Patrick, such additions as he makes are made from his wide store of Irish antiquarian knowledge.

As a briefer example of recensional differences, here is a short extract from the Life of St Aed:

---

[14] F. J. Byrne, 'Derrynavlan: The Historical Context', *JRSAI* 110 (1980), 116–18.

[15] P. Ó Riain (ed.), *Corpus Genealogiarum Sanctorum Hiberniae* (Dublin, 1985), §§191.1, 612.

[16] Ibid. §§191.2, 722.59; the nickname uses his mother's name.

Aed S §29: Alio tempore uenit rex Thethbe cum grandi exercitu ad uastandas plebes Midi. Que rogauerunt Aidum episcopum ut ab inimicis sibi pacem quereret. Qui confestim abiit rogare pro eis pacem. Hoc audiens rex Tethbe surrexit et ait comitibus suis: 'Surgite, eamus, priusquam ueniat episcopus Aidus.' Et egredientes omnes, precedebant equites ad fluuium qui diuidit inter duas plebes. Et intrantes in illum, statim equi eorum steterunt immobiles in flumine, nec huc illucque pedem mouere potuerunt.

Aed O §23: Alio tempore uenit princeps terre illius que Tedpha dicitur cum grandi exercitu ad deuastandum fines Midentium. Cuius impetum timentes illi, miserunt ad episcopum Aydum ut rogaret eum ne noceret eis. Cumque filius pacis properaret ut uerbum pacis inter plebes illas seminaret, timens superbus regulus ne uir Dei conatum suum impediret, ait ad suos: 'Surgite, eamus, priusquam ueniat Aydus.' Ad cuius imperium properantes ceteri implendum, equites multi antecedebant ad flumen quod diuidit inter duas plebes, et intrantes illud, equi eorum steterunt immobiles quasi lapides, nec mouere se potuerunt.

The latter is linguistically more polished, but clearly follows the older S-text very closely. The redactor as often has avoided the word *rex*, preferring *regulus*, though here he also uses the more elaborate 'princeps terre illius'. The redactor of **D**, whom we know to avoid the term *rex* where it does not refer to the ruler of a major territory, predictably uses *dux* here. But his assessment of political implications is less superficial than that of the **O**-redactor.

Aed D §21: Venit aliquando dux Tedbe deuastare quandam plebem in regione Midhi; et rogatus ⟨est⟩ sanctus Edus ab incolis illius plebis occurrere ei et pacem ab eo querere. Hoc audiens dux, ait exercitui suo: 'Eamus uelociter priusquam sanctus Edus episcopus ad nos ueniet.' Hoc sciens uir Dei signauit contra illos. Illi autem ingredientes in quendam fluuium in confinio illius plebis et regionis Tedbe, equi eorum steterunt immobiles in uado, donec peruenit ad eos sanctus episcopus.

If the ruler of Tethbae is downgraded from *rex* to *dux*, so his power could not be sufficient to devastate the *plebes* of Meath, and his attack is therefore reduced to one against 'quandam plebem' in that region.[17] The river which formed the boundary between Tethbae and Meath was no longer of direct relevance to the story, and this too is changed to 'quendam fluuium' on the border.

---

[17] Compare in his Life of St Brigit, II 50 and n. 158.

From the same text, here is another and shorter example of minor differences:

Aed **S** §34: Alio autem die sanctus abiit ad quemdam regem Baiethene ut de manibus eius liberaret ancillam.

Aed **O** §28: Alio quoque tempore peruenit homo Dei ad regulum quendam ut de manibus eius uirginem unam quam captiuam habebat liberaret.

Aed **D** §25: Beatus senex Edus episcopus perrexit ad ducem Baithenum ut liberaret quandam feminam liberam quam dux cogebat ut esset ancilla.

The progress *rex, regulus, dux* appears again; the redactor of **O** has even suppressed the king's name. From the story in the original we learn no reason why the woman should be released from the king's service, but both the later redactors have reworded the text to imply that she was unjustly detained.

Another example of the recensional relationship, this time at its closest, is taken from the Life of St Cainnech:

Cain. **S** §8: Alio quoque die, sanctus Kannechus iter agens in Italia inuenit ibi in deserto armentarium cuiusdam regis, et ipse letatus est in aduentu eius et inuenit gratiam in oculis illius. Tunc sanctus Kannechus dedit ei aliud munusculum auri quod secum habuit. Audiens autem rex ille crudelis et immitis ab aliis nunciantibus sibi quod sanctus Kannechus aurum dedisset seruo et rustico, iratus est ualde, et displicuit ei donum regi congruum seruo dari, et dixit: 'Reus est mortis qui hoc opus insolitum ausus est facere.' Tunc rex ille iussit rogum magnum incendi et sanctum Kannechum in illum mitti. Quod ita iuxta preceptum factum est, sed statim ignis ille a Deo extinctus est, non audens tangere sanctum Dei.

Cain. **O** §7: Alio quoque die, cum esset uir Dei in Ytalia iter agens, inuenit armentarium cuiusdam regis qui in aduentum uiri Dei letatus est atque humanitatis obsequia sibi fecit. Tunc sanctus Kynnecus diiudicans eum beneficio dignum dedit ei munus quoddam de auro quod pro necessitatibus uie a quodam fideli Deum timente accepit. Audiens uero rex quod tale donum datum fuit rustico quod dignum esset dari regi, iratus est ualde et dixit: 'Reus est mortis qui hoc opus insolitum ausus est facere.' Tunc rex iussit rogum magnum incendi et sanctum Kynnicum immitti. Cumque in ignem mitteretur, statim flamma ignis extinguebatur, nec in aliquo ipsi Kennico nocuit. Qui enim Danielem cum sociis suis in fornace ignis custodiuit, ipse hunc uirum sanctum illesum ab hac flamma seruauit.

The reviser once again has changed little but the words, though he apparently thought it odd for the saint to carry gold and so has given an explanation of why he had it and how he came by it. He also adds his favourite signature, a biblical parallel to the story. The redactor of **D** has kept even closer to the text of **S**:

Cain. **D** §6: Alio quoque die sanctus Kainnicus, in Ytalia iter agens, inuenit armentarium cuiusdam ducis, qui letatus est in aduentu eius, et inuenit gratiam in oculis eius. Tunc sanctus Cainnicus munusculum auri dedit illi armentario. Audiens ⟨dux⟩ ille crudelis et immitis, aliis sibi nunciantibus, quod sanctus Cainnicus aurum dedisset armentario suo, iratus est ualde, et displicuit ei donum regi congruum seruo dari, et dixit: 'Reus est mortis, qui opus insolitum ausus est facere.' Tunc dux ille iussit rogum magnum incendi, et sanctum Cainnicum in illum mitti. Quod ita est factum iuxta preceptum ducis. Ideo hoc fecit dux quia putauit sanctum Cainnichum plus habere de auro. Set statim ignis ille a Deo extinctus est, non audens tangere sanctum Dei.

The almost inevitable use of *dux* is practically the only change made by the redactor, apart from his speculation as to the ruler's motives.

For a brief final example, I return to the Life of St Aed:

Aed **S** §45: Quadam autem die uenit sanctus Aidus ad sanctum Riocc insule Bo Finne, quem sanctus Riocc cum magno gaudio suscepit.

Aed **O** §39: Quodam tempore uenit sanctus ad uisitandum sanctum Riocum qui fuit sancti Patricii nepos; erat enim filius sororis eius. Qui eum cum magno gaudio hospicio suscepit.

Aed **D** §31: Venit sanctus Edus episcopus ad insulam Bo Finde, id est Vacce Albe, que est in stagno Righ. Suscepit eum sanctus Ryoch, abbas illius loci, honorifice. Monasterium enim clarum in illa insula est quod ex nomine insule nominatur.

The redactor of **O** flourishes a little knowledge of the Patrician legend, as he did in the extract quoted above from the Life of St Ailbe. St Patrick's sister Darerca was indeed supposed to be the mother of St Rióc of Inis Bó Finde, as also of fourteen or so other bishops.[18] The redactor of **D** prefers topography, and tells us a little about the monastery of Inishboffin, whose name is omitted by the **O**-text.

This procedure could be carried on for many pages, but it is

---

[18] Ó Riain, *Corpus*, §722.16.

obviously out of the question here to illustrate the whole of the nine texts in three recensions. The only deviations from this pattern are presented by the Lives of St Munnu and St Molua, the latter in particular, where versions very close to the O-texts are also found in S. I shall discuss the particular problems these present at a later stage. Meanwhile, it is sufficient to have established for the O'Donohue group a general pattern of recensional relationship.

The relationship between these Lives is consistent in all essentials. In each case Plummer considered that the S-text was the most nearly original; that O followed the original almost as closely as S, so that these two are often verbally alike; and that D omitted much, revised more, but retained some points from the original omitted by S. The stumbling-block for this argument—one might almost call it Plummer's blind-spot—was the failure to realize that the passages peculiar to D and O consistently conform with the interests of the redactors, and were their own additions to the S-text.

This result is of major significance, since it means that for nine Lives we have ascertained that we have in S the original on which the other recensions depend, and not merely a recension close to but indefinably different from a putative common original. Obviously, therefore, if we wish to study what the authors of these Latin Lives wanted to put across about their saintly subjects, it is not necessary to look any further than S. It is also of interest, though perhaps less so, that we now have a considerably larger number of texts where comparisons will reveal exactly what the late medieval redactors were doing. In the annotation of *Vita IV S. Brigitae* I took advantage of this to indicate by asterisks where comparisons were on such firm ground.

Having established now the recensional relationships which explain the differences in form of these Lives in S, D, and O, we may return to consider their status as a group. Is one justified in supposing that nine consecutive Lives in S which show a consistent pattern of relationship with Lives in D and O form a group of Lives available to all three compilers? Perhaps not on this argument alone. The argument derives some support from the fact that the pattern of recensional relationship of these Lives applies to none of those other dossiers which are represented in each collection. But for stronger reasons, we move on from recensional relationships to textual ones.

10.2. *Textual Connexions in the O'Donohue Group*

The redactors of **D** and **O** both worked from Lives of the S-recension for these nine Lives. The relative dates which we have established for the collections exclude the possibility that they could have used **S**, which was first assembled at the time that the *Codex Salmanticensis* was written in the late fourteenth century. We must deduce, therefore, the existence of an archetype (Φ), earlier than the redaction of **D**. Following the different lines of descent from that parent manuscript, we must distinguish between its textual legacy, that is what was *copied* from it, and its recensional legacy, that is what was *adapted* from it.

Where **S** and **O** or **S** and **D** are verbally identical, the secondary recension has copied its archetype, and textual comparisons are straightforward. Where they are not verbally the same, it may still be possible to infer textual comparisons where the **D**- and **O**-texts appear to be rewording to avoid a corrupt passage which may be seen undisguised in **S**.

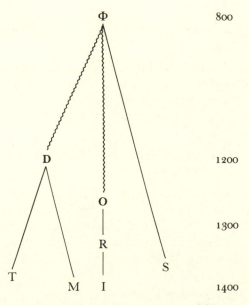

Fig. 5 Textual Descendants of Φ

But it is quite possible for **D** and **O** to agree on a reading against **S** at the textual level. Our copy of the **S**-texts, though its scribes attempted to reproduce the archetype more closely than the redactors of the other collections, may none the less contain errors of transcription not found in **D** and **O**. This is shown as a stemma. **D**, **O**, or **S** may each have misread Φ as they revised or copied from it, so they may each have peculiar errors. The agreement of any two against one is therefore possible. It is also possible that Φ contained errors of its own. If we can find them, then we can prove textually the existence of an archetype for the three recensions of the Lives in this group. On the other hand, a true reading in any one recension against two agreeing in error would invalidate this stemma, as we should have to add an intermediate archetype to explain the pair in error. More than one such pair could not be accommodated, and would therefore disprove textually the existence of Φ.

Plummer was well on the way to proving the existence of the archetype in the case of the Life of St Cainnech, though he may have thought himself to be arguing textually towards an error in the common original, which he thought all three witnesses had reworked. At **S** §44, he noted the reading:[19]

Laicus de illis, lucernam sancti circa se tenens, celesti igne ardens, pene consumptus est.

This *lucerna* was one of his *uestimenta linea* which the *laici* 'brigands' had stolen from the saint; it must therefore represent a miscopying of 'lacernam' and the story is similar in this detail to one told by Muirchú.[20] The reading of **D** betrays the same error:

Nocte autem ueniente, sanctus Cainnicus lucernam celesti igne ardentem habuit; et uidentes illi laici ipsam lucernam, uenerunt ad eam, et tunc unus de illis pene mortuus fuit.

The redactor has read 'lucernam', and in the same way that he modified that wording in *Vita IV S. Brigitae* II 83 to make sense of the corrupt 'moram iugulationis', so he has made sense of the corrupt reading here. Unfortunately, the redactor of **O** has here obscured the evidence. His text reads:

---

[19] *Vitae*, vol. i, p. xliv.
[20] Muirchú, *Vita S. Patricii*, I. 20 (ed. L. Bieler, *The Patrician Texts in the Book of Armagh* (Scriptores Latini Hiberniae, 10; Dublin, 1979), pp. 92–7).

Et cum unus illorum ueste sancti indueret, celesti igne ardens, pene consumptus est.

He has got rid of the illatinate phrase 'laicus de illis' for 'one of the brigands', and has also changed the noun we are interested in into 'ueste'. He may have had 'lacernam' in his exemplar and chosen an easier substitute, or he may have read 'lucernam', realized that this was nonsense, but been unable to emend, and so substituted a non-specific equivalent which gave adequate sense. The latter alternative seems to me the more likely: *lacerna* is not so difficult or rare a word that he would avoid it. Palaeographically the two words are close enough to be confused; and one might even hazard here that the archetype Φ was in eighth-century script with 'open' *a*. Furthermore, the word *lucerna* had just been used in S §42, D §35, and was perhaps still in the mind of the scribe of Φ.

Plummer gives other examples of misreadings from the same text. In S §48, the text runs:

Nos festinamus ad contentionem anime alicuius uiri diuitis hi Mollib Muscrigi.

D has the sentence almost verbatim:

Nos festinamus ad contendendam animam unius diuitis in regione Muscraighi.

The O-text was clearly following S:

Nos festinamus ad animam cuiusdam diuitis rapiendam nobiscum qui Maeldubh uocatur.

This, I suggest, is a misinterpretation, not a misreading. The redactor of O has taken the Irish construction 'hi Mollib' (preposition with dative plural) as '.i.' followed by the man's name. For 'Mollib' he has substituted a recognizable name, Maeldubh, a rash conjecture.[21] The S-text contains no error, so this is not evidence in our textual argument.

Plummer's third example is taken from §47 of the S-text, where we read:

'Scio quod ad Colmanum tibi amicum ad liberandum festinas. Sed tibi non prodest, quia non inuenies eum nisi cadauer eius iugulatum et

---

[21] It seems likely that the redactor took *Mollib* as an attempt to represent the pronunciation of *Maeldub* and regularized the spelling accordingly.

combustum igni.' Cui Kannechus dixit: 'Scit Filius Virginis quod est aliud carius quam quod cogitas. Nam antequam ad cellam tuam peruenias, mortuus eris.'

The difficulty is in the sentence, 'The Son of the Virgin knows that it is something dearer than what you think.' The man who predicts the death of Colmán will himself die, not Colmán. The simplest emendation might be to omit 'carius': 'The Son of the Virgin knows that it [*sc.* the fact] is different from what you think'. The reading of **O** has a different sense, but is grammatical:

Scit Filius Virginis quod est alius tibi carior in periculo maiori quam ille.

Plummer thought that this was 'a recasting of the sentence due to the false reading of S'.[22] He believed that **D** had the true reading: 'Scit Filius Virginis quia est uerius aliud quam quod dicis.' But this is nonsense: the man's words are not true at all. This represents a poor guess by **D** to interpret 'carius' in the exemplar. I would not say that 'carius' is right, but I think it was probably the reading in Φ.

From the two cases here, therefore, we find that **S** preserves a problem reading, 'lucernam' (an error) and 'carius' (perhaps an error?); **D** has recast in the first case, and tried an emendation in the second, but in both has missed the true sense; **O** has got the true sense, in each case with a simple paraphrase. With a little persuasion, the textual evidence appears to bear out the existence of Φ in the case of the Life of St Cainnech.

One would certainly prefer harder evidence, such as a clear misreading retained in all three recensions. But it is hardly likely that such a reading would get past the attentions of the redactors both of **D** and **O**. The one case where Plummer thought this had happened he mentions only in his notes.[23] At §12 of **S**, and the matching chapter in **O** and **D**, all three recensions agree that the skull which Cainnech makes speak belonged to someone dead for thirty years (xxx); Plummer thought that this may have been a shared error for three hundred (ccc). The latter reading makes better sense of the story, but if 'xxx' is a misreading, it is certainly not a clear one. We must accept the kind of evidence available. So far, however, we have only considered the Life of St Cainnech. What of the other Lives in the O'Donohue group?

If one were to believe Plummer's text of the Life of St Ailbe **D** § 13, there is a common error in M, S, and R. He prints the text as:

Multi erant ex ipsis unius nominis, id est duodecim Colmani, et duodecim Comangeni, et sancti duodecim Fintani.

The word 'sancti' is not in M or S or R. Plummer has taken it from T, but it has no business in the text and should be excised as a casual error in T. M, S, and R agree on the true reading, which is of no help to us.

An ill-founded editorial text can be a real peril. For example, in the Life of St Fintán of Clonenagh, S § 20, the manuscript reads:

Veniens quoque, Deo ducente, ad domum in qua uinctus erat, similiter illius aperta est.

Heist emended 'illius' to 'illis', De Smedt and De Backer to 'illi', but either of these would leave the feminine 'aperta' awkwardly construed with *domus* as the implied subject. The reading of **O** is, 'Et mox domus illa similiter ultro aperta est eis'; possibly a conjecture, but certainly a better one. I suspect, however, that **D** § 17 has in fact kept the original construction:

Et perueniens ad domum in qua erat iuuenis cathenatus in uinculis, similiter aperta est et ianua illius.

The omission of *ianua* may easily have been an error in the manuscript S, so the reading of Φ may be restored: 'similiter ⟨ianua⟩ illius aperta est'. In the same chapter, S reads:

Et statim occurrit ei multitudo uirorum, inter quos erat filius, qui uolebat iugulare uirum nuper resolutum.

'Filius' on its own is insufficient; Heist prints 'filius ⟨Belial⟩' without saying that this is taken from **D**:

Et occurrit ei in uia multitudo militum, inter quos erat filius Belial de genere regali qui uolebat Cormacum, quem absoluit sanctus, occidere.

The redactor has here changed several minor details, and it must be recognized that his 'filius Belial de genere regali' could easily be an interpretative treatment of the reading preserved in **O**:

Ecce occurrit eis filius regis cum turba magna qui statim uoluit prefatum uirum occidere.

Heist has too readily looked to Plummer's edition of the **D**-text without considering the existence of other textual evidence. The most economical reading here, proposed by De Smedt and De Backer, is to supply 'regis' after 'filius' in **S**. If this were the reading of **Φ**, we can see how **O** and **D** paraphrased in their different ways, while the scribe of our **S** omitted the word. In both these instances, therefore, one is looking at an individual error in the present manuscript **S**, not an error transmitted from the archetype **Φ**. Unfortunately, most of the errors in the Lives preserved in **S** fall into this category.

Occasionally, however, one feels that it is possible to detect omissions in the text of **Φ**. In the Life of St Aed, for example, at **S** §2, we read:

Erat autem sanctus Aidus in domo matris sue alitus in terra Munnensium puerulus. Denique adhuc iuuenis factus, gregem porcorum in siluis querens, sanctum Brandanum Birra inuenit in aliquo secreto loco scribens [*corr.* scribentem] euuangelium, et Kennechus sanctum Aidum nuper uenientem loquentes autem et salutantes sancti inuicem, uiderunt puerum proximantem.

Something has to be wrong somewhere. The two saints, Brendan of Birr and Cainnech, appear to have just met, and their conversation has disturbed St Brendan's writing, even before they see the young Aed. But the later recensions do not help to emend the text. In **O**, Aed is said to come 'ad locum in quo sanctus Brandanus Birra et sanctus Kynnecus erant'; the text of **D** reads:

Quodam die ambulans beatus puer Edus solus in heremo, inuenit[a] in quadam cellula ⟨in⟩ secreta[b] et remota insula duos sanctos seniores abbates, silicet Brendanum Byrra et Kainnicum, legentes euangelium sub umbra arborum et, loquentes sibi inuicem, sancti uiderunt sibi proximantem puerum.

[a] inuen M inuenit T *edd.*   [b] ⟨in⟩ secreta *Plummer, rejected by Grosjean*

Neither of these readings picks up all the clues of the **S**-text, and I suspect that both are attempts to avoid a problem in the exemplar **Φ**, undetected by the scribe of **S**. While the editors of the **S**-text have noticed the difficulty, only Plummer has attempted surgery.[24]

---

[24] De Smedt and De Backer conjectured that some words had dropped out after 'uenientem', and were followed in this by Grosjean and Heist. Plummer (in his own copy of De Smedt and De Backer) proposed to emend the text to read, 'et Kannechum sanctum ad eum nuper uenientem. Loquentes . . .', which is neat.

Likewise, in S §46 of the Life of St Cainnech, the text runs:

Colmanus filius Feradichi rex Ossirgi sancto Kannecho amicus erat, quia ipse rex magnum ⟨...⟩ de seculo propter celum Kannecho in commercium dedit.

Whatever agrees with 'magnum' is omitted, and the gift is left unspecified. The text of **O** has 'Erat quidam regulus in terra qui Ossrigia dicitur, Colmanus nomine, qui sancto uiro ualde deuotus erat', perhaps an evasive paraphrase. The redactor of **D** has indulged his own whim somewhat more:

Colmanus filius Fearaidhe, dux regionis Osraidhe, sancto Cainnico amicus erat, et ipse multas uillas dedit ei, in quibus sanctus Cainnicus edificauit monasteria et ciuitates.

It is possible that the reading of Φ underlying **D** here was 'magnum agrum', but there are familiar phrases here, and it is more likely that the redactor has elaborated on an incomplete 'magnum' in the exemplar. Another apparent omission in Φ occurs in the Life of St Molua, where at S §5 we read:

Cumque pater quereret illum, inuenit eum in campo dormientem, sed tamen propius accedere ad illum non ausus est, quia uirum in uestibus albis stantem iuxta illum uidit, et odor ex ore pueri egrediens patrem inebriauit per nouem ⟨...⟩. Tunc Carthachus perrexit...

For nine what? 'Horas', perhaps? The reading of **D** shortens the sentence, going straight from 'ante eum stantem uidit' to 'tunc'. The text of **SO** omits the whole chapter.

Two readings, however, add greater weight to the theory that Φ existed, not only for the Life of St Cainnech but for the whole O'Donohue group. First, in the Life of St Fintán of Clonenagh, S §8, the original reading 'per octo dies' was altered by the scribe to 'per iiii^{or} dies'; the reading of **O** is 'per iiii dies', that of **D** 'post uii dies'. It would appear, therefore, that the numeral in the exemplar Φ was indistinct, presumably four minims. Second, and perhaps most conclusive, is a misreading noted by Heist in the Life of St Fínán Cam, at S §§4–5:

Dixit autem sanctus Brendanus maccu Alte ad parentes eius: 'Magnus erit filius uester coram Domino.' Deinde uenit ad Brandanum, ut legeret et disceret regulam cum eo. Fiebat autem apud Brandanum contra fornacem.

Alio autem die, traxit secum de silua materiam baculi sine permissione abbatis sui Brandani. Videns autem Brandanus, proiecit illud lignum in fornacem .uii. annis. Et non solum non tetigit ignis lignum, sed formauit ignis baculum sicut uoluit Finanus.

In the **D** text, the first paragraph ends, 'dimiserunt eum ad sanctum Brendanum, ut legeret et disceret apud eum in monastico habitu'. In the second paragraph, the second sentence reads, 'Videns hoc sanctus pater Brendanus proiecit in fornace ignis, et fuit ibi ille baculus multo tempore'. The words 'multo tempore' obviously stand for '.uii. annis' in **S**. But Heist observed that '.uii. annis' is misplaced; it should follow 'contra fornacem', but by an error of transcription it follows 'in fornacem' three lines below. The reading of **D** proves that it was so in Φ. The redactor of **O** has evaded the problem by removing any reference to time.

None of the textual evidence is clear and decisive, but this would hardly be likely when two of our three witnesses were in the habit of detecting and avoiding textual difficulties. Our attempts to peer through their efforts amount to a considerable case for saying that we can detect errors in Φ in the light of our three witnesses. The existence of a single manuscript source for all three recensions seems highly likely.

10.3. *The Linguistic Evidence of Irish Names*

In changing the wording as they worked, both redactors give some indication of the linguistic gulf between them and the authors of their models. Where this is merely at the level of stylistic taste, it is not of much interest. In matters of vocabulary, however, their usage can be instructive. Often enough we find an obscure word in the **S**-text, which the later redactors either avoid by substitution or occasionally misunderstand. Plummer noted a passage in the Life of St Fintán of Clonenagh, **S** § 18:

Unus de fratribus scire uolens ubi Fintanus orabat, quesiuit eum et non inuenit eum in reliquis sanctorum.

Here *reliquiae* is used in the same sense as its loan-word in Irish, *reilic* 'cemetery'. The redactor of **D** has realized this and written 'in cemeterio sanctorum'; the redactor of **O** has not understood, perhaps misled by the contracted 'reliquis' (= *reliquiis*), and he has written 'non inuenit eum cum aliis qui orabant', treating 'in

reliquis sanctorum' as 'in reliquis sanctis'. This usage of *reliquiae*
had presumably become obsolete between the period when the
original *uita* was composed and that of the redactors.

A number of years ago, I discussed the use of the Latin word
laicus in the sense of Irish *díbergach*, a brigand bound by an evil
vow.[25] This usage is found in *Vita I S. Brigitae* and, adjectivally, in
Adomnán's *Vita S. Columbae*, as well as in several Lives in Φ.
When confronted with it, the redactors of **D** and **O** usually
substituted a word such as *latro* or even *miles*, knowing that *laicus*
would not be generally understood in this sense. The striking
difference between the standard meaning of the word and its use
in the older Hiberno-Latin Lives, combined with the apparent
antiquity of the custom it referred to, perhaps hints that these
Lives from Φ may be very much older than the later recensions.
Yet the fact that the redactors were generally able to understand
such usage, whether by familiarity with older texts or through
guessing from context, diminishes the utility of such linguistic
evidence for dating texts. A word met with in an older text can be
reused long after it had become obsolete, so that these points of
vocabulary, like the detailed, circumstantial form of these Lives,
and the so-termed 'primitive' aspects of the content, give the
impression of antiquity without actually permitting the dating of
the texts. The evidence of Irish names, however, is potentially
more informative.

One significant feature of **S** which Plummer noted is 'the early
form in which many of the Irish names of persons and places
appear'.[26] Plummer did not go on to say that these early forms are
found chiefly in those long, detailed Lives which alone retain a
high density of incidental place and personal names—in other
words, in the O'Donohue group.[27] The other Lives in **S** tend to be
short and to lack names, or to be long, literary, and equally lacking
in names. So the very fact of there being so many place and
personal names in the O'Donohue Lives argues for their antiquity.

The occurrence in these texts, especially as preserved in **S**, of

[25] R. Sharpe, 'Hiberno-Latin *laicus*, Irish *láech*, and the Devil's Men', *Ériu*, 30
(1979), 75–92.

[26] Plummer, *Vitae*, vol. i, p. xxii, quoted above, pp. 84–5 and 243.

[27] The argument of this part of the present book was first advanced in a paper
on 'Vernacular Evidence in the Dating of *Vitae Sanctorum Hiberniae*' at the Sixth
International Congress of Celtic Studies, Galway, in July 1979.

place-names which became obsolete at an early date adds further weight to the case. Père Grosjean had intended a study of these names to form part of an elaborate onomastic index to the edition of **S** brought out by Heist.[28] Alas, it was never written, and without such a study, this is difficult and dangerous territory. A few examples will have to serve for our present purposes. In the passage already quoted from the Life of St Ruadán, **D** §25, we are told that Daire Ethnech had changed its name to Daire na Fland. In the Life of St Cainnech, **S** §17, a place is mentioned, 'in quodam loco propinquo ad Tollum Ruaid', for which **D** §13 substitutes 'apud Eas Ruaidh', the later name (Anglicized as Assaroe, Co. Donegal), while **O** §17 avoids the name with 'prope mare'.[29] The ridge of hills referred to several times in the O'Donohue group as 'mons Sinoir' (or sometimes 'mons Smoir', a misreading) is always given its later name of 'mons Bladma' in the **D**-texts, sometimes added to the earlier name, sometimes in place of it.[30]

Early names may indicate that the texts of the O'Donohue Lives were composed at an early date, but to appreciate their evidence one needs a detailed study of the historical topography of Ireland, which is not available. But if the *form* of names—any names, obsolete or not—is early, this is a tool which is easier to use and more informative.

Here too there are problems. Names do not provide the most readily datable criteria, which in Irish are the form and syntax of verbs and pronouns. The inflexion of nouns is sometimes preserved where Irish names are embedded without Latinization. Take, for example, this sentence from the Life of St Munnu, §25:

---

[28] Heist, *Vitae*, p. 414.

[29] I note in passing that in the Life of St Crónán, **D** §§2, 3 have 'Tullum Ruaidh' where **S** §1 has 'iuxta gurgitem Ruayd'. In **S** §2 the corrector of the manuscript has added the place-name in its later form, 'silicet Eas Ruaydh' (which Heist has admitted to the text).

[30] *Lug.* **S** §31 'montem Sinnoir' has become in **D** §28 'montem Smoil qui modo dicitur mons Bladma' (while **SO** §16 has 'in monte Smoyr'); *FinC.* **S** §9 'ad montem Sinoir' has become in **D** 'ad montem Smoir qui modo dicitur mons Bladhma'; *FintC.* **S** §3 'in monte Sinor' (and compare the closely related passage in *ColT.* **S** §14 'in montem Smoir') has become in **D** §3 'per montem Bladhma'. *Cain.* **S** §52 'iuxta montem Smoir' is omitted by **D**. Elsewhere in **D** we find *CiS.* **D** §20 'ad montem Smoil alias Bladhma'; *Com.* **D** §3 'montis Bladhma'; *Mchg.* §11 'in monte Bladhma'.

Tunc Cruindmael, assumpto exercitu omnium Lagenensium, uenit et conclusit Fothartu in Inso Bairri for Loch Edidach.

First, the form *Fothartu* is correct.[31] This is the accusative of plural *Fothairt*, declined as an *o*-stem noun, as in Old Irish. It is of particular interest to remember that in the Middle Irish period this name came to be treated as an *ā*-stem, with the plural *Fotharta* in both nominative and accusative.[32] The form 'in Inso Bairri' is more difficult: the preposition *(h)i n-* takes the dative, which would give 'i nInsi Bairri'; *inis* is a feminine *ī*-stem, and 'inso' is not an acceptable dative at all.[33] Is this morphological confusion or a simple misreading? The phrase 'for Loch Edidach' must be corrected to 'for Loch Echdach', which was surely the reading of Φ.[34] The impression from this is that the original Φ-text used Old Irish forms, but these have been ignorantly corrupted rather than modernized.

Where so few linguistic tests based on inflexion are available, one may extend the study to consider variations in orthography. For example, the capital of the heroic kingdom of Ulster might be written *Eamhain Mhacha* in Modern Irish, but in Middle Irish (say between 900 and 1200) it would be written *Emain Macha*; in Old Irish the second element is not standardized but appears as *Machae*, and in the earliest texts of the seventh or early eighth century it is written *Mache*. As a guide to dating, Irish orthography is a fairly blunt instrument, but it should help to distinguish between texts of the early Middle Ages and those of the twelfth or thirteenth century.

[31] De Smedt and De Backer erroneously report the manuscript reading as 'Forthartu', and falsely emend to 'Fothartum', a grotesque error.

[32] Compare, in the genealogies, Rawl. 125a51, 126a4, 137b47, 139b32, 140b35, etc. (*Fothairt*), 126a36 (*la Fothartu*), with ibid. 140b9 = LL 318b55, etc. (*Fotharta*). Heist, incidentally, mistakenly restores the *a*-stem nominative/accusative in genitive plural position, 'in regionibus Fothart⟨a⟩' (§18), though elsewhere in the text he leaves the correct genitive plural, 'de optimatibus Fothart' (§25).

[33] The declension of *inis* varies in Old Irish: as a feminine *ī*-stem the genitive singular is *inse*, dative singular *insi*, but as an *i*-stem the genitive singular is *inso*, becoming *inseo* as palatalization affects the consonant cluster. The Book of Armagh uses both declensions side by side. It hardly seems possible that our form is a Latin ablative termination added to an Irish noun; *inis* and *insula* are both feminine, so the change of gender would be a further step from plausibility.

[34] The **D**-text has 'Eachtach', with vowel harmony, as one would expect. The misreading *di* for *ch* occurs again in this text, S §15 'nepotes Barridie', cf. §29 'rex Ua mBarriche'.

THE TEXTUAL EVIDENCE

It is fairly obvious, on the one hand, that **D** and **O** both write names in the spelling of their own time. This is particularly the case with the scribes of M, who regularly used the mark of lenition and whose spelling was sometimes influenced by phonetic confusion in late medieval Irish, e.g. Osraighi and Osraidhi.[35] But there are inconsistencies. In the Life of St Ruadán, the scribe of T writes *Ruadanus* always, a spelling of indeterminate date (eighth to thirteenth century); M occasionally writes *Ruadanus*, more often *Ruadhanus* and sometimes *Ruanus*, a phonetic spelling, though in these cases the corrector has often made it *Rua'dha'nus*. The degree of uniformity in **S** is very much less: by the same token that the compilers of **S** imposed no editorial unity, they made no attempt to harmonize the spelling of Irish words.

We have already noted that Heist argued from certain bungled names that the scribes of **S** did not know Irish at all. If the scribes were genuinely ignorant of the language, they would have made very many elementary mistakes. But on the whole the names of **S** are not mishandled. There is, however, sufficient confusion to suggest that they were not accustomed to writing Irish. In fact, it seems likely that they were unable to impose on the spelling of names the practice of their own time. There is certainly no sign of markedly late features such as the extension of vowel harmony to broad as well as slender vowels or the widespread use of *h* to mark lenition (both shown in *Eamhain*). It is, however, possible that they were deliberately conservative. For example, in the **S**[1] Life of St Munnu §11 'Tech Tailli Maicc Segeni' is the corrector's reading; the original scribe seems to have modernized the vowel in OIr. *maicc* (genitive) to MIr. *meicc*, but the corrector restored the older spelling. If one could establish that this conservatism took the form of keeping faithfully to the orthography of the exemplar, then one might have a basis for estimating the date when the exemplar was written which would provide a *terminus ante quem* for the Lives in question.

How well established, then, are the linguistic tests based on orthography? The primary basis for linguistic dating in Irish is the

---

[35] The confusion of *dh* and *gh* becomes frequent in thirteenth-century and later Irish; T. O'Rahilly, 'Middle Irish Pronunciation', *Hermathena*, no. 44 (1926), 152–95 (at pp. 164–7, 187–94). K. H. Jackson, 'Common Gaelic', *Proceedings of the British Academy*, 37 (1951), 71–97 (at p. 83), dates the beginning of the confusion to the early twelfth century.

gradual change in the morphology and syntax of the language from the earliest texts available in archaic or early Old Irish, through a whole series of phases until early modern Irish is reached, when for a time the language appears more stable. But the habits of redactors and copyists were sometimes to modernize the language of their exemplars, sometimes to archaize, and there is very little firm ground in the dating of texts throughout the Middle Irish period.[36] For the Old Irish period, the evidence is more secure because of the extensive glosses in manuscripts of the eighth and ninth centuries which have formed the basis of all descriptions of Old Irish grammar. Even here 'standard Old Irish' is less changeless than it is sometimes represented as being.[37]

In the case of the orthography of names, the evidence available for the eighth century is better than one might have expected. Not only have we evidence for the language of the period in the Würzburg glosses, but we have many Irish names preserved in a Latin context in Adomnán's Life of St Columba and in the early Patrician texts, works for which the manuscripts have firm dates at the beginning of the eighth century and the beginning of the ninth. Better still, the evidence is of the same type as that with which we want to compare it, so that our comparisons for the early period are well founded. It is especially fortunate, since it is the early forms that we are most interested in investigating, that between the late seventh and early ninth century there were considerable changes in orthographic practice.

These orthographic features were used as a dating criterion by Eoin MacNeill.[38] He hoped to distinguish between the earlier and later strata of the Patrician texts, a refinement beyond the scope of applying a few linguistic tests to a small sample of text. Our aims are less ambitious, namely, to see whether the early forms of names which Plummer observed amount to enough to suggest

[36] G. S. Mac Eoin, 'The Dating of Middle Irish Texts', *Proceedings of the British Academy*, 68 (1982), 109–37; K. H. Jackson, 'The Historical Grammar of Irish: Some Actualities and Some Desiderata', in *Proceedings of the Sixth International Congress of Celtic Studies, Galway 1979*, ed. G. S. Mac Eoin (Dublin, 1983), pp. 1–18.

[37] K. McCone, 'The Würzburg and Milan Glosses: Our Earliest Sources of "Middle Irish" ', *Ériu*, 36 (1985), 85–106.

[38] E. MacNeill, 'Dates of Texts in the Book of Armagh Relating to St Patrick', *JRSAI* 58 (1928), 85–101 (at pp. 85–90).

that some of the texts in **S** were written in the Old Irish period rather than in the twelfth or thirteenth century. It is not clear why Plummer himself did not follow up his observation. Anyone reading his brief comment would probably think little of it, since a scatter of Old Irish spellings in strata preserved from that period would be expected by anyone who, like Kenney, imagined the Lives to be made up of such layers. It would not add greatly to the value of a text, for the dissection of a text into its component strata has never been successfully accomplished. But all the evidence which we have considered here suggests that redaction did not take this 'layer cake' form. The late redactors we can see at work in **D** and **O** overlay what they take from their model with their own stamp. Early forms of names tend not to survive as fossils in older strata. So we should expect to find the early forms noticed by Plummer used reasonably consistently through an individual text. I propose to try and show that there is such reasonable consistency in the use of Old Irish forms in the long and detailed Lives of our **Φ** group, and that this provides prima-facie evidence for supposing that the exemplar **Φ** itself was written in the Old Irish period.

As an example I shall present as concisely as possible the evidence of the name-forms in the Life of St Molua.[39] A large proportion of the names is Latinized, and there are also a few names where Latin forms were readily available.[40] In all cases, here given in the order of their first occurrence in the text, the basic form to which a Latin ending is added need not be later than the Old Irish period:

Lugidius (6), Lugiduus (2), Lugidus (*passim*); Carthachus; Felanus; Fintanus; Comgallus (27), Comgellus (2); Benchorensis (1), Benchurensis (1); Finnianus; Munensis; Lagnensis (2), Lagensis (2), Lagenus (1); Beldenus (dat. Bledno); Berachus (gen. Beraky); Conanus; Aidus (9); Dauid; Brandubus; Gobanus (1), Gopbanus (1); Cronanus; Gabrenus; Deganus; Lugerus; Lactenus; Scellanus; Machenus; Tulchanus.

In a few instances, the original form appears to be in early Old Irish spelling: *Comgell* rather than *Comgall*, *Aid* rather than *Aed*.

---

[39] On this Life, it has been remarked, 'It is especially valuable for place and personal names, and for many pictures of conditions and customs in secular and monastic life'; Kenney, *The Sources*, p. 398.

[40] Roma, Britannia, Hibernia, Grigorius, Petrus.

For the rest, without Latin terminations, most of the names are written in Old Irish spelling, though there is some characteristic inconsistency in the use of the unsounded *i* before a palatal consonant or *a* between a neutral consonant and a slender vowel:

Corchode, Carthach, Daigre, Sochla, Dal Birnn Osrigi (2), Luger, Iohain, Dimma (2), Gylla na Tri Nonbur, Druim Snechti, *stagnum* nEchach, *stagnum* hErne, Cluain hIraird, Bleden, Ros Bilech, Bacan, Luigse (but also Lygese and Lygisi), Erthech, Cluain Ferte, Setne, Segri (gen.), Niall, *ecclesia* Muini, Lugid mac Coche, Ferna (gen.), cruimther Lugdech (gen.) cf. *presbytero* Lugdech, Corcho Luigde, Emne Ban (acc.), Milsail, Benchuir (gen.), Fiachrach (gen.) (2), Osrigi, Crilline mac Erce, *plebs* Eugenachte, Dare *niger*, i nDolab Glas (dat. pl.), i nAchthib Critri (dat. pl.), Maeldub, Maelandich, na nDesse (gen. pl.), Berchan, Documini mac Male-Anfith, Maidoc, Ath Dagain, Sen Ros.

Some names show features of the older spelling system of the early manuscripts.

The features to which I would particularly draw attention are those which distinguish the names in the Schaffhausen Adomnán and the Book of Armagh from the orthography of the Old Irish glosses, features which belong to the early Old Irish of the late seventh and early eighth centuries. These are:

(*a*) Preservation in spelling of original vowels in unaccented closed final syllables where in standard Old Irish there was a levelling of orthographic practice to *a* between neutral consonants, *ai* between neutral and palatal, *e* between palatal and neutral, and *i* between palatal consonants.

(*b*) Preservation of the spellings *o* and *e* (from original long vowels /oː/ and /eː/) which in standard Old Irish were replaced by the digraphs *ua* and *ia* (for the diphthongs /uːə/ and /iːə/); MacNeill drew attention also to the digraphs *uo* and *ie* ('intermediate diphthongs'), which he regarded as belonging to the actual period of the diphthongization. I note also the occurrence of some strange intermediate trigraphs.[41]

(*c*) The archaic use of *oo* and *ee* to represent these long vowels where the pronunciation had not diphthongized.

---

[41] Baiethene (between *ai* and *ae*, Aed S §34), 'i nAirbriu apud Cuoanum' (between *uo* and *ua*, *Mun.* S¹ §24), 'Dimma filium Aiedi Croin' (between *ai* and *ae*, ibid. §25) alongside 'Dimma filius Aidi Croin'.

These three features are all diagnostic of a period before the so-called standard Old Irish of *c.* 800. Supplementary evidence comes from a fourth feature, one which may be early but which is not such a consistent indicator.

> (*d*) In early Old Irish -*th* (/θ/) and -*d* (/δ/) are distinguished at the end of syllables; by *c.*700 these are confused, and in standard Old Irish sound and spelling are levelled to -*d*.

The place-name Achad Bó hÉle occurs in the Life of St Cainnech S §46 in Latin disguise, 'a Campulo Bouis', and at §54 in a perfectly acceptable Old Irish dative construction 'in Achuth Bo' (so Heist, though one might read 'i nAchuth Bo' as an Irish phrase), with confusion of final *th* and *d*, and the Old Irish dative inflexion. In the first Life of St Molua S §55, it is 'ad locum qui dicitur Acheth Boo Hele', showing three of our early Old Irish features: (*a*), (*c*), and (*d*). These features appear in the Life of St Molua in the following names:

> (*a*) *Coilboth* §§5, 7 (nom. *Colboth*); cf. *Colbath* §11.
> *Acheth* §55.
>
> (*b*) *Toim Domnich* §§37, 65, 68 (for later *Tuaim Domnaig*).
> *Ochtar nArde* §44.
>   Examples of MacNeill's 'transitional' vowels:
> *Cluoin Ferte*, *Cluoin Ferta* §§34, 68. Cf. *Cluain hIraird* §29,
> *Cluana Ferta* §§40, 49, *Kainer Cluana Clarith* §12.
>
> (*c*) *Acheth Boo Hele* (but not *Heele*) §55.
> *insula Cree* §67, *ros Cree* §68 (cf. *Cain.* §§48–52).
>
> (*d*) *Fithgente* §§1, 30, 53.
> *Lugith* §§1, 18.
> *Colboth* (see under (*a*)).
> *Acheth* (see under (*a*) and (*c*)).

In the same text, one finds two examples of the early spelling *már* for Old Irish *mór* 'great'; *Scanlain Mair* (gen., m., §52) and *Ferna Mare* (gen., f., §43). If this pattern were maintained consistently through the nine Φ Lives, one would have reason to conjecture that the exemplar was written in the eighth century. The full presentation of the linguistic evidence would take a great deal of space, and it is not my intention here to provide a linguistic commentary. I shall give only some key points.

In the group as a whole (including, for present purposes, the

Life of St Columba of Terryglass), we find that the name-element
achad 'field' (*o*-stem) occurs twelve
times:[42]

nom. sg. *acheth* (2), *aicheth* (1), *aiketh* (2), *aketh* (1).
gen. sg. *achith* (2).
dat. sg. *achuth* (2), *achud* (1); pl. *achthib* (1).

The choice of this example depends solely on the fact that its uses
illustrate more inflexions than any other noun used as a name-
element in the *uitae*. The etymologically 'correct' early spellings
would be nom. *ached*, gen. *achid*, dat. *achud*, but most of our
examples show confusion of -*d* and -*th*. In the only plural
example, early and standard spelling are indistinguishable; in the
singular, there are nine examples of an early spelling to one of the
standard. The preservation in three instances of a dative singular
with *u*-colouring confirms that these forms do not arise as scribal
eccentricities far outside the Old Irish period.[43] In the case of *tuaim*
'hillock', we find seven examples of the early form *tōim* and none of
the standard spelling.[44] With other name-elements, this extreme
preponderance of early spellings is not maintained. *Cluain*, for
example, is found twelve times, *cluoin* twelve times, but the older
clōin only four times. Where the word occurs in the genitive, all
thirteen examples inflect in -*a* rather than the older spelling -*o*:
clona (1), *cluona* (1), *cluana* (11). The -*uo*- form of the digraph is
dominant in the name of St Ruadán but the standard spelling in
-*ua*- is rare by comparison with the early -*o*-: *Rodan(us)* (29),
Ruodan(us) (63), *Ruadan(us)* (4).

The establishment of precise dates from this sort of evidence
cannot be accomplished; there are not nearly enough dated
examples for a statistical analysis to be of much use. The materials
best used for comparison are the early manuscripts of Adomnán's
Life of St Columba and of the Lives of St Patrick, and the annal-
records, in particular the Annals of Ulster. Although these

---

[42] (Nom.) *Lug.* §55, *Mun.* §§9, 18, *Ail.* §36, *ColT.* §20, *FintC.* §19; (gen.) *Cain.*
§39; (dat.) *Cain.* §§46, 54, *Mun.* §3, *Lug.* §57. It is worth noting that **D** failed to
recognize the form *achith* at *Cain.* §32.

[43] The '*u*-coloured' dative singular in *o*-stem nouns became obsolete in the
early Middle Irish period; J. Strachan, 'Contributions to the History of Middle
Irish Declension', *Transactions of the Philological Society* 1903–6, 202–46 (pp. 213–
15) (a reference I owe to Dr Paul Russell).

[44] *Toim*: *Lug.* §§37, 65, 68, *ColT.* §15; *thoim, thom*: *Ail.* §40 (twice), *Lug.* §68.

328 THE TEXTUAL EVIDENCE

manuscripts furnish additional examples, they also present different problems. The Schaffhausen manuscript may be taken to represent the practice of Iona about 700, and is likely to differ little from Adomnán's own spelling.[45] The Armagh texts have the difficulty that a century or more elapsed between the composition of the texts and the penning of the Book of Armagh. The large incidence of early forms, however, suggests that the scribe was careful to retain the forms of his exemplar. Fergus Kelly's analysis leads to a linguistic date in the eighth century for the source of the Irish items in the Book of Armagh.[46]

The Annals of Ulster should certainly be the best source for a study of these name-forms, for here very many place- and personal names are accurately transcribed from sources of the seventh, eighth, and ninth centuries. On this basis, Tomás Ó Máille set up a chronological framework within which orthographic and phonetic changes could be dated.[47] But the annals proved in many ways unsatisfactory. For example, he found that -th was 'pretty frequent' until AU 732, when it disappeared, to be 'revived' in the ninth century; but Uloth was used for Ulad (gen. pl.) very frequently and seems to have been a deliberate archaism.[48] The levelling of original -e- in closed, unstressed final syllables, Ó Máille suggests, 'took place very early in the eighth century', but he found that etymologically correct spellings occur in the Annals of Ulster well into the ninth century.[49] The change of ó to ua Ó Máille also considered to have happened in the first half of the eighth century but again found instances of the etymological spelling until the ninth century.[50] In these cases one cannot learn when pronunciation changed from the change in orthographic

[45] The form of his Irish names is discussed by A. O. Anderson and M. O. Anderson (edd. and trans.), *Adomnan's Life of Columba* (London and Edinburgh, 1961), pp. 124–51.

[46] See Kelly *apud* Bieler, *The Patrician Texts*, pp. 241–8. MacNeill's analysis might have arrived at the same conclusion if he had not attempted more precisely to distinguish by this method strata in the texts, and so separately to date individual paragraphs. The linguistic data do not sufficiently permit distinctions to be drawn within the period 700–800.

[47] T. Ó Máille, *The Language of the Annals of Ulster* (Manchester, 1910). Ó Máille considered that contemporary entries begin in the late seventh century, and that from about 740 or 750 the annals represent '*bona fide* contemporary language' (p. 18). [48] Ibid., pp. 115–16.

[49] Ibid., p. 55. [50] Ibid., p. 75.

practice; for that one must depend on the occasional use of non-orthographic representations.[51] The difficulty from our point of view—since we are concerned with spelling rather than pronunciation—is that the annalists may have continued to use forms which they found in earlier entries and so prolonged the apparent life of a particular spelling.[52]

The determination of a close date for Φ is thus impractical. The Lives in S are not so archaic as either Adomnán or the Book of Armagh in the treatment of Irish names, but features are preserved which became obsolete in the eighth century. I incline, therefore, to adopt a date for the writing of Φ in the broad range 750 to 850. This date does not relate to the composition of the Lives, but to their transcription as a collection. I have not attempted here to take account of internal evidence bearing on the dates of composition, but offer the linguistic evidence for the date of Φ as a basis for further study. The proposed early date of transcription unfortunately cannot be tested on palaeographical grounds: we were not able to pinpoint many textual errors in the archetype and none of these were of a kind necessarily to be explained as arising from a late medieval copyist's misreading of an early insular hand. There is, however, one error that may be explained in this way, namely the confusion of *lacerna* and *lucerna* in the Life of St Cainnech. It is possible that the correct reading, *lacerna*, was written with 'open' *a*, such as one finds in manuscripts of the eighth century, leading easily to its being read as *u*.[53]

Some apparently much later features are problematical, and some individual names require special attention. For example, in the Life of St Fintán of Clonenagh S §19, Bishop Brandub arrives

---

[51] For example, *calad/calath* in Adomnán, *Vita S. Columbae*, ii 10, has the etymologically 'incorrect', levelled vowel *-a-* in the last syllable. The 'correct' spelling would be *caleth* from the prehistoric /kaleton/. If the scribes had written this, we should not have known whether they pronounced the word etymologically /kaleθ/ or in the standard manner /kaləð/. Their 'error' shows that around 700 the spellings *caleth* and *calath*, *caled* and *calad* were phonetically interchangeable. The levelling of closed final syllables and the confusion of final /θ/ and /ð/ must have happened before this date, even though etymological spellings continue to be used in the eighth century.

[52] Ó Máille, p. 116.

[53] See above, p. 313. In other circumstances an early open *a* could be misread as *ci*, as in the B-text of Adomnán, *Vita S. Columbae* i 9, *Micitorum* for *Miatorum*; Anderson and Anderson, *Adomnán's Life*, p. 228 n. 6.

from Leinster and finds St Fintán 'in loco qui dicitur Aketh Harclayss'. The equivalent passage in **D** §19 reads 'in monasterio quod dicitur Achadh Firghlais in plebe Hua Drona contra ciuitatem Lethgleann in orientali parte fluminis Berbha'. *Aketh* is all right: there is still the original final vowel and the confused *-th* for /ð/ as against the standard Old Irish *achad*. The *k* is a minor problem; the letter does not occur in Irish at all, but it is common in both **S** and **O** and not infrequent in **D**, regularly substituted for *c* before *i* or *e* to prevent a Latinist from treating *c* as soft. It also occurs for lenited *c* or *ch*. Plummer appears to regard 'Harclayss' as a corruption, and identifies the place on the basis of the geographical gloss in **D**. If he is right, **S** could not have copied the form from Φ. The **O**-text omits the name. But what most persuades me that **D** has interpreted the place-name and thereby misled Plummer is that in the Life of St Columba of Terryglass **S** §20 we read 'Usque ad locum qui dicitur Aiketh Arglass'. This second example strongly suggests that in the first case it is **S** that has preserved the reading of Φ. The redactor of **D**, with his keenness for identifying places, has made the name into one phonetically quite similar which he could locate.

Secondly, there are individual features which are likely to date from later than the ninth century. These features are not great in extent, but we must consider whether they *could* be compatible with our date of around 800, whether they may be explained in another way, or whether they undermine the whole argument for an early date for Φ. The definite article in Old Irish, *in*, has the genitive plural *inna*, which in early Middle Irish became *na*. In the Life of St Ailbe, **S** §40, 'Inis ina nDam' shows the Old Irish genitive plural, causing nasalization of the following noun; Plummer and Heist sensibly read 'Inis in⟨n⟩a nDam', assuming the loss of a suspension-mark.[54] In the Life of St Molua, however, **S** §19, the nickname Gylla na Tri Nonbur 'servant of thrice nine men' has the Middle Irish article *na*. This in itself is not a major problem, but personal names formed with *gilla* 'boy, servant' are not generally found in the Old Irish period; they came into use in the ninth century.[55] The story of how the saint, consistently called by the radical name Lugidus in preference to the hypocoristic

---

[54] Plummer, *Vitae*, i. 59 n., Heist, *Vitae*, p. 128.
[55] B. Ó Cuív, 'Aspects of Irish Personal Names', *Celtica*, 18 (1986), 167.

Molua, served thrice nine men always gives him the nickname *Maccán* 'little son', a name not otherwise recorded for him. Could it be that the last sentence, 'Hinc illi nomen datum est Gylla na Tri Nonbur', was a marginal addition in Φ?

A worse problem is the use of the name Odo for Aed. A certain Aed Sláine (not the Uí Néill king of that name, but an otherwise unknown son of Cruindmael mac Rónáin (d. 656), king of Uí Chennselaig) is mentioned as 'Odo Slane filius Cruindmail', in the Life of St Munnu, a Life which is otherwise consistent in using Old Irish spelling with a light admixture of early and transitional Old Irish spellings. Even in the chapter where *Odo* is used, *Cruindmael* is twice given in standard Old Irish spelling, and again in the genitive *Cruindmail*, and once in the older spelling *Cruindmel*. But Odo is a Norman name of Scandinavian origin, and one could hardly expect to find it used in Ireland before the late twelfth century. One might perhaps make an excuse, and guess that the fourteenth-century scribe had come across this usage of *Odo* for *Aed*, and employed it when he recognized the name of Aed Sláine—but nowhere else does he modernize even familiar names. In the Life of St Aed, it is always *Aidus*.

The same name *Odo* is used frequently in the Life of St Ruadán, S §12. The most frequent spelling of *Aed* in the O'Donohue group is *Aidus*, reflecting the early spelling *Aid*. In the Life of St Aed, the genitive is even sometimes found as *Aidui*, in recognition of the name's Old Irish *u*-stem. But here in the Life of St Ruadán, Aed Guaire appears first as *Ed Guori* and thereafter as *Odo Guori*. While *Guori* looks like a transitional spelling, and is found in the Life of Munnu, S §16, *Odo* must be late. As a whole, the Life of St Ruadán is no different from the other Lives in the group in its treatment of names; indeed, Professor Byrne took its spellings as suggesting a date as early as the eighth century.[56] This chapter includes old spellings such as 'i Pull Ruodan': the dative inflexion of *poll* is shown, but not the genitive *Ruodain*; compare the Latinized 'juxta Pollum Ruodani' later in the chapter. The chapter corresponds to the tale of St Ruadán and the cursing of

---

[56] Byrne, 'Derrynavlan: The Historical Context', p. 118. The date is based not only on the spelling of Irish names, but also on the use of Latin *cortex* 'bark' in the sense 'vessel' (see above, p. 305). Byrne thought that the topography of the **D**-text suggested a date for that no earlier than the tenth century and 'probably a good deal later'.

Tara, which was transmitted as an independent story in Irish.[57]
The explanation for its anomalous forms in **S** may be that this
story was translated into Latin at a comparatively late date and
inserted as an extra leaf or two in Φ; it was in the same place in the
exemplar when it was used by the compilers of **D** and **O**. The latter
even gave the story a special heading, 'Qualiter maledixit
Temoriam'. Some spellings may have been preserved from a
vernacular source, while others were altered at the time of the
translation into Latin.

The most forceful argument against this whole thesis is the
suggestion that the spelling of the text may reflect the fluctuating
usage of Anglo-French scribes, ignorant of the correct orthography of Irish. To such scribes, a form such as *acheth* might be a
phonetic equivalent of *achad* and not an early spelling. The most
frequent sign of such late medieval spelling is the use of *k* and *y*,
but these in themselves do not interfere with the underlying forms.
I would counter this argument by pointing to the frequency with
which names are given their correct Old Irish inflexions, both in
Latin constructions and in occasional Irish phrases. The use of
Irish prepositions, *(h)i* 'in', *oc* 'at', and *for* 'on' before place-names
is found quite widely, from Adomnán's Life of St Columba to the
Tara episode in the Life of St Ruadán; but if these are
accompanied by Old Irish inflexions, such as the dative uses of
achad, then we may be sure that Anglo-French scribes could not
accidentally arrive at them. The use of nasalization after Latin
neuter nouns, as if they were Old Irish neuters, similarly would
not happen with scribes who made up their spelling as they went
along in the fourteenth century.[58]

But perhaps the most secure evidence that the scribes of S were
attempting faithfully to reproduce the names as they found them
in Φ is the fact that a quatrain in Irish is reasonably well preserved
in the **S**-text of the Life of St Ailbe.[59] Professor Byrne has suggested
that this Life may have been composed about 784.[60] The quatrain

---

[57] Plummer, 'A Tentative Catalogue', no. 174.

[58] mare nIcht, stagnum nEchach.

[59] *Ail.* **S** §50; commented on by Zimmer, *Göttingische gelehrte Anzeigen* (1891),
p. 168.

[60] 'Derrynavlan: The Historical Context', p. 119, where he says that the Life
'may possibly have been composed on the occasion of the proclamation of the
Law of Ailbe over Munster in 784 (AI)'.

is Old Irish, and could not be understood by the redactor of **D**, for all his antiquarian knowledge, who reduced the language to gibberish, and then provided a 'translation'.[61] In editing the **D**-text, Plummer printed the quatrain from **S**. The redactor of **D** not only knew Irish but was familiar with Irish genealogical and topographical material; and yet he could not cope with the infixed pronouns nor the Old Irish verbs. How much less could Anglo-French scribes have preserved it intelligibly unless they were copying faithfully from an Old Irish exemplar.

Since my argument supposes that this early exemplar was still available hundreds of years later and was used by the compilers of all three later medieval collections, one may well wonder whether the copyists would have had difficulty in reading the ancient manuscript in insular minuscule. Signs of misreading the older script might be expected to turn up in any or all of the witnesses to Φ. I have, however, noted only one misreading of this kind: *lucerna* for *lacerna*, in the Life of St Cainnech **S** §44, already discussed. Another error which one might look for is the confusion of the compendium for *autem* with some part of *hic*, *haec*, *hoc*, common among early modern students of insular manuscripts. Errors of this kind are not inevitable, and their absence need not indicate that Φ was less ancient than the orthography of its names. When all books were manuscripts, readers were often familiar with several forms of script. In particular, one should remember that insular script was the basis of the later medieval Irish hand, and may have been perfectly familiar to Irish readers , even to those who did not normally read texts in the vernacular.

The case that the archetype Φ was written in the late eighth or early ninth century may have to be modified if a persuasive case could be made out that the higher proportion of early Old Irish forms such as *acheth*, *töim*, or *clöin* in some Lives than in others reflected the dates of composition and not transcription. The manuscript Φ was a collection. It is possible that it was written, say, about 900, from copies of individual Lives written during the eighth and early ninth centuries, and that it preserved forms from the sources it was copied from. This sort of refinement would be difficult to establish, since statistics of proportions can carry little weight when the data on which they are based are so limited.

[61] Plummer, *Vitae*, i. 62 n. 1.

With or without such niceties, the linguistic evidence strongly supports the view that in the O'Donohue group we have nine or ten Lives preserved largely as they were known in the Old Irish period. Their composition should almost certainly be dated earlier than about 800. It is possible that some may be as early as the Lives of SS. Patrick, Brigit, and Columba, but only historical argument from the content of the several texts will be able to establish the dates of composition. That argument lies beyond the scope of this study.

10.4. *The Lives of St Munnu and St Molua*

We have twice passed over the problems presented by the several recensions of these two saints' Lives. For each of them, there is a full and detailed Life in the O'Donohue group in **S**, a Life revised by the redactor of **D**, a Life in **O**, and a second Life in **S**. As analysed by Plummer, the relationship between the four recensions for these texts appears very complex, but verbal comparisons reveal that the difficulties are by no means insuperable. The main reason for the complexity is that the two versions in **S** apparently witness to Lives of St Munnu and St Molua in both of our conjectured collections, Φ and Θ.

We may conveniently begin with the Life of St Munnu, of which Plummer writes:[62]

Of the four lives S[1] is clearly the fullest and most original. But it and the M recension have a common source. S[2] is closely allied to M, agreeing with it in omissions and arrangement as compared with S[1]; S[2] also agrees with M in calling the virgin to whom Munnu abandoned Tehelly, Emer, whereas S[1] and R call her Ciar (Kera, Kyear). The R recension is nearly identical with S[2], but is still further abbreviated in certain parts, and has not been padded with moral and religious commonplaces as is the case with many of the lives in R. It cannot, however, have been taken direct from S[2], as in some cases it has preserved a better reading; and, as has been stated above, in an important point it agrees with S[1] against M and S[2].

The notion that **S**[1] and **D** need a 'common source' has already been disposed of, since it should by now be recognized that the redactor of **D** will add as well as excise in his revision of a text. The

---

[62] Ibid., vol. i, p. lxxxv.

D-text of St Munnu's Life, as for other Φ-texts, depends on the archetype from which the longer S-text was copied:

S¹ §5 Post hec uenit Fintanus ad scolam sancti Columbe Kylle, qui erat hi Kyll Mair Diathrib, et ibi legit apud Columbam diuinam scripturam.

D §5 Deinde *accepta licentia a sancto Comgallo* uenit beatus Munnu ad scolam sancti Columbe, qui *tunc* erat *magister in loco qui dicitur Scotice* Ceall Mor Dhithraimh, *id est cella magna remota*. Et ibi sanctus Munnu legit apud *uirum sapientem* Columbam.

Here we have one common formula of the D-redactor, 'accepta licentia', and his characteristic gloss on the place-name. The word *magister* spells out the interpretation of the passage. Though this is not one of the Lives in which the redactor of D shows any special interest, we may be sure he worked from Φ. Plummer was quite right to observe that the S²-text and the D-text are closely allied. In fact, D was the source of S²:

S² §5 Post hec transtulit se sanctus Munnu, habita licentia sancti Comgalli, ad sanctum Columbam, ut ab eo informaretur.

The place-name is now entirely omitted, but the preservation of St Comgall's *licentia* establishes the dependence.

It is clear that we have a sequence of recensions, each based on the previous one. Indeed, we can extend that sequence to include the O-text:

S¹ §1 Fintanus sanctus, summi Dei sacerdos, filius Tulcani, de Nepotibus Neill, de genere Conalli ortus fuit. Mater uero eius, nomine Fethelin, de genere Maini filii Neill. Domus in qua sanctus Fintanus natus est fundata erat super lapidem magnum, et, deficiente domo, lapis ille magno honore ab omnibus honoratur, et super lapidem illum usque hodie nix non fuit, propter gratiam sancti infantis qui super ipsum lapidem natus est.

D §1 Fuit uir uite uenerabilis, nomine Munnu, de claro genere Hibernie, id est de Nepotibus Neill. Pater eius uocabatur Tulchanus, qui de semine Conalli filii Neill ortus fuit; mater quidem sancti Munnu nominabatur Fedhelyn, que de eadem gente nata est, id est de semine filii Diua filii Neil. Sanctus siquidem Munnu super lapidem genitus ⟨est⟩, qui magno honore ueneratur ab hominibus regionis illius propter gratiam sancti infantis qui natus est super eum. Mirabilia enim perficiuntur in ipso lapide; ab illo iam die usque hodie non manet nix super illum lapidem.

S² §1 Fuit uir uite uenerabilis, nomine Munnu, de claro genere Hybernie, id est de Nepotibus Neill, cuius pater uocabatur Tulcanus, mater uero Fedelni dicebatur. Hic sanctus super unum lapidem natus fuit, qui in reuerentia non modica in populo habetur, nam nix desuper cadens mox liquescit nec ad horam indurescit.

O (R f. 192ᵛᵃ) Fuit uir uite uenerabilis, nomine Munnu, de claro genere Hibernie insule, id est de Nepotibus Neyl, cuius pater uocabatur Tulcanus, mater uero Fedelnia dicebatur. Hic natus fuit super unum lapidem, ⟨qui⟩ in reuerentia non modica apud incolas illius regionis habetur. Nam nix desuper cadens mox liquescit nec ad horam permanet sed euanescit.

One could hardly ask for a clearer illustration. The original text is that of S¹. The redactor of **D** cut out the reference to the house but retained the stone; he added his more detailed genealogical account, and the opening formula. This last, together with the phrase 'de claro genere Hibernie', is taken over in S², confirming its dependence on **D**; the rest, however, is much abbreviated and surplus names are cut out. The redactor of **O** has taken over S² almost verbatim, avoiding only the poor phrasing *in populo* and the ambiguous use of *indurescit*. There may even be a textual indicator: it is hardly likely that the scribe of Φ would write *Fethelin* for *Fethelm*, but it must have looked like that, to have been so copied in both Δ and S, producing a chain of corrupt spellings.

The relationship between S¹ and **D** is simple. That between S² and **O** is so close as to suggest that we are dealing with another text from Θ which S has preserved exactly while the redactor of **O** introduced some very minor changes. The obvious dependence of S² on **D** presents no difficulty since we know from the Lives of St Ciarán of Saigir and St Maedóc that **D** was available to the compiler of Θ. The stemma for the four recensions is straightforward. S¹ witnesses to Φ, S² to Θ.

Plummer, however, drew attention to an additional problem: he noted that the virgin in S¹ §13 is called *Kyear*, in **D** §12 *Emher*, in S² §13 *Emer*, and in **O** *Kera*. This makes it appear that **O**, in revising Θ a little, has referred back to Φ rather than accept the name introduced in **D**. This is perfectly possible, of course, since we know that Φ was used by the compiler of **O**. Yet it seems unlikely that the compiler of **O**, who shared with the compiler of Θ a want of interest in names, should have bothered to 'correct' this Θ-reading by consulting Φ, while not adding anything else from

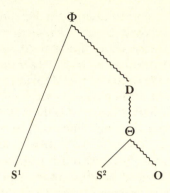

Fig. 6 Life of St Munnu

the fuller text. There could be another explanation. Perhaps in Φ
there was one reading in the text and the other in the margin or
between the lines; using Φ, the redactor of D kept both, and so did
the compiler of Θ in using Δ; any choice would presumably have
been uninformed anyway. The scribe of M has chosen *Emer* in
copying from Δ, as did the scribe of the primary manuscript of O
in copying from Θ; the scribe of S chose the curious spelling *Kyear*,
which may come closest to the reading of Φ.[63] Although both
possibilities seem implausible, neither is impossible, and neither
entails any serious modification in the stemma.

Turning now to the Life of St Molua, we may approach the
different recensions in the same way. First, Plummer's observations:[64]

The relation between the three texts is curious. S[1] and M each contain a
good deal that is not in the other. Where they cover the same ground they
resemble each other strongly, S[1] being as a rule the more original. It is
probable, therefore, that they are independent recensions of a common
original. The S[2] R text is a much abbreviated recension, evidently made
for homiletic purposes (cf. §§21, 35, 41). But it cannot be taken from
either S[1] or M, for it contains several of the sections which are peculiar to
S[1] and M respectively. It has also preserved one or two things which are
not either in S or M. It may be an independent epitome of their common
original.

---

[63] Assuming that *k* and *y* are late, an earlier spelling *Ciear* would epitomize
those unusual trigraphs found elsewhere in Φ.

[64] Plummer, *Vitae*, vol. i, p. lxxxiii.

Again Plummer's interpretation of the relationship between S^1 and **D** can be reinterpreted quite easily; the redactor of **D** has simply revised the text in front of him in Φ, as he did with eight others. Plummer's treatment of 'S^2 R' as a single text can also be easily translated into new terms: the **SO**-text of the short Life of St Molua derives from Θ, and has already been considered as such in Chapter 9. The problem remaining is the link between these two pairs. There is no easy solution. One might readily have expected the **SO**- or Θ-text to derive from the **D**-text, as with St Munnu. This cannot be the case, however, for the **SO**-text contains several sections found in the **S**-text but not in the **D**-text.[65] The possibility opens up that the compiler of Θ had access, if not to Φ, then to another copy of the same Life of St Molua, or one based on it. The arrangement of the Θ-text differs to a considerable extent from that of the **S**- and **D**-texts; much more than is the case with the Θ-text of the Life of St Maedóc, where the redactor's work can be compared with his model. I incline, therefore, to conjecture that the immediate source of Θ in this case was not Φ but an already reorganized text. This and the extremely summary treatment the Life receives make the **SO**-text of St Molua's Life of little interest. One may wonder why the compiler of **O** preferred to copy this meagre text rather than produce his own version from Φ, or why the compiler of Θ did not follow the version available to him in **D**. One cannot answer. In terms of the recensional relationships within the O'Donohue group, **S** still preserved the text of Φ, which was used by the compiler of **D** after his customary fashion. The **SO**-text stands apart because an unknown, intermediate version seems to have come between the compilers of Θ and **O** and their usual sources.

For several reasons, the O'Donohue group of Lives is remarkable. Chiefly, one must welcome the preservation of so much hagiographical writing from before or around 800—a major addition to the corpus. The survival of the codex Φ from the ninth to the late fourteenth century perhaps should not surprise, since manuscripts of that date and older have lasted down to the present. These latter, however, are almost exclusively precious gospel-books or

---

[65] **SO** §§ 19, 21, 25, 28, 29, 36, corresponding to S §§ 36, 38, 54, 52, 44, 43, in that order.

their equivalent such as the Book of Armagh. Other early fragments, such as the Cathach or *Codex Usserianus Primus*, survived because they were enshrined. We know of no other literary manuscript, in Latin or Irish, which survived over this period in Ireland itself—yet clearly survival was possible, a point which has implications for the transmission of other texts: late copies may have followed an ancient exemplar. The fact that the same manuscript Φ was used by the compilers of **D**, **O**, and **S** over a period of 150 years suggests that it was quite well known to hagiographers, and says something for the possibilities of circulation for early texts. The use made of it by these compilers greatly enhances our scope for studying exactly how they worked. For these reasons, I propose in future to publish afresh the text of the O'Donohue Lives, fully annotated.[66] These texts will form the basis of further advances in the use of hagiographical evidence for the history of early medieval Ireland.

---

[66] It is expected that this will appear in the series *Scriptores Latini Hiberniae*, published by the Dublin Institute for Advanced Studies.

11

The Value of the Textual Evidence

THE presentation of textual arguments has taken many pages, but the body of texts under examination is so large that it is not possible to attempt an item-by-item analysis of the textual evidence for the whole of the three collections. As each Life is studied, new points will perhaps emerge about the textual relationships between the different recensions for particular texts. I cannot claim to have considered how a comparison of the version of every *uita* in the collections might lead to a complete textual stemma, covering all the connexions between the three collections and showing how many lost sources might have to be postulated. Throughout, it has been my primary intention to establish the general characteristics of each collection.

This has been best done where the source text used by each of the compilers is known, so that comparison between versions rests on a secure foundation. It was desirable to do this first without begging any questions about the cross-currents running from collection to collection. No comparison of recensions in **D** and **O** could lead to a well-founded understanding of the work of either compiler, still less to a conjectural archetype. Where a text is found in three versions, such comparisons must appear even shakier. But the identification of external sources enabled us to find a way out of this problem. Thus *Vita IV S. Brigidae* provided the kind of test that was needed for the **D**-collection. With the **S**-collection, the problem was less pressing because of the existence of several external checks, but I was reluctant to extrapolate from the treatment of texts such as Lawrence's Life of St Brigit or the anonymous Life of St Mochuille to the conclusion that the compiler of **S** did no more than copy his sources. In the absence of any identifiable editorial style, it seemed that there was room to imagine that he might copy some texts but revise others. Comparisons between **S** and **O**, however, and then between **S** and its derivatives in **D** and **O**, in Chapters 9 and 10, have confirmed the conclusion that I drew from a few texts in Chapter 7. The confidence this gave in the stability of the S-texts was essential to gaining a clear insight into the redactor of **O**, and enhanced our appreciation of the work of the redactor of **D**.

It is perhaps remarkable that such textual evidence has never been presented before. Although Plummer discussed his comparisons of the several versions, Life by Life, it is not possible to learn from that discussion to what extent the different compilers copied their sources verbatim. Nowhere does he present two or three texts side by side. Instead he will say that two recensions 'cover much the same ground'.[1] Occasionally he is more confident: 'often very close together', 'sufficiently alike to make it certain that they have some common source or sources', 'nearly coincident in matter and arrangement', 'they resemble each other strongly'.[2] Nowhere, however, does he mention that different recensions often use the same words, nor does he quote extracts side by side. Yet without literal comparisons of this kind, any comparison of recensions admits a large area of uncertainty. Where two or three texts are the same in substance but have very few actual words in common, recensional comparisons will only lead to a general impression of the relationship between the three, and cannot eliminate the need for lost common originals. The recognition that texts in the three collections can be compared verbatim to a significant degree changes the whole character of recensional comparisons.

Where whole sentences, or if not whole sentences, parts of sentence after sentence, show verbatim parallels, then one knows there must be an archetype at the textual level. This gives a greater element of security to comparisons than does the inference of a common original from community of substance. In changing the level of comparisons from one of speculation about the stages through which a Life was revised to one in which it can be known that the reviser had one text in front of him which he reworded or copied at whim, the opportunity for understanding the work of revision is greatly increased.

---

[1] *Vitae*, vol. i, pp. xxxi (*Ba.*), xlix (*CiC.*), liii (*CiS.*, re Irish Lives), lvi (*Coem.*, re Irish Lives), lxxiii (*Ita*), lxxxii (*Mol.*, 'covers the same ground but . . . gives a very different version'), lxxxiii (*Lug.*).

[2] Ibid., vol. i, pp. xxvii (*Aed*), lvii (*ColE.*), lxxv (*Maed.*), lxxxiii (*Lug.*).

It was the knowledge gained from an examination of the treatment of the Life of St Brigit in **D**, where textual comparisons could be made, that allowed us to see exactly the same treatment applied in other Lives of the **D**-collection. At this point in the argument, it became clear that this collection at least had to be studied as a unity, because only that way was it possible to learn about the redactor's methods. Knowing for each text where the wording appeared to be his and where it did not was essential for the move from textual comparison against independent sources to textual comparisons within the circle of the collections. A clearer understanding of the work of the compilers of the collections emerged.

This has consequences of considerable importance. For a large number of Lives, a comparison of the various versions shows only how a source text was manipulated in the hands of the redactors of **D** and **O**. For some texts, such as those of the Θ-group, we have had to hypothesize another collector whose aim seems to have been the production of an abbreviated lectionary. Whatever interest these collectors have themselves or however revealing their methods may be, the study of their editorial activity is a very different exercise from a comparison of recensions of a *uita* progressively reworked by the saint's publicists. In other words, we have shown that the medieval collectors' role was essentially one of *transmission* of an existing text, more or less edited; they were not producing new recensions to meet new domestic needs. In almost all cases, the work of textual comparison will reverse the process of transmission, leading to the choice of a particular version as being the original on which the other Latin versions depend; or, failing that, of the version which is the fullest and least interfered with. When that is established, the historian need concentrate only on that version, and can avoid being misled by the contribution of the redactors.

It is to be hoped that our study of the collections will enable historians to begin a soundly based investigation of what these *uitae* reveal about the people who composed them, their interests, and their intentions. So far as the study of the *uitae* is concerned, this is only the beginning. For the study of the late medieval collections, however, we have still to draw together what we can learn about their compilation. When were they assembled? In what milieu? While each individual *uita*, by which I mean the original or best preserved witness to the original, has still to be fitted into its place in the history of hagiography in Ireland, the study of the compilers will allow us to improve on the previous very sketchy outline of Latin hagiography in the thirteenth and fourteenth centuries.

PART III

THE COLLECTORS AND THEIR SOURCES

12

The Compilation of the Dublin Collection

THE value which students from Ward, Colgan, and Ussher to Plummer and Kenney have consistently put on the Lives of the D-collection was not based on a textual or critical examination of their relationship to the other collections. Often enough, Plummer like Reeves had recognized that S preserved a more original version of some Lives, yet he still found the versions in D so interesting that he printed them, even though the more original text was already published. The reason for this must surely lie in the fact that the work of the redactor was itself the occasion of interest. Countless details—his concern to identify places, to explain place-names, to fill in historical or genealogical background—all make his versions of special interest to the student. Not all these additions are to the point, some are even mistaken, but they show an antiquarian mind collecting and imposing on his text material which a similar scholar in the modern era would have confined to his notes.[1]

His attention to such details should be for us only a part of the interest of his collection. Though Ward and Colgan thought the collection was all the work of St Euinus, they did not ask themselves whether there were any general principles, any consistent interpretation, detectable throughout the collection, but concerned themselves with individual Lives. Plummer hardly recognized the role of the collector, and Kenney not at all; their interest in the work of the D-redactor was aroused anew with each separate Life. Knowing now, however, that there was one mind collecting the texts, studying them, and reworking them, one must ask what can be said about the compiler: where and when did he work, how did he come by his sources, both for Latin *uitae* and for Irish antiquarian information, what were the motives directing his work and the influences acting upon it?

---

[1] De Buck, as we have seen, above, p. 73, took these additions for the explanatory notes of a seventeenth-century translator.

The evidence now available for approaching these questions is considerable. In Chapter 5, it was established that the redactor's work on St Brigit can be compared with his model, and in Chapter 6 this was shown for the Lives of St Patrick and St Maedóc. Our examination of Φ in Chapter 10 added nine further Lives where the redactor's work can be studied alongside his base-text. The same is also true of his version of *Nauigatio S. Brendani*. So for twelve entire texts and fragments of a thirteenth, a comparison will reveal precisely what contribution the redactor made to his texts. With the Lives of SS. Columba, Malachy, Lawrence, and Senán, comparisons show that the redactor made no substantial changes at all. For the remaining twelve Lives in the collection, one is less well placed to assess his work, but the inevitable uncertainty need not be a disabling factor. In two cases—St Mochoemóc and St Declán—no comparisons can be made, for these Lives are peculiar to the **D**-collection; the style of the redactor is apparent throughout both of them. Although Irish Lives are known for both, these too are only translations of the **D**-texts.

For the remaining ten Lives, one can make some comparisons, either with texts in **S** (SS. Abbán, Mochutu, and Crónán), **O** (St Finnbarr and St Íte), both **S** and **O** (St Ciarán of Clonmacnoise), and Θ (SS. Ciarán of Saigir, Coemgen, Comgall, and Moling). Setting aside for the present the question of the twelfth-century Austrian witnesses to the Lives of St Coemgen and St Íte, we may note that in all cases the **D**-text is fuller than the others, and that in some it can be shown to be the source.[2] For the others, there are three possibilities: first, that **D** again served as source but the revision and abbreviation have obliterated the traces of the **D**-redactor; second, that the **D**-text is based on the other; and third, that both depend on the same source, perhaps at more than one remove. Even without attempting to determine the relationship for each Life, it is feasible to detect passages of special interest to the **D**-redactor in his versions of these texts. While some of his contributions will go unnoticed, those which most clearly reflect his overall interests should be apparent from their similarity with the other Lives, and it is these overall interests which now concern us.

---

[2] Certainly in the case of St Ciarán of Saigir, as we saw in Chapter 9, and of St Abbán, which I shall discuss shortly; probably also in the case of St Comgall.

12.1. *When was the Collection Made?*

No attempt has ever been made to ascertain dates for individual Lives in the collection, but the collection as a whole ought by rights to be later than the latest text in it. The reality, however, may not be so simple. Apart from the Lives of St Anthony and St Louis, which we have excluded from further consideration, the latest text in **D** is the Life of St Lawrence O'Toole. Here, at the end of the *uita* proper, the author has given an account of the saint's enshrinement in 1186, of the miracles which led to his canonization, and of his canonization by Pope Honorius III on 11 December 1226. The bull of canonization is included in the text, between *uita* and *miracula*. At first sight, the compilation of **D** must therefore be placed no earlier than 1227. Since the Life of St Lawrence is one of those which show no trace of the personal style of the redactor, the possibility must be left open that this text was added to the collection after the time of the redactor himself but before the archetype from which M and T were copied received its arrangement.

The *terminus post quem* may thus be somewhat earlier than 1226, but it can hardly be earlier than 1185. This is the date which Gerald of Wales gives for the *inuentio et translatio* of the relics of SS. Patrick, Brigit, and Columba, an event mentioned in one of the redactor's additions in his Life of St Brigit. Allusions which can so easily be dated are extremely unusual in the collection, so that one must allow that the redactor had no particular interest in referring to modern events.

Of his identifiable sources, we know that *Vita I S. Brigitae* was already some four or five centuries old when the redactor used it, and some of the Lives he took from Φ may have been as ancient. The Life of St Declán, on the other hand, may have been much more recent, since it appears to maintain a case for Ardmore as the episcopal see of the Déisi, a case which makes most sense in the late twelfth century. So much of the Life is taken up with themes of special interest to the redactor, however, that with no other texts for comparison it is not possible to draw any clear inferences about the underlying text.

A very interesting argument has been put forward for dating the Life of St Abbán.[3] The argument is applied to the 'original form' of the *uita*, the lost common source which Professor Ó Riain sees

[*See p. 350 for n. 3*]

behind the three surviving texts, the Latin *uitae* in **D** and **S** and the Irish *betha* in the collections of Dinneen and O'Clery. I should question this view of the relationship of the three texts, principally because there are unmistakable signs that the **S**-text is derived directly from the **D**-text.[4] The Irish text may derive from either, or conceivably from a lost source; but all the passages that are important for Professor Ó Riain's general case are absent from the Irish text. I shall treat his argument, therefore, as referring to the **D**-text.

St Abbán's most notable foundation was the historically obscure church of Moyarney, but Ó Riain points out that the *uita* bespeaks an interest in one of the major churches of Leinster. Abbán's name is linked with those of Coemgen and Moling as the three principal saints of Leinster, but several references to Uí Chennselaig suggest a particular concern with south Leinster. The writer—whether the author of the original *uita* or our redactor is hard to tell—identifies himself as descended from a king mentioned in the Life (**D** §26, **S** §21), whom Ó Riain with much probability locates in Fir Chell. The writer also shows a strong interest in the church of St Evins at Ross and in other minor churches. Of Ross he says:

magnum siquidem monasterium prope flumen Berbha, quod uocatur Ross meic Treoin [Ross mac Troin S], in quo iacet beatissimus abbas sanctus Emenus.

Whether or not this was part of the original, the redactor has taken note of the information, for in the Life of St Molua he changes the original reading of **S** §45 'ad salutandum uirum Dei, silicet Emne Ban' into this:[5]

---

[3] P. Ó Riain, 'St Abbán: The Genesis of an Irish Saint's Life', in *Proceedings of the Seventh International Congress of Celtic Studies, Oxford, 1983*, ed. D. E. Evans *et al.* (Oxford, 1986).

[4] For example, the simple but habitual formula of **D** §28 'ex eo cellas et monasteria per circuitum eiusdem loci construxit' appears in **S** §23 'et multa monasteria et cellas per circuitum edificauit'; at **D** §9 the redactor indulges in one of his favourite themes, that St Ibar 'unus erat egregius dispensator diuini dogmatis de prioribus predicatoribus, quod elegit Deus ut Hibernienses de gentilitate ad fidem Christi conuerterent', cf. **S** §5 'fuit autem de primis predicatoribus qui Hyberniam ad Christum conuerterunt', and notes on *Vita IV S. Brigitae*, I 49 n. 86, II 23 n. 116, II 53 n. 162.

[5] **D** §39. Plummer on both occasions mistakenly prints the name as Ernenus instead of Emenus. Fleming, *Collectanea Sacra*, p. 376 (§41), read Einenus, but in

Aliquando sanctus Molua uisitauit sanctum Emenum abbatem in regione Cennselach, non longe a flumine Berua, in monasterio Ross meic Treoin, quod sanctissimus senex Abbanus fundauit, habitantem.

The redactor may have been responsible for both passages, or he may already have known the Life of St Abbán when he worked on the Life of St Molua. Either way, Ross was not a great monastery, but a minor church, overshadowed from the early thirteenth century by William Earl Marshall's foundation of New Ross, a town with a large new parish church. Ó Riain detects in this a reference to a conflict of property between the Leinster church which was using the name of St Abbán, somewhere presumably more important than Moyarney, and the Anglo-Norman invader. Such a conflict is documented: in 1218 Ailbhe O Maelmhuaidh, alias Albinus O'Mulloy, bishop of Ferns (c.1186–1223), brought a claim against William Earl Marshall, in an ecclesiastical court in Dublin, concerning two unnamed manors.[6] One manor, Templeshanbo, was successfully recovered.[7] Templeshanbo is almost certainly 'Seanboith Ard' mentioned in the *uita*, D §47, as being given to St Abbán. Ross, and other places mentioned as belonging to St Abbán in the *uita*, may all have been in dispute in the years immediately preceding 1218, and it makes good sense to suppose

---

his side-note added 'rectius Eminum'. The name was correctly read by FitzSimon (or White), for in his 'Auctuarium' (Oxford, Bodleian Library, MS Add. c. 299, f. 123 *invers.*) he gives 'Emenus Ab. in Vita S. Albani'.

[6] The principal account of the dispute is in Matthew Paris (H. R. Luard (ed.), *Matthæi Parisiensis, Monachi Sancti Albani, Chronica Majora* (Rolls Series, 57; London, 1872–89), iv. 492–5), where it is told retrospectively as explaining the demise of the Marshall family owing to William Marshall's dying (in 1219) under excommunication by Albinus. The case had been taken by Albinus to the archbishops of Dublin and Tuam, who reported it to Pope Innocent III in 1216. Honorius III in 1218 maintained the bishop's claim (M. P. Sheehy (ed.), *Pontificia Hibernica: Medieval Papal Chancery Documents Concerning Ireland 640–1261* (Dublin, 1962–5), no. 98), but Marshall in Apr. 1218 obtained from the king (the infant Henry III) a prohibition, stopping the archbishops from hearing Albinus's plea (*Patent Rolls of Henry III 1216–1225*, pp. 148–9, 173–4; cf. H. S. Sweetman (ed.), *Calendar of Documents Relating to Ireland Preserved in Her Majesty's Public Record Office, London* (London, 1875–6), §§823, 825). The case is discussed by G. H. Orpen, *Ireland under the Normans 1169–1333* (Oxford, 1911–20), iii. 29–31. After Marshall's death at Caversham in May 1219, Albinus travelled to England to petition the king in person, and, according to Paris, also visited the earl's grave.

[7] Orpen, *Ireland under the Normans*, iii. 29.

that the Life was written at Ferns as supportive background to the bishop's case.

Ó Riain goes on to suggest that Albinus O'Mulloy was himself the author. His origins, like the writer's, were in the territory of Fir Chell, and he may have regarded Abbán as a personal patron.[8] The best argument, however, for this attribution comes from **D** §14, 'in illo die quo sancti uiri in ciuitatem que dicitur Abbaindun uel Dun Abbain uenerunt'. This place, in pagan country in southern England, is surely meant to be Abingdon. That monastery certainly included in its chronicle that:[9]

Verumtamen tunc temporis fuit quidam religiosus monachus, Abbenus nomine, qui ex Hibernia Britanniam ueniens, uerbum Dei, prout Spiritus Sanctus dabat eloquii illi, fideliter predicabat. ... Obtinuit autem memoratus Abbenus a rege Brittonum, ad precum suarum instantiam, maximam partem Berrocensis prouincie, in qua de consensu regis et consilio regni monasterium feliciter fundauit, cui nomen Abbendoniam, uel a nomine suo uel a loci uocabulo, alludenter imposuit. Secundum enim idioma Hibernensium, ut ex relatione modernorum accepimus, Abbendon mansio Abenni interpretatur; secundum uero idioma Anglorum Abbendun mons Abenni uulgariter nuncupatur.

Ó Riain draws attention to the fact that Albinus had 'travelled extensively in southern Britain'.[10] Abingdon may even have been known to him earlier: in 1180, Archbishop Lawrence O'Toole was kept waiting there for three weeks before he followed Henry II to Normandy.[11] Lawrence did not return from Normandy, but Albinus had been a disciple and companion, and would surely have known the events preceding the archbishop's death; he may even have been in the entourage. Albinus also had a copy of

---

[8] In its Latin occurrences *Abbanus* is often written *Albanus* (so *passim* in **S**, but in the manuscripts of **D** the word is sometimes divided at line-ends as *Ab | banus*; Plummer, *Vitae*, i. 3 n. 1). *Albinus* may have connected this with his own name. (As Ó Riain notes, 'St Abbán', p. 164, the possibility that Abbán is genuinely a hypocoristic form of Ailbe would not have been recognized in the twelfth or thirteenth century.)

[9] J. Stevenson (ed.), *Chronicon Monasterii de Abingdon* (Rolls Series, 2; London, 1858), i. 2–3.

[10] 'St Abbán', p. 170 n. 85, mentions his crossing England on his return from Rome, and his visiting the Cistercian abbey of Waverly.

[11] *Vita S. Laurentii* §25 (ed. C. Plummer (ed.), 'Vie et miracles de S. Laurent, archevêque de Dublin', *AB* 33 (1914), 152).

Bishop Malachy's *liber de miraculis*, written in the 1180s to promote the canonization of St Lawrence, and was himself one of five bishops who wrote to Innocent III in 1207 in support of the canonization.[12]

Few details are known of Albinus's career, and less of his personal interests.[13] He was a Cistercian, and is favourably mentioned by Matthew Paris.[14] In Lent 1185, while still abbot of Baltinglass before becoming bishop of Ferns, he preached at length at a synod in Dublin, 'de continentia clericorum', in which he denounced the English and Welsh clergy arriving in Ireland as a corrupting influence on the Irish clergy. This is reported briefly by Gerald of Wales, who goes on to quote at length his own address in reply, denouncing the laxity of the native clergy.[15] Ó Riain draws attention to the fact that the Life 'champions the Irish, and by implication their clergy, in the introductory chapter', which is clearly intended for a non-Irish audience. He suggests that Abbán's claim to have founded Abingdon was intended as a vindication of the Irish saints in the face of such criticism from Britain. Whether or not there was an underlying nationalist reason for writing the Life, this argument convincingly provides a datable context for its completion in or shortly before 1218. The Life of St Abbán appears to run that of St Lawrence a close second for being the latest text in the collection.

To go from the dating of a single Life to the date of the collection is not easy. Even within this Life, it is impossible to say whether the passages relevant to the dating were written by the author or by the redactor. The reference to Ross, for example, with its parallel in the D-text of the Life of St Molua, may well be taken for the work of the redactor. It might perhaps prove possible to dispense, in the case of this Life, with the distinction between author and redactor.

[12] M. V. Ronan, 'St Laurentius, Archbishop of Dublin: Original Testimonies for Canonization', *IER*[5] 27 (1926), 350.

[13] The outline of his career is given by Sheehy, *Pontificia Hibernica*, no. 67 n. 1. His death is reported in 1223 (AU, ALC, AFM).

[14] 'Ipse episcopus fuit episcopus de Fernes, monachus Cisterciensis ordinis, natione Hibernicus, sanctitate precipuus'; *Chronica Majora*, ed. Luard, iv. 493. The editor mistakenly identifies the bishop as Geoffrey St John, who occupied the see 1254–8.

[15] Gerald of Wales, *De Rebus a se Gestis*, II 13–15 (J. S. Brewer *et al.* (edd.), *Giraldi Cambrensis Opera* (Rolls Series, 21; London, 1861–91), i. pp. 65–72).

12.2. *Ferns and Uí Chennselaig*

Albinus was bishop of Ferns for close to forty years. For many years the monastery of Ferns had been the principal church of south Leinster, a region very frequently mentioned in the **D**-collection, sometimes as 'australes Laginenses', sometimes as Uí Chennselaig, and sometimes simply as Cennselach or 'regio Cennselach'.[16] Such references, however, are more than merely frequent; they are sometimes pregnant. In the Life of St Moling, of St Mullins, another leading church of south Leinster, **D** § 1:

De australi Laginensium plaga que dicitur Kennselach, et ipsa est illustrior pars Laginensium, inde iam regnum eorum fortiter regnat, . . .

Or in the fragmentary Life of St Patrick, **D** fr. 24, in an addition by the redactor:

Fyacha . . . qui iussione beatissimi Patricii gentem Ceanselach ad fidem conuertit et baptizauit, que gens maior atque potentior pars Laginensium est.

Or in the Life of St Fintán of Clonenagh, **D** § 19:

Quidam sanctus episcopus . . . a regione Kennselach, que est celebrior pars Laginensium . . .

This compliment is not found in the corresponding section of the **S**-text, a Life taken from Φ; it is the redactor's own. He does not make such statements about other regions, and one is tempted to suspect that the redactor had a special concern for this district.

Uí Chennselaig was for centuries the weaker of the two principal lineages of Leinster. From the beginning of the seventh century until the middle of the eleventh, the Uí Dúnlainge of north Leinster were able to control the entire province. But changing political circumstances allowed Diarmait mac Mael na

---

[16] 'australes Laginenses' at *Ab.* §§ 50, 51, *Cain.* § 10, *Coem.* § 25, *FintC.* § 7, *Mol.* §§ 1, 12, *Lug.* § 53; Uí Chennselaig at *Ab.* §§ 2, 9, *Cain.* § 34, *Maed.* §§ 20, 21 24, *Mun.* § 14; (as *plebs*) *Maed.* § 24; (as *regio*) *Ab.* §§ 28, 47; Cennselach (for people), *Coem.* § 19, *Com.* § 42, *Mol.* § 8; (as district) *Coem.* § 25, *Lug.* § 53, *Maed.* § 19, *Mol.* § 1, *Mun.* § 7; (with *regio*) *Coem.* §§ 21, 42, *FintC.* § 19, *Lug.* § 39, *Maed.* § 24; (with *regnum*) *Mun.* § 15; (with *rex*) *Mun.* § 22. Apart from Brandub, King Cormac mac Diarmada of Uí Chennselaig is mentioned, at *Ab.* §§ 3, 33, *FintC.* § 17, and *Com.* § 42.

mBó, king of Uí Chennselaig, to establish himself as the dominant ruler in both Leinster and Munster. After his death in 1072, the family remained prominent, and often dominant. The most famous of the line was Diarmait Mac Murchada: born about 1110, he fought his way to power in the years after 1126, and remained for many contentious years one of the most powerful rulers in Ireland. In 1166, however, his own territory was invaded by his rivals, his castle at Ferns was destroyed, and the town burnt. Diarmait fled to England where he made agreements with a number of Anglo-Norman lords. The story of how they helped restore Diarmait need not be recounted here. Richard fitz Gilbert, earl of Pembroke, and better known as 'Strongbow', was the most important. Diarmait married his daughter to him in 1170, before marching on Dublin. Diarmait died in May 1171, leaving Strongbow his heir. He soon came to terms with Diarmait's nephew, Muircheartach Mac Murchada, who retained Uí Chennselaig. His position, however, was insignificant in relation to Strongbow or Strongbow's heir, his son-in-law, William Earl Marshall. The period of Albinus's episcopate and the years immediately following saw Anglo-Norman control consolidated in Leinster and much of Ireland.

None the less, the redactor of **D** was still ready to proclaim Uí Chennselaig as 'gens maior atque potentior Laginensium', as though there were no rivals on the scene. The Life of St Maedóc, patron of Ferns and the Uí Chennselaig, exhibits this tendency more than other Lives. For example, in the Life of St Maedóc, **V** §24, a story is told of how St Maedóc protected the *munera* ('treasure' ?) of the people of Cluain Mór against Aed mac Ainmirech, supreme king of Uí Néill. We have already shown that the **V**-text was probably translated into Latin from Irish and that it formed the principal source of the **D**-text. Into this story the redactor of **D** introduces a number of significant changes. First, we may note the explanation of the place-name, which would appear to be wrong. The church of Cluain Mór Maedóc in Co. Carlow was associated in the Martyrology of Tallaght with an obscure Leinster saint called Maedóc Ua Dúnlaing, commemorated on 11 April. This church is mentioned several times in the annals, and in the late tenth and eleventh centuries it was disputed between rival branches of Uí Chennselaig. In 1040, according to the Annals of the Four Masters, King Diarmait mac Mael na mBó plundered

Cluain Mór Maedóc. This fact is used by Doherty in an argument towards dating the original Irish text of which we have a translation in **V**.[17] The name given in the **D**-text, Cluain Mór Dícholla Gairb, is Clonmore near Enniscorthy, Co. Wexford, a place of no importance. There are grounds for thinking that in specifying the minor church the redactor was deliberately seeking to mislead rather than merely making a faulty guess at a place-name. St Maedóc Ua Dúnlaing was still recognized as a different saint from Maedóc of Ferns in the eleventh century when the Middle Irish tale *Bórama* reached its full development.[18] This tale was well known to the *litterati* of Leinster, and seems to have influenced the redactor of **D** in his changes to the story here; for the conflict between Brandub and Aed mac Ainmirech has a prominent place in *Bórama*. Doherty has suggested that the two Maedócs were being deliberately merged into one in the original text of the Life; in **D** the process is taken further, so that Maedóc of Ferns and Brandub are seen in a specially close relationship. Following *Bórama* the redactor has introduced Brandub here to oppose Aed, and then advanced **V** § 29 to a position soon after this story in order to reinforce the impression of Brandub's successes. Both chapters are rewritten to the greater glory of Brandub, who was the only ancient ruler of Uí Chennselaig to have been recognized as king of Leinster. For centuries after his death in 605, the kingship of the province was held by the ruling dynasty of north Leinster, the Uí Dúnlainge.

V § 24 Alio autem tempore, cum esset sanctus Aidus in loco illo qui dicitur Cluain Mar, homines plebis istius ueniebant ut sua munera apud sanctum Aidum in custodia commendarent. Cumque Rex nepotum Neill, Aidus filius Ainmereth, cum suo exercitu in illam uenisset regionem, nunciatum est illi quod multa munera plebis in custodia apud sanctum Aidum essent. Venit ergo rex cum suis satellitibus, ista munera auferre uolens. Tunc sanctus Aidus posuit uestigium sui baculi inter hostem et locum in quo erant munera deposita. Quidam autem preco uenit trans uestigium baculi, dicens: 'Non est clericus qui me prohibere possit transire'. Et cum hoc dixisset, statim mortuus est. Hoc autem ceteri

[17] Doherty, 'The Irish Hagiographer', pp. 14–18. The closest range of dates he adopts is 1042 × 1059 (p. 20).

[18] The text is printed in *The Book of Leinster*, ed. Best *et al.*, v. 1268–1318. This recension was also edited with an English translation by W. Stokes, 'The Borama', *Revue Celtique*, 13 (1892), 32–124.

uidentes, non ausi sunt uenire; set nimio timore perterriti, reuersi sunt, preconem mortuum secum portantes, et sanctum Aidum glorificantes.

D §24 *Multa monasteria per circuitum regionis Cennselach sanctus Moedhog construxit.* Et cum esset in uno eorum quod dicitur Cluain Mor *Dicholla Gairbh (qui Dicholla erat sanctus abbas ipsius loci sub cura patris Moedhog*), collegit Edus filius Ainmirech, rex Hybernie, agmen maximum ad deuastandam plebem Hua Cennselach. *Brandubh enim filius Ethach, rex Hua Cennselach, erat contra eum.* Multi homines illius regionis cum substanciis suis fugerunt ad sanctum Moedhog manentem in predicto loco, sperantes defensionem per sanctitatem uiri ⟨Dei⟩. Hoc audiens rex Temorie, uenit tollere predam de loco illo. Exiuit sanctus Moedhog foras contra exercitum, et signauit cuspite bacculi sui contra eos. Vnus autem miles, qui erat prior ceteris, uolens transire signum, ait: 'Non est qui me prohibere potest suo signo'. Et cum hec dixisset, cecidit, et mortuus est. Ceteri iam ualde timentes, reuersi sunt ad regem. Et corpus exanime secum ducebant, narrantes regi que gesta fuerant, et glorificantes sanctum Maedhog. *Tunc rex cum exercitu suo reuersus est, dicens: 'Non iam possumus contra Deum certare.' Ipse enim rex Temorie, Edus filius Ainmireach, iterum alia uice de aquilonali parte Hybernie, et de regionibus Connachtorum et Muminensium et Hua Neyll, ad aquilonalium Laginensium* [sic; ? l. *ad ⟨deuastandam regionem⟩ aquilonalium Laginensium*] *multos exercitus collegit. Et uenit deuastare eandem regionem Hua Cennselach, et expellere inde regem eorum, silicet eundem Brandubh. Ipse uir astutissimus, et ualde probus in milicia erat. Et agens astute, intrauit audacter in castra inimicorum, et occidit ipsum regem Hybernie, Edum filium Ainmireach, et maximam cedem nobilium 'uirorum' tocius Hybernie cum eo fecit.*

A minor incident in **V** is thus turned in **D** into a story of how Brandub defeated and killed the king of Tara (*rex Temorie*), as the supreme king of Uí Néill is often called by the redactor. In **D** §26 we are then told how Brandub himself became the ruler of all Ireland 'usque ad Calla Ruaidh', a phrase which I take to be a corruption of 'usque ad Tollum Ruaidh',[19] and to imply that he ruled all of Ireland except Ulster.

V §29 Alio autem tempore uenit rex Brandub, filius Eochae, cum armento magno per litus Echdromo. Et ecce quidam leprosus ueniens, aliquid ab eo postulabat. Cui rex Brandub ludarium caluum et fuluum dedit. Rex autem cum armento ad amnem qui dicitur Slane perrexit; ibique in illa nocte manens, grauissimus dolor pene usque ad mortem super ipsum cecidit; et in ipsa doloris grauitate uisionem uidit. Portatus

---

[19] See above, p. 320.

est enim ad infernum, et omnes bestias inferni ore, labiis apertis, uidit inhiare; aliamque bestiam magnam in porta inferni ore aperto uidit, cuius anela ad se regem trahebat. Cum pene deglutisset eum bestia, quidam clericus amoenus superueniens, ludarium caluum et fuluum in os bestie proiecit. Et cum bestia ludarium deuorasset, interim rex ab ore ipsius retro reuersus est. Et iterum anela bestie post regem ueniens retraxit, et pene deglutiuit eum. Tunc idem clericus amoenus baculo suo bestie percussit capud, et os eius ignitum clausit; et sic rex Brandub inferni periculum euasit, et portatus est rex in dolore ad locum qui dicitur Inber Crimthain, ibique in graui dolore fuit. Tunc amici eius dixerunt ei: 'Quidam uir, nomine sanctus Aidus, in hac plebe consistit; mitte ergo, ut ab ipso aqua benedicta aportetur tibi.' Quibus rex ait: 'Ego potius ipse uadam ad hominem Dei.' Ascendensque ⟨currum⟩ uenit ad locum sancti Aidui. Cumque rex Brandub de longe uidisset sanctum Aidum ad se uenientem, dixit suis: 'Hic est clericus qui me de inferno liberauit.' Tunc rex ad pedes sancti se prostrauit, et dixit: 'Penitet me omne malum quod feci; et omnia quecunque mihi dixeris, in omni uita mea ego implebo. Tu enim me de penis inferni et eius bestiis soluisti.' Et in illa hora rex ab omni dolore, sancto benedicente, sanatus est. Et contulit Brandub sancto Aido multam terram, et in tota uita sua amici fuerunt inuicem.

D §26 *Quodam die rex supradictus Branndubh, accepto regno omnium Laginensium non solum set totius Hybernie usque ad Calla Ruaidh post occisionem Edani filii Ainmireach,* ueniebat per littus quoddam, habens magnas predas ante se de regionibus aquilonis. Occurrit ei quidam leprosus, petens ab eo elymosinam. Cui rex ludarium caluum et fuluum dedit in elymosinam. Postea rex in terram suam uenit, et castrametatus est iuxta flumen Slane; et magno dolore ibi comprehensus est. Et uidit hanc uisionem ibi. Vidit se portari ad infernum, et omnes bestias inferni labiis apertis occurrere ei. Viditque unam magnam et ferociorem ceteris in porta inferni aperto ore, que erat parata se deuorare. Cuius hanela regem ad se traxit, et pene deglutiuit eum. Cumque deglutis⟨s⟩et eum bestia, quidam clericus pulcer et letus uenit ad eum, et ludarium talem qualem dedit rex ipse leproso, posuit in ore bestie, et rex ab ore bestie reuersus est. Et iterum bestia traxit eum ad se, et pene deglutiuit eum. Tunc idem clericus baculo percussit capud bestie, et os eius ignitum clausit, et sic rex periculum inferni euasit; et reductus est spiritus eius ad corpus suum, et postea de extasi surrexit. Et narrauit suis familiaribus quod uidit. Deinde rex in dolore possitus, ductus est ad locum qui dicitur Inber Crumthin; ibi mansit infirmus. Tunc amici eius dixerunt ei: 'Est quidam uir sanctus, nomine Moedhog, in terra tua, qui facit magna mirabilia. Mitte ergo ad eum, ut ab ipso aqua benedicta feratur tibi.' Quibus rex ait: 'Non ita fiet; set ego pocius ad hominem Dei uadam.' Statimque

ascendens rex currum, uenit ad sanctum Moedhog. Audiens autem
beatus Moedhog quod rex ad se ueniret, exiuit in occursum eius.
Cumque rex de longe uidisset sanctum ad se uenientem, dixit: 'Iste
sanctus me liberauit de ore bestie, et de omni pena infernali. Cognosco
iam formam eius.' Tunc rex se prostrauit ad pedes sancti, dicens:
'Penitet me, quia multa feci mala, et quecumque dixeris mihi pro
remedio anime mee, in Dei nomine implebo.' Et tunc, orante sancto,
sanatus est 'rex' ilico ab omni infirmitate sua. Et 'ait' ad uirum Dei:
'Sanasti me ab infirmitate, et soluisti de inferno.' Et narrauit ei uisionem
suam. *Postea iterum rex ait sancto Meodhog: 'Ecce offero me ipsum tibi, ut
sepeliar in cimiterio tuo, et genus meum semper apud te sepelietur.' Et magnas dedit
rex oblaciones sancto Moedhog, et agrum, in quo uir Dei construxit monasterium,
quod dicitur Ferna. In quo sanctus Moedhog sepultus est; et rex Brandubh et genus
eius post eum ibi semper sepelitur. Et magna ciuitas in honore sancti Moedhog ibi
creuit, que eodem nomine uocatur, id est, Ferna. Deinde facta synodo magna in
terra Laginensium, decreuit rex Brandubh, et tam laici quam clerici, ut archiepiscopus omnium Laginensium semper esset in sede et cathedra sancti Moedhog. Et
tunc sanctus Moedhog a multis catholicis consecratus est archiepiscopus.*

The redactor has gone all out to establish a link between Brandub,
whose reign marked the apogee of the power of Uí Chennselaig in
the early Middle Ages, and Maedóc's principal church of Ferns.
In the perspective of the collection as a whole these changes take
on a larger significance.

Elsewhere in the work of the redactor of **D**, we find evidence for
the same interests, where they are less expected. If such accounts
have a place in the Life of St Maedóc, this aside is surely dragged
into the Life of St Coemgen, **D** § 19:

Quodam quoque die uenator regis Laginensium, Brandubh filii
Eathach, de semine Enna a quo nominatur gens Cennselach, qui
innumerabilem cedem in maxima plaga super aquilonales Hybernie
prouinchias in bello magno fecit (et ille Brandubh regnum multarum
Hybernie regionum, postquam ipse regem Temorie et Aileach, id est
Edum filium Ainmireuch, occidit in bello, tenuit), sequens canes suos
aprum persequentes . . .

Similarly, in the Life of St Moling, **D** § 8, we find this explicit
linking of Brandub with the same exaggerated status for Maedóc's
church at Ferns as we have just read in the **D**-version of his own
Life:

Cum esset ciuitas sancti Aedani, qui uulgo Moedhog uocatur, post
obitum episcopi sui sine pastore, miserunt ciues illius cum rege

Laginensium ex consilio principum prouinchie ad sanctum Molyng, ut ipsum ad episcopatum supradicte ciuitatis, siue uellet siue nollet, ducerent. Et adductus sanctus Molyng ad predictam ciuitatem, constitutus est ipse archiepiscopus in sede et in cathedra sancti Moedhog. A rege iam Laginensium, Brandubh filio Eathach, constitutum est ut archiepiscopatus Laginensium in ciuitate sancti Moedhog esset. Ipsa ciuitas uocatur Ferna, que est in terra gentis Kennselach, que gens in antiquis temporibus dicebatur Fyr Gailyan, usque ad Enna a quo Kennselaydh dicuntur, eo quod ipse aspersus ualde cruore et sanguine inimicorum in facie et in toto corpore de cede aquilonalium uictor uenit.[20]

The significance of this episode in the career of St Moling is rather uncertain,[21] but it once again clearly demonstrates the redactor's strong commitment to a somewhat extreme and unusual view of the position of Ferns. He further maintains this position in §55 of the Life of St Maedóc, where the saint helps Brandub to defeat the Uí Néill once again. Where V §54 simply says, 'Tunc•rex Brandub exiit ad salutandum Aidum', D §55 reads, 'Tunc rex Laginensium uenit ad sanctum archiepiscopum suum Moedhog', a title used again at §59. Similarly, in the Life of St Molua, S¹ §43, the Φ-text reads, 'Sanctus Aidus, abbas Ferna Mare, uoluit ire trans mare ad Dauid ecclesie Muini', but D §38 has:

Beatissimus archiepiscopus Laginensium Moedhog uoluit ire trans mare in Britaniam ad sanctum magistrum suum, Dauid episcopum.

The maintenance of this point of view, both unhistorical and idiosyncratic, through Lives other than that of Maedóc himself shows that it was no casual fantasy, inspired by that Life. Rather it was a theme which mattered to the redactor. If it were simply designed to give prominence to Brandub, the ruler of Uí Chennselaig who achieved the greatest position in Ireland, then one might suppose this was meant to express support for the Mac Murchada family, the displaced and degraded rulers of Uí Chennselaig. The interest in establishing the link with Ferns, their principal seat by the twelfth century, would perhaps be an expected accompaniment in an ecclesiastical author. Yet this setting out of pretended archiepiscopal status for Ferns must

---

[20] As Plummer notes, *Vitae*, ii. 193 n. 1, the redactor derives the nickname Énda Cennselach from *cenn* 'head' and *salach* 'dirty'.

[21] See Plummer, *Vitae*, vol. i, p. lxxxii, Colgan, *Acta*, pp. 407–8, and cf. V §57.

imply that the redactor was not only committed to the Uí
Chennselaig—perhaps even a member of the lineage—but was
also closely connected with the church of Ferns.

Is it possible that Albinus O'Mulloy was responsible for all this?
It looks unlikely, for, although the Life of St Abbán reflects many
of the redactor's interests—especially, for example, in the roles of
St Patrick and St Ibar—it is in conflict with the other Lives over the
status of St Maedóc. Yet the very passage which is most in conflict
appears well suited to a collection of the Lives of Ireland's saints:

In occidentali plaga tocius orbis est insula possita, cuius nomen
Hybernia dicitur. Eadem uero insula est magna et clara atque amena
terra, in qua continentur maxime quinque prouinchie, in qua etiam
nulla bestia uenenosa, nec genus ullum serpentinum habitat; set terra
sana est, morbis carens, habitabilis ualde, fructifera in diuersis fructibus,
tam in aquis quam in terris et lignis. Habitatores autem eius bino
nomine nominantur; id est ab Hibero flumine Hibernia uocatur, et ab
Hibernia Hibernienses uocantur. Scoti uero a Scota, matre eiusdem
gentis, dicuntur, que fuit filia regis Egypti. Quomodo de Egypto ipsa
uenit ad Hiberniam, causa breuitatis omittimus, quia satis inuenitur de
illa in libris, qui narrant quomodo in primis habitata est Hybernia.
Cultores uero Hybernie probati sunt in fide catholica et in dogmatibus
ecclesiasticis; et plus omnibus nacionibus hospitalitatem sectantur.

De illa scilicet gente maximum sanctorum agmen sibi Deus elegit;
sicut ueritas in euangelio ait: 'Alias oues habeo, que non sunt ex hoc
ouili'. Et alibi: 'Multi uenient ab oriente et ab occidente, et recumbent
cum Abraham', etc. De quorum collegio fuit uir uite uenerabilis,
Abbanus nomine, quem Deus preelegit, antequam natus fuisset; quia
multi sancti uiri per multa tempora, antequam natus esset, predicauerunt ipsum nasciturum. De quibus sanctus Patricius archiepiscopus, tenens portum in australi parte Laginensium, id est Hua
Cennselaidh, cum uenisset ad predicandum in Hibernia, dixit: 'Tres filii
uite eterne de gente Laginensium nascentur, quorum nomina uoca-
buntur Abbanus, Coemgenus, et Molyng. Ipsi maiores sanctorum
Laginensium erunt; et per merita eorum, quamuis nondum nati sunt,
Deum modo rogabo, quia illi uenturi sunt lucerne clarissime hominibus,
pia opera et Deo placita clarificaturi, et propter eos conuertam
Laginenses ad Christi fidem, set non modo; quia Deus predestinauit
mihi prius ire in aquilonales partes Hybernie, et postea ociosius uenire
ad Laginenses, quia ipsi belligeri sunt.' Nomina uero aliorum, et
quomodo predicauerunt de sancto Abbano, propter breuitatem omittimus, nisi quomodo in hora natiuitatis eius predicauit de eo sanctus
Ybarus episcopus. . . .

The whole introductory passage *could* be the work of the redactor, and one may compare his description of Ireland in the Life of St Patrick, **D** fr. 11. There are some indications to this effect: the word *plaga*, the reference to the five provinces, the mention that the inhabitants 'probati sunt in fide catholica et in dogmatibus ecclesiasticis', the allusion to the custom of hospitality. Familiarity with *Lebor Gabála hÉrenn* 'the Book of Invasions of Ireland', however, could be expected of most educated Irishmen from the twelfth century on. None the less, the two paragraphs taken together—one introducing Ireland, the other her 'maximum sanctorum agmen'—suggest that this passage was intended for the beginning of a national legendary; perhaps more specifically for a Leinster legendary. Its author introduces St Patrick at an early stage, and goes on to make him prophesy of three great Leinster saints, Abbán, Coemgen, and Moling. It is certainly an idiosyncratic list—including the little-known Abbán, but excluding St Brigit of Kildare and St Maedóc of Ferns—and it hardly seems possible that this could have been written by our redactor, to whom St Maedóc was of such great importance. It is even somewhat surprising that he has allowed the list to remain unchanged in his revision.

On the available information, however, a highly speculative compromise seems possible. If we accept that Albinus of Ferns was responsible for the Life of St Abbán, and that he intended to follow this up with other Lives—Coemgen and Moling, presumably, but perhaps a more extensive and national collection—he may have decided that he needed to call in an assistant, someone to do most of the work. Our redactor may have begun his task at the instigation of Albinus, though he did not complete the work until at least a few years after Albinus died in 1223. Moreover, he organized the collection in his own way, so that instead of beginning with St Abbán he began with St Patrick and St Brigit. If our earlier comments are accepted, St Columba may or may not have come next, and the first saint after these national patrons was St Maedóc.[22] Although Albinus was bishop of Ferns, he appears to have been much less devoted to St Maedóc than was the redactor, for whom south Leinster must surely have been native territory.

---

[22] See above, pp. 113–14.

This compromise would provide a date for the redactor's work around the 1220s. Professor Ó Riain's study of the Life of St Abbán has provided one limit, but we have no *terminus ante quem*. I should venture to say, however, that before the thirteenth century was much older, a collection of this kind would already have been out of step with current taste. As we shall see in the next chapter, the collections of the later thirteenth century were concerned to abbreviate and tailor to liturgical or edificatory use. While the redactor of **D** loves local detail, his successors constantly avoid it. Where he writes expansively, they will shorten the narrative and fill up the space with devotional commonplaces. In this sense, the development of the hagiographical taste must itself restrict the period within which **D** could have been written. Therefore, even if the redactor had no personal connexion with Albinus, and treated the Life of St Abbán as just one of the many texts he was editing, the period of his work could still not have been much later than the 1220s or 1230s.

Picking up what we said in Chapter 1 about hagiography in this period, Albinus and the redactor of **D** represent a development from Phase IV. Sharing the local commitments and interests of a writer like the author of *Vita S. Declani*, they rise above them to take a national view. If the **D**-collection were to be assigned to a fifth phase, on available evidence it would be its only representative.

12.3. *The Purpose of the Collection*

The national scale of the collection has been obvious from the outset. From the point when it was recognized that there was a single redactor shaping the texts in this collection, it must have been clear that Kenney's locally centred approach to each *uita* had to be mistaken, for the redactor of a national collection could hardly be expected to make each Life a political statement in the interests of whatever church was most relevant. An extreme aspect of Kenney's critical method is his use of the phrases *patronus noster*, *pater noster*, *senex noster* as a touchstone proving that a Life in **D** was composed in the particular saint's own foundation.[23] This inference is demonstrably false, because it can be shown that the

[23] Kenney, *The Sources*, pp. 392 n. 69, 422.

redactor inserts such references to *patronus* impartially in several different Lives.[24] Similarly the method of comparing the various recensions of a Life in search of historical clues to changed conditions is not applicable where the secondary recensions were not the product of local revision. It must surely be nonsense to imagine that in revising so many Lives our redactor could have had any specific interest, Life by Life, in the individual patrons of different churches. One specific element in Kenney's line of argument can be shown to rest on a misconception. Discussing the Life of Fínán, he writes of the Life in **D** that its version, 'though older' [than other texts] 'is farther removed from the original—yet it preserves the "pater noster", "patronus noster", which indicate the source in a composition of Fínán's community'. Again, of the life of St Ruadán, he notes that one passage in the **D**-text 'preserves the formula "noster senex", pointing to composition in Ruadán's community'.[25] Kenny's expression is itself forumlaic, and his use of 'preserves' rests on assumptions about the survival of early strata in later texts and not on a textual understanding of the different recensions. He had not realized that the redactor of **D** habitually adds the phrases *pater noster, patronus noster*, and as the saint grows older *senex noster*.[26] In this way he identifies himself with the cult of

---

[24] A list of occurrences is given n. 26. Where these can be checked against other recensions, the word *patronus* and the notion it implies are demonstrably the contribution of the redactor of **D**.

[25] Kenney, *The Sources*, pp. 422, 392 n. 69. Elsewhere he uses the same argument from other lives: p. 396 and n. 94 (Comgall); it is perhaps implicit at p. 460 (Crónán).

[26] In the following examples *patronus* is used: 'nostrum sanctum et patronum' *Abb.* **D** §50; 'sanctissimus noster patronus Carthagus' *Car.* **D** §45; 'sanctus patronus noster Mochutu' ibid. §68; 'sanctissimus noster patronus Mochutu' ibid. §69; 'sanctus Kiaranus patronus noster' *Cic,* **D** §31; 'sanctissimus noster patronus Kiaranus' ibid. §32; 'sanctus patronus noster Kyaranus' ibid. §38; 'ad patronum suum sanctum Kyaranum' *Cis.* **D** §16; 'beatissimus patronus noster Patricius' *Coem.* **D** §22; 'sanctum patronum nostrum Coemgenum' ibid. §47; 'beatissimus noster patronus Patricius' *ColE.* **D** §25; 'in honore nostri patroni Comgalli' *Com.* **D** §58; 'sanctus senex noster Declanus et patronus' *Decl.* **D** §39; 'gens . . . uenit ad suum patronum sanctum Finanum' *FinC.* **D** §16; 'sanctus Finanus patronus noster' ibid. §29; 'post obitum beatissimi Moedhog patroni nostri' *Maed.* **D** §58; 'sanctus et patronus noster Moedhog' ibid. §59; 'patronus noster beatissimus Mocoemog' *Mchg.* **D** §35; 'de sanctitate beatissimi nostri patroni, sancti silicet Molyng' *Mol.* **D** §29; 'beatissimus noster patronus Molua' *Lug.* **D** §54; 'patronus noster Ruadhanus' *Rua* **D** §30. In every case where the text can be compared with its source the phrase is shown to be an addition in the **D**-

saint after saint impartially. It has justly been argued that historical texts composed in Ireland down to the twelfth century tend to reflect the contemporary concerns of the writer.[27] One must, however, beware of too simple assumptions that the Life of a particular saint could reflect the concerns only of his own church, or that those concerns should necessarily have a context in the realities of the time. There was never a time when Ferns had any realistic pretensions to archiepiscopal status; such a notion was irrelevant in the time of Brandub, and from the twelfth century, when it may have meant something, Ferns can hardly have hoped to supplant Dublin as the metropolitan see of Leinster. Diarmait Mac Murchada had ambitions to rule Dublin, but not to transfer the metropolis to Ferns. Rather, it was the redactor who dreamt of a Leinster, powerful and famous, ruled by the Uí Chennselaig from Ferns, without rivals in Dublin. This moulded his version of the careers of St Maedóc and King Brandub, giving the dream reality in the imaginary past.

The redactor was essentially an antiquary. Although his religious outlook balked at some of the content of the older texts, he was not seriously out of sympathy with their authors; he could still read their work with an intelligent understanding and revise it in a manner responsive to the tradition of eighth-century hagiography. He brought to his interest in the past a sense of Ireland's history, traditions, and customs, which one could almost

text. The same is the case with the following examples of *noster pater*: 'noster pater Coemgenus' *Coem.* **D** §36; 'sanctus noster pater' *Decl.* **D** §37; 'pater noster Fintanus' *FintC.* **D** §24; 'beatissimi patris nostri Colmani Ela' *ColE.* **D** §36; 'beati patris nostri Colmani' ibid. §37; 'sancti patris nostri Findbarri' *Com.* **D** §30; 'sanctissimi patris nostri Finani' *FinC.* **D** §29. I also add a number of examples showing *noster senex*: 'noster senex et uenerabilis pater' *Abb.* **D** §51; 'sanctus noster senex Mochuda' *Car.* **D** §59; 'noster senex Coemgenus' *Coem.* **D** §36; 'sanctissimi senis nostri Cronani' *Cron.* **D** §28; 'sanctus senex noster Declanus' *Decl.* **D** §38; 'sanctus senex noster Declanus et patronus' ibid. §39; 'noster senex Finanus' *FinC.* **D** §24; 'sanctus senior noster' *Mchg.* **D** §4; 'sanctissimus noster senex Ruadhanus' *Rua.* **D** §30. I add a single example of *noster sanctus*: 'noster sanctus Cronanus' *Cron.* **D** §29. The phrases *sanctus pater, sanctus senex*, and *sanctus senior* occur very frequently without the possessive adjective; at a rough count their frequency amounts to about 400, 200, and 100 repsectively. The redactor habitually progresses *puer, pater, senex* as a saint grows older.

[27] D. Ó Corráin, 'Historical Need and Literary Narrative', in *Proceedings of the Seventh International Congress of Celtic Studies, Oxford, 1983*, ed. D. E. Evans *et al.* (Oxford, 1986), pp. 141–4 and 153.

describe as nationalist. He was familiar with *Lebor Gabála*, and with the 'synthetic' version of Irish history, in which ancient kings had ruled all Ireland from Tara. He knew other historic tales such as the Expulsion of the Déisi and *Bórama*, and draws on them. He was able to add digressions on the battles in which one province had triumphed over another, or in which the kingship of Tara had changed hands. He could fill in genealogical background. His knowledge of Irish places and place-names must have been considerable for him to have had the confidence to identify and locate places named in his sources; the fact that he sometimes went wrong hardly matters. Very occasionally he adds a story to a place-name, so that it seems likely that his topographical knowledge was based on *dindsenchus* rather than travel. None of this is remarkable in an Irish man of learning: history, genealogy, and place-name tales were the very substance of Irish learning, summed up in the one word *senchus*.[28] What is remarkable is the use to which it was put.

The redactor systematically gathered some twenty-nine Lives of saints in Latin. Some of them apparently came from the Continent, though we need hardly imagine that they were brought to Ireland solely for the redactor's use. A manuscript such as Φ he must have sought out in whatever libraries he had access to, while more recent texts such as the Lives of St Abbán or St Declán, or those of St Malachy and St Lawrence, may have been fresh and readily available. Having gathered these materials, he studied them carefully, smoothing inconsistencies within individual texts, and cross-referring from one Life to another. He was even able to synthesize information from the different Lives and create a new thesis about the earliest period of Irish Christianity. I drew attention at the end of Chapter 4 to the evenness of language used in different Lives when writing about four bishops who supposedly carried on a limited mission in Ireland during the thirty years before St Patrick began his work.[29] In another place I have argued in detail that the role of these four bishops is a historical construct, inferred by the redactor from the *uitae* of St Ailbe and St Ciarán of Saigir and developed by him. Having

---

[28] F. J. Byrne, 'Senchas: The Nature of Gaelic Historical Tradition', *Historical Studies*, 9 (1971), 137–59.

[29] See above, pp. 115–16.

founded his view on these sources, he then wrote it into other Lives as he revised them, giving a view of the period which is almost wholly consistent throughout the collection.[30] He shaped each text more or less to a pattern, excepting four which were hardly revised at all, and rewrote them in his own identifiable style. The scale of the project is considerable, the vigour with which it was accomplished admirable.

As a literary achievement, the work of the redactor of **D** is the most substantial piece of Latin writing by an Irishman, still preserved, between the time of Eriugena and the end of the Middle Ages. It represents a personal interpretation of a sizeable corpus of older *uitae*. The comparison between the old and the new is instructive, but it must be admitted that the redactor revised so extensively that, unless one can compare his work with his source, it is difficult to tell how much he has altered his text. Even with a lively awareness of his methods and interests, one cannot read a text which he revised and pretend to determine its original form. The student of early medieval Ireland must regret the loss of the redactor's models, but it would be churlish not to praise his ambitions and efforts.

---

[30] Sharpe, '*Quattuor sanctissimi episcopi*', pp. 385–97.

13

The Milieux of the Later Collections

THERE is no parallel in the later collections to the grand literary design conceived and executed by the redactor of **D**. Indeed, with the exception of only one text, the elaborate *Vita et nauigatio S. Brendani* in **O**, the pattern of hagiographical activity appears to be downhill all the way, at any rate in Latin. By the thirteenth century, throughout Europe, the trend in hagiography was for legendaries to grow larger, but for the *uitae* in them to be cut shorter and made less detailed, less specific. While the *Legenda Aurea* became a best-seller among abbreviated legendaries, everywhere saints' Lives were being reduced to potted versions for easy reading. In England, early in the fourteenth century, John of Tynemouth's *Sanctilogium* was a veritable *summa* of brief Lives for numerous saints of Britain and Ireland.[1] His Irish sources have yet to be investigated, but the taste for abbreviated *uitae* had already led to the production of compendia of brief Lives. Although neither **O** nor **S** is strictly a compendium of such Lives, both bear witness to the practice of abbreviating texts for reading aloud. This is declared in the much abbreviated second Life of St Brendan in **S**, § 17:

Hactenus de plurimis pauca diximus. Nunc uero lectionalis modus ultra cogit nos transilire.

So saying, the abbreviator jumps to the last three days of St Brendan's life, leaving the *uita* a mere stump, from which almost all reference to the saint's voyaging is omitted. From what we know of the conservative methods of the compiler of **S**, we must take it that his text had already been subjected to this drastic abbreviation. Other texts in **S** were clearly intended for homiletic

---

[1] The content of John's *Sanctilogium*, but not its original calendar arrangement, is accessible in C. Horstman (ed.), *Nova Legenda Anglie: As Collected by John of Tynemouth, John Capgrave, and Others* (Oxford, 1901). On the Irish saints represented, see ibid. i, p. xxvi.

use. The Life of St Fintán of Dún Bléisci, for example, begins with a homiletic prologue which leads into the Life thus:

Ipse enim est qui facit mirabilia magna solus; multi uero sunt sancti et amici eius per quos aperte facit mirabilia sua. De quorum numero est ille de quo locuturi sumus, silicet Fintanus . . .

Some of the texts common to both **O** and **S** appear to have been quite heavily abbreviated by the compiler of Θ. In the case of St Molua, more than half of the original text was omitted, sometimes overtly.[2] The liturgical intention is in some cases very obvious: the Life of St Coemgen, for example, begins, 'Adest nobis, fratres, gloriosi abbatis Caymgini ueneranda festiuitas', while that of St Molua ends, 'Nos itaque, fratres, in tanti patris festiuitate superis congaudeamus ciuibus et collaudemus filium Dei, qui . . .'. The tendency to remove names and to add pious phrases and biblical asides, which we observed in both Θ and **O**, indicates that saints' Lives were being treated as edifying reading in the most generalized way. There was no serious concern to remind the audience of the saint's associations with particular places, people, or even events. All that was necessary was ample reference to miracles and to the saint's devout life and holy character. Efforts were also made to improve the Latin style of the texts, or at least to avoid what the revisers regarded as grammatical solecisms. This was the feature most often singled out by Colgan as distinguishing the **O**-collection—which he regarded as 'latinior et recentior'—from the **D**-collection, whose less regular grammar he took as a sign of its great antiquity.

Between the work of the redactor of **D** and the compilation of the later collections, then, there was a considerable change in the literary expectations brought to the saints' Lives. There may be more than one reason for this. It is possible that there was a marked change of taste soon after the completion of the **D**-collection. Another factor may have been that the later collections were produced for an entirely different audience in a different social context. Whatever the reason, the Lives of what we might call Phase VI are generally disappointing.

[2] See *Lug.* SO §§ 21, 35.

13.1. *The Dates and Origins of the Later Collections*

The anodyne nature of the house-style in Θ and O, and the absence of any editorial interest in S, make it impossible to establish dating criteria for these collections. It is necessary to fall back on the relative chronology discussed in Chapter 9.

The S-collection can be dated palaeographically because we have ascertained that the state of the codex bears witness to the actual process of compilation. This belongs to the late fourteenth century. The earliest known copy of the O-collection was probably written in the early fourteenth century; that was likely to have been a fair copy, but there is no cause to think that its archetype was assembled any earlier than about 1300. Both of these collections used the conjectured collection Θ, which in turn had access to the D-collection. The latest possible date for D is not certain, but I have suggested about 1230. Within the date range 1230 × 1300, it seems probable that Θ is later rather than earlier. It is markedly different in approach from D and very similar in style to O, so the turning-point lies somewhere in the later half of the thirteenth century.

Where the collections were compiled is far from certain. In the case of the S-collection, we have inferred that the compiler belonged to a religious house in Ireland but *inter Anglos*, and that neither he nor his scribes knew much of the Irish language. Geographically a group of Lives peculiar to this collection deals with saints of south-east Ulster: SS. Daig, Mochta, Eogan, Mac Nisse. The Life of St Tigernach has been associated with this group.[3] Since this Life occurs in a different part of the codex, was derived from a different textual source, and is known from other copies including one written as far south as Waterford, its connexion with the group is questionable. Moreover small groups of texts could and did travel considerable distances in manuscript. I doubt, therefore, whether we have any evidence more precisely to place the compilation of S.

The O-collection contains a number of Lives peculiar to itself: SS. Berach, Molaisse of Devenish, Énda of Aran, Gerald, Fechin, Mochua of Timahoe, Samthann, and Buite, whose centres of cult

---

[3] K. McCone, 'Clones and her Neighbours in the Early Period: Hints from Some Airgialla Saints' Lives', *Clogher Record*, 11 (1982–4), 305–25.

lie scattered widely, from Devenish in the north to Timahoe in Co. Laois, from Aran in the west to Monasterboice in the east. These do not indicate any likely place of compilation, nor should one necessarily expect them to. When a collection has reached thirty-nine Lives, it can no longer be strictly tied to one locality. The edificatory character of the editing, and the apparent tendency of the O-redactor to adopt and extend the methods of the compiler of Θ, should probably lead one to suppose that the collection was made in a religious house *inter Anglos*, where Irish details were of little interest. Yet there are signs of occasional attention to the Irish vernacular, while one at least of the manuscripts we have was written by an Irish scribe and spent much of its existence in a house where Irish was the everyday language. The milieu of this collection seems to me, therefore, indeterminate.

Both collections are large enough to be regarded as national rather than local in their interest; even though St David is admitted to O and St Catherine to S, they are in all other respects Irish legendaries, and the two outsiders can be explained.[4] Both collections are much more varied in the form of Lives contained than is D. Long Lives such as Jocelin's St Patrick or the redactor's own St Brendan have their place in O, while many others are brief, and some of them distinctly homiletic. In S too, a fair proportion of the Lives is of the same brief character, although others are long and full. In literary terms, S is beyond consideration because of its indiscriminate conservatism. The redactor of O, apart from his indulgence in the Life of St Brendan, shares the stylistic tastes of the latest stage of editorial activity, which we have seen probably dates from the late thirteenth century.

Some texts which survive outside the three collections will help to fill out the picture of this phase of hagiographical writing in Ireland.

---

[4] St David visited Ireland himself, and was much visited by Irish saints. His Irish cult is attested, for example, in the *Kalendarium* (ff. 1–32) of Dublin, Trinity College, MS 97 (B. 3. 5) (s. xiii/xiv) from St Thomas's Abbey, Dublin; W. Hawkes, 'The Liturgy in Dublin, 1200–1500: Manuscript Sources', *Reportorium Novum: Dublin Diocesan Historical Record*, 2 (1958–60), 63. Another Welsh saint, Cadoc, is also included here. St Catherine's cult was popular in fourteenth-century Ireland; see above, p. 241 n. 42.

13.2. *Lections and Offices for Irish Saints*

Liturgical verses, not found in the **D**-collection at all, occur at the end of several Lives in the **O**- and **S**-collections. The Life of St Berach, for example, concludes with a brief collect headed 'Oracio'.[5] The Life of St Fechin ends with two hymns.[6] These are both in the **O**-collection only. The Life of St Mochutu in **S** ends with an antiphon.[7] The Life of St Tigernach is of special interest on this account, and also in respect of the transmission of *uitae* in late medieval Ireland. In addition to the copies in **O** and **S**, both derived from Θ, there are two witnesses outside the main collections. One of these, unknown to Plummer, is now bound in Cambridge, Corpus Christi College, MS 405, a composite of several pieces from the Hospital of St John of Jerusalem at Waterford (W). Its contents include a thirteenth-century calendar of saints (many of them Irish) and a fourteenth-century *sanctorale*, containing offices for four Irish saints: Patrick, Brigit, Tigernach, and Barmedinus. Two hymns from the office for St Tigernach are also given at the end of his Life in the **O**-collection, confirming the liturgical character of such passages appended to other Lives.[8] The Life of St Tigernach in this office is textually very close to that in Θ, but there are some passages not found in that text. The fourth witness is the edition published by the Bollandists, which was itself based on three sources: **S**, which was in their own library, a text supplied by Hugh Ward which was almost certainly **O**, and a text from Fr. Henry FitzSimon.[9] Plummer noted that 'Fitzsimon's MS must have differed markedly from the others. In particular it contained one chapter peculiar to itself.'[10] This chapter is not peculiar to FitzSimon's text, but is found also in W, with minor differences of reading, and appears probably to have belonged to the archetype. Its omission from Θ can be explained simply as an error in copying.[11] 'Markedly different', in the context of these

---

[5] Plummer, *Vitae*, i. 86.

[6] Ibid. ii. 84–6.   [7] Heist, *Vitae*, p. 340.

[8] Plummer, *Vitae*, ii. 268–9. The end of this text is missing in **S**, so that one cannot tell whether the hymns were in Θ.

[9] *Acta Sanctorum*, Apr. I (1675), p. 401.

[10] Plummer, *Vitae*, vol. i, p. lxxxix.

[11] As Plummer observed, ibid. ii. 264 n. 12, the omitted passage begins 'Deinde ad' and ends 'baptizati sunt'; §8, which follows, begins and ends with the same

Lives, is an overstatement, since in general the four witnesses are very close, forming two textual pairs.

This sheds a little light on Θ, but leads also to an awareness of still greater areas of darkness. If W and FitzSimon had access to a better witness than Θ, then obviously the text as we have it was not the work of the compiler of Θ. It was taken into that collection, with minimal deliberate revision, from another source. That source was presumably similarly intended for lectionary or liturgical use, since its text is found in W, a liturgical manuscript. The compiler of W has confined himself to four offices, and one might expect therefore that it would be easy to work out where this book was originally intended for. St Patrick and St Brigit are both saints of national status and so provide no guide. 'Barmedinus' is a saint derived from the place-name Kilbarrymedan, *Cell Bairre Mittíne*, a local manifestation of St Finnbarr, reflecting perhaps the local devotion of a compiler from Co. Waterford.[12] Yet St Tigernach's principal church, Clones, is almost at the other end of the country, and I can suggest no locality where the cult of Bairre Mittíne might be found alongside Tigernach. His four offices were presumably drawn from some sort of pool, since special offices for certain saints were required by episcopal constitutions, to which we shall shortly turn.

The offices of a few Irish saints are known from other sources. That of St Patrick is naturally enough the most widely distributed.[13] Kathleen Hughes drew attention to Brussels, Bibliothèque royale, MS 8590–8598, ff. 166–190, a booklet from the *collectanea* of the early Bollandists, containing offices for St Patrick (incomplete), St Columba, the Feast of the Translation of SS. Patrick, Columba and Brigit, St Finnian of Clonard, and St

---

words, and §9 also begins 'Deinde ad'. It would be only too easy for the whole of §8 to have been omitted by eye-skip; it is less easy, but still quite possible, for the passage preceding §8 to have been lost.

[12] P. Grosjean, 'Les Vies de S. Finnbarr de Cork, de S. Finnbarr d'Écosse et de S. Mac Cuilinn de Lusk', *AB* 69 (1951), 326 n. 1, promised a study of this text which he did not live to achieve.

[13] Offices of St Patrick are found in Cambridge, Corpus Christi College, MS 405 (s. xiv), pp. 104–21, and Dublin, Trinity College, MS 80 (B. 1. 5) (s. xv), ff. 122–124. T. Messingham (ed.), *Officia SS. Patricii, Columbae, Brigidae* (Paris, 1620), and the Brussels manuscript mentioned here likewise have offices for him. The only printed edition is Messingham's.

Camnech.[14] Different but related offices of these saints, and also of St Brigit, were published by Thomas Messingham, but his texts provide fewer lections drawn from the *uitae*.[15]

Hughes has examined the lections in the office of St Finnian, showing that they are not dependent on either of the known Latin Lives, in **S** or **O**, nor on their immediate source, our **Θ**; she suggests they were based on the fuller text which was the source of **Θ**.[16] In her view, the Latin style of the opening lections reflects that original, and on this basis she supposes the source-text to have come from an Anglo-Norman milieu. I cannot see how this can be maintained, since it is impossible to say whether the lections have preserved more than incidental words from the source. I suspect rather that the rhetorical manner of the first lections, degenerating into very basic, summary narrative in the later ones, was the work of the liturgical compiler. His effort is datable to the period when Thomas St Leger was bishop of Clonard (1287–1320); it was St Leger, according to lines in the *hymnus ad uesperas* of the office, who placed St Finnian in the calendar.[17] His implied absence before that date indicates that the background is one of Anglo-French revival of native cults.

The office of St Cianán of Duleek, also discussed by Hughes, is known from two sources. London, Lambeth Palace Library, MS 357, ff. 72^v–77^r, presents the full office in a large hand of the fifteenth century.[18] British Library, MS Lansdowne 387, ff. 1–41, a slim volume of 'Lectiones in festis sanctorum', has the office at ff. 35–41, and at ff. 11^v–14^r copies of some of the lections.[19] The provenance of both manuscripts is probably Lanthony Secunda

---

[14] K. Hughes, 'The Offices of St Finnian of Clonard and St Cíanán of Duleek', *AB* 73 (1955), 342–72 (at p. 343).

[15] Messingham, *Officia*.

[16] Hughes, 'The Offices', pp. 346–9. One should perhaps allow the possiblity that the liturgical compiler has taken a free hand.

[17] Ibid., pp. 345 and 357. The lines of the hymn are: 'Presul Midensis inclitus, Thomas de Leodegario / uirtute Sancti Spiritus hunc rexit annuario'.

[18] Ibid., pp. 349–50. The office was recopied by William More in July 1656 for Sir James Ware; the copy survives in one of Ware's notebooks, now London, British Library, MS Lansdowne 418, ff. 105^r–110^v.

[19] The office of St Cianán was first printed from this manuscript by W. H. Hart, *Lectionarium Sanctae Mariae Virginis, Sancti Thomae Cantuariensis, Sanctae Kyneburgae Gloucestrensis, et Sancti Kenani de Hibernia* (London, 1869). It was printed from both copies by Hughes, 'The Offices', pp. 363–72.

near Gloucester; the priory had property at Duleek, while the combination of saints in the Lansdowne manuscript points strongly to somewhere near Gloucester. Evidently the local patron of the priory's Irish estates was remembered in the liturgy of the mother house. More interesting, however, is the fact that the same lessons are known also from Brussels, Bibliothèque royale, MS 8953–8954, ff. 299[v]–300[r].[20] This is a volume of the Bollandist *collectanea*, containing Lives intended for publication under 23 and 24 November—dates still not reached, 350 years after the material was assembled. The text is headed, perhaps in Papebroch's hand, 'Ex MS. P. Fitzimon'.

13.3. *Texts Preserved by Henry FitzSimon*

We thus have two *uitae*, St Tigernach and St Cianán, known both as lections in offices and among the texts communicated to the Bollandists by FitzSimon. There are more of the latter category in the Bollandist *collectanea*. Grosjean, in 1942, published *Vita S. Secundini* from Brussels, Bibliothèque royale, MS 8957–8958 (Lives for 27–8 November), ff. 25[r]–27[v], 'Ex MS. P. Fitzimon'.[21] In 1959, he published *Vita S. Commani* from MS 8972–8973 (Lives for 12–13 December), ff. 6–7, 'Ex MS. P. Fitzimon',[22] and while correcting the proofs of that[23] he discovered by chance a Life of St Ibar in MS 7773 (texts residual from the volumes for April), ff. 550[r]–551[v].[24] This text was copied by the same assistant as the Life of St Commán; it was marked '23 Apr.' by Bolland, and 'Ex MS. P. Fitzimon' by Papebroch, who added, 'Vide cetera in manuscripto Fitzimon'. Unfortunately this direction to what was presumably the master-copy of the FitzSimon texts cannot be followed up. One should not complain that Bolland and Papebroch were disorderly in their filing of material according to the calendar, but the stage preceding these copies is generally obscure, while reordering, rebinding, and loss make it impossible to reconstruct what was available in the seventeenth century. As a

---

[20] Ibid., p. 351.

[21] 'Une Vie de S. Secundinus, disciple de S. Patrice', *AB* 60 (1942), 26.

[22] 'Notes sur quelques sources des Antiquitates de Jacques Ussher', *AB* 77 (1959), 183–5.

[23] Ibid., p. 169 n. 2.

[24] 'Deux textes inédits sur S. Ibar', *AB* 77 (1959), 439–41.

consequence, Grosjean was unable to pursue more systematically what remained of FitzSimon's material. The possibility still exists that further discoveries will be made from this source.

Bollandist editors over the years have repeatedly acknowledged their debt to FitzSimon. In the first volume of January, Bolland remarked on FitzSimon's experience of Irish hagiographical material and his general advice.[25] In the next volume, the Life of St Fechin was edited from **O** (supplied by Ward) and a manuscript communicated by FitzSimon, which lacked **O** §§ 7–9 (missing also from the Irish text) and paraphrased § 13.[26] To what extent it differed in other detail is not apparent. In 1675, the Lives of St Tigernach and St Lasrén of Leighlin were published. The former came, as we have seen, from **S**, **O**, and FitzSimon's text. The latter they had from **S** and from FitzSimon's text; the two present the same Life with some differences in wording, FitzSimon's text adding a little to the other. In 1680, the Life of St Comgall was published, again from **S**, collated with the **O**-text supplied by Ward, and with FitzSimon's manuscript, which here, according to Plummer, was closer to **S** than to **O**. Since the differences between these two are slight enough, it would seem that, as with St Tigernach's Life, FitzSimon's text closely resembled Θ.

The later Bollandists seem to have treated FitzSimon's texts, where they had them, with more circumspection. Already, when working on April, Henskens and Papebroch had rejected those for St Commán and St Ibar. In the third volume of June, the Life of St Moling was printed from **S**, but extracts were also given from a text supplied by FitzSimon. To Plummer, these represented a very inaccurate **D**-text. At 4 August, the editors of the *Acta* rightly chose to print the **S**[1]-text of *Vita S. Lugidi*, mentioning also the shorter **S**[2]-text and Fleming's edition of the **D**-text; they also had a copy 'in MS. non admodum antiquo' from FitzSimon, but no information is available about its text.

There is not really enough information here for us to form a clear sense of FitzSimon's source or sources. The Lives now known only from the Bollandist papers—SS. Commán, Ibar, and Secundinus—are all brief, lectionary-style Lives. The same is true

---

[25] 'De Sancto Mochua alias Cuano', *Acta Sanctorum*, Jan. I (1643), p. 45, quoted in part by Plummer, *Vitae*, vol. i, p. xciii n. 7.

[26] *Acta Sanctorum*, Jan. II, 329; Plummer, *Vitae*, vol. i, p. lxv.

of St Cianán; and of SS. Comgall, Tigernach, and Lasrén, where texts in S or Θ are very close to those of FitzSimon. One might suppose that he had a volume similar to Θ in its intention, and to some extent in its contents. Indeed, it may only be the text of his Life of St Moling that is against this, for the Life of St Fechin, with its liturgical verses, is of such character as to fit in this context, while the unknown Life of St Molua may have been close to the Θ-text.

We have not yet exhausted this matter. Grosjean has shown that Ussher knew a number of the very same texts which FitzSimon supplied to the Bollandists.[27] He quoted, for example, from the Life of St Lasrén of Leighlin, though he did not know the S-collection; indeed, already in 1627, he must have had a copy of this Life, which was recopied in his library by Dr Thomas Arthur.[28] He cited the Life of St Commán in the addenda to the first edition of the *Antiquitates*. The Lives of St Ibar and St Secundinus are referred to only in the addenda to the second edition, suggesting that he learnt of them at a still later stage. The Life of St Cianán, also cited here, appears to differ slightly from that known from the Bollandist files and the saint's office. Grosjean, observing that the passage is a paraphrase, 'une adaptation humaniste', conjectured that Ussher 'met à profit une notice biographique communiquée par quelque correspondant', and guesses at FitzSimon.[29] To my mind, Ussher was capable of paraphrase himself.

Although there is no direct evidence on this point, Grosjean repeatedly infers that these and other texts reached Ussher's hands from his kinsman FitzSimon. While this may be so, he does not produce any evidence to support the view, and the conjectures on which it rests are often mere wishful thinking.[30] It is perhaps unfortunate that Grosjean was concerned to discover sources used by Ussher, and therefore did not attempt to present a coherent account of the material associated with FitzSimon, some of which was also known to Ussher. As far as the Life of St Lasrén is concerned, this was known to Ussher before FitzSimon returned to Ireland in 1630. But most evidently came to Ussher's attention during or after the printing of the *Antiquitates*.

[27] 'Notes sur quelques sources', pp. 160–1, 166–72.
[28] Maynooth, St Patrick's College, MS 3 G 1.
[29] Grosjean, 'Notes sur quelques sources', p. 171.
[30] Ibid., pp. 160, 168, 170.

There is one other item, unknown to Grosjean, which is in line with his conjectures. Ussher's addenda to the second edition of the *Antiquitates* include a reference to a Life of St Brendan of Birr, of which Grosjean could find no trace in Latin or Irish. Instead, he compared an Irish anecdote in the Book of Leinster, which presents a different version of the same episode.[31] He suggested that this was communicated by FitzSimon in a Latin translation, again characterized as 'humaniste'.[32] The citation hardly admits such speculation on the basis of its style, but FitzSimon's own 'Auctuarium' to his *Catalogus* includes mention of a Life of St Brendan of Birr.[33] This text, not traced, should join the list of those known to both Ussher and FitzSimon. It does not, however, add weight to Grosjean's theory that FitzSimon was supplying information to Ussher. That depends principally on the fact that Ussher did not know these texts until 1639 or later.

What matters more is that Ussher and FitzSimon both had access to a source or sources, now lost to us, which contained brief Lives or more likely lections, suitable for liturgical use, relating to minor saints for whom no other hagiographical material remains. What we can read of such texts, in the Bollandist *collectanea* and elsewhere, suggests that they were the product of a revival of interest in native saints, which appears to date from the late thirteenth or early fourteenth century. The Life of St Tigernach is now known from a liturgical context, as lections in the Waterford manuscript; in our hypothetical collection of abbreviated Lives, Θ, where some liturgical verses were appended; and from references to FitzSimon's text in the *Acta Sanctorum*. There are no differences of recension. The Life of St Lasrén of Leighlin is known from S, from the text FitzSimon supplied to the Bollandists, and from Arthur's paraphrase of a copy in Ussher's library. From these two cases we may infer that no great gulf separated the hagiographical interest and the liturgical interest. While it would be an over-simplification to suppose that Θ, O, and S all arose from exactly the same interest as lections in known offices, the likelihood is that one primary motivation—the renewal of interest in the cult of

---

[31] P. Grosjean, 'Hagiographica Celtica', *AB* 55 (1937) 96–108.

[32] 'Notes sur quelques sources', pp. 166–7.

[33] R. Sharpe, 'The Origin and Elaboration of the *Catalogus praecipuorum Sanctorum Hiberniae* Attributed to Henry FitzSimon SJ', *Bodleian Library Record*, 13/3 (1989), p. 221, s.n. 'Locranus princeps in V. S. Brandani Bir:'.

native saints—led to the collection of their Lives in an 'improved'
form such as we see in Θ and O and to the preparation of
lectionary Lives. The fact that some texts are found in the same
form in both the hagiographical and the liturgical context may
indicate that these were recently drafted to suit both needs at once.
Need is not an inappropriate word. At times the need seems to
have been quite desperate, as in the remarkable case of the Life of
St Maculinus or Mac Cuilind of Lusk. This text is known from two
sources. A transcript which once belonged to Ussher is now
Dublin, Trinity College, MS 580 (E. 3. 8), ff. 128–130.[34] A copy
supplied by FitzSimon to the Bollandists was recopied in what is
now Brussels, Bibliothèque des Bollandistes, MS 150, ff. 6–8.[35]
The text takes the form of nine lessons and has been described by
Plummer as 'an impudent forgery'.[36] It is, in fact, closely based on
a Life of St Finnbarr of Cork with the names of the saint and his
church changed. In many passages it very nearly resembles the
lections for St Finnbarr copied in 1624 from a breviary at Cork.[37]
The resemblance was sufficient for Bolland himself to regard
Maculinus as another name for St Finnbarr.[38]

If the clergy of Lusk had felt a desire to know more about the
original founder of their church, they would surely have been
more diligent in researching, or more ingenious in devising,
something to say about him. This cavalier forgery springs from no
particular interest in the patron of Lusk but from the need to fill a
gap. The explanation, I suggest, lies in the insistence on the
commemoration of particular native saints set out in some Irish
episcopal constitutions.

---

[34] Grosjean, 'Les Vies de S. Finnbarr', pp. 343–7.

[35] *Acta Sanctorum*, Sept. VII (1760), p. 144; Plummer, 'A Tentative Catalogue',
p. 249.

[36] Ibid., p. 249.

[37] The latter survive in Brussels, Bibliothèque des Bollandistes, MS 150, f. 120.
The two texts are both printed by Grosjean, 'Les Vies de S. Finnbarr', pp. 333–6
(St Finnbarr from Cork breviary) and pp. 338–43 (St Maculinus).

[38] On the letter from Bernard Mede, dated 19 Apr. 1624, which accompanies
the transcript of the Cork lections for St Finnbarr in the *collectanea*, Bolland has
written, 'Eadem 'S. Barri' Vita habetur in MS. P. Fitzimon sed sub nomine
Maculini Episcopi pag. 19'; Grosjean, 'Les Vies de S. Finnbarr', p. 327 n.

13.4. *Calendars and Constitutions*

The principle that episcopal constitutions or statutes should include some prescriptions for the liturgical observances of a diocese was well known and accepted in medieval England: a thirteenth-century set of constitutions of Worcester is particularly full on the subject.[39] The principle allowed an individual bishop or archbishop to impose his private devotional enthusiasms on his diocese. In Ireland, however, hardly any bishops' registers survive from the Middle Ages, and very few diocesan or provincial constitutions are preserved. It is necessary, therefore, to extrapolate from fragmentary evidence.

The earliest statute of this kind from Ireland occurs at the end of the constitutions promulgated by the provincial council held by Alexander de Bicknor, archbishop of Dublin, about 1320. This provides a full statement of the intention:[40]

In medio pectoris nostri beati Patricii Hibernie apostoli et patroni memoriam reuoluimus qui diuina disponente clemencia populum Hibernicanum ad fidem conuertit, nonnulla eciam monasteria et ecclesias suis construxit temporibus et multimodis choruscauit miraculis; cuius doctrina uita et sanctitate Hibernicana fulget ecclesia aliisque multis insigniis decoratur et priuilegiis. Ipse nos fouet, ipsiusque meritis et intercessionibus assiduis indies iuuamur et refocillamur, et digne ad sui honoris gloriam et laudem quilibet catholicus oculos sui cordis et mentis conuertere astringitur. Idcirco dignum prorsus arbitramur ut fidelis populus prona uoluntate tam excelsi, tam gloriosi patroni nostri memoriam cordialius rememoret ad diuinam misericordiam pro peccatis impetrandam. Sacri presentis approbacione concilii ordinamus et statuimus quod qualibet hebdomada extra quadragesimam solempnis fiat commemoracio sanctissimi Patricii patroni nostri per totam prouinciam Dublin' in aliqua feria uacante cum regimine cleri; et quod dies exitus sui ab hoc ergastulo sanctissimus sub duplici festo perpetuis temporibus celebretur.

Further, the same statute provides for the celebration of the feasts of the patron saints of the other dioceses within the province of

---

[39] F. M. Powicke and C. R. Cheney, *Councils and Synods with Other Documents Relating to the English Church*, ii: AD *1205–1313* (2 parts; Oxford, 1964), pp. 321–5. This statute is datable to 1220 × 1266.

[40] A. Gwynn (ed.), 'Provincial and Diocesan Decrees of the Diocese of Dublin During the Anglo-Norman Period', *Archivium Hibernicum* 11 (1944), 82–3; cf. id., *Anglo-Irish Church Life: Fourteenth and Fifteenth Centuries* (Dublin, 1968), p. 43.

Dublin: St Brigit of Kildare, St Cainnech or Canice of Ossory, St Lasrén or Laserian of Leighlin, St Maedóc or Aidan of Ferns, all were to have double feasts throughout the province, as were Archbishop Lawrence O'Toole and the Translation of St Patrick. The statute ends:

Item ordinamus quod ubi est seruicium proprium dictorum patronorum copia per diocesim ad quamlibet ecclesiam cathedralem mittatur, ut dyocesani possint facere de illis distribucionem inter illas ecclesias prout decet.

The intention is to commemorate the native saints regarded as of importance in the province at this date, around 1320, without reference to their significance at an earlier date. Even St Coemgen or Kevin is omitted, though the former see of Glendalough was incorporated into that of Dublin. It is particularly notable that steps were taken to insure the availability of copies of these saints' offices, though the statute does say 'ubi est servicium proprium'; presumably where none was available, steps would be taken to create one.

Later constitutions do not alter this list significantly. In 1352 St Catherine was added by Archbishop John of St Paul, and in 1367, this was amended by Archbishop Thomas Minot, who reduced the status of St Anne, St Catherine, and the Translation of St Thomas the Martyr, but increased that of St Mary Magdalene.[41]

Turning from these prescriptive statements to the liturgical books of the province, we find the importance of episcopal constitutions borne out by *Kalendaria*. For example, in the fifteenth-century antiphonary from St John the Evangelist, Dublin, now Trinity College, MS 79 (B. 1. 4), the calendar originally included St Patrick and St Brigit, the Translation of SS. Patrick, Columba, and Brigit, and the patrons of other suffragan dioceses, St Laserian and St Aidan. St Coemgen or Kevin has displaced St Cainnech, but in other respects the constitutions of Archbishop Bicknor are observed.[42] Around 1500, this calendar was extended with the addition of more than twenty further Irish saints and some foreign patrons of Dublin churches such as St Audoen. In another manuscript, a portable breviary,

---

[41] Gwynn, 'Provincial and Diocesan Decrees', pp. 85, 103–5.

[42] Hawkes, 'The Liturgy', p. 45. The manuscript in question once belonged to Ussher.

now Dublin, Trinity College, MS 88 (B. 3. 13) (s. xvⁱⁿ), the patrons of the suffragan sees are fully represented, and in three cases, the entries and offices are said to be 'per constitutiones Dublin.'; these are St Laserian, St Lawrence O'Toole, and the Translation of SS. Patrick, Brigit, and Columba. A few other Irish saints with Dublin connexions are included.[43] The names in the calendar of another Dublin breviary, now Cambridge, Emmanuel College, MS I 3. 11 (s. xv), are similar.[44] The two manuscripts last mentioned include St Maculinus in their calendars at 6 September: commemoration demanded an office, and this surely was the motive for the transference of lections from St Finnbarr to him. He is also included in the larger number of Irish saints included in the calendar of a Dublin antiphonary, Trinity College, MS 78 (B. 1. 3) (s. xv^{ex}); here many of the saints named are marked 'per constitutiones'.[45]

Here, I suggest, is the essential background to the revision of Latin saints' Lives in the late thirteenth century and onwards. The patchy survival of episcopal statutes and of liturgical books from medieval Ireland prevents systematic examination of the connexion between Lives and liturgy. There is, however, ample evidence in these few cases to demonstrate the connexion, which is corroborated by the Lives themselves, in the liturgical nature of the revisions in some *uitae*, particularly references to the feast-day, and by the overlap in the transmission of Lives and liturgical lections.

The renewal of interest in native saints would appear, on this evidence, to have been somewhat artificial. Some of the Lives which found their way into both **O** and **S** smack of the same half-hearted revival—the short **SO**-Life of St Molua is an obvious case in point. The compiler of **O**, however, was prepared to put some work into preparing what he regarded as suitably modified texts of some older and longer Lives. Moreover, the compiler of **S**, without making any effort to revise his texts, was evidently willing to seek out *uitae* of any description, and even to transcribe Lives of positively antique, 'primitive' taste. It seems unlikely that either compiler could have felt the commitment to his task which shows throughout the work of the **D**-redactor. Both, after all, were heirs

---

[43] Ibid., pp. 49–51.   [44] Ibid., p. 53.   [45] Ibid., pp. 48–9.

to the generalizing taste of the late thirteenth century, and were also accustomed to the perfunctory commemoration of some of these Irish saints. If all the Lives in both collections were like the Θ-texts, these compilations would be dull indeed. Fortunately, both managed to do rather better in some of their work: both deserved credit, in particular, for their use of Φ.

14

Conclusions and Continuations

IN Chapter 1, I set out a brief outline of the history of hagiographical writing in Ireland. Now we may consider what changes
can be made to that outline in the light of our textual study of the
three collections.

First, and most importantly, the O'Donohue group of Lives
must be added to the list of Latin texts from what I called Phase I,
the period roughly between 650 and 850. These texts each have
their own individual features, but in form they more nearly
resemble *Vita I S. Brigitae* than any other definitely early *uita*. The
conjectured manuscript Φ, which transmitted these Lives for
some five centuries, appears to have been assembled as a
collection of the Lives of native saints in the ninth century. The
occurrence of a tiny proportion of Middle Irish forms does not
demand a date for the manuscript significantly later than 800 or
850, so that we may assume that the collection as well as the
composition belongs to Phase I. This is an early date for the
collecting together of saints' Lives into a legendary,[1] and an exceptionally early date for the compilation of a legendary devoted—if it
was so devoted—to the Lives of national saints. One cannot now
know whether the native saints were only a few among a host of
universal saints in Φ, disregarded by all three of the late medieval
compilers; but it seems rather unlikely. The fact that nine Lives
are represented in all three collections, and that the one possible
tenth—St Columba of Terryglass—is lacking only from **D**, suggest
that our compilers used everything from Φ that was to their purpose: in the case of **S** in consecutive order. One may wonder as to
the nature of this early collection, which seems to have excluded
the most famous names—SS. Patrick, Brigit, and Columba—and
to have no unifying theme except that its contents were all of native
origin.

[1] G. Philippart, *Les Légendiers latins et autres manuscrits hagiographiques*,
Typologie des sources du moyen âge occidental 24–5 (Turnhout, 1977), p. 30.

We have found nothing in the collections which can be dated to the three hundred years or so after the date of Φ. The hiatus in the extant Latin literature of Ireland between the mid-ninth and the eleventh century is thus unchanged. The possibility, however, still exists that future research on individual Lives transmitted in **D** may suggest that some of the *uitae* used as base-texts by that redactor may have been composed in this period. What we know of the methods of the compiler shows that, at the date when he worked, there must have been more than twice as many Lives available to him from before *c.* 1230 as now survive in their original form. The range of possible dates, however, is such that I think it more likely that a fair proportion of those models were composed in the twelfth century than at an earlier date. Some, such as the Life of St Mochutu, show signs of an eighth-century origin. Not one, so far as the present state of research permits one to say, originated in the period when I have suggested that Latin was little used in Ireland for original writing.

The compilation of the **D**-collection itself, whether or not it was inspired by Albinus O'Mulloy, was the crowning achievement of hagiography in Ireland. The redactor has brought together some twenty-five Lives (besides a few outliers), effectively knitting them into a single statement that Ireland was justly to be regarded as *insula sanctorum*. It is no wonder that Ward and Colgan so admired his work, which may have been originally intended to declare the virtues of Ireland's saintly past to its critics among the Anglo-French, English and Flemings, who arrived in Ireland in the decades before and after 1200. The Latin hagiography produced in the English lordship or under Anglo-French influence in the later thirteenth century and after is pale and insignificant in comparison with this last great work of native Latin learning.

After 1230, there is little of intrinsic interest in the Latin *uitae*. Both of the later compilers achieved nothing to compare with the work of **D**. Such interest as these collections have is mostly incidental—the preservation of some early texts in **S**, some utility as a control for the other collections, the textual help to be derived by comparing **S**- and **O**-texts, their witness to the liturgical commemoration of Irish saints. Sense, however, could not have been made of the collections as a whole just by focusing attention on the interesting work of **D**, or the obviously circumstantial Lives at the centre of **S**. The flaw which undermined previous studies of these Lives was the failure to take account of the interdependence of the collections and to treat them as a whole. It has been a long labour to do this, but inevitably so. Without this framework, no advance could be made on a secure foundation.

Such conclusions as have proved possible could not have been reached if there had not been a substantial degree of inter-dependence between the three collections. In the case of some *uitae* I have been able to relate all the extent texts to one another stemmatically. This may yet be possible for others where I have not attempted it, but in not a few cases it has been impractical to establish textual relationships. The processes of transmission involving individual *uitae* and intermediate collections are complex, often differing from saint to saint: it is inevitable that in many cases our study of the textual relationships must remain open-ended. The degree of overlap between the three extant collections is more likely to be a matter of undeserved good fortune than an indication that the pool of texts available in the thirteenth and fourteenth centuries was not much more extensive than what survives. What we know of the Lives preserved in the *Magnum Legendarium Austriacum*, or by FitzSimon and Ussher shows that there was a considerable volume of Latin hagiography that has not survived. The number of texts to be conjectured in understanding textual relationships for certain *uitae* further adds to their volume. This must have a cautionary influence on any inferences which we make about hagiographical interests in Ireland in the later Middle Ages.

This problem is compounded when the large quantity of Lives written in Irish is taken into account. A few of these, such as the Lives of St Declán and St Mochoemóc, are closely dependent on Latin texts which survive. In most cases, however, the relationship between Irish and Latin Lives is more remote than can be approached textually in the way I have discussed Latin Lives. The *bethada* may be divided broadly into three groups: those written in the tenth and eleventh centuries; those written or redacted later in the medieval period but still surviving in manuscript collections of the fifteenth century; and those known only from late transcripts. The study of this material has been much neglected and must come high on a list of priorities for future work on the Irish saints. Lives, however, are no more than a part of the voluminous saint-lore of Ireland, and there remains much to be done on the genealogies of the saints, the other listing texts in the Book of Leinster, and on the anecdotes scattered through Irish manuscript collections. These are likely to add considerably to our understanding of the literary context of hagiographical writing; they are certain to deepen our appreciation for the developing role of saints in the Irish churches' perception of themselves and their history.

The historical study of individual texts has advanced in recent years but it is still in large measure dominated by the handful of *uitae* from the seventh century. The Lives of St Patrick and St Columba have provided the materials for an approach to the history of the early church in which Armagh and Iona may be perceived as playing a disproportionate role. Study of the Lives of St Brigit has not sufficiently modified that historical perspective. It is to be hoped that the new availability of other Lives of early date will allow historians to write into the picture the interests of other churches. By the end of the eighth century a good many centres had developed cults of their own local saints. The evidence for cult takes many forms—a very large number of native saints were commemorated in the Martyrology of Tallaght around the year 800, and the practices of cults are to some extent illustrated by archaeological evidence. All of this evidence, however, provides too little information about particular saints or particular churches to write their histories in such a way as to give a truer perspective on the role of churches such as Armagh and Iona. The O'Donohue group of lives has now increased the number of *uitae* threefold from the pre-Viking period, and it may be hoped that some of these will contribute to that change in perspective. The nature of the hagiographical narrative does not readily lend itself to the rewriting of history, but the techniques of studying individual Lives have been developing and one may for the moment take an optimistic view. It is certainly the case that these Lives, like the anonymous *Vita I S. Brigitae*, have much to add to our perception of early Irish society. The social and economic history of early medieval Ireland is an area in which we may look forward to major advances as the legal texts are increasingly opened up.[2] The Lives of saints provide the best narrative accounts we have to complement this prescriptive material.

---

[2] An excellent introduction is now available in F. Kelly's *A Guide to Early Irish Law* (Dublin, 1989).

Plummer, in his introduction to *Vitae Sanctorum Hiberniae*, tried to index this material: this aspect of his book remains useful provided that one recognizes the limitations of the texts so treated.[3] His approach to the Lives also included a good deal of rather primitive study of what he called 'heathen folk-lore and mythology'[4] as well as the collection of a wide range of parallel stories from the vernacular tales of early medieval Ireland. The study of saints' Lives both as folk-lore and as stories has advanced beyond recognition since Plummer's time. In 1910 he was criticized for naïve speculations on the divine attributes of saints. That criticism may have been in some measure motivated by a desire to perceive the saints of the *uitae* in the light of an attitude to holiness and the holy life which would have been quite alien to their authors. Plummer was seen as trying to make pagan gods out of minor heroes of modern Christianity. His methods were misguided, but his recognition that the *uitae* illuminate aspects of how the authors of the *uitae* and their audience perceived the spiritual aspects of their world has still to be followed up.

It is not my intention in these closing paragraphs to expatiate on how much the surviving hagiography of Ireland still awaits the application of modern methods of hagiographical study, although that is so. The volume of the material is large enough, and the labourers so few, that it will probably be more than a generation before it has been reduced to order. The next steps, however, in the continuing study should include, first, more detailed textual studies of the Lives with which this book has been concerned and similar studies of the corpus of vernacular Lives. Second, it is essential that we should have a new inventory to supersede Plummer's 'Tentative Catalogue' and Kenney's chapters—an inventory which attempts to set out the relationship between the recensions of individual *uitae* and considers the historical evidence for dating the earliest recoverable stage. The possibilities for studying the information in individual texts are wide, and there is a need for further comparisons at many levels. There is room for a much more thorough study of the redactor of **D** than I have achieved here. An exhaustive study of the changes in an individual Life from one recension to another would deepen our understand-

---

[3] Plummer, *Vitae*, vol. i, pp. xcv–cxxix.
[4] Ibid., pp. cxxix–clxxxviii.

ing of matters I have been able only to sketch—the Lives of St Munnu, St Molua, and St Maedóc seem particularly promising for this approach. Some individual Lives, especially of the early period, present a great diversity of valuable information and demand a study drawing in detailed evidence from elsewhere: in the new edition which I propose of the O'Donohue Lives, it will be my intention to provide a wide-ranging commentary on the texts. As and when all this is accomplished, it may be possible to embark on a synthesis, unravelling what Irish hagiography means for Irish hagiology: for some fifteen hundred years the native saints, living and dead, have exercised a profound influence on the *mentalités* of Ireland, *insula sanctorum*. This book is a belated introduction to the major collections of their Lives.

Bibliography

VITAE

In this listing I have not referred to older editions in Colgan's *Acta* or the work of the Bollandists unless there is no more modern printed text. References to these older works may be had from Plummer's 'A Tentative Catalogue of Irish Hagiography', in his *Miscellanea Hagiographica Hibernica* (Brussels, 1925), pp. 234–54. I have not given references to *Bibliotheca Hagiographica Latina* for the Lives in the collections because its information on these is too slight to be of value.

ABBÁN (Abbanus) [16 March, 27 October]. The fullest surviving Life is that in **D**, Plummer, *Vitae*, i. 3–33. The Life in **S** is derived from this; printed by Heist, pp. 256–74. The Irish Life in Plummer, *Bethada*, i. 3–10, is not directly related to either.

AED MAC BRICC (Aidus, Edus) [10 November]. The Life in **S** is a Φ-text; Heist, pp. 167–81. Plummer, *Vitae*, i. 34–45, prints the derivative **D**-text. Both of these were also edited with notes by Grosjean, *Acta Sanctorum*, Nov. IV (1925), 504–17 and 525–31. The **O**-text, also derived from the Φ-text, was edited by Grosjean, ibid. pp. 517–24. There is no Irish Life.

AILBE (Albeus, Elueus) [12 September]. The Life in **S** is a Φ-text; Heist, pp. 118–31. Plummer, *Vitae*, i. 46–64, prints the derivative **D**-text; the **O**-text, also derived from Φ, is unprinted. The only Irish Life, according to Plummer, is an abbreviated translation of the **D**-text; printed in *Irish Rosary*, 16 (1912).

ATTRACTA [11 August]. Known only from a seventeenth-century transcript in the Franciscan collections, whence printed by Colgan, *Acta*, pp. 278–81.

BAITHÉNE (Baithinus) [9 June]. Short Life from Θ, printed from **S** by Heist, pp. 379–82; the text in **O** is uncollated.

BERACH (Berachus) [15 February]. Unique to **O**, whence printed by Plummer, *Vitae*, i. 75–86.

BLATHMAC (Blaithmacus) [24 July, 19 January]. Walahfrid Strabo's poem (*BHL* 1368) on his martyrdom in 825 has been printed many times; there is no evidence that it was known in medieval Ireland.

BRENDAN (Brendanus) [16 May]. The late eighth-century *Nauigatio S. Brendani* is most readily accessible in the edition by C. Selmer (Notre Dame, Ind., 1959; repr. Dublin, 1989). It is incorporated into a *uita* of uncertain origin in **D**; P. F. Moran, *Acta Sancti Brendani* (Dublin, 1872), prints the *uita* but merely reports the readings of the **D**-text of *Nauigatio* in his textual notes. The whole text is printed by Grosjean, *AB* 48 (1930), 99–123. A different recension also merging *uita* and *Nauigatio* is preserved in **S**, printed by Heist, pp. 56–78. This text formed the basis of a more elaborate conflation in **O**, printed by Plummer, *Vitae*, i. 98–151. There is also in **S**, Heist, pp. 324–31, a late abbreviation of the *uita* which does not include text introduced from the *Nauigatio*. Plummer, *Vitae*, ii. 262–92, also printed a quite different recension, a Latinization of the Anglo-French poem by Benedeit, ed. I. Short and B. Merrilees (Manchester, 1979), which was itself based on the *Nauigatio*.

BRIGIT (Brigita, Brigida) [1 February]. *Vita I S. Brigitae* is best edited by Colgan, *Trias*, pp. 527–42; Cogitosus's *Vita II* by Colgan, *Trias*, pp. 518–24 or by Bolland, *Acta Sanctorum*, Feb. I (1658), 135–41. The relationship between these two and the Old Irish *Bethu Brigte*, ed. D. Ó hAodha (Dublin, 1978), is the subject of debate. *Vita III (metrica)* was edited by D. N. Kissane, *PRIA* 77 C (1977), 57–192, but the related prose Life attributed to Donatus of Fiesole has never been printed. *Vita IV*, edited in this volume, pp. 139–208, is a revision of *Vita I* by the compiler of **D**. Of the other Irish collections **O** contains an abbreviated text of *Vita I*, **S** the completely recast Life by Lawrence of Durham, Heist, pp. 1–33 (with defects; see above, p. 33).

BUITE (Boecius) [7 December]. There is one Life only of St Buite of Monasterboice, printed from **O** by Plummer, *Vitae*, i. 87–97.

CAINNECH (Kannechus, Cainnicus) [11 October]. The life in **S** is a Φ-text, Heist, pp. 182–98; passages based on Adomnán's *Vita S. Columbae* provide a *terminus a quo* for its date. Plummer, *Vitae*, i. 152–69, prints the derivative **D**-text; the **O**-text, also derived from Φ, has never been printed. There is no Irish Life.

CARTHACH. See Mochutu.

CIARÁN OF CLONMACNOISE (Kyaranus, Queranus) [9 September]. No primary text survives, but three Latin and one Irish recension bear some witness to a lost original. The fullest is that in **D**, Plummer, *Vitae*, i. 200–16, though its fulness may have as much to do with the redactor as the source. The text in **O** was printed by Macalister, *Lives of St Ciarán*, pp. 172–83, and the very abbreviated text in **S** by Heist, pp. 78–81. The Irish Life was printed from the Book of Lismore by Stokes, *Lismore Lives*, pp. 117–34. All the versions are discussed by Macalister, but his conclusions are not well founded.

CIARÁN OF SAIGIR (Keranus, Piranus) [5 March]. The Life in **D** bears many marks of the compiler's interests; printed by Plummer, *Vitae*, i. 217–33. This was the source of the Θ-text, printed from **S** by Heist, pp. 246–53; the text in **O** has not been collated. Of the two Irish Lives printed by Plummer, *Bethada*, i. 103–12 and 113–24, the latter may bear witness to the source used by **D** but the former is an abbreviated translation of the **D**-text. See above, pp. 294–5.

COEMGEN (Coemgenus, Caymginius) [3 June]. The earliest Latin witness is the unprinted fragment (*BHL* 1868) in MS Rein, Stiftsbibliothek 51, ff. 28ᵛ–31ʳ (s. xii) and in MSS of the Austrian Great Legendary. It is related in an indeterminate way—perhaps both based on the same text—to the *uita* in **D**, Plummer, *Vitae*, i. 234–57. The text in **S** and **O** is from Θ, printed from **S** by Heist, pp. 361–5. Grosjean discovered an abbreviated text in the Bollandist *collectanea*, printed and discussed by him, *AB* 70 (1952), 313–15; see also *AB* 63 (1945), 122–9.

COLMÁN OF DROMORE (Colmanus) [7 June]. A short and late Θ-text, printed by Heist, pp. 357–60; the copy in **O** is uncollated.

COLMÁN ÉLO (Colmanus) [26 September]. A text from Φ survives in **S**, Heist, pp. 209–24. The derivative **D**-text is printed by Plummer, *Vitae*, i. 258–73; the **O**-text, also derived from Φ, is unprinted.

COLUM CILLE (Columba) [9 June]. Only a fragment survives from the *Liber de uirtutibus S. Columbae* by Cumméne, abbot of Iona; this text is one of the sources lying behind Adomnán's *Vita S. Columbae*, ed. A. O. and M. O. Anderson (London and Edinburgh, 1961), from which the extant Latin tradition descends. There are two ninth-century abridgements of Adomnán's work, the so-called Ps.-Cumméne, ed. G. Brüning, *Zeitschrift für celtische Philologie*, 11 (1916–17), 291–304, and the 'shorter recension' of Adomnán, ed. H. Canisius, *Antiquae Lectiones* (Ingolstadt, 1601–4), vol. v.2, pp. 559–621. The text in **D** is a slightly revised form of the latter; it has never been printed separately. This **D**-text was the only form of Adomnán's *uita* known to Manus O'Donnell who in 1532 commissioned a major complete Life in Irish. The other principal source used here was a homiletic Life in Middle Irish, written at Derry about 1160, ed. M. Herbert, *Iona, Kells, and Derry* (Oxford, 1988), pp. 211–88. In **S** there is a *uita* based on Adomnán's work, Heist, pp. 366–70, followed immediately, pp. 370–8, by a series of miracle-stories closely based on Adomnán. The text was probably taken from Θ, since the same material was used by the compiler of **O**, who inserted the latter series into the former; the text in **O** has not been collated.

COLUMBA OF TERRYGLASS (Columba) [13 December]. The text in **S** agrees very closely with that in **O**: text-historically therefore it could be regarded as a Θ-text. In its spelling of names and its general tenor it more nearly resembles the Φ-texts, but there is no derived version in **D**. The text is printed by Heist, pp. 225–33. At §§12–13 there is a passage closely related to §3 of the Φ-text Life of St Fintán of Clonenagh. See also Grosjean, *AB* 72 (1954), 343–7.

COLUMBANUS [23 November]. Jonas's Life of St Columbanus of Bobbio (*BHL* 1898) lies outside the range of this study.

COMGALL (Comogellus, Comgallus) [10 May]. The earliest reference to a Life is found in Jocelin's *Vita S. Patricii*, but the earliest and fullest version now surviving is a **D**-text, Plummer, *Vitae*, ii. 3–21. The other collections have a Θ-text, printed from **S** by Heist, pp. 332–4, complemented from **O** by Grosjean, *AB* 52 (1934), 343–56.

COMMÁN (Commanus) [26 December]. A short text was communicated by FitzSimon to the Bollandists; it was discovered and published by Grosjean, *AB* 77 (1959), 183–5.

CRÓNÁN (Cronanus) [28 April]. The earliest text known is that in **D**, Plummer, *Vitae*, ii. 22–31. In **S** there is a text apparently abbreviated from this, Heist, pp. 274–9.

CUANNA (Cuannatheus) [4 February]. Fragments only survive in **S** from a Latin Life, apparently translated from Irish for the compilers; Heist, pp. xxi–xxii, 407–10. See above, pp. 236–8. No Irish text remains.

DAIG (Daigeus) [18 August]. A very much abbreviated *uita* survives only in **S**, Heist, pp. 389–94.

DARERCA. See Moninne.

DECLÁN (Declanus) [24 July]. The *uita* is known only from **D**, a full and fascinating text, Plummer, *Vitae*, ii. 32–59. There is an early modern Irish translation of this text, ed. P. Power (London, 1914).

ÉNDA (Endeus) [21 March]. A Life is known only from **O**, Plummer, *Vitae*, ii. 60–75. The present text cannot date from earlier than the thirteenth century.

EOGAN (Eugenius) [23 August]. There is a short life in **S** only, Heist, pp. 400–4.

FECHIN (Fechinus) [20 January]. A late thirteenth-century text from an office for St Fechin was included in **O**, Plummer, *Vitae*, ii. 76–85. The Bollandists had a copy of this from FitzSimon.

FÍNÁN CAM (Finanus) [7 April]. There is a text from Φ in **S**, Heist, pp. 153–60. The derived text in **D** is printed by Plummer, *Vitae*, ii. 87–95; the text in **O**, also derived from Φ, is not printed.

FINNBARR (Barrus) [25 September]. There are two Latin and two Irish Lives, of which the Life in **D**, Plummer, *Vitae*, i. 217–33, is related to the Irish Life printed by Plummer, *Bethada*, i. 11–22. The Life in **O**, printed in parallel with the **D**-text by R. Caulfield (London, 1864), may be based on that in **D**. According to Plummer, there is a second Irish Life, unprinted, which he described as a later expansion of the former. Three short, homiletic Lives have been edited by Grosjean, *AB* 69 (1951), 324–43, and discussed by him, *Journal of the Cork Historical and Archaeological Society*, 58 (1953), 47–54. One of these had been borrowed and used for a different saint, Mac Cuilinn of Lusk.

FINNIAN (Finnianus) [12 December, 23 February]. The Life in **S**, Heist, pp. 96–107, is an abridgement of an older text, now lost. The Life in **O** is the compiler's revision of the **S**-text, suggesting that the latter may have belonged to Θ. The Irish Life edited by Stokes, *Lismore Lives*, pp. 75–83, is fuller than either of the Latin texts.

FINTÁN OF CLONENAGH (Fintanus) [17 February]. There is a text from Φ in S, Heist, pp. 145–53, which is in part closely related to the Life of St Columba of Terryglass (q.v.). The derived text in D is printed by Plummer, *Vitae*, ii. 96–106; the derived text in O is unprinted.

FINTÁN OF DÚN BLÉISCI (Fintanus) [3 January]. A short, homiletic Life in S is printed by Heist, pp. 113–17.

FINTÁN/MUNNU OF TAGHMON (Fintanus, Munnu) [21 October]. S preserves an original *uita* from Φ, printed by Heist, pp. 198–209. The text in D is derived from this in the usual way; printed by Plummer, *Vitae*, ii. 226–39. The shorter Life in S conforms to the style of *uitae* from Θ, but the Life in O in this case shows further editing by the compiler; the version printed by Heist, pp. 247–56, represents the text of Θ, at one remove from Φ; the unprinted text from O is based on this but stands at a further remove from the original. See above, pp. 334–7.

FLANNÁN (Flannanus) [18 December]. The original twelfth-century text is preserved in S, although imperfectly due to the loss of one leaf; printed by Heist, pp. 280–301. This Life was also known among the Lives of Irish saints circulating in southern Germany and Austria. The text in O is based on it and appears to be the compiler's own edition; printed by Grosjean, *AB* 46 (1928), 124–41. The fragment in D is related to the same original but is too brief to admit much analysis; printed by Grosjean, ibid., pp. 122–3. See above, pp. 268–9.

FURSU (Furseus) [16 January]. The primary Life, written in the third quarter of the seventh century, was edited from many manuscripts by Krusch, *MGH Scr. rerum Meroving.* iv. 423–49 (omitting the visions). Two of the Irish collections contain copies of a Life abbreviated from this which I have suggested belonged to Θ; the text is printed by Heist, pp. 37–55. The text in O is further revised, though to no great extent; it is unprinted. See above, pp. 287–8.

GERALD (Geraldus) [13 March]. The O-collection contains a Life apparently dating from the thirteemth century, printed by Plummer, *Vitae*, ii, 107–15. There are no other witnesses.

IBAR (Ybarus) [23 April]. FitzSimon supplied a brief lectionary Life of St Ibar to the Bollandists; printed by Grosjean, *AB* 77 (1959), 439–41. The same text was also known to Ussher.

ÍTE (Ita) [15 January]. The primary Life, written no later than the twelfth century, does not survive. The unpublished Life in the Austrian Great Legendary is a revision of this text; see *AB* 17 (1898), 50, 159. There are sufficient verbal parallels between this text and the *uita* in the D-collection to suppose that the latter was based on the same original; the D-text is printed by Plummer, *Vitae*, ii. 116–30. Each of the two derivatives has added to and changed the reading of the original in a number of identifiable places. There is a further abbreviated text in **O**, not printed, which appears to be based on the **D**-text. There is another abbreviated text in Horstman's *Nova Legenda Anglie*, ii. 543, and a very short abbreviation of the Bavarian text in Munich, MS cgm. 2928 f. 147^v.

LASRÉN/MOLAISSE OF DEVENISH (Lasrianus) [12 September]. The only known version of this Life is the text in **O**, printed by Plummer, *Vitae*, ii. 131–40.

LASRÉN OF LEIGHLIN (Lasrianus) [18 April]. The short Life in **S** is incomplete due to the loss of a leaf; printed by Heist, pp. 340–3. It is closely related to the Life supplied to the Bollandists by FitzSimon and printed by them in *Acta Sanctorum*, Apr. II (1675), 544–7. The text was probably composed for liturgical use in the late thirteenth century when 'Laserianus' was regarded as patron of one of the suffragan sees in the province of Dublin.

LORCÁN Ó TUATHAL (Laurentius Dublinensis) [14 November]. A *liber de miraculis* was written by Malachy, bishop of Louth, between 1181 and 1191; it is referred to in contemporary letters supporting his canonization (cited above, p. 28 n. 104) but it does not survive. The earliest surviving text, forming a booklet now Paris, Bibliothèque de l'Arsenal, MS 938 ff. 81^r–96^v (s. xiii), has been attributed by Dr Roche to Henry of London, archbishop of Dublin (1213–28). The completed *uita* was composed by a canon of Eu soon after 1226 and a copy of it was included in **D**; the text has been edited by C. Plummer, 'Vie et miracles de S. Laurent, archevêque de Dublin', *AB 33* (1914), 121–86. There is a single paragraph devoted to St Laurence's miracles in **S**, printed by Heist, *Vitae*, p. 280.

LUGUID/MOLUA (Lugidus, Molua) [4 August]. There is a Life from Φ in **S**, printed by Heist, pp. 131–45. The text derived from this in **D** is printed by Plummer, *Vitae*, ii. 206–25. A short Life in **S**, printed by Heist, pp. 382–8, is very closely related to the unprinted text in **O**; they probably reproduce the text of Θ, which appears to have been an abbreviation of the Life in **D**. See above, pp. 337–9.

MAC CAIRTHINN (Maccartinus) [15 August, 24 March]. A short Life survives (with some loss of text) in **S** only; printed by Heist, pp. 343–6.

MAC NISSE [3 September]. A very short lectionary Life is preserved in **S**, printed by Heist, pp. 404–7.

MAC CUILINN. See Finnbarr.

MAEDÓC (Aidus, Edanus) [31 January]. The earliest Latin Life is that preserved in Wales in MS Cotton Vespasian A XIV, printed by Plummer, *Vitae*, ii. 295–311. Obscurities in its otherwise rudimentary Latin may indicate that it was a translation from Irish, made in the late eleventh or early twelfth century. This text was the basis of the redaction in **D**, printed by Plummer, *Vitae*, ii. 142–63. The **D**-text was then used by the compiler of Θ, whose version survives in **S**, printed by Heist, pp. 234–47. The unprinted text in **O** is in turn a further revision based on the Θ-text. One thus has four Lives in direct sequence. See above, pp. 223–7, 289, 295–6.

MAEL MAEDÓC Ó MORGAIR (Malachias) [3 November]. The Life of St Malachy was written by St Bernard of Clairvaux soon after 1148 and was widely read. Manuscript copies are very numerous. Copies of this Life were included in **D** and **S**, but these witnesses were not used in the edition by J. Leclercq and A. Gwynn in *Opera S. Bernardi*, ed. J. Leclercq *et al.* (8 vols.; Rome, 1957–77), iii. 295–378; the **S**-text was printed by De Smedt and De Backer, *Acta*, cols. 551–640.

MOCHOEMÓC [13 March]. The only surviving text is the version in **D**, printed by Plummer, *Vitae*, ii. 164–83. There is an unprinted Irish translation of this among O'Clery's transcripts; Plummer, 'A Tentative Catalogue', p. 192.

MOCHTA (Mocteus) [24 March, 19 August]. A short Life survives among the abbreviated *uitae* in the last section of **S**, printed by Heist, pp. 394–400.

MOCHUA [24 December]. Only one text of this Life is known, that in **O**, printed by Plummer, *Vitae*, ii. 184–9.

MOCHUTU (Carthagus) [14 May]. The oldest and fullest surviving text is that in **D**, but the material is very circumstantial and it seems likely that the model used by the compiler was a full *uita* of somewhat earlier date. The text in **S** is an abbreviation of the **D**-text, apparently made for liturgical use; printed by Heist, pp. 334–40.

MOCHUILLE (Mochulleus) [12 June]. The Life was written by the same author as the Life of St Flannán. A large part of it was printed from the Austrian Great Legendary by Poncelet, *AB* 17 (1898), 136–54 (compare *BHL* 5978). A fragment of this text remains in **S**, printed by Heist, pp. 410–13.

MOLING [17 June]. The oldest and fullest surviving text is the **D**-recension of a lost original; printed by Plummer, *Vitae*, ii. 190–205. A derivative text in Θ was printed from **S** by Heist, pp. 353–6; the copy in **O** has not been collated.

MOLUA. See Luguid.

MONINNE, DARERCA (Monenna, Moninna) [6 July]. The Life of St Monenna by Conchubranus may perhaps date from the late eleventh or early twelfth century. It was edited by Esposito, *PRIA* 28 C (1910), 202–38, and more recently by the Ulster Society for Mediaeval Latin Studies in *Seanchas Ard Mhacha*, 9 (1978–9), 250–73, and 10 (1980–2), 117–41, 426–54. This text does not appear to have been the direct source of the Life of St Darerca or Moninna in **S**, printed by Heist, pp. 83–95, but it is not clear whether one should conjecture a common source or an intermediary recension. The Life by Conchubranus survives in a single manuscript from Burton, where it was used by Geoffrey of Burton, writing his Life of St Modwenna (*BHL* 2097) in the second quarter of the twelfth century; the changes he introduced make this more than merely a recension of the Life. Geoffrey's work is unprinted: copies in British Library, MS Royal 15 B IV, ff. 76–88; Add. 57533 (formerly Mostyn 260), ff. 81^r–113^v.

MUNNU. See Fintán of Taghmon.

PATRICK (Patricius) [17 March]. Of the early Lives of St Patrick, Muirchú's survives in the Book of Armagh and two fragmentary copies elsewhere, Tírechán's only in the Book of Armagh. The link or links between the collection of Patrician material in this manuscript and the later tradition cannot be exactly determined. The vernacular Tripartite Life, ed. K. Mulchrone, *Bethu Phátraic* (Dublin, 1939), and the three Latin Lives termed by Colgan *Vitae II, III*, and *IV* are clearly dependent on a lost link. Of these, *Vita III* was the only one to achieve wide circulation. These three together with the Life by Probus have been edited by Bieler, *Four Latin Lives of St Patrick* (Dublin, 1971). Other derivative or fragmentary texts from the later Middle Ages were also edited by him and are now collected in his *Studies on the Life and Legend of St Patrick* (London, 1986). I have shown that a copy of *Vita III* served as the basis of a now fragmentary Life in **D**, whose remains were collected by Bieler, *Four Latin Lives*, pp. 235–45. Of the other collections, **O** contains the Life of St Patrick by Jocelin of Furness, and **S** probably did so though these leaves are lost. Jocelin drew extensively on earlier material, including the Tripartite, reworking the text into more stylish Latin. His Life is printed by Colgan, *Trias*, pp. 64–108, and by Papebroch, *Acta Sanctorum*, Mart. II (1668), 540–80; my quotations are taken from a text prepared by L. Bieler and revised by me, which I hope will shortly be published.

RÓNÁN (Ronanus) [18 November]. A fragment survives in the Austrian Great Legendary from a Life of St Rónán, printed by Poncelet, *AB* 17 (1898), 161–6. The earliest manuscript dates from the twelfth century but the style of the Life resembles the much older Lives in Φ.

RUADÁN (Ruadanus, Ruadhanus, Ruanus) [15 April]. A text from Φ survives in **S**, printed by Heist, pp. 160–7; I have suggested that §12 may be a later addition. The derivative text from **D** is printed by Plummer, *Vitae*, ii. 240–52; the version in **O** is unprinted.

SAMTHANN (Samthanna) [19 December]. The only Life of St Samthann is the short life in the **O**-collection, printed by Plummer, *Vitae*, ii. 253–61.

SECHNALL (Secundinus) [27 November]. A short lectionary Life of St Secundinus survives among the Bollandist *collectanea*. It was supplied by FitzSimon and has been printed by Grosjean, *AB* 60 (1942), 26–34.

SENÁN (Senanus) [1 March, 8 March]. A thirteenth-century Life in ₒctosyllabic verse was included in all three collections. Heist, pp. 301–24, prints a text based on all three (the collation was done by Grosjean) but he does not discuss their textual relationship. There remain some lacunae in the text as transmitted. The Irish Life, printed by Stokes, *Lismore Lives*, pp. 54–74, contains much of interest; there is also a group of late medieval *miracula* in Irish, printed by Plummer, *Zeitschrift für celtische Philologie*, 10 (1914–15), 1–35.

TIGERNACH (Tigernacus) [4 April]. A thirteenth-century Life designed for liturgical use survives from Θ in both S and O; it was printed from S by Heist, pp. 107–11 (imperfect at the end) and edited from both by Plummer, *Vitae*, ii. 262–9. The Bollandists printed a nearly identical text supplied by FitzSimon, *Acta Sanctorum*, Apr. I (1675), 402–4; a copy in a liturgical manuscript, Cambridge, Corpus Christi College, MS 405, agrees with the Bollandist text, being slightly superior to that from Θ which had lost a chapter as a result of a copying error. See above, pp. 372–3.

OTHER WORKS

ANDERSON, A. O., and ANDERSON, M. O. (edd. and trans.), *Adomnan's Life of Columba* (London and Edinburgh, 1961).

BERNARD, E., *Catalogi librorum manuscriptorum Angliae et Hiberniae* (2 parts; Oxford, 1697).

BERNARD, J. H., and ATKINSON, R. (edd. and trans.), *The Irish Liber Hymnorum* (2 vols., Henry Bradshaw Society 13 and 14; London, 1898).

BEST, R. I., 'The Oldest Fragments of the Senchas Már: Addenda and Corrigenda', *Analecta Hibernica*, 10 (1941), 301–3.

—— et al. (edd.), *The Book of Leinster, formerly Lebar na Núachongbála* (6 vols.; Dublin, 1954–83).

BETHAM, Sir W., *Irish Antiquarian Researches* (2 vols.; Dublin, 1827).

BIELER, L., 'An Austrian Fragment of a Life of St Patrick', *Irish Ecclesiastical Record*, 5th ser., 95 (1961), 176–81.

—— 'The Celtic Hagiographer', *Studia Patristica*, 5 (1959), *Texte und Untersuchungen zur Geschichte der altchristlichen Literatur*, 80 (Berlin, 1962), 243–65.

—— *Codices Patriciani Latini* (Dublin, 1942).

—— (ed. and trans.), *Four Latin Lives of St Patrick* (Scriptores Latini Hiberniae, 8; Dublin, 1971).

—— (ed. and trans.), *The Irish Penitentials* (Scriptores Latini Hiberniae, 5; Dublin, 1963).

—— 'Jocelin von Furness als Hagiograph', in *Geschichtsschreibung und geistiges Leben im Mittelalter: Festschrift für Heinz Löwe* (Cologne, 1978), 410–15.

—— 'John Colgan as Editor', *Franciscan Studies*, 8 (1948), 1–24.

—— *The Life and Legend of St Patrick: Problems of Modern Scholarship* (Dublin, 1949).

—— (ed. and trans.), *The Patrician Texts in the Book of Armagh* (Scriptores Latini Hiberniae, 10; Dublin, 1979).

—— 'Recent Research in Irish Hagiography', *Studies*, 33 (1946), 230–8 and 536–44.

—— [Review of Anderson and Anderson, *Adomnan's Life of Columba*], *Irish Historical Studies*, 13 (1962–3), 175–84.

—— 'Studies on the Text of Muirchú, II: The Vienna Fragments', *Proceedings of the Royal Irish Academy*, 59C (1959), 181–95.

—— 'Tírechán als Erzähler', *Sitzungsberichte der bayerischen Akademie der Wissenschaften*, phil.-hist. Kl. 1974, Nr. 6.

—— 'Trias Thaumaturga', in *Father John Colgan, OFM*, ed. T. O Donnell (Dublin, 1959), 41–9.

—— and BISCHOFF, B., 'Fragmente zweier frühmittelalterlicher Schulbücher aus Glendalough', *Celtica*, 3 (1955), 211–20.

—— and CARNEY, J. (edd. and trans.), 'The Lambeth Commentary', *Ériu*, 23 (1972), 1–55.

BINCHY, D. A., 'Patrick and his Biographers, Ancient and Modern', *Studia Hibernica*, 2 (1962), 7–173.

—— 'A Pre-Christian Survival in Mediaeval Irish Hagiography', in *Ireland in Early Mediaeval Europe*, ed. D. Whitelock *et al.* (Cambridge, 1982), 165–78.

BINDON, S. H., ['MSS of Irish Interest in Brussels], *Proceedings of the Royal Irish Academy*, 3 (1845–7), 477–502.

BISCHOFF, B., *Anecdota Novissima* (Quellen und Untersuchungen zur lateinischen Philologie des Mittelalters, 8; Stuttgart, 1984).

BLUME, C., 'Hymnodia Hiberno-Celtica', *Analecta Hymnica*, 51 (1908), 264–343.

BRADSHAW, B., 'Manus "the Magnificent": O'Donnell as Renaissance Prince', in *Studies in Irish History presented to R. Dudley Edwards*, ed. A. Cosgrove and D. McCartney (Dublin, 1979), 15–36.

BRAY, D. A., 'Motival Derivations in the Life of St Samthann', *Studia Celtica*, 20/21 (1989–6), 78–86.

BREWER, J. S., *et al.* (edd.), *Giraldi Cambrensis Opera* (8 vols., Rolls Series, 21; London, 1861–91).

BROOKE, C. N. L., *The Church and the Welsh Border in the Central Middle Ages* (Studies in Celtic History, 8; Woodbridge, 1986).

—— 'St Peter of Gloucester and St Cadog of Llancarfan', in *Celt and Saxon: Studies in the Early British Border*, ed. N. K. Chadwick (Cambridge, 1963), 258–322; rev. repr. in Brooke, *The Church and the Welsh Border*, 50–94.

BRÜNING, G., 'Adamnans Vita Columbae und ihre Ableitungen', *Zeitschrift für celtische Philologie*, 11 (1916–17), 213–304.

BUICK KNOX, R., *James Ussher, Archbishop of Armagh* (Cardiff, 1967).

BURY, J. B., 'Sources of the Early Patrician Documents', *English Historical Review*, 19 (1904), 493–503.

—— 'The Tradition of Muirchú's Text', *Hermathena*, no. 28 (1902), 172–207.

BUTLER, J., 2nd Marquess of Ormonde (ed.), *Vita Sancti Kennechi a Codice in Bibliotheca Burgundiana Transcripta* (Kilkenny Archaeological Society extra volume, Kilkenny, 1853).

BYRNE, F. J., 'Derrynavlan: The Historical Context', *Journal of the Royal Society of Antiquaries of Ireland*, 110 (1980), 116–26.

—— *Irish Kings and High Kings* (London, 1973).

—— *1000 Years of Irish Script: An Exhibition of Manuscripts at the Bodleian Library* (Oxford, 1979).

—— 'Senchas: The Nature of Gaelic Historical Tradition', *Historical Studies*, 9 (1971), 137–59.

CANISIUS, H. (ed.), *Antiquae Lectiones* (6 vols.; Ingolstadt, 1601–4).

CARNEY, J., 'Aspects of Archaic Irish', *Éigse*, 17 (1977–9), 417–35.

—— 'On the Dating of Early Irish Verse', *Éigse*, 19 (1982–3), 177–216.

—— [Review of Selmer, *Nauigatio Sancti Brendani Abbatis*], *Medium Ævum*, 32 (1963), 37–44.

—— 'Three Old Irish Accentual Poems', *Ériu*, 22 (1971), 23–80.

CAULFIELD, R. (ed.), *The Life of St Fin Barre* (London, 1864).

CHADWICK, N. K. (ed.), *Celt and Saxon: Studies in the Early British Border* (Cambridge, 1963).

CHARLES-EDWARDS, T. M., 'The *Corpus Iuris Hibernici*', *Studia Hibernica*, 20 (1980), 141–62.

COLGAN, J. (ed.), *Acta Sanctorum Veteris et Majoris Scotiæ seu Hiberniæ*, vol. i (Louvain, 1645).

—— (ed.), *Triadis Thaumaturgæ seu Divorum Patricii, Columbæ, et Brigidæ . . . Acta* (Louvain, 1647).

CONNOLLY, S., 'The Authorship and Manuscript Tradition of *Vita I Sanctae Brigidae*', *Manuscripta*, 16 (1972), 67–82.

COSGROVE, A. (ed.), *A New History of Ireland*, ii: *Medieval Ireland 1169–1534* (Oxford, 1987).

CROSTHWAITE, J. C. (ed.), *The Book of Obits and Martyrology of the Cathedral Church of the Holy Trinity* (Dublin, 1844).

D'ARBOIS DE JUBAINVILLE, H., [Review of Zimmer, *Göttingische gelehrte Anzeigen* (1891)], *Revue celtique*, 12 (1891), 393–7.

DE BUCK, V., 'L'Archéologie irlandaise au couvent de Saint-Antoine de Padoue à Louvain', *Études réligieuses historiques et littéraires de la Compagnie de Jésus*, 4th ser., 3 (1869), 409–37 and 586–603.

—— (ed.), 'De SS. Abbanis Kill-Abbaniensi et Magharnuidhiensi', in *Acta Sanctorum*, ed. J. Bolland *et al.*, Oct. XII (Brussels, 1867), 270–93.

DELEHAYE, H., *L'Œuvre des Bollandistes à travers trois siècles* (2nd edn.; Subsidia Hagiographica, 13A²; Brussels, 1959).

DE SMEDT, C., and DE BACKER, J. (edd.), *Acta Sanctorum Hiberniae ex Codice Salmanticensi nunc primum integre edita* (Edinburgh and London, Bruges and Lille, 1887/8).

DIMOCK, J. F. See BREWER, J. S., *et al.*

DOHERTY, C., 'The Irish Hagiographer: resources, aims, results', in *The Writer as Witness: Literature as Historical Evidence*, ed. T. Dunne, *Historical Studies*, 16 (Cork, 1987), 10–22.

DUMVILLE, D. N., 'Latin and Irish in the *Annals of Ulster*, AD 431–1050', in *Ireland in Early Mediaeval Europe*, ed. D. Whitelock *et al.* (Cambridge, 1982), 320–41.

—— 'Two Approaches to the Dating of *Nauigatio Sancti Brendani*', *Studi Medievali*, 3rd ser., 29 (1988), 87–102.

ESPOSITO, M. (ed.), 'Conchubrani Vita Sanctae Monennae', *Proceedings of the Royal Irish Academy*, 28C (1910), 202–38.

—— '*Lour Darg*' [Notes on Latin learning and literature in mediaeval Ireland, part I: viii], *Hermathena*, no. 45 (1930), 259–60.

—— 'On the Early Latin Lives of St Brigid of Kildare' [Notes on Latin learning and literature in mediaeval Ireland, part IV], *Hermathena*, no. 49 (1935), 120–65.

—— 'The Sources of Conchubranus' Life of St Monenna', *English Historical Review*, 35 (1920), 71–8.

EVANS, D. E., *et al.* (edd.), *Proceedings of the Seventh International Congress of Celtic Studies, Oxford, 1983* (Oxford, 1986).

F., G. (pseud.), *Hiberniae sive Antiquioris Scotiae Vindiciae . . . Authore G. F. Veridico Hiberno* (Antwerp, 1621).

FABRÉ, P., and DUCHESNE, L. (edd.), *Le Liber Censuum de l'Église romaine* (3 vols. in 7 fasc.; Bibliothèque des Écoles français d'Athènes et de Rome, 2nd ser., 6; Paris, 1910, 1889–1952).

FERGUSON, M. C., *Life of the Right Rev. William Reeves, DD* (Dublin, 1893).

FITZSIMON, H., *The Justification and Exposition of the Divine Sacrifice of the Masse* (Douai, 1611).

FLEMING, P. (ed.), *Collectanea Sacra seu S. Columbani Hiberni Abbatis . . . Acta et Opuscula*, ed. T. Sirinus [Sheeran] (Louvain, 1667).

FLOWER, R., 'Manuscripts of Irish Interest in the British Museum', *Analecta Hibernica*, 2 (1931), 292–340.

FRASER, J., *et al.* (edd.), *Irish Texts* (5 vols.; London, 1930–4).

FRYDE, E. B., *et al.* (edd.), *Handbook of British Chronology* (3rd edn.; London, 1986).

GEC, *The Complete Peerage*, ed. V. Gibbs *et al.* (13 vols.; London, 1910–59).

GIBLIN, C., 'Hugh McCaghwell, OFM, Archbishop of Armagh († 1626): Aspects of his Life', *Seanchas Ard Mhacha*, 11 (1984–5), 258–90.

GILBERT, Sir J. T., 'The Manuscripts of the Former College of Irish Franciscans, Louvain', *HMC 4th Report* (1874), appendix, 599–613.

GOUGAUD, L., 'The Isle of Saints', *Studies*, 13 (1924), 363–80.

—— 'The Remains of Ancient Irish Monastic Libraries', in *Féilsgríbhinn Eóin Mhic Néill*, ed. J. Ryan (Dublin, 1940), 319–34.

GREENE, D., 'Archaic Irish', in *Indogermanisch und Keltisch*, ed. K. H. Schmidt (Wiesbaden, 1977), 11–33.

GROSJEAN, P., 'Catalogus Codicum Hagiographicorum Latinorum Dubliniensium', *Analecta Bollandiana*, 46 (1928), 81–148.

—— (ed.), 'De Sancto Aido, Episcopo Killariensi in Hibernia', in *Acta Sanctorum*, ed. J. Bolland *et al.*, Nov. IV (Brussels 1925), 495–531.

—— (ed.), 'De Sancto Greallano, Confessore in Hibernia Occidentali', in *Acta Sanctorum*, ed. J. Bolland *et al.*, Nov. IV (Brussels, 1925), 483–95.

—— 'Deux textes inédits sur S. Ibar', *Analecta Bollandiana*, 77 (1959), 426–50.

—— 'Édition du *Catalogus praecipuorum Sanctorum Hiberniae* de Henri Fitz-Simon', in *Féilsgríbhinn Eóin Mhic Néill*, ed. J. Ryan (Dublin, 1940), 335–93.

—— 'Édition et commentaire du *Catalogus Sanctorum Hiberniae secundum Diuersa Tempora* ou *De Tribus Ordinibus Sanctorum Hiberniae*', *Analecta Bollandiana*, 73 (1955), 197–213 and 289–322.

—— 'Hagiographica Celtica', *Analecta Bollandiana*, 55 (1937), 96–108.

—— 'Narratiuncula de S. Columba Hiensi', *Analecta Bollandiana*, 55 (1937), 96–108.

—— 'Notes d'hagiographie celtique (nos. 37–40)', *Analecta Bollandiana*, 75 (1957), 373–419.

—— 'Notes sur quelques sources des Antiquitates de Jacques Ussher', *Analecta Bollandiana*, 77 (1959), 154–87.

—— 'Relations mutuelles des Vies latines de S. Cáemgen de Glenn dá locha', *Analecta Bollandiana*, 63 (1945), 122–9.

—— [Review of C. McNeill, 'Reports'], *Analecta Bollandiana*, 48 (1930), 361–8.

—— (ed.), 'S. Comgalli Vita Latina', *Analecta Bollandiana*, 52 (1934), 343–56.

—— 'Un soldat de fortune irlandais au service des *Acta Sanctorum*: Philippe O'Sullivan Beare et Jean Bolland (1634)', *Analecta Bollandiana*, 81 (1963), 418–46.

—— 'Une Vie de S. Secundinus, disciple de S. Patrice', *Analecta Bollandiana*, 60 (1942), 26–34.

—— 'Les Vies de S. Columba de Tír Dá Glas', *Analecta Bollandiana*, 72 (1954), 343–7.

—— 'Les Vies de S. Finnbarr de Cork, de S. Finnbarr d'Écosse et de S. Mac Cuilinn de Lusk', *Analecta Bollandiana*, 69 (1951), 327–47.

—— 'Les Vies latines de S. Cáemgen et de S. Patrice du manuscrit 121 des Bollandistes', *Analecta Bollandiana*, 70 (1952), 313–15.

—— 'Vita S. Brendani Clonfertensis e Codice Dubliniensi', *Analecta Bollandiana*, 48 (1930), 99–123.

GWYNN, A., *Anglo-Irish Church Life: Fourteenth and Fifteenth Centuries* (A History of Irish Catholicism ii. 4, Dublin, 1968).

—— 'Archbishop Ussher and Father Brendan O Conor', in *Father Luke Wadding Commemorative Volume* [ed. B. Millett] (Dublin, 1957), 263–83.

—— (ed.), 'Provincial and Diocesan Decrees of the Diocese of Dublin During the Anglo-Norman Period', *Archivium Hibernicum*, 11 (1944), 31–117.

—— *The Twelfth-Century Reform* (A History of Irish Catholicism ii. 1, Dublin, 1968).

—— and HADCOCK, R. N., *Medieval Religious Houses: Ireland* (London, 1970).

GWYNN, J. (ed.), *Liber Armachanus: The Book of Armagh* (Dublin, 1913).

HAND, G. J., *The Church in the English Lordship 1216–1307* (A History of Irish Catholicism ii. 3, Dublin, 1968).

—— 'The Psalter of Christ Church, Dublin (Bodleian MS Rawlinson G. 185)', *Reportorium Novum: Dublin Diocesan Historical Record*, 1 (1955–6), 311–22.

HANSON, R. P. C., 'The Date of St Patrick', *Bulletin of the John Rylands Library*, 61 (1978–9), 60–77.

—— *Saint Patrick, His Origins and His Career* (Oxford, 1968).

HARDY, Sir T. D. (ed.), *Descriptive Catalogue of Materials Relating to the History of Great Britain and Ireland* (3 vols. in 4 incomplete, Rolls Series 26; London, 1862–71).

HARRIS, S., 'The Kalendar of the *Vitae Sanctorum Wallensium*', *Journal of the Historical Society of the Church in Wales*, 3 (1953), 3–53.

HART, W. H., *Lectionarium Sanctae Mariae Virginis, Sancti Thomae Cantuariensis, Sanctae Kyneburgae Gloucestrensis, et Sancti Kenani de Hibernia* (London, 1869).

HARVEY, A. J. R., 'The Significance of *Cothraige*', *Ériu*, 36 (1985), 1–10.

HAWKES, W., 'The Liturgy in Dublin, 1200–1500: Manuscript Sources', *Reportorium Novum: Dublin Diocesan Historical Record*, 2 (1958–60), 33–67.

HAYES, R. J. (ed.), *Catalogue of the Manuscript Sources of Irish History* (11 vols.; Boston, Mass., 1965, with suppl., 3 vols.; Boston, Mass., 1979).

HEIST, W. W., 'Over the Writer's Shoulder: Saint Abban', *Celtica*, 11 (1976), 76–84.

—— (ed.), *Vitae Sanctorum Hiberniae e Codice olim Salmanticensi nunc Bruxellensi* (Subsidia Hagiographica, 25; Brussels, 1965).

HENNIG, J., [Review of Koch, *Sankt Fridolin*], *Irish Ecclesiastical Record*, 5th ser., 95 (1961), 136–8.

HENRY, F., and MARSH-MICHELI, G. L., 'Manuscripts and Illuminations 1169–1603', in *A New History of Ireland*, ii: *Medieval Ireland*, ed. A. Cosgrove (Oxford, 1987), 781–815.

HERBERT, M., *Iona, Kells, and Derry. The History and Hagiography of the Monastic* Familia *of Columba* (Oxford, 1988).

—— and Ó Riain, P. (edd.), *Betha Adamnáin: The Irish Life of Adamnán* (Irish Texts Society, 54; London, 1988).

HOGAN, E., *Distinguished Irishmen of the 16th Century* (Dublin, 1894).

—— (ed.), 'Documenta de S. Patricio', *Analecta Bollandiana*, 1 (1882), 531–83, and 2 (1883), 35–68 and 213–38; continued in *Irish Ecclesiastical Record*, 3rd ser., 7 (1889), 846–53. Also separately with corrigenda and indices, *Documenta de S. Patricio* (2 vols.; Brussels, 1882–9).

—— 'Irish Historical Studies in the Seventeenth Century, II: Hugh Ward', *Irish Ecclesiastical Record*, 2nd ser., 7 (1870–1), 56–77.

—— 'Irish Historical Studies in the Seventeenth Century, III: Patrick Fleming, OSF', *Irish Ecclesiastical Record*, 2nd ser., 7 (1870–1), 193–216.

—— 'Life of Father Stephen White, SJ', *Journal of the Waterford and Southeast of Ireland Archaeological Society*, 3 (1897), 55–71 and 119–34.

—— (ed.), *Onomasticon Goedelicum Locorum et Tribuum Hiberniae et Scotiae* (Dublin, 1910).

—— 'Sketch of Father Fitzsimon's Life', in *Words of Comfort to Persecuted Catholics by Henry Fitzsimon*, ed. E. Hogan (Dublin, 1881), 200–84.

HORSTMAN, C. (ed.), *Nova Legenda Anglie: As Collected by John of Tynemouth, John Capgrave, and Others* (2 vols.; Oxford, 1901).

HOSTE, A., 'A Survey of the Unedited Work of Laurence of Durham, with an Edition of his Letter to Aelred of Rievaulx', *Sacris Erudiri*, 11 (1960), 249–65.

HOWLETT, D. R., 'Penance for an Editor', *Celtica*, 18 (1986), 150.

HUGHES, K., 'British Museum MS Cotton Vespasian A XIV ("Vitae Sanctorum Wallensium"): Its Purpose and Provenance', in *Studies in the Early British Church*, ed. N. K. Chadwick (Cambridge, 1958), 183–200.

—— *The Church in Early Irish Society* (London, 1966).

—— 'The Historical Value of the Lives of St Finnian of Clonard', *English Historical Review*, 69 (1954), 353–72.

—— 'A Manuscript of Sir James Ware: British Museum Additional 4788', *Proceedings of the Royal Irish Academy*, 55C (1952–3), 111–16.

—— 'The Offices of St Finnian of Clonard and St Cíanán of Duleek', *Analecta Bollandiana*, 73 (1955), 342–72.

HUNTER BLAIR, Dom D. O., *John Patrick Third Marquess of Bute, KT: A Memoir* (London, 1921).

JACKSON, K. H., 'Common Gaelic', *Proceedings of the British Academy*, 37 (1951), 71–97.

—— 'The Date of the Tripartite Life of St Patrick', *Zeitschrift für celtische Philologie*, 41 (1986), 5–45.

—— 'The Historical Grammar of Irish: Some Actualities and some Desiderata', in *Proceedings of the Sixth International Congress of Celtic Studies, Galway, 1979*, ed. G. S. Mac Eoin (Dublin, 1983), 1–18.

JAMES, J. W. (ed. and trans.), *Rhigyfarch's Life of St David: the Basic Mid-Twelfth-Century Latin Text* (Cardiff, 1967).

JENNINGS, B. (ed.), 'Brevis synopsis provinciae Hiberniae FF. Minorum', *Analecta Hibernica*, 6 (1934), 139–91.

—— (ed.), 'Documents from the Archives of St Isidore's College, Rome', *Analecta Hibernica*, 6 (1934), 203–47.

—— (ed.), *Louvain Papers 1606–1827* (Irish Manuscripts Commission; Dublin, 1968).

—— *Michael O Cleirigh, Chief of the Four Masters, and his Associates* (Dublin, 1936).

—— (ed.), *Wadding Papers 1614–38* (Irish Manuscripts Commission; Dublin, 1953).

KENNEY, J. F., *The Sources for the Early History of Ireland: Ecclesiastical* (Records of Civilisation; New York, 1929).

KISSANE, D. N. (ed.), '*Vita Metrica Sanctae Brigidae*: A Critical Edition', *Proceedings of the Royal Irish Academy*, 77C (1977), 57–192.

KNOWLES, M. D., *Great Historical Enterprises* (London, [1962]).

KOCH, M., *Sankt Fridolin und sein Biograph Balther* (Zurich, 1959).

KRUSCH, B. (ed.), *Ionae Vitae Sanctorum Columbani, Vedastis, Iohannis* (Hanover and Leipzig, 1905).

LAPIDGE, M., and SHARPE, R. (edd.), *A Bibliography of Celtic-Latin Literature 400–1200* (Dublin, 1985).

LAWLOR, H. J., 'The Cathach of St Columba', *Proceedings of the Royal Irish Academy*, 33C (1916–17), 241–443.

—— 'A Fresh Authority for the Synod of Kells, 1152', *Proceedings of the Royal Irish Academy*, 36C (1921–4), 16–22.

—— *The Rosslyn Missal* (London, 1899).

—— (trans.), *St Bernard of Clairvaux's Life of St Malachy of Armagh* (London, 1920).

LECLERCQ, J., *Recueil d'études sur Saint Bernard et ses écrits* (3 vols.; Rome, 1962–9).

—— 'Un recueil d'hagiographie colombanienne', *Analecta Bollandiana*, 73 (1955), 193–6.

—— *et al.* (edd.), *Opera S. Bernardi* (8 vols.; Rome, 1957–77).

LEERSSEN, J. T., 'Archbishop Ussher and Gaelic Culture', *Studia Hibernica*, 22/23 (1982–3), 50–8.

LEVISON, W., *England and the Continent in the Eighth Century* (Oxford, 1946).

LOMBARD, P., *De Regno Hiberniae Sanctorum Insulae Commentarius* (Louvain, 1632).

LUARD, H. R. (ed.), *Matthæi Parisiensis, Monachi Sancti Albani, Chronica Majora* (7 vols., Rolls Series 57; London, 1872–89).

MABILLON, J., *Acta Sanctorum Ordinis S. Benedicti* (9 vols.; Paris, 1668–1701).

MAC AIRT, S. (ed. and trans.), *The Annals of Inisfallen* (Dublin, 1951).

—— and MAC NIOCAILL, G. (edd. and trans.), *The Annals of Ulster (to AD 1131*, part I (Dublin, 1983).

MACALISTER, R. A. S. (trans.), *The Latin and Irish Lives of Ciaran* (London, 1921).

MAC CANA, P., 'The Influence of the Vikings on Celtic Literature', in *Proceedings of the International Congress of Celtic Studies, Dublin, 1959*, ed. B. Ó Cuív (Dublin, 1962), 78–118.

MACCARTHY, B., *The Codex Palatino-Vaticanus 830* (Todd Lecture Series, 3; Dublin, 1892).

MACCARTHY, C. J. F., 'St Finbar and his Monastery', *Journal of the Cork Historical and Archaeological Society*, 40 (1935), 57–61.

McCONE, K., 'Brigit in the Seventh Century: A Saint with Three Lives?', *Peritia: Journal of the Medieval Academy of Ireland*, 1 (1982), 107–45.

—— 'Clones and her Neighbours in the Early Period: Hints from Some Airgialla Saints' Lives', *Clogher Record*, 11 (1982–4), 305–25.

—— 'An Introduction to Early Irish Saints' Lives', *The Maynooth Review*, 11 (1984), 26–59.

—— 'The Würzburg and Milan Glosses: our Earliest Sources for Middle Irish', *Ériu*, 36 (1985), 85–106.

MAC DONNCHA, F., 'Dáta Vita Tripartita Sancti Patricii', *Éigse*, 18 (1980–1), 124–42, and 19 (1982), 254–72.

—— 'Middle Irish Homilies', *Proceedings of the Irish Biblical Association*, 1 (1976), 59–71.

MACDONNELL, C., 'Notice of Some of the Lives Which Seem to have been Ready, or in Preparation, for the Continuation of the "Acta Sanctorum Hiberniae", at the Death of Colgan', *Proceedings of the Royal Irish Academy*, 7 (1857–61), 371–5.

MAC EOIN, G. S., 'The Dating of Middle Irish Texts', *Proceedings of the British Academy*, 68 (1982), 109–37.

—— (ed.), *Proceedings of the Sixth International Congress of Celtic Studies, Galway, 1979* (Dublin, 1983).

MACERLEAN, J. C., 'Synod of Rath Breasail: Boundaries of the Dioceses in Ireland', *Archivium Hibernicum*, 3 (1914), 1–33.

McNEILL, C., 'Reports on the Rawlinson Collection of Manuscripts', *Analecta Hibernica*, 1 (1930), 12–178, and 2 (1931), 1–92.

MacNEILL, E., 'Dates of Texts in the Book of Armagh Relating to St Patrick', *Journal of the Royal Society of Antiquaries of Ireland*, 58 (1928), 85–101.

—— 'The Earliest Lives of St Patrick', *Journal of the Royal Society of Antiquaries of Ireland*, 58 (1928), 1–21.

[MACRAY, W. D.], *Catalogus Codicum Manuscriptorum Bibl. Bodl.*, v. 1 (1862).

MESSINGHAM, T. (ed.), *Florilegium Insulae Sanctorum seu Vitae et Acta Sanctorum Hiberniae* (Paris, 1624).

—— (ed.), *Officia SS. Patricii, Columbae, Brigidae* (Paris, 1620).

MEYER, K. (ed. and trans.), *Betha Colmáin maic Luacháin* (Todd Lecture Series, 17; Dublin, 1911).

MILLETT, B., 'Dioceses in Ireland up to the 15th Century', *Seanchas Ard Mhacha*, 12 (1986–7), 1–42.

MGH (Monumenta Germaniae Historica). *Scriptores*, i–xxx (Hanover and Leipzig, 1826–1934). *Scriptores rerum Merovingicarum*, i–vii (Hanover and Leipzig, 1885–1920).

MOONEY, C., 'Colgan's Inquiries about Irish Place-Names', *Celtica*, 1 (1946–50), 294–6.

—— 'Father John Colgan', in *Father John Colgan, OFM*, ed. T. O Donnell (Dublin, 1959), 7–40.

—— 'Irish Franciscan Libraries of the Past', *Irish Ecclesiastical Record*, 5th ser., 60 (1942), 215–28.

MOORE, N., [Review of Plummer, *Vitae*], *English Historical Review*, 24 (1911), 562–3.

MORAN, P. F. (ed.), *Acta Sancti Brendani* (Dublin, 1872).

MULCHRONE, K., 'Die Abfassungszeit und Überlieferung der Vita Tripartita', *Zeitschrift für celtische Philologie*, 16 (1926–7), 1–94.

MURPHY, G., 'On the Dates of Two Sources Used in Thurneysen's Heldensage', *Ériu*, 16 (1952), 145–56.

NÍ BHROLCHÁIN, M., 'The Manuscript Tradition of the Banshenchas', *Ériu*, 33 (1982), 109–35.

—— 'Maol Íosa Ó Brolcháin: An Assessment', *Seanchas Ard Mhacha*, 12 (1986–7), 43–67.

Ó BRIAIN, F., 'Brigitana', *Zeitschrift für celtische Philologie*, 36 (1977), 112–37.

—— (alias F. O'Brien), 'Irish Franciscan Historians of St Anthony's College, Louvain: Father Hugh Ward', *Irish Ecclesiastical Record*, 5th ser., 32 (1928), 113–29.

—— 'St Brigid of Ireland', unpublished typescript in the library of the Franciscan House of Studies, Killiney (n.d. [1930s]).

O'Brien, M.A. (ed.), *Corpus Genealogiarum Hiberniae*, i (Dublin, 1962).

Ó Buachalla, B., '*Annála Ríoghachta Éireann* agus *Foras Feasa ar Éirinn*: An Comhthéacs Comhaimseartha', *Studia Hibernica*, 22/23 (1982–3), 59–105.

Ó Cléirigh, T., *Aodh Mac Aingil agus an Scóil Nua-Ghaedhilge i Lobháin* (Dublin, [1935]).

Ó Corráin, D., 'Foreign Connections and Domestic Politics: Killaloe and the Uí Briain in Twelfth-Century Hagiography', in *Ireland in Early Mediaeval Europe*, ed. D. Whitelock *et al.* (Cambridge, 1982), pp. 213–31.

—— 'Historical Need and Literary Narrative', in *Proceedings of the Seventh International Congress of Celtic Studies, Oxford, 1983* , ed. D. E. Evans *et al.* (Oxford, 1986), 141–58.

—— *et al.* (edd.), *Sages, Saints and Storytellers: Celtic Studies in honour of Professor James Carney* (Maynooth Monographs, 2; Maynooth, 1989).

O Cróinín, D. I., 'A Poem to Toirdhealbhach Luimnech O Néill', *Éigse*, 16 (1975–6), 50–66.

—— 'A Poet in Penitential Mood', *Celtica*, 16 (1984), 169–74.

Ó Cuív, B., 'Aspects of Irish Personal Names', *Celtica*, 18 (1986), 151–84.

O'Curry, E., *Lectures on the Manuscript Materials of Ancient Irish History* (Dublin, 1861).

O Daly, M. (ed. and trans.), *Cath Maige Mucrama* (Irish Texts Society, 50; [London], 1975).

O'Doherty, D. J., 'Students of the Irish College, Salamanca (1595–1619)', *Archivium Hibernicum*, 2 (1913), 1–36.

O Donnell, T. (ed.), *Father John Colgan, OFM, 1592–1658. Essays in Commemoration of the Third Centenary of his Death* (Dublin, 1959).

O'Donovan, J. (ed. and trans.), *Annals of the Kingdom of Ireland by the Four Masters* (2nd edn., 7 vols.; Dublin, 1856).

O'Grady, S. H. (ed. and trans.), *Silva Gadelica* (2 vols.; London, 1892).

Ó hAodha, D. (ed. and trans.), *Bethu Brigte* (Dublin, 1978).

Ó hInnse, S. (ed. and trans.), *Miscellaneous Irish Annals (AD 1114–1437)* (Dublin, 1947).

O'Kelleher, A., and Schoepperle, G. (edd. and trans.), *Betha Colaim Chille* (Urbana, Ill., 1918).

Ó Máille, T., *The Language of the Annals of Ulster* (Manchester, 1910).

O'Rahilly, T. F., *Early Irish History and Mythology* (Dublin, 1946).

—— 'Middle Irish Pronunciation', *Hermathena*, no. 44 (1926), 152–95.

Ó Riain, P. (ed.), *Corpus Genealogiarum Sanctorum Hiberniae* (Dublin, 1985).

—— 'St Abbán: The Genesis of an Irish Saint's Life', in *Proceedings of the Seventh International Congress of Celtic Studies, Oxford, 1983*, ed. D. E. Evans *et al.* (Oxford, 1986), 159–70.

ORLANDI, G., *Navigatio Sancti Brendani, I. Introduzione* (Testi e documenti per lo studio dell'antichità; Milan, 1968).

ORPEN, G. H., *Ireland under the Normans 1169–1333* (4 vols.; Oxford, 1911–20).

O'SULLIVAN BEARE, P., *Historiæ Catholicæ Iberniæ Compendium* (Lisbon, 1621).

O'SULLIVAN, W., 'Medieval Meath Manuscripts', *Ríocht Na Midhe*, 7 (1980–6), part 4, 3–21, and 8 (1987–), 68–70.

—— 'Ussher as a Collector of Manuscripts', *Hermathena*, no. 88 (1956), 34–58.

OULTON, J. E. L., 'Ussher's Work as a Patristic Scholar and Church Historian', *Hermathena*, no. 88 (1956), 3–11.

PHILIPPART, G., *Les Légendiers latins et autres manuscrits hagiographiques*, Typologies des sources du moyen âge occidental, 24–5 (Turnhout, 1977).

PICARD, J.-M., 'The Purpose of Adomnán's *Vita Columbae*', *Peritia: Journal of the Medieval Academy of Ireland*, 1 (1982), 160–77.

—— 'The Schaffhausen Adomnán: A Unique Witness to Hiberno-Latin', *Peritia: Journal of the Medieval Academy of Ireland*, 1 (1982), 216–49.

PLUMMER, C. (ed. and trans.), *Bethada Náem nÉrenn* (2 vols.; Oxford, 1922).

—— 'The Miracles of St Senán', *Zeitschrift für celtische Philologie*, 10 (1914), 1–35.

—— (ed.), *Miscellanea Hagiographica Hibernica* (Subsidia Hagiographica, 15; Brussels, 1925).

—— 'On the Colophons and Marginalia of Irish Scribes', *Proceedings of the British Academy*, 12 (1926), 11–44.

—— 'On Two Collections of Latin Lives of Irish Saints in the Bodleian Library, Rawl. B. 485 and Rawl. B. 505', *Zeitschrift für celtische Philologie*, 5 (1904–5), 429–54.

—— 'Some New Light on the Brendan Legend', *Zeitschrift für celtische Philologie*, 5 (1904–5), 124–41.

—— 'A Tentative Catalogue of Irish Hagiography', in *Miscellanea Hagiographica Hibernica*, ed. C. Plummer (Brussels, 1925), 171–285.

—— 'Vie et miracles de S. Laurent, archevêque de Dublin', *Analecta Bollandiana*, 33 (1914), 121–86.

—— (ed.), *Vitae Sanctorum Hiberniae* (2 vols.; Oxford, 1910).

[PONCELET, A.], 'De Magno Legendario Austriaco', *Analecta Bollandiana*, 17 (1898), 24–216.

POWICKE, F. M., and CHENEY, C. R., *Councils and Synods with Other Documents Relating to the English Church*, ii: AD 1205–1313 (2 parts; Oxford, 1964).

REEVES, W., 'The Irish Library, 1: Colgan's Works', *Ulster Journal of Archaeology*, 1 (1853), 295–303.

—— 'The Irish Library, 2: Fleming's *Collectanea Sacra*', *Ulster Journal of Archaeology*, 2 (1854), 253–61.

—— (ed.), *The Life of St Columba by Adamnan* (Irish Archaeological and Celtic Society, Dublin, 1857; Bannatyne Club, Edinburgh, 1857).

—— 'Memoir of Stephen White', *Proceedings of the Royal Irish Academy*, 8 (1861–4), 29–38.

—— 'On a Manuscript Volume of Lives of Saints (Chiefly Irish), Now in Primate Marsh's Library, Dublin, Commonly Called the Codex Kilkenniensis', *Proceedings of the Royal Irish Academy*, 2nd ser., 1 (1870–9), 339–50.

ROCHE, M. F., 'The Latin Lives of St Laurence of Dublin Edited with a Critical Introduction' (University College, Dublin, Ph.D. thesis, 1981).

ROIRK, D. *pseud.* See ROTHE, D.

RONAN, M. V., 'St Laurentius, Archbishop of Dublin: Original Testimonies for Canonization', *Irish Ecclesiastical Record*, 5th ser., 27 (1926), 347–64, and 28 (1926), 247–56, 467–80, and 596–612.

ROSWEYDE, H., *Fasti Sanctorum quorum Vitae in Belgicis Bibliothecis Manuscriptae . . .* (Antwerp, 1607).

—— *Martyrologium Romanum* (Antwerp, 1613).

—— *Vitae Patrum: De Vita et Verbis Seniorum Libri X Historiam Eremiticam Complectentes, Auctoribus suis et Nitori Pristino Restituti* (Antwerp, 1615; rev. edn., Antwerp, 1628).

[ROTHE, D.], *Hibernia Resurgens sive Refrigerium Antidotale adversus Morsum Serpentis Antiqui in quo . . . Hiberniae Sancti sui Vindicantur, Auctore Donato Roirk* (Rouen, 1621).

RYAN, J. (ed.), *Féilsgríbhinn Eóin Mhic Néill: Essays and Studies Presented to Eoin MacNeill* (Dublin, 1940).

SCOTT, J., and WHITE, N. J. D. (edd.), *Catalogue of Manuscripts Remaining in Marsh's Library, Dublin* (Dublin, [1913]).

SELMER, C. (ed.), *Nauigatio Sancti Brendani Abbatis* (Notre Dame, Ind., 1959; repr. Dublin, 1989).

SHARPE, R., Hiberno-Latin *laicus*, Irish *láech*, and the Devil's Men', *Ériu*, 30 (1979), 75–92.

—— 'The Origin and Elaboration of the *Catalogus praecipuorum Sanctorum Hiberniae* Attributed to Henry FitzSimon SJ', *Bodleian Library Record*, 13/3 (Oct. 1989), 202–30.

—— 'Palaeographical Considerations in the Study of the Patrician Documents in the Book of Armagh', *Scriptorium*, 36 (1982), 3–28.

—— 'The Patrician Texts', *Peritia: Journal of the Medieval Academy of Ireland*, 1 (1982), 363–9.

—— '*Quattuor Sanctissimi Episcopi*: Irish Saints before St Patrick', in *Sages, Saints and Storytellers: Celtic Studies in honour of Professor James Carney*, ed. D. Ó Corráin *et al.* (Maynooth, 1989), 376–99.

—— 'Some Problems Concerning the Organization of the Church in Early Medieval Ireland', *Peritia: Journal of the Medieval Academy of Ireland*, 3 (1984), 230–70.

—— '*Vitae S. Brigitae*: The Oldest Texts', *Peritia: Journal of the Medieval Academy of Ireland*, 1 (1982), 81–106.

—— 'Were the Irish Annals Known to a Twelfth-Century Northumbrian Writer?', *Peritia: Journal of the Medieval Academy of Ireland*, 2 (1983), 137–9.

SHEEHY, M. P. (ed.), *Pontificia Hibernica: Medieval Papal Chancery Documents Concerning Ireland 640–1261* (2 vols.; Dublin, 1962–5).

—— *When the Normans Came to Ireland* (Cork and Dublin, 1975).

SMITH, J. T., 'Ardmore Cathedral', *Journal of the Royal Society of Antiquaries of Ireland*, 102 (1972), 1–13.

STANTON, P., 'The Life of St Finbar of Cork', *Journal of the Cork Historical and Archaeological Society*, 2 (1893), 61–9 and 87–94.

STEVENSON, J. (ed.), *Chronicon Monasterii de Abingdon* (2 vols., Rolls Series 2; London, 1858).

STOKES, W. (ed. and trans.), *Félire Oengusso: The Martyrology of Oengus the Culdee* (Henry Bradshaw Society, 29; London, 1905).

—— (ed. and trans.), *Lives of Saints from the Book of Lismore* (Anecdota Oxoniensia, Mediaeval and Modern Series; Oxford, 1890).

—— (ed.), *On the Calendar of Oengus* (Dublin, 1880).

—— (ed. and trans.), *Three Middle-Irish Homilies on the Lives of Saints Patrick, Brigit, and Columba* (Calcutta, 1877).

—— and STRACHAN, J. (edd. and trans.), *Thesaurus Palaeohibernicus* (2 vols. and suppl.; Cambridge, 1901–10).

STUBBS, W. (ed.), *Chronica Magistri Rogeri de Houedene* (4 vols., Rolls Series 51; London, 1868–71).

—— (ed.), *Gesta Regis Henrici Secundi Benedicti Abbatis* (2 vols., Rolls Series 49; London, 1867).

STYLES, P., 'James Ussher and his Times', *Hermathena*, no. 88 (1956), 12–33.

SURIUS, L. (ed.), *De Probatis Sanctorum Historiis* (6 vols.; Cologne, 1576–81, and later editions).

SWEETMAN, H. S. (ed.), *Calendar of Documents Relating to Ireland Preserved in Her Majesty's Public Record Office, London* (5 vols.; London, 1875–6).

THOMAS, [A.] C., *Christianity in Roman Britain to AD 500* (London, 1981).

ULSTER SOCIETY FOR MEDIEVAL LATIN STUDIES (edd.), 'The Life of St Monenna by Conchubranus', *Seanchas Ard Mhacha*, 9 (1978–9), 250–73, and 10 (1980–2), 117–41 and 426–54.

USSHER, J., *Britannicarum Ecclesiarum Antiquitates* (Dublin, 1639; 2nd edn., Dublin, 1686).

—— *A Discourse of the Religion Anciently Professed by the Irish and British* (Dublin, 1631).

—— *An Epistle Concerning the Religion Anciently Professed by the Irish and Scottish*, in C. Sibthorp, *A Friendly Advertisement to the Pretended Catholickes of Ireland* (Dublin, 1622).

—— (ed.), *Veterum Epistolarum Hibernicarum Sylloge* (Dublin, 1632).

—— *The Whole Works*, ed. C. Elrington and J. H. Todd (17 vols.; Dublin, 1847–64).

VAN DEN GHEYN, J., *Catalogue des manuscrits de la Bibliothèque royale de Belgique*, v (Brussels, 1905).

WALKER, G. S. M. (ed. and trans.), *Sancti Columbani Opera* (Scriptores Latini Hiberniae, 2; Dublin, 1957).

WALSH, P. (ed.), *Genealogiae Regum et Sanctorum Hiberniae by the Four Masters* (Maynooth, 1918).

—— *Irish Men of Learning* (Dublin, 1947).

WARD, H., *Sancti Rumoldi Martyris Inclyti . . . Acta, Martyrium, Liturgia Antiqua, & Patria*, ed. T. Sirinus [Sheeran] (Louvain, 1662).

WARE, J., *De Scriptoribus Hiberniae* (Dublin, 1639).

[——] *Librorum Manuscriptorum in Bibliotheca Jacobi Waræi, Equitis Aur., Catalogus* (Dublin, 1648).

—— *S. Patricio Adscripta Opuscula* (Dublin, 1656).

WATT, J. A., *The Church and the Two Nations in Medieval Ireland* (Cambridge, 1970).

—— *The Church in Medieval Ireland* (Dublin, 1972).

WEBSTER, C. A., *The Diocese of Cork* (Cork, 1920).

WHARTON, H. (ed.), *Anglia Sacra* (2 vols.; London, 1691).

WHITE, S., *Apologia pro Hibernia adversus Cambri Calumnias*, ed. M. Kelly (Dublin, 1849).

WHITELOCK, D., *et al.* (edd.), *Ireland in Early Mediaeval Europe: Studies in Memory of Kathleen Hughes* (Cambridge, 1982).

WINTERBOTTOM, M., 'Variations on a Nautical Theme', *Hermathena*, no. 120 (1976), 55–8.

ZIMMER, H., 'Die frühesten Berührungen der Iren mit den Nordgermanen', *Sitzungsberichte der königlichen Preussischen Akademie der Wissenschaften zu Berlin* (1891), 279–317.

—— 'Keltische Beiträge, III', *Zeitschrift für deutsches Alterthum*, 35 (1891), 1–178.

—— [Review of De Smedt and De Backer, *Acta*], *Göttingische gelehrte Anzeigen* (1891), 153–200.

Index of Manuscripts

General Index